"The father, wife and son of Company Havildar-Major Chhelu Ram, V.C., 4 Battalion (Outrams) 6 Rajputana Rifles."
—*From the painting by Simon Elwes*

FOURTH INDIAN DIVISION

by

LIEUT-COLONEL G. R. STEVENS OBE.

The Naval & Military Press Ltd

Published by

The Naval & Military Press Ltd
Unit 10 Ridgewood Industrial Park,
Uckfield, East Sussex,
TN22 5QE England

Tel: +44 (0) 1825 749494
Fax: +44 (0) 1825 765701

www.naval-military-press.com
www.military-genealogy.com
www.militarymaproom.com

In reprinting in facsimile from the original, any imperfections are inevitably reproduced and the quality may fall short of modern type and cartographic standards.

I wish to acknowledge the great help freely proffered by Lieut-General Sir Francis Tuker KCIE CB DSO OBE, who supplied private papers and advice upon many matters: by Brigadier A. Anderson DSO MC, without whose guidance the chapter upon the fall of Tobruk could not have been written: by Lieut-Colonel A. E. Cocksedge DSO, Historical Section, Simla, who answered a multitude of questions: by Lieut-Colonel W. W. Stewart MC, and Lieut-Colonel P. S. Mitcheson DSO OBE, each of whom as GSO 1 of Fourth Indian Division rendered unfailing assistance.

Special mention should be made of Brigadier (afterwards Major-General) D. R. E. R. Batemen CIE DSO OBE, whose meticulous memory was no small factor in arriving at accuracy in this history.

Among those whose checking and criticism threw light on dark places were Major-General the Hon. P. G. Scarlett CB MC and Brigadier H. F. C. McSwiney CBE DSO MC, original officers of Fourth Indian Division: Lieut-General H. R. Briggs CB CBE DSO: Major-General A. W. W. Holworthy DSO MC: Major-General G. C. Evans CB CBE DSO: Major-General O. de Lovett CB DSO: Brigadier R. B. Scott DSO: Brigadier J. C. Saunders-Jacobs DSO: Brigadier H. W. D. McDonald DSO: Brigadier Claude Goulder DSO: Colonel Roger Peake DSO OBE: Colonel H. A. Hughes DSO MBE: Colonel Unni Nayar MBE: Lieut-Colonel Arthur Noble DSO: Lieut-Colonel L. B. Jones DSO: Lieut-Colonel K.Shepheard DSO: Lieut-Colonel J. A. C. Greenwood OBE: Lieut-Colonel A. V. MacDonald MC: Major D. A. Beckett DSO: Major J. A. C. Harley MC: Capt. G. W. Hawkes MC: Mr. Dennis Cox DSO: and others.

The chart of SUPERCHARGE operation at the battle of El Alemein is reproduced by the kind permission of Field-Marshal Lord Montgomery of Alemein; the Frontispiece by kind permission of the Government of India.

Finally, to Major-General T. W. Rees CB CIE DSO MC, the last commander of Fourth Indian Division under the old dispensation, and to Miss Audrey Knighton, Research Assistant, the writer's grateful acknowledgments for their share in the making of this book.

G. R. S.

ILLUSTRATIONS

FRONTISPIECE

Between Page 22-23

EARLY COMMANDERS . . . . SIDI BARRANI

DESERT TERRAIN . . . . KEREN BATTLEFIELD

ITALIAN PRISONERS—KEREN

Between Pages 86-87

CYPRUS SCENES . . . . TOBRUK PERIMETER

SIWA OASIS . . . . BENGHAZI

BATTLE OF LIBYAN OMAR . . . . ROYAL SIGNALS

ROYAL INDIAN ENGINEERS

Between Pages 182-183

DIVISIONAL COMMANDERS . . . . . . SAPPER OFFICERS

ROYAL ARTILLERY COMMANDERS . . . CAPTURE OF VON ARNIM

TUNISIAN ROUTE LINE . . . . DIVISIONAL MEMORIAL, TUNIS

DIVISIONAL RECEPTION—TOUR OF BRITAIN

Between Pages 214-215

FOR SUPREME VALOUR

FOR SELFLESS SACRIFICE

ILLUSTRATIONS—Continued

Between Pages 246-247

THE FIGHTING RACES

Between Pages 278-279

VISIT OF HIS MAJESTY THE KING	ARTILLERY IN NORTH AFRICA
OTHER DISTINGUISHED VISITORS	ARTILLERY IN ITALY
CONTACTS WITH ALLIES	INDIAN MEDICAL SERVICES

Between Pages 310-311

BRIGADE COMMANDERS	CENTRAL ITALY
CASSINO	SAN MARINO
LOWER ITALY OPERATIONS	GOTHIC LINE

URBINO PRESENTATION WOODCUT

Between Pages 342-343

COMMANDERS IN GREECE	VISIT TO MOUNT ATHOS
LANDING AT SALONIKA	DURBAR IN GREECE
FIGHTING AT PIRAEUS	BAILEY BRIDGE—ALIAKMON RIVER

RETURN TO INDIA

CONTENTS

CHAPTER		PAGE
1.	THE BEGINNINGS	1
2.	SIDI BARRANI	15
3.	ADVANCE TO KEREN	27
4.	BATTLE OF KEREN—CONQUEST OF ERITREA	37
5.	ROMMEL ARRIVES—"BATTLEAXE OPERATION"	57
6.	THE SYRIAN CAMPAIGN	67
7.	1941—THE TURN OF THE TIDE	82
8.	"CRUSADER" OPERATION—ADVANCE ON TOBRUK	90
9.	THE CLEARING OF THE DJEBEL ACHDAR	109
10.	RETREAT FROM BENGHAZI	124
11.	BENGHAZI—7 BRIGADE BREAKS OUT	146
12.	THE STORM GATHERS	160
13.	DESTRUCTION OF 11 BRIGADE IN TOBRUK	167
14.	5 BRIGADE—MERSA MATRUH, RUWEISAT AND ALAMEIN	177
15.	THE DOLDRUMS	200
16.	MATMATA MOUNTAINS	207
17.	WADI AKARIT	217
18.	DJEBEL GARCI AND ENFIDAVILLE	231
19.	THE END IN AFRICA	248
20.	AFTERMATH OF VICTORY	256
21.	ITALY—THE FIRST PHASE	269
22.	CASSINO—THE LINE UP	274
23.	CASSINO—THE FIRST ASSAULT	280
24.	CASSINO—THE SECOND ASSAULT	292
25.	LOWER ADRIATIC	317
26.	CENTRAL ITALY AND "VANDAL" OPERATION	325
27.	THE GOTHIC LINE	340
28.	GREECE—THE BACKGROUND	361
29.	7 BRIGADE IN MACEDONIA	366
30.	5 BRIGADE IN ATHENS	373
31.	GREECE—11 BRIGADE IN THE PELOPONNESE	381
32.	GREECE—THE LAST PHASE	389
33.	EPILOGUE—"PUNJAB BOUNDARY FORCE"	401

CHARTS AND DIAGRAMS

	PAGE
SIDI BARRANI	17
SUDAN AND ERITREA	26
KEREN BATTLEFIELD	38
BATTLEAXE OPERATION	58
ADVANCE ON DAMASCUS	68
SALUM—TOBRUK	88
THE DJEBEL ACHDAR	110
ASSAULT ON TOBRUK	168
THE BATTLE OF EL ALAMEIN	194
TUNISIAN CAMPAIGN	205
MARETH LINE OPERATIONS	212
WADI AKARIT	218
ARTILLERY COMMUNICATIONS	242
ASSAULT ON CASSINO	281
CASSINO HILLSIDE BATTLEFIELD	294
CENTRAL ITALY	328
THE GOTHIC LINE	344
NORTHERN GREECE	388
THE PUNJAB	404

It is fitting that the history of the Fourth Indian Division should have been written, and so well and attractively written. For the fame of this Division will surely go down as one of the greatest fighting formations in military history: to be spoken of with such as The Tenth Legion, The Light Division of the Peninsular War, Napoleon's Old Guard.

A mere summary of its record is impressive: in five years it fought nine campaigns, travelled more than 15,000 miles, suffered over 25,000 casualties, captured upwards of 150,000 prisoners. Its campaigns include the great victory of Sidi Barrani, that began the destruction of Graziani's army; the storming of the natural fortress of Keren and the clearing of the Italians from their colony of Eritrea; the capture of Damascus, which was a turning-point in the struggle for Syria; a wonderful fighting retreat from Benghazi when less confident and well-trained troops might have despaired and succumbed; a share in the El Alamein Victory; a more decisive rôle in forcing the Mareth Line, and again in the final victories of Tunisia; a gallant costly assault at Cassino against defences even more formidable than at Karen or Mareth; the successful breaching of the Gothic Line; and finally a task in Greece of composing civil disturbance that called for diplomacy and discipline as much as for fighting. And the discipline of the Division, based on the pride all felt in themselves and their achievements, was outstanding. It expressed itself by staunchness in battle and by good behaviour and smartness of appearance off the battlefield. It withstood even the supreme test of the period of communal troubles in the Punjab in 1947, when the Division strove impartially to prevent the massacres and to restore order. This was its last and its hardest service.

The Fourth Indian Division has a claim on history even beyond its fighting reputation. It represents the culmination of one of the finest warrior forces ever created, the old Indian Army, with its mixture of British and Indian units. The brigades of the Fourth Indian Division had throughout each one British battalion, and the artillery of the Division was British. Between British and Indians was a true spirit of comradeship, of mutual trust in battle, of fellowship in camp and bivouac. Many instances of this will be found recorded in this book.

The old Indian Army, in which all creeds and races of Indians served together with British in mutual trust and concord, is gone for ever. But its memories and traditions will remain, and its proud history in many countries and on many fields. The record of the Fourth Indian Division in this volume will show that Indian Army at its highest and finest.

Those who fought under the sign of the Red Eagle will always be justly proud of it; and those commanders who, like myself, have known the worth in the field of that magnificent Division, will be the first to acknowledge their debt of gratitude, and to salute one of the greatest bands of fighting men who have ever served together in this troubled world of wars and warriors.

August 1948.

Wavell F-M

AUTHOR'S NOTE

This history begins with Fourth Indian Division as a mobilization skeleton. It ends when its constituent units have been absorbed in the Armed Forces of India and Pakistan. That the book closes with the termination of British Command of Indian forces is coincidental.

Chapter 1

THE BEGINNINGS.

AS the unmistakeable clouds of the Fascist menace began to loom on the world horizon, the Committee of Imperial Defence requested the Government of India to accept additional responsibilities and in event of emergency to designate two brigade groups for overseas service.

In response to this request an earlier deployment scheme, known as PINK PLAN evolved during 1934/35 into SCHEME HERON (the despatch of 11 Ahmednagar Infantry Brigade to Egypt) and SCHEME EMU (the movement of 12 Secunderabad Infantry Brigade to Malaya). Fourth Indian Division — at this time no more than a paper formation, a mobilization skeleton — was selected as foster parent of these expeditionary forces. Thus a name destined to win enduring fame on the battlefield came into existence to satisfy a routine necessity.

The Government of India previously had undertaken to underwrite certain Imperial commitments. These commitments were widespread. The original memorandum of the Committee of Imperial Defence designated (1) Singapore (2) Burma (3) Persian Gulf (4) Egypt and (5) "elsewhere" as areas which it might be necessary to reinforce at top speed. Two plans for mobilisation and despatch of troops were prepared. It is interesting to note that the planners were prepared to find the seas unsafe. An alternative routing for the movement of Indian troops to Egypt had been devised by way of ship to Basra, rail to Baghdad, and lorries across the Arabian deserts.

These plans were no more than in the egg when on the evening of September 28th, 1938, a thunderbolt came over the wire into Headquarters, Deccan District, the home territory of the newly hatched Fourth Indian Division. It was the agreed signal for a state of emergency. The startled officers sat in conference far into the night, intent on conjuring men, arms and equipment out of thin air. Even as the wheels began to turn a stand-down order arrived. In the breathing space which followed, planning continued. "SCHEME HERON" evolved to "R PLAN" and Egypt became "R4" destination. The projected garrison force for Middle East was increased to two brigades and a Divisional Headquarters. 5 Jhansi Infantry Brigade was designated as the second formation for Egypt. Unfortunately chronic shortages of equipment prevented the immediate mechanisation of 5 Brigade and frustrated plans for its speedy preparation for overseas service.

In May 1939, Major-General the Hon. P. G. Scarlett, MC, commander-designate of Fourth Indian Division, attended a conference in Middle East at which details of the employment of Indian troops in that theatre were discussed. General Scarlett was on his way to England at the time and few in India knew of this meeting. In midsummer the tension in Europe mounted and on July 26th the critical signal once more flashed to Ahmednagar. This time there was no retraction. The first brigade group of Fourth Indian Division was given four days in which to make ready for overseas. On July 30th, when packs and limbers had been squared for travel, an innocuous message concerning NAAFI stores contained the significant word "Egypt" *

On July 31st, Brigadier A. B. McPherson, MVO, MC, led out 2 Cameron Highlanders (Lieut-Col. A. Anderson, MC), 1/6 Rajputana Rifles (Lieut-Col. L. S. Bell-Syer), 4/7 Rajput Regiment (Lieut-Col. A. B. Blaxland) and 4 Field Regiment R.A. (Lieut-Col. L. F. Thompson, MC) — the original units of 11 Indian Infantry Brigade Group. On August 2nd, three transports sailed from Bombay. Eleven days later, through the shimmering heat, the sepoys saw the desolate Egyptian ridges closing up on one bow, the bleak Sinai wastes on the other. Next morning the transports dropped anchor in Port Tewfik. Within a few hours the Brigade Group had settled under canvas at Fayid Camp.

The peace had but nineteen days to live. Nevertheless on September 3rd, when the momentous message came, only the principal enemy took the field. Four hundred miles to the west of the Nile, in their camps along the Libyan frontier, the Italian garrisons continued to saunter through their customary routines. On September 19th an advance reconnaissance party from 11 Brigade proceeded to Western Desert. They took the road so many came to know so well, turning north at the Pyramids across a hundred miles of hard sand to the causeway over the magenta lagoons behind Alexandria, thence west through the rolling dunes which skirted the bright thunderous Mediterranean, past scattered date oases and fig plantations, until beyond the dusty hamlet of Burgh el Arab the road rose to the crest of the dunes and along the easy valley inland a train snorted up to a sun-bitten drought-stricken halt whose name, (which did not matter then), was El Alamein. Forty miles farther on at El Daba Divisional officers met for the first time the bronzed and cheerful officers and men of 7 Armoured Division, who had kept watch for years in the sandy wastes; who knew more about the desert and its ways than anyone alive; who having taken as their emblem the Libyan jerboa, were destined to be known as The Desert Rats as long as memory remains.

*12 Indian Brigade, the most advanced unit of Fourth Indian Division in training, proceeded to Singapore on the outbreak of war. There it later achieved a magnificent fighting reputation. For purposes of record this brigade consisted of 2 Argyll & Sutherland Highlanders, 5/2 Punjab Regiment, 5/14 Punjab Regiment, 4/19 Hyderabad Regiment, under command of Brigadier A.C.M. Paris, MC, who was drowned at sea during escape from Malaya.

THE BEGINNINGS

Thus Fourth Indian Division came to a battlefield on which it was destined to find fame. Western Desert, between Nile Delta and the Gulf of Sirte, once a naked and desolate expanse, was no longer empty upon the maps. British officers in search of adventure and against the day of battle had charted its maze of age-old trails, had plotted its contours and had defined even its most insignificant features. Of the traditional soft burning sand of the Sahara, they had found little, save in the Great Sand Sea far to the south. But there were vast stretches of hard sand and of stony ground raddled with black basaltic slabs; there were bony ridges and ribbed escarpments and deep depressions; there were flat pans which held water after the rains, where gazelles cropped the coarse grass in midsummer. There were wadi-fed flats which sprang over-night into flowery glory in spring; there were endless undulating sand and gravel dunes whose crests marched in rhythm, like waves at sea.

To the tyro these wastes held no landmarks, but desert-worthy soldiers used their compasses only to check their navigation. They steered by the *birs,* the curious cisterns of antiquity, the *alems,* the Senussi direction cairns, the *gabirs,* the reputed tombs, the *ghots,* the circular potholes and the *mengers,* the kopje-like mounds which the mirage sometimes lifted into mid-air. These features gave the desert character and harsh habitation though it remained, there are few who lived and fought there who have not forgotten its worst and remembered its best. On many it cast a spell which did not pass. The days of burning heat and intolerable glare, while the mirage blocked the horizon with Braille-like formations; the cool dark nights, with the incomparable pageant of the heavens wheeling overhead; the choking sandstorms, the marrow-sucking *khamsins,* the intolerable pestilence of flies, the clammy fingers of night mists, all played their part in moulding the character of the desert soldier. Skins might burn, lips might crack, eyeballs might sear, throats might parch, but amid the sandy wastes life flowed with riotous vigour. The code of social intercourse was simple. An Indian Army officer wrote:

"Your chief concern is not to endanger your comrade."

"Because of the risk that you may bring him, you do not light fires after sunset."

"You do not use his slit trench at any time."

"Neither do you park your vehicle near the hole in the ground in which he lives."

"You do not borrow from him, and particularly you do not borrow those precious fluids, water and petrol."

"You do not give him compass bearings which you have not tested and of which you are not sure."

"You do not leave any mess behind that will breed flies."

"You do not ask him to convey your messages, your gear, or yourself unless it is his job to do so."

"You do not drink deeply of any man's bottles, for they may not be replenished. You make sure that he has many before you take his cigarette."

"You do not ask information beyond your job, for idle talk kills men."

"You do not grouse unduly, except concerning the folly of your own commanders. This is allowable. You criticise no other man's commanders."

"Of those things which you do do, the first is to be hospitable and the second is to be courteous. The day is long in the desert and there is time to be helpful to those who share your adventure. A cup of tea, therefore, is proffered to all comers — it is your handshake and your badge of association. Over the tea mugs the good-mannered guest transacts his business expeditiously, gossips shop for a little, and gets him gone."

"This code is the sum of fellowship in the desert. It knows no rank nor any exception."

As 11 Brigade savoured this new world, back in India "R" PLAN was changed to "K" Force and Fourth Indian Division rapidly completed its establishment. Within a fortnight of the outbreak of war Divisional Headquarters and a second Brigade Group awaited movement orders. General Scarlett was already in Egypt. His staff comprised Brigadier N. M. de la P. Beresford-Peirse, DSO, as CRA, Colonel W. L. Lloyd, MC, as GSO.1, Colonel D. F. Murphy, MC, as ADMS. Lieut.-Col. R. V. Cutler, MBE, MC, was in command of the Sappers and Miners, Lieut-Col. C. M. F. White, DSO, in charge of the Royal Signals. Colonel H. F. C. McSwiney, DSO, MC, was the Division's first A.A. & Q.M.G.

On September 23rd Divisional Headquarters and 5 Indian Brigade group from Jhansi assembled to take ship at Bombay. Under Brigadier T. J. Ponting, MC, 1 Royal Fusiliers (Lieut-Col. C. R. Johnston), 3/1 Punjab Regiment (Lieut-Col. J. B. Dalison) and 4/6 Rajputana Rifles (Lieut-Col. W. A. L. James) filed aboard. With them came 1 Field Regiment, R.A. thus inaugurating a proud and happy association with an outstanding unit which lasted throughout the war. No animals were taken, but by dint of special efforts the Divisional troops and 5 Brigade embarked fully equipped with motor transport and weapons. *

Nevertheless substantial adjustments were necessary to meet the needs of desert warfare. These changes on more than one occasion called for patience and ingenuity. Thus when Lieut-Colonel White's Signals establishment expanded overnight from six to twenty-six despatch riders, he was highly pleased, but when he was sent twenty muleteers in lieu of trained motor cyclists, his experienced personnel

*The preface to "The Tiger Strikes" implies that Indian troops reached Middle East with little more than rifles and bayonets. This was not the case. 11 Brigade had drawn transport in Egypt and when Fourth Indian Division coalesced as a striking force it was well-found and well-armed.

were much too busy instructing the newcomers to carry his messages. Specialist weapons, such as mortars and anti-tank rifles and specialist services, such as water points, recovery sections, blood banks and pick-up vans, were very new and strange. But the basic training of Indian troops had been sufficiently flexible to afford easy comprehension of new devices and quick mastery of the technique of their employment.

Fourth Indian Division, two brigades strong, mustered under the shadow of the Pyramids, with headquarters in the famous Mena House and with Divisional units strung out as far as Beni Yusef, five miles away. With a static front in Europe and the Italians still uncommitted, there was time to train and to organise. First to be considered were the implications of soldiering in boundless wastes of thirsty sand. Army housekeeping was transformed into Navy housekeeping, with the vehicle, like the ship, the paramount concern of its crew. The warfare likewise was naval warfare, in which mobility was everything and location a minor consideration. New concepts of distances and of speed of movement became inevitable. In this readjustment experience gained in decades of bickering along the North West Frontier proved invaluable. The Indian brigades were able to develop new routines without undue delay or dislocation.

The particular difficulties of the supply and transport services should be recorded. In Egypt the importance of these ancillary units burgeoned overnight. This evolution was not achieved without certain growing pains. The sepoy driver, often a new hand at the wheel, had been dropped in a strange land, where he was compelled to drive on what was to him the wrong side of the road. He also had to drive where there were no roads, over soft sand, hard sand, quicksand, scrabbly ridges and naked rock. He had to learn to navigate on a compass bearing, to steer by almost imperceptible landmarks, to keep formation and direction by feel, to be miserly with liquids both for himself and for his vehicle, to devise safe and easy ways of leaguering and of taking cover, to learn the tricks of air-spotting and of evasion under air attack. He had to extricate himself from every manner of mischance by the aid of his native wits and with such home-made devices as might be conjured out of nothing. Moreover he had to work for endless hours at a miscellany of tasks — a very different routine to the easy division of labour to which he had been accustomed. All difficulties, however, were eventually overcome and the grant of combatant status to the RIASC brought home to all ranks the proud assurance that the supply services hereafter would be full partners in the business of battle.

The infantry and the other combatant arms required less radical adjustments. The desert afforded terrain on which problems of man management and organised encounter could be worked out under almost ideal conditions. The ever-altering face of war never obscures its basic principles; in such principles the officers and men of Fourth Indian Division had been drilled and disciplined to a high standard of efficiency. Much was still to be learned—the problems of artillery and air co-operation, the mechanics of combined infantry-armour operations, the tactics of fluid defence. When exercises began in the desert the sepoys and their officers proved equally versatile and adaptable. With toughened bodies came toughened minds, capable of coping with the tensions and variations of modern warfare. The keenness and adaptability of all ranks was so marked that in a remarkably short time Fourth Indian Division was in shape to take the field as a mechanised formation.

A glance through the routine orders of these early months in Egypt reveals the ease and alacrity with which the newcomers settled into harness in a strange country. Serious crime was non-existent. (From the beginning to the end of the Middle East campaign only the South Africans vied with Indian troops in model behaviour). Early admonitions dealt with trivia. Sepoys were forbidden to buy the ornate rather than lethal Egyptian stilettoes. Joy-riding on flat cars and on the tops and steps of trains, a universal Egyptian pastime, likewise was put under ban. Stones were not to be gathered or moved without permission of the Mamour of the area. When the ardent sun-worshippers from Australia and New Zealand arrived and stripped to the buff, Indian units were warned that such exposure would not be tolerated. "The chest will not be bared" said an instruction, "and troops proceeding on leave to the Pyramids will do so in the recognised recreation dress of the unit."

The Egyptian populace quickly recognised the correct and soldierly behaviour of the Indians and reacted in friendly fashion. Moslem troops were first to find friends, but after acquaintance the bond of religion proved a minor tie; the Indian Mussalmans discovered their Egyptian brethren to be anything but austere in the Faith. Numerous prominent Egyptians, notably Sayed Bakri Bey, head of the Sufi sect, organised entertainment for the strangers in their midst and laid the foundation for a comprehensive programme of amenities. These hospitable efforts were supplemented by Divisional officers who promoted games, wangled leave transport, installed camp cinemas and arranged hostelry accommodation for Indian personnel in Cairo. Many of these facilities had not been available in India, a circumstance which created a favourable impression of foreign service in the minds of the sepoys and contributed substantially to their high morale.

On December 12th, 1939, the War Office designated that "the left mudguard of vehicles of Fourth Indian Division shall carry a red eagle, painted on a black background."* Thus originated a symbol which became famous around the world.

*The War Office, curiously enough, has no record of the origin of the Red Eagle. It was the custom of units at this stage to select their own signs, afterwards submitting them for approval. There are a number of theories of origin: that the first design was taken from a newspaper advertisement, from a beer bottle label, that it was drawn by one Private Page, a clerk in "Q" Branch, that the colour was chosen because of General Scarlett's name. At a later date General Tuker personally improved the design of the eagle.

On January 26th General Scarlett relinquished command to Major-General Philip Neame, VC. On March 16th Brigadier R. A. Savory, MC, assumed command of 11 Brigade. During this month Divisional training began to spread afield. Australians and New Zealanders were attached to Fourth Division units and in turn undertook to give Indian formations training in newly-arrived specialist weapons. The Camerons of 11 Brigade inherited a fifth company from the Egyptian Army and platoons of 4/6 Rajputana Rifles moved to Mersa Matruh as instructors to newly-raised Arab legionaries. 1 Royal Northumberland Fusiliers were taken under command as the Divisional Machine Gun Battalion and 3 Royal Horse Artillery joined as the Divisional Anti-Tank Regiment. At the beginning of May 4/7 Rajputs and the Sappers and Miners Companies moved to Baqqush, where Western Desert Force Headquarters was in course of construction. A fortnight later 5 Indian Brigade took over lines of communication duties between Amiriya aerodrome, 15 miles west of Alexandria and Sidi Haneish station, 30 miles east of Mersa Matruh, thus assuming responsibility for 150 miles of coastal dunes. 11 Brigade, less 4/7 Rajputs, remained at Mena under GHQ command — the only reserve troops in all Egypt.

These moves were in rhythm with the times. Spring was at hand and spring was Hitler's hour. His Italian henchmen waited while Norway, Denmark, Holland and Belgium were struck down. Then with France reeling and the British Expeditionary Force backed against the Channel, Mussolini appeared on a balcony above the Piazza Venezia in Rome. An hysterical crowd had gathered, clamouring for war. On the evening of June 10th General Neame while dining with 5 Brigade Headquarters at El Daba received a telegram which sent him hurrying back to Cairo through the night. Africa was aflame.

On paper the odds in the Mediterranean theatre were appalling. From south and from west Egypt and the vital Suez artery was menaced by well over a half million enemy troops. Abyssinia and Eritrea were crammed with ten Italian divisions. In Libya Marshal Graziani marshalled over 300,000 men. Lieut.-General O'Connor, commanding Western Desert Force, could array against this host one incomplete armoured division, two brigades of Fourth Indian Division, together with scattered elements of British, Australian and New Zealand formations which barely comprised a division in all. The odds were more than five to one.

With Germans in command or with a leavening of German troops to stiffen them, the Italian armies might have converged on Egypt in overwhelming force, crushing the defenders by sheer weight of numbers. Cairo was a hive of Fifth Columnists and spies; the Italian High Command must have known to a man the strength of the British forces in Egypt. Fortunately the enemy's resolution failed to keep pace with his ambitions. From the beginning Marshal Graziani's attitude was that of a commander who must ponder profoundly and must move warily, as though pitfalls abounded everywhere. The strutting Duce might bellow "Avanti" from every balcony in Italy, but his generals in the field had no intention of making a dash for it. On the Libyan frontier the British screens were first on the move, probing and pin-pricking. This circumstance confirmed the Italian commanders in their caution and established a psychological advantage for their assailants which eventually influenced the issue of the campaign.

5 Indian Brigade in its scattered encampments along the coastal dunes was first to experience the alarums of war. Five wounded prisoners were brought into Daba dressing station on June 14th — the first enemies to be seen. 11 Hussars shortly afterwards passed back a second party of Italians from the Frontier which included a general and a number of women, one of whom gave birth to a child soon after capture.

On June 19th 4/6 Rajputana Rifles reported a queer find on the coast — a ship's raft which bore 34 pairs of waterproof trousers, 28 heavy tweed coats, a bale of white gloves and a roll of rubber tubing containing rockets. No clue to the origin of this miscellany was ever discovered. Air warnings were of daily occurrence, but nothing was seen until June 22nd, when two small bombs, one a dud, were dropped within a few hundred yards of the Indian encampment at El Daba. Camel patrols every now and then dashed back from the dunes with news of submarines offshore, warships on the horizon, mines washed up; but only empty seas and bare beaches confronted the investigators.

As Fourth Division squared away for the sterner tasks in view, a number of changes occurred. Early in June Brigadier Ponting had fallen ill and had been succeeded in command of 5 Brigade by the GSO.1, Brigadier W. L. Lloyd, MC. Colonel T. W. Rees, DSO, MC, replaced Brigadier Lloyd on Divisional Staff. When the Italian threat in East Africa developed, 4 Field Regiment R.A. left for Somaliland and 31 Field Regiment R.A. began its long association with Fourth Division. On August 5th Major-General Neame was called to another appointment. As its new commander the Division reclaimed one of its own in Major-General N. M. de la P. Beresford-Peirse, DSO, who had gone to Cairo on a staff appointment in June. At that time he had handed over command of the gunners to Brigadier P. Maxwell, MC. In September Brigadier W. H. B. Mirrlees, MC, succeeded Brigadier Maxwell as artillery commander.

Major-General Beresford-Peirse, who was destined to lead Fourth Indian Division in its first battles, was a Gunner of long family association with India, his father having served in the Royal Berkshire Regiment during the Afghanistan campaign of 1879. In the Great War of 1914-1918 he himself had served with 7 Indian Division. In 1939 his appointment was BRA Southern Command, India. Fourth Indian Division was indeed fortunate in securing such an outstanding officer as its first battle commander. He established the tradition of thoroughness and attention to detail which was to mean so much in the years to come. Possessing great drive he was withal an intensely human and sympathetic personality, inspiring a family feeling among the troops under his command.*

The stage was now set for the move forward. In the third week of August Captain Walter Hingston, GSO.III of the Division, was instructed to demarcate a tar barrel track between Kilo 42 on the Alexandria Road and Nagamish Nala, seven miles east of Mersa Matruh. On August 19th the Divisional convoys navigated across the desert for the first time. Keeping open formation and wary eyes on the sky, fleets of vehicles plodded all day across flat stony wastes intersected by abrupt ridges strewn with tilted rocky slabs. By nightfall 144 miles had been traversed and a watchful R.A.F. pilot had flashed some kind words on march discipline. By August 21st the Division had concentrated in its new area around the old Roman wells at Baqqush. A check-up reported ninety-nine out of every hundred vehicles to have arrived; only two per cent required repairs en route. With such propitious performance the Red Eagles took the field.

The first task was to continue work on the Baqqush-Naghamish defences. Fourth Division shifted to Naghamish where 16 British Infantry Brigade (Brigadier C. E. N. Lomax, DSO, MC), consisting of 1 Queen's Regiment, 2 Leicesters and 1 Argyll and Sutherland Highlanders, were taken under command. The first New Zealand battalions to arrive in Middle East had moved up to share in the task and at Naghamish began a long and memorable association with the dogged and dynamic men who wore the Silver Fern. While digging was in progress, Major Jennings-Bramley, a retired British officer who had chosen the dust-bitten hamlet of Burg el Arab as his retreat, drew the attention of Divisional officers to the possibilities of the El Alamein bottleneck as a defensive position. Initial reconnaissance disclosed the importance of this area, with profound results in years to come.

At Naghamish a deep nullah was transformed into an anti-tank ditch and a fortified "Box," designed to cover the coastal road, provided a "keep" position or bastion upon which mobile forces would pivot in a battle of manoeuvre. From this fortress troops might sally to attack any enemy operating against Mersa Matruh. While the British and Indian troops dug and trained earnestly, intelligence officers sifted the prodigious chaff of Rome Radio in search of grains of solid fact. Transport units pushed forward across the waterless wastes beyond Mersa Matruh for training with forward troops along the Libyan frontier. The returning RIASC drivers patronised their sepoy comrades who had not yet been within one hundred miles of the enemy.

The behaviour of that enemy still requires elucidation. For three months no attempt was made to invade Egypt. British armoured cars reconnoitred the chief camps on the crest of the Libyan escarpment

*After leaving Fourth Indian Division, General Beresford-Peirse served as Commander, Western Desert Force, Kaid in the Sudan, Corps Commander against the Japanese in Eastern Bengal in 1942, and as Army Commander Southern Command, India, 1942-44.

and reported no less than eight divisions to be concentrated there. In the Capuzzo and Salum areas strong defensive positions were being built. Why did the Italians fail to exploit their great numerical superiority? It seems possible that Hitler propounded some such enquiry to his Ally, for early in September a Hussar unit, piquetting the perimeter of one of the escarpment camps, reported characteristically. "Things" said the message "are beginning to hot up." On September 13th, long lines of transport defiled down the switchback at Salum and over the rugged trail at Halfaya. The invasion of Egypt had begun. Four days later Graziani wrote grandiloquently to Mussolini. He praised his own strategy highly. He had feinted with his right and had struck in the best Fascist fashion by the shortest route. He had gained a victory and now held Sidi Barrani, forty miles inside Egypt, on the road to Cairo. He said nothing of prisoners taken or casualties inflicted. They were few; but the invading forces had sustained substantial losses in brushes with British rearguards. The imperturbable young men of 7 Armoured Division counted noses and reported the advancing enemy to consist of two regular Italian divisions, two colonial divisions and one Blackshirt division.

Next day the war came for the first time to Fourth Indian Division. A group of Italian bombers strewed the Baqqush and Naghamish areas with thermos flask and shaving-stick anti-personnel bombs — vicious little contrivances which exploded when moved. An unwary officer and four other ranks were killed in picking up these missiles. Rough harrows towed by carriers were devised to deal with them but for some time natural curiosity took its toll and these booby traps retained considerable nuisance value.

When training entered the operational stage Fourth Indian Division discovered that it had been committed to a varied repertoire. Its first and immediate responsibility was the defence of Egypt, which called for training in mobile defence and the construction of fortifications. But should the enemy drive eastwards, the defenders did not propose to stand siege. Instead they would sally in an offensive-defensive operation, designed to intercept and destroy the invaders in the Mersa Matruh area. There was also the possibility that the Italians would stand fast along the Libyan frontier. Should this occur, the British forces would not tolerate stalemate but would advance to the attack. Thus three different strategical possibilities existed which postulated three different types of training — a circumstance which laid the foundation for the flexibility and all-round efficiency destined to characterise Fourth Indian Division thereafter.

Extensive schemes, practised by night and by day, inculcated the purposes of desert manoeuvres. 7 Royal Tank Regiment (Lieut.-Colonel R. M. Jerram, MC) with troops of the new heavy Infantry Assault tanks, was attached for combined exercises which supplied the rough shape of battles to be. Central India Horse (Lieut-Colonel J. G. Pocock), had arrived in Middle East in August as Divisional Cavalry, and after a spell of digging moved forward to learn the routine of

"Jock Columns" from those expert mentors, 11 Hussars. Central India Horse at this juncture only had soft-skinned vehicles. Nevertheless, Lieut.-Colonel Pocock and his men accepted the hurly-burly and risks of "Jock Column" outings with the same gusto and enthusiasm as their armoured comrades.*

Towards the end of September news came through that 7 Indian Brigade was on the water and would soon join the Division. With Brigadier H. R. Briggs in command, 4/11 Sikhs (Lieut-Col. J. J. Purves, MC), 3/15 Punjabis (Lieut-Col. A. H. Pollock, MC) and 4/16 Punjabis (Lieut-Col. S. S. Lavender) had sailed from Bombay on September 24th. 3/15 Punjabis, dropped at Aden as a garrison battalion, was destined to see early action in the Somaliland campaign. On arrival of the Indian units at Suez on October 12th, 1 Royal Sussex (Lieut-Col. J. M. H. Edye, DSO, MC) began its long and auspicious service in 7 Brigade. 25 Field Regiment R.A. completed the Brigade Group.

For some weeks, it seemed as though the seizure of the fishing village of Sidi Barrani had sufficed the Italians as a victory. British reconnaissance forces reported the enemy to be fortifying their new positions, instead of preparing to push on. In the arc of 40 miles between Sidi Barrani and the broken ground to the south-west where the Libyan escarpment sinks into the desert, groups of camps had sprung up. Deep inland the old Egyptian frontier cantonments of Sofafi formed the hub of a number of defended localities. Twenty miles to the north-east, Nibeiwa was held by a strong force. Due south of Sidi Barrani and less than five miles from the coastal road, Tummar West, Tummar East and Point 90 swarmed with busy workers, erecting entanglements, digging trenches and dugouts, emplacing guns and constructing vehicle shelters. Between the coastal road and the seashore Maktila Camp covered the approaches to Sidi Barrani from the east. Around the village itself and among the dunes at Buq Buq, fifteen miles to the rear, other substantial forces were stationed.

These camps were well stocked with ammunition, water and food, and their perimeters (except for certain inexplicable gaps) bristled with defensive obstacles. But as a whole their security depended upon mutual support, upon maintained communications, and upon the ability to reinforce rapidly any camp which might be assailed. The freedom with which 7 Armoured Division's fighting patrols probed and harassed these encampments, moving boldly among them and even penetrating their perimeters, exhibited the patent weakness of the Italian dispositions. As a result, General Wavell did not hesitate. Early in October he began to plan for an outright offensive against the enemy.

*Central India Horse throughout its period of overseas service maintained an admirable News Letter of a chatty yet informative type, which will be quoted frequently in this narrative. As an historical record it is unique in the Division.

As a preliminary to this operation infantry detachments began to find their way along the road already so familiar to Central India Horse and the RIASC — the 80 miles of dreary wasteland between Mersa Matruh and the watchful screen of 7 Armoured Division to the east of Sidi Barrani. On one such visit the Division drew first blood. On the night of October 21st, Lieutenant Cochrane debussed a raiding party of 2 Camerons on the outskirts of Maktila Camp. The Indian transport drivers, armed only with bayonets cajoled from the Highlanders, joined in the raid. Unfortunately the alarm was given prematurely and although eight vehicles were destroyed, the Camerons suffered seven casualties.

The pace began to quicken. British strength grew in the desert and at long last in the sky. On October 31st, when a substantial force of Italian planes attacked Naghamish, a group of Gladiators swam out of the east and engaged them. A highly spectacular and satisfactory dogfight ensued; the troops went mad with excitement. Nor was the excitement all on the ground; two British planes in the heat of manoeuvre rammed each other, the pilots parachuting to safety. Nine Italian machines were shot down for the loss of the two Gladiators.

Early in November the build-up for the attack on Sidi Barrani began. The essence of this bold enterprise, in which an outnumbered force advanced one hundred miles across waterless desert for an assault upon fortified positions, was secrecy and deception. Had 7 Armoured Division mounted the attack, the establishment of forward dumps and leaguers would have revealed its intentions. But if the enemy could be made familiar with training movements a hundred miles away, such routine exercises might lull his suspicions. Then at an appropriate moment the rehearsal might become the performance. Early in November large-scale manoeuvres began in the desert to the south of Mersa Matruh, for the double purpose of concealing General Wavell's plans and of training his men for the battle-to-be.

Throughout that month, when autumn brought a brave sting to the air, Fourth Indian Division re-enacted the assault on the Italian positions. The scheme possessed the simplicity of genius. Nibeiwa in the centre of the arc of camps would be first assailed. If this assault proved lengthy or costly, the offensive would be reduced to the dimensions of a raid and the operation terminated.* While Fourth Indian Division dealt with Nibeiwa, 7 Armoured Division would "keep the ring", containing the enemy in the Sofafi camps to the south and preventing reinforcements from Italian reserve positions on the Libyan escarpment. It was rightly assumed that an assault on Nibeiwa would not lead Graziani to shift his forces inland from Sidi Barrani and the Tummars and so weaken his grip on the vital coastal road. Should Nibeiwa fall, without delay Fourth Division

*A limit of 4 days and 50 per cent casualties was set in the early planning.

would swing north against the Tummar camps. Concurrently 7 Armoured Division would pivot on the left of the infantry battle and would strike to the north-west to cut all lines of retreat to Salum. The fall of Tummars would isolate the Maktila position and permit the investment of Sidi Barrani from three sides.

Months of tough training in the desert had given the Indian units every confidence in their ability to deal with enemy forces in battle. The approach march rather than the assault proper provided the conditional factors. Should the initial concentration be spotted and correctly interpreted, should 30,000 men in 5,000 vehicles be detected anywhere on the hundred mile trek forward, should the Italians be on the alert when the British and Indian troops deployed in battle positions, success would be jeopardized and the attacking forces assured of a warm welcome. A single enemy air patrol which read the evidence aright might make the difference between defeat and victory.

Nevertheless the odds against surprise were shorter than the situation deserved. The wellnigh complete mastery of the desert outside the encampment by the harriers and raiders of the support group of 7 Armoured Division had compelled the enemy commanders to rely upon the Regia Aeronautica for intelligence and reconnaissance. Undoubtedly they were badly served. Italian air observers had cried "Wolf!" until they had bred sceptics. It was afterwards discovered that on the crucial day of the approach to Sidi Barrani an enemy airman had returned to render true report, only to be told incredulously "to put more water in his wine next time".

British intelligence—thanks again to the ubiquitous Desert Rats—was comprehensive. Regular Italian divisions were identified at Sofafi and in reserve at Buq Buq, twenty-five miles behind Sidi Barrani. Nibeiwa was held by a mobile group of divisional strength under General Pietro Maletti, Graziani's expert in desert warfare. The Tummar camps were defended by 2 Libyan Division, which likewise provided the garrison for Point 90. Maktila was held by 1 Libyan Division, while Blackshirt divisions supplied battle and area reserves at Sidi Barrani and Salum. Two brigades of light and medium tanks (120 in all) were distributed among the camps, together with 250 guns of various calibres. The defending force totalled 80,000 infantry, of which 63,000 were Italians.

General Wavell could muster a striking force of 31,000 men, 120 guns and 225 tanks, including 50 of the heavily armoured Infantry Assault tanks. Against four enemy divisions on the immediate battlefield one British and two Indian brigades would advance to the assault. 11 Indian Brigade would open the battle by storming Nibeiwa. When a decision had been reached at this key camp, 5 Indian Brigade would move with all speed to attack the Tummar camps. Thereafter 16 British Brigade under Fourth Divisional command would follow through and drive on Sidi Barrani. On the coastal flank of the Division, Selby Force, an independent group from Mersa Matruh consisting of 3 Coldstream Guards, 7 Hussars, with elements of 1 Durhams, 1 South

Staffordshires and machine-gunners from 1 Northumberland Fusiliers and 1 Cheshires, would demonstrate against Maktila Camp in a not too convincing manner. (It is perhaps worth noting that for the first time in Western Desert Selby Force employed the useful device of dummy tanks). In the early stages of the action Central India Horse would keep touch with Selby Force: after the capture of Nibeiwa and the Tummars the Divisional cavalry would switch swiftly to the opposite flank as a mobile reserve to maintain contact with 7 Armoured Division when the Desert Rats advanced to effect a *coup de grace* by cutting the coastal road behind the Italian positions.

The artillery available for the attack—1, 25 and 31 Field Regiments RA together with 7 Medium Regiment RA, would remain mobile, travelling as a 'circus' and moving speedily from place to place to support the successive assaults. Having opened the ball with all available guns at Nibeiwa, Brigadier Mirrlees would shift his regiments as soon as the infantry assault went in, in order to array the artillery in support of 5 Brigade at the second objective.

7 Infantry Brigade would not arrive in the forward zone in time to participate in the battle. Its sole representative would be the anti-tank platoon of 4/16 Punjabis, which had been brought forward as Divisional troops. The remainder of Brigadier Briggs men took over lines of communications duties and protection of dump areas, with a forward battalion at Charing Cross, 7 miles west of Mersa Matruh.

On November 27th a conference under presidency of General O'Connor put the finishing touches to the battle plan. 'CORPS EXERCISE' was promulgated as the name of the real thing. Only essential divisional officers and brigade commanders had been put in the picture: the rendez-vous area was sealed off and officers forward were not allowed to return. Supply dumps were established along tracks known to be used by 7 Armoured Division. As far as possible the overworked R.A.F. squadrons piquetted the sky. The season was propitious, since the turn of the year promised low cloud ceilings with limited visibility. High winds might provide sandstorms and dust cover. Each of these possibilities shortened the odds. Given the luck, the long shot might come home.

The troops themselves were not troubling about odds. High adventure was in the air. This was 1940, when Britain and her Commonwealth associates stood alone against the might of the Fascist powers. London and the homeland were under fire and British civilians were enduring the malice of the enemy with a dour and indomitable courage which won the admiration of the world. The spirit of the Elizabethans once more stalked abroad and nowhere in greater ardour than among the 30,000 comrades of Wavell's striking force, soon to be committed to the supreme ordeal of battle. The months of isolation in the desert had bred a kinship between officer and man, between sepoy and British soldier, which dedicated their utmost strength to the common task. With high hearts and unshakeable confidence they awaited zero hour.

Chapter 2

SIDI BARRANI

AT first light on December 6th Fourth Indian Division moved out of its defensive positions west of Baqqush and headed into the open desert. Dawn broke chill and overcast, with a rising wind which whipped spinneys of sand across the plain. By mid-forenoon the dust had thickened into a veil which cloaked the flat wastes. Through the murk long lines of vehicles in diamond formation plodded forward. By 1500 hours the Division had reached Bir Kenayis on the Siwa trail 30 miles to the south-west of Mersa Matruh. Here the units dispersed over 30 to 40 square miles and remained at rest for 36 hours. Their advance had been undetected. When at rest the widely scattered formations suggested troops on routine exercises rather than arrayed for a quick and imminent stroke.

On December 7th the secret was out. Junior officers and men learnt that the rehearsals were over and that the curtain was about to rise. As the Division would be on the move at dawn next day, (Sunday, December 8th), Padre Walters with HQ 5 Brigade held early Communion on the Saturday morning. The service, in the open desert was well attended. Half way through, an Italian aircraft appeared overhead. There was a moment of hesitation; should all remain still or take to slit trenches? All remained still. The service continued and the Italian aircraft proceeded on its course. That morning General O'Connor arrived, bringing special messages of encouragement and good wishes from the Prime Minister and from the Commander-in-Chief. General Beresford-Peirse visited each Brigade Headquarters with last minute instructions and advice. Tense excitement gripped all ranks.

The night of December 7th was bitterly cold. At dawn the men drew their chilled and cramped limbs from slit trenches and from under vehicles. The wind had fallen and the bowl of the sky was clear. Now came the crucial hours of the approach. Sixty miles of bare desert separated Fourth Division from its deployment area. No reconnaissance plane could miss the cruising pattern of 5,000 vehicles. The R.A.F. had sent up every available machine to pin down enemy observation flights, yet it seemed incredible that throughout the day no specks appeared in the west, to bank sharply and to streak home with the momentous tidings. Hour by hour the formations crawled forward, avoiding used tracks in order to keep down dust. In the afternoon the sky clouded over and at 1530 hours the Division concentrated without incident 15 miles to the south-west of Nibeiwa.

Here 5 and 16 Brigades settled down to wait. The remainder of the Division paused only until dusk fell, when guides from 7 Armoured Division arrived to lead the infantry of 11 Brigade, the four artillery regiments, and the tanks of 7 Royal Tank Regiment to their battle positions. 4/7 Rajputs were detached to demonstrate in a feint attack against the eastern perimeter of Nibeiwa. The remainder of the brigade group swung into the north-west through the Bir Enba gap, in a detour which carried the striking force about 5 miles to the south of their objective. Here the artillery regiments were dropped, to move up and align in their gun positions. The infantry and tanks continued their march until two hours before dawn, when they halted within four miles of the north-west entrance to the camp. Quietly, rapidly, the columns redeployed in battle order. Thanks in part to low flying aircraft which droned overhead, in part to the tumult and fireworks display which from 0300 hours onwards 4/7 Rajputs evoked along the eastern perimeter, and in part to the casualness of the Italian sentries, who dismissed the noises in the night as those of routine reconnaissance by 7 Armoured Division, 44 tanks, 72 guns and 5,000 men had closed undetected upon their quarry. An hour before dawn General Beresford-Peirse and Brigadier Savory moved forward and took position on a small hillock. At 0630 hours the grey tide of dawn flooded upwards in the eastern sky. 2,000 yards away Nibeiwa lay sleeping. Lieut.-Colonel A. Anderson, MC., of the Camerons, so described the objective:

"The camp was roughly rectangular in shape, and covered an area of approximately 2,400 by 1,800 yards. The defence perimeter was complete all the way round, except for a small gap in the north-west corner, and built up in the form of a wall with sangars. The absence of loose rock probably accounted for the shortage of 'Dragons' Teeth' around the camp. A special type of anti-tank obstacle had been constructed on the eastern and southern faces. Anti-tank minefields were laid all around the camp except on the north-western face. There were no wire obstacles. Machine gun and anti-tank gun emplacements were built in every twenty-five yards of perimeter, about a hundred and fifty in all—twice as many emplacements as any other camp possessed. The centre of the camp was a mass of earthworks with a few tents and about 250 vehicles widely dispersed".

On such scene the Divisional artillery at 0700 hours began to register. Simultaneously the British armour moved forward with a battery of 25 Field Regiment under command, to snipe or cast smoke shell as required. Only then did the Italians come to life, rushing to man their weapons. It was too late: rank on rank of tanks came rolling out of the desert, with Bren carriers out-riding on their flanks, their machine guns uptilted in high angle fire. Gathering momentum as it closed, this modern commando charge thundered into the north-western gap in the defences.

The rush won home with unexpected ease. No guns had been laid to cover the western approaches of Nibeiwa, the perimeter in that sector was unmined, the ramps and ditches easily negotiable. The heavily

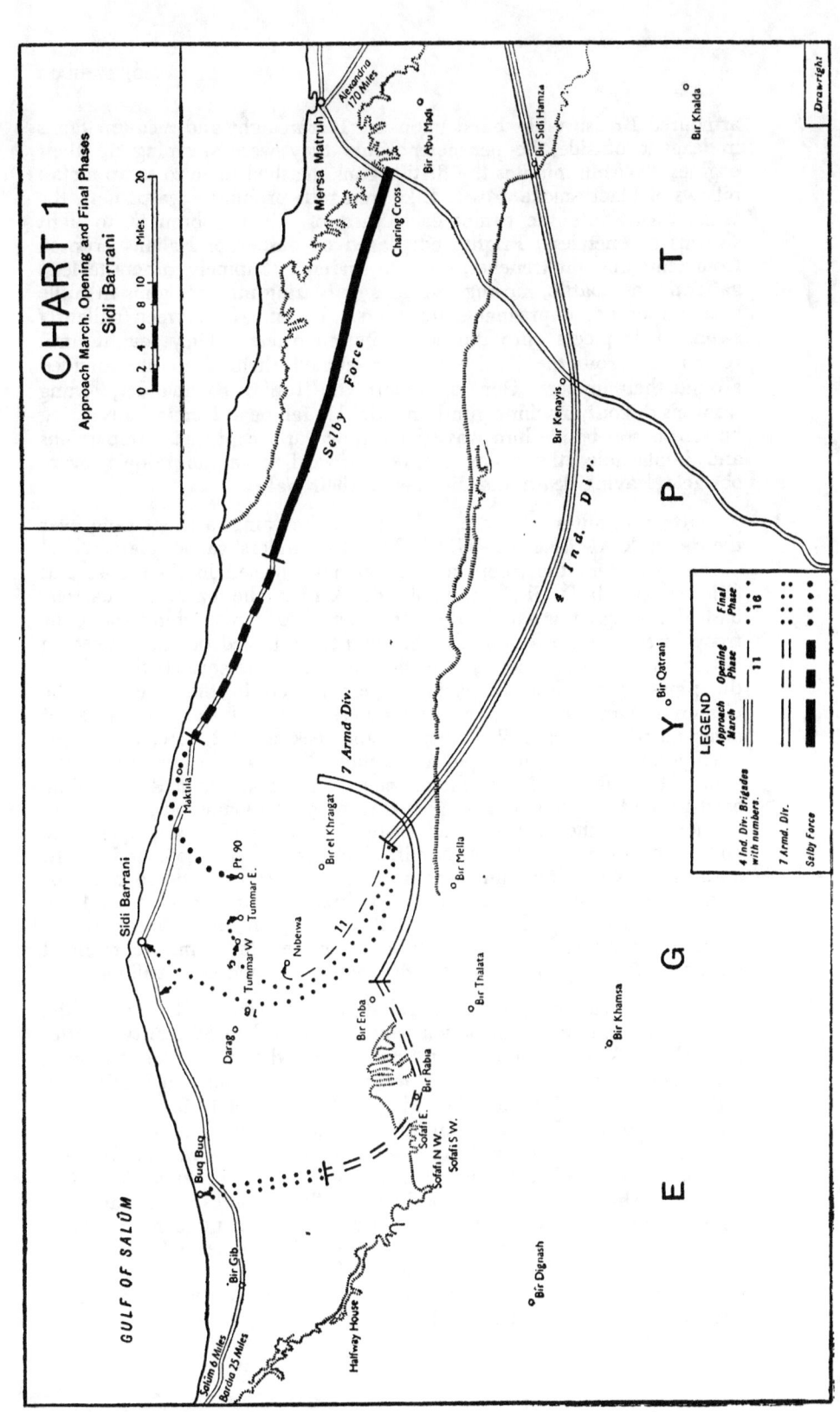

armoured British tanks burst upon the Italian light and medium tanks in leaguer outside the perimeter while they were warming up their engines. Within minutes the British guns smashed them to scrap metal: billows of black smoke arose. Like iron rods probing a wasps nest, the tanks thrust into the camp; each yard of advance brought to light swarms of enemies. Frightened, dazed or desperate Italians erupted from tents and slit trenches, some to surrender supinely, others to leap gallantly into battle, hurling grenades or blazing machine-guns in futile belabour of the impregnable intruders. Italian artillerymen gallantly swung their pieces onto the advancing monsters. They fought until return fire from the British tanks stretched them dead or wounded around their limbers. General Maletti, the Italian commander, sprang from his dugout, machine-gun in hand. He fell dead from an answering burst; his son beside him was struck down and captured. Impervious and implacable, the tanks ground forward, trampling down every obstacle, leaving death and disorder in their wake.

Fifteen minutes after the tanks struck the camp, a shout rang over the radio: "CAMERONS—GO!" The Highlanders' carrier platoon shot ahead in screen; the troop-carrying lorries wheeled in their dust and followed on the trail. Gradually quickening the pace, the carriers flashed through the gap in the perimeter; 500 yards behind them the troop lorries whipped about. The infantry tumbled out and raced in hotfoot with the bayonet; above the noise of battle shrilled the skirl of the pipes as the gravely pacing pipers played in the charge. The Camerons burst upon a scene of indescribable confusion, as masses of demoralised Italians milled about, some seeking to escape, others belatedly endeavouring to organize resistance. Hundreds threw up their hands at the first flicker of the bayonets. 1/6 Rajputana Rifles, riding hard to the hunt, followed in, passed through the Camerons, and began to mop up in the northern and eastern expanses of the camp. Here and there brave or hysterical handfuls refused the summons and fought until shot down, but within an hour resistance was over. Some hundreds of dead and wounded lay among the débris and litter; more than 4,000 prisoners, including 80 officers, huddled in sullen and shaken groups. 23 tanks, together with some scores of lorries and guns, represented material captures. British and Indian casualties had been trifling.

From his vantage point General Beresford-Peirse had followed the progress of the tide of destruction which engulfed Nibeiwa. Fifty minutes after the tank onset the decision was secure; whereupon the Divisional Commander hastened to set the remainder of his men in motion. 5 Indian Brigade, which had followed up in the wake of 11 Brigade, moved off as pre-arranged in a détour to the west of the Tummar group of camps. 16 Brigade followed to a reserve position to the west of Nibeiwa. 7 Royal Tank Regiment, eager for the next encounter, endeavoured to break out through the camp perimeter. Seven tanks shed tracks on mines. Sergeant Scobie of the Camerons Pioneer platoon, who had never examined a mine in his life, came to the rescue and cleared the way, raising several mines personally before allowing his men to deal with them. The undamaged tanks wriggled through the gap, refuelled and hurried off on the trail of 5 Brigade.

General Beresford-Peirse had called for the next assault to go in at 1100 hours—a time table which reflected the optimism in the air. This programme, if carried out, might have ended the battle of Sidi Barrani in a single day. As the columns swung into the north-west, the Italian Air Force arrived and lost several machines in rash dive-bombing attacks. One of the Divisional artillery reconnaissance parties, on passing Tummar West, reported the parapet of that camp to be lined with soldiery peering into the south, aware from the columns of dust and smoke that something had occurred but still ignorant of the menace at hand. The rising wind had thickened the air with sand, which while blinding the Italians also reacted unfavourably on the attacking forces. All reconnaissance groups had difficulty in locating their objectives. Both Brigadier Lloyd and Brigadier Mirrlees, emerging from the murk to find large camps spread before them, could not be certain whether Tummar West, Tummar East or Point 90 confronted them. Nevertheless by 1200 hours 5 Brigade was in correct position to the north-west of Tummar West. At the same hour the "I" tanks arrived, laden with stores from Nibeiwa and bearing chalked notices in Italian on their sides inviting surrender. 25 Field Regiment likewise joined 5 Brigade, while the remainder of the artillery took up battle positions as at Nibeiwa, to the south of the camp. By 1330 hours all was in readiness. Five minutes later a concentration of all available guns crashed upon Tummar West.

This encampment was an oyster-shaped expanse about two miles in length, with a tongue of ground running into the west. An anti-tank ditch encircled its low parapet, but there were many gaps; neither ditch nor ramps presented serious obstacles. Once again the British tanks bored in, shooting up vehicles, strong points and dugout entrances. Once again the Italian artillerymen fought with extreme valour, dying around their guns. Twenty minutes behind the tanks New Zealand lorries of 4 Reserve M.T. Company, bearing 1 Royal Fusiliers, closed up. Coming under distant machine-gun fire the troop carriers stepped up their speed to thirty miles an hour and raced to within 150 yards of the camp. Out sprang the infantry; to a man the Kiwi drivers deserted their vehicles and charged beside the Fusiliers, thus inaugurating the long and memorable association in battle of Fourth Indian and 2 New Zealand Divisions.*

As the British troops hurdled the ramps a blaze of small arms fire swept many to ground. Captain J. W. Fisher, leading the foremost company, was struck down. At a string of dugouts near the centre of the camp bitter fighting ensued. Lieut.-Colonel C. R. Johnston was mortally wounded; Captain MacDonald and his subaltern were slain by a Libyan who threw a grenade after surrendering. The Fusiliers battled steadily forward, but in the north-east and south-east corners of the camp resolute groups stood at bay. 3/1 Punjabis, arriving on schedule twenty minutes after Royal Fusiliers, sprang into the fray.

*Lieut. Lomax, a New Zealand medical officer who accompanied the troop carrying section, entered Tummar West and offered his services, which were gratefully accepted by 17 Indian Field Ambulance.

After overcoming fierce opposition, 'A' Company (Sikhs) reached the south-eastern perimeter of the camp, having captured a general and thirteen senior officers who emerged, booted and spurred, from a concrete dugout. Scrimmages continued until the carrier platoons arrived to reinforce the mopping up squads. By 1600 hours resistance had ceased. 2 Libyan Division had been destroyed and 2,000 prisoners taken, again with negligible losses to Fourth Indian Division.

A great victory was in the air. Within forty minutes of opening the attack on Tummar West, Brigadier Mirrlees pushed forward a few sniping guns to aid the mopping-up, swung the remainder of his artillery thirty degrees and began to register on Tummar East. Having ploughed through their first objective, the remaining "I" tanks, sixteen in number, lumbered off to support 4/6 Rajputana Rifles who had been designated to head the assault on the next objective. As the infantry in cruising formation rounded the north-east corner of Tummar West, a substantial enemy force sallied from Tummar East and bore across the gap of open desert between the camps. Two light tanks, followed by a considerable body on foot, swung against the right-hand company of the Rajputana Rifles, while six lorry-loads of Italians escorted by six light tanks continued across their front, heading for the eastern perimeter of Tummar West. In an instant the desert resounded with the crackle of small arms fire; a platoon of Northumberland Fusilier machine gunners attached to 5 Brigade brought their weapons to bear and mowed down the unprotected infantry. Three lorry loads of these Italians managed to reach Tummar West where they hurled themselves against 'A' Company 3/1 Punjabis. A well-placed Bren gun caused havoc among these reinforcements. This fruitless excursion cost the enemy 400 killed and wounded in less than ten minutes.

As the survivors fled, 4/6 Rajputana Rifles resumed their advance on Tummar East. The "I" tanks, approaching their battle positions by a different route, missed the scrimmage on the plain and arrived first at the rendezvous; whereupon they opened the attack unsupported, wreaking characteristic destruction. Dusk was closing rapidly, and through casualties and mechanical ailments less than a dozen runners remained in action. At 1730 hours armour and mopping-up squads were recalled into leaguer for the night, 500 yards to the north-east of Tummar West.

Thus, ten hours after the opening salvoes of the battle, the Italian forces in the coastal area faced destruction. At Nibeiwa the Camerons guarded more than 7,000 prisoners. Several hundred dead lay sprawled amid the wreckage of the camps and more than a thousand wounded enemies had been picked up. Forty tanks had been knocked out, over a hundred guns and several hundred vehicles captured. In the destruction of two enemy divisions, Fourth Indian Division had lost 5 officers and 17 men killed, 5 officers and 47 men wounded.

General O'Connor, the Corps Commander, arrived at Fourth Indian Division Headquarters, now in Tummar West, at 1700 hours. In conference with General Beresford-Peirse he recast the battlefield. It was obvious that the key to decisive victory lay in blocking the roads leading westwards from Sidi Barrani. As soon as dawn broke 16 Brigade was ordered to move against these objectives. 11 Brigade would assist if necessary. 5 Brigade would complete the reduction of the Tummars and afterwards of Point 90.

During the night General Beresford-Peirse concentrated his Division for the next phase. 16 Brigade, now due to enter the battle, had moved up to within five miles of Sidi Barrani. With 1 and 31 Field Regiments under command Brigadier Lomax waited for daylight to open his attack. 11 Brigade together with 7 Medium Regiment and Central India Horse had been moved into Divisional reserve. 5 Brigade was concentrated at Tummar West, with 25 Field Regiment in support, and with seven "I" tanks still in action; from their leaguer outside the camp, 4/6 Rajputana Rifles, with the remaining five runners of 7 Royal Tank Regiment, contained Tummar East. At Maktila 1 Libyan Division continued to be engrossed by the attentions of Selby Force. For the present stage Point 90 was ignored. All strength was concentrated against Sidi Barrani.

At first light, in a heavy sandstorm, 16 Brigade moved to the north in lorries, with Argyll and Sutherland Highlanders (Lieut.-Col. R. C. B. Anderson, MC) leading.* Brigadier Lomax was not entirely happy. Neither his artillery nor his tanks had established contact, although they were known to be in the vicinity. (All three missing units had leaguered within a thousand yards of his headquarters during the night). The objective lay 3½ miles ahead. Less than half this distance had been covered when the columns came under heavy close-range shell fire. Debussing, the Highlanders went to ground. As day broke, Italian gunners could be seen from Brigade Headquarters firing over open sights. Many vehicles were hit, and 2 Leicesters, hurrying up on the flank of the Highlanders, likewise were pinned down. The British anti-tank guns, coming into action in the open, fought back gallantly, but were no match for the fully dug-in Italian artillery. 2 Queens lapped around the opposition on the left, and with them went the "I" tanks, which had been guided to the scene by the noise of the battle. At 0830 hours British artillery opened fire, but before its effect could be felt Colonel Anderson called for the Argylls to clear a series of small knolls on their front. Pipe Major Hill attempted to sound the charge but the flying sand had choked his pipes. The Argylls swept forward in fine style and in spite of the loss of the commanders of both forward companies established themselves in a position so close to the leading wave of Italian artillery that the field guns could not be brought to bear upon them.

At 1015 hours, with the British guns in full blast, 16 Brigade struck. The Leicesters broke into the southern perimeter of the Sidi Barrani defences. A formidable body of men emerged from their trenches and moved forward, as if in mass attack; but they came stumbling, with their

*17 Field Ambulance accompanied the Scotsmen.

hands up. 2,000 Blackshirts had had enough. A rot set in. At 1230 hours the Argylls after brisk fighting reported all objectives taken, with many prisoners coming in. (The Highlanders' casualties in this spirited advance were the heaviest of any unit in the battle; 9 officers and 144 men). On the left the Queens were more or less in open country; a series of foot and lorry charges scattered the opposition. The southern main road was reached and blocked, and a solid 16 Brigade line was refused in the rear of Sidi Barrani, facing east. 11 Brigade advanced and rapidly boxed in the battlefield on the south-east. Between the Tummars and the sea a constricting investment began. When this cordon had been drawn, General Beresford-Peirse, who had been in the forward areas all morning, decided to complete the capture of Sidi Barrani that night.

Behind 16 Brigade he had built up a Divisional reserve of 2 Camerons, 4/6 Rajputana Rifles and Central India Horse. 7 Armoured Division loaned 2 Royal Tank Regiment and two squadrons of 11 Hussars to support the handful of remaining "I" tanks. (In one of his last runners sat Colonel Jerram of 7 Royal Tank Regiment, in action at last after chafing for two days in an administrative capacity at Headquarters). At 1615 hours, with the Camerons on the sea flank and astride the northern road and with the Queens to the south of the road, the attack on Sidi Barrani from the west went in.

The enemy, already staggering under the assault on the southern perimeter, was in no condition to cope with a drive from another direction. With the Hussars pinching out the Italian posts along the beaches and with armour and guns rendering yeoman service to the rapidly moving infantry, resistance soon collapsed. When dark fell the advance had swept through Sidi Barrani and a line had been established 2,000 yards to the east of the small shattered village. A large number of prisoners had been rounded up, including a party of officers in charge of Captain Cope of 1 Field Regiment, who had been captured while on reconnaisance during the previous night. . Shaken by fairy tales of Indian ferocity, these Italians had exacted a promise that they would not be mutilated on surrender.

Thus thirty-six hours after the battle had opened, four of the five principal camps had fallen. (Tummar East had surrendered without resistance at 0730 hours that morning). The remaining Italian forces in the coastal area were cut off and compressed between the walls of 16 and 11 Brigades, advancing from the west, and the screen of Selby Force, advancing from the east. 1 Libyan Division in Maktila Camp had not waited for the onset; as ominous noises grew in the west the colonial forces fell back on Sidi Barrani. To complete the encirclement Central India Horse on the night of December 10th rapidly skirted the battlefield and closed up from the south-east. By dawn on December 11th all enemy forces at liberty in the coastal area were pinned against the Mediterranean in an enclosure less than ten miles long and five miles deep.

EARLY COMMANDERS

Major-General the Hon. P. G. Scarlett CB, MC.

Major-General (afterwards Lieut-General) Philip Neame VC, CB, DSO.

Major-General (Afterwards Lieut-General) N. M. de la P. Beresford-Pierse CB, DSO.

Major-General (afterwards Lieut-General) Frank Messervy CB, DSO.

Brigadier A. McPherson MVO, MC.

Brigadier T. S. Ponting CIE, MC.

Brigadier (afterwards Lieut-General)
H. R. Briggs CBE, DSO.

Brigadier (afterwards Lieut-General)
R. Savory DSO, MC.

Brigadier (afterwards Major General)
W. L. Lloyd CBE, DSO, MC.

Brigadier A. Anderson DSO, MC.

Brigadier (afterwards Major General)
D. Russell CBE, DSO, MC.

Brigadier (afterwards Major-General)
D. R. E. R. Bateman DSO, OBE.

THE SOFT DESERT.

THE HARD DESERT.

THE STONY DESERT.

DISPERSAL—
NIGHT LEAGUER.

"Better to Live a Day as a Lion than a Hundred Years as a Sheep."
Fascist Slogan on Wall at Sidi Barrani

"The Italian troops at Sidi Barrani, well clothed and armed, in good physical condition, seemed in no mood for fighting after the first hours of the encounter."
Official Report

Eighteen days before the destruction of the Italian forces at Sidi Barrani 21 Regiment of Engineers unveiled a Pylon to its Third Company, which:

"*in spite of the menaces of the enemy and under the sapient leadership of General Negroni, had tamed the burning sands between Salum and Sidi Barrani and had united the Libyan and Egyptian highways.*"

KEREN BATTLEFIELD AS SEEN FROM HOGS BACK.

BRIGS PEAK — SANCHIL — CAMERON RIDGE

KEREN—FRONTAL APPROACH TO ITALIAN POSITIONS.

KEREN—ITALIAN PRISONERS DESCENDING THE MOUNTAIN.

Only at Point 90 did a legion of 2 Libyan Division maintain cohesion and defiance. Elsewhere the Italian formations had resolved into isolated masses of bewildered men shifting aimlessly, ready to lift their hands at the first challenge. 7 Medium Regiment had its meed of takes. Captain Bray captured a Libyan battery single-handed, with 300 prisoners. Major Snook of the same regiment, having bracketed a large force of Italians approaching his observation post, discerned white rags waving, regretfully discontinued his shoot, went out and brought in 2,000 captives. Indeed one of the principal concerns of the day was not how to take more prisoners but how to be rid of them. The constricting box had closed sufficiently to make the employment of artillery hazardous, lest 'overs' harm British troops advancing from the opposite direction. Orders therefore were issued to maintain pressure but wherever possible to avoid battle. It was nevertheless still necessary to deal with Point 90, which continued to shell the Tummars sporadically. Brigadier Lloyd sent a captured Italian officer under a flag of truce with a demand for surrender. The Point 90 commander reiterated his resolve to die fighting. Whereupon 1 and 25 Field Regiments registered and 3/1 Punjabis escorted by 5 "I" tanks moved forward. (By dint of feverish exertions, two crocks from workshop caught up with their hale brethren and seven actually waddled to the attack). The Punjabis advanced in skirmishing order and closed on Point 90 to find 2,000 Libyans lined up with kitbags and suitcases packed for travel. Honour had been satisfied.

Of cohesive formations only 1 Libyan Division remained. Most of its units had camped philosophically among the dunes between the coastal road and the beaches and were waiting for someone to take them away. As 16 British Brigade and Selby Force advanced to meet each other, Selby Force as the more mobile formation claimed the bulk of the prisoners.

When tidying-up operations had been placed in train, General Beresford-Peirse shifted his forces for the next stroke. At 1530 hours on December 11th, 5 and 11 Brigades with attendant artillery were ordered to concentrate three miles south-west of Nibeiwa for the purpose of a blow against the southern group of camps. The striking force would march throughout the night, in order to fall at dawn upon Rabia, twenty-five miles to the south-west. When the Divisional commander and his staff reached headquarters of 7 Armoured Division that evening, the new move was in full swing. There disappointing news awaited them. The birds had flown. That morning 1 KRRC heading the Support Group 7 Armoured Division, had occupied both Rabia and Sofafi. During that day 7 Armoured Division had fallen on the disorganized columns scrambling westwards from Buq Buq and had raked in 14,000 prisoners. Egypt was clear of the enemy, and the Indian brigades, unbriefed for long range pursuit, regretfully turned back to the Sidi Barrani battlefield to organize the routine tasks of salvage and of evacuation of unwieldy masses of prisoners of war.

The news of Sidi Barrani electrified the world. The march of the hitherto invincible Axis powers had been halted by a devastating defeat.

At a cost of under 700 casualties Fourth Indian Division had destroyed four Italian Divisions and had taken more than 20,000 prisoners. It was such tonic as the free peoples craved. Nowhere was its effect more profound than in the United States. This great victory gave quietus to the "Too Late to Save Britain" argument, with which isolationist groups sought to substitute Western Hemisphere defence for President Roosevelt's interventionist policy. A nation which when under siege at home and without allies abroad could strike with such vigour, must be kept alive at all costs. Mr. Churchill's sober declaration that Britain had proved her ability to defend Egypt was too tame for American commentators. "Give Britain continued help and she will knock Italy out of the war!" cried Raymond Daniell. "The Old Country is in there, pitching!" exulted Walter Winchell, the most widely-read of columnists. In the Western Hemisphere nothing succeeds like success. American correspondents poured in spate into Cairo. Fourth Indian Division had put Western Desert on the Front Page.

Certain commentators have taken exception to the predominant rôle accredited to Fourth Indian Division in nearly all the narratives of the battle of Sidi Barrani. It has been declared that the rôle of 7 Armoured Division has not received due recognition. In their own short history the Desert Rats cover their activities in this battle with a single characteristic sentence:

"After a short action against Italian artillery in the sandhills in which one squadron of 3 Hussars suffered heavily, being caught on a salt march in front of enemy guns, acres of Italians surrendered".

Fourth Indian Division can elaborate this modest report. It was 7 Armoured Division which reconnoitered the camps minutely and found the entrances and the weak spots on the perimeters. It was 7 Armoured Division which cordoned the battlefield and held reinforcements from the hapless enemy garrisons. Fourth Indian Division also feel that their bays should be shared in full by 7 Royal Tank Regiment, whose magnificent work in the van of the advance proved a decisive factor in the battle.

Military critics (save in Axis countries, where Italy was condoled on "the glorious burden" she was bearing) were singularly reticent. Perhaps as technicians they re-echoed Lieut.-Colonel A. Anderson's pithy conclusion in a later lecture to staff officers: "Aye, and had ye done such a thing in your Promotion even three years ago, ye'd never have passed it."

Of such implications, of such plaudits, the officers and men of Fourth Indian Division knew nothing. They only knew that in three days they had fought a battle which had progressed with the smoothness of a tactical exercise; that the enemy had crumpled under their blows; that they were tired and could do with rest. But when nature had been restored it occurred to many that the operation was little more than an introduction to a new syllabus of military science. The ease of the victory bred no false confidence. The voluminous reports of General Beresford-Peirse, Brigadier Mirrlees and other administrative officers, betrayed no complacency. Instead they dwelt on the need for more and new equipment and tools and greater training in their uses; on the necessity of more elaborate security precautions, on the problems of inter-communication and administration on the fluid desert battlefields. They wrote as dispassionately as though an exercise was under review instead of one of the most complete victories of all time. This attitude on the occasion of Fourth Indian Division's first baptism of fire was an earnest of the attention to detail and the desire ever to improve its performance which was destined to characterise this great fighting formation in campaigns to come.

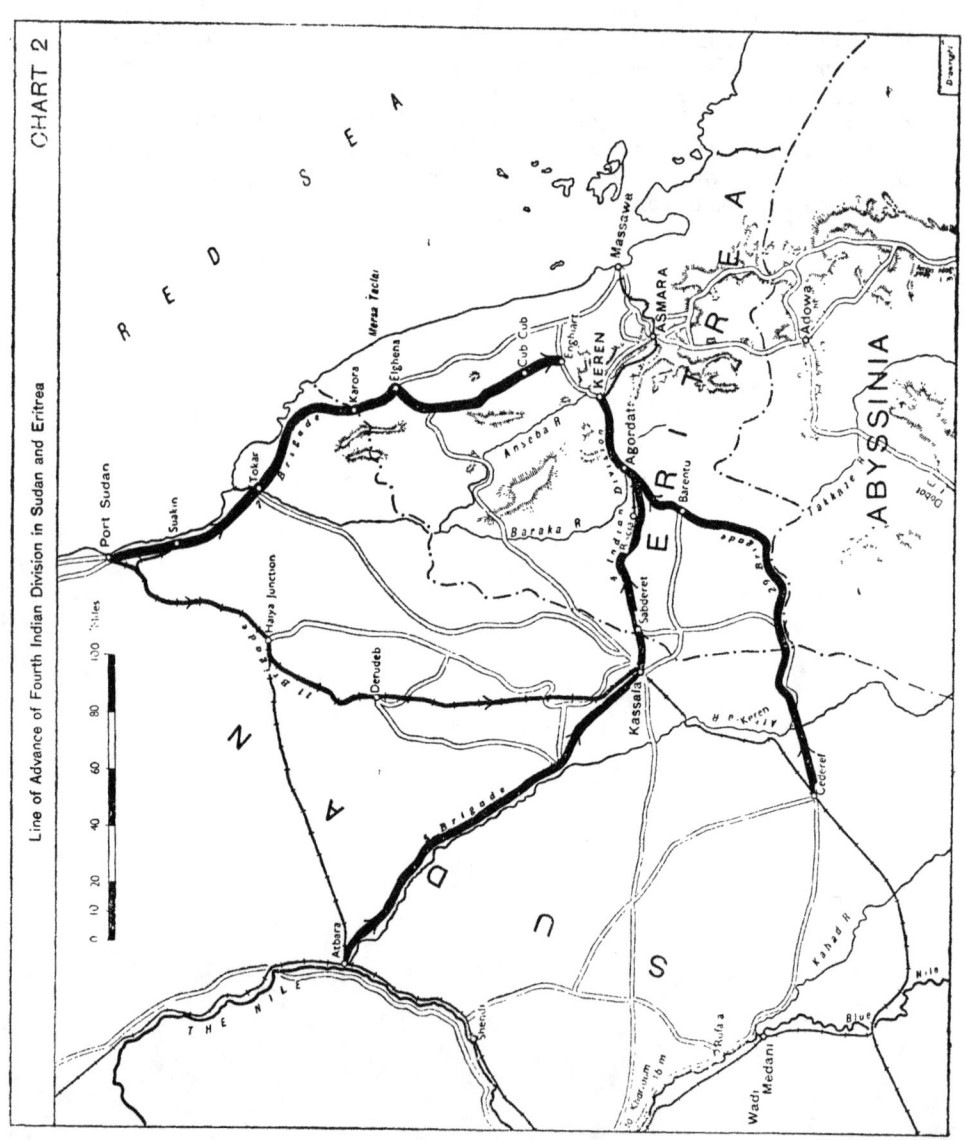

Chapter 3

ADVANCE TO KEREN

To men of Fourth Indian Division it seemed a strange thing that they should be halted and recalled when in full stride upon a battlefield. They had put their enemies to flight, yet the pursuit was entrusted to others. The ninety miles of coastal road between Sidi Barrani and Mersa Matruh was thronged with fresh troops flooding into the Desert, intent upon the chase. Fourth Division, busy with the disposal of prisoners and the assembly of spoil, watched them pass. But when Lieut.-Colonel Cutler, who as CRE was in charge of salvage, counted noses on the morning of December 15th, one-third of his strength was missing. 11 Brigade had left and was threading its way through the traffic on the road to the Nile. 7 Brigade had moved eastwards from Mersa Matruh a day earlier, to recuperate (as the Brigade chronicler put it sardonically) "after the rigours of the campaign". Twenty-four hours later Divisional Headquarters received orders which put an end to rumours. Fourth Indian Division would proceed to the Sudan immediately. 16 British Brigade took over the chores and good comrades parted as the sepoys piled into troop carriers. Four days later the Division had concentrated at Mena and at Amiriya Camps.

On the outbreak of war even heavier odds confronted Britain on the Sudanese than on the Libyan frontier. Four years had passed since Abyssinia had been struck down, but in its hinterland the Duce's writ still ran precariously. To hold fierce intractable tribesmen in check the cream of Italy's fighting men had been shipped to East Africa. Among the quarter million in garrison were her finest colonial service brigades, Alpini, Bersaglieri, Grenadiers—well-disciplined soldiers hardened by the rigours of irregular warfare. From concentration areas in the temperate Eritrean highlands these forces were in position to strike in overwhelming strength against British possession on three sides—against Kenya to the south, Somaliland to the east, and Sudan to the west.

Each of these colonies was woefully unprepared. In Kenya a few battalions of King's African Rifles held a piquet line in the waterless wastes of Jubaland. Until the South Africans could arrive, there were no other defenders. Somaliland was garrisoned by a camel corps, little more than militarised police, together with whatever sparse reinforcements the garrison of Aden might spare. In the Sudan a brigade of Sudanese and three British battalions represented the blocking force on a frontier 1,200 miles in length. Against any or all of these defenders the Italians might have struck in overwhelming strength.

In East Africa as in Libya, however, the enemy leaders failed to seize their opportunity. It is not known what orders they received from Rome; but even a commander-in-chief of the House of Savoy, and a good soldier to boot, proved to be chained to caution. On the outbreak of war, British forces were first on the move. The back door to Abyssinia had been under investigation for some time and without delay intelligence officers on fleet camels crossed the frontier and disappeared in the uplands, to blow the embers of revolt into flame. In July the Italians moved sluggishly down the canyons of the Ascidera valley, following the line of the Keren-Biscia railway. They fanned out gradually over the blunt cape of high ground which thrusts into the cotton savannahs to the east of the Nile. The thin British screen gave ground and several border towns fell to the enemy. The seizure of Kassala, on the eastern frontier, cut the railway and gave the invaders access to the principal routes leading to Khartoum and to the northern and southern provinces of Sudan.

Had this thrust been staged at the outbreak of war, or with greater determination, it might have reached the line of the Nile and so severed communications with Egypt. Or had the enemy advanced into the north along the Red Sea littoral, Suakin and Port Sudan might have fallen, isolating the African hinterland. But while the Italians loitered the seasonal rains came and turned the Sudan, except for the coastal strip, into a greasy and sodden morass. A second time the enemy overlooked the possibility of a stroke to the north; instead, the Duc d'Aosta despatched two divisions to chase the Camel Corps, a battalion of Black Watch and 3/15 Punjabis out of British Somaliland. Before this game was won a greater was lost, for during September 5 Indian Division reached Port Sudan. When the rains ended this vigorous formation had fortified the coast, garrisoned the upper line of the railway to Khartoum, and had moved two brigades against the mud-bound Italians along the eastern frontier of the Sudan.

Two hundred miles south of Kassala, at road's end on the Abyssinian boundary, stands the small frontier post of Gallabat. Thence a trail winds along the gorge of the Atbara river into the remote highlands where revolt was simmering. In order that the chieftains might know that help was at hand, 5 Indian Division early in November ejected the Italians from Gallabat. Further north, in the Gash Delta, "Gazelle Force", a mobile column of varying constituents, went on the prowl and made life miserable for outlying Italian garrisons. These preliminary evidences of aggressive intention were sufficient to dismay the enemy. The Italians ceased to regard their Eritrean stronghold as a base for the subjugation of Africa, but instead began to think of it as a fortress for a last stand.

There are few less accessible spots on earth. Only the port of Massawa offers entry from the Red Sea, and this harbour is ringed by miles of coral reef, blocked by clusters of offshore islands and served only by a tortuous channel—an impossible site for an amphibious operation. Behind the bleak and desolate foreshore stands the central keep of the mountains, the eastern wall high and grim, its bare rocks slashed only by precipitous ravines which bear a spate of storm water for three months in each year and are bone dry thereafter. From Massawa a railway in endless spirals climbs a winding gorge until it emerges on the green and fruitful highlands where at a height of 7,000 feet the trim capital town of Asmara snuggles among the peaks. Thence the railway feels into the north-west, dropping steadily for 60 miles until confronted by the inner wall of the Eritrean keep, a formidable mountain range which supports the interior plateau high above the broken lands and sandy wastes which spread westwards towards the Nile. In a hundred miles there is only one crack in this wall. At Keren, a small dusty upland town where the trails come in from the north, a deep gash in the mountain face provides a twisty passage through which the railway and motor road drop sharply into the Ascidera valley and follow along the canyon to Agordat and on to the Sudanese frontier.

With the Massawa and Keren gorges blocked, unscaleable heights awaited the invader on all approaches to Eritrea save on the south, where passable roads follow the grain of the ground into Abyssinia. The security of such an eyrie influenced Italian strategy profoundly. After the disaster at Sidi Barrani and the headlong flight of the Italian forces from Kenya, the enemy prepared to sustain his resistance in East Africa by retirement behind these mountain walls, which he deemed to be impregnable. In British high-level planning, however, the cleansing of Africa held first priority. Even before Sidi Barrani revealed how shakily the Italian military structure stood, it was decided to seize Eritrea. With scarcely less disdain of odds than he had exhibited in Western Desert, General Wavell entrusted two Indian divisions with the task.

On Christmas Day 1940, 7 Brigade led Fourth Indian Division's move, embarking at Suez and arriving at Port Sudan a week later. On New Year's Day 11 Brigade followed from Port Said. On January 4th the road party of 5 Brigade started down the Nile on an adventurous journey overland. Excellent time was made in spite of dubious roads and some faulty navigation. Atbara, nine hundred miles to the south, where the railway from Port Sudan meets the Nile, was reached on the fifth day out of Cairo. On January 7th, after a quick sea voyage on a luxurious South American liner, Divisional Headquarters was established at Derudeb, half way to Kassala on the railway from Port Sudan and General Beresford-Pierse and his GSO 1 Colonel Rees accompanied General Wavell to Khartoum to discuss plans with the Kaid (General Platt).

The Eritrean picture unfolded forthwith. The capture of Kassala would reopen the railway, would retrieve control of the diverging highways, and would permit the link-up of scattered defence forces in the Sudan. Thereafter it would be possible to concentrate for a major offensive. Fourth Indian Division was briefed to seize this junction and was given Gazelle Force as a reconnaissance and pursuit group. This mobile column consisted of Skinner's Horse from 5 Indian Division, No. 1 MMG Group Sudan Defence Force, two British batteries and some frontier scouts. 4/11 Sikhs were brought down from Port Sudan to join Gazelle Force as lorry-borne infantry. The Gazelle Force Commander, Colonel F. W. Messervy, was destined to be better known to Fourth Indian Division in days to come.

At this stage Fourth Division consisted of Divisional Headquarters plus 11 Brigade. 5 Brigade was concentrating at Gaderef, to the south of the Gash Delta, under command of 5 Indian Division. 7 Brigade, busied with coastal defences around Port Sudan, had come under command of Sudan Force Headquarters. All three brigades were short a battalion. 4/7 Rajputs had been left in Egypt and the replacement, 3/14 Punjabis, was yet to arrive. 4/6 Rajputana Rifles were still en route down the Nile.

The arrival of British and Indian reinforcements had not gone unmarked by the enemy. As Sudan Force drew together for the stroke, the Italians flinched from it. In mid-January signs of their uneasiness multiplied. Fourth Division had been ordered to prepare for battle by the first week in February. When it became evident that the enemy proposed to withdraw, the timing was stepped up. On January 14th, 11 Brigade moved down to a concentration area 15 miles north of Kassala. The Italians speeded their preparations for departure; on January 17th Intelligence reported their withdrawal to be imminent. The Indian divisions in turn expedited plans for pursuit. From Kassala two roads led into the east—a first-class motor road through Barentu and a dry-weather track to Agordat by way of the terminus of the Eritrean railway at Biscia. Fourth Division was alloted the latter and more northerly route as its line of advance and immediately prepared to attack the enemy positions at Kassala. But as the advanced troops moved up for the assault the Italians withdrew and avoided contact.

On January 19th, Kassala was reported to be clear of the enemy. Gazelle Force led the pursuit, with 2 Camerons and guns of 25 and 31 Field Regiments in support. The dusty road led across cruel African terrain—a desolate rolling plain scarred by dried watercourses, cicatrized by rocky shelves, with scattered patches of thorn scrub which afforded poor shelter from the glare and no cover from the air. Culvert demolitions and occasional mines gave the Sappers and Miners their first taste of rigours to come. During the afternoon the lorry-borne Sikhs in the van caught up with the enemy near Wachai, 40 miles east of Kassala; an exchange of shots, and the Italian rearguard slipped away. That night Gazelle Force pressed on, while 11 Brigade closed up and leaguered five miles east of Wachai, with the Camerons well forward and 1/6 Rajputana Rifles twenty miles behind at Sabderat. All next day Gazelle Force hung on the enemy's rear and finally caught an Italian column scrambling through a defile near Amiem. The guns swung into action and mauled this target; Gazelle Force pushed on through a litter of broken and burning vehicles, of dead and wounded enemies. The Regia Aeronautica was active, and on several occasions pelted the pursuers; 2 Camerons, caught in the open, suffered 12 casualties. When night fell the advance screen was nearing Keru, where the fair-weather track passed through a narrow gorge with commanding heights on either side. Gazelle Force probed the position under cover of darkness and discovered that Keru village had been evacuated, that the road through the defile had been blocked and mined and that substantial enemy forces occupied the crests above the ravine. 4/11 Sikhs at once came forward to test the mood of the enemy. The remainder of Fourth Division had camped along the road, with Gazelle Headquarters and the guns only a few miles behind Keru. On this night 3/14 Punjabis (Lieut.-Colonel J. N. Shute) joined 11 Brigade at Wachai, having received a rough welcome en route. They had been bombed in the train from Derudeb, suffering a number of casualties. Thereafter they had footslogged forward at the rate of twenty miles per day. They reported "I" tanks from 4 Royal Tank Regiment to be on the way up.

The advance into Eritrea had begun with more than twenty miles of open country between Fourth and 5 Indian Division columns. A number of enemy reconnaissance groups, misjudging the speed of the advance, loitered sufficiently to fall behind the Indian screens. This circumstance led to the only cavalry charge of the African campaign. At 0700 hours on January 21st, while Colonel Messervy was engrossed with the situation at Keru, a nearby patch of scrub erupted. With shrill yells a squadron of Eritrean horsemen, 60 in number, raced on the gun positions in front of Gazelle Force Headquarters. Kicking their shaggy ponies to a furious gallop, the cavalrymen rose in their stirrups to hurl small percussion grenades ahead of them. With great gallantry they surged on, but the gunners brought their pieces into action in time to blow back the horsemen from the muzzles of the guns. Clerks and orderlies opened fire from slit trenches and from under thorn bushes; a troop of Skinner's Horse joined the scrimmage, thrusting the audacious intruders from the camp. Only a handful of the raiders regained the shelter of the scrub. 25 dead and 16 wounded were left on the ground.

Having dealt with this daring incursion, Gazelle Force returned to the business of the day. Before dawn on January 22nd 4/11 Sikhs had begun to climb the heights to the south of Keru Gorge. On contact, the Italians stood firm; as the Indian infantry scrambled up the seamed and boulder-strewn slopes, they came under heavy if inaccurate harassing fire. The Sikhs worked forward until they had cleared the immediate ridge. They then discovered their positions to be commanded by higher crests across a deep and exposed valley. Several attempts to seize these heights failed. Meanwhile Skinners Horse occupied the low ground on the right and the Camerons came up to lend a hand, eventually taking over from the Sikhs who had sustained considerable casualties, including Lieut.-Colonel Purves, who was wounded. Throughout the day Gazelle Force inched forward, but night fell with the stouthearted colonial troops clinging to their positions. A midnight patrol detected withdrawal, and when morning broke the crests on both sides of the gorge had been evacuated. This strong position was relinquished less because of immediate pressure than because 5 Indian Division, bowling along rapidly on the motor road to the south, had despatched 10 Indian

Brigade to the north-east along a fair-weather track which led into the rear of the Keru positions. Throughout the morning Sappers and Miners worked diligently in opening the defile; that afternoon 1/6 Rajputana Rifles, who had come forward to relieve 4/11 Sikhs as motorised battalion with Gazelle Force, led the way through. The Eritrean railhead at Biscia was reached during the forenoon of January 24th and occupied without resistance.

On that same day, 10 Indian Brigade, pressing through rolling lands to the south-west, found its way barred by five colonial battalions. After severe fighting 2 Highland Light Infantry and 4/10 Baluchis broke through, taking 700 prisoners and driving the remnants of the Eritrean brigade northwards into the screen of Gazelle Force. 300 prisoners represented Fourth Division's share of the mopping-up. In spite of pestiferous air attacks (even the R.A.F. visited a few bombs on Gazelle Force), the advance screen made good headway and by noon on January 25th had closed up on Agordat and had cut the road to Barentu.

At Agordat Fourth Division was confronted with its first major obstacle. This colonial marketing town lay in the plain a mile south of the Baraka river bed, with bunkers of high ground on all sides. To the south-west the approach was barred by the long steep ridge of Laquetat, with forts on either tip. To the north, across the sandy palm-clad watercourse (itself an obstacle), the terrain rose in a series of jumbled terraces. To the east, four abrupt hillocks stood sentry over the road to Keren. In the south, four miles across the plain, these moderate eminences were dwarfed by Mount Cochen, a steep and involved ridge system which sprang to a height of 1,500 feet, its rugged barrier extending into the east until it ended above a defile four miles long through which the road to Keren passed. From the northern shoulder of Mount Cochen a long tongue of high ground, known as Gibraltar, thrust into the plain. The low ground between Laquetat and Gibraltar was defended by a line of trenches and an anti-tank ditch. The position therefore offered serried obstacles near at hand, while on the southern and eastern horizons the misty outlines of the main Eritrean massif stood into the sky, revealing the Agordat terrain to be the shape of more ominous things to come.

4 Colonial Division, consisting of three brigades and three supplementary Blackshirt units, (sixteen battalions in all), held the Agordat bunkers and Mount Cochen. Gazelle Force spread to flank and reconnoitred; no route passable for wheels was discovered on either side. The long straggling skyline of Mount Cochen dominated the scene; there the first blow fell. On January 27th, 1 Royal Fusiliers and 3/1 Punjabis came forward from Kassala. 1/6 Rajputana Rifles rejoined 11 Brigade and 4/11 Sikhs completed 5 Brigade. Four of the seven "I" tanks which had left Port Sudan arrived to represent armour. Next morning the Indian formations began to trickle across the dusty plain. On the right 3/14 Punjabis led, while the Sikhs closed up on Laquetat on the opposite flank. After nightfall patrols investigated Laquetat

and a company of Sikhs established themselves on the crest of the ridge. The intruders drew heavy fire, revealing the presence of a substantial enemy force. Rather than waste strength on a secondary objective, General Beresford-Peirse before dawn ordered 5 Brigade to sideslip into the re-entrant plain between Laquetat and Mount Cochen, thus massing his forces against the Italians' vulnerable left flank. Gazelle Force moved up to contain the enemy at Laquetat and on the western approaches to the town.

Soon after dark on January 29th, 3/14 Punjabis began the steep and difficult ascent of the rocky slopes of Mount Cochen. No opposition was encountered. When the Punjabis reached the frontal tip of the crest, a dark and ominous summit stretched before them into the east. 1/6 Rajputana Rifles followed up, passed through and advanced along the ridges. The night burst into flame as the leading company stumbled on enemy outposts. Seeking to break through or to by-pass, the Rajputana Rifles pressed forward, only to find themselves in the midst of a strong position. Bitter and confused fighting followed as defender and intruder grappled in the dark. By dawn the enemy had thickened upon the crest, and the advance was held up.

Early in the day Italian reinforcements arrived on the northern or inner hillsides; later, fresh colonial troops were encountered on the opposite slopes. Six battalions were identified. Captain Haddon's "A" Company of Rajputana Rifles, which had led the advance, struggled against a crescent of enemies; although reinforced by a second company early in the afternoon, the Italians lapped around the Indian flanks, until contact with the Punjabis was broken. Pack guns began to shell the Rajputana Rifles from close range. This serious situation brought Brigadier Savory forward to establish battle headquarters on the frontal tip of the mountain. Lieut.-Colonel Shute of the Punjabis was evacuated and Lieut.-Colonel Skrine of Rajputana Rifles assumed command of both battalions. Ammunition ran low and it became necessary to despatch two companies to porter supplies up the mountain-side. The stubborn enemy closed around the thinning Rajputana Rifles with bombs and petrol grenades. The assailants were beaten back and night fell with the Indians dourly sticking it. After dark 31 Field Regiment came to the aid of the infantry by sniping at the flashes of the pack batteries.

During the evening Brigadier Savory withdrew his tired and battered men from the crest of Mount Cochen onto the south-eastern slopes. Here he organized a fresh assault. At 0500 hours on January 31st, while the night mists still enveloped the mountain, Punjabis, Rajputana Rifles and 4 Field Company Sappers and Miners charged uphill and flung themselves at the summit. As the rush reached the peak, the enemy broke and fled. Dogged tenacity had won the day.

While battle rang on Mount Cochen, 5 Brigade had moved into action on the plains below. During the preceding forenoon (January 30th), Royal Fusiliers had reached their start line in the re-entrant between Laquetat and Mount Cochen. An audacious reconnaissance by Lieut. C. R. V. M. Adams revealed the trench system which crossed the front to be strongly held. The trenches ended against Gibraltar escarpment, which protruded into 5 Brigade's right flank. Here an enemy force occupied the tip of the high ground. 2 Camerons were loaned to Brigadier Lloyd to deal with this obstacle. "A" and "B" Companies, under Captain David Douglas and Major Hugo Haig, took advantage of natural cover, cleverly infiltrated into the position and brought the spit under control. The enemy with perfect observation from Laquetat shelled the Camerons viciously, but high boulders and deep nullahs provided excellent shelter; whereupon the Italians thrust down the line of the escarpment in two determined counter-attacks, each of which was blown back by steady fire. Snipers and machine-gun nests continued to harass the Camerons during the night, but failed to retard preparations for the next phase of the attack.

At 0520 hours next morning, when the musketry of the battle on the heights above crackled through the cloak of mist, the Divisional artillery crashed a heavy shoot on Gibraltar and the lower slopes of Mount Cochen. With two companies on the top of the escarpment and two companies skirting its base, the Camerons swept forward. Having cleared the promontory of high ground, the Highlanders charged with the bayonet and secured a knobbly kopje which stood about 500 yards out on the plain. This capture established a firm shoulder for the Royal Fusiliers' attack. The Divisional artillery switched onto the Italian trenches; four "I" tanks emerged from cover and escorted by the brigade carriers led the advance. Behind came the infantry in skirmishing order. Manning their low parapets the Italians gallantly met the challenge; in a blaze of small arms fire the adversaries closed. A brief deadly hurly-burly and the bayonets of Royal Fusiliers put an end to resistance. A gap had been punched in the Agordat defences.

While the Fusiliers were consolidating, the Camerons reported to Brigade Headquarters that enemy tanks had been discovered lurking in the defile behind Mount Cochen. One of these tanks, reconnoitring along the skirt of high ground, had been despatched by a lucky shot from a Cameron anti-tank rifle. Brigadier Lloyd immediately recalled his quartette of tanks from their freebooting behind the trenches on the plain, attached them to the Camerons' carriers and sent Major Colin Duncan to find and to destroy the enemy armour. Major Duncan cannily sent the carriers ahead, while the heavy tanks remained hidden in the lee of thorn copses. The little caterpillars skirmished up to the suspected position, where the bait was taken with a vengeance. Eighteen Italian tanks burst from cover and raced to destroy the flimsy intruders. Then the "I" tanks barged into the open, their guns playing on their Italian adversaries at point blank range. Six medium and five light tanks went up in flames. The survivors scuttled frantically into covert. Following up, the British tanks and carriers thrust across the north-eastern haunches of Mount Cochen and came upon a Blackshirt battalion lying doggo until 5 Brigade's attack had progressed sufficiently for a pounce upon its flank. As Major Duncan's force bored in, panic seized the Italians and they bolted in all directions. Instead of seeking safety in the broken ground above, many doubled downhill into the plain, giving target practice to Brigade machine-gunners and to Royal Fusiliers, who had renewed their advance. The Camerons, conforming in a wide right wheel to the swing of the Fusiliers into the north, rounded up the Blackshirt survivors and threw "C" Company across the Keren road, to trap stragglers and to seal up that line of retreat.

Meanwhile the battle had ended in most spirited fashion on the crests of Mount Cochen. When the mist lifted that morning, the forces on the high ground, like spectators in a stadium, could follow the fortunes of the fighting beneath them. As the Royal Fusiliers and Camerons swept forward, the Italian commander on Mount Cochen realized his position to be precarious, and despatched a company of Eritrean infantry to contain the Indian troops on the peak while the remainder of his men withdrew. This masking force clashed with a covering party of "A" Company, 1/6 Rajputana Rifles and 4 Field Company, Sappers and Miners under command of Major Holloway. On the impact two score Punjabis and Sappers and Miners leapt downhill with the bayonet. They fell upon the Eritreans like furies, plying the steel and leaving a wake of dead and wounded behind them. The survivors scattered in frantic flight. 104 bodies afterwards were counted along the slopes.

No further resistance was encountered as 11 Brigade advanced along the heights and made good the eastern end of the Cochen ridge system overlooking the Keren road.

The wheel into the north confronted 5 Brigade with the four hillocks —Tinker, Tailor, Soldier and Sailor—which guarded the rear of Agordat. These pimples had been fortified, if not with the subterranean halls and heavy artillery reported by Intelligence, at least with well-sited slit trenches and concrete emplacements. A resolute garrison could have held open the jaws of the trap through which the guns and supply echelons in Agordat might have escaped. But the cloak of resolution had slipped from Italian shoulders. At 1430 hours 3/1 Punjabis deployed, passed through Royal Fusiliers and moved to the assault. A brief but savage bombardment demoralised the defenders; within two hours the Punjabis had taken all objectives with negligible losses, and were winkling the last recalcitrants from their hideouts. Two "I" tanks lumbered up the Keren road, shouldered their way into the defile behind Mount Cochen and smashed a long traffic jam into flaming wreckage. The débàcle was complete.

On the night of January 31st the garrison of Laquetat threw in its hand and slipped away along camel tracks into the broken land to the north of Agordat. The Indian troops entered the town next morning. The streets were strewn with guns and vehicles, the square piled high with military stores. Looting engrossed the civilian population. 4/11 Sikhs took charge and restored order, while 1/6 Rajputana Rifles combed the outskirts for stragglers. As the remainder of his men hurried forward in the pursuit, (including 4/6 Rajputana Rifles who had arrived during the battle), General Beresford-Peirse may have paused to cast up a very satisfactory account. In 24 hours 1,000 prisoners together with great spoil, had been taken. Several hundred dead awaited burial. Two Indian brigades had destroyed 4 Colonial Division at a cost of less than 150 casualties.

Twelve miles beyond Agordat the Keren highway crossed the Baraka watercourse on a four-span steel bridge. This bridge had been damaged and its by-pass heavily mined. It took the Sappers and Miners eight hours to clear the ground and to prepare crossings. This delay allowed remnants of the enemy to make their way back to their main position in front of Keren where they occupied fortifications astride Dongolaas Gorge and along the mountain wall. On February 1st Gazelle Force covered only twenty of the forty miles to this all-important gap in the defences. At 1000 hours next morning the leading troops of Skinner's Horse reached the southering bend in the Ascidera valley, two miles south of the entrance to the Gorge. From the canyon came dull booms; clouds of smoke and dust curled upwards in the still, hot air. The last Italian rearguards had passed through and on a stretch of several hundred yards demolition squads were blowing away the retaining walls which pinned the road to the cliffsides.. Two "I" tanks crossed the valley to reconnoitre and reported the ravine to be blocked by barricades of huge boulders covered by anti-tank and machine guns. The eastern gateway of the Eritrean fortress was bolted and barred.

Chapter 4

BATTLE OF KEREN — CONQUEST OF ERITREA

ON the evening of February 2nd, the soldiers of Fourth Indian Division surveyed for the first time the scene that they were to know so well.

Along the northern slopes of the Ascidera rose the grim ramparts of the Eritrean fortress. The valley itself was less than a mile in width and its expanse offered little cover except for boulders and occasional clumps of thorn trees. Along the face of the mountain wall the railway ran, diving into a tunnel before turning into Dongolaas Gorge. From the neighbourhood of this tunnel, a spur of high ground began to stand out from the mountainside. At a height of 1,000 feet it flattened into a platform, half way to the crest of the peaks. This platform was destined to become famous as Cameron Ridge. Beyond a chasm cut out of the deep hillside (like a wedge out of a cake) the massive abutment continued to rise until a mile along the face of the mountain it fused into a protuberant outcrop nearly as high as the main range. This feature was called Flat Top. Immediately behind Flat Top a high transverse ridge marked the beginning of a parallel mountain parapet whose crest rose into the opposite direction. To the north this high knoll looked across the twisted and tangled terrain of Bloody Hell Hollow to the great cones of Mount Amba and Mount Samana; to the south it adjoined the rising crests of Brig's Peak, a narrow feature crowned by three sharp pinnacles. On the right of these rocky spires the summit rose gradually to the solid and imposing mass of Mount Sanchil, whose flank towered high above the Col, the narrow throat of Dongolaas Gorge.

Although the mountain wall was less regular to the south of the Gorge, the lie of the land was no more favourable for attack. Across the ravine from Cameron Ridge a rugged bluff stood 1,500 feet above the valley. A switchback road from Keren Vale wound up to Fort Dologorodoc on the crest of this feature, which protruded sufficiently to command the entrance into the Scescilembi valley, a sac-shaped basin which continued the Ascidera valley beyond Dongolaas Gorge. Behind Dologorodoc a rough plateau gashed by chasms and warty with knolls rose gradually for a mile, until Mount Falestoh and Mount Zebar sprang into the air to a height of 2,000 feet. On the right of Mount Falestoh, a gap between the peaks offered a comparatively easy climb onto the upland plateau by way of the dried watercourse of Acqua Col. Beyond this hollow the Sphinx, a rocky bastion 1,000 feet in height, squeezed the Scescilembi valley into a narrow defile. The trapped and exposed basin between Dologorodoc and the Sphinx was known sardonically as "Happy Valley".

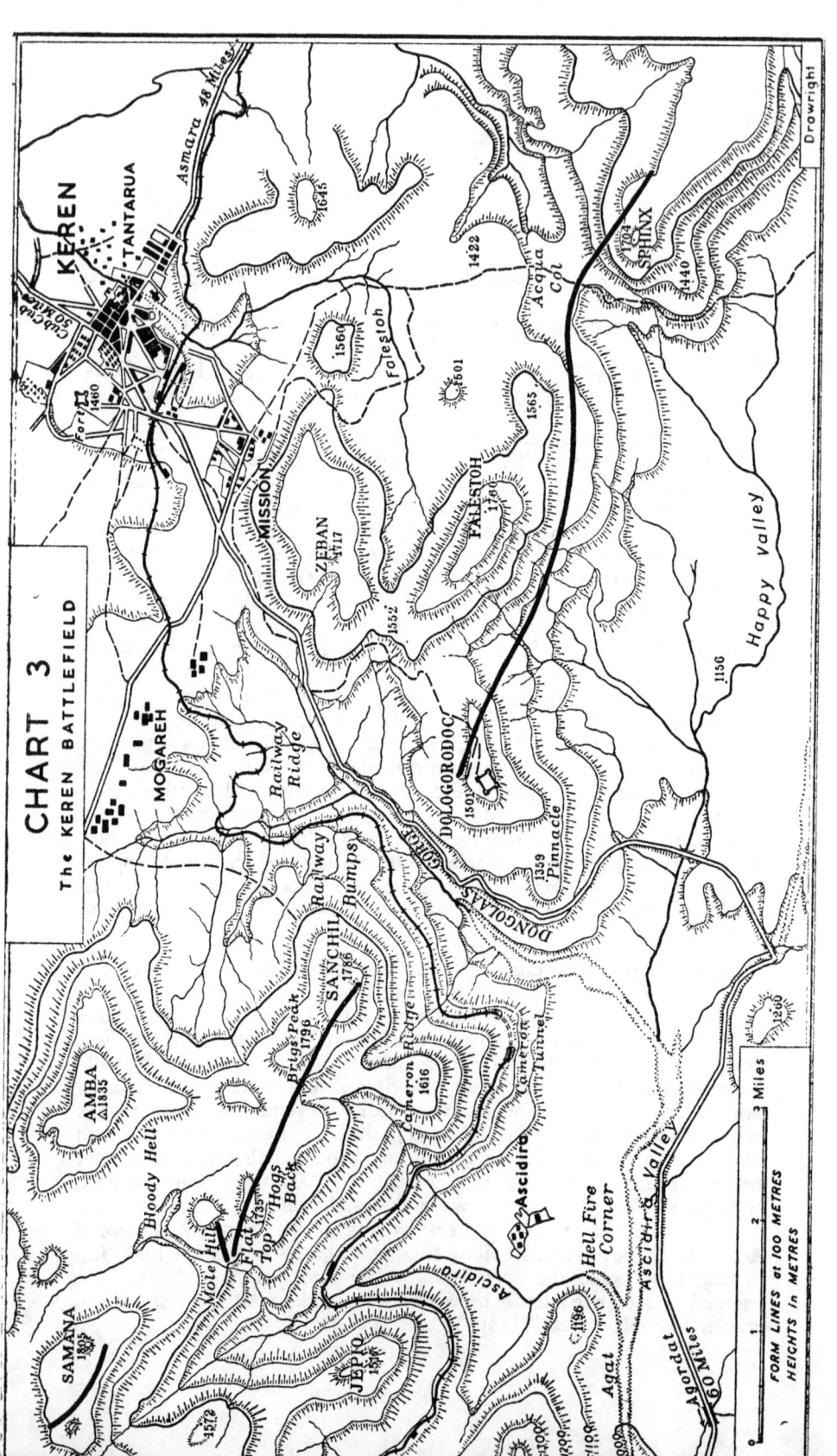

Such were the salient features of the formidable position which confronted Fourth Indian Division. For the attackers the mountain wall was as the ramparts of a fortress; for the defenders, its battlements. Keren Vale stood at a height of 1,500 feet above the Ascidera valley and in most places the reverse slope of the mountain wall offered gradual and easy approach. It had even been found possible to pipe water to Mount Sanchil. The natural advantages of the position had been increased by extensive fortifications. The summits of the peaks on both sides of the Gorge constituted a continuous defence line, with sangars and emplacements joined by belts of wire. Intercommunicating trails permitted rapid reinforcement of any threatened peak. Mule tracks led to almost all sectors. The possession of animal transport on such terrain was a final and almost decisive advantage to the Italians. To be asked to storm mountains with only backs to bear loads was particularly galling to Indian troops, who had left the best mule transport in the world at home.

On February 3rd a second reconnaissance by "I" tanks confirmed Dongolaas Gorge to be impassable. Skinner's Horse explored the hills to the south and returned to report no feasible passage. There was nothing for it but to fight it out on the summits. 2 Camerons on the left of Dongolaas, 1/6 Rajputana Rifles on the right, investigated the approach ground and the lower slopes. The Rajputana Rifles found no jump-off positions; the Camerons, however, decided that it was possible to seize the platform above the railway tunnel as an intermediate objective before assaulting Brig's Peak and Mount Sanchil. On February 4th the Highlanders opened the battle for Keren. "C" Company under Lieutenant A. G. Cameron crossed the valley and began to toil up the hillside, reaching the line of the railway without encountering much resistance. "D" Company passed through; the climb stiffened. Numerous machine-gun nests and bomb squads disputed the approach, but by using the cover of ledges and boulders, the Camerons gradually drew up to the crest of the ridge. "C" Company after a rest had swung to the right and had discovered an alternative line of approach. The converging companies managed to pinch out the defenders and within four hours the tabletop of Cameron Ridge was won.

That night 3/14 Punjabis toiled up the mountainside, passed through the Camerons, crossed the ravine which lay like a moat around the base of Brig's Peak, and worked up the steep and difficult slopes. Enemy outposts disputed the advance, but against light opposition the Punjabis reached the crest and established themselves on a bare hundred yards of summit. When light broke the Indian troops from the pinnacles gazed down on the terrain beyond the mountain ramparts—over the long easy fall to the Anseba valley, where the trim white-walled town of Keren stood on a low knoll against the opposite hillside.

The view from this lofty lookout confirmed Mount Sanchil as the key to the defences. Its commanding position and excellent communications provided the enemy with a bastion from which the rest of the mountain front could be controlled. Proof came quickly; on the afternoon of February 5th elements of Savoy Grenadier Division, one of the finest Italian formations, mustered on the reverse slopes of Mount Sanchil and after bombardment dashed with overwhelming strength and great elan down the narrow hogs back which connected Sanchil with Brig's Peak. The assault hurled the Punjabis from the crest and down the slopes; for a time it seemed as though Cameron Ridge might be in danger. 1/6 Rajputana Rifles hastily clambered to the platform and took over the left of the position; the enemy, his strong fighting patrols repulsed, seemed to be content with the recapture of Brig's Peak. 3/14 Punjabis were withdrawn to reserve positions in the valley and 3/1 Punjabis came forward from Agordat to assist in the defence of Cameron Ridge.

This vigorous counter-stroke suggested that Italian strength had been concentrated around Mount Sanchil and that the easy contours of Acqua Col might be more lightly defended. To reach this position the assault troops must cross Happy Valley, a bare basin which lay under intimate observation and almost under the muzzles of the guns on the summit of Dologorodoc. Nevertheless in view of the rough handling of 3/14 Punjabis on Brig's Peak, it was felt that Acqua Col should be investigated. If a quick thrust were to penetrate the gut of low ground on the extreme right of the battle front, it might be possible to burst onto the upland plateau and so turn the Keren defences. 5 Brigade therefore came forward to test this sector.

The Acqua Col project gained in attractiveness as the situation deteriorated to the north of the Gorge. The enemy was in full strength on the peaks above Cameron Ridge. No full scale attack was attempted, but Italian bomb squads sallied down the mountain side to harry the outposts and to take toll of the exposed Indians and Highlanders. In these troublesome assaults the small Italian percussion grenades proved the master weapon. They could be hurled with great accuracy for more than twice the distance of the heavier Mills grenade. They killed few but their fine fragmentation wounded many. From hide-outs behind boulders on the slopes, lurking grenadiers pelted the troops below them without respite. These badgering tactics did not pass without retribution. British and Indian stalkers wriggled out, and sometimes closed with their tormentors with gratifying results. During a melee on the night of February 6/7, Havildar Khani Zaman fell after accounting for 5 enemies with the bayonet. 12 enemy dead were picked up on his platoon position at daybreak. Lance Naik Bhaira Ram of 1/6 Rajputana Rifles, with two sepoys, intercepted a strong assault group, attacked with bomb and bayonet and slew eleven. A stubborn and indomitable spirit imbued all ranks of this magnificent battalion, which the Camerons, their admiration conquering native pride, admitted at the conclusion of this tour to be just as canny as themselves*

*Colonel Skrine, wounded in Eritrea in command of 1/6 Rajputana Rifles, (Wellesley's) later was killed leading them in "Battleaxe" Operation at Halfaya in June, 1941. The Camerons' Pipe-Major played at his burial the march With Wellesleys Rifles at Keren. The Camerons had composed this tune in their honour and had presented it to the 1/6 Rajputana Rifles with due ceremony at Keren, not many weeks before.

General Beresford-Peirse likewise has recorded:

"The Raj Rifs had been through a particularly sticky time in which they had endured extreme discomfort and suffered many casualties. Finally they came out for a week's rest. The morning after leaving the line every man in the battalion turned out as smartly dressed in clean shirts and starched shorts as if he were on a party in Cairo".

On the afternoon of February 7th the Divisional artillery switched onto Mount Dologorodoc and pounded the enemy gun positions there. This pummelling was preliminary to the move of 5 Indian Brigade into "Happy Valley". Without challenge all three battalions defiled past the menacing height in the early hours of the evening. Royal Fusiliers and 3/14 Punjabis sought sparse cover on the far side of the valley, while 4/6 Rajputana Rifles swung to the left into battle positions fronting the low curve in the skyline between the peaks. The leading Rajputana Rifle company had reached the haunches of high ground which rose on both sides of the entrance to the gap, when heavy mortar and machine-gun fire opened. The company commander fell wounded, but Subedar Richpal Ram sprang to the front and headed the rush which carried the leading platoons over the crest. In hand to hand fighting a dozen Italians fell. Richpal Ram's men, by now no more than 30 in number, effected a lodgment in the enemy's main position. An immediate counter-attack swept against them. With their leader shouting fire orders and indicating targets, the Rajputana Rifles blew back the assault. In the next four hours five similar attacks were smashed by the bombs, bullets and bayonets of the dauntless handful. An hour before dawn, their last cartridges expended, the gallant Subedar with 9 survivors fought back through an enemy block in the rear and rejoined the main body of the battalion, which had dug in under the shelter of a low crest, afterwards known as Rajputana Ridge. This position afforded little protection and when day broke harassing artillery and mortar fire searched the area. The Regia Aeronoutica, in a series of dive-bombing attacks, inflicted casualties. Making the best of sparse cover the advanced troops clung grimly to their isolated and uncomfortable positions, with the enemy massed in strength before them and with the bare and fire-swept basin of Happy Valley behind them.

Plans were laid immediately for a fresh assault on Acqua Col. As a preliminary to the second try it was determined to neutralize the enemy's artillery fire by more effective counter-battery. This necessitated the establishment of an observation post overlooking the Italian gun positions on the interior plateau. Brig's Peak seemed the obvious location. On the afternoon of February 10th, Divisional artillery crashed a heavy shoot on the mountain top while 3/1 Punjabis swarmed upwards from Camerons Ridge. Bitter fighting followed. By nightfall the leading companies had established themselves on the upper slopes of Brig's Peak and were investing the pinnacles. At dawn they struck again. They swept over the spires, destroyed the garrisons, surged across the low hollow, up the easy hog's back and seized the near slopes of Mount Sanchil. This splendid feat of arms might have proved prelude to victory had 11 Brigade been able to consolidate and to provide sufficient garrisons for the summits, and had pack trains been available for their replenishment. Unfortunately men were scarce and mules non-existent. The Punjabis had suffered heavily; Lieut.-Colonel Whitehead had been wounded and Major Proctor, who had taken over command, was missing. (Casualties among commanding officers were high in Eritrea. Lieut-Colonel Purves of the Sikhs, Edwards of Royal Fusiliers, Skrine of 1/6 Rajputana Rifles and Scott of Skinner's Horse all had been wounded). Throughout the morning of February 11th enemy artillery and mortar shoots swept Mount Sanchil with increasing intensity. In order to conserve their dwindling strength the Punjabis withdrew from the highest ground and established defensive positions on the crests and southern slopes of Brig's Peak. Divisional observation groups came forward, strung their wires and prepared to direct their guns in support of the assault on Acqua Col.

As infantry reinforcements 2/5 Mahrattas (Lieut.-Colonel M. Chambers) arrived to join 11 Brigade. Central India Horse, which had been operating far out on the southern flank, exploring the mountains in search of possible by-passes, came into Happy Valley in close support of 5 Brigade. In addition Sudan Defence Headquarters ordered 5 Indian Division, which had completed its mopping up in the Southern Sudan, to despatch 29 Brigade as an exploiting force should 5 Brigade punch a hole. Should 5 Brigade fail to establish itself on the neck of Acqua Col and on the high ground on either side, 29 Brigade would not be committed to the assault.

By the afternoon of February 11th Fourth Divisional Headquarters had placed the battle in train and the issue remained with the adversaries who would clash in the darkness. That night was destined to be long remembered by General Beresford-Peirse and his staff. Soon after dark Sudan Defence Headquarters reported an enemy colonial brigade accompanied by tanks, to be advancing down the Baraka valley twenty-five miles in Fourth Division's rear. Central India Horse and a group of tanks were despatched to contain this force. Four hours later a small R.A.F. wireless interception party reported the enemy to be nearing Ponte Mussolini on the Keren road. (The signallers had mistaken the carriers of Central India Horse for the advance screen of the Colonial Brigade, but this Divisional Headquarters was not to know.) Two hours later, while Headquarters Staff hung anxiously on the wire to the rear, the battle which had been simmering around Brig's Peak burst into fury. A heavy attack swept down from Mount Sanchil while a second enemy force struck at the opposite flank of 3/1 Punjabis. The battalion was swept from the pinnacles and driven down the slopes, to rally on Camerons Ridge. Casualties had been heavy. Two commanding officers, three company commanders and 280 other ranks had fallen. An equally serious loss were the gunner observation groups which had taken station on Brig's Peak to control the artillery fire for the imminent Acqua Col assault.

In spite of these misfortunes, 5 Brigade's attack went in as timed. At 0530 hours a heavy shoot crashed on the gap between the mountains and the slopes which rose above it. The leading companies of 4/6 Rajputana Rifles dashed uphill. The ground rose in a series of knife-edged false crests whose abrupt reverse slopes supplied parapets for the defenders. Only high angle weapons could search such ground; the Italians lay low and when the barrage passed they sprang to the lip of the ridges to shower grenades on the sepoys below them. One false crest carried, another barred the way; again and again the Rajputana Rifles were pinned down on ground newly won. In some astonishing fashion individual groups filtered through and seized the Col, the entrance between the peaks. These indomitable handfuls were submerged in a sea of enemies. Among those struck down was the dauntless Subedar Richpal Ram, now as ever in the van, leading and exhorting his men. As he lay dying he kept command and cheered them on. A Jat from Barda Village, Narnoul Tehsil, Patiala State, his superb gallantry earned for his regiment and division its first Victoria Cross of the war.

As the Rajputana Riflemen struck for Acqua Col, 4/11 Sikhs advanced against the Sphinx, a steep kopje-like feature which rose on the right of the gap. A swift rush carried the lower slope; one platoon, thrusting through under heavy fire, reached the enemy line and leapt in with the steel. In a grim deadly grapple the Sikhs destroyed their enemies, but a hail of grenades made progress impossible. Only the low explosive content of these bombs saved the Indian troops from decimation.

The attack had failed. Neither Sikhs nor Rajputana Riflemen could make headway. Rather than commit Royal Fusiliers, the only available reserve, the assault was abandoned. That night all troops were withdrawn from Happy Valley. In silence the columns stole to safely past the frowning heights of Dologorodoc. After 48 hours for rest and reorganization, 5 Brigade relieved 11 Brigade in a holding capacity on Cameron's Ridge. At this juncture Gazelle Force was disbanded, since the mobile phase was over. Fourth Indian Division parted with these willing and capable British and Sudanese comrades with deep regret.

Failures on both sides of Dongolaas Gorge called for a review of the situation. In the initial assaults Fourth Indian Division had endeavoured to compensate for shortages of the tools of war by a lavish display of courage and endurance. More mobility or more weapons might have put a quick end to the defence of a narrow mountain wall and a ravine less than two miles in length. Given a single brigade on a pack mule basis, given 500 aircraft to pattern bomb the heights on either side, given 400 guns to blast a passage through the gorge, and the battle for Keren might have ended in a morning. In the absence of such auxiliaries the terrain had proved too difficult, the defenders too tenacious. On ground of their own choosing the crack Italian formations were no mean adversaries. In a pithy paragraph General Beresford-Peirse summarized his impressions of his opponents:

"The enemy troops, both Italian and colonial, have fought with bravery and determination. The colonial battalions are an odd mixture. Half a company may desert in a night but the other half will fight magnificently next day, possibly followed by more desertions and another great fight by the remainder during the night. Their small light percussion hand grenades are tremendously effective in preventing troops from getting to close quarters on these hills. They have many heavy mortars which are boldly and skilfully used and which outrange our three-inch mortar. They are able to get their packguns and their mules onto the hills where they move freely, while our 25-pounders are forced to remain on motorable ground in the valleys below".

Before the next battle could be mounted Fourth Division must rest, 5 Indian Division must complete a refresher course of training in mountain warfare, and improvisations must be devised which would give better tactical balance to the battlefield. Throughout the ensuing four weeks of preparation two battalions garrisoned Cameron Ridge, while Central India Horse provided flank guards and mobile reserves. Reliefs at short intervals released the infantry from the tension of front-line duty. For other elements of the Division there was little rest. The artillerymen snatched precarious sleep beside guns trained on the peaks. The transport services drove all day and far into the night on endless journeys over the single crowded highway to Agordat, in order to build up new dumps of food and munitions.

For the Divisional Sappers and Miners these weeks were an education and a revelation. They had never imagined that they could work so many hours at so many diverse enterprises. Each morning brought new problems, fresh urgencies; yet by nightfall rule of thumb and innate ingenuity had devised workable expedients. At the end of February the CRE proudly enumerated no less than thirty-one tasks successfully undertaken by his men. The list included the construction of water points, the boring of water holes and the clearing of deep wells; the survey, marking and construction of mountain tracks; the building of defilade walls under fire to protect the infantry on mountainsides; the reconstruction and operation of sabotaged steam engines, of electricity, water and ice plants; the removal of burning and wrecked vehicles from blocked roads under shell fire; the repair and operation of a wide variety of captured machinery and equipment; the recruitment and control of local labour.

Without specialists to assist or technicians to advise, the Indian sappers had transformed themselves into railway construction and railway operation companies. A score of ingenious makeshifts contributed to the re-opening of the line to Agordat. This narrow gauge railway abounded in steep gradients which had been blocked by the removal of rails, the demolition of culverts and bridges, and by rolling stock crashed in the tunnels. Yet within six weeks the line was open and regular services were delivering supplies in the battle area. New piers were built for steel bridges, new retaining walls constructed, the crashed rolling stock tumbled down the mountain side. (As many as ten wrecked trucks were dragged out of one tunnel). A motorcycle installed on a platelayer's trolley provided a useful runabout for sappers and senior officers. Lorries were fitted with wheels which ran outside the rails: in low gear they dragged strings of goods vans uphill. A captured diesel vehicle was transformed into a passable locomotive. The tops of railway trucks were sawn off and their platforms equipped with skids to carry guns and equipment. Captured water tanks were fitted with trolley axles. A signal system was devised.

Pride in their handicraft suffused the Sappers and Miners. They had never owned a railway before. A year later some of these men were sent to the New Zealanders to learn the routine of railway construction. Within a few weeks they were laying greater daily yardages of track than their mentors. Yet in spite of such multifarious accomplishment, the proudest contribution of all were those many occasions when, as at Mount Cochen, the Indian engineers fixed bayonets and joined the infantry in the forefront of the battle.

While the new operation was in the plans stage, an unexpected but extremely welcome reinforcement provided the Divisional Commander with the opportunity to widen his battlefield. To the north-west of Brig's Peak a number of features were approachable if supply difficulties could be solved. The capture of 40 mules at Agordat and the arrival of 2 Cypriot Pack Transport Company provided Fourth Division with the beginnings of a mountain train. Thereafter infantry could be deployed against the spine of the massif anywhere between Mount Sanchil and Bloody Hell Hollow. These same mules permitted a still greater extension of front when 51 Palestine Commando, a tough and aggressive agglomeration of Jews and Arabs under British officers, were taken under command. Outposts were established at Points 1702 and 1710, two miles to the north of Brig's Peak, covering the front and flanks of Mount Samana. These threats to the extreme right of the Italian position drew an enemy force estimated at two battalions from the main battlefield.

Meanwhile the plan for the combined assault by Fourth and 5 Indian Divisions had been worked out. This plan required 5 and 11 Brigades to seize a series of dominating summits on the left of Dongolaas Gorge, while 5 Indian Division in similar fashion would storm Mount Dologorodoc on the right of the ravine. 11 Brigade would deploy on Cameron Ridge while 5 Brigade would muster on a start line around the base of Mount Samana, 4,000 yards to the north-west. In view of the gravity of 11 Brigade's task, 1 Royal Fusiliers and 4/6 Rajputana Rifles were held on call in Divisional reserve. 5 Brigade's striking force therefore consisted of 4/11 Sikhs, 3/1 Punjabis, a Sudanese Motor Machine Gun unit and 51 Palestine Commando.

The Camerons drew Brig's Peak and Mount Sanchil as their portion of the mountain wall. 1/6 Rajputana Rifles were directed onto Hog's Back, the high ground adjoining Brig's Peak to the north-west. 2/5 Mahrattas were allotted Flat Top and Mole Hill, buttresses of the main massif on the left of the Rajputana Rifles' objective. A gap of 3,000 yards intervened between the Mahrattas and the western slopes of Mount Samana, where 4/11 Sikhs, with the Palestine Commando as flank guard, would head the assault. The attack was set down for 0700 hours on March 15th. This timing gave the assault troops a full night's rest and a morning meal before the battle opened. It was also hoped to catch the Italians off guard as it was known that after dawn stand-to only sentry groups remained in their forward positions. The daylight attack likewise was designed to assist artillery observation and to permit effective intervention by the R.A.F., whose squadrons had laboured indefatigably for several weeks to establish air superiority.

Yet in spite of all that had been done, the new battle remained a desperate venture. "We have too little of everything", wrote an officer in a candid summary. Too few fighting men—the enemy held the peaks with 42 battalions and there were only 19 battalions available for the attack. Too few guns—the British artillery force mustered 124 pieces; the enemy many more, with the inestimable advantage of perfect observation. Too tenuous communications—a handful of radio sets which seemed to go wrong on many critical occasions, and land lines continually cut by mortar and artillery fire. Too little transport—only backs could bear loads up precipitous slopes and every man-pack meant one less fighting man. Each of these factors contributed to the hazard of the enterprise, and it says much for the morale and courage of British and Indian troops that they advanced to attack well-nigh impregnable positions in high heart and unshaken in confidence.

At 0700 hours on March 15th a shoot by 96 guns opened on Fourth Division's objectives. For ninety minutes the artillery searched the mile of crests from Mount Sanchil northwards. The Camerons, who had marched eight miles from rest billets on the previous evening, scrambled from cover along the platform of Cameron Ridge, crossed the ravine and clambered upwards. "B" Company headed for the highest ground of all, the tip of Mount Sanchil which stood above Dongolaas Gorge. "C" Company struck for Brig's Peak and the intermediate features, Centre Bump and Sugar Loaf. From the outset intense opposition was encountered. The preliminary bombardment had failed to reach the enemy in his rocky lairs, and as the Camerons struggled up the sheer mountainside, Savoy Grenadiers emerged from the shelter of giant boulders and poured machine-gun fire, mortars and grenades down the slopes. Officers and men fell fast, but the survivors climbed steadily on. "A" and "D" Companies followed up to reinforce the firing line. As the dogged advance closed around the pinnacles, extensive belts of wire blocked the way. Dauntless groups fought through, gained and even crossed the crests, but in too few numbers to seize and to hold. Twenty-four hours later Captain D. Douglas DSO, and 12 men, sole survivors of "C" Company, gave up the struggle and returned by way of Brig's Peak. Lieutenant Peter Cochrane MC actually broke through with the remnants of his platoon onto the reverse slopes before being struck down and taken prisoner. At a cost of 8 officers and 280 men, the attack failed to win the summits. After the Italian surrender the bodies of Camerons were found in the heart of the defences, on the tips of the rocky spires.

With the Camerons' attack held, 1 Royal Fusiliers came forward, climbed to the jump-off platform and followed up the precipitous slopes of Brig's Peak. This battalion, whose resolute demeanour under fire had excited the admiration of Indian troops at Agordat, again moved calmly and steadily to the assault. Its leading companies encountered a storm of missiles. Each yard of climb took its toll, and when the Fusiliers reached the crests they were too weak for the decisive effort. The leading company had only eight men standing. Throughout the day gallant handfuls of Scotsmen and Englishmen continued to press the attack, and even after dark little groups far up on the mountain side fought on. Success seemed so near that 10 Indian Brigade came forward from Corps reserve to punch through and to exploit onto the high plateau to the west of Keren. 4/10 Baluchis and 3/18 Garhwalis climbed the mountain side and joined the battle. These substantial reinforcements failed to make headway. The Garhwalis suffered heavily, losing all but one of their British officers. On the summit of Mount Sanchil the Savoy Grenadiers stood like the rocks themselves.

The left wing of 11 Brigade's attack had plunged into a battle of equal vehemence, but with rather more success. 1/6 Rajputana Rifles in a powerful and impetuous thrust against well prepared positions swept the enemy from Hog's Back, 600 yards on the left of Brig's Peak. It was a dearly bought victory; when the battalion reorganized on the summit, half of its riflemen were down. Artillery and mortar fire raked the position, and two counter-attacks developed during the afternoon, from north and from east. The Rajputana Rifles met these assaults with a blaze of fire which threw back the enemy in disorder. Two companies of 4/6 Rajputana Rifles came forward to reinforce the sister battalion; by nightfall Hog's Back was firmly held. The capture of this position proved a boon to the artillery, since it gave observation over Keren Vale. Thereafter counter-battery fire gained greatly in effectiveness.

In similar fashion 2/5 Mahrattas in a most spirited attack drove the enemy from Flat Top, the high protruding spur beyond the Hog's Back feature. Again the cost of winning home was high and only a few unwounded men remained to consolidate the position. The Italians struck back vigorously. From hastily prepared cover the Mahrattas threw back one counter-attack after another. They were too reduced in strength to attempt the scheduled follow-up attack on Mole Hill, but it was discovered that this feature could be commanded from Flat Top. Night fell with the men from the Deccan well established on their objective and awaiting the next challenge.

3,000 yards away, across Bloody Hell Hollow, 4/11 Sikhs had been less successful in their assault on Mount Samana. Working up along the western slopes they had stormed the first of the three crests of this triangular feature. Middle Bump, the second and principal peak, proved to be a fortress, with a palisade of huge boulders linked by knife rests of wire. Three times the Sikhs threw themselves at this obstacle; each time as they closed to bombing range, progress became impossible. As a result of their experience on Acqua Col, some of the Sikhs had constructed bucklers of corrugated iron, which although heavy to carry afforded sufficient protection against the splinters of the light percussion grenades. One rugged warrior declared that during the assault no less than six bombs detonated against his shield, with no worse effects than bruises and a headache from the blasts.

With the leading companies pinned down before the barricade of boulders, Lieutenant Mohammed Sadiq brought forward the reserves in a final effort to win the key position. The garrison refused to give ground and night fell with all of Samana except the western tip in enemy hands. During the evening Lieutenant Sadiq led a fresh assault and although twice wounded, headed the rush which reached the first sangars. Once again stubborn Indians and dour Alpini battled toe to toe. The defence held and thereafter no further attempt was made to seize Middle Bump. The footing gained by the Sikhs on the western tip of the mountain provided the requisite flank protection for the main battle.

A sombre picture confronted the British Corps commander when he examined the over-all situation on the night of March 15th. Of Fourth Division's seven battalions, five had suffered severely. Of their objectives, the one which really mattered seemed to be beyond reach. On 5 Division's front the morning attack on Dologorodoc had failed. The Indian divisions seemed to be committed to costly slogging matches, without reserves to fill even the wastage of the first day's fighting. In a protracted struggle supply difficulties would progressively increase. Carrying parties had already become a serious problem. All rear formations had been organised as reinforcements and even corporal clerks at brigade headquarters had been sent to the firing line.

The Italian commander at the same hour saw the picture in a different light. A successful day's fighting had given him confidence. He therefore hastened to strike a heavy blow while the battle was fluid. As soon as night fell a fresh colonial brigade moved across from a concentration area behind Mount Samana and deployed against 11 Brigade's positions. In the early hours of the morning fierce attacks swept against the British and Indian troops all along the mountain parapet. Fortunately two companies of 4/6 Rajputana Rifles had been brought forward to Cameron Ridge to make yet another try for Brig's Peak. They arrived on the upper slopes in time to intercept the assault which swept down on the thin screen of Camerons and Fusiliers—not more than one hundred men in all—who clung like limpets to their hard-won ground. The thrust of the Rajputana Rifles met the counter-thrust from above and no progress was made by either side.

Concurrently fighting broke out on Hog's Back and Flat Top. The enemy sorely resented the loss of the latter feature and in an effort to regain it had massed two battalions against the Mahrattas. The assault flooded over the crest and breached the forward Indian positions. Captain J. A. Oldham, Mahratta adjutant, who had gone forward to investigate, took command, re-grouped the defenders, collected all men near at hand and launched a bayonet charge which drove the intruders down the slopes. More than one hundred enemy dead were left behind. On Hog's Back 1/6 Rajputana Rifles were less severely tested and without much difficulty repelled several enemy attempts to re-establish posts on the high ground.

This ordeal on Fourth Division's front paid dividends elsewhere. After heavy all-night fighting 3/5 Mahrattas, 3/12 Frontier Force Regiment and 2 West Yorkshires of 9 Indian Brigade (5 Indian Division) stormed Mount Dologorodoc. This victory changed the course of the battle. Although Mount Sanchil towered high above, possession of Dologorodoc brought the road blocks in Dongolaas Gorge under control. Thereafter the assailants need not disperse their strength in battering at the summits but could concentrate for a decisive smash through the gap. Fourth Division was ordered to maintain sufficient pressure against the dominating heights to contain the enemy forces and so ease the task of 5 Indian Division in driving home the knockout blow.

Except for feints and demonstrations, the remainder of the Keren operation was 5 Indian Division's battle. That great-hearted fighting formation crowned the edifice of victory with a magnificent capstone. They would be the last to deny the claim of Fourth Indian Division to having laid the corner stones. 5 and 11 Brigades had borne the brunt, had pinned down and exhausted the tenacious defenders. The refusal of British and Indian units to accept any failure as final profoundly depressed the Italians, who now strove only to hold out until the seasonal rains might bring respite. Fed on the pap of false news they believed the war to be all but won in Europe. Consequently they saw less reason for dying in Eritrea. The seeds of disillusion sown by Fourth Indian Division bore fruit on the morning of March 25th when 9 and 10 Brigades (the latter now commanded by Brigadier Rees, promoted from GSO 1 Fourth Division) in a powerful assault burst through Dongolaas Gorge. Resistance cracked. On Acqua Col Central India Horse relieved a 5 Division battalion which hurried into the battle; Sappers and Miners of both Divisions rushed forward to clear the canyon. During the afternoon the enemy made a last bid. A heavy counter-attack, supported by tanks and artillery, struck at Railway Ridge at the top of the Gorge. Lest the forces on Mount Sanchil intervene and trap the assault brigade between two fires, Royal Fusiliers demonstrated from Cameron Ridge and engrossed the garrison of the peaks. Other Fourth Division patrols probed along the front and pinned down the defenders. These small clashes were the last encounters. Enemy artillery and mortar fire fell away. By the afternoon of March 26th the Sappers and Miners by prodigious labours had opened the roadway through the Gorge. A mobile force for pursuit was organised, to which Fourth Division contributed Central India Horse and the carriers of 3/1 Punjabis. As the first columns began to wind through the ravine a white flag appeared on the crest of Mount Sanchil. Royal Fusiliers and Camerons effected contact with 2 Highland Light Infantry and 4/10 Baluchis of 10 Brigade, who scaled the heights from the east. Together they climbed the slopes which had cost so much and accepted the surrender of the valiant Bersaglieri garrison.

In the van of Fletcherforce (the pursuit group) Central India Horse entered Keren at 1050 hours on March 27th. Passing through onto the Asmara road the cavalrymen bowled eastwards, disarming hundreds of bewildered Italians and askaris, and instructing them to walk into captivity at Keren. The Asmara highway—a magnificent road—wound backwards and forwards in a pattern of loopy whorls as it climbed the central plateau. Simple demolitions might have delayed the advance indefinitely, but no obstacle intervened until half way to Asmara, where in a winding valley road blocks were encountered, covered by infantry and pack artillery. As Central India Horse deployed to force this position the Italians fled. At Ad Teclesan elaborate demolitions delayed the advance for 24 hours, and it was not until a set piece attack with artillery had been mounted by 5 Indian Division that the enemy pulled out.

At dawn on the morning of April 1st, Central India Horse, now with 10 Indian Brigade, took over the pursuit from 9 Indian Brigade. Near Asmara, in a motor bus, Brigadier Rees received the surrender of the city from the Italian military and civil officials. Central India Horse led the victorious troops into the capital.

Having installed General Heath, Commander 5 Indian Division, in the Governor's palace, the Divisional cavalry set out to patrol eastwards along the road to the port of Massawa. In a gorge ten miles from Asmara an impassable road block was encountered. After capture of an Italian pack battery of 250 men and 100 very useful mules, Central India Horse returned to Asmara. Here another expedition was organised to follow up elements of the Eritrean forces which had retreated southwards in the hope of reaching sanctuary in Abyssinia. With the Sudanese motor machine-gunners under command the cavalrymen sped down the first-class highway which led to the frontier. At Addi Ugri, 50 miles south of Asmara, numbers of British and Indian prisoners were liberated. After crossing into Abyssinia the pace slowed owing to bad roads and demolitions. On occasion the enemy laid ambushes and hit back. 230 miles to the south of Asmara, in the heart of the highlands, the road climbed for 2,000 feet to encircle the giant mass of Amba Alagi. Here the Duc d'Aosta and the remnants of his once proud forces stood at bay. Skinner's Horse arrived cross country to take over reconnaissance duties and Central India Horse retraced its steps, with the distinction of being the only Fourth Division unit to have penetrated into Abyssinia. In this foray 2,000 prisoners, including a complete lorry-borne battalion, had been added to the cavalrymen's game book.

While 5 and 11 Brigades tidied Keren battlefield, there came news of absent friends. 7 Brigade had been in at the kill at Massawa. Two months before Brigadier Briggs and his men had been relieved from routine duties at Port Sudan for the purpose of participating in the Eritrean campaign. This move had been well advertised with a view to detaching enemy forces from Keren. In the desert south of Port Sudan, 1 Royal Sussex had devoted themselves to deception, constructing dummy camps, dumps and air strips for the cameras of the Italian reconnaissance planes. The enemy took the bait and their bombers strafed daily. Bored by this routine (a Royal Sussex officer in a letter described his day as "all sand storms and air raids—neither lethal") the South Country men filibustered into the south in an attempt to seize Karora, an Eritrean border post, by surprise. When the enemy garrison proved alert, the raid was reduced to a reconnaissance in force.

On January 27th Brigadier Briggs, accompanied by Lieut.-Colonel Roger Peake (a liaison officer whom Fourth Division was to know well in days to come) carried out an aerial reconnaissance of Massawa for the purpose of selecting a landing area for an attack from the sea. Preparations for this operation began, but higher authority changed its mind. On February 5th Brigadier Briggs was instructed to advance southward along the Red Sea littoral with a view to relieving pressure on Keren and of seizing a sea base in Eritrea.

In the first week of February Briggs Force, comprising 7 Brigade plus 8 guns of 25 Field Regiment, 12 Field Company Sappers and Miners, 3 Battalion Chad Regiment Free French Forces, a battalion of the French Foreign Legion, a motor transport company of the Sudanese Defence Force, and 170 Field Ambulance took the field. Across the waterless scrub-covered waste the columns made good progress. The Eritrean border, 125 miles south of Suakin, was reached on the second day. At dawn on February 9th Royal Sussex seized Karora and Mersa Taclai, a small roadside 30 miles inside the frontier. 100 prisoners were taken in this operation. The tiny haven of Mersa Taclai held possibilities for supply by dhows and coasters—a valuable acquisition in view of the vast petrol consumption entailed by columns operating over soft sands and trackless dunes. Concerning the improvisation of a supply base Captain H. A. Hughes (2/11 Royal Sikhs) Staff Captain 7 Brigade wrote:

"The problem was a curious one as we had to cater for food for British, French, Indians, West Africans and Sudanese. Native dhows had to be used and as there was no standard tonnage our loading was not planned on Staff College lines. Escorts were provided by Punjab Mussulmans of 4/16 Punjabs. Some dhows were never seen again and presumably were lost at sea. Others arrived with the escort so seasick they had to be carried ashore".

(Captain Hughes, with the high audacity which invariably pays dividends, placed an order on personal recognisance with Shell-Mex in Port Sudan for 100,000 gallons of petrol, which were duly delivered).

Unfortunately no road connected Mersa Taclai with the rough track which followed the mountain wall southward along the foreshore, and the intervening countryside was well-nigh impassable. Leaving a few Sappers and Miners to open up a trail, Briggs Force pressed on. If it could not live on the country, it could live on the Italians, once it caught up with them.

At Elghena, fifty miles to the south-west of Mersa Taclai, a rough track left the coastal road and wound up into the foothills. Fifty miles beyond, this track divided, and its left fork bore into the south along the mountain escarpment, across desolate hillsides and through bleak boulder-strewn gorges. When twenty miles to the north-west of Koren, it turned sharply down a ravine to emerge on the coastal plain forty miles to the north of Massawa. This elbow in the road constituted a prime strategic objective. If occupied it threatened both Massawa and the rear of the Keren defences.

On February 10th Royal Sussex, still in the lead, seized Elghena, 30 miles inland from Mersa Taclai. Three days of rugged navigation brought the columns to Cub Cub, 80 miles farther south on the Keren road. 3 Chad Battalion had been ferried down the coast to Mersa Taclai and had closed up to within six miles of Cub Cub. The Italian blocking force consisted of a colonial battalion with a number of guns holding a ring of low hills behind the village. Brigadier Briggs determined to manoeuvre the enemy out of his positions. He despatched a mobile column consisting of "C" Company of 1 Royal Sussex and a carrier platoon on an encircling move to cut the Italian lines of communication, while the Chad Battalion sent two companies round the right flank. The Sussex were delayed for 48 hours by soft sand, impassable *khors* (dried river beds) and because of inaccurate handkerchief maps. They eventually cut the road three miles south of Cub Cub, one of their first captures being an Italian field cashier with two large chests of lire. On the morning of February 22nd the attack on the enemy positions began. The guns of 25 Field Regiment and elements of 4/16 Punjab Regiment, which had arrived from Elghena, supported the Frenchmen. That evening resistance ended, the victors claiming 430 prisoners, a number of pieces of light artillery and a large supply dump. Briggs Force had sustained 40 casualties.

Stepping up the pace, the flying column drove on Chelamet, bursting through the ravine before demolitions could block the gap. Another twenty miles brought Briggs Force to Mescalit, only 15 miles by air line from Keren. The remainder of 4/16 Punjabis, who had remained at Mersa Taclai because of shortage of transport, now came forward. On March 1st this battalion climbed the steep slopes and chased the enemy from the crests above the pass. The strategic objective, the bend in the road, now had been reached. Should Briggs Force turn to the right and strike at the rear of Keren or wheel left, advancing against Massawa? Events in the west unmistakably indicated the proper choice. A frontal assault on Keren was in course of preparation. 7 Brigade would press into the south-west and attempt to unbar the back door. Zero hour for the renewed offensive was still a fortnight away—a fortunate circumstance for men who had been on the trek through wild country for more than three weeks. For Briggs Force the next ten days passed quietly and pleasantly. Despite the heat the district had its attractions. Water was plentiful and the countryside abounded in game. Every evening found savoury stews bubbling over the fires.

Liaison with the gallant Frenchmen had its lighter moments. Both the Lake Chad battalion and the Foreign Legionaries fought with characteristic elan and consummate courage. (It is interesting to note that the 9 Italians in the Foreign Legion all fell in this campaign against their countrymen). Of the French commander Captain Hughes wrote:

"General Montclar was constantly afflicted with hiccoughs which I regret to say caused us amusement at conferences. He was also incredibly brave. In battle he was never at his headquarters but would be found leading the forward sections into action. Brigadier Briggs' schoolboy French mixed with Urdu was masterly. Strange though it may seem, he was understood."

Administration of the mixed forces provided snags. The colonial Frenchmen always seemed to be hungry and were not averse to helping themselves from unwatched dumps. On at least one occasion they consumed three days' rations in one. On another occasion a Lake Chad fatigue party, sent to draw water from the only available well, drank up their entire loads on the way back to their battalion.

For the cross country move to the west, 600 camels were collected. This train supplied the necessary mobility and on March 13th Briggs Force began to close up against the rear Keren defences. Monte Gegghiro, commonly known as Big Willie, barred the way to Enghiart, six miles to the south. 4/16 Punjabis seized an adjoining feature while the Foreign Legion moved around the flank of the position. The Frenchmen bumped a strong enemy force and sustained 50 casualties. 4/16 Punjabis, having exerted pressure in a clever enveloping movement, seized Point 1967 after a climb of 5,000 ft. On March 15th the barrage on the Keren peaks could be clearly seen. Brigadier Briggs advanced to break into Anseba valley, and again 4/16 Punjabis led the attack. The Enghiart position, consisting of a series of mountain spurs with narrow approaches and fortified to a depth of nearly a mile, proved too strong. The difficult terrain and the shortage of supplies precluded assault on the grand scale; the operation therefore was restricted to a holding attack which would pin down all forces in the neighbourhood and prevent reinforcement of the main Keren front. No particular ground was gained and no solid thrusts were attempted; but during the critical days of the Corps assault, Briggs Force's harassing tactics contained eight battalions of colonial infantry and a substantial group of field guns in the environs of Enghiart.

On May 26th, when the end came at Dongolaas Gorge, resistance immediately slackened around Enghiart. 12 Field Company Sappers and Miners cleared a way through road blocks and minefields in the Anseba valley, and the Foreign Legionaries advanced to effect contact with the victors at Keren. Three days later Brigadier Briggs received instructions to wheel into the east, and to close up on Massawa from the north. The move of the Foreign Legion would protect his right flank. As the columns organised for this advance, news arrived that Asmara had fallen. A general surrender in Eritrea appeared to be imminent. Whereupon Briggs Force was ordered to expedite the advance on Massawa in order to prevent the destruction of the port installations.

On April 2nd a light column of three companies of the Royal Sussex and the guns of 25 Field Regiment took to the road. Captain Hughes was despatched ahead, with the chaplain's surplice for use as a white flag. He was given a letter addressed to the admiral in command at Massawa, calling upon him to surrender. He found the coastal road blocked by demolitions. The dash therefore was abandoned and Briggs Force was placed under the command of 5 Indian Division, whose 10 Brigade had begun the descent to the coast by way of the winding switchback road from Asmara. Admiral Bonetti, Italian naval commander in East Africa, had referred the terms of surrender to Rome and had been instructed to resist to the last man. With more than 10,000 troops under his command in Massawa, a battle appeared to be imminent. Briggs Force was ordered to move on the port from the north as the left claw of 5 Division's pincer movement.

On April 4th the Royal Sussex, still in the van of the advance, encountered Italian artillery in a belligerent mood near Embergin. After some delay these gunners were chased from their positions. By April 7th Briggs Force was in contact with a solid line of defences on the north-west perimeter of Massawa. Explosions in the town told of demolitions in progress. Ships were seen leaving the harbour. It was determined to attack simultaneously from both sides. Shortly after dark, 2 Highland Light Infantry and 3/18 Garhwalis of 10 Indian Brigade seized hills which overlooked the town to the south west. At midnight Royal Sussex and 4/16 Punjabis advanced on Massawa from the north.

In the early stages only light opposition was encountered on 7 Brigades front. Italian warships shelled the advance heavily but inaccurately. Two belts of wire held up the infantry until the carrier platoons wriggled through. Beyond these obstacles Royal Sussex were attacked by a troop of tanks which, for some remarkable reason, sheered off when pelted with small arms fire. The 4/16 Punjabi carriers, sallying well ahead, overran a battery of naval guns. Nevertheless enemy groups on Briggs Force front continued to fight stoutly until the "I" tanks which had accompanied 10 Brigade forced their way into the town. Resistance then collapsed and the Punjabi carriers won the infantry race into Massawa. The port had been extensively damaged, some twenty ships (which were afterwards raised by American engineers in a magnificent feat of salvage) being sunk at their anchorages.

In the late afternoon of April 8 the square outside Italian headquarters in Massawa was packed with enemy officers waiting to surrender their men. (40 German merchant seamen ignored the capitulation, barricaded themselves in a house and gave battle. They were quickly overcome). General Heath of 5 Indian Division had arrived and Captain Hughes was instructed to arrange for the reception of the prisoners. After discussion it appeared as though the aerodrome would be the only area large enough to accommodate them. Next morning all roads leading to the airfield were thronged with smiling Italians on foot, on bicycles and in lorries, flocking to surrender. By 1000 hours 550 officers and 10,000 Italian and native troops with their arms and equipment had presented themselves and were taken into custody by a small Indian guard.

For a fortnight Briggs Force were busied with the routine tasks of salvage, prisoner collection, restoration of order and pacification of the neighbourhood. On April 23rd, prior to taking ship for Suez, they said goodbye to their good friends of the Foreign Legion and the Lake Chad battalion, whom they were destined to meet again two years later in a great battle two thousand miles away.

Fourth Indian Division had reached journey's end in East Africa. In a campaign of 66 days duration they with their comrades of 5 Indian Division, and 1 South African Division in Abyssinia, had smashed their way to complete victory. The great Eritrean fortress had fallen, Sudan had been made secure. The operation had cost 3,273 casualties, but fortunately the death toll was light—approximately one-tenth of the total. A tough and tenacious enemy, with mountain walls to guard him, had been overthrown.

As the campaign ended, more of Europe was sucked into the maelstrom of war. On April 6th the gallant Greeks, who had been driving the Italians before them in Albania, found a deadly foe at their backs. German forces had crossed into Macedonia. Treaty obligations and common decency compelled the British Commonwealth to hasten to the aid of the only ally which had stood firm. Western Desert was denuded as British, Australian and New Zealand divisions took ship. To fill the void, Fourth Indian Division was ordered to hasten back to Middle East while 5 Indian Division remained to mop up in Eritrea. On March 30th 5 Brigade led the move to the Sudan. 11 Brigade followed a week later, together with Central India Horse and the artillery. 3/14 Punjabis remained on garrison duties in East Africa. By April 28th all other elements had arrived in Egypt and two days later Fourth Indian Division concentrated in the familiar Baqqush-Sidi Haneish area.

Before leaving Eritrea, Lieut.-Colonel D. R. Bateman, long to be identified with the Division, became GSO 1,—a promotion from the rank of Brigade Major of 5 Indian Brigade. On arrival in Middle East, General Beresford-Peirse was selected to command Western Desert Force—an appointment which gave pleasure to all ranks. On April 27th Major-General F. W. Messervy DSO succeeded him in command of Fourth Division. General Messervy was no stranger. From Hodsons

Horse he had came to Africa as GSO 1, 5 Indian Division. After arrival in the Sudan he had been given command of Gazelle Force, whose exploits already have been narrated. All who served under him recognised his aggressive leadership and determination. At Keren he had commanded 9 Indian Brigade, which had stormed the vital bastion of Fort Dologorodoc. A cavalryman for most of his service, he had attained a wide grasp of his profession while serving as an instructor at the Staff College for more than three years, with Colonel (now Field-Marshal) Montgomery as his senior. With his great knowledge of Indian troops and acquaintance with all their current problems, his selection as Divisional Commander was welcomed by all ranks as again they turned towards Western Desert.

Chapter 5

ROMMEL ARRIVES — "BATTLEAXE OPERATION"

ON the journey from Eritrea officers and men congratulated each other on a return to civilisation. It was anticipated that the amenities of Cairo and Alexandria would be available during the period of refitment and training. This illusion was quickly dispelled. Fourth Indian Division arrived back in Middle East at a grave hour. In his headquarters in Cairo General Wavell sat balancing his onerous commitments against his pitifully few assets. From Greece and Crete only 30,000 men had returned out of an expeditionary force of twice that number. In Iran and Iraq enemy agents were fomenting revolt; every available mobile unit had been hurried eastwards to cover the vital oilfields. In Syria Vichy complaisance invited the Germans to leap across the Greek islands, to take Cyprus in their stride and to establish themselves in the crossroads of Middle East. In Western Desert a major menace loomed. During March, April and May, while the Royal Navy was engrossed with the Grecian operations, no less than nine enemy divisions had been ferried to Africa. Six Italian divisions had arrived, together with the formidable reinforcement of General Erwin Rommel and his Afrika Korps. With two British divisions besieged in Tobruk, 2 Armoured Division destroyed during the retreat through Cyrenaica, and 7 Armoured Division without tanks since February, the Middle East Commander-in-Chief, by scraping the bottom of the barrel, could muster five infantry brigades and part of one armoured brigade to defend Egypt—a corporal's guard to do the work of an army.

Only to the south was the sky clear. The rapid conquest of East Africa had freed Fourth and 5 Indian Divisions and 1 South African Division to reinforce Middle East. If these troops could be moved quickly, if the tank replacements from Britain were not sunk en route, if the promised transport from America arrived in time, if the enemy delayed his stroke, the odds might be shortened. These conditional factors might have disheartened General Wavell. He might have said as Mary Tudor said of Calais, that they would find tanks and transport engraved upon his heart. Instead, the essential courage of leadership emerges in his despatch covering this period;

"In the middle of May, before the reinforcements (of tanks) could be unloaded, there seemed to be a fleeting opportunity of attacking enemy forward troops on the Egyptian border near Salum in favourable circumstances".

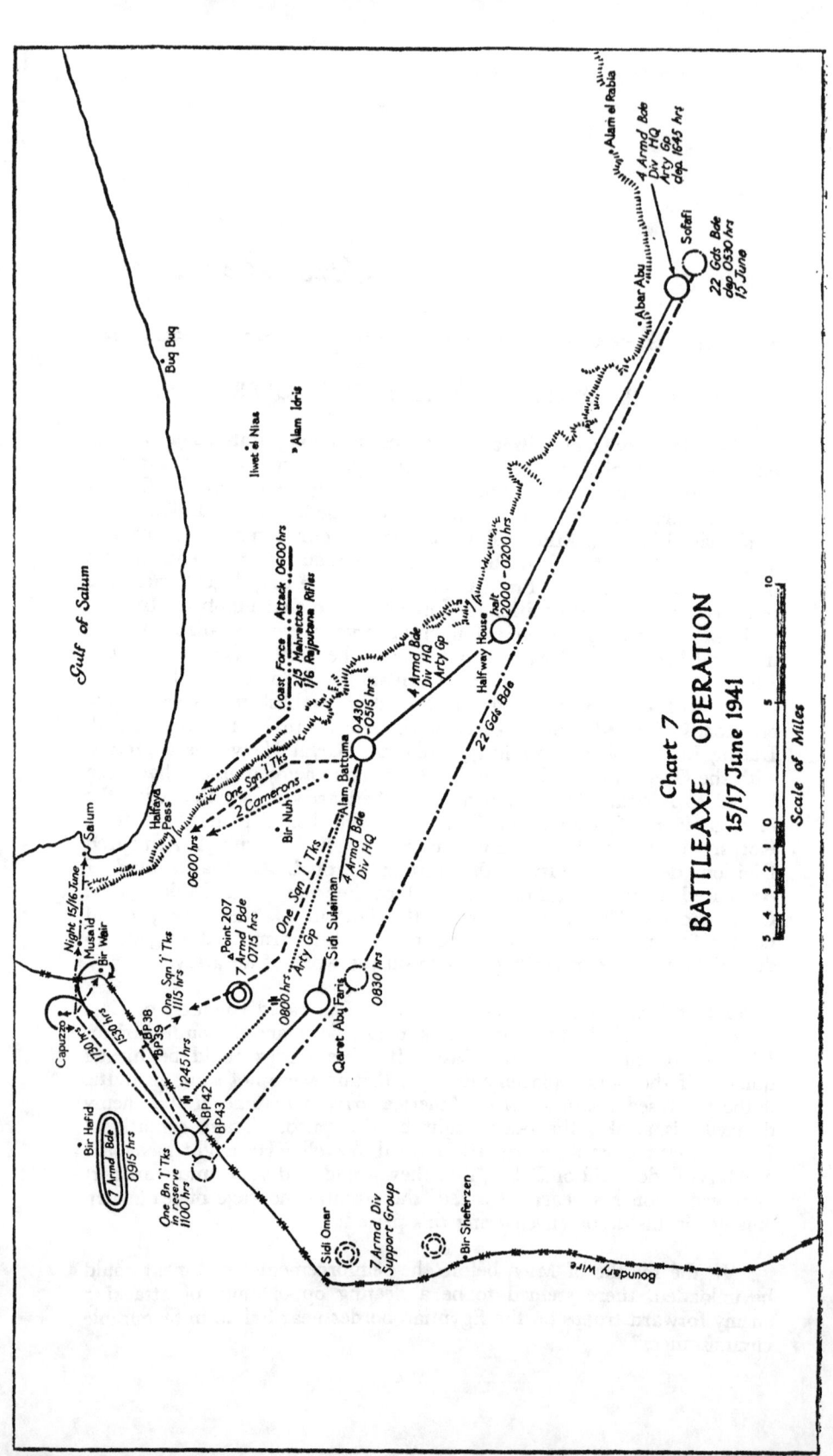

No one knew better than General Wavell how fleeting the opportunity, yet no one could have seized it more audaciously. On May 15th 1941 a force of 55 cruiser and "I" tanks spearheaded a surprise invasion along the top of the Libyan escarpment. Salum and Capuzzo were captured and the garrisons destroyed. Enemy armour in overwhelming strength compelled an immediate withdrawal, but substantial losses had been inflicted. On balance the foray had proven a profitable enterprise.

That Rommel did not take the offensive immediately on arrival in Africa suggests that Afrika Korps had been sent to Libya as an insurance rather than as a threat. By this time the most momentous decision in history had been reached and scores of German divisions were shifting towards the Russian frontier. For the time being the British Empire had been relegated to a secondary objective. The Nazis however had no illusions about their Mediterranean Ally. They were quite aware that if left to themselves the Italians speedily would be driven out of Africa. This would bring British troops into contact with French forces in Tunisia, a development which might prejudice German plans to maintain the paralysis which had stricken France since her surrender. Another consideration probably influenced the top Wehrmacht technicians. They knew that German tank design led the world and that the tactics of armoured warfare had not kept pace with mechanical progress. Sooner or later the endless tug-of-war between armour and fire power would produce a weapon which would compel the tacticians to redraft the principles of tank function. There could be no better theatre in which to keep ahead of the times than the vast open spaces of Western Desert, where the value of any weapon was in ratio to its mobility. The employment of panzer divisions in Africa therefore promised to pay dividends in military advantage, in the support of a wavering confederate and in future preeminence in a decisive arm.

After the battle of Sidi Barrani, when Western Desert Force had pursued the demoralised Italians to the borders of Tripolitania, and had been hustled back at almost equal speed, a mixed British and Australian garrison had been thrown into Tobruk to hold the port as a fortress on the flank of the enemy forces pressing towards Egypt. Thus began the dramatic incident of the siege and the glorious annals of the naval occasion which is remembered as the Tobruk Passage. It was obvious that a sound commander like Rommel would give Tobruk top priority for attention, and this circumstance led General Wavell to instruct Western Desert Force to hurry preparations for another attack. The conditional factor was the date at which 7 Armoured Division could take the field. Its tanks, less one lost shipload, arrived at Alexandria on May 12th. Thereafter precious days flitted by, with delays in unloading, in reconditioning for the desert, in breaking in crews. When the date of the offensive was set for June 10th, the commander of 7 Armoured Division, General O'Moore Creagh, pleaded for a week in which his tanks and men might become acquainted with each other. He was given five days.

Of the enemy forces in Libya, two-thirds besieged Tobruk, one-third kept guard on the Egyptian frontier. At the end of May the Bardia-Capuzzo-Salum triangle held 13,200 infantry, 70 field guns and 100 tanks. There were two Germans for every three Italians. Western Desert Force could put an equal strength into the field save in the item of tanks. Armour in the Tobruk area had to be counted in the enemy potential, since tank forces could traverse the intervening 60 miles in a night. General Wavell hoped to overrun the frontier garrisons in a *coup de main* and thereafter to settle accounts with the Tobruk reinforcements as they rushed to the rescue. A decisive victory would be exploited by raising the siege of Tobruk and by driving the enemy back to the line Derna-Mechili.

The plan of battle called for a three-pronged operation—an assault on the Egyptian plain, a main attack on the top of the escarpment and an outriding thrust by a roving armoured force still further to the west, which was designed to intercept and to destroy the reinforcements from Tobruk. The infantry battle would develop along the line of the escarpment. For this encounter 11 Indian Brigade and 22 Guards Brigade comprised Fourth Indian Division's command. 11 Brigade would be committed to a frontal assault on Halfaya Pass; 22 Guards Brigade would accompany 4 Armoured Brigade in the capture of the Capuzzo-Salum positions. It is necessary to note that the primary intention was an armoured battle; indeed, the operation orders stated:

"It is essential to bring to battle the enemy armoured forces in order that our own armoured divsion may defeat them decisively and move freely on Tobruk."

This plan seems to have been unduly optimistic. Two armoured brigades were available and each consisted of two regiments. 4 Armoured Brigade had "I" tanks, a slow but hitherto impregnable type, with a cruising radius of 40 miles and a speed in action of not much over 5 miles an hour. 7 Armoured Brigade had cruiser tanks, with a radius of 100 miles and a speed in action of 20 miles an hour. Such diverse types could only co-operate to a limited extent; it was like coupling monitors and destroyers at sea. The function of the "I" tanks was to protect infantry, yet should the cruisers find themselves out-gunned or out-numbered, they naturally would sound the horn and summon their heavily armoured brethren. Such a move would disintegrate the attacking forces and leave the infantry naked on the plain.

On June 2nd General Messervy received the plan of battle. He apparently received little else, for in his report he states:

"In making his plans the Commander had no knewledge of the country except what could be gleaned from maps and from a short previous visit to the area. Air photographs did not become available until June 11th and a general issue of maps compiled from these photographs was not available until three days before the battle".

The two prongs of the attack which embodied infantry formations were known as COAST FORCE and ESCARPMENT FORCE. It was decided that in view of the difficult nature of the ground, only two of 11 Brigade's battalions would attack along the glacis of the escarpment. 2 Camerons would accompany ESCARPMENT FORCE in the early hours of the advance and would enter the battle on the higher ground. Below the escarpment a mixed force of Central India Horse, 25 Field Regiment and a number of "I" tanks would contain the enemy in the heavily fortified wedge of plain which covered the port of Salum.

On June 4th, 11 Brigade moved by train to Mersa Matruh, accompanied by 1 Buffs, who were to join 22 Guards Brigade for this operation. From Matruh the four battalions foot-slogged forward in the intense heat of midsummer. In four days they covered 70 miles to a bivouac area ten miles east of Sidi Barrani. After two days' rest 1/6 Rajputana Rifles and 2/5 Mahrattas dribbled forward across the sand dunes, while the transport moved warily by night. Security precautions identified the move with a routine relief. The approach proceeded in leisurely fashion, and by the evening of June 13th the two battalions were less than 15 miles from their objective. On that date 2 Camerons proceeded by bus to Sofafi, where ESCARPMENT FORCE had concentrated. The timing of the attack required the Camerons to leave their start line at Bir Nuh, five miles to the south of the entrance to Halfaya Pass, at the same time as the Rajputana Rifles and the Mahrattas commenced to work along the slopes. In order to avoid minefields and flanking fire from enemy covering troops on the Egyptian plain, COAST FORCE selected jump-off positions some distance to the south of the bottom of Halfaya Pass. Command of the Camerons reverted to 11 Brigade as from hour of entry into battle.

The belated air photographs resulted in a change of plan which proved calamitous to 11 Brigade. On these photographs an unusual anti-tank obstacle consisting of heavy concrete slabs was detected between Musaid and the crest of the escarpment. It was through this five mile gap that 4 Armoured Brigade had planned to burst ahead of the infantry. Had this plan been followed, 11 Brigade's attack would have been more or less a mopping-up operation. The presence of this obstacle, however, was interpreted as denoting that the enemy expected an attack from this direction. 4 Armoured Brigade therefore was ordered to swing wide, approaching Capuzzo and Musaid from the west. No detour was possible for 11 Brigade. The infantry was invited to walk into the lion's jaws and an escort of a few "I" tanks was provided to cushion the bite.

On the late afternoon of June 14th ESCARPMENT FORCE moved off from Sofafi in desert formation. 4 Royal Tank Regiment led, with the Camerons on the right flank and 7 Royal Tank Regiment deployed on the left. 8 Field Regiment followed with medium batteries and some anti-tank and anti-aircraft guns. Battle headquarters of Fourth Indian Division moved with the artillery group. 22 Guards Brigade advanced separately and by a different route. At dusk the columns halted for a six hours' rest near Half Way House, 16 miles south-west of Halfaya, where a rough but usable track descended over the escarpment. At Alam Battuma, 10 miles beyond Half Way House, the routes diverged. The Camerons with tanks and a battery of 31 Field Regiment plodded on into the north, while the remainder of ESCARPMENT FORCE swung to the west.

At 0600 hours the Camerons' screen of 12 "I" tanks approached the top of Halfaya Pass. A sudden blaze of artillery fire sent tank after tank reeling out of line in flames or as shattered wrecks. The Germans had unmasked one of their most effective surprises of the war. The long-barrelled 88 millimetre anti-aircraft gun had been fitted with a flat mounting for desert use. Its low trajectory, heavy shell and high velocity made it the deadliest of anti-tank weapons. These guns had been dug in on concrete emplacements covering the entrance to the Pass. They held their fire until the armour screen approached to point-blank range. Eleven of the twelve "I" tanks brewed up in a twinkling. In that ambuscade the fate of the operation was decided.

This startling disaster failed to discompose the Camerons. They opened out into artillery formation, advanced steadily between the wrecks of the tanks and closed on their objective. Major Hugo Haig's leading company reached the mouth of the pass. Following up, the next two companies swung left to cover the consolidation. Then from the shelter of a low ridge a squadron of panzers lurched into the open and charged into the midst of the Highlanders. One company was overrun and destroyed and the remainder pinned down on the bare desert by machine-gun fire. Two anti-tank guns and the remaining "I" tank fought on; in the confusion many of the Camerons managed to slip away to safety over the edge of the escarpment. At 1100 hours, a thousand yards short of the objective snatched from their grasp, the Highlanders reorganized in the heads of the wadis which furrowed the steep slopes. Neither tanks nor gunfire could reach them; on the other hand it was impossible to advance from these positions until the remainder of 11 Brigade had gained its ground along the lower skirts of the escarpment. The Camerons sat like spectators on a grandstand, surveying the battle which raged below them.

At 0730 hours 2/5 Mahrattas and 1/6 Rajputana Rifles had advanced from a start line three miles south of the Pass. The Mahrattas moved along the base of the escarpment with the Rajputana Rifles on the slopes above them. The broken ground provided a measure of cover, and by short rushes the Indians crossed wadis and cutbanks for the first thousand yards with little loss. On the plain below, Central India Horse with two troops of "I" tanks kept flank guard; 25 Field Regiment followed in close support. The infantry had covered less than a mile when the curve of the escarpment exposed the attacking troops to the enemy on the crests ahead. Under heavy fire both battalions pressed on gallantly. The opposition stiffened; in rocky sangars and along wadi beds outposts fought to the death. Every dried watercourse and intervening ridge took its toll. By the afternoon, after hours of tense fighting, both battalions were within 1,000 yards of the twisty Halfaya wadi which carried the road down the escarpment. The Rajputana Rifles had one officer and 103 riflemen standing; the Mahrattas were in little better case. The tank escort had run on an uncharted minefield and four out of six machines had been disabled. Lieutenant N. R. Thomas of 4 Field Company came forward with his Sappers and Miners and under intense fire cleared a path for the recovery of the tanks.

At 1600 hours Brigadier Savory held a conference at Lieut.-Colonel Skrine's headquarters. Lieut.-Colonel Eastman, 25 Field Regiment, Major Saunders of the Camerons and Major Lancaster of the Mahrattas reported. In spite of the heavy losses it was decided to persevere with the attack. From the main battlefield the news was good. 4 Armoured Brigade had beaten the enemy from a dominating ridge and had captured Capuzzo. 22 Guards Brigade had arrived to consolidate the gains, freeing the armour for the anticipated tank battle. This success enhanced the value of 11 Brigade's operation; the opening of Halfaya Pass would greatly improve the tactical situation. An assault was ordered for 1930 hours that evening when 1/6 Rajputana Rifles behind a barrage of all available artillery would make an all-out bid to cover the last thousand yards and to seize the neck of the pass

Fifteen minutes before zero hour, as Lieut.-Colonel Skrine arrayed his thin groups for the attack, he was killed. This bitter blow failed to deter his men, who swept to the assault in splendid style. Five hundred yards were gained; the coveted gap was almost in their grasp when unbearable fire beat the Rajputana Riflemen into the ground. Major Boulter, now in command, organized his survivors into two companies under Jemedars Rampat Ram and Harnarain Ram and took up defensive positions for the night in the wadi heads, where contact was established with "D" Company of the Camerons.

The sunset air patrols brought tidings of long columns of enemy tanks and motor transport heading eastwards from Tobruk. In the last hours of the afternoon fighting began between 7 Armoured Brigade and the first panzers to arrive on the battlefield. Fourth Divisional Headquarters from night leaguer watched the clash against the fading light. At 2000 hours 100 panzers were reported to be approaching Capuzzo; whereupon 4 Armoured Brigade moved out to intercept them. With the British armour all committed the combined infantry and tank assault on Salum, which had been arranged for next morning, was cancelled and a silent night attack by unsupported infantry substituted. At 0230 hours 1 Scots Guards motored to within a few hundred yards of Musaid, a garrison post half way between Capuzzo and Salum. Dashing in with the bayonet the guardsmen killed or captured 90 Italians for the loss of 7 of their own number. In the forenoon they advanced against Salum. Under cover of a heavy artillery shoot a second bayonet charge seized the barracks which stood on the cliffs above the harbour, again with negligible losses.

The tactical situation was now extremely interesting. The Guards Brigade had secured the main infantry objectives. If Tobruk reinforcements could be held off, it would be possible for the British formations to turn down the line of the escarpment and so trap the defenders of Halfaya between two fires. It all hung on what was happening in the desert. Unfortunately the armoured action which had begun at sunset on June 15th revealed the pattern which was to complicate so many battles to come. The British cruiser tanks, finding themselves outranged, endeavoured to close. Detecting this intention the panzers led their lighter opponents onto anti-tank guns, which inflicted severe damage. The enemy formations manoeuvred with greater precision, concentrated their fire power more effectively, and avoided stand-up slogging matches. At an early stage in the battle an enemy outflanking group surprised and disabled many cruiser tanks while refuelling. When fighting ended for the night, 7 Armoured Division had lost heavily, was outnumbered, and was unable to cope with the south-eastern drive of the Tobruk reinforcements. At midnight an urgent message reached 4 Armoured Brigade, asking that "I" tanks and artillery should move to the support of the cruisers with a view to protecting the Halfaya position from the south. This message in effect admitted that the British tanks had failed to destroy or even to contain the panzers.

Such move would have left 22 Guards Brigade uncovered in the Salum-Capuzzo triangle. 4 Armoured Brigade therefore compromised. 4 Royal Tank Regiment with 15 runners and 8 Field Regiment moved south to take station on the left of 7 Armoured Brigade, while 7 Royal Tank Regiment with 16 sound tanks remained on guard in the north. As 4 Royal Tank Regiment reached its new area, 12 panzers suddenly swooped out of the desert against Fourth Indian Division's Headquarters in the Bir Nuh area. According to the Divisional diarist, the attack was "impressive", since it was heralded by a "thin slow-moving barrage" from Mark IV tanks in the rear of the enemys armoured screen. Divisional Headquarters shifted camp with "unprecedented alacrity".

This narrow escape was precursor to a day of black tidings. At 0915 hours 7 Armoured Brigade revealed its cruisers to be in action near Sidi Suleiman, 20 miles to the east of the battlefield of the night before, 12 miles to the rear of the Guards Brigade at Salum, and only 8 miles from the line of the escarpment below Halfaya. Within an hour a heavy attack drove in 4 Armoured Brigade, now the right instead of the left flank of the tank battle. This withdrawal left a corridor of not more than 5 miles open along the top of the escarpment. During the forenoon another enemy column, consisting of 75 tanks and artillery, was discovered moving to the north-east from the Omars area. Thus three enemy forces, each of greater strength than 7 Armoured Division could muster, were converging on the rear of the Salum-Halfaya position. A most critical situation had developed. ESCARPMENT FORCE was threatened with destruction.

General Wavell had spent an anxious night on June 16/17 with General Beresford-Peirse at Sidi Barrani. In the forenoon he flew to

7 Armoured Division headquarters. Before his arrival General Messervy had ordered 22 Guards Brigade to disengage and to withdraw with the utmost expedition. At 1100 hours 1 Buffs, which had been roughly handled in Capuzzo, led the retirement, with Coldstreams and Scots Guards close behind. Their corridor of escape was 20 miles in length, from 4 to 5 miles in width. 200 panzers were thrusting to cut them off on a front of ten miles; like pebbles in the path of the tide a handful of "I" tanks and guns strove to maintain the passage. Fortunately the R.A.F. had put up a dozen squadrons of fighter bombers who intervened to good effect, smashing at the advancing panzers in audacious low level attacks. 8 and 31 Field Regiments spread out in the open plain between Bir Nuh and Point 207 and by their boldness kept the enemy at a distance. The screen yielded but did not give, and by 1530 hours the Guards Brigade Group had reached Half Way House and safety without the loss of a gun or a man.

Throughout these critical hours, 11 Brigade had clung grimly to the face of the escarpment on the approaches to Halfaya. COAST FORCE had been warned during the morning of June 17th of the battle in the Sidi Sulamein area; with enemy tank forces less than 7 miles away it was useless to continue the attack. When withdrawal became imminent, Central India Horse moved forward in the Egyptian plain, to contact and contain the enemy between the escarpment and the sea. At 1430 hours a liaison officer arrived with instructions at 11 Brigade Headquarters. Forward positions would thin out at 2100 hours. As dusk closed the few remaining runners of 4 Armoured Brigade and the artillery limped away, followed down the plain by a vicious Stuka attack which caused 70 casualties. Enemy light forces raced to the lip of the escarpment in the rear of 11 Brigade and began to work down the crests of the spurs, raking the wadis which sheltered the Camerons and Rajputana Rifles. A battery of 25 Field Regiment at the bottom of the slopes swung its guns in quarter circle and blasted back the armoured cars; Subedar Feroze Khan of the Rajputana Rifles made good shooting with his three-inch mortars. Simultaneously an enemy force emerged from the Salum port defences and fell on the right flank of the Mahrattas. One company was cut off but adroitly led in the darkness by Subedar Pandurang Chawan, made its way to safety. With the infantry clear, only the Camerons' carriers remained on the crest of the escarpment. Unable to negotiate the slopes, Lieutenant A. G. Cameron MC during the night shepherded his runners for a dozen miles through the midst of the enemy, arriving at Sofafi next morning.

Thus ended "Battleaxe" operation. The high ground had not been held, the panzers had not been defeated. Tobruk had not been relieved. British losses totalled 1,000 killed and wounded and 96 tanks destroyed. Yet this gallant enterprise had not altogether failed. Its very daring paid dividends in morale and confidence. As a holding or delaying action it prevented an early attack on Tobruk. In spite of every advantage of armour, gunpower and cruising radius, 50 panzers had been destroyed. Rommel had something to think about.

This first clash with Afrika Korps brought to a head strong controversy over tank tactics and tank function. Many considered the British cavalry regiments, now mechanised, to be wedded to the tradition of the *arme blanche*. They were disposed to regard their tanks as iron horses, expendable as battle offered. Others considered the tank as a specialized weapon of auxiliary and limited function, only to be employed in conjunction with other arms. A great deal of acrimonious yet valuable discussion ensued over the proper integration of infantry, armour, anti-tank guns, artillery and air forces. The common ground for agreement was the rueful admission that the enemy had better tanks and a new and devastating anti-tank gun and that Rommel's men had been trained for armoured combat in accordance with definite tactical theories. Until British forces could produce equal weapons and equal training, the panzers promised to remain masters of the desert.

Chapter 6

THE SYRIAN CAMPAIGN

ON the evening of May 18th 1941, General Catroux, Free French Commissioner, advised the Commander-in-Chief, Middle East, that he believed Syria to be about to be handed over to German forces.

Next to Western Desert, this ancient land was General Wavell's most pressing preoccupation. Its strong garrison was dominated by General Dentz, who was known to be anti-British and completely subservient to the Vichy collaborationists. Certain of his officers who did not share his views had managed to communicate with General Catroux. These contacts fostered the impression that the Syrian forces were sufficiently restless to welcome Allied intervention. Six battalions of Free French infantry had been assembled in Palestine and General de Gaulle was telegraphing in imperious language from West Africa, enquiring why these troops were not already on the march to Damascus. Moreover the British War Cabinet, well aware of the manifest eagerness of the Germans to follow the conquest of Crete with entry into Middle East, continued to urge General Wavell to make Syria secure. A suggestion came from London that if British troops could not be found for the operation, the six Free French battalions should be allowed to filibuster independently over the Palestinian frontier.

The Commander-in-Chief, Middle East, in no degree shared the optimism of the impetuous French commanders; nor did he consider the War Office suggestion to be a serious proposal. It seemed likely that Frenchman would oppose Frenchman with the utmost bitterness. Before taking action he insisted that General Catroux personally should investigate the situation. As a result of this investigation, General Catroux admitted his earlier advices to have been erroneous, reported that a campaign in Syria would involve substantial forces, and that it was out of the question for the Free French troops to act without British support. General Wavell's staff estimated a corps, including an armoured division, to be the minimum effective force for an invasion.

In the light of this conclusion many commanders would have abandoned the project. But the making of bricks without straw was no new employment for General Wavell. German planes already had been identified on Rayak airfield, in the Baalbek valley between Beirut and Damascus. Any day enemy ground forces might arrive. By denuding Nile Delta and Palestine it was found possible to add two brigades

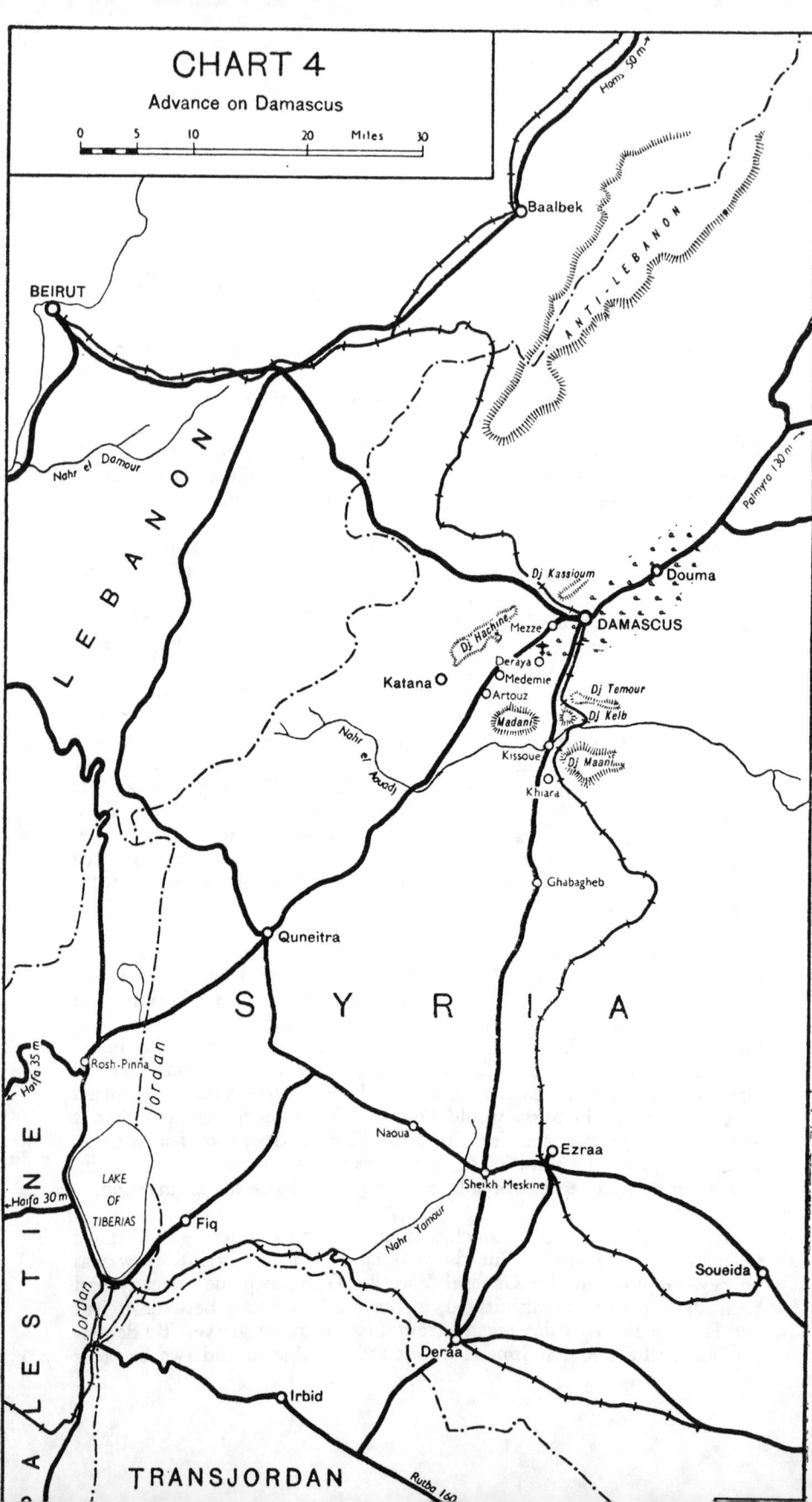

of 7 Australian Division and 5 Indian Brigade to the six Free French battalions. By the last week in May these formations had concentrated in northern Palestine and Transjordania along the Syrian frontier, with the Australians on the sea flank, the Free French in the centre, and 5 Indian Brigade on the right, on the fringe of the desert.

Southern Syria consists of two mountain ranges and an intervening bountiful valley, caught between the sea and the waste lands. Out of the Mediterranean thrusts the towering mass of the Lebanons. On tiny spits running into the sea stand small fishing villages which bear resounding names of old time—Acre, Tyre and Sidon. Behind them a series of great cones spring to heights of over 6,000 feet. Thirty miles inland the Jordan, no more than a brawling burn, rises in a valley which spreads into the north until it becomes the spacious vale which separates the Lebanons and the Anti-Lebanons. The latter mountain spine is less precipitous than the Lebanons; its crests rise in the centre of the massif to a height of 4,000 feet. This rugged range stands as a barrier against the desert, which stretches eastwards to the great rivers of antiquity. On the eastern slopes of the Anti-Lebanons the city of Damascus, famed in song and story, nestles in an oasis of orchards and gardens. Seventy-five miles to the west, a stubby promontory abutting into the Mediterranean bears the thriving city of Beirut, whose substantial commerce has stippled the gracious terraces of the mountainside with the villas and summer homes of the wealthy colonists. Strategically, Damascus and Beirut were Syria. The seizure of these cities would constitute a *de facto* conquest of the country.

From Palestine there were four roads reaching into the north. A first-class highway, clinging precariously to the mountainside and barely evading the sea, followed the coast along the western haunches of the Lebanons. From the Sea of Galilee, the easy corridor of the Marjayun valley provided a second passage. The main road to Damascus, after crossing the Jordan at the bridge of Jacob's Seven Daughters, wound over the southern spurs of the Anti-Lebanons by way of Quneitra, a seedy and sombre-looking village built of black basaltic stone on a bleak lava-strewn plateau under the majestic pile of Mount Hermon. Finally, there was the open desert to the east, where a serviceable road joined Damascus with Deraa, the rail junction which for so long had evaded Lawrence and his Arabs in the First World War. This sand-bitten, drought-stricken frontier village was allotted to 5 Indian Brigade as its preliminary objective.

By the beginning of June Brigadier Lloyd's men were organised in four columns, of which three were to be directed on Deraa, while the fourth would move to the north-west to secure Quneitra. Thereafter Free French forces under General Legentilhomme would pass through and strike for Damascus. Column "A" under command of Lieut. Colonel L. B. Jones, DSO, comprised 4/6 Rajputana Rifles with detachments of Sappers and Miners and anti-tank guns. Its mission was to isolate Deraa from the north, while column "B" under Brigadier Lloyd, with 3/1 Punjabis as its principal component, would attack the town from the south. Column "C", consisting of one company of 1 Royal Fusiliers, was ordered to cut the railway to Damascus, while the remainder of this battalion (Column "D") under Lieut.-Colonel A. D. G. Orr, DSO, with Australian gunners in support, moved to secure Quneitra.

On June 5th the "stand ready" signal came, but without definite date, as every effort was made to conceal the impending invasion from the inhabitants. At 2100 hours on June 7th, "A" Column, led by Captain Adam Murray's "C" Company of 4/6 Rajputana Rifles, moved off into the north. As a preliminary objective Captain Murray was ordered to seize and to prevent damage to an important viaduct which carried the railway across the Wadi Meidane, a dried watercourse exactly on the boundary. Accompanied by Company Havildar-Major Goru Ram and a Free French officer Captain Murray crept across the frontier, stalked and destroyed a sentry post, thus giving the signal for his men to lead the invasion. The viaduct, which had been mined, was captured intact.

At 0530 hours next morning a pourparler party from Brigadier Lloyd's column, consisting of a Transjordanian political agent and the Brigade Major, approached Deraa under cover of a white flag. Their vehicle was struck by a shell from a field gun which fortunately failed to explode. The summons to surrender was rejected and at 0700 hours 1 Field Regiment opened fire on the town. Concurrently Lieut.-Colonel Jones' column had raced off into the north covering more than 45 miles in the night to reach its debussing point. This area, which had been selected by map reference, proved to be an enemy outpost zone garrisoned by infantry and armoured cars. The Rajputana Rifles immediately attacked and rounded up 4 officers and 135 men. Unfortunately a trainload of troops from Deraa slipped through before the railway could be cut.

By 0830 hours the investment of Deraa was complete. As the attack closed in from all sides, part of the enemy garrison escaped to the east. 3/1 Punjabis had taken 250 prisoners while the Rajputana Rifles rounded up 50 mounted gendarmerie. Sheikh Meskine, 15 miles on the road to the north, was the next objective. 4/6 Rajputana Rifles moved off at 1100 hours with their carrier platoon in screen. Throughout the day Vichy aircraft and armoured cars harassed the line of march. Captain Venkiea of 17 Field Ambulance was killed when his Red Cross vehicle was machine-gunned from the air. To counter these nuisances a platoon of anti-tank guns advanced with the leading company. In mid-afternoon Sheikh Meskine was sighted. A battalion attack was mounted immediately. The enemy retaliated with heavy machine-gun and artillery fire which held up the frontal approach. At 1650 hours "D" Company under Major Roosmalecocq was despatched to turn the position by seizure of a ridge to the north-west of the village. A sharp encounter ensued in which Naik Bhopal Singh and his platoon wiped out a series of machine-gun nests manned by Foreign Legionaries. By 1900 hours "D" Company had secured its objective. Enemy armoured cars and artillery joined in the fray but failed to affect the issue. An attack on the village was planned for dawn but when morning broke the garrison was gone.

The first day's fighting was typical of the bitterness with which the Vichy forces contested the Allied advance. In what was little more than a series of skirmishes, the defenders had lost 90 killed and wounded against 5 Brigade casualties of less than half that number. On the morning of June 9th 4/6 Rajputana Rifles occupied Ezraa, six miles east of Sheikh Meskine and from there despatched patrols south-east towards Es Souida, on the extreme right flank 20 miles further east, where an enemy battalion with armoured cars and guns in support constituted a potential menace. At this juncture the Fighting French contingent passed through 5 Brigade and pressed on. By June 12th its leading elements were within ten miles of Damascus. Whereupon strong Vichy forces from the coastal area were despatched eastward into the Anti-Lebanons. Wheeling to the south they worked down over secondary tracks and trails through the Djebel Druze and fell on the rear of the Allied line of advance. Well screened by armoured cars, groups of medium tanks attacked with customary French dash. The Australians were held up on the sea coast, and lost Marjayun in the central Syrian valley. On June 15th a substantial enemy force estimated at 2,000 infantry with eleven tanks, as well as armoured cars and artillery, closed around Quneitra, which Royal Fusiliers had seized on June 9th without fighting. "C" Company of this battalion was absent on patrol, and the garrison consisted of 575 men with one Breda anti-tank gun. At 0345 hours on June 16th the Vichy troops attacked. Tanks broke into the town and cruised the streets. The gallant Fusiliers blew back the mopping-up squads but by 1045 hours they had been driven into a group of houses surrounding Battalion Head-quarters. At 1730 hours the Vichy commander under a flag of truce demanded surrender, threatening to attack again at nightfall. With ammunition exhausted, Lieut.-Colonel Orr had no option but to comply.

1 Royal Fusiliers had reported their predicament to Brigadier Lloyd in time for forces to be despatched to their relief. Unfortunately 3/1 Punjabis and 4/6 Rajputana Rifles, after four days rest in the Deraa-Sheikh Meskine areas, had moved forward on the night of June 14/15 to assist the Free French, who were facing substantial Vichy forces along the line of the Nahr el Aouadi, an insignificant stream twelve miles south of Damascus. General Legentilhomme had been wounded and Brigadier Lloyd had taken over battle command. (Lieut.-Colonel Jones of 4/6 Rajputana Rifles succeeded him in the leadership of 5 Brigade.) The decision hung on the left flank of the position where the village of Kissoue sat in a narrow bottleneck, with the high Djebel Maani feature on the right, a rough and almost impassable lava floe on the left, and a crescent of high ground in the rear. A small stream looped in front of the village like a moat. The low ground along its banks was heavily cultivated in small holdings in the style of Damascus Gardens, with a maze of irrigation ditches intersecting the cactus zarebas and the tiny orchard enclosures of lemon,

nectarine and fig trees. The Free French forces had avoided a frontal attack on Kissoue, declaring it to be impregnable. Captain J. A. C. Harley MC of 3/1 Punjabis, in his lively account writes:

"While the conference between commanders was in progress, we Company Commanders were given the opportunity of liaison with the Free French Battalions which had carried out the attack the night before and which were licking their wounds in a woody area immediately to the east of the hill. Our impressions of our Allies were not very good, particularly as when the suggestion of an attack against Kissoue cropped up, we saw those semi-naked, unshaven and ragged Legionnaires shake their heads in argument with their own officers and reply 'Les Anglais sont foux!' "

"Kissoue village was built on the south-east slopes of Jebel Kissoue, approximately triangular in shape, its apex to the north on the main Deraa-Damascus road, its eastern side guarded by the river which flowed from the north through the village and on to the south-west, and its southern side along the line of the river to the south-east slopes of the Diebel Maani. In all the southern side—or breadth of the village—was some 500/600 yards, and its depth from south to north some 400 yards. Green woods and vines grew along the river banks, making the village look very cool and pleasant, with its mud houses and its mosque peeping over the tree tops. As we surveyed it in the boiling heat of that hot June day, it seemed very welcoming, with ample promises of water—of which we were very short, our ration being a half gallon a day per man for all purposes."

A first reconnaissance by Lieut.-Colonel Jones seemed to confirm the French opinion. The approach ground narrowed in a re-entrant which afforded no opportunity for turning movements. A deep and wide anti-tank ditch had been dug along the front of the gardens area. Among the orchards wire defences were covered by machine-gun nests. In the absence of armour, and with little more than sniping artillery, a surprise night attack seemed to offer the only prospects of success. As the presence of the enemy at Es Souida remained a threat, Lieut.-Colonel Jones instructed the Free French detachments on the right to carry out intensive patrolling and to make as much noise as possible to cover the assembly of 5 Brigade in front of Kissoue.

On the evening of June 14th Brigadier Lloyd sent an inspiring message to all ranks:

"In the attack on Kissoue I have asked you two Indian battalions to carry out the impossible. I know you will achieve the impossible and I am confident that only you are able to accomplish this task. Good luck to you all!"

At 0400 hours on June 15th, 13 Free French Brigade and 5 Indian Brigade moved forward to battle positions. The Batallion d'Infanterie de Marine* advanced under 5 Brigade command. "C" Company, Royal Fusiliers, which had escaped disaster in Quneitra, kept flank guard on the left. The Deraa-Damascus road provided a dividing line, the Frenchmen to its east, the Indian units to its west. The plan called for 3/1 Punjabis to open the attack with a four company assault, in which "A" and "B" Companies advanced directly against the village, while "C" and "D" Companies headed into the re-entrant low ground below the high conical feature of Madani. The forces attacking the village carried wooden ladders prepared overnight by 18 Field Company Sappers and Miners, for use in crossing the anti-tank ditch.

By a stroke of luck the Vichy garrison of the village was due for relief at dawn, and many impatient troops (Moroccans and Tunisians) had left their posts and embussed before their reliefs arrived. Harassing fire by 1 Field Regiment began at 0415 hours; soon afterwards, in a swift rush out of the darkness, the leading Punjabi platoons swept across a wadi and established themselves in the gardens along the eastern outskirts of the village. Although caught off their guard, the Vichy troops stood their ground and fierce hand-to-hand fighting ensued. "C" Company, having burst through to its objective on Madani, wheeled to the right downhill and fell on the flank of the defenders of the village. By 0900 hours Kissoue was firmly held, and numbers of dripping prisoners had been fished out of the irrigation ditches, where they had hoped to be overlooked by the mopping-up squads.

As the attack on Kissoue village went in, 1 Field Regiment lifted its fire onto Tel Kissoue, a round knoll immediately behind the village. With "A" and "B" Companies leading, 4/6 Rajputana Rifles passed through the Punjabis and advanced up the slopes. Crossfire from the extreme left flank proved troublesome, but the crest of the knoll was seized and held with light losses. "C" and "D" Companies of the same battalion by-passing Tel Kissoue, advanced on Tel Afair, the next high ground to the north. When Vichy tanks appeared Major R. B. Scott, in charge of the attack, ordered his carrier platoon to intervene. Under cover of this diversion the infantry seized Tel Afair without difficulty but four carriers were lost in an unequal skirmish with French armour. On the extreme left of the battle front Free Frenchmen and "C" Company of the Royal Fusiliers cleared and held the tiny hamlet of Mouquilibe. All Brigade objectives had been secured at low cost.

It was now the turn of 13 Free French Brigade, to the east of the Damascus road. At 1100 hours the Frenchmen dashed to the attack and stormed a number of preliminary objectives before meeting embittered resistance on the last high ground covering the open plain to the north. Within two hours the advance was at a standstill. Encouraged by this success, the enemy threw a quick counter-attack

*Lieut.-Colonel Jones comments: "This battalion consisted of various naval ratings and personnel and could better be described as 'mariners'."

with infantry and tanks at "A" Company of the Punjabis on the right of the battalion position, and at "C" and "D" Companies of the Rajputana Rifles on Tel Afair. The Punjabis, ensconced securely in the glades and orchards, met the threat resolutely. Naik Bachan Singh, firing the only anti-tank rifle available, disabled the leading tank when it was only 20 yards from the Indian positions. Sepoy Karam Singh picked off three officers heading the attack. When Colonel Greatwood came racing up with a Bren carrier laden with ammunition, the counter-attack disintegrated, leaving behind a number of prisoners. Consequent on this success 3/1 Punjabis prepared to move ahead to secure the Madani hillock to the northwest of the village. Once again Vichy tanks interposed their threat and the operation was abandoned.

That afternoon disturbing news arrived from the rear. An enemy raiding column of infantry, armoured cars and artillery had cut across country and was threatening the small Transjordan Frontier Force garrison in Sheikh Meskine. A mobile column was detached to deal with these intruders. In the early hours of the evening 3/1 Punjabis silently renewed their thrust against Madani. The quick follow-up caught the enemy unawares, and when day broke the jawns, from the hilltop, surveyed the verdant mantle of Damascus Gardens flung around the minarets and spires of the city eleven miles to the north. 4/6 Rajputana Rifles, who had been relieved during the night by 4 Bataillon de Marche, passed through the Punjabis and thrust across the plain, seizing Djedeide-Artouz, on the Quneitra road, nine miles from the outskirts of the city. These quick thrusts imposed a severe strain upon administration and supply. By dawn on June 17th the advanced infantry had been without water for 24 hours—a circumstance which reveals high morale in sustaining the offensive. The French "mariners" followed the Indian battalions into the north but when coming into alignment on the right flank sustained heavy casualties from vicious air and tank sorties. Nevertheless 13 Free French Brigade moved to the attack, three miles to the east, on the line of Djebel Kelb. Here it was thrown back in assault after assault. The fall of Kissoue had failed to shake the enemy's grip on Damascus.

5 Indian Brigade therefore remained in an exposed position at the apex of the line of advance, with Vichy forces established on both flanks and in its rear. It was the moment for a radical decision; either to face about, conform with the alignment of the frustrated Free French and to consolidate a defensible position, or else to press on, crash through the centre and seize Damascus behind the backs of its defenders. Brigadier Lloyd without hesitation chose the bolder, decisive alternative.

Two miles to the north-east of Djedeide-Artouz, Damascus Gardens began, the glades and orchards of the oasis gradually spreading until they filled the triangle between the Deraa and the Quneitra roads. The Quneitra road ran along the base of the Anti-Lebanons under the forts which commanded the entrance to Damascus by way of Mezze, a detached suburb at the mouth of the gorge which carries the main road and the railway through the mountains to Beirut. The capture of Mezze would isolate Damascus from the west and south and would compel the Vichy forces to fight a decisive battle for the possession of the city.

Such thrust could only succeed if a high degree of surprise could be effected and if reinforcements could reach the striking force within a matter of hours. These conditional factors caused the proposed operation to hover on the borderline between a forlorn hope and a speculative yet justifiable undertaking. Fully realizing its chancey nature, Lieut.-Colonel Jones had suggested as alternative a drive into the north-west across the foothills of the anti-Lebanons, for the dual purpose of establishing the assault forces on commanding ground and of cutting the road from Damascus to Beirut. Unfortunately it was not found possible to adopt this plan. It therefore was necessary to strike into the heart of the Vichy defences and after the tactics of Arnold von Winkelreid, to draw every spear into a single breast.

Throughout June 17/18 3/1 Punjabis and 4/6 Rajputana Rifles rested, while details of the new operation were perfected. It was estimated that not more than 24 hours should elapse before reinforcements would fight through to Mezze and relieve the striking force. Brigadier Lloyd had been promised a fresh battalion of the Queens Regiment which might turn up at any time. It was known that the Australians had by-passed Quneitra and were driving up from the south-west. The remnants of the Royal Fusiliers and the rather battered B.I.M. Battalion would be used as local reserves and sent into Mezze to stiffen the garrison as soon as the success signal was received. . Concurrently with the departure of the Indian battalions, 13 Free French Brigade would advance once more, in an endeavour either to break through or to slip past the Vichy forces in its path and thereafter to fight its way into Damascus on the opposite side of the city from Mezze. At 2000 hours on June 18th, therefore, 3/1 Punjabis and 4/6 Rajputana Rifles moved out in the gathering dusk, well aware that although committed to a critical enterprise, the key to complete victory might rest in their hands.

Lieut.-Colonel Greatwoods Punjabis led the advance, detaching its Sikh company first to mask and then to capture the fortified village of Medemie, five miles from Mezze on the approaches to Damascus airfield. The Rajput company was ordered to work along the anti-Lebanon ridges in order to guard the left flank of the advance. The remainder of the brigade column halted well off the road to await the seizure of Medemie before driving on the main objective.

At 2200 hours, in the orchards surrounding Medemie, the Sikhs encountered intense opposition. Artillery fire searched the road and it was apparent that a strong force blocked the approach to Damascus. The Rajput company on the hillside could follow the progress of the Sikhs by the yellow splashes of the grenades among the fruit trees. Yard by yard the gardens were cleared and a number of enemy tanks destroyed. A charge swept through the village and the Sikhs had completed their alloted task, but with only 27 men of the company standing.

On the lower side of the main road, below the Rajput line of advance the Hazara company worked forward until a line of machine gun posts was encountered. (It seems possible that these were the small ground-level concrete cupolas which guarded Damascus airfield.) In spite of considerable resistance the infantry filtered past these obstacles. Meanwhile the Brigade transport column, bearing reserve supplies of ammunition, food and medical stores, and believing infantry to be in screen, bowled briskly forward on the main road. In the dense darkness the vehicles fetched up against an enemy road block which opened fire at a few yards range. A sapper officer found the Rajput company on the hillside, and besought assistance in saving the precious stores. By the time the surviving supply vehicles had been extricated, the remainder of the brigade column had passed on and had been swallowed up in the night.

At midnight, having escorted the vehicles into safe harbour, the Rajput company contacted the remnants of the Sikh company in Medemire. It was then decided to disregard all minor objectives and to march directly on Mezze. At 0200 hours the two companies, with 18 Field Company Sappers and Miners, advanced along the main road. Night began to thin as the column neared Mezze; above them the Punjabis detected the dim shapes of two small forts on the crest of the ridge. Leaving the survivors of the Sikh Company and the Sappers behind, the Rajputs clambered uphill and in a surprise attack seized the nearer fort. They charged along the crest of the ridge in an attempt to secure its companion, but intense small arms fire swept them to ground and they were obliged to fall back and reorganize. Concentrated mortar and artillery fire searched the ridge; with the enemy alert and in force the Rajputs withdrew down the hillside and rejoined the column. Captain Harley, the last British officer on his feet, had been wounded in the attack on the forts. Major Stuart of the Sappers and Miners took command. Crossing the road, the remains of the Rajput company took cover in the groves and reported their position by wireless to Brigade Headquarters.

Meanwhile the battle had opened at Mezze. The main brigade column, brushing aside minor opposition along the airfield, approached the south-eastern outskirts of the village at 0415 hours, after a twelve mile march across unreconnoitred country. The infantry immediately deployed and hurried into the assault. While the Hazara company of the Punjabis advanced up the hillside on the left of the village, "B" and "C" Companies of the Rajputana Rifles struck frontally, and "A" Company of the latter battalion worked through the groves on the right flank. The enemy was standing ready and intense fighting developed. Field guns in front of the village pinned down the centre companies until Subedar Mohammed Akbar of the Punjabis dashed in and destroyed the crews at point blank range with his tommy gun.

For an hour a vicious mêlée reigned. Two enemy ammunition lorries blew up; their flames revealed a Vichy tank; the Indians stalked it with petrol grenades and destroyed it. Mezze was cleared and 40 prisoners taken.

"A" Company of the Rajputana Rifles meanwhile had burst through the gardens in the rear of the village and had raced hotfoot for the mouth of the gorge which carried the road and railway through the Anti-Lebanons. An enemy cavalry piquet pulled out rapidly and the Beirut road was reached and cut. An infantry battalion emerged from Damascus in close order and was blown back by steady musketry. A large petrol dump was fired, and a train endeavouring to escape into the Anti-Lebanons was turned back. At 0900 hours a squadron of heavy tanks sallied from Damascus against the intruders, and "A" Company, well content with its morning's work, fell back on the main force in Mezze.

In the village all worked feverishly to consolidate and to fortify against the imminent attack. With the fort on the ridge still in enemy possession, with neither artillery nor armour available, the only salvation lay in a delaying action. Road blocks were hurriedly constructed and dispositions made to defend the village street by street. During these preparations Lieut.-Colonel Greatwood of the Punjabis was seriously wounded and carried into Brigade Headquarters, which had been established in Mezze House, a large square edifice surrounded by spacious gardens and a high thick wall. The headquarters of both battalions were brought into this building and a "keep" defence organised. Walls were loopholed and barricades built.* The four infantry companies were distributed in mutually self-supporting groups around the perimeter of the village.

The challenge soon came. Early in the forenoon the force of heavy tanks which had chased "A" Company of 4/6 Rajputana Rifles from the road and rail junction, advanced against the eastern and northern faces of the village. Lurching over the flimsy obstacles, the French armour barged up and down the streets, shooting up centres of resistance. From windows and doorways, cellars and lofts, the sepoys blew back the mopping-up squads, dodged the tanks, and rallied in new coverts when ejected from former positions. At 1400 hours "A" Company's area was overrun, but a number of men managed to make their way to Brigade Headquarters. The heavy walls of Mezze House garden held in spite of attempts to open breaches by cannon fire, but the front gateway was battered down, and tanks shelled the chateau at 200 yards range. The road to Quneitra was cut, and the supply train, rescued on the previous evening, could not enter. Lieut.-Colonel Desmond Young MC,

*Unfortunately the Sappers and Miners had not arrived and the absence of tools made it impossible to construct effective barriers. Indeed the road blocks were of such an unsubstantial nature as to puzzle the enemy. Instead of driving over them immediately, the Vichy tanks shelled them for some time before advancing. There was only one pickaxe in Mezze House and bayonets were used to loophole the walls.

Indian Army Public Relations Officer, with two American correspondents—Robert Low of Liberty Magazine, and Kenneth Downes, International News Service— endeavoured to reach the garrison. A Vichy tank blew their vehicle to pieces and they were taken prisoner by an infuriated French officer who with difficulty was dissuaded from shooting them out of hand.

From hour to hour the Mezze garrison scanned the south. The success signal had been put up several times and Lieut.-Colonel Jones sparse reserves, the surviving company of Royal Fusiliers and the French "mariners", were expected to arrive at any moment. Unfortunately these signals were never picked up. After daybreak a helio party had continued to call for help until shot off the roof of Mezze House.

By nightfall the situation was desperate. Ammunition was running low, medical supplies were exhausted. The manor house sheets had been torn up for bandages; under heavy fire the trees in the orchard had been stripped of fruit to eke out the scanty rations. At dusk Lieut.-Colonel Jones selected three officers to run the gauntlet to Brigadier Lloyd at Syrian Force Headquarters. Captain Andre Brunel of the Free French Forces, Lieutenant Cordwell and Jemadar Hoshiar Singh of 4/6 Rajputana Rifles, managed to slip away. After an adventurous night in which they crawled through gardens, crept over roofs, swam streams and burst through cactus zarebas, they arrived at 0500 hours and reported the critical situation.

Brigadier Lloyd already had gathered up his remnants and had despatched them with instructions to reach Mezze at all costs. Under Major Burke of 1 Field Regiment a composite column of the available artillery, the carrier platoons of the Rajputana Rifles and Punjabis, the remaining company of Royal Fusiliers and a few anti-tank guns, had advanced from Medemie. This force battered its way forward against stiff opposition and by evening had contacted the Sikh and Rajput companies of the Punjabis, which had remained throughout the day under cover of the groves. After consultation it was decided to deal with the forts on the ridge above the village before attempting to smash through to Mezze. An assault on these objectives was arranged for next morning.

Had Burke Force, with the audacity characteristic of this operation, endeavoured to reach Mezze that night, it might have achieved the rescue of the garrison. During the hours of darkness the enemy thickened around Brigade Headquarters, and sought to make a speedy end to resistance. The dawn assault on June 20th was particularly severe. The assailants closed to bombing range; every door and window became a target. Field guns over open sights systematically began to batter down the house. A top corner collapsed, burying many wounded including Lieut.-Colonel Greatwood, who later died of his injuries. The building caught fire and it was necessary to carry the wounded outside; from the hillside the tanks continued to rake the grounds, so that men were struck again and again. In the forenoon the defenders saw shells bursting around the forts on the ridge and knew that help was near. With ammunition exhausted, it was decided to ask for a truce to move the wounded to safety; it was hoped that the relief columns would arrive during the armistice. At the sight of the white flag the enemy came rushing from all sides. "D" Company of the Rajputana Rifles under Major Roosmalecoq, which was holding the northern perimeter, endeavoured to cut its way through with the steel but encountered overwhelming forces dug in along the garden ditches. The defence of Mezze House had ended.

Captain S. N. Chatterjee, IMS, Medical Officer of Rajputana Rifles, describes the surrender:

"The enemy rushed in, shouting, snatching arms and field glasses from the officers and men. They were absolutely mad, threatening to shoot an officer and keeping him covered with their guns. Even after surrender some continued firing and killed two men. This was stopped by a French captain who seemed to be a very nice man. The officers were made to fall in in one place and the other ranks in a different place. A party of the enemy were ordered by the French captain to carry the wounded to the hospital. The officers and men were marched away while the wounded were being helped out. They were behaving very ruthlessly towards our wounded, paying no attention to their wounds and pain. One man with a gunshot wound in the abdomen was simply being dragged along. I could not stand the sight so I carried him on my shoulders for a distance of two miles."

Burke Force failed to save the Mezze garrison by less than three hours. At 0700 hours that morning, under cover of an artillery shoot, the Punjabi companies emerged from the woods and clambered up the hillside against the fort which they had captured two nights before. By 0900 hours the first objective had been taken, but the enemy clung obstinately to the second fort and was not dislodged until 1400 hours. At 1600 hours the leading companies of 2/3 Australian Infantry Battalion, force-marching on the sound of the battle, arrived and went over from column of route into the attack. One company stormed enemy positions on the second and commanding ridge behind the Punjabis, while the other company joined Burke Force in the assault on Mezze village. Led by the guns of 1 Field Regiment with muzzles down, blasting their way through, the relief column crashed into Mezze, only to find shattered and empty ruins. The Vichy forces with captives in hand had withdrawn hurriedly into Damascus. Dispositions were taken for the night with the Royal Fusiliers in the village, the Punjabis on the hillside on the left, and the Australians holding the crests of the ridges above the gorge and the road to Beirut.

Against these positions a strong counter-attack swept at 0400 hours next morning. The weight of it fell on the right flank, and after confused fighting the enemy broke into Mezze village. Within an hour the Royal Fusiliers had ejected the intruders, had regained their ground, and had released a number of British and Indian prisoners. At 1100 hours the Australians with artillery support swept across the Beirut road and seized the heights to the north. From the east came sounds of heavy firing. While the Mezze battle had engrossed the defenders, 13 Free French Brigade had eluded the blocking force around the Djebel Kelb, had fought its way through the Gardens and had penetrated to the centre of the city. Among the terraced villas of the summer colony on the slopes of Djebel Kassioum the Vichy forces made their last stand. Here "B" Company of 3/1 Punjabis, brought forward from Madani, put an end to the resistance. For Fourth Indian Division the Syrian campaign was over.

Little remained of 5 Brigade. Royal Fusiliers mustered 100 men, 4/6 Rajputana Rifles 240 of all ranks, while 3/1 Punjabis had sustained over 200 casualties. Fortunately most of the prisoners were soon recovered, being freed at Aleppo after the signing of the Armistice on July 14th. A number of senior officers, however, toured Europe before release. Lieut.-Colonel Calvert Jones, RA, Lieut.-Colonel Jones and Major Scott of the Rajputana Rifles and Major Partridge of Royal Fusiliers, were flown to Salonika, where a number of Viceroy's Commissioned Officers and British NCOs later arrived by ship. After a month's imprisonment on a French liner in the harbour, the prisoners spent an enjoyable week in a slow moving train through Yugoslavia, the Austrian Tyrol, Bavaria and Southern France. It was captivity with a difference. German guards played "Tipperary" and "Roll out the Barrel" on their harmonicas for their charges. On French railway platforms girls surreptitiously exhibited small Union Jacks on the reverse of their lapels. The British Government had addressed a stern note to Vichy, demanding the return of these captives under threat of imprisonment of French collaborators. After a few days in a fortress in Toulon the prisoners were placed on ship for Beirut. While passing through the Messina straits, several of the officers occupied themselves in charting enemy minefields with the aid of a compass and wristwatch. The Royal Navy later gave its thanks. On September 6th Lieut.-Colonel Jones and Major Scott rejoined their battalion.

The reunion necessitated a long inland journey. On the outbreak of hostilities in Syria 21 Indian Brigade of 10 Indian Division had despatched columns as far as Deir Ez Zor on the upper Euphrates. Little opposition but a good deal of argument was encountered from Vichy officials who wished to save their faces. The sheikhs were restless and the area required a firm hand. On the signing of the Syrian armistice 21 Brigade whirled in its tracks and raced eastward to participate in the invasion of Iran. On August 4th 5 Brigade moved into north-eastern Syria by way of Palmyra and Deir Ez Zor, covering the 372 miles between Damascus and Raqqa Fort in three days. Major R. Lawrenson of 4/16 Punjabis had taken over 4/6 Rajputana Rifles pending return of their officers. Major A. V. McDonald, MC, from 5/13 Frontier Force Regiment, had been appointed to command 3/1 Punjabis.

In its new area 5 Brigade settled down to keep the peace between the bickering tribesmen. During this tour both junior and senior officers gained experience in the tricky business of controlling unreasonable people by the arts of diplomacy. Visitors were plentiful. General de Gaulle, General Auchinleck, General Maitland Wilson, the Jam Sahib of Nawanagar and Brigadier Tuker, Director of Military Training in India, all managed to find their way to this out-of-the-way spot.

On September 5th Brigadier Lloyd left for India to take up a staff appointment and was succeeded by Brigadier Dudley Russell, OBE, MC. Thus began an association destined to bring fame to both leader and led. The positive and highly individual "Pasha" had commanded 6/13 Frontier Force Rifles in Eritrea before appointment as GSO I, 5 Indian Division. He brought to his new command a cool and sagacious brain and a marked flair for doing the right thing in the rough-and-tumble of desert fighting.

Free French officials and formations gradually took over 5 Indian Brigade's responsibilities. On September 14th orders arrived for return to Egypt. It is interesting to note that the rear parties on quitting Deir Ez Zor handed over to 1/4 Essex—a battalion destined afterwards to make a great name in 5 Brigade. Moving by easy stages the 800 mile journey to Cairo was covered in nine days. In the second week of October 5 Brigade rejoined Fourth Indian Division in the Libyan frontier area. 1 Buffs (Lieut.-Colonel J. .E. King) replaced the virtually destroyed Royal Fusiliers and training for the autumn offensive began.

Chapter 7

1941 — THE TURN OF THE TIDE

AFTER the Halfaya operations Fourth Indian Division and 7 Armoured Division withdrew from the front, the former returning to Baqqush, the latter to the Delta. Small mobile columns of infantry and artillery kept watch on the frontier. For some months both divisions worked steadily on fortifications in the rear areas. Minefields were laid to cover the port and airfield of Mersa Matruh. The Baqqush "Box" was extended and elaborated. Sixty miles farther east the bottleneck between El Alamein and the Qattara Depression was surveyed and demarcated for defences. On account of the dispersal of the formations on these tasks, training was difficult, and the Indian brigades saw little of each other.

In July General Wavell returned to India. He was succeeded as Commander-in-Chief, Middle East, by Sir Claude Auchinleck, GCIE, CB, DSO, OBE. This appointment thrilled all ranks of Fourth Indian Division. General Auchinleck's life-long association with Indian troops had earned him outstanding recognition. Few if any commanders have known Indian soldiers more intimately; none has stood higher in their esteem. His powerful and sympathetic personality had equipped him with the requisites of leadership; his tall, soldierly figure, quick appraising eye, stern yet kindly greeting, will never be forgotten by those who have served under him.

In August 7 Brigade, which had seen little of the Division to date, was given another outing. With Central India Horse, 12 Field Company Sappers and Miners and 17 Field Ambulance under command, Brigadier Briggs moved to relieve Australian troops in the Siwa and Giarabub oases. These settlements of great antiquity are situated on the Egyptian-Libyan frontier, two hundred miles deep in the desert. From earliest times they have exercised a peculiar fascination over the minds of soldiers, although at no period could they have possessed any particular strategic value. Alexander the Great visited the Siwa oracle before starting on his march to India. More than one army has been engulfed in negotiating the treacherous soft dunes of the Great Sand Sea.

On arrival at Siwa the 4/16 Punjabi diarist wrote:

"The green of the oasis was a welcome sight after 200 miles of desert. The men soon made themselves very comfortable in the date gardens. Each garden had a pond which provided ample water for washing—a luxury almost forgotten. The Sikhs were particularly delighted and wallowed in the unlimited water."

On 7 Brigades return many stories of life in the oases regaled the remainder of the Division. There is the story of the Royal Sussex private who, bored to tears by flies, brackish water and the unending monotony of dry ration diet, opened his first parcel from home in six months and found it to contain delicate dates from Siwa. *The Tiger Kills* sponsors another favourite:

"In the gunner mess it was a rule that every officer before he could drink or dine should kill 30 flies. The late arrivals sometimes had difficulty in complying. One day the Commanding Officer returned late—hot, dirty and tired—and wearily picked up the fly swatter. At that moment his batman entered the dugout and handed him a plate with the words 'Your flies, Sir'."

On August 6th 4/11 Sikhs were despatched to Giarabub, seventy miles further west, where they occupied a modern fort built by the Italians to prevent their restless Senussi subjects from escaping into Egypt. Until Bagnold began his invaluable surveys, the desert beyond Giarabub had been unknown; now the daring young men of Long Range Desert Group crossed and re-crossed regularly on their missions behind the enemy lines. 7 Brigade varied the monotony of garrison duties with patrols of sufficient range and strength to annoy the enemy. Giarabub was bombed on several occasions; on August 17th the Sikhs suffered 17 casualties. The greatly venerated shrine of Mohammed Ben Senussi, the founder of the sect, received damage which the Moslem soldiers of the garrison undertook to repair. During their stay they served as custodians of the Holy Place.

Meanwhile the miseries of summer—heat, glare, *khamsin,* and above all the filthy and intolerable plague of flies—vexed and tormented the British and Indian garrisons in Western Egypt. The Sappers and Miners had never worked under such pressure before. The demand for fresh fortifications, new minefields, better roads, seemed insatiable. The new RAF squadrons on arrival borrowed guards and sappers; each airstrip required buildings, fluid installations and plane bunkers. In July the commander of 4 Field Company wrote glumly that there was enough work on hand to keep his men busy until Christmas. The vagaries of local labour presented problems. (Libyan refugees and Egyptians, when placed on the same water ration as the Sappers and Miners, promptly went on strike). There was great joy when New Zealand engineers brought the first machines to replace picks and shovels. "We now have 2 bulldozers, 2 rooters, 1 backacter and 1 autopatrol," boasted a Sapper diarist proudly. The greatest preoccupation remained mines—their raising and their laying. The Indians quickly became proficient but not without cost; on July 28th a party of 2/5 Mahrattas engaged in arming mines was blown up, 10 being killed and 6 wounded. The Field Companies competed in speed of sowing these lethal instruments; over 3,000 in a night was deemed worthy of mention. The monotony of the mine laying was illustrated by a reference in 4 Field Company's diary. A New Zealand lorry by chance backed over an armed mine. "It gave us confidence" said the commentator. "Mines really work. We have laid so many, and have never seen one go off before." The arrival of the first radio mine detector likewise was a memorable occasion, and sappers quarrelled vigorously for the privilege of testing the new device and of hearing the hum in their ears. Sandwiched among regular tasks were a never-ending host of minor jobs which often were interrupted by the sound of enemy aircraft overhead. When the passing silhouettes identified Junkers 52 troop carriers, picks and shovels were dropped, rifles seized, and the Sappers and Miners rallied at appointed stations to deal with parachutists, who were always expected but who never came.

At the beginning of September Fourth Division Headquarters moved forward and assumed command of all troops in the frontier area. These included 22 Guards Brigade, 7 Support Group from 7 Armoured Division, and 4 South African Armoured Car Regiment. At the same time its own wanderers returned to the fold—7 Brigade from the oases, 5 Brigade from Syria. At this juncture 11 Indian Brigade changed its commander. When Brigadier Savory was posted to an appointment in Eritrea, to the delight of all an officer of one of the battalions of 11 Brigade was selected to succeed him.* Brigadier A. Anderson, DSO, MC, 2 Camerons, had risen from private to lieutenant-colonel in his regiment. This pithy and characteristic Scot had endeared himself to all by his outstanding courage and resource. "A couple of tanks and the Colonel" had been the Camerons' recipe for victory.

In the four months since the Halfaya operations, the tide had turned in Middle East. The Eastern march of the Axis powers had been halted. Syria, Iran and Iraq had been pacified. Malta and Tobruk, still under seige, resisted stoutly. The Anzac and British divisions which had been mauled in Greece and Crete had been re-equipped and were ready for fresh employment. The supply build-up to some extent had been retarded by diversions to Russia, but a trickle of cargoes, soon to swell into spate, delivered weapons from the new American arsenals—Tomahawk and Kittihawk planes, Stuart tanks, and above all else, the light trucks which were the common carriers of Western Desert. Expansion was in the air. On September 27th Western Desert Force breathed its last in giving birth to Eighth Army. General Beresford-Peirse took over as Kaid, Sudan Command, and General Sir Alan Cunningham, KCB, DSO, MC, came from East Africa as Army Commander. 13 Corps under Lieutenant-General A. R. Godwin-Austen, CB, OBE, MC, and 30 Corps under Lieutenant-General C. W. Norrie, CB, DSO, MC, were new intermediate forma-

---

*Brigadier Savory afterwards became, in succession, G.O.C. 23 Indian Division on the Burma front, Director of Infantry Training at G.H.Q. India, G.O.C. in Iraq, and Adjutant-General, India.

tions. Middle East Command, a boy on a man's errand a year before, now had grown up.

The relentless war at sea now took toll of two of every four enemy ships which dared the Mediterranean passage. At this juncture Axis forces in Africa consisted of eleven divisions. Rommel's Afrika Korps comprised 15 and 21 Panzer Divisions and 90 Light Division. Two Italian corps included the Pavia, Bologna, Brescia, Savona and Sabrata infantry divisions; the Ariete armoured division; Trieste and Trento motorised divisions. Four of these divisions were employed in the siege of Tobruk. The remainder of the enemy forces (barring Sabrata on lines of communication in Tripolitania) garrisoned a great encampment, whose crescent swung twenty to thirty miles into the desert between the horns of Halfaya and Tobruk. The perimeter was guarded by minefields and strong points along the ridges and escarpments which paralleled the sea; on the outer arc, substantial concentrations at the Omars in the frontier areas, at El Gubi in the deep desert, at Sidi Rezegh and El Adem on the outskirts of Tobruk, provided anchor strongholds competent to endure siege and to provide bastions for the protection of mobile forces. In the desert as the armour battle went, so went the victory. The enemy's panzers therefore gave cohesion and fortress status to an encampment area covering 3,000 square miles.

As long as Axis tanks could rove at will, the enemy remained in a strong strategic position. His back was secured by the sea, his eastern flank by the frontier escarpment. Invading forces could approach only through a narrow entrance; whatever the direction of the attack or choice of battlefield, the advantage of terrain remained with the defenders. In tanks as in their tactical employment, Rommel held a marked advantage. His three armoured divisions represented 505 runners of which more than half were of the heavy Mark III and Mark IV types, superior in gun power and armour to anything that Eighth Army could put in the field. On paper the British force possessed 665 armoured fighting vehicles, but 90 of this number were locked up in Tobruk with 32 Army Tank Brigade. Of the remainder, 1 Army Tank Brigade mustered 120 Matildas and Valentines, and the three brigades of 7 Armoured Division 455 tanks, of which 165 were light Stuarts and the remainder mostly Crusaders. None of the British tanks mounted a heavier gun than a two-pounder; the lightest German cannon fired a shell of 4½ pounds, the heaviest enemy projectile weighed 14 pounds. In a fleet action all the dreadnoughts would be on one side.

Nevertheless the Commander of Eighth Army had resolved to seize the initiative and to attack at the earliest opportunity. This decision was spurred by the knowledge that Rommel was preparing for a major assault on Tobruk. While preparations for the new offensive proceeded, Fourth Indian Division entered on its tour of duty on the frontier. On September 24th 11 Brigade relieved 22 Guards Brigade on the coastal plain below Halfaya. The guardsmen in best Desert Rat tradition had pinned down and harassed the enemy, a routine entirely to the taste of their successors. Nightly British and Indian raiding groups infiltrated, snatched prisoners, identified gun positions, laid mines and rigged booby traps. Small patrols would penetrate deeply, lie doggo in inconspicuous coverts throughout the day and return on the following night with intimate details of the enemy dispositions. On one occasion Captain Kirke of 1/6 Rajputana Rifles led a patrol nearly three miles into enemy territory and blazed off Verey lights to provoke retaliation. Captain J. McA. Haddon, DSO, of the same battalion, who had won a very fine award as a subaltern in Eritrea, was killed on a similar daring expedition. These reconnaissances fitted piece after piece into the picture of the enemy's defences, and gave British planners the necessary information to organize counter-measures.

The enemy did not always accept these demonstrations tamely. On September 15th South African armoured cars reported columns to be advancing rapidly along the top of the escarpment towards Divisional Tactical Headquarters in Straffers Wadi. Wireless intercepts confirmed a full scale reconnaissance in force by 21 Panzer Division. An exciting twelve hours followed, during which Divisional forward elements withdrew some twenty miles. The panzers penetrated as far as Rabia Fort. By this time air groups from both sides were participating in the action and during a refuelling halt the panzers received a thorough plastering by Maryland bombers. An Italian Stuka squadron remaining aloft too long, ran out of petrol and landed in twos and threes in the forward area. For several days thereafter armoured car clashes continued as the advance screens sought to rescue or to capture the grounded aircraft.

To Central India Horse this was only one of many adventurous and exciting outings. Lieut.-Colonel George and his men had a parish of 30,000 square miles. The armoured cars often covered 300 miles in a night. It became a matter of pride to find gaps in wire and minefields by blind navigation during the hours of darkness. Investigating dust clouds, shadowing convoys, rescuing baled-out airmen, searching for hidden dumps, demarcating trails, strewing mines in likely spots, cutting off straggling transport, shooting up enemy outposts, cheekily reconnoitring enemy concentration points, but always with a wary eye overhead for Stukas which might slide out of the sun—so ran the tale of the cavalrymen's days. Because they were mobile they were popular, and it fell to them to play desert hosts to every manner of visitor—soldiers, sailors, airmen, distinguished neutrals, war correspondents, broadcasters, and other daring and inquisitive civilians who had wangled their way to the front. They taught desert ways to Polish cavalrymen who became their firm friends. These impetuous and gallant exiles, great comrades all, were introduced to "Whisky Buq Buq", the splash being the brackish fluid from the local wells. The Poles in a *lingua franca* of Arabic, French, English and gesticulation, talked endlessly of the three K's which mattered—Kon, Kobeita and Kognac—which translated into Horses, Women and Wine.

CYPRUS

FAMAGUSTA--CATHEDRAL CONVERTED INTO A MOSQUE BY ADDITION OF A MINARET.

RUINS—HILARION CASTLE, CYRENE.

VILLAGE SCENE.

SIWA OASIS.

GENERAL MESSERVY AND BRIGADIER BRIGGS FOLLOWING THE PROGRESS OF THE BATTLE OF LIBYAN OMAR.

NEAR ALAM HAMZA—STUKA STRIKE ON HEADQUARTERS GROUP.

TOBRUK PERIMETER—ROAD BLOCK.

TOBRUK PERIMETER—ANTI-TANK DITCH.

BENGHAZI WATERFRONT—FORMER GERMAN HEADQUARTERS IN BACKGROUND.

SOUVENIR.

ROYAL SIGNALS

LINE LAYER.

PORTABLE WIRELESS.

DESPATCH RIDER.

COMMUNICATION UNIT.

ROYAL INDIAN ENGINEERS

MINE-DETECTING—THE OLD METHOD.

MINE-DETECTING—THE FIRST SWEEPS.

ROYAL INDIAN ENGINEERS

ROAD BUILDING—ERITREA.

ROAD BUILDING—BEN ZELTEN DEFILE, TUNISIA.

On November 3rd details of the invasion of Libya were disclosed to senior officers. The general scheme contemplated a more ambitious version of "BATTLEAXE" operation. Two corps would enter Libya by the southern route, where the escarpment sank into the desert forty miles to the south-east of Salum. 13 Corps, comprising Fourth Indian and 2 New Zealand Division, together with 1 Army Tank Brigade, would strike north along the line of the escarpment, to contain the enemy in the frontier area, and to protect the lines of communication of 30 Corps, which as the predominant partner in the operation would drive across the desert, would bring the enemy armour to battle and would relieve Tobruk. 7 Armoured Division, 1 South African Division and 22 Guards Brigade were entrusted with this task. At the right moment the garrison of Tobruk would burst out to link up with the relieving forces.

13 Corps would not be committed to battle until the hostile tank forces had been met and dealt with. Thereafter the Indian and New Zealand divisions would root out the enemy garrisons in the frontier area and would link up with 30 Corps for an advance to Tobruk along the coast. Only one Indian brigade would participate in the early stages of the battle. 7 Brigade, which had moved up to Sofafi on November 11th, would cross the frontier at zero hour and would advance in conformity with the New Zealanders as far as the Omars, where it would mask that strong position and await the outcome of 30 Corps' endeavours to bring the panzers to battle. 11 Brigade would continue to engross the enemy beneath the Salum escarpment. 5 Brigade would remain on lines of communication until troop-carrying transport became available. 5 Brigade Headquarters however would take command of the southern escarpment area as soon as the invasion had been launched.

The deployment of Eighth Army was delayed until the last moment in the hope that the enemy would believe the manifest preparations to represent no more than those of a reconnaissance in force. Only a few hours before the battle did 7 Brigade move forward to its start line, five miles north-west of Conference Cairn. 1 Royal Sussex under Lieut.-Colonel G .C. Evans had been left behind on guard duties until such time as the enemy forces had been located and engaged. 2 New Zealand Division came up on the left of 7 Brigade and to ensure effective liaison placed a squadron of its Divisional Cavalry Regiment under Brigadier Briggs command. Elsewhere among the rolling dunes, on the bleak salt pans and scrabbly wastes, 100,000 men and over 10,000 vehicles stood ready.

On November 17th in a special Order of the Day General Messervy addressed his men in words of pride:

"On the eve of this great battle in which this Division has the honour to take part, I wish to stress a few points of major importance to all ranks.

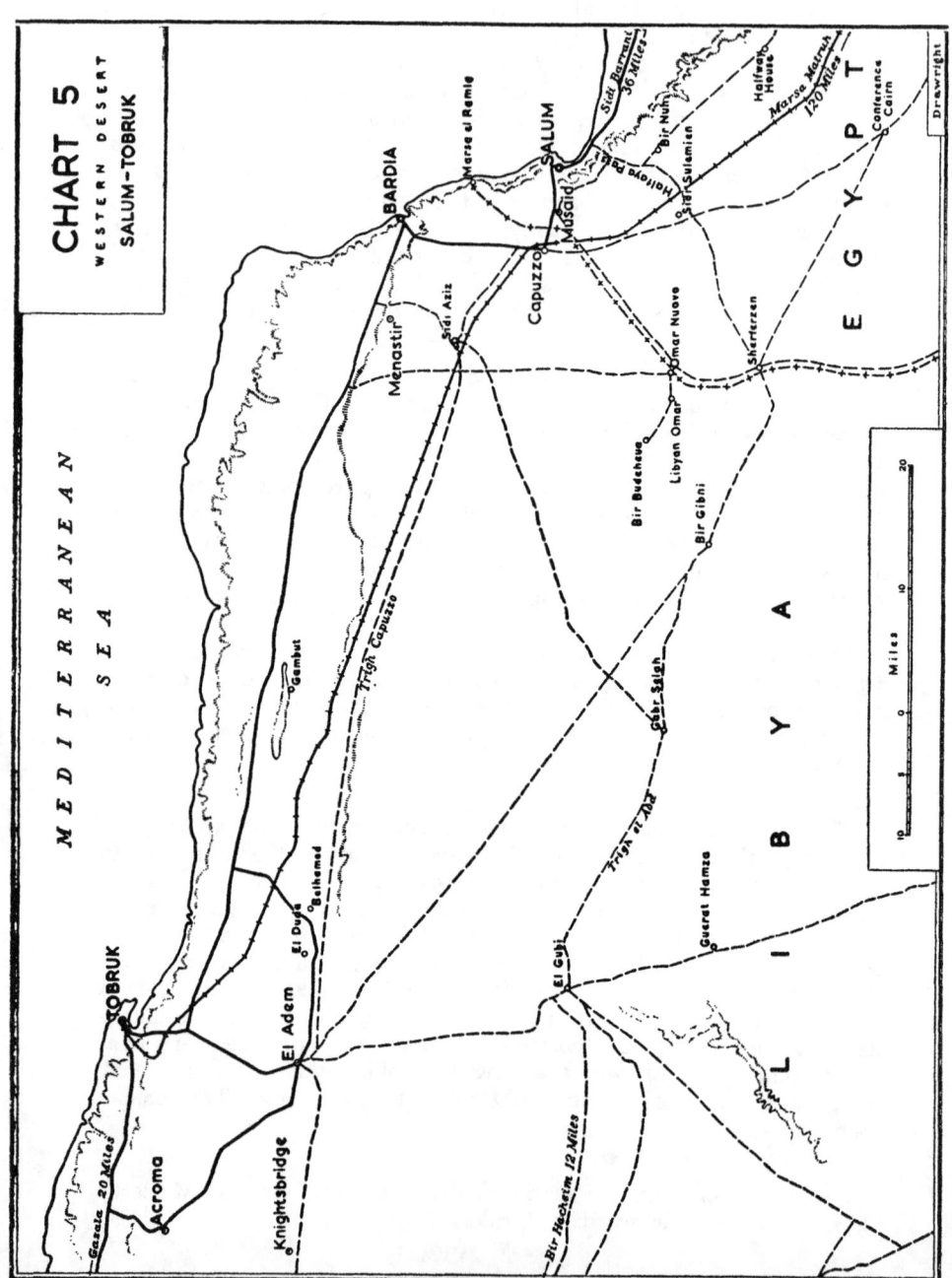

"We are now in full strength in our supporting arms. We have in the Division no less than 102 anti-tank guns, with 64 South African anti-tank guns behind them; 56 twenty-five pounders, 36 40 mm. guns, a total of 258 guns in the Divisional area, (quite apart from any 'I' tanks allotted), with which we can kill the German panzers if they should come our way. With such armament and such staunch men behind the guns, we can only hope that the fortunes of the days to come will give us the chance of helping in the issue of the battle by providing us with some good 'panzer shikar'.

"Similarly we are all ready and trained for a good Stuka shoot. Let us keep cool, swing boldly ahead of our birds, and let them have it with every weapon we possess. The bag will be good.

"Finally, if we close in on the enemy, I know that every man in the Division by his skill and courage and dash will play his part in achieving the great success in which I am confident.

"I would have liked to have been able to have visited you all personally, to wish you all the best of luck and to reiterate to you the pride I feel in having under my command such a fine body of troops. But time and distance will not permit me to do so. I have, therefore, resorted to the written word, to wish you Godspeed and good fortune."

Next morning, after a night of heavy rain, a great armada of vehicles sailed in fleet formation north and north-westwards to find and to engage the enemy. By dawn 7 Brigade had advanced twenty miles to Bir Sheferzen. As the first patrols went out, a heavy rumble of artillery came from the west. The battle had been joined.

Chapter 8

"CRUSADER" OPERATION — ADVANCE ON TOBRUK

For Fourth Indian Division the early days of the new offensive were uneventful. After a heavy night's rain the sun on November 18th shone blithely—a superb and stimulating day. When no enemies showed, the rumour spread that the panzers were bogged down in their harbours along the coast. At noon 1 Royal Sussex hurried forward, in high spirits at rejoining their Indian comrades before the battle opened. That evening 7 Brigade were ordered to concentrate in the Bir Bu Deheua area, five miles to the north-west of the Omars. This move was made on November 19th without encountering the enemy. The New Zealanders conformed, advancing in the open desert on the left.

Throughout that day thunder grew in the west. 7 Armoured Division was trailing its coat in the enemy's bailiwick. Near Gabr Taleb El Essem, eighteen miles beyond the frontier wire, a running fight occurred between 4 Armoured Brigade and 100 panzers. 22 Armoured Brigade fell on Ariete Division near Bir El Gubi and destroyed 45 out of 60 tanks. Thereafter the British columns wheeled and drove on Sidi Rezegh, on the rim of the desert escarpment. Late in the afternoon of November 19th tanks trundled across the airfield to seize this strong position, within ten miles of the main coastal road and only twenty miles from Tobruk. Next morning 5 South African Brigade arrived to consolidate the gains, and the signal was flashed to the Tobruk garrison to stage its breakout on November 21st.

Heavy fighting ensued in the Sidi Rezegh area throughout November 20th, but that evening Army Headquarters was sufficiently sanguine to unleash 13 Corps. 2 New Zealand Division pushed on into the north for twenty miles and reached the line of the Trigh Capuzzo. 7 Brigade had reconnoitred the Omars and had discovered the garrison to be mining the northern perimeters. Central India Horse moved to the north-east to cut communications with the enemy strongholds on the frontier. These preliminaries completed, Fourth Indian Division turned to the main business in hand and prepared for battle against the Omars. The attack was timed to begin at 1200 hours on November 22nd.

This fortified area consisted of three encampments which had been dug around Libyan Omar and Omar Nuovo, mounds in the plain fifteen miles south of Capuzzo, and Got Adhidiba, shewn on military maps as the Cova position. The Omars were slightly over two miles apart, Omar Nuovo being due east of Libyan Omar. Cova, a boomerang-shaped feature of inconspicuous height, was five miles to the north-east. The Omars fortified areas were roughly circular in shape and approximately two miles in diameter. Around the central humps, which afforded excellent observation over a wide expanse of level plain, well-sited trenches and gun positions had been prepared flush with the ground. The slit trenches were straight-faced and narrow, dug by mechanical drills and lined with rock. They were organized in radial groups which gave each strong point additional protection from shell fire. The overhead cover was sufficient to thwart field artillery. There was no spoil to betray the locations, and the camouflage harmonized with its surroundings sufficiently to render the strong points almost invisible. Belts of wire and minefields encircled the perimeters. All three encampments were garrisoned by the Savona Division, with headquarters at Bir Ghirba, four miles to the north of Cova. A number of specialist German units were nominally under Italian command.

Brigadier Briggs allocated one of his battalions to each of the fortified localities. Royal Sussex was directed to open with an assault on Omar Nuovo. As soon as success was assured, 4/16 Punjabis would attack Libyan Omar. 4/11 Sikhs were ordered to mask Cova. 5 New Zealand Brigade undertook to keep the ring in the north, with special attention to Bir Ghirba. The similarity to Sidi Barrani tactics should be noted. Omar Nuovo like Nibeiwa represented the keystone of the enemy structure.

On the morning of November 22nd, 1 and 25 Field Regiments, 7 Medium Regiment and a group of R.A.F. bombers, opened a softening-up programme on Omar Nuovo. A smoke screen was laid along the eastern perimeter of Libyan Omar to mask the artillery in that camp. 1 Royal Sussex embussed and moved off on a two company front, with two squadrons of "I" tanks from 42 Royal Tank Regiment in support. Lieut.-Colonel Desmond Young MC, Indian Army Public Relations, has supplied a vivid story of the approach and subsequent action:

"As we crossed the desert that morning, we could hear the rumble and crashes as the artillery and bombers laid on. The little carriers of Royal Sussex led, followed by the tanks with their pennants flying. Immediately behind the tanks came the leading companies of the infantry in lorries. Behind them, Brigade Headquarters. Then came the remainder of the Royal Sussex, and following, more tanks, lorries and carriers for the 4/16 Punjabi attack, until as far as the eye could reach the plain was filled with fighting machines speeding into battle. I had just said 'Trafalgar must have been like this' when a whizz and a crash showed the enemy to be ranging on us. On the horizon upright black streaks marked the telescopic ladders of his artillery observers. We had no hope of concealing ourselves on a plain as flat and bare as a billiard table."

As the Royal Sussex neared Omar Nuovo, Lieutenant D. W. Gaylard with his carriers dashed for a previously reconnoitred gap in the minefield. It proved a trap; a hedge of mines had been sown; four tanks and three carriers were blown up. With the infantry pressing behind, Lieutenant Gaylard rallied his remaining carriers and charged across the minefield. The tanks followed; the Royal Sussex tumbled out of their lorries, formed up and raced in. A magnificent surge carried them into the enemy positions, 500 yards ahead. In a short fierce hurly-burly, the attack won home. From deep slit trenches and heavily manned strong points Italians emerged, their arms upraised. Here and there groups fought on, but within two hours the main resistance had been broken and 1,500 prisoners had been taken.

This superb feat of arms had not been without loss. 11 officers and 103 men had paid the price of victory. Let Lieut.-Colonel Young continue his narrative:

"Thirty men, all that remained of one company, took 300 prisoners armed with mortars, anti-tank and machine-guns. 14 men of another company took a further 300 prisoners. At every step I saw gallantry beyond praise. Corporal A. Talmey, wounded several times, continued to lead his section. When weakness stopped him, he gave covering fire with a Bren gun, enabling his two remaining men to capture yet another post. Lieutenant C. H. Covington, hit in the knees, hobbled on until killed against a strong point, just as his men took it. Corporal Brennan, with his stretcher-bearers right up with the forward troops, picked up the wounded as they fell. A gunner officer, observation over, led another section, waving his cap and cheering madly. Another corporal, badly wounded, lay under the muzzle of a silenced gun, but raised himself painfully to say 'I put that bastard out, Sir, with a couple of bombs'. No storm troops in the world could have bettered those South Country men."

"In the twilight of that winter evening I walked over the battlefield with Brigadier Briggs. I saw a sad number of our dead, but never one who had not fallen with his face to the enemy. Action had ceased but a sniper was paying us some attention and a machine-gun was firing at close range. 'We must get those birds out before dark', said the Brigadier. Two tanks were despatched to sweep the ground, with infantry accompanying them. In the dusk their tracer bullets splashed red and green against the apparently deserted trenches. Then came the bright yellow flashes of grenades thrown into dug-outs by the infantry. Back came the tanks with their tails behind them—tails of 200 more prisoners, who trudged in as night fell."

The minute by minute sitreps give a succinct yet dramatic description of the action:

    1140   Our bombers plaster the Omars.

    1155   23 of our own fighters over enemy positions.

1200   Zero hour. Artillery barrage opens. Cloud of dust completely covers enemy area.

1220   Royal Sussex start.

1221   Briggs reports "All Well."

1235   Sussex CO reports tanks went in late but all going well. Some shelling.

1250   6 our tanks up on mines. Main advance continuing. Sussex have debussed pushing right in.

1300   20 our fighters over area. Tanks have smashed through inner wire and advanced into enemy positions.

1305   Companies still advancing. Enemy fire weakening.

1310   Advancing under heavy shell fire.

1321   Left position penetrated. Think right also.

1342   First objective taken with many prisoners. Moving on to second phase.

1358   31 Field Regiment ordered up and Brigadier going forward to contact tanks.

At 1400 hours an exultant message flashed from General Messervy: *"Royal Sussex and 42 Tank Regiment. Shabash Gora Paltan. Shabash tanks".*

As the Royal Sussex won home, 4/16 Punjabis closed up and waited for the word. While deploying on their start line, their leading vehicles fouled a minefield, and it was decided to bring the infantry to jump-off positions through Omar Nuovo. The Royal Sussex were still mopping-up when the Punjabi troop carriers filed through the encampment and deployed 4,000 yards east of their objective. The Indian attack swept in under cover of bombardment with tanks in the van heading for a narrow gap in the minefield. When within 800 yards a trap was revealed. This gap was covered by a battery of 88 millimeter guns, dug in flush with the ground. At such range they could not miss. The leading tanks reeled out of line broken and burning. A second squadron, swinging away from the unbearable fire, blundered into a known and wired minefield; here a dozen tanks, disabled by mines, were blown to pieces by the deadly artillery. When 4/16 Punjabis arrived on their debussing line, only five tanks remained in action.

Yet as at Omar Nuovo the spirit of the infantry prevailed. Dashing through gaps in the wire, the Punjabis fell with the bayonet on the first enemy trenches and cleared them. A brilliant operation followed, in which platoons and sections, methodically stalking enemy weapon pits and strong points, destroyed post after post. Moving always to the flank and skirting resistance, the Indians quartered the ground like terriers, ferreting out the defenders. The sepoys had packed their pockets with captured Italian grenades. As in East Africa, these small, light missiles proved an excellent weapon. Hurling them high, the Punjabis, under cover of their bursts, raced in with the steel. When night fell, the eastern section of the camp had been cleared to a depth of several hundred yards. 500 prisoners had been taken, together with several guns, in return for 147 casualties of all ranks. But without armour it was impossible to overwhelm the defenders and piecemeal mopping-up promised to be prolonged. On the morning of November 23rd, Brigadier Briggs informed Lieut.-Colonel Lavender of the Punjabis that it was unnecessary to work to schedule. In the afternoon the artillery put down a shoot and the Punjabis, reinforced by one company of 4/11 Sikhs, resumed their nibbling tactics, slipping between the enemy posts, harassing them and eventually winkling out the occupants. By nightfall more than 1,000 prisoners had been taken as against 35 Indian casualties, and the Punjabis held one-third of the area of Libyan Omar.

Meanwhile the demonstration by 4/11 Sikhs had proved the Cova position to be strongly held. The enemy plastered the Sikh forming-up area with shell fire. Lieutenant Mohammed Sadiq MC, having stormed an outpost in a brisk encounter, found it difficult to disengage. 2 New Zealand Division, on the other hand, encountered little or no opposition to its advance into the north, and by the nightfall on November 23rd was some twenty-five miles ahead. With 7 Brigade's flank uncovered, General Messervy ordered 5 Brigade to hasten to the battle area. Brigadier Russell, who was busily concentrating his men from dispersal on various tasks under nominal command of 2 South African Division, received two different sets of instructions within a matter of minutes— General Messervy's orders and a fresh task set by Army Command. The battle need seemed greater. Leaving the remainder of his men to follow, the Brigade Commander hurried forward with 3/1 Punjabis.

Before he could arrive, tragedy had supervened. Everywhere November 23rd had been a day of resounding defeats. The Tobruk sortie, executed with the utmost gallantry by 70 British Division, had been pinned down with heavy casualties at El Duda, less than five miles from the relief columns. After 48 hours of terrific fighting, a bull's rush by 100 panzers smashed through the covering armour and destroyed 5 South African Brigade at Sidi Rezegh. At Gambut, on the line of the escarpment twenty miles farther east, the New Zealanders, having captured Capuzzo, Salum and Sidi Azeiz, were held up. 13 Corps and 30 Corps had lost touch. Rommel's armour was calling the tune in the battle.

The optimistic outlook which had characterized the opening days of the operation had to be reconsidered. On November 22nd a high staff officer was quoted as saying: "We have the beast's head in the bag but he is still lashing his tail". Unfortunately it was part of 30 Corps that was about to go in the bag and those remaining outside were lashed by the flail of incessant tank attacks. Indeed the situation appeared so ominous that General Cunningham advised Commander-in-Chief Middle East that the battle should be abandoned. General Auckinleck immediately flew to Advanced Headquarters, assumed command of operations personally for a short period, and subsequently entrusted the command of Eighth Army to his Deputy Chief-of-Staff, Major-General Neil Ritchie. 30 Corps was relieved from its Tobruk commitments and 13 Corps was ordered to push forward and to raise the seige. With the frontier area under control, it appeared possible to drive on Tobruk along the main road and the coastal escarpment. In this operation the New Zealanders would strike while Fourth Indian Division kept their backs.

Unfortunately this plan ignored, and not for the last time, the mathematical relationship of the arc and the chord. The long northwesterly swing of 13 Corps' communications was vulnerable from any point in the desert. Disengaging from Sidi Rezegh, Rommel despatched a strong filibustering force to strike at Eighth Army's rear echelons as they plodded across the wastes.

On November 24th, while General Messervy prepared to continue the Omars operation, groups of transport, having passed through one of the gaps in the wire fence marking the Libyan frontier, began to stream past Advanced Divisional Headquarters at Bir Sheferzen. This unorganized movement increased throughout the day, until it became obvious that something had happened in the west. South African vehicles brought news of the disaster at Sidi Rezegh and wireless intercepts from armoured cars revealed panzers to be only a few miles distant. Headquarters of 30 Corps arrived late in the day, bringing the first authentic news of events. Rommel's armour was loose and was heading east; all soft-skinned transport was being withdrawn. To the confusion of such a large-scale withdrawal the R.A.F. added its quota. On news of the German thrust, all available planes had been sent out on ground strafing missions. On 1,000 square miles of desert pursued and pursuers were inextricably intermingled. Pinpointed positions meant nothing. Bombs fell on friends and foes alike. At nightfall hundreds of vehicles were heading into the south-east for safety. 7 Indian Brigade supply echelons drew into close leaguer and refused to be infected by the motoring craze.

With little information except 30 Corps intercepts, General Messervy made dispositions for defence. Central India Horse and 31 Field Regiment moved east to cover the supply dumps on the frontier wire. Instructions to 1 Royal Sussex and to 4/11 Sikhs to continue to probe the Cova position were countermanded. The Sikhs and 1 Field Regiment were sent to escort a New Zealand supply column into Capuzzo. A bit of welcome news was the relief of 11 Brigade in front of Salum, a development which promised to unite Fourth Division in the field. The sun sank with black dots crawling against it all over the western plain. Darkness, strangely enough, threw light on the situation. German leaguer flares identified the lines of advance of the enemy columns. Divisional Headquarters seemed to be in the midst of the panzers, for the Axis signal lights soared and fell on all sides. One of the two main German armoured columns had crossed the frontier wire about a mile south of Divisional Headquarters just as the sun was setting. These raiders then moved to the north-east. Had the enemy chosen the gap in the wire immediately opposite to Bir Sheferzen, one mile farther north, he inevitably must have blundered into the Indian night leaguers. Before midnight it was deemed advisable to move Divisional Headquarters into Omar Nuovo. 7 Brigade despatched patrol screens to cover the shift, and the seven miles of enemy-infested desert was covered, as Lieut.-Colonel Bateman, GSO 1 of the Division, wrote in his excellent account, "almost on tiptoe".

Never in the history of the Division was the ether so cluttered with hopes and fears as on the night of November 24th. A stolid signaller logged the justifiable comment, "Seems to be a flap everywhere". Groups under chase seeking sanctuary, despairing detachments identifying the enemy on all sides, reports from convoys off bearing, of shellfire out of nowhere, of panzers emerging and disappearing, continuous appeals for guidance, identification and direction—minute by minute a spate of first impressions and wild guesses swelled the intelligence summary into a mass of misinformation. Unit commanders read, weighed the probabilities, sighed and waited for daylight to see what really had happened.

With the enemy swarming in the area, a clash was not long delayed. The panzer columns, having crossed the frontier wire south of the Omars, turned into the north in a wide sweep, intent on destruction. Supply columns were shot up and dispersed, the vehicles fleeing in all directions. At 0700 hours on November 25th 4/11 Sikhs and 1 Field Regiment, having completed their escort duties, had returned to their masking positions to the south-east of Cova. An armoured car raced up and reported an enemy tank force to be approaching. One troop of 11 Battery accompanied the Sikhs into the Omars; the remainder of 1 Field Regiment prepared for action.

At 0730 hours 25 tanks appeared in the south, fired a few ranging rounds and withdrew. 1 Field Regiment deployed its batteries in echelon, dug slit trenches and waited. At 0840 hours the panzers reappeared on the horizon and slowly crept forward. Twenty-eight heavy Mark III and Mark IV types advanced in fleet formation in lines five abreast, with 30 yards interval between tanks and 70 yards between ranks. The much debated clash of tank versus field gun was imminent.

At 2,000 yards the panzers opened fire, halting to lay their cannon and maintaining long-range machine-gun fire while in movement. They closed from the south-east and concentrated on 52 Battery on the left of 1 Field Regiment's position. The gunners, lying beside their pieces and waiting for the word, suffered heavily. The tanks crept closer and closer; one gun after another was struck. Still the dour artillerymen waited. When the panzers were only 800 yards away and the final rush imminent, the gunners sprang into action. The sharp bark of the twenty-five pounders cut against the crack of the 75 millimeter cannon as tanks and field guns belaboured each other. For ten minutes, in close deadly encounter, the adversaries swapped punches. The tanks flinched first, broke away and lumbered to the west for 400 yards, where a low dune afforded hull-down protection. Ten tanks in line, the battle continued. When the artillery fire grew unbearable the panzers charged 52 Battery head on. Among the strewn bodies of their comrades the gunners, working like mad, held the enemy armour from the close. At 300 yards the panzer line broke and scrambled away to the south-east, with the vengeful guns buffeting them. Seven smashed tanks dotted the plain, and troops of South African anti-tank gunners, which had arrived too late to join the action, finished off another as it hobbled away.

(Water-Carrier Rattan Singh of the Sikhs, whose imperturbability on the slopes of Samana in Eritrea had earned him mention, was preparing breakfast for his comrades in a slit trench when the tanks appeared. The guns and panzers fought it out over his head. The battle over, he emerged to announce that tea was ready).

This magnificent stand in the open and without support, cost 1 Field Regiment 18 killed and 42 wounded. 52 Battery sustained 42 casualties out of 73 of all ranks in action. The discipline and courage of the artillerymen had halted the panzer foray before it could reach the supply routes to the north of the Omars. This trouncing, however, failed to satisfy the enemy, and during that afternoon another 28 tanks crawled upon the southern perimeter of Omar Nuovo. The purpose of this approach remains a mystery, as the enemy must have known that he was advancing against his own minefields. At 4,000 yards the tanks opened fire. Receiving no response, they continued to close. The drama of the encounter drew the infantry from their slit trenches; every vehicle became a miniature grandstand. For a mile the panzers crept up, firing, halting, studying their targets, firing anew and steadily closing in. The gunners of 1 Field Regiment crouched and bided their time until the first tanks topped a low contour 1,000 yards away. Then artillery commander sprang to his feet with a shout and a salvo from the twenty-five pounders crashed home. Furiously plying shell, the gunners blew the leading tanks to pieces. The panzers tacked to the west under punishment, circling the perimeter and providing a target for every gun in Omar Nuovo. Even 7 Medium Regiment depressed muzzles and pumped heavy shell at the German armour. Five tanks reeled to a stop and six more were disabled as they fled. Many others carried heavy damage out of range.

Towards sunset 4/16 Punjabis reported a number of tanks to have entered the western perimeter of Libyan Omar, where the enemy still held out. Under the direction of Subedar Ghulam Rasul MC, artillery fire searched the area and no attack developed. That evening detachments from 4 Field Company Sappers and Miners blew up all disabled tanks with land mines.

So ended a proud day for the gunners whose casualties in the second encounter had been negligible. 5 German Tank Regiment had lost 19 panzers and had been held from the close. This day's test of tank versus field gun may have had important repercussions. The ability of British artillery to endure heavy punishment while waiting for targets must have suggested to Rommel's realistic mind that his favourite bull's rush might prove an expensive manoeuvre. From then onward his armour grew more cautious in its attempts to overrun British positions; self-propelled guns and other artillery were enrolled in support of the German tanks. It is perhaps not too much to claim that another stage in the evolution of mechanised warfare was reached on that exciting day at Omar Nuovo.

Although Rommel's blow at Eighth Army's lines of communications was less than twenty-four hours old and its results as yet unascertained, General Auchinleck had decided to adhere to the classical axiom—"Maintain the Objective". 2 New Zealand Division less 5 New Zealand Brigade and the Divisional Cavalry Regiment would continue to drive on Tobruk along the coastal road. Fourth Indian Division as from noon of November 25th would assume command of the frontier area as far west as the line Sidi Azeiz-Bardia. This commitment carried responsibility for the maintenance of the Kiwi garrisons at Capuzzo and Salum—an undertaking which gave Divisional Headquarters some anxious hours. Neither food nor ammunition convoys as yet had reached the Omars.

By the morning of November 26th the situation was clearing. The raiding panzers, blocked from replenishment at Eighth Army dumps, were less fancy-free and more or less footbound as they moved to rendezvous with their own supply columns. The British air forces had continued their indefatigable if sometimes over-generous intervention: for ninety minutes before dawn on November 28th Albacores of the Fleet Air Arm gave Omar Nuovo a thorough plastering. Mr. Quentin Reynolds, American war correspondent, shared this ordeal, afterwards describing his stay with Fourth Division in a brilliant narrative captioned "There were Giants in those Days".

7 Brigade sent out patrols throughout the morning along the line of the frontier wire towards Capuzzo without encountering the enemy. Later in the day the New Zealand Cavalry Regiment, which had lost touch with its Division, entered the Omars and asked for instructions. While quiet reigned on the frontier, two New Zealand brigades had battered their way forward along the coastal escarpment and on November 25th had stormed Sidi Rezegh and Belhamed, within five miles of the Tobruk garrison at El Duda. The relief of Tobruk appeared

imminent until the enemy struck venomously out of the desert at New Zealand lines of communication. After fierce fighting a strong panzer force overran 5 New Zealand Brigade Headquarters at Sidi Azeiz, twenty miles north of the Omars. Thus a stab in the back countered a blow at the breast. In such confused encounter the battle continued. No one knew what the desert held. Every dust cloud must be scanned until it yielded either friend or foe. Roving forces bumped each other, sheered away or closed in a blaze of gun fire. A storeman who lived in a *bir*, one of the cistern-shaped silos of antiquity, emerged one morning to find an enemy troop of armoured cars replenishing at his dump. Ducking down the ladder, a quick S.O.S. caught South Africans less than a mile away. They raced to the kill. Neither Germans nor South Africans had previously known of the dump nor of each other's presence in the neighbourhood.

On the morning of November 26th, 17 Field Ambulance reported in at Conference Cairn after thirty-six hours' captivity. Two evenings before, a German light tank and armoured car had arrived at the main dressing station in the shelter of a low ridge to the south of Bir Sherferzen. The personnel were lined up, informed that they were prisoners and instructed to continue work under directions of an Italian doctor. In the middle of the night a lost British gunner officer walked into the surgical ward to enquire his whereabouts. Fortunately the guard's back was turned. On being advised *sotto voce* of the situation by Major Aird, who was operating, he tiptoed out and away. Next morning the dressing-station was in the midst of the tide of battle which flowed up and down the plain. The tank groups mauled by 1 Field Regiment passed through the ambulance lines. In the afternoon the dressing-station caught part of the storm of shells and salvoes of bombs which sped the discomfited panzers on their way. Colonel von Stephan, commander of 5 German Panzer Regiment and mortally wounded at the Omars, was brought in for treatment. Late in the evening a German officer who spoke English called and collected his personal effects. During the night the battle passed and Central India Horse arrived early next morning to escort the Field Ambulance to a more secure location.

When the Germans captured the medical unit, they also netted two of the Division's chaplains—the Reverend Philip Daniels and Father O'Flynn. Father O'Flynn made a dramatic escape in a 15-cwt. truck on the morning before the unit was liberated.

With Rommel's raiders occupied elsewhere, Fourth Indian Division could now re-apply itself to its appointed task. At dawn on November 27th, after a ten-minute shoot, 4/16 Punjabis with a company of 4/11 Sikhs under command moved against the stubborn survivors who continued to resist in the south and west sections of Libyan Omar encampment. The artillery barrage proved ineffective and after 300 yards penetration the attack was pinned down by resolute opposition. 44 Punjabi and 35 Sikh casualties were sustained in this unsuccessful operation. The Punjabi anti-tank platoon bagged a careless panzer for the sole trophy of the day. It was later learned that a German named Schoen had been responsible for the well-integrated and obstinate defence of Libyan Omar. A fanatical fighter, this officer had been told by Rommel to hold fast until relieved. He was a brutal if indomitable man, shooting cowards and weaklings out of hand and using Italians as a screen to protect his Germans.

Chagrin at failure to make headway at Libyan Omar was ameliorated during the morning by good news from the west. New Zealanders and the Tobruk garrison had established contact, with a narrow corridor opened along the El Adem road. This junction had been effected in the face of the utmost German resistance. Such achievement in the west marked the end of the enemy filibuster along the frontier. At noon on November 27th a panzer count from the air reported no German tanks east of the frontier wire except odd runners limping westwards. The counter stroke had ended in failure. The refusal of General Auchinleck to be discountenanced or deterred by defeat at Sidi Rezegh was the turning point of the battle. Fourth Indian Division, by storming the Omars and so denying the raiders a fortress for replenishment, had played a leading part in the discomfiture of the enemy.

The destruction of 5 New Zealand Brigade Headquarters had left a number of orphan formations in Fourth Division's northern area. A New Zealand battalion was withdrawn from blocking the bolt hole of Bardia and brought into Capuzzo to set up an emergency brigade headquarters. It then became necessary to feed and munition this formation—no easy task in view of the chronic shortage of vehicles. On the morning of November 29th the first Fourth Division supply convoy reached the Kiwis. Their pleasure was unbounded as they were very short of liquids. When the grinning Indian drivers handed out not only petrol and water but also a generous issue of rum, an intimate link was forged in the chain of comradeship.

5 Indian Brigade was now concentrated on the battlefield and available for employment. 3/1 Punjabis were ordered to attempt a surprise attack on Libyan Omar from the north in conjunction with an assault by 4/16 Punjabis from the east. The remainder of the Brigade, with Central India Horse, 1 and 31 Field Regiments under command, moved north to Sidi Azeiz and relieved 5 New Zealand Brigade, which immediately embussed for the west. Brigadier Russell's instructions were to block all routes by which the enemy garrisons in Halfaya, Salum and Bardia might escape. In the course of this move to Sidi Azeiz, an air report of a large tank force on his flank impelled Brigadier Russell to despatch Major Sykes of 57 LAA Regiment to investigate. A terrifying concentration was discovered, which after painstaking reconnaissance was identified as British dummy tanks which had been emplaced and forgotten.

On November 29th the welcome news came through that 11 Brigade was approaching Bir Sheferzen. As Fourth Division drew together, thoughts turned to the next task; but first it was necessary to put an end to Libyan Omar. The garrison had been compressed into an area of less than a square mile but continued to resist obstinately. Shortly after 1800 hours 3/1 Punjabis left Sidi Omar for an assembly position to the north of Libyan Omar, on the opposite side to the sector held by 4/16 Punjabis. It was arranged that the latter battalion, by means of signal flares and war cries, should provide the newcomers with a bearing for their deployment and that 31 Field Regiment should give directional fire. The night was dark and intensely cold. By 0230 hours the numbed troops had debussed and all four companies were moving forward on foot. At 0515 hours the enemy wire was reached, the gap found, and the infantry passed through. Lieut.-Colonel A. V. McDonald MC and his headquarters remained outside the wire, to effect contact with artillery liaison officers due to arrive at dawn.

It would appear that fire was opened prematurely. (Due to losses in Syria, 3/1 Punjabis contained a high percentage of recruits). An eye-witness wrote: "Within ten minutes Libyan Omar appeared ablaze, a shrieking inferno. A torrent of flashes swayed towards the left, then to the centre and over to the right—a frenzy of small arms fire and bursting bombs". No messages came back from the companies. As soon as dawn broke, Battalion Headquarters was detected on the open plain and heavily shelled. Captain Charles Boulter passed through the wire and minefield and found the attack held up in front of heavily manned and unapproachable positions. Captain J. A. Robertson MC had taken command of the confused and intermingled companies and was organising small groups in a desperate endeavour to infiltrate. Subedar Fateh Singh died gallantly in leading one such attempt. A few parties wriggled forward for short distances, but sustained advance was impossible. The assaulting troops remained pinned down and in desperate circumstance.

At 1100 hours, while endeavouring to join his men by way of a gap in the minefield further east, Lieut.-Colonel McDonald encountered Brigadier Briggs, who declared that a second attack must go in at 1420 hours, when tank support would be forthcoming. Only three Matildas and a number of carriers were available, but behind this meagre spearhead 3/1 Punjabis, together with Captain McKinley's company of 4/16 Punjabis, leapt to the assault in gallant style. Two strong points were mopped up in quick succession, yielding 170 prisoners. The tanks under heavy punishment veered off to the right flank, and the infantry again was exposed to galling fire. Many of the carriers had been smashed by sniping guns and one of the tanks was disabled. A smoke screen was put down to assist in its recovery. With quick perception Captain Robertson took advantage of this cover, dashed forward at the head of his men and stormed a strong point which had been holding up the advance. By nightfall the end was in sight, but approximately 100 Germans still stood at bay. Plans were made to complete the mopping up on the morrow, but when dawn broke the enemy had disappeared. In a final effort to escape the Germans had crept out into the desert singly and on foot. A troop of South African armoured cars were sent in pursuit and speedily rounded them up. At a cost of 356 casualties the entire garrison of Libyan Omar, totalling 3,000 of all ranks, had been wiped out. In their day's fighting 3/1 Punjabis had lost 4 officers and 88 men.

On December 1st 15 Panzer Division, supported by lorry-borne infantry from 90 Light Division, smashed at the New Zealanders at Sidi Rezegh and Belhamid, recapturing the airfields and cutting the corridor. 5 New Zealand Brigade hurried forward to join in the fighting. 5 Indian Brigade followed into the north, taking over New Zealand responsibilities. On November 30th Central India Horse, with 31 Field Regiment and detachments of 65 Anti-Tank Regiment and 57 LAA Regiment, initiated a patrol along the Trigh Capuzzo, a desert track which skirted the coastal escarpment about ten miles south of and parallel to the main road to Tobruk. Strong enemy forces were known to be roving in this area. By the evening of December 2nd, the cavalrymen and their guns had pushed a screen forward as far as Bir El Chleta, forty miles from Capuzzo and only some fifteen miles east of Sidi Rezegh. The day had been profitable. "C" Squadron under Captain Turner had taken 150 prisoners, had liberated a captured field hospital and had snatched a baled-out R.A.F. pilot from an enemy patrol.

On the morning of December 3rd while Central India Horse endeavoured to effect contact with 11 Hussars in the desert to the south, eight panzers suddenly appeared over a ridge and charged the cavalrymen. A column of 300 enemy motor transport followed the tanks. From headquarters of the column twelve miles behind, Lieut.-Colonel Claude Goulder, 31 Field Regiment, instructed Captain Turner to delay the advance without becoming committed and if possible to decoy the Germans onto his guns. A running fight which was just short of a chase developed. As the enemy barged into the trap, Central India Horse swung to flank to lop off stragglers and to take advantage of the confusion. The manoeuvre proceeded like an exercise. The enemy tanks lumbered over the ridge in full pursuit and came face to face with the twenty-five pounders. Four panzers were reduced to blazing wrecks as they frantically dived for dead ground. The field guns lifted onto the auxiliary transport and sent it scurrying. Central India Horse raced in, bringing down vehicle after vehicle. 50 prisoners were taken for a loss of 1 killed and 3 wounded.

(The enemy at this stage of the battle was singularly rash. Eight miles to the north on the same day 28 Maori Battalion ambushed a column of German infantry, killing and wounding 300 and taking 150 prisoners in return for one killed and 5 wounded.)

As Lieut.-Colonel Goulder's force retraced its steps on the following morning, another enemy column of 15 tanks with attendant lorried infantry was encountered. On this occasion the enemy failed to respond to the lure and the tanks kept a cautious distance; whereupon a fire fight developed between guns and panzers, under cover of which Central India Horse continued to nibble at flanks and rear. When the enemy finally managed to disengage, he was poorer by 100 killed and 100 prisoners.

As illustrative of the swiftly changing fortunes of this desert battle, two sappers of 4 Field Company returned from captivity on the morning of December 3rd. They had been detailed to escort prisoners of war from the Omars to Sofafi. Raiding panzers intercepted the column near Sheferzen, released the Italians and captured the Indians, who were taken to a nullah near Halfaya where approximately 300 prisoners had been collected. On the second day of captivity, at the instigation of a British lieutenant-colonel, the prisoners had overpowered their weak German guard and had scattered into the desert in all directions.*

On this same morning 7 Brigade at the Omars was deeply gratified by a visit from the Commander-in-Chief. To Indian troops General Auchinleck was always a field commander and he received a fighting soldier's welcome. He expressed pleasure concerning the progress of the battle. The next phase had begun to unfold. The New Zealanders after their great drive on Tobruk were to be relieved and Fourth Indian Division would move forward to take up the battle under command of 30 Corps. 2 South African Division in turn would take over responsibilities on the frontier. 11 Brigade would lead the move into the west under orders of 7 Armoured Division, for the purpose of securing Bir El Gubi area, fifty miles west of the Omars and forty miles south of Tobruk. 5 and 7 Brigades would concentrate some fifteen miles south of El Gubi in conjunction with 22 Guards Brigade. When 11 Brigade had cleared El Gubi, Fourth Indian Division would move to the north to contact the main body of the enemy.

The Bir El Gubi position was a heritage from Graziani's days when this trail junction on the Trigh El Abd (The Road of Slaves) had been the site of a fortified camp. The surrounding desert was wavy rather than ridgey, and offered cover in successive expanses of dead ground. Such terrain afforded scope for armoured manoeuvre; the 24 miles between the fortress positions of El Adem and Bir El Gubi gave Rommel's tanks ample elbow room for their favourite raiding and cutting out tactics. It therefore was not feasible to send supply convoys across the desert, or to carry the battle to the west of Tobruk until El Gubi had been reduced and the panzers denied their hunting grounds.

On December 3rd, just before nightfall, 11 Brigade with 31 Field Regiment and 6 Valentine tanks from 8 Royal Tank Regiment under

---

* One ambulance load of wounded from this battle took a wrong bearing and drove into Bir Ghirba, still occupied by Germans. Not wanting any extra mouths to feed, the Germans mended two punctures, dressed the men's fresh wounds and sent them on to the Omars.

command, formed up at Bir Duedar, twelve miles to the south-east of El Gubi. The plan of battle called for attack from the north-west after an encircling night march. Captain Robertson, Brigade Intelligence Officer, took charge of navigation, and the columns moved off for thirty miles by compass bearing over unreconnoitred ground. The approach was carried out with exceptional skill and at 0400 hours 11 Brigade was astride the Trigh El Abd, three miles in the rear of the El Gubi encampment. The Brigade deployed with 2/5 Mahrattas facing Point 182 to the north of the trail while 2 Camerons confronted Point 174 to the south-west.

At 0700 hours the artillery opened fire. Ten minutes later, infantry and tanks moved to the assault. In the midst of a heavy dust storm the Mahrattas swept forward for nearly two miles without great difficulty, capturing 10 officers, 100 men and an Italian field hospital. An important prize was a dump containing 50,000 gallons of petrol and diesel oil which had served as a refuelling point for roving clumps of Rommel's panzers. Many of the chance encounters of the next few days developed from enemy vehicles searching for this replenishment centre.

No such good fortune awaited 2 Camerons in their assault upon Point 174. This area comprised the focal point of enemy resistance. From the outset the Highlanders were harassed by heavy small arms fire from well-sited slit trenches. Mortar concentrations were exceptionally severe and the tanks encountered a hedge of anti-tank guns. Captain Palande's company of Mahrattas wheeled to the right and drove on the flank of Point 174 in an endeavour to aid their Scottish comrades. A curtain of machine-gun fire and mortar fire enveloped the company; Captain Palande was killed and his men pinned down. When the first attack petered out, 11 Brigade organised a fresh assault with the uncommitted companies. At 1500 hours the Camerons advanced from the south while the Mahrattas again endeavoured to close down from the north. The little carriers gallantly dashed ahead. Five were knocked out immediately. Mahrattas and Highlanders came steadily across the open under a hail of fire until mounting casualties drove the men to ground. When it became apparent that none could stand and live, the assault was abandoned.

Nevertheless Brigadier Anderson's orders had been explicit. El Gubi must be taken. At 0600 hours next morning companies of Camerons and Mahrattas crept forward in an endeavour to penetrate the position by surprise. When the enemy was found to be alert the attack was not pressed home. One Mahratta platoon missed the withdrawal signal and having wiped out an enemy machine-gun nest, established themselves in the post and held it throughout the day. During the morning a Stuka squadron which attacked at a height of 100 feet lost five machines. At 1245 hours the artillery laid a smoke screen on the southern approaches to El Gubi; behind it two companies of 1/6 Rajputana Rifles moved to the attack. Four "I" tanks accompanied the assault, but owing to wireless failures fought independently and were not on call by the infantry. After initial progress the Rajputana Rifles were held up. A company of Camerons joined the fray on the left flank. At 1430 hours Lieut.-Colonel Butler (Rajputana Rifles) reported that he had reached the outskirts of a comprehensive defence position organised in depth. His tanks and carriers had penetrated the outpost line but were unable to deal with the enemy in their deep and narrow slit trenches. A number of tanks had been knocked out by Molotoff cocktails. A similar report came from the Camerons, who added that enemy machine-gun squads had occupied one of the disabled "I" tanks and were enfilading them. At 1600 hours the Rajputana Rifles' commander again reported the situation as stalemate. One company was slowly worming its way forward under heavy fire, but the remainder could do no more than hold their present positions. A few minutes later Lieut.-Colonel Butler was killed by a mortar — the second commander of this fine battalion to fall in Western Desert.

During the day 4 Armoured Brigade, which had been covering 11 Brigade against panzer attack, moved northward towards Sidi Resegh. As a result of this withdrawal at 1730 hours a column of enemy tanks with attendant transport approached the Mahrattas positions from the north-west. Simultaneously a similar group appeared from the east. Each force, comprising 25 tanks with lorried infantry in close support, charged. As the rush went in the Mahratta anti-tank gunners met the surge with excellent marksmanship, but the odds were too great. One by one the guns were knocked out. "A" Company was overrun and destroyed. Night fell while the panzers searched for further victims. Under cover of darkness the Deccan men fought on with the enemy tanks in their midst; led by Subedar Laxuman Chawan and Jemadar Govind Desai, they blew back the mopping-up squads until lorry-borne troops closed in a flood over them. This spirited stand allowed Major Cocksedge to withdraw the reserve company of the Mahrattas to a safer position, and also gave the Camerons time to extricate their left flank from peril. The battered infantry rallied around Brigade Headquarters while the 25-pounders rushed up to engage the intruders at close range. The night was filled with fireworks as anti-tank tracer cut patterns on all sides; the noise was so great that Brigade control vehicles were obliged to move out of Headquarters leaguer in order to use their wireless sets. Signalmen repaired lines within fifty yards of the German tanks and Lieut.-Colonel Lancaster of the Mahrattas gave the Division a running commentary in Hindustani on the ever-changing situation. On one occasion his report was interrupted while two German officers, who had driven up in a staff car, were overpowered.

During these tense hours, while the enemy wolf packs sniffed for prey in the night, the minute-by-minute sitreps of 11 Brigade reveal an odd mixture of excitement and prosaic unconcern. A great deal of shouting has been heard in the darkness. The Mahrattas have neglected to say in what language. After some thought, the Mahrattas decide it is German. Dumdum ammunition has been found in the shot-down Stukas; it is imperative that specimens should be sent out by safe hand. An artillery officer is incensed when a column of motor transport passes through his vehicle lines. He approaches to protest, and three stick genades are thrown at him. The Mahrattas report parties marching south-east with shovels on their shoulders and thereafter the noise of stakes being driven into the ground. Brigade Headquarters is very interested and wishes to know more about this. Dogs are barking all over the desert. Is it possible that these are accompanying enemy patrols? Would Corps be good enough to acknowledge receipt of fifteen lorry-loads of prisoners, crediting 11 Brigade? After a day of bitter disaster and in the midst of imminent danger, this calm absorption in the business of battle reflects the unbroken morale which carried British and Indian troops over so many rough places.

At 2200 hours Brigadier Anderson was ordered to make rendezvous with the Corps Commander. At that meeting 11 Brigade was instructed to disengage and to withdraw southward towards Fourth Indian Division's concentration area. 22 Guards Brigade would supply a screen to cover the withdrawal. When dawn broke 11 Brigade was organised for the move, but there was no sign of the promised screen. At 0730 hours enemy columns were identified on all sides. The situation seemed so hazardous that all secret documents were destroyed. Led by the Mahrattas, 11 Brigade headed into the south. As the move began, artillery and long-range mortars shelled the Indian columns in somewhat desultory fashion. The Germans made no attempt to close, and unit after unit passed safely through their midst into the open desert. Last to shift were 1/6 Rajputana Rifles. As the Indians left their battle positions and scrambled towards their vehicles, a group of panzers and lorried infantry headed for them. It was a tense moment; had the troop-carriers panicked the battalion would have been lost. The British RASC drivers faced the threat with great coolness, drove towards the enemy, picked up their loads, and moved off through a rearguard of tanks and guns. Six miles south of El Gubi the columns passed through the Guards screen.

The El Gubi action had cost 11 Brigade 25 officers and 450 men. The Camerons had been particularly unfortunate, losing 16 officers. Some 380 Italian prisoners were captured and a number of tanks destroyed. (In the first assault upon the Mahrattas, a Bofors troop had disabled no less than 16 panzers). To the participants the battle remained a confused memory. The sandstorms, the enemy here, there and everywhere, the breakdown of communications, the impossibility of manoeuvre, the final withdrawal while the enemy sat idly by, combined to give events an air of frustration and unreality. The failure to win El Gubi had arisen from faulty intelligence, lack of reconnaissance, hit-and-miss relationship between infantry and armour, and undue optimism in believing that Italians were always waiting to surrender.

At 1030 hours on December 6th, 11 Brigade reached its concentration area. For the first time since Eritrea, all brigades of Fourth Indian

Division were together. 22 Guards Brigade also was under command and at first it seemed probable that the El Gubi action would be continued as a Divisional operation. To the north the desert was aflame as throughout December 6/7th 4 Armoured Brigade and the German tanks struggled for mastery. Mobile columns emerged from driving dust storms, battered each other and disappeared in flight or in chase. In one of these mêlées Major-General Neumann-Silkow, commander of 15 Panzer Division, was mortally wounded. The El Gubi-El Adem panzer playground now was menaced on both flanks by substantial forces. It became clear that while the enemy would turn snarling if pushed too hard, he might be nudged westwards if his own tactics were adopted and raiding columns unloosed to harass his communications.

For the next phase Fourth Division was organized into brigade groups comprising infantry, tanks and guns. Central India Horse and 31 Field Regiment returned from service with the South Africans and by the afternoon of December 7th the Division was ready to move off. 7 Brigade was allotted a route to the east of El Gubi directed on El Adem, the important road junction and airfield thirty miles to the north. 5 Brigade advanced towards Acroma, an old fort on the coastal escarpment eighteen miles west of Tobruk. On the left flank Central India Horse linked up with 4 Armoured Brigade. 11 Brigade moved in Divisional Reserve. Just before the advance began, news arrived of the incredible treachery of Pearl Harbour and all hearts were buoyed with the knowledge of a great new Ally.

As the columns worked into the north, the area so lately crowded with enemies was found to be empty. On the afternoon of December 9th 7 Brigade's screen reached the edge of the desert escarpment three miles south of El Adem airfield. 4/11 Sikhs occupied the landing ground. That evening contacts were established with patrols of 23 British Infantry Brigade from Tobruk. 5 Brigade, having rounded El Gubi, crossed the Trigh el Abd and moved through the heavily tracked desert to the north-west. Here the plain ended in hummocky and rolling wasteland, with low ridges and flat pans. Throughout the first day good progress was made, with no hostile formations nearer than fifteen miles to the south-west. At Knightsbridge, on the Bir Hacheim trail thirteen miles south of Acroma, the brigade columns closed up on the screen of Central India Horse, which had encountered enemy rearguards. "C" Squadron of the cavalry managed to slip past on the right flank, and as night fell reached the edge of the escarpment immediately above the El Adem-Acroma by-pass. Below them in the coastal corridor the road was packed bonnet to tail with enemy vehicles heading west. Central India Horse armoured cars and trucks carrying machine-gunners bounced down the slopes, swept into the traffic jams, shot them up and stampeded the transport in wildest confusion. The flood of panic-stricken vehicles engulfed some of the assailants and the strange spectacle was seen of intermingled enemies swept along together. When out of ammunition most of the cavalrymen broke away, bringing, as Central India Horse Newsletter put it, "the best of our prisoners, to wit,

150 Germans". Lance-Daffadar Janak Singh however, with two trucks, was still involved in the enemy columns when day broke. Being discovered, a battle and chase in the best Hollywood tradition ensued. He escaped to rejoin his regiment five days later.

During the night the enemy rearguards had pulled out from south of Acroma. The delay, however, had cost 5 Brigade its objective. In a spirited cross-country race the Divisional Commander on reconnaissance outdistanced the fighting troops. General Messervy and Brigadier Mirrlees were first to reach the old fort, where a sleeping Italian proved the sole trophy. Four miles beyond Acroma a strong enemy covering force was encountered on a low ridge whose hummocks were described as Points 208 and 209. A quick attack by 4/6 Rajputana Rifles on the right and 1 Buffs on the opposite flank broke into the enemy's position, capturing 200 prisoners. 3/1 Punjabis passed through and secured a commanding position above the coastal road. The remainder of 5 Brigade followed up and occupied a front of eight miles along the rim of the escarpment.

The enemy had not lingered when the Tobruk battle went against him. With great dexterity Rommel extricated his forces and dropped back before the trap could close. On December 10th Central India Horse, probing far to the west among the broken spurs of the escarpment, could only collect 150 stragglers in a full day's search. Poles and New Zealanders were advancing in the coastal corridor below the cavalrymen. On the desert flank 7 Armoured Division was replenishing for a long chase.

The battle was over, the pursuit about to begin.

Chapter 9

THE CLEARING OF THE DJEBEL ACHDAR

ON the evening of December 10th, General Messervy outlined plans for the next phase. It was possible that the enemy would stand at Gazala, where the coastal escarpment created a bottleneck against a shallow arm of the sea. If so, the New Zealanders would deal with the resistance. 7 Armoured Division would follow the panzers across the desert while Fourth Indian Division pursued the battered and disorganised 21 Italian Corps along the Via Balbia, the main Djebel highway. Only two brigades would participate. Vehicles were scarce and 11 Brigade needed a rest: it therefore would move into garrison in the Tobruk area. The Division would advance in three groups—Divisional Headquarters forming the third group, with Central India Horse, 1/6 Rajputana Rifles and 12 Valentine tanks from 8 Royal Tank Regiment under command. The order of march would be 5 Brigade on the right, 7 Brigade on the left with Headquarters Group echeloned between them in the rear. The first objective would be Bir Halegh-el-Eleba on the Tmimi-El Mechili trail, twenty miles to the south-west of the entrance to the Djebel.

The advance was timed to start at 1430 hours on December 11th. That morning the Buffs were still bickering with stubborn enemy pockets around Point 209. At noon they disengaged and joined 5 Brigade in the move to the west. After a short trek, the columns went into early leaguer. In dense darkness at 0500 hours next morning, the pursuit continued. The flat desert was now behind; undulating and broken land cut by innumerable dried watercourses, with ridges and hummocks jumbled higgledy-piggledy, rose slowly towards the west; everywhere desert tracks converged, reaching for the fruitful Djebel Achdar. Desert vegetation thickened, with scattered patches of scrub, low bushes and coarse grass on the pans which caught the seasonal floods. When light broke Divisional Headquarters found itself no longer in echelon but spear-heading the advance. There had been some delay over petrol supplies and neither brigade was in sight. 7 Brigade came into its correct position during the forenoon and 5 Brigade arrived soon after midday.

During the afternoon 7 Armoured Division patrols were encountered on 7 Brigade's front. They reported contact with a substantial body of the enemy only a few miles ahead, on Fourth Division's axis of

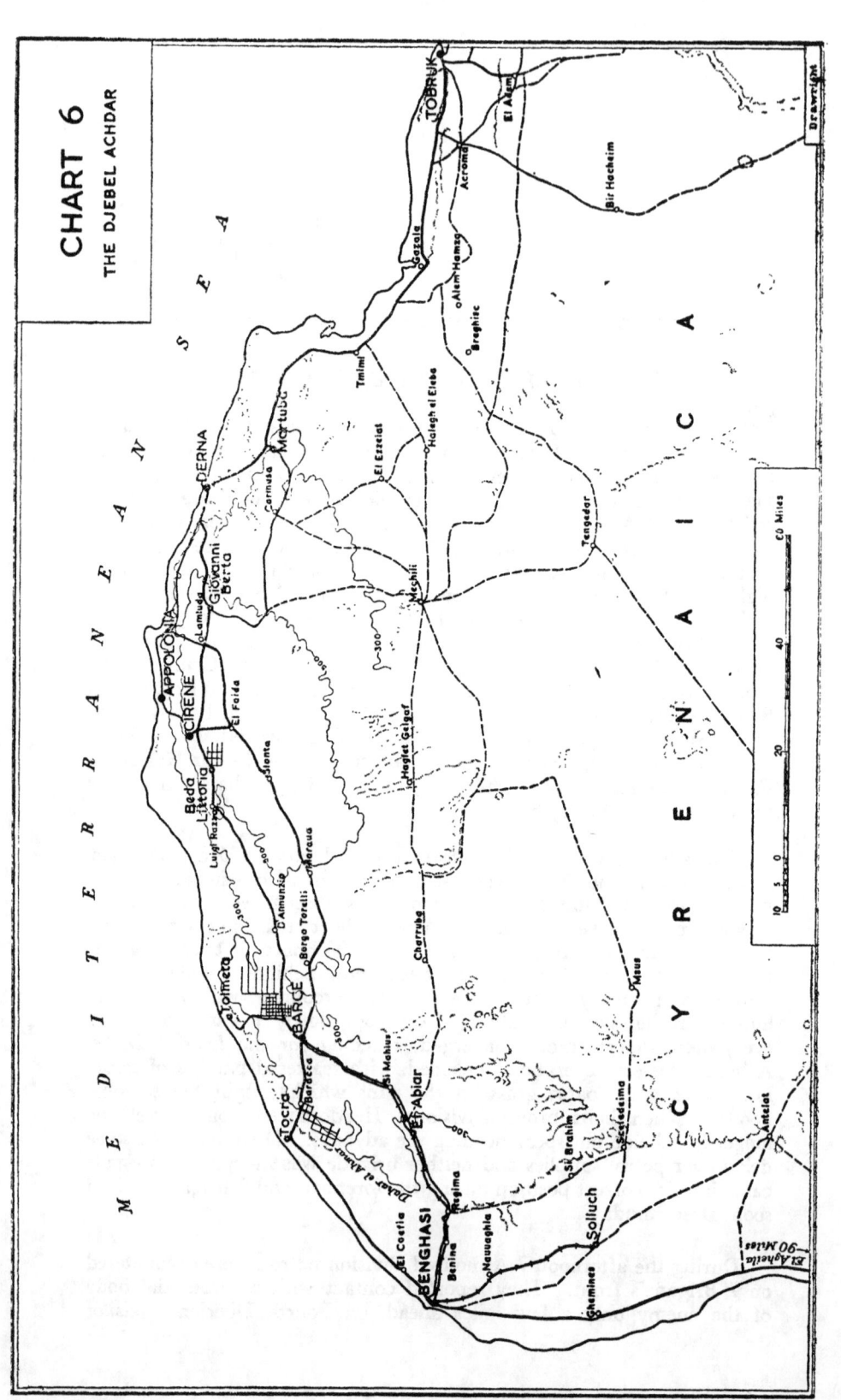

advance. The presence of hostile forces near at hand had been suspected, since the Stukas, birds of ill omen, had been active. No less than eleven dive-bombing attacks had been sustained by Divisional Headquarters group. These raids were exciting rather than dangerous. Divisional Signals incurred a number of casualties, but many bombs fell so wide of the mark that it was surmised that Italian pilots might be flying German machines. Another guess was that 57 LAA Regiment, which had now reached the top of its form, had made precision bombing too dangerous. It was noticed that the Stukas no longer screamed down in their familiar long dive but dropped their missiles from a height and hurried away. In one day the crack Divisional gunners knocked seven planes out of the sky. Nevertheless on some occasions the Stukas all but scored bulls-eyes. Lieut.-Colonel Peter Gray, Divisional Signals officer, looked up to see a heavy bomb descending on him: he dived from his vehicle seconds ahead of the strike.

In the afternoon 5 Brigade was in touch with the enemy on a front of three miles. The defensive position had been cleverly chosen to cover both the route to the Djebel and the westering desert trails. It was difficult to by-pass, for the defenders had dug in on high ground which fell away both to the north and to the south. At 1100 hours "B" and "D" Companies of 4/6 Rajputana Rifles advanced two miles west of Alam Hamza trig point. "D" Company, after initial penetration, was pinned down. "B" Company overran a number of positions, including a battalion headquarters, before encountering a blaze of machine-gun fire from three sides. Captain Arthur Knowles, a gallant officer previously wounded in Eritrea, was struck down. He ordered his men back, bidding them leave him. They refused to retire, and it was only after dark, in response to a direct order from Lieut.-Colonel Lawrenson, that the platoons under Subedar Sukh Ram reluctantly came in, bringing their wounded with them. Captain Knowles died before reaching the dressing-station. Casualties in this assault amounted to 4 officers and 69 men. 15 enemy officers and 300 men were captured, together with a number of light guns and considerable equipment.

While this assault was in progress, "A" and "C" Companies of the same battalion mounted an attack against Points 205 and 208, on the right flank of 5 Brigade's front. This attack was timed to coincide with a demonstration by 1 Buffs against Point 204 on the extreme left of the Brigade's sector. On closing up, the Rajputana Rifles came under heavy fire from front and left, and were pinned down a mile short of their objective. The Buffs were more fortunate and turned their demonstration into the seizure of a key position. On encountering no resistance they moved forward and established themselves on Point 204. Why this locality was unoccupied remains a mystery. There had been a slip-up somewhere, as later in the afternoon a German column approached Point 204 in convoy formation as if expecting to find friends there.

While 5 Brigade was endeavouring to penetrate the enemy's defences on the right, 7 Brigade had probed along the line towards Sidi Breghisc, searching for a soft spot and favourable terrain for attack. The enemy line swung in an arc and after reconnaissance it was decided to commit 4/11 Sikhs to an assault against the northern face of the re-entrant. 25 Field Regiment, escorted by guns from 65 Anti-Tank Regiment, had begun to register, when the Bren carriers came racing in to report 40 tanks approaching supported by artillery and lorried infantry. The Sikhs, who had not debussed, withdrew. Brigade Headquarters hurried forward 10 Valentine tanks and another company of anti-tank guns. Platoons of infantry covered field gun positions. 25 Field Regiment took station for action with 16 guns in echelon facing north-west, with the tanks on their left flank and covering detachments of anti-tank guns on both sides. A mile to the west, 31 Field Regiment swung its guns in half circle and stood ready to intervene at long range.

As the gunners crouched waiting, 2,000 yards away a dust column grew. The panzers poured over a low ridge and opened fire, the Mark IVs laying a barrage in the path of the lighter tanks. Enemy self-propelled guns and lorried infantry swung to flank. The heavy mass rolled on through seething dust and smoke, flailing the silent British group with cannon shells and machine-gun fire. At 1,200 yards the gunners smashed back. There followed a fierce and stubborn grapple. John Hetherington, Australian war correspondent, who witnessed the encounter, wrote:

"The enemy's armour fleet looked like ships fighting their way through a storm at sea, surrounded by flying sand and stones. The leading tanks reeled out of action, broken and burning, but the rest rolled on in a great gray wave."

Over the Gun Position Officer's radio came a graphic description as the artillerymen hurled shell as long as any man stood to work the guns. The panzers flooded over 31/58 Battery; Major Newell, the battery commander, served the last piece single-handed. 12/25 Battery swung its guns at point blank range on to the milling tanks as they reached the sister battery and blew them back before they could seize either guns or prisoners. Ranging backwards and forwards under the unbearable fire, like wild beasts in torment, the enemy armour once more hurled itself upon its quarry. 31 Field Regiment, 65 Anti-Tank Regiment and the guns of the Valentines joined in pounding the enemy with an inferno of shell. Suddenly the German lorried infantry wheeled and drove away into the north. The tanks slowly followed, leaving a dozen wrecks behind. 7 officers and 58 men of 25 Field Regiment had fallen around their guns. Eight guns had been knocked out but all were recovered. Once again the bull's rush had failed to win home in the face of gallantry and discipline beyond praise.

In the course of this short, fierce encounter, it was learned that the Germans had discovered that tanks were not enough to deal with field artillery. A Valentine officer whose tank was disabled baled out and lay on the ground feigning death. He brought back an interesting story of German battle organisation. In this action the tanks had been relegated from battleship to cruiser status. Behind the dust screen of the panzers, fast moving tractors towed batteries of guns, both field and medium, which were designed to intervene at any point in the battle where the tanks might be getting the worst of it. The lorry-borne infantry and anti-tank guns hung about the outskirts, to follow in as mopping-up squads when the panzers had broken the opposition. These tactics revealed that the enemy planners had recognised that in armour battle the integration of all arms was essential to secure victory.

Fighting was now in progress on a comprehensive front between Sidi Breghisc and the Mediterranean, a distance of upwards of 20 miles. 5 New Zealand Brigade had seized the Gazala airfield and the Polish Carpathian Brigade had closed up on the right of Fourth Division to drive into the north-west. The Polish-New Zealand line lay back at an angle of about 130 degrees to the Sidi Breghisc-Alam Hamza positions, a circumstance which made the hinge at Point 204, held by the Buffs, the key to the battlefield. Due to late arrival of ammunition, 7 Brigade did not pursue its plan for assault on December 14th, but 5 Brigade made a further attempt to establish itself on the Point 205-208 positions. On attempting to advance 4/6 Rajputana Rifles were greeted with extremely heavy machine-gun fire and made no progress. About noon a number of panzers, followed by lorried infantry, appeared before the Buffs' position at Point 204. The excellent marksmanship of 31 Field Regiment discouraged a close approach. Three hours later a more serious thrust probed this vital sector. 15 tanks approached the Buffs, followed by a body of infantry. Again the alert gunners crashed an accurate shoot on the panzers, which stood their ground and struck back. A tense struggle ensued, which grew critical as 31 Field Regiment's ammunition ran low. Fortunately quads arrived in time with fresh supplies of shell and after losing a number of tanks the assailants withdrew.

The manifest strength of the enemy on the Sidi Breghisc-Alam Hamza line made it essential to mount a full-scale attack. For December 15th an ambitious operation was projected. 7 Armoured Division was ordered to despatch 4 Armoured Brigade on a wide detour around the right flank of the enemy, in order to seize Bir Halegh El Eleba, 20 miles in the rear of Sidi Breghisc. This force, by continuing a further 18 miles to the north-west, could block the entrance to the Djebel Achdar at Tmimi. The hour of arrival of the armour at Bir Halegh El Eleba would coincide with a general infantry assault. On the Gazala-Sidi Breghisc line the New Zealanders and Poles would advance north-westwards on the left of Gazala. 5 Indian Brigade again would assault Points 205-208. 7 Brigade would secure Point 201, to the rear of Sidi Breghisc. To strengthen Fourth Division's assault, 32 Army Tank Brigade sent 30 "I" tanks forward from Tobruk. From this reinforcement each assault brigade was allotted 12 machines. 1/6 Rajputana Rifles from Headquarters Group joined 5 Brigade with instructions that should the day assault on Points 205-208 fail, the newcomers would lead a night attack.

On the morning of December 15th 5 Brigade continued pressure on the right sector of its front. 3/1 Punjabis advanced to assist 4/6 Rajputana Rifles, who had been pinned down for two days. As soon as movement was detected, a heavy enemy shoot opened. The Punjabis were caught on their start line and mauled. A number of their supporting "I" tanks were knocked out. Throughout the forenoon enemy artillery fire intensified and heavy vehicle movements were reported behind the Axis lines. "C" Squadron of Central India Horse, which had been reconnoitring on the right flank, was driven into Point 204. 1200 hours had been set provisionally for the main Divisional attack, as it was hoped that by then 4 Armoured Brigade would be making its presence felt in the German rear. At noon, however, disappointing news came through. The British armour was barely under way and still had 30 miles to cover to Bir Halegh El Eleba. Before the Divisional Commander could learn whether he should adhere to the original plan and await tank intervention, or should keep timing with the New Zealanders and Poles in an unsupported infantry attack, the mounting fury of the enemy's bombardment on 5 Brigade's front presaged an early and heavy counterstroke. A German scout picked up by the Buffs had boasted that he would be a prisoner for less than a day. All available reserves were hurried to reinforce the critical sector and at 1400 hours the garrison of Point 204, in addition to 1 Buffs, consisted of 31 Field Regiment, "C" Squadron of Central India Horse, a battery of 73 Anti-Tank Regiment, a troop of 57 LAA Regiment, a section of 18 Field Company and ten "I" tanks.

At that hour a cannonade of terrifying intensity burst on the Divisional positions. No equal concentration of fire power had been previously encountered. Mark IV tanks crept up to within 3,000 yards and added their weight to the artillery bombardment. The action which followed was a classical example of sound tactics against unsound dispositions. The artillery force at the disposal of the defenders was stronger than that which broke the panzer rushes at the Omars and at Sidi Breghisc. Unfortunately the field guns were not dug in. The anti-tank and anti-aircraft guns were not arrayed to protect them, nor was covering infantry provided. In the face of an armour attack the infantry could only live as long as the guns lived. At these guns the enemy struck with all his fury.

When the devastating bombardment drove back the "I" tanks the panzers began to creep forward. Simultaneously three battalions of 115 Lorried Infantry Regiment advanced, two swinging to flank accompanied by self-propelled guns. 31 Field Regiment, under heavy pressure from the front, could not prevent the approach of these forces, which debussed within machine-gun range, mounted their weapons and pelted the unprotected gunners with a sleet of steel. The gun crews thinned until single men fired on. When no one was left, from all sides the enemy closed for the kill. The tanks crashed into the Buffs' positions with tommy gunners riding outside and infantry swarming behind. The Buffs passed gloriously, meeting the Germans with a blaze of fire and fighting bitterly in small grim groups until the flood closed over them.

The climax was well described by Lieut.-Colonel Desmond Young MC, Indian Army Public Relations:

"A few thousand yards behind the battle, in a little group of vehicles dispersed on a wind-swept plain, Brigade Headquarters heard the tale of disaster unfold. Over the wireless Lieut.-Colonel King of the Buffs gave a running commentary. Minute by minute well planned and perfectly executed manoeuvres exploited every weakness of the Buffs' position and dispositions. The Brigade Staff listened in full realisation that gallantry was confronted with ruthless efficiency and that there could only be one end. 'I am afraid that this is the last time that I shall speak to you', said Lieut.-Colonel King. 'They are right on top of my headquarters'. The shout of the Sikh signaller came through. 'Last message, Sahib. I am breaking the instrument'. A war cry, a crash, and silence."

A few survivors escaped in the confusion of mopping-up. 31 Field Regiment found enough gunners for one battery. 100 men of Headquarters Group of the Buffs managed to escape. Enemy losses likewise were substantial. At least 12 panzers were destroyed. An intercept from the commander of 115 Lorried Regiment revealed that he was unable to continue with his allotted task of breaking through at Point 204 and rolling up the remainder of the Indian front.

While 5 Brigade suffered the shock, 7 Brigade had made valiant attempts to fasten its teeth in the left sector of the enemy defences. At 1330 hours 4/16 Punjabis moved to attack Point 201 on a three-company front. When within a mile of their objective, intense fire crashed upon them. The battalion pressed gallantly on until within 700 yards of the enemy. Owing to casualties and non-arrival of drafts Lieut.-Colonel Lavender had only been able to put 180 rifles into action. Such sparse force could accomplish little and after 44 casualties had been incurred the assault was abandoned. Upon news of the Buffs' disaster, 7 Brigade threw back its right flank and with the remainder of 5 Brigade refused a continuous line around the bulge created by the loss of Point 204. Anti-tank formations were stationed to cover the new positions and next morning 42 Royal Tank Regiment arrived to stiffen the defences. 1 South African Infantry Brigade was placed under Divisional command and an assault was organised to smash the Sidi Breghisc flank of the enemy's positions.

The day however was won elsewhere. On December 16th, in a magnificent attack, the Poles had burst through in the Gazala corridor. Next morning they were exploiting along the road which wound up the coastal escarpment on to the grass-clad approaches to the Djebel. 4 Armoured Brigade had reached Bir Halegh El Eleba, had raided into Tmimi and had turned south-east on the enemy's rear. For a few hours it appeared as though the victory over the Buffs might have cost the enemy encirclement of all his forces east of Tmimi. As had happened before, by means of an abrupt disengagement Rommel slipped his head out of the noose. He despatched the remnants of 21 Italian Corps into the Djebel through the closing door and withdrew hastily with the remainder of his Germans by the open route across the desert. Of the eight divisions which had opposed Eighth Army's advance, 27 days' fighting had left the Axis Commander with 30 tanks, 35,000 infantry and 3,000 vehicles.

Pursuit of the enemy was hurriedly organized and at 1000 hours on December 17th a fresh advance began. 42 Royal Tank Regiment and 1 South African Brigade remained under Divisional command. 3 South African Reconnaissance Unit joined Central India Horse in screen. Unfortunately the weather had worsened and the first stages of the chase led over ground which the winter rains had converted into greasy bogs. 5 Brigade struck extremely bad going and made little more than twenty miles before nightfall. 7 Brigade on the left passed through Bir Halegh El Eleba and leaguered for the night at El Ezzeiat, on the edge of a shaggy basin with the stony boss of the Djebel rising in the north.

An interesting possibility now presented itself. The Italians were flooding eastward along the main Djebel highway, which ran across the rocky headland above the Gulf of Bomba. It seemed possible that in order to avoid congestion on the main road, part at least of the retreating enemy forces would avoid the bottleneck of Derna by withdrawal along a secondary track which by-passed that port by way of Carmusa and Lamluda. From 7 Brigade's overnight position a trail led into Carmusa. Should Brigadier Briggs and his men mount into the Djebel by this route, it might be possible to surprise and cut off the retreating columns. It was therefore arranged that 7 Brigade should work up this track, and having cut the by-pass at Carmusa, should wheel east and seize Martuba, where extensive airfields were located, thereafter exploiting across the high plateau towards Derna. 5 Brigade on reaching the by-pass would strike in the opposite direction towards Giovanni Berta, a market town 23 miles from Carmusa, thereafter thrusting on for seven miles to Lamluda crossroads, from whence two main highways led through the Djebel. This short cut involved both brigades in difficult treks across rocky and broken terrain, in vehicles rickety and crotchety after a hard campaign. Nevertheless the sight of rolling uplands, of grass and trees, the presence of abundant water and of fruitful ground, was sufficiently stimulating to launch everyone on this adventure in good heart. The Germans were known to be in full retreat and the Italians, after their heavy battering, were not expected to provide serious opposition.

At 1000 hours on December 18th the Divisional advance continued with 5 Brigade on the right bearing towards the Bir El Chaualat escarpment which represented the beginning of the high ground. The going was exceedingly bad and the columns twisted and turned in constant meanders along nullahs and around ridges. The Stukas were out in force and on a number of occasions both brigades received unwelcome attentions. Plodding steadily into the north, 5 Brigade made thirty miles before nightfall. 7 Brigade found easier going along a re-entrant of flat pans which intruded for nearly twenty miles into the rising ground and by 1000 hours had reached the Mechili trail five miles south of Carmusa. Pushing on rapidly the advanced elements cut the by-pass an hour later. Without pause, 1 Royal Sussex in the lead wheeled to the right and thrust down the road for 10 miles to Martuba. En route a certain amount of transport, including an Italian tank and a few guns, were mopped up. At Martuba airfield the astounded Italians could scarcely believe their eyes as the lorries swept in upon them. A number of aircraft were seized. In a large hutted encampment midday dinner swung over the fires; the Royal Sussex, their chores completed, sat down and ate with relish. Following hard behind, 4/11 Sikhs passed through and raced for the junction of the by-pass and main Djebel road, two miles to the north. This highway was jammed with transport fleeing towards Derna. A narrow defile gave a troop of light Italian tanks the opportunity to hold up the Sikhs briefly, but two companies having been dropped to block exit from the east, the remaining Sikhs managed to scramble around the obstacle and to emerge on the flat table-top which stretched to the brink of the cliffs above Derna.

Ahead a long line of transport choked the road. Five miles away planes could be seen circling over Derna airfield. The Sikhs dashed at their prey, swinging down either side of the road and shooting up the enemy transport in Wild West fashion. 300 prisoners, five 88 millimeter guns and many vehicles were captured. By early afternoon the Sikhs were beating up traffic as it fled along the road between the air strips. Four small Italian tanks undertook to cover the retirement, but with their carriers leading the Sikhs rushed the landing ground, riddling and bombing the planes while the panic-stricken ground crews fled. In the midst of this busy scene twelve Junkers 52 troop-carriers appeared in the north. Failing to detect anything unusual, they swung in and landed. The Sikhs, scarcely believing their luck, waited until all had rolled to a stop. Eight of the Junkers, which were carrying war material from Crete, were crippled before they could take off; two crashed in endeavoring to escape and two made their getaway. The troop-carriers' Messerschmidt escort swooped and machine-gunned, but without result. These Derna landing grounds were the main forward air supply centres for the Axis forces. No less than 183 aircraft, in whole or in part, were bunkered around the strips. Among the wrecked planes a huge six-engined aircraft, as well as many gliders, were found. Ammunition, petrol and food dumps were stacked high on all sides of the airfield.

Sikh patrols by nightfall had covered the remaining four miles to the crest of the escarpment. Seven hundred feet below, the blue Mediterranean was flung in a gleaming loop around Derna, built on a tiny promontory. The road descended the escarpment by a series of hairpin bends, all of which had been blown. 4 and 18 Field Companies came forward to work throughout the night. Above them the Sikhs rested, well content with their day's work.

Meanwhile 5 Brigade, on their divergent axis of advance, had continued to find heavy going. The Stukas had been pestiferous and from time to time rearguards had caused delay. At nightfall the Brigade crossed the Mechili track and made camp amid rocky, grass-clad ridges, with narrow intervening valleys. The sepoys chattered and congratulated each other, for this greenery was new and pleasant and the *birs* were filled with water. 1 South African Brigade, still under Divisional command, had made a late start that morning, having been held up for want of petrol, but once under way it sped forward and by evening had reached Sidi El Meheigen, six miles south of Carmusa. During the evening, advanced Divisional Headquarters and 42 Royal Tank Regiment likewise had reached Carmusa. As 5 Brigade was unable to proceed further that night, two companies of 4/16 Punjabis under Captain Pelly were despatched to the west along the by-pass with instructions to explore as far as possible. After covering 19 miles, and when only six miles short of Giovanni Berta, the Punjabis came up with the carrier platoon of Central India Horse, which was held up by a road block in a rocky defile. At dawn the Punjabis simulated attack and drew heavy fire. This demonstration having proved the position to be held in force, the Punjabis returned to rejoin their battalion at Carmusa.

Early next morning 5 Brigade was on its way, working across country on a bearing towards Giovanni Berta. At 1145 hours, on the line of a twisty ravine, 1/6 Rajputana Rifles bumped into the forces encountered by the Punjabis on the previous evening. Contact was made with Central India Horse on the left, and the flanks of a continuous enemy position determined. It was decided to turn the defences by simultaneous moves. 1/6 Rajputana Rifles would attack and endeavour to work around the right or eastern flank, while 4/6 Rajputana Rifles would move westwards, would cross the Carmusa road and strike into the north for Lamluda crossroads, seven miles to the west of Giovanni Berta. Under such plan, the more sustained the resistance the more certain the fate of the enemy.

At 1330 hours 4/6 Rajputana Rifles, lorry-borne by 309 G.T. Company, RASC, and accompanied by 52 Battery, 1 Field Regiment and a troop of anti-tank guns, moved off on a memorable trek. The distance was 9 miles, the bearing 356 degrees N.W. The terrain was a higgledy-piggledy mass of hummocks, ridges, rocky ledges and deep nullahs, in places heavily timbered and nowhere offering open vistas or unencumbered ground. The passage is well described in *The Tiger Kills*:

"Within a mile of leaving the road the carriers in the lead encountered a strong and cleverly devised line of tank obstacles which the natural difficulty of the terrain made almost impassable. (Fortunately the apron of mines protecting it was found to be unfused). The Rajputana Rifles located a gap and wriggled through in single file. The country steadily grew more precipitous, with deep wadis and steep hillsides strewn with giant boulders. It was impossible to advance in fighting formation, but carriers, trucks, guns and lorries plunged on like elephants in underbrush, dropping into holes, perching on stones, smashing through scrub, sometimes no more than moving but never quite held up. The heavy troop-carrying lorries rolled and pitched like smacks in a running sea; now tilted till it seemed certain that they must topple over, with the men inside hanging on or thrown into heaps; now inching downhill with the brakes hard on, skidding and slithering over ground that had never seen a wheel before."

At 1600 hours a Central India Horse carrier patrol, which had slipped past the road block in the defile during the morning, was startled by threshing and floundering in the heavy undergrowth near Abiar Haddah, five miles to the south-east of the vital Lamluda crossroads. The head on Rajputana Rifles' column lurched into the open; to the astonishment of both parties, Indian confronted Indian. The cavalry gave position; without delay the leading company thrust on. At 1700 hours the main highway at Lamluda was packed with westbound enemy transport. Suddenly the Rajputana Rifles raced up the trail from the south. Taken completely by surprise, the transport drivers and their loads threw up their hands. The vehicles were shepherded off the roads and the prisoners locked in a large building. Road blocks covered by anti-tank guns were constructed on the main highway 500 yards on each side of the crossroads. One rifle company was detailed to cover each block, while 1 Field Regiment took position to bring fire to bear on Giovanni Berta, where the 3/1 Punjabis were about to attack.

As it was known that considerable transport was on the road east of the road blocks, the Rajputana Rifles remained alert after darkness fell. At 2100 hours an enemy column headed by a heavy tank achieved a measure of surprise, the tank crashing through the road block before the anti-tank guns could be brought to bear. The tank escaped but the Rajputana Riflemen sprang out of the scrub onto the running boards of the lorries, forcing the vehicles to halt. A considerable number of Italians sought escape in the undergrowth. At dawn a cordon was drawn and the glades searched. This highly satisfactory ambuscade yielded 650 prisoners, the only casualties being Major Williams of the anti-tank gunners (who unfortunately was killed in a scrimmage in the dark), and four Indian other ranks wounded.

On the morning of December 19th, 4/11 Sikhs worked their way down the cliffside and took possession of Derna without resistance. The townsmen received the bearded warriors nonchalantly. The Arabs crowded round with pouches of eggs, demanding pounds of tea but quite willing to accept spoonfuls in payment. The Union Jack went up over the tiled and chromium-plated bank building which had been German headquarters. Derna had been extensively used for the evacuation of prisoners and wounded. The graves of two German divisional commanders were discovered in the Christian cemetery. 100 Indian wounded were recovered from the hospitals. 4 Field Company, having raised 800 mines in an afternoon on the outskirts of Derna airfield, descended into the town and began to restore public services. The water supply had been sabotaged, but with the help of a local plumber it was again functioning within twenty-four hours.

Patrols passed through the town and began to work westwards along the main road. The rolling uplands were studded with small Italian farms, and the Arabs had begun to wreak vengeance upon the colonists. Ousted families stood by the roadside weeping and appealing for help against the looting Senussi. In a number of instances a few long shots sent the thieves scurrying. Occupied Enemy Territory Administration officials had not yet arrived and the care and protection of civilians devolved upon the fighting forces. Other responsibilities slowed down the pursuit, particularly the assembly and repair of salvaged weapons and vehicles which might be employed against their former owners. Moreover, the weather had worsened; the winter rains were streaming down and it was necessary to get as many men as possible under cover. To British officers and men the recurrent showers and drizzles were reminiscent of home; to the sepoys they were less welcome. The rather clayey loam of the Djebel quickly turned to mud and cross-country navigation became chancey when not impossible. When one brigade was ordered to surrender its troop-carrying transport for maintenance tasks, the enemy had every opportunity of making a stand. Fortunately there was little fight left in 21 Italian Corps. The blocking force at Giovanni Berta held back the 3/1 Punjabis throughout December 20th, but at dusk a bayonet charge overran the last stubborn defenders. 110 prisoners were taken and 40 dead picked up on the battlefield.

7 Brigade, having surrendered its transport, remained in Derna area on security and salvage duties. 1 South African Brigade, to the disappointment of all, reverted to its own Division, but 3 South African Reconnaissance unit remained with Fourth Division as part of the advance screen. From Lamluda crossroads 5 Brigade columns pressed down the parallel highways ten miles apart which traverse the Djebel plateau as far as the Barce valley. On December 21st the advance reached the highest point in the uplands. There on a lip of the escarpment four miles from the sea, stood the ruins of Cyrene, famous city of antiquity. Below, the old Roman road wound down to Apollonia on the coast, with the grooves of chariot wheels still showing in the stones of the roadway. In this area an ugly situation prevailed. 15 Italians had been killed in Cyrene and the village ransacked. Detachments from 4/6 Rajputana Rifles were dropped to restore order and the pursuit swept on into the well settled wine-growing area of Beda Littoria, a pleasant green countryside dotted with small white farmhouses which bore the favourite Fascist cliches painted upon their eastern and western walls.

Beyond Lucia Razza, where the trim fields of Italian experimental farms brought an air of civilization with them, a demolition in a deep cypress-clad canyon held up the advance on the north road until 12 Field Company arrived. On the southern road nightfall (December 21st) found forward elements at Maraua, roughly halfway to Barce. This was a memorable night for Central India Horse; two squadrons slept under roofs for the first time since they had left Abyssinia eight months before. The 1/6 Rajputana Rifles' diarist, on the same day, boasts of "old-fashioned open fireplaces and plenty of logs" at their billets in the El-Faida area, where they kept a watchful eye on Arabs intent on bushwhacking the Italian colonists.

On December 22nd, on the northern road, 5 Brigade advanced only about fifteen miles. The weather had broken completely and it was impossible to progress except on the main highway, which traversed a series of picturesque canyons winding down to D'Annunzio. On the lower road better time was made. That night the advance screen had reached El Gsur, seven miles short of where the highway debouches from the hills into the broad and fruitful Barce valley. Here extensive demolitions were covered by a rearguard which included several guns. Infantry and artillery closed up to force the road block. On the approach of the assault party the defenders withdrew. Detachments of 12 Field Company, aided by Arab volunteers, repaired the damage in an afternoon. At 1500 hours, while the road blows were still under repair, "C" Squadron of Central India Horse, with a detachment of South African armoured cars, arrived at Barce by the upper road. This market town was in turmoil. The Central India Horse News Letter describes the situation:

"The Italians in the town were being besieged by the Arab population, who murdered, raped, robbed and looted. Everything of value had been taken by them and such things as furniture which they could not carry they destroyed. The Arabs were completely out of hand. The Italian police, therefore, were allowed to keep their arms, pending the arrival of more of our troops. Immediately upon receipt of this order an Italian police sergeant shot an Arab in front of the Hotel. The Hospital was a shambles, Arabs having murdered the Italian wounded and staff. One Free French major in the hospital escaped by feigning death until rescued by one of our chaps. Detachments were sent at once to outlying Italian settlements to stop the same sort of thing."

Resistance had now ceased. The remnants of Rommel's forces had reached sanctuary among the salt marshes to the south of Agheila, at the foot of the Gulf of Sirte. 7 Armoured Division, having ended the pursuit, had despatched a mobile force northwards to secure Benghazi. Central India Horse had been entrusted with the same mission, but found Tocra Pass, where the main Barce-Benghazi road descends the escarpment into the coastal plain, to be blown and impassable. On encountering this block, two squadrons remained in the Baracca area, ten miles west of Barce. Here the colonists, grateful for protection, supplied voluntary labour for the clearing and improvement of the roads. Another squadron followed a fair weather track westwards along the line of the railway and on December 24th emerged from the low scrub-covered hills near Benina aerodrome, twelve miles east of Benghazi. On Christmas morning General Messervy received an intriguing message: "C.I.H. patrols reached Benghazi 1800 hours yesterday. Dancing girls arrived three hours previously." The "dancing girls" were neither an ENSA pantomime troup nor those Italian official entertainers whom only the Long Range Desert Group ever had the luck to capture. They were stalwarts of the King's Dragoon Guards who had driven in from the south. One detects a certain frustration and acerbity in that signal.

Benghazi offered a dismal appearance. The R.A.F. bombing had shattered and blocked the streets. A large blue edifice of Moorish design on the waterfront, which had served as German headquarters, was one of the few main buildings which had escaped damage. Approximately 300 Italians, 300 Jews and 50,000 Arabs remained in the town. Fortunately the power installations had not been destroyed. The Sappers and Miners immediately restored the electricity and water supply services. Scores of enemy food, ammunition and equipment dumps lined the main roads. One observer enthusiastically wrote of "a mile and a half of petrol drums". It was substantially less, but nevertheless an important haul of fuel.

Christmas Day found Fourth Indian Division dispersed in bits and pieces over 150 miles of desert and the Djebel Achdar, with 11 Brigade less 1/6 Rajputana Rifles in Tobruk, 5 Brigade spread out between Giovanni Berta and Barce and 7 Brigade packing up in Derna for the move to Benghazi. Rations were scanty and the weather atrocious. Nevertheless all units honoured the festival with good cheer and high spirits. Nearly everybody was under cover and beside a warm fire. NAAFI was able to supply a certain amount of seasonable fare, and officers returned from excursions as far as Egypt with supplementary supplies. Inspection of the captured dumps revealed that the Italians ate and drank well, so that the enemy contributed considerably to the feasts. For the sepoys' Rich Food the Arabs provided goats and rice, bought with part of the generous tea ration. (It is feared that the wheeze of peddling re-dried leaves was not unknown). The return of comrades retrieved from the clutches of the enemy enlivened the festivities.*

In the messes the year's accounts were cast up with justifiable pride. In Eritrea, in Syria, and now in Cyrenaica, the Division had marched in the van and had struck resounding blows. The game book of the

*Among those rescued (though not actually from enemy hands) was Lieut.-Colonel Laycock, later to become well known as Director of Combined Operations. He had been behind the enemy lines since the beginning of the offensive in November, having landed with the Commando force which raided Rommel's headquarters.

Division showed that between the Omars and Benghazi, 6,000 prisoners had been taken, 51 tanks and 27 aircraft had been destroyed, in addition to heavy casualties inflicted on the enemy. The campaign had cost the Division 178 officers and 2,455 other ranks in killed, wounded and missing. Some units had been withdrawn because of casualties but their replacements had carried on in the spirit of their predecessors. As General Messervy said in his Christmas message, "Your speed and forward drive has earned for you the code name of NONSTOP. I cannot express to you adequately my pride in, and my admiration for, your deeds which have brought us so far on the road to victory."

Except for farewell, this was destined to be the last message from the Divisional Commander. General Messervy had been selected to command an Indian armoured division, but before leaving Western Desert he was entrusted with the leadership of 1 British Armoured Division, which was about to begin the relief of 7 Armoured Division in the Agheila area. On December 30th, Major-General F. I. S. Tucker, DSO, OBE, arrived to take command of Fourth Indian Division.

A year had wrought great changes. When General Messervy brought Fourth Indian Division to the Western Desert for the second time many in high places doubted if Indian troops, despite their success against heavy Italian odds, were of the calibre to deal with the picked German formations of Afrika Korps. This foreboding Fourth Indian Division had dispelled in no uncertain fashion. The advance from the Omars to Benghazi was more than a battle and a chase. It was proof positive of the ability of Indian Army formations, properly led and equipped, to meet the fiercest challenge of the greatest professional army in the world.

Chapter 10

RETREAT FROM BENGHAZI

FOR a number of years before the war, provocative articles under the pseudonyms "John Helland" and "Auspex" had been appearing in various Service publications, articles which were remarkable for their acute and positive prophecy of things to come. The earliest of these commentaries are to be found only in the files of the Regimental News Letter of 2nd Goorkha Rifles. Tall, light-haired Captain F. I. S. Tuker found an unorthodox outlook on the problems of policing the North West Frontier to be compatible with an equal interest in polo, shooting and the routine recreations of a junior regimental officer. He had first seen service in the war of 1914-1918 in Iraq, Assam, and against the Bolsheviks in Northern Iran. He entered Camberley at the age of thirty. There he expressed himself as dissatisfied with the standard of the teaching. In 1936 he assumed command of the 1st Battalion of his regiment, 2nd King Edward's Own Goorkha Rifles. After service in Waziristan he was appointed to General Headquarters, New Delhi. With the war only a few months away, he endeavoured without success to persuade the financial advisers to anticipate necessities and to float a loan of thirty crores of rupees for the expansion of ordnance factories and arsenals. In October 1940 he became Director of Military Training, perhaps to the consternation of some of his colleagues. There he continued to dwell on the implications of modern warfare, particularly mountain and jungle fighting and combined operations. Fourteen months later came the opportunity to test his theories. His appointment to command Fourth Indian Division in the field occasioned wide interest in the military hierarchies and a considerable degree of speculation.

On arrival at Benghazi he was confronted with a picture whose technical interest did not make it any more to his liking. On the map Cyrenaica is the shape of a skull with a receding forehead. Tobruk, which supplied the British forces, sat at the point of the chin; Tmimi stood at the eye-holes. The crescent plateau of the Djebel Achdar, reared above the Mediterranean, represented the brain box. Benghazi

---

*In 1934 United Services of India Magazine returned a contribution by Colonel Tuker on "blitz" warfare with air and armoured forces as "controversial and against the settled policy of the day". In 1941 this article was published anonymously by the same Magazine under the caption "Found in a Bottle".

was on the cerebellum, and Agedabia, where Rommel waited, at the nape of the neck. The rival forces strove for mastery of the complete head. The configuration, however, was complicated by an escarpment which created a coastal corridor to the south of Benghazi, gradually curving away from the sea until at Antelat, 80 miles below the seaport, it died into the desert 40 miles inland. This long wall created a funnel-shaped approach to Benghazi northwards along the Gulf of Sirte, with only a few negotiable passes between the coastal corridor and the desert to the east. Consequently it served as a barrier to protect the right flank of any force which advanced into Cyrenaica from the south-west.

No similar feature protected the brain box of the Djebel. Numerous age-old trails led northwards from the great wastes into the fruitful lands and left them all but indefensible by forces based on Egypt. The chord of the Desert could always amputate the arc of the Djebel, and in any battle of manoeuvre the Djebel must dance to the Desert's piping.*

The problem of the defence of the Djebel was intensified by the Japanese attack on Pearl Harbour and Britain's declaration of war in support of the United States. Reinforcements immediately had been diverted to meet the threat to British possessions in the Far East. Even Western Desert contributed: 7 Armoured Brigade, refitting at the base after hard knocks around Sidi Rezegh, was shipped to Burma. Australia requested the early return from Middle East of two of her three divisions. To counterbalance these withdrawals 1 Armoured Division, consisting of 2 Armoured Brigade and 1 Support Group, had moved forward to relieve 7 Armoured Division, sorely in need of rest and re-equipment. The newcomers took over the piquetting of Rommel's lair in the south, but because of the shortage of men, tanks and guns, this relief amounted to no more than the exchange of support groups. The British armoured force in Western Desert, therefore, consisted partly of troops unblooded in battle and partly of units exhausted physically and mechanically by the rigours of 400 miles of pursuit.

In addition, a tendency to underestimate Axis strength and particularly Rommel's recuperative powers undoubtedly coloured Eighth Army's appreciation of enemy potential at the end of the long chase. The Agedabia position was not particularly strong and the fact that Afrika Korps took refuge there was construed as a sign of weakness.

*General Tuker stated his strategical convictions in a galloping cadence in his book of verse, *The Gebel Stakes*:

> "So stand on the gas and stuff her along,
> Stick to the Desert, you'll never go wrong.
> Chase through the Gebel, you're just a mad fool,
> Through the slush and bogs of Akdor,
> You'll stick in its twisty mined ways and you'll
> Miss your quarry once more, once more;
> He'll slip away once more.
> And back you'll cast one anxious look
> At the Dannaert and mines around Tobruk."

When the panzers battered 22 Armoured Brigade near Antelat on December 28/30, destroying 65 tanks, this serious British defeat induced Intelligence to claim that because Rommel had failed to exploit his victory he realised his limitations. When at about the same time the German commander withdrew to his "keep" position at El Agheila, once again the story ran of a last stand and imminent liquidation. The truth was simple and far different. Rommel was waiting for replenishment. He was certain that he would be able to take the field before Eighth Army was in position to resume the offensive. On January 5th nine ships had arrived at Tripoli bringing him tanks and men. Before the middle of the month Littorio Armoured Division and the Subrata Infantry Division were on their way to join him. A still larger convoy was about to put to sea from Italian ports. When these reinforcements arrived, the Axis commander would know when and how far he could go. 24 enemy ships were discovered by the R.A.F. off the Tripolitanian coast on January 23rd. Although attacked from the air, 22 ships made harbour. Rommel's supplies were assured.

Throughout January Eighth Army continued to plan for an early resumption of the offensive. An assault by one brigade group of Fourth Indian Division on Mersa Brega, 25 miles east of El Agheila, would coincide with a similar attack by 1 Armoured Division against Maaten-Gofer, 20 miles further south. The tank attack was designed to roll up the enemy's right flank. Thereafter the armoured group would advance to the west to meet a second brigade of Fourth Division, which would be landed from the sea well in the enemy's rear near Marble Arch. If caught between these forces, Rommel's remnants were doomed.

Although apprised of its rôle in the new operation, Fourth Division continued to be dispersed on multifarious duties. On January 4th, Divisional Headquarters moved from Barce into Benghazi. Here the Divisional engineers laboured steadfastly under command of the Royal Navy at repairs to the harbour. 2 Camerons and 2/5 Mahrattas of 11 Brigade remained at Tobruk. 1/6 Rajputana Rifles had passed under 13 Corps command for protective duties in the Antelat district. 5 Brigade, in the Derna area, was complete once more; on January 1st 1/1 Punjabis (Lieut.-Col. W. M. C. Wilson) had relieved 3/1 Punjabis, and 1 Welch Regiment (Lieut.-Col. V. J. L. Napier, MC) had arrived to replace the remnants of 1 Buffs. Brigadier Russell's men continued to have a busy time; police duties in a wild countryside with colonists and Arabs at each other's throats produced a succession of interesting missions. Major R. B. Scott with two companies of 4/6 Rajputana Rifles and some guns occupied the troublesome Cyrene and Beda Littoria townships. Soon after arrival, an Arab brought a message from an R.A.F. pilot who was held prisoner by a group of Italians hiding in the woods to the east of Apollonia. A patrol which beat the district returned with 18 rescued airmen and 84 prisoners. On January 12th Brigade Headquarters was warned that 500 stragglers of Brescia Division were making their way westwards through the Djebel disguised as colonists. Dispositions were made to intercept them. On January

21st 200 men bombed in the principal hotel in Cyrene were dug out. 149 Anti-Tank Regiment sustained 50 casualties in this mishap. On the same day these miscellaneous chores ended when the Polish Carpathian Brigade arrived to take over.

In Benghazi 7 Brigade group had been entrusted with the opening stage of the Agheila operation. Central India Horse, 25 Field Regiment, the remaining battery of 31 Field Regiment and 65 Anti-Tank Regiment were under command. It was believed that by the beginning of February the port of Benghazi would be functioning and British supply services would be in position to support a full-scale offensive. On January 11th Divisional Headquarters returned to Barce. On January 18th, when Divisional and Brigade commanders went forward on an operational reconnaissance, abnormal Stuka activity was noted—usually a sign of something afoot. There seems however to have been no premonition of Rommel's intentions until January 21st, when enemy forces drove back British patrols along the El Agheila-Agedabia road. Intelligence reports treated the occurrence lightly, regarding it as a reconnaissance in force. Yet that evening formidable columns of guns and tanks with upwards of 3,000 attendant vehicles were identified in the Saunnu-Antelat area, 40 miles north-east of their reported location that morning. In the face of such threat 13 Corps Headquarters had withdrawn to Msus, 45 miles to the north-east, and Fourth Indian Division had suffered its first loss. A company of 1/6 Rajputana Rifles under Captain Mahbaksh Singh, on outlying guard duties under 13 Corps near Antelat, did not receive its troop-carrying transport until the northering trails had been cut. Endeavouring to escape by a détour, the Indian lorries bogged down in soft sand. In this defenceless condition they were rounded up by the enemy.

In its first directive after Rommel's advance, Eighth Army defined Fourth Indian Divisions tasks as control of the coastal corridor and the protection of Benghazi. General Tuker immediately despatched a force under Lieut.-Colonel Goulder of 31 Field Regiment to delay the enemy advance west of the escarpment and to secure the passes at Scheledeima and Si Brahim, respectively 35 and 48 miles south of Benghazi. The force consisted of Central India Horse, the remaining battery of 31 Field Regiment and some anti-aircraft and anti-tank guns. The Divisional Commander also asked that 11 Brigade be sent forward with the utmost expedition from Tobruk. 1 Field Regiment (lately under 13 Corps command), 144 Field Regiment, 4 South African Field Regiment, 149 Anti-Tank Regiment and 32 Valentines of 8 Royal Tank Regiment were placed under Divisional command. The tanks and a company of troop-carrying transport were allotted to 7 Brigade, which immediately occupied defensive positions along the Nauuaghia minefield, fourteen miles south of Benghazi. When 1 Welch Regiment arrived from Barce two companies were despatched to occupy the escarpment passes seized by Lieut.-Colonel Goulder's men. The remainder of the Welch remained as garrison in Benghazi.

Divisional Headquarters likewise moved into the outskirts of Benghazi. On arrival General Tuker held a conference with local commanders and service representatives, explaining the situation and advising them to prepare outline schemes for evacuation and demolition. Having taken these precautions, on the afternoon of January 23rd he proposed to 13 Corps that Fourth Division should strike immediately at the enemy's rear in the Agedabia area, with 7 Brigade as the spearhead of the attack. A mobile force thrusting against enemy lines of communication could scarcely fail to influence the imminent encounter between 1 Armoured Division and Rommel's panzers. Unfortunately that battle, which began on January 23rd and continued throughout the next day, went badly. 21 Panzer Division seriously mauled 2 Armoured Brigade. 13 Corps therefore decided that until the armour situation clarified, Fourth Indian Division should not be committed to the offensive; moreover if 1 Armoured Division gave further ground and the German forces continued their push beyond Msus, 26 miles to the east of Scheledeima Pass, it would be necessary to consider the evacuation of Benghazi. Should such contingency arise, I Armoured Division would retire through the desert as far as Mechili and would give a firm flank to Fourth Division on the line Derna-Martuba-Carmusa. The code word MERCURY was designated to convey that Msus had been evacuated and that the withdrawal to this line should begin.

During these days detached Indian columns found good hunting at the foot of the coastal corridor. The enemy was streaming past into the north-east and a variety of targets presented themselves. A series of ambushes resulted in numerous captures, all the prisoners being German. (22 Guards Brigade had previously reported 90 Light Division to be holding Agedabia). 57 LAA Regiment had maintained its sniping prowess, knocking down three Stukas out of a dive of four. Lance Daffadar Attar Singh of Central India Horse had distinguished himself by shadowing the Axis forces in an open truck, playing tag with their armoured cars, clinging like a limpet to the dusty columns and faithfully reporting all moves. A Divisional patrol picked up Lieutenant Lord Jellicoe and 10 Coldstream guardsmen, all but spent after walking 80 miles in a gallant escape from the enveloping advance.

On the morning of January 25th 13 Corps considered the situation sufficiently stable to advise General Tuker that he now might despatch 7 Brigade group to the south for the purpose of establishing a defensive line between Sidi Abd el Aati and the sea-coast. This plan involved the construction of defended localities at Beda Fomm, Antelat and Saunnu, upon which mobile forces might pivot. It represented the beginnings of a cordon drawn across the enemy's rear and astride his lines of communication.* The Divisional Commander and reconnaissance parties left immediately for the south, but they were no more than under way when out of a clear sky flashed the code word MERCURY. In view of 13 Corps' sanguine hopes of the morning,

* General Tuker disagreed with this proposal. It repeated Graziani's mistake of establishing field defensive positions in enemy territory while weak in the mobile arm.

nothing was less expected. Reconnaissance parties immediately were withdrawn and instructions issued for the evacuation of base and administrative details from Benghazi. Artillery and tank units on their way forward to reinforce 7 Brigade were halted at key positions throughout the Djebel.

During the evening of January 25th 13 Corps advised General Tuker that 1 Armoured Division had disengaged from the enemy and was rallying at Charruba, 35 miles south-east of Barce on the edge of the Djebel. These rapid bounds backward aroused anxiety concerning the fate of the remainder of 1/6 Rajputana Rifles, who had already lost a company and were without troop-carrying transport. A patrol of Central India Horse crossed Scheledeima Pass but was unable to learn anything. The desert to the east was alive with enemy columns and it was feared that the Rajputana Rifles had been lost. Fortunately Lieutenant Mehbub Singh, the battalion transport officer, had shown praiseworthy ingenuity. While the Rajputana Rifles took cover in a wadi, he stripped the few battalion vehicles to springs and floorboards. He drew petrol while the enemy was replenishing from the other end of the dump. Abandoning all equipment, packing 50 men to each truck, and covered by 12 Lancers of 1 Armoured Division the Rajputana Rifles slipped away to Charruba and eventually withdrew via Mechili to Tmimi.

That same evening at 2120 hours the Army Commander discussed the situation with General Tuker by telephone. General Tuker stated that in his opinion the opportunity for offensive action in the coastal corridor had passed and that the soundest course was withdrawal to the Derna-Martuba line as ordered by 13 Corps. The Army Commander did not agree. He stated that he was sure that there were only Italians on Fourth Division's front. As a result of this conversation General Tuker was advised that as from 1000 hours next morning his Division would come directly under Eighth Army command; that the MERCURY order was cancelled and that harassing operations by mobile columns would continue. The greatest offensive action was to be taken together with the greatest risks. 1 Armoured Division would deny the enemy entrance into the Djebel.

General Tuker stated that his present tactical dispositions were insecure and that in his opinion an offensive-defensive operation with further dispersal of forces was not the way to destroy Rommel. Nevertheless orders for the evacuation of Benghazi were cancelled and 7 Brigade was organized into a number of gun-cum-infantry columns to sally southwards. 4/6 Rajputana Rifles and 1/1 Punjabis of 5 Brigade moved forward to cover the lower road into Benghazi until 11 Brigade arrived.

At 0915 hours on January 26th a staff officer arrived from Eighth Army to put General Tuker comprehensively in the picture. He stated that Army Headquarters viewed the present enemy advance not as a counter-offensive but as a rather reckless foray. Rommel had overreached himself.* If a bold and aggressive attitude was maintained, Fourth Indian Division could wreak sufficient destruction on the enemy's rear to halt his advance.

In return General Tuker asked that his views might be represented to the Army Commander. He doubted if 1 Armoured Division in its present state was capable of containing the enemy panzers. Fourth Indian Division had intercepted two messages from General Messervy's headquarters. The first gave the tank strength of 2 Armoured Brigade at 0600 hours on January 26th as 33 runners. The second message, in acknowledging the Corps Commander's instructions to protect Fourth Indian Division's flank, replied that it would be quite impossible for 1 Armoured Division in its present strength to undertake such duties over a front of 35 miles. The blocking of nearby trails entering the Djebel would be as much as could be guaranteed. If these signals were accepted at face value it meant that under present instructions Fourth Indian Division would be committed to attack 90 miles in the enemy's rear, with supporting armour out of reach. Sound tactics demanded that the infantry and armour should fight together. The original 13 Corps plan had merit—a quick disengagement followed by a rally for a counterstroke from a defensible position. But if in the Army Commander's opinion it was inexpedient to give ground General Tuker suggested that Fourth Division should concentrate at Maraua, 90 miles east of Benghazi and 30 miles north of 1 Armoured Division's position on the outskirts of the Djebel. Here the British, French and Polish forces which were moving into the Mechili-Tengeder-Bir Hacheim areas would give substance to the always fluid southern flank.

The liaison officer returned to Army Headquarters that afternoon. On his arrival a signal flashed to Fourth Indian Division ordering the continuance of offensive operations based on Benghazi. Meanwhile General Tuker had been busily elaborating his project. That evening he submitted additional details to the Army Commander. He proposed that 11 Brigade should move southward from Maraua to support 2 Armoured Brigade in a head-on clash with Rommel's advancing columns. Concurrently 7 Brigade, moving rapidly across the Scheledeima Pass, would engage the enemy's left flank and drive him from Msus. General Ritchie arrived at Benghazi next morning (January 27th) and after discussion accepted these proposals. 11 Brigade group would include 1 and 144 Field Regiments, 149 Anti-Tank Regiment, a squadron of 8 Royal Tank Regiment and sections of 4 and 18 Field Companies, Sappers and Miners. 1 Armoured Division would not be ready for battle for 48 hours. The attack therefore was set down for the morning of January 30th.

*One of the chief difficulties during the Benghazi operations was the confusing intelligence. Obviously 13 Corps had the same sources of information as its component divisions, but something seems to have happened in the sifting of the intelligence. 1 Armoured Division, the R.A.F. and Central India Horse all provided positive identifications which for some reason or other Eighth Army refused to accept.

At 1745 hours, soon after the termination of this conference, a report was received that the track Msus-Scheledeima was packed with enemy transport moving west. 7 Brigade was ordered to reinforce the escarpment passes, which were to be held at all costs. (Shortly afterwards Brigadier Briggs confirmed that the passes had been reinforced and that no enemy elements were within six miles of Scheledeima).

At this juncture "P" Force was improvised under command of Lieut.-Colonel Roger Peake of the Royals, an old friend of Eritrean days, for the purpose of defending Benghazi against enemy forces which might strike across the escarpment or along the fair weather road from Barce. This force consisted of 8 Royal Tank Regiment, a battery of 7 Medium Regiment, 4 South African Field Regiment, two companies of the Welch Regiment, two batteries 57 LAA Regiment and the carrier squadron of Central India Horse. The medium guns and the tanks were in the Barce area; before they could move forward heavy rain began to fall and they were bogged down. In the early evening General Tuker sent a personal message to the Army Commander which suggested that 1 Armoured Division should not wait until January 30th but should at once strike at the rear of the forces moving on Scheledeima.

This message crossed an appreciation of the situation from Eighth Army. The enemy (said the report) had divided his forces. One group continued eastwards towards Mechili, the other moved westwards towards Solluch and Benghazi. The groups were more or less of equal strength, but the bulk of the panzers appeared to be accompanying the eastbound force. When the thrust on Mechili had developed sufficiently, 1 Armoured Division would fall on its rear. Fourth Indian Division would deal with the westbound force single-handed, without armour and without flank protection.

Thus once again the anticipated battle resolved into dispersed forces operating individually, with the British armour attacking in one direction, the Indian infantry defending in another. General Tuker doubted whether Eighth Army would have approved such plan had it received his proposal by which the enemy would be caught between two forces, with 1 Armoured Division playing hammer to 7 Brigade's anvil. At midnight, therefore, GSO II Fourth Division, called BGS Eighth Army, asking for confirmation of arrangements. He was relieved to hear that 1 Armoured Division would strike in concert with 7 Brigade, as suggested by General Tuker.

The wet weather had prevented the bulk of 7 Brigade from crossing Scheledeima on the previous evening, but early in the morning of January 28th two mobile columns moved off with instructions to find and to engage the enemy's forces to the east of the Pass. Gold Group, under command of Lieut.-Colonel C. Goulder, DSO, of 31 Field Regiment, consisted of 4/11 Sikhs, 31 Field Regiment, anti-aircraft and anti-tank guns, together with a squadron of Central India Horse. Silver

Group, under command of Lieut.-Colonel G. C. Evans DSO, comprised 1 Royal Sussex, a battery of 25 Field Regiment, 65 Anti-Tank Regiment, two troops of 57 LAA Regiment and a second squadron of Central India Horse. Brigade Headquarters Group, which included the undetached companies of 4/16 Punjabis, a squadron of Central India Horse, two troops of 57 LAA Regiment and 12 Field Company Sappers and Miners, remained in reserve at Solluch.

The dawn patrol from Benina airfield identified strong enemy columns to the south of El Abiar, which is situated on the fair-weather road through the Djebel, thirty-five miles east of Benghazi. These columns were moving north rather than west, a circumstance which did not affect 7 Brigade's expedition; instead of meeting them head on at Scheledeima, Brigadier Briggs' force would fall upon their flank and rear. During the morning the enemy advance struck heavy going among the rocky outcrops of the Dahar El Ahmar, the most westerly buttresses of the Djebel. The R.A.F. bombed and machine-gunned the advancing columns to good effect. Gold and Silver Groups were on their way to Scheledeima when they encountered Central India Horse patrols withdrawing in the coastal corridor. The cavalrymen reported two enemy columns, each consisting of 40 tanks, a number of guns and many attendant vehicles, to be moving up the corridor only a few miles behind them. One enemy force was following the line of the escarpment, the other exploiting along the main coastal road. If unobstructed, these columns would reach Benghazi in a few hours.

It was therefore out of the question for Gold and Silver Groups to proceed on their missions. Benghazi was now menaced from two directions and Fourth Indian Division possessed only one blocking force. Everything depended upon the intervention of 1 Armoured Division. 7 Brigade columns were ordered to engage the enemy in the coastal corridor while General Tuker organised the defence of the port. 8 Royal Tank Regiment, with Divisional Headquarters, one company of 2/5 Mahrattas and 11 Brigade Anti-Tank Company, were ordered to move eastward from Benghazi in all haste to meet and delay the advance screen of the enemy approaching by way of El Abiar. In Benghazi plans were laid for a "keep" defence. Petrol, water and ammunition dumps were established in the centre of the town. The port would be defended street by street.

At noon Brigadier Briggs reported a serious situation in the coastal corridor. Heavy Stuka attacks and roving clumps of panzers were making disengagement difficult. Gold Group which had leaguered at Magrun and Sidi Abd el Aati on the night before, had dropped back steadily throughout the morning, under pressure but keeping cohesion and taking toll. When 21 enemy aircraft passed overhead at Magrun, 57 LAA Regiment added five notches to its score. Shortly after midday Colonel Goulder's columns reached the defensive zone 13 miles south of Benghazi.

Silver Group had arrived at Scheledeima at first light, and had immediately despatched Major Pope of 25 Field Regiment with eight guns to reinforce the garrison. While the gunners were seeking positions, enemy groups approached from the east and along the top of the escarpment. The blocking force in the Pass was assailed from three sides. Concurrently scout cars came racing in from the south to announce the approach of enemy forces along the base of the escarpment. Under the circumstances Silver Group had no alternative but to withdraw. Major Pope's battery covered the retirement, extricating the guns at the last moment. Throughout the forenoon Lieut.-Colonel Evans' men dropped back towards Benghazi, holding the enemy at arm's length but unable to disengage. 24 panzers were reported at Solluch directly in their rear, but keeping well to the east of this danger spot Silver Group avoided a clash and slowly made its way towards the rallying line of Nauuaghia minefields.

The garrison of Scheledeima, under command of Lieut.-Colonel Napier, consisted of Battalion Headquarters and "B" Company of 1 Welch Regiment, a company of 4/16 Punjabis and an anti-tank platoon. Throughout the forenoon the defenders sustained severe casualties as the enemy ring closed around the Pass. When at 1400 hours the Divisional Commander's instructions to withdraw to Benghazi were received, there followed a gallant attempt to break out. Six officers and approximately 150 men of the Scheledeima garrison slipped away on foot through the enemy cordon to the north and took cover among the rolling scrub-clad ridges. In two nights this party covered 25 miles, suffering greatly from lack of water and scanty rations. On January 30th it had dwindled to 70 strong and had reached an area south of the Benghazi railway stiff with enemy formations. Here, while Lieut.-Colonel Napier was organising his men into small parties which stood better chances of escape, mobile forces closed in and compelled surrender.

"C" Company of the Welch, stationed at Si Brahim Pass, was not engaged by the enemy, and upon receipt of instructions withdrew into Benghazi.

Immediately on receipt of Brigadier Briggs' report, General Tuker telephoned the Army Commander, reporting the situation and anxiously enquiring for news of 1 Armoured Division. He then learnt to his dismay that 1 Armoured Division was not following up Rommel's westbound columns, but, as in terms of the earlier Eighth Army plan, was moving eastward in the rear of the enemy forces which were thrusting against Mechili. As the situation stood, there was no hope of reinforcements from Barce arriving ahead of the main body of the enemy. It was therefore not a matter of holding Benghazi until Rommel could be brought to battle; instead, it was a question of whether there was any way by which the forward elements of Fourth Indian Division could escape destruction.

Making an instantaneous decision, General Tuker told the Army Commander that it would be necessary to evacuate Benghazi immediately. Both 90 Light Division and 21 Panzer Division had been identified in the coastal corridor and it was useless to contend that only Italians were involved in the enemy advance. After some hesitation General Ritchie consented to the evacuation of the seaport. 7 Brigade columns immediately were ordered to withdraw behind the Nauuaghia minefields. 5 Brigade was sent to hold Tocra Pass * on the coastal road and Si Mahius, ten miles east of El Abiar on the fair-weather track. Lieut.-Colonel Peake's "P" Force was given the task of covering the main road through Benghazi and the by-pass around the town along which 7 Brigade columns must pass. Demolitions were put in hand including 6,000 tons of captured enemy ammunition. The plan of withdrawal called for the improvised Benghazi defence force and all "B" Echelon vehicles to be clear of the port by 1800 hours. 7 Brigade would follow through two hours later. 8 Royal Tank Regiment would fall back at dusk on Si Mahius. **

At 1530 hours, when Divisional Headquarters left for Barce, it looked like a tight squeeze. Until that hour Lieut.-Colonel Peake's patrols to the south and east of Benghazi had not encountered the enemy. Divisional Headquarters, however, were no more than on the road when Lieutenant Willis of 4/11 Sikhs, attached to Lieut.-Colonel Peake's force, reported that he had been fired on by Mark III tanks in the pass at Regima above Benina airfield. Lieut.-Colonel Peake at once sent one company of the Welch Regiment to cover the Benghazi by-pass and gave an authorisation to the remaining fighter squadron to evacuate Benina. At 1730 hours the covering company of the Welch Regiment reported enemy scout groups to have reached the outskirts of the town. Its commander was instructed to keep the by-pass open at all costs.

All that afternoon 7 Brigade's command vehicle had called in clear, "You are to withdraw behind main minefields repeat main minefields." The outlying wireless sets dutifully replied, "We are withdrawing behind main minefields repeat main minefields." The minefields at Nauughia were incomplete, but the ruse served and the enemy followed up circumspectly. When day closed with thunderous blasts of demolitions along the waterfront, long lines of "B" Echelon vehicles began to defile along Benghazi by-pass on to the raised causeway which marked the beginning of the coastal road to the east.

Out of the gathering night the enemy struck. Apparently German tanks and armoured cars had made their way northwards along the rim of the escarpment and so escaped detection by 8 Royal Tank Regiment on the fair-weather track. In the dusk Stukas swept along the

---

*Teucer, Teucrum, Tocra, Tuker—the old Latin word for battle-axe persists in many guises.

** Fortunately, after the first MERCURY signal for evacuation much heavy equipment had left Benghazi and had not been brought back.

roads, shooting up transport. Behind them enemy armoured fighting vehicles emerged from the scrub and plunged down over the escarpment onto Benina airfield. Here the attacking force split, part pressing into Benghazi, eleven miles away, while the remainder cut across country towards the coastal road. The first group plunged head on into the covering party of the Welch, who by great good fortune had 171 LAA Battery in close support. These gunners stood ready; as the panzers lurched down the road from the airfield the Bofors opened at point blank range. Four tanks and an ammunition waggon burst into flames. The survivors sheered off in the darkness. The by-pass remained open and the traffic continued to file through.

Shortly after 1900 hours, as streams of transport poured past el-Coefia, on the coastal highway eight miles north-east of Benghazi, intersecting lines of tracer announced the arrival of the enemy. The road was raised above the brackish foreshore, with deep ditches on either side. The closely packed vehicles halted, endeavoured to scurry to safety and jammed in a tangle of reversing and ditched lorries. 7 Brigade was already following along the by-pass, led by 4/16 Punjabis. Lieut.-Colonel Lavender hurried forward to find enemy armoured cars sweeping the road with their machine-guns in order to screen the construction of road blocks. A more perfect site for an ambuscade could not have been found anywhere. On the coastal side the lagoons came up to the causeway; on the inner side a raised road running into Coefia village provided the enemy with a frontal rampart. Captain Chase of the Punjabis brought forward two Breda guns and a troop of anti-tank guns, but owing to the narrow causeway and lack of firm footing it was found impossible to dislodge the enemy or to burst through his barricade.

At approximately the same hour Lieut.-Colonel Peake despatched an officer to Brigadier Briggs to inform him that he could no longer guarantee safe passage along the by-pass or through the town. Brigadier Briggs sent back word of his intention to break out to the south. Lieut.-Colonel Peake then learned of the road block at Coefia. He at once proceeded to the scene with his two companies of the Welch Regiment and four carriers of Central India Horse. He found the road blocked by transport and it was with great difficulty that his fighting troops worked forward. On reaching the ambush he gave over command of the Welch companies to Lieut.-Colonel Lavender, whose first attack had failed to shift the enemy. The Welch deployed and joined in the attempt to open the road; but by this time the blocking forces had thickened. One enemy field gun had been brought up to sniping range; panzers could be heard milling in the darkness; signal flares constantly soared and fell along the escarpment and on the foreland, announcing the arrival of fresh bodies of the enemy; from the high ground guns began to harass the roads and the approaches to the port. The situation was hopeless. At dawn all caught in such a *cul de sac* would be doomed. Lieut.-Colonel Lavender ordered the forward groups to destroy their vehicles, to disperse, and to endeavour to make their way out of the trap individually. Some of the men melted into the darkness across the foreland, seeking sanctuary in the Djebel undergrowth. Others turned back into Benghazi and were picked up by cool-headed drivers who had extricated their vehicles. (Most of the "B" Echelon transport of 25 and 31 Field Regiment had managed to escape). Before dawn the enemy forces moved into Benghazi, where they rounded up the demolition engineers, who had accepted capture in order to complete the destruction of the port.

Sixty miles away, in Barce, Divisional Headquarters waited for news with the utmost anxiety. 7 Brigade had gone off the air and the last situation report placed enemy forces in Regima, 17 miles to the east of Benghazi. At 2115 hours General Tuker reported the situation to the Army Commander. General Ritchie reiterated that there were only Italian troops approaching Benghazi. He suggested that 7 Brigade might remain there, or at least might leave a battalion group behind. Through the long night Divisional Headquarters waited, straining at the earphones. At 0500 hours a message came over a 4/16 Punjabi set, reporting the road block at Coefia, announcing Lieut.-Colonel Lavender's force to be in action there and that the arrival of Brigadier Briggs at Barce would be delayed. The message likewise revealed the blocking forces to be German. General Tuker immediately instructed 5 Brigade to despatch strong fighting patrols along both highway and fair-weather track in an endeavour to contact 7 Brigade. A last appeal was sent to 1 Armoured Division to move on Benghazi. With the utmost good will this formation could do no more than despatch contact patrols, since its strength in runners was less than that of a single armoured regiment.

On the morning of January 29th, with a curtain of silence drawn across the west, General Tuker received instructions from Eighth Army to give as little ground as possible with a view to an early resumption of the offensive. Fourth Indian Division was ordered to stand on the line d'Annunzio-Maraua, twenty-five miles east of Barce. Should further withdrawal be necessary, an additional 35 miles to the Cyrene-el-Faida crossroads was authorised. At 1040 hours, in a telephone conversation, General Ritchie amplified these instructions. The Commander-in-Chief, Middle East, would not consent to any attempt to regain Benghazi. Losses must be cut and no troops employed to the west of Barce. 5 Brigade therefore withdrew its forward patrols and preparations were made to blow up Tocra Pass.

At this juncture additional artillery arrived in the form of 1 Field Regiment, lately returned from 13 Corps, and 144 Field Regiment, which was remembered from Eritrean days when it served under 5 Indian Division. The most pressing necessity, however, was to find more infantry. No one seemed very sure of the thrust lines of Rommel's eastbound columns. To cover the withdrawal it was essential without delay to garrison layback positions along the Djebel roads. In addition Fourth Division must guard its flank by blocking the numerous trails from the south. General Tuker requested the Army Commander to supply reinforcements for these purposes. He was told that no troops were available to cover his flank and rear, but that 3/1 Punjabis and 1/6 Rajputant Rifles might be brought forward from Tobruk to strengthen his brigades. (Neither of these battalions at this stage was fit for active operations). The only other troops in the Djebel consisted of the King's Dragoon Guards, a detachment of 7 South African Recce Regiment and a battalion of the Libyan Arab Force. At this critical juncture a small but welcome reinforcement arrived from an unexpected quarter. In the previous November Brigadier Denys Reid of 29 Indian Brigade had led a mixed Indian and South African group ("E" Force) to the capture of Jalo oasis, 230 miles deep in the desert to the south of Benghazi. On January 15th this expedition had been called in. On moving to the north it found itself in the midst of Rommel's advancing columns. After an exciting trek "E" Force, consisting of 1/2 Punjabis, six 25-pounders, one Bofors gun and eight armoured cars, arrived at Maraua on January 28th. The men had been on half rations for weeks and their transport was no more than hanging together. Yet everyone was in good heart and General Tuker was thankful to have even this handful. "E" Force was placed under command of 11 Brigade.

The plan for Fourth Division's withdrawal called for 5 Brigade to fall back on the north road and 11 Brigade on the south road. At noon on January 29th enemy armoured cars had reached Tocra village at the bottom of the Pass. At 1400 hours the Pass was blown. The same afternoon Barce was evacuated and the entrances to the defiles in the eastern escarpment blocked by extensive demolitions. The rains had ceased and the ground was drying rapidly, a circumstance which drew General Tuker's attention to his open flank. 1 Armoured Division had undertaken to deny Charruba to the enemy until noon on January 30th. Hagfet Gilgaf, 25 miles south of Maraua, which covered the first of the layback positions, would be held for 36 hours longer. General Messervy, however, sent General Tuker a personal message in which he stated that his desire might exceed his capacity. He doubted if his Division could oppose more than 25 panzers with any hope of success. Eighth Army Headquarters apparently had reached a similar conclusion, for during the night of January 29/30 Fourth Division was instructed not to stand on the d'Annunzio-Maraua line but to withdraw to the second layback position covering the road junctions at Cyrene-el-Faida.

At 0700 hours on the morning of January 30th a faint call out of the desert rang as exultantly as a hunting horn. 7 Brigade was loose and was enquiring if it was safe to put into Mechili. Gaily the answer sped—"Many friends there". With such invigorating tidings 5 and 11 Brigades began to drop back along the Djebel roads. The enemy was reported as coming on fast, but without interference the brigades reached Maraua and d'Annunzio that night. 4 Field Company found time to turn into Lucia Razza and to blow up a number of dumps as well as 13 captured tanks.

The timing of the withdrawal called for this layback position to be held for 48 hours. On the morning of January 31st clashes occurred on both roads, as enemy screens probed and attempted to by-pass the brigade positions. The forward battalions—4/6 Rajputana Rifles on the upper, 2 Camerons on the lower road, were on the alert, and the intruders received a rough welcome. Lorried infantry which endeavoured to cut the road in the rear of the Highlanders suffered such a thorough shooting-up that the attempt was not renewed. At d'Annunzio a similar force reconnoitred the Rajputana Rifles' positions. The sepoys held their fire until the Germans approached to point-blank range. Anti-tank guns and small arms then wiped out the party, 50 Germans being killed. These sharp thrusts at the Divisional positions suggested that it would be asking for trouble to delay withdrawal for the set period of 48 hours. That afternoon, therefore, the Army Commander was asked to relax his instructions in order that the road demolition plan might be put into effect immediately and that the Divisional units might reach a stabilised line as soon as possible. Assent to move at discretion was forthcoming.

That evening "E" Force hurried back to el-Faida, 34 miles to the rear of Maraua, where a trail offered access to the Djebel from the desert. Enemy forces were reported to be advancing along this track. With Brigadier Reid's blocking force covering the danger point, 5 and 11 Brigades withdrew the same evening as far as Caf Tartagu on the upper road and Slonta on the lower road, or approximately half way between the first and second layback positions. The oncoming enemy had remained in close contact with the Divisional rearguards and as 4/6 Rajputana Rifles disengaged, a force of lorried infantry and tanks burst from cover and endeavoured to disrupt the withdrawal. The veterans again blew back the rush from close range, destroying one tank.

Next morning (February 1st) 3/1 Punjabis arrived to reinforce 11 Brigade. During the forenoon the enemy pressed strongly against Brigadier Anderson's rearguards and it became apparent that Axis forces were thickening on the desert flank. As they disengaged at Slonta, 2/5 Mahrattas had considerable difficulty in preventing the enemy from lapping around into their rear. By noon, however, the Deccan men had passed through 2 Camerons at el-Faida, where the Highlanders hastily prepared a holding position.

At 1530 hours a force of lorried infantry approached the Camerons, who had dug in on the forward slopes of a hillside overlooking a densely wooded valley. A reconnoitring tank and an armoured car were disabled, but the Germans, under cover of mortar and shell fire continued to close. Fighting ensued throughout the afternoon, but every attempt to penetrate or to infiltrate was defeated by steady musketry and canny positioning. Sergeant S. Grey, DCM, MM, of the Camerons has provided a lively account of this action:

"About 1530 hours they arrived. An armoured car and a tank, followed by lorries, came streaming over the top. Twenty Kittyhawks paid no attention and cruised above us as if on Bank Holiday. The lorries stopped on the top and the tank and armoured cars came on, watched breathlessly by everyone, until they got neatly picked off by an anti-tank gun as they came round the last corner—nicely within Bren range. The crews only ran a yard or two!

"Then the party started. The Germans deployed well out of range, got their mortars, machine-guns and a battery going, and rushed stuff over and into our hill without stopping. Meanwhile one could see the infantry dodging about in the bushes on the hillside. Things looked ugly, as presumably we were on a last-man-last-round racket, and it was going to be a night party. No wire and five hundred yards to each platoon front!

"But as dusk fell word came to thin out at 1915 hours and leave by 1930 hours — a big relief as there seemed to be a lot of Germans. By 1930 hours it was dark and I went out to bring in one of the forward sections.

"I went off down the hill and saw some people coming my way. So I shouted 'Is that McKay's section?' 'Yes!' came the answer. So I went on to tell them to sit on top of the hill. When I came nearer I felt that something was wrong. Something was! A large German jumped out from behind a bush and pinned me before I could think. Then a German and an Italian officer came running up, took my rifle and equipment off me, stuck automatics in my stomach and back, while the Italian, speaking perfect English, said 'Lead us to your comrades; tell them to surrender and you will be well treated'. I feigned sickness and stupidity and asked for water, but got kicked in the stomach by the German. There seemed no alternative, so I pointed to my left and the German ordered his platoon to go off in that direction, presumably to do a flanking movement. I started off up the hill, with the officers on either side, and stumbling in the dark managed to bring my platoon well onto my flank. Then I aimed for their position, which I could just distinguish in the dark. I heard a Jock say 'Here the b - - - - s come'. Then the Italian said 'Shout to them to surrender!' So I shouted 'McGeogh, McGeogh!' (I knew he was a good shot), got within ten yards of them, shouted 'Shoot!' and fell flat. The boys shot and got the German in the head and the Italian in the stomach. Grand! So off I ran and rejoined the platoon. By then we were long past our withdrawal time; so back we went, and after a bit of bayonet work by the rear platoon, jumped into lorries and drove off with the Germans lining the road behind us, popping at us at point-blank range.

"When we left Faida we reckoned that by tea-time to-morrow we would be busy again."

While the Camerons were under pressure an enemy force had appeared on 5 Brigade's front on the upper road, but without attempting to attack. Brigadier Russell's men were now covering Derna, where the evacuation of naval installations, the destruction of dumps and essential demolitions, retarded withdrawal. 5 Brigade therefore could not keep pace with 11 Brigade, but 11 Brigade dared not withdraw further east until 5 Brigade had cleared Derna and had passed through Martuba, where the two Djebel roads joined before descending the eastern escarpment to Gazala. This unavoidable delay promised to offer Rommel his last and greatest opportunity to trap Fourth Division. The Axis columns had by-passed Mechili, and were thrusting northwards in the rising ground south of Derna, where the Djebel massif narrows to a headland only about 15 miles in depth. Here Martuba was easily approachable from the desert side.

While the Army Commander on the morning of February 2nd had given assent to complete withdrawal from the Djebel, he was anxious that Fourth Indian Division should conform in timing with the eastern movement of 1 Armoured Division through the desert, the withdrawal of French forces from Mechili and the arrival of reserves in the Gazala positions. To this end he promised that should the threat to Fourth Division's flank and rear become too marked, "L" Force, consisting of French and Polish units based on Mechili, would strike northwards to harass and delay the enemy. He still hoped that Rommel would prove to have overreached himself and that the next canter of the Djebel Stakes would begin immediately, and to the westward. This sanguine view underestimated the Axis Commander's capacity and the sparse margin of safety on which Fourth Indian Division operated. A single well-blocked road might bottle up everybody. General Tuker, not wishing to occupy any position in which he could not fight advantageously, urged that the withdrawal to a defensible position should be expedited.

His views received striking support on February 2nd when events all but wrote "finis" to the retirement. 5 Brigade was making slow time through the Derna bottleneck, where Arab looters were adding their quota of difficulty. Precious hours passed in which 11 Brigade dared not drop back, although enemy forces were closing in on its flank and rear. Keeping a wary eye on all sides, Brigadier Anderson and his men settled down to hold Carmusa, a trail junction 13 miles west of Martuba. 11 Brigade deployed with two companies of 3/1 Punjabis and 52 Battery of 1 Field Regiment in a covering position seven miles west of the junction; two companies of 2/5 Mahrattas two miles west of Carmusa, astride the road; 2 Camerons with the remainder of 1 Field Regiment and 144 Field Regiment, at the Carmusa cross tracks; two companies of 3/1 Punjabis three miles to the north of Carmusa, on the trail to Derna; the remainder of the Mahrattas with 18 Field Company further east, on the track to Martuba. The Punjabis and Mahrattas to the west of Carmusa had been dropped as rearguards until the remainder of the Brigade had prepared defences in which it could meet attacks from any side. A position had been organised and Brigadier Anderson had despatched officers to recall the covering companies when the blow fell.

After heavy losses in the Syrian campaign and at the Omars, 3/1 Punjabis had recently received the equivalent of two companies of recruits, men not yet versed in the wiles and precautions of desert warfare. During the morning they had laboured at a screening position to the south of the road. They were resting at noon, apparently without a covering party, when a fleet of British lorries headed by a cruiser tank appeared from the west. This column was permitted to drive up without challenge. Out sprang Germans, covering the two companies and securing them with scarcely a shot fired. A group of enemy tanks which had crept up under cover of the undergrowth burst into view and swung around the northern flank against 52 Battery positions. The British gunners were alert and instantly went into action, but heavy mortar and machine-gun fire cut them down. In 15 minutes the position had been overrun. One gun fortunately escaped destruction, a circumstance which perhaps saved everybody. Racing eastward its crew encountered 11 Battery of 1 Field Regiment, which had been moving forward to support the Punjabis when the catastrophe occurred. Major Kitcat, the battery commander, wirelessed for reinforcements, seized the first available position, and swung his guns westward. At the head of the fleet of 400 vehicles carrying the pursuers came into view, the 25-pounders slashed at them. Swinging to flank the vehicles sought to by-pass the tiny blocking force. 11 Battery dropped back to conform, snatched fresh positions and as the enemy again hove into sight, crashed shell into the massed transport. A troop of 65 Anti-Tank Regiment and a Bofors gun came racing up to join 11 Battery. In four successive positions the gunners met the challenge. 11 Field Battery fired over 1,000 rounds during the afternoon.

This fighting had occurred to the south of the road, and the forward companies of 2/5 Mahrattas were only involved in the fringe of the battle. They dropped back on the main Brigade position, covered by a rearguard in which Naik Narayan Surwase distinguished himself. With a captured Breda gun he knocked out a Mark III tank and several vehicles. At Carmusa 11 Brigade drew together to take the shock. The Divisional Commander had made it clear, in a signal passed in Urdu for the sake of security, that the position must be held at all costs. At 1600 hours the attack developed against the Camerons, to the south and west of the crossroads. Until dark fell the enemy under cover of shell fire endeavoured to penetrate the position. The commander of 18 Field Company Sappers and Miners offered his men as infantry, and they were sent to reinforce the firing line on the left flank of the Camerons. By 1800 hours the fighting had died away with no appreciable gain for the enemy and negligible casualties for the defenders.

Orders now arrived from the Divisional Commander for 11 Brigade to effect junction with Brigadier Denys Reid's "E" Force to the south and with 5 Brigade to the north, for the purpose of establishing a continuous defensive position in front of Martuba. Withdrawal to this line began at 2020 hours. At Martuba there was no sign of 5 Brigade, but from passing transport Brigadier Anderson learned that the demolitions had been completed in Derna and that 1/1 Punjabi rearguard party might be expected at any time. At this juncture fresh orders instructed both brigades to continue their withdrawal to Tmimi, 30 miles to the south-east, on the first Djebel spurs above the Gazala corridor. Lieut.-Colonel Wilson of 1/1 Punjabis arrived at the cross-roads as well as a representative of "E" Force, which had spent an exciting day in the midst of the enemy without incurring attack. Details of the subsequent withdrawal were arranged. Throughout the night the tired groups plodded on. Before dawn the troop carriers filed in to take their places in the Tmimi perimeter, with 5 Brigade holding the north-western and western faces, 11 Brigade commanding the south-western approaches and "E" Force completing the ring to the Mediterranean on the south-east. 1/6 Rajputana Rifles were despatched ten miles south to El Aleima to make contact with "L" Force, the Franco or Polish group which was expected to arrive from Mechili that afternoon.

At Tmimi, to the delight of all, there was news of absent friends. 31 Field Regiment, which had broken out of Benghazi with Gold Group, still had six workable guns. Declining the opportunity to rest and refit in Tobruk the gallant artillerymen came posting forward to take up the battle again. That forenoon it appeared as though employment might be imminent. Enemy columns thrust down the road from the Djebel against 5 Brigade's perimeter. All guns were swung on to this front and the intruders received a plastering. Lorried infantry engaged 1/1 Punjabis but were easily discouraged from pressing home the assault. Panzers appeared late in the afternoon, but only to demonstrate at a safe distance.

Orders now reached Fourth Indian Division to complete the withdrawal to the Gazala line that night and to take station on the Acroma plateau, the rugged shelf of rock which stood above the coastal corridor to the west of Tobruk. Here a defensive line would be established. At the hour of disengagement 1/1 Punjabis staged a small counter-attack, under cover of which "E" Force took on rearguard duties. To avoid congestion Divisional Headquarters dropped back along the main road while 11 Brigade turned south over the rocky ridges and abrupt nullahs of the bad lands where the eastern horn of the Djebel sinks into the desert.

That night will be long remembered by Brigadier Anderson's men for its nightmare march across all but impassable country. One column negotiated no more than ten miles in the first six hours. Another group was followed by panzers, but even the tracked vehicles were foiled by the topsy-turvy terrain. Lorries crashed into nullahs, bellied with wheels in the air, snagged sumps and differentials on boulders, and yet in some fashion managed to right themselves and to keep moving. A number of guns and vehicles blew up on mines and booby traps while crossing the Alam Hamza-Sidi Breghisc battlefield. Nevertheless by dawn 11 Brigade was bumping over the open desert, and "E" Force had defiled down the escarpment at Gazala with South African sappers standing by to blow the last bridges. By noon Fourth Division was concentrated in its new area and in touch with 7 Brigade columns at El Adem and Tobruk.

The final tally showed Fourth Indian Division to have extricated itself from the clutches of the enemy at a cost of about 600 men out of Divisional strength of approximately 12,000 of all ranks. These moderate losses reflected the skill and energy with which the withdrawal had been conducted. Had everyone not risen to outstanding performances when confronted with successive emergencies, the story of the Djebel might have been a black tale. The Divisional Commander, with his ability to keep a play ahead of the board, captained a steadfast side. In Brigadiers Briggs, Russell and Anderson, he possessed a trio of tough and wily field leaders unsurpassed in any army. But as always the chief merit rested with the rank and file, who met every challenge of circumstance with a clear reply. They struck at enemies on their flank and turned to meet others at their backs. They kept food, water and ammunition moving to wherever the fighting men might be. They toiled with picks and shovels, laying them aside to seize their rifles as their adversaries closed. They strung the wires and repaired the breaks at every hour of the day and night. They picked up the wounded where they fell. Task by task they surmounted every obstacle, frustrated every enemy intention. *The Tiger Kills* pays a well-deserved tribute to the work of the supply services:

"In retirements in which units are hopelessly mixed up and scattered over wide distances, it is the supply columns which carry the greatest strain. A dozen times each day 'Q' services find themselves with almost insuperable problems. Units come out of nowhere, to be placed under command, to be fed and watered. There is never enough transport to supply all; the shuttling of vehicles takes on the intricacy of a jig-saw puzzle. Supply dumps are constantly shifting. Officers go on reconnaissance in search of them, and never come back. Units struck off ration strength as captured walk in next day demanding supplies. Above everything else looms the liquid problem. There are never enough water tins to go round, and never petrol tins which do not leak. (After this war some sardonic essayist will find a fruitful subject in the British Army's determination to capture enough 'Jerry cans' to serve, rather than to manufacture non-leakable water and petrol tins of its own). Then when supply columns have been sent up to units which have given a reliable map reference, too often such convoys run into the enemy before they can reach their destination; or having reached the map reference, they find no one there; or having found someone, they arrive in the middle of a battle, or of a hasty withdrawal. All this adds up to a hundred nightmares for the hard-working 'Q' services, and that they continue to function efficiently is a supreme tribute to their patience and endurance".

Of all crises in the Djebel none was more protracted, more arduous, than that of the transport services. Eighth Army was always hungry for vehicles, Fourth Indian Division invariably in a state of acute starvation. Only fantastic improvisation coupled with desperately hard work far into the night, when fitters tied rickety bodies together and teased failing engines to a last spurt, kept the Division mobile. Even then each vehicle did the work of four. Every unit could re-echo the cry of 18 Field Company:

"We have only 38 vehicles and we need 100. We have 13 different types, which make spares hard to obtain. 13 of our lorries are over two years old and completely worn out. 7 are relics which formerly towed trucks up the Keren railway. Their engines are finished, their steering deplorable, their frames out of alignment. The remainder are veterans of Sudan, Syria and Libya. Their mileage over rough desert is in scores of thousands, and they are constantly in the workshops. One is a captured French lorry that no one knows anything about. Another was picked up in a minefield and repaired by our own LAD. A third had a shell burst under it and is a mass of holes".*

General Tuker issued a detailed report on the Cyrenaican operation to his staff officers and unit commanders. His summary is sufficiently succinct to allow quotation in full:

"The reason why Rommel was successful against 13 Corps was because when he counter-attacked from Agheila, 13 Corps was spread out from the sea right round to the south of Agheila in small groups of columns. This was a dispersion of effort, for these columns were not able to concentrate to join 1 Armoured Division in the main battle south-east of Antelat.

"The first principle of war is concentration at the decisive time and place. The result was that 2 Armoured Brigade, Guards Brigade and Support Group, were beaten in detail. Fourth Indian Division had no troop-carrying transport at first, and when it got it, it was not sent to the help of 1 Armoured Division. The result was that 1 Armoured Division was attacked without a shot being fired by Fourth Indian Division, and Fourth Indian Division was attacked without a shot being fired by 1 Armoured Division.

"When control of the desert area was lost by 13 Corps, Fourth Indian Division had an extremely difficult withdrawal to make because the Germans were in a position not only to follow it up but to hit at it from the desert, in flank and almost in rear. The Division piquetted its route all the way back as in Frontier warfare, in order to hold enemy attacks from its rear and flank. This succeeded, and the enemy was held every time except once, 12 miles west of Carmusa, when the stubborn fighting of 11 Brigade kept the way clear for 5 Brigade to draw out.

*To accentuate the discontent with exhausted, senile and temperamental vehicles, the first jeeps had been seen in the land. The reports of their performance ran like wildfire and filled every heart with longing. A jeep corps would have been invincible if only because of the morale of its drivers.

"You will notice also that the principle of security was neglected, for nowhere west of Tobruk was there a firm base on which 13 Corps could fall back, or behind which it could rally for a counter-offensive. In modern war these firm bases are an essential part of one's method of advance.

"There is no doubt that Fourth Indian Division showed up very well in the extremely difficult conditions of this deliberate withdrawal. There was never a single sign of panic. Without sufficient transport and with other difficulties, the withdrawal went through most smoothly. This was a great credit to our Brigade Commands and Staffs, and to our Signals and Administration Services."

It will now be necessary to return to Benghazi and from there to trace the fortunes of 7 Brigade, trapped by the enemy on the evening of January 28th.

Chapter 11

BENGHAZI — 7 BRIGADE BREAKS OUT

WHEN the enemy cordon closed around Benghazi on the evening of January 28th, it was indeed fortunate that 7 Brigade was organised in mobile columns on a more or less self-sustaining basis. It was also a happy circumstance that the leaders of these columns—Brigadier Briggs of Headquarters Group, Lieut.-Colonel Goulder of Gold Group and Lieut.-Colonel Evans of Silver Group, were all men of wide desert knowledge and great determination. It is interesting to note that although Brigadier Briggs issued only general instructions for this operation, all columns adopted similar tactics in making their getaway. Finally, the break-out proved once again the soundness of the old adage that fortune favours the audacious. The escapees had good luck because they took long chances.

In spite of the destruction of documents it has been possible to piece together the story of the 4,100 men who broke out with the three principal groups. 200 others got away, many turning up long afterwards, having endured great hardship and extraordinary advantures. It will not be possible to include all the latter individual narratives in this history, but representative instances will be cited which must stand for all.

Tidings of the ambush on the Coefia road reached Brigadier Briggs soon after 1900 hours at El Guarscia, 9 miles south of Benghazi. The situation has been graphically described in *The Tiger Kills*:

"Night had closed over a wild scene. Heavy clouds scurried across the sky and a shrill blustery gale whipped in from the sea. Winter rain fell in torrents. Along the black streets transport raced furiously. Thunderous blasts shook the waterfront, where the tireless demolition engineers worked on. From the north-east came a crackle of gunfire, as Lieut.-Colonel Lavender with his Welch and Punjabis valiantly strove to break out. To the east along the escarpment the leaguer flares of the Germans rose constantly, as more men and guns closed round the doomed town. Only to the south was the darkness unbroken. Here at the airfield beside the Agedabia road Brigadier Briggs sat in his staff car in the beating rain and pieced together the situation.

"The booming guns at Coefia, the soaring flares along the line of the escarpment, told the 7 Brigade Commander all that he needed to know. He was cut off, surrounded, and in the gravest peril. As he studied his map, the desert called with no uncertain voice. If the enemy could be dodged in the coastal corridor, his brigade might escape.

"This night of storm was made for adventure. The pelting rain drove the enemy into close leaguer and blurred the sentries' eyes. The darkness was a dense curtain, although later there would be a moon. If dawn broke with the columns beyond the Agedabia-Antelat trails, the danger would be over. That meant 75 miles before daybreak across rough country.

"At 2000 hours all plans had been laid. A message was sent to Lieut.-Colonel Lavender at Coefia asking him to arrange his own route if he could break away. A similar message went to Lieut.-Colonel Peake of the Royals. (A message likewise was despatched to Divisional Headquarters but was never received.) The following signal then sped to Gold and Silver Groups: *"Road cut. Groups must make own way over desert. Carry only personnel and weapons. Conserve petrol by destroying surplus vehicles. Good luck everyone"*.

"In the darkness and rain the word passed from vehicle to vehicle. The distance to safety was three hundred miles. A check-up showed that there was not enough petrol for all vehicles. Private kit and all stores except food, water, fuel and ammunition were ruthlessly jettisoned. All documents, codes, files and maps were destroyed. Most of the Bren carriers, because of their high petrol consumption, were drained of oil and their engines raced until they seized. Fire or explosive could not be used, so pickaxes and bayonets were plied on radiators and tyres. A signaller recounts in a letter his sadness when obliged to use a hammer on his wireless transmitter-receiver. By 2300 hours all was in readiness. The columns of Headquarters Group formed up and wheeled about on the airfield. As an omen of good fortune, the moon elected to show for a moment through the clouds. The break-out was under way".

It will be necessary to trace the movements of the various groups individually.

HEADQUARTERS GROUP

Commander—*Brigadier H. R. Briggs, DSO.*

7 Brigade Headquarters
7 Brigade Signal Section
Headquarters 25 Field Regiment
Headquarters 65 Anti-Tank Regiment and 8 guns
Headquarters 171 LAA Battery
3 Companies 4/16 Punjab Regiment
1½ Companies 1 Welch Regiment
Headquarters Central India Horse
12 Field Company, Sappers and Miners

During the hour in which Brigadier Briggs organised his column for escape, the garrison of Si Brahim, the lesser and more northerly of the escarpment passes, arrived, having successfully withdrawn before encirclement by enemy columns. This force consisted of a company of 1 Welch Regiment, the carrier platoon of 4/16 Punjabis and a few anti-tank guns. Other detachments of Punjabis and Welch joined the column from Benghazi, so that Headquarters Group moved off at a strength of about 1,200 men and 300 vehicles. On advancing through the Nauuaghia minefield it was discovered to everyone's relief that the enemy had not closed up around the gap. The column passed through in single file, spread out into desert formation and headed into the south about half-way between the coastal road and the line of the escarpment.

Rough ground held the group to a low cruising speed, but the column kept admirable cohesion and plodded on without incident. At 0230 hours a halt was called for the first of the periodical check-ups. A number of straggling vehicles were destroyed. At 0400 hours the steady rise and fall of leaguer flares on the right front identified a large enemy encampment. A mileage check-up showed the leaguer area to be Solluch, thirty miles south of point of departure. This identification made it certain that Headquarters Group would be forced to negotiate the dangerous Antelat-Saunnu area by day.

Beyond Solluch the space between the sea and the escarpment widened until there was approximately twenty-five miles for manoeuvre. The moon broke through the clouds and navigation grew easier. The columns edged away from the main coastal road. An hour after passing Solluch they were negotiating the overlay of fertile soil which from time immemorial has been washed down from the desert through Scheledeima Pass. Across this stretch the vehicles made excellent time, and through good fortune escaped detection by the numerous nomadic encampments. While crossing this cultivated strip an amusing incident occurred. The Brigade Major and Staff Captain, Major H. A. Hughes and Captain T. C. W. Roe, were gingerly feeling out the route with rather tense nerves when they heard a cock crow. "Damn!" said Captain Roe. "Why must we run into a village when we particularly want to avoid one?" Direction was altered, but a few minutes later another lusty chanticleer broke on the night. "It can't be another village," said Captain Roe. Major Hughes darkly suggested that they might be navigating in circles. The column halted while Captain Roe reconnoitred. He returned chuckling. A sepoy in the vehicle behind was carrying next day's dinner in the feather.

Dawn broke with Headquarters Group making good progress through easy country. The Beda Fomm-Antelat track, 65 miles south of point of departure, was crossed soon after daylight. The vehicles spread out widely in an endeavour to assume the guise of casual groups. They were now in the danger zone, since all of Rommel's supplies moved to the north-east along the Agedabia-Antelat trails. Shortage of petrol would not permit detour of this area; the fugitives must swing sharply around the southern end of the escarpment. For 15 miles the desert would be swarming with the enemy. Everything depended upon luck and cool heads.

As the columns approached the gap, dust clouds crossing the front marked continuous movement of transport. The leading vehicles drew up to the first of the trails to find enemy traffic passing in both directions. A large German convoy escorted by panzers appeared from the south. The story of these exciting minutes is well told in the Central India Horse News Letter:

"Vehicles appeared on the crest of the rise over which we had to pass. Coming down the slope they turned along the track to Agedabia. A small convoy also was seen coming in the opposite direction towards Antelat. Three Axis aircraft flew very low over the valley just ahead. After watching the enemy lorries for a few minutes, the Brigade Commander went back to his car and said: 'Cross the road'.

We set off on what all regarded as the critical phase of our journey. Nearing the trail we could see four tanks, about 800 yards away, with men working on them. A motor-cyclist passed along the track 200 yards ahead of our leading truck. A staff car coming from the opposite direction halted for a few minutes beside the tanks and then went on. Just as we crossed the road, two big lorries which had been moving towards us apparently became suspicious, and also halted near the tanks. A big gun on tow, a straggler from one of the enemy convoys, was only fifty yards away from us. Its driver was quite oblivious of us, and he pulled up to allow one of our three-tonners to pass in front.

"In one of our vehicles were five German prisoners. The sowars stood over them, with the butts of their rifles held ready to bash their heads in if they attempted to give the alarm. One prisoner started to pull himself to his feet, but was quickly hauled down by his comrades."

Headquarters Group had passed through the midst of the enemy, but not without loss. While crossing this dangerous locality, three light anti-tank guns, escorted by a platoon of 4/16 Punjabis, bogged down. In the scurry to reach dead ground beyond the ridge, their absence was not detected. Apparently the enemy tanks moved up to extricate them and discovered their secret.

Steadily the columns plodded on without challenge. Each mile raised the co-efficient of safety as the vehicles bowled briskly across hard sand through featureless wastes. All day with periodic halts for check-ups Headquarters group fled into the east. Again the News Letter of Central India Horse provides an interesting picture:

"Driving all day in a shallow depression of the desert, with a rim of high ground extending many miles round the horizon, we might have expected to be observed from many of the numerous, but distant, view points. But neither on this day nor the next did we see any further sign of enemy movement, either on the ground or in the air. Halts were few and short, but at dusk we had a longer break when we got into night formation. The remaining petrol reserves were then issued, to give all vehicles an equal share. On this second of our sleepless nights, between which was sandwiched a long day's driving, fatigue began to produce hallucinations. In the slanting rays of a low moon, the play of shadows on a mass of vehicles moving over the flat, horizonless desert produced visions of mosques and houses, palm trees, pools of water, and even leafy English lanes down which one appeared to be wandering. Keeping awake called for a strong mental effort. Many did not succeed, but no serious accident occurred."

At dawn on January 30th, Brigadier Briggs felt his columns to be sufficiently secure to permit of a long halt and a hot breakfast. Headquarters Group now was 80 miles south of Mechili, far off the beaten track. It was necessary to obtain petrol, food and water as soon as possible. The problem was whether to risk going into Mechili or chance stranding for want of fuel by proceeding an additional hundred miles eastward to El Adem. It seemed certain that Axis forces must be on seach, and radio communication consequently would be dangerous. Nevertheless at 0700 hours Brigadier Briggs decided to make cautious enquiries. In clear he asked if there were "friends in Mechili". Both 13 Corps and Fourth Division Headquarters picked up the message. The answer immediately flashed back: "Many friends". Corps then asked Headquarters Group for its location. Brigadier Briggs was too canny to advertise his whereabouts, but in his column were several New Zealand signallers who had served with 13 Corps. The Kiwis remembered that each operator with Corps had a number. For the four figures of the map reference they signalled the corresponding names. Corps interpreted and acknowledged the extempore cipher.

Believing danger to be past, Headquarters Group struck off into the north-east, on a bearing for Mechili. Then came an alarm. Some miles behind, armoured cars appeared on the horizon. It was impossible to increase the cruising speed, and throughout the morning the dust puffs in the rear crept nearer. Other shadowers showed along the northern flank, but made no attempt to close. Could these be enemy scouts, holding the Group under observation while other forces moved to cut off the escape? Fortunately a keen-eyed observer identified the silhouettes. Headquarters Group halted until patrols from the Royals, which had been deeply suspicious of this large formation, raced up. With this last alarm dissipated the columns rolled on, until at 1500 hours they encountered French and Polish outposts at Mechili.

The break-out had been accomplished at the cost of no more than a score of vehicles and men.

GOLD GROUP

Commander—Lieut.-Colonel Claude Goulder, DSO.

31 Field Regiment
4/11 Sikh Regiment
"A" Squadron Central India Horse
One troop 169 LAA Battery
One troop 171 LAA Battery
258 Anti-Tank Battery

After reaching the Nauuaghia minefield in the early afternoon of January 28th, Gold Group waited its turn to withdraw through Benghazi. At 1930 hours it began to move to the north along the congested highway. At El Guarscia airfield Lieut.-Colonel Goulder learnt that the coastal road had been cut. Brigadier Briggs' instructions to break out by way of the desert followed immediately. In a short conference with his unit commanders Lieut.-Colonel Goulder decided on a plan similar to that of Brigadier Briggs.

As the column was turning at El Guarscia a number of groups joined up from Benghazi. These included a detachment from 12 Field Company, a platoon of 4/16 Punjabis and the "B" Echelon transport of 25 and 31 Field Regiments. The latter luckily carried some spare petrol. This was distributed and approximately 300 vehicles moved off at 2300 hours.

Negotiating the gap in the minefield without difficulty Gold Group followed the main Agedabia road for ten miles before taking to the desert on a bearing which would carry the columns midway between Ghemines and Solluch. Both these villages were known to be occupied by the Germans.

When dawn approached, the columns were still 20 miles short of the Antelat gap. Shortly before daybreak Gold Group had picked up a lame duck from Headquarters Group. A sergeant of the Welch Regiment in this vehicle told Lieut.-Colonel Goulder that he estimated Brigadier Briggs' Force to be about two hours ahead. Lieut.-Colonel Goulder decided that for two columns to attempt to pass the Antelat bottleneck in daylight within two hours of each other would be asking for trouble. He therefore decided to risk lying up for the day in dispersed formation east of Beda Fomm. When dawn broke, the columns were in view of Magrun to the north. Side-stepping to the south, a dispersal area offering a certain amount of cover was found. Gold Group settled down to lie low until nightfall and to hope for the best. Strict orders forbade movement, fires, digging and any firing at hostile aircraft.

The morning passed without incident although enemy planes circled the area on two occasions. During the forenoon a gunner artificer sergeant-major joined the group bringing with him two Italians whom he had wounded in the course of his escape. Soon after midday enemy forces were reported to be approaching the area from the north-west. The hostile column fortunately changed direction and although it passed within a mile failed to detect Gold Group.

At 1530 hours a dust storm blew up. Taking advantage of this cover Gold Group, after a tense day characterised by magnificent individual discipline, moved off.

The march proceeded without incident until the column had crossed the Beda Fomm trail and were swinging through the Antelat-Saunnu gap. In the heart of the danger zone 19 troop-carrying lorries in the rear of the column bogged down in soft sand. But again luck held. An RASC driver, with a four-wheel drive vehicle, pulled them out single-handed, a feat which saved nearly 300 men from capture.

The Antelat-Saunnu gap proved a busy thoroughfare that evening. Enemy reinforcements were moving up; flares and camp fires showed on all sides. For an hour in stealthy fashion Gold Group felt its way across the critical miles. Emerging without challenge the vehicles found hard sand and gathered speed for the run to the south-east. When at 0800 hours on January 30th a short halt was allowed for breakfast the column was about 30 miles south-east of Antelat. Here the signallers picked up the good news that Headquarters Group had broken out and were at that moment some distance to the east heading for Mechili. The situation at Mechili appeared uncertain so Lieut.-Colonel Goulder decided to make for Tengeder which was known to be free of the enemy.

A small party of extremely lucky men shared Gold Group's morning brew up. They were Major Turner* and a number of Rifle Brigade other ranks from 1 Armoured Division Support Group who had missed connections during the withdrawal from Agedabia. After walking 40 miles along the coastal road their feet gave out. When a German staff car came by, one of their number appeared on the roadway with hands raised. When the German occupants sprang out to take him, the others emerged with drawn pistols from behind the car. Leaving the owners stranded they drove off into the desert, heading east by blind reckoning. With less than a half gallon of petrol in their tanks they had blundered into Gold Group in the middle of the night.

Breakfast was no more than over when armoured cars of Central India Horse reported a group of vehicles to be approaching from the north-east. A few minutes later four panzers were identified at the head of a column of transport. Gold Group rapidly embussed while the 25-pounders of 31 Field Regiment, two troops of anti-aircraft guns and one troop of anti-tank guns deployed in the path of the advancing

*This officer later was destined to win a magnificent Victoria Cross while commanding a battalion of the Rifle Brigade.

force. Unfortunately the anti-tank guns opened fire at extreme range; whereupon the enemy column wheeled off into the north-west and disappeared. Gold Group's whereabouts must have been reported as throughout the day enemy aircraft examined the columns closely and on one occasion opened fire. Eliciting no response the planes circled in puzzled fashion and disappeared.

Lieut.-Colonel Goulder's chief worry now was petrol. A number of vehicles had been destroyed in order to save fuel and the troop carriers were laden with an average of 35 men to each lorry. Everything except rations, water and arms had been jettisoned.

The columns were going well about 20 miles from Tengeder when Lieut.-Colonel Goulder received a report from a scout vehicle that a troop of armoured cars were approaching. A message was flashed back "Investigate further probably friends". This assumption proved correct. After an anxious moment contact was made with a troop of the Royals who were searching for breakout parties. The cavalrymen brought the cheerful news that there was plenty of petrol less than 10 miles away.

The columns leaguered for a well earned rest, filled up at first light and reached Tengeder soon after midday. The march was resumed next morning by way of Bir Hacheim. Gold Group arrived at El Adem at 1600 hours on February 1st having incurred no casualties and with the loss of only 31 vehicles.

SILVER GROUP

Commander—*Lieut.-Colonel G. C. Evans, DSO.*

1 Royal Sussex Regiment
"C" Squadron Central India Horse
31 Battery 25 Field Regiment
2 troops 171 LAA Battery
259 Battery 65 Anti-Tank Regiment.

Lieut.-Colonel Evans' Silver Group, on receipt of Brigadier Briggs' instructions, assembled along the main coastal road to the south of the El Guarscia airstrip. Moving in single file it crossed to Nauuaghia station where it picked up its squadron of Central India Horse. At 0100 hours it negotiated the minefield and veering towards the line of the escarpment worked into the south. By 0700 hours the Group had covered 40 miles. Halting for breakfast at Got es Saeti, 25 miles to the north-west of Antelat, it was discovered that during the night a platoon of the Royal Sussex and a troop of 25-pounders had strayed and that a troop of anti-aircraft guns and a number of men of the Welch Regiment had joined the columns.

At 0845 hours the columns moved off on the critical stage of their journey. An error in navigation led them too far to the east and Gold

Group struck the line of the escarpment at Eluet Abdalla, four miles north of Antelat. The column swung right-handed in a sharp detour, but as direction was altered, Royal Sussex carriers, outriding on the left flank, spotted a string of enemy vehicles descending the escarpment towards them. Two tanks led the procession, followed by a number of staff cars and lorries. Lieut.-Colonel Evans ordered the carriers to attack. The six tiny caterpillars lay low until the panzer escort had descended the escarpment and was traversing the plain well ahead of the soft-skinned vehicles. They then dashed in. The convoy, consisting of 20 lorries, two staff cars, and a number of motor-cyclists, wheeled about and fled uphill. One enemy truck turned, dropped its tailboard and opened fire with a storm gun. A fortunate shot from a Boyes rifle killed the gunner. Seven lorries were cut off before they could reach the crest of the ridge; 14 Italians were killed and 28 taken prisoner. The Royal Sussex suffered no casualties. Having lost an hour in this successful foray, the carriers hurried on to rejoin the main column.

In spite of this small battle almost within sight of Antelat, no general alarm was given. Silver Group crossed the trails and negotiated the dangerous gap without discovery. Retribution however was in the air. Shortly after 1300 hours, two enemy planes investigated the columns. Against orders an anti-aircraft gun opened fire, hitting one of the aircraft. The other plane machine-gunned a number of vehicles and wirelessed for aid. At 1400 hours two flights of Italian machines dive-bombed the Group. An hour later a third low-level attack by Messerschmidts raked the column. These air attacks cost 13 killed and 25 wounded—a high price for a single act of disobedience. Enemy armoured cars likewise appeared and hung around the flanks. The Sussex carriers caught up in the nick of time and drove them off, taking one prisoner.

These harassing attacks drove Silver Group off bearing. At 1800 hours when a halt was called, Lieut.-Colonel Evans and his men were deep in the desert, 60 miles to the south-east of Saunnu. Radio communication had not been established, and the Group commander was unaware of the situation at Mechili and at Tengeder. He therefore proposed to continue the march eastward in his present latitude. If the enemy had overrun Libya he would strike for Giarabub Oasis, 210 miles further east on the Egyptian frontier.

At 1945 hours an all-night march began under a bright moon and over hard sand. In the next ten hours 120 miles were covered. At 0530 hours on January 30th the Group halted for breakfast and to prepare for the long trek to Giarabub. Because of their high petrol consumption the carriers had been destroyed at the previous halt. Preparations were now made to bury the guns, jettison all but essential equipment and strip the vehicles. While this work was in progress a patrol was sighted in the north. It proved to be a detachment from 150 Infantry Brigade which was then stationed at Qaret el Auda in the Menny Massiv, to the east of Tengeder. That afternoon, without further incident, Silver Group arrived at the Tynesiders' headquarters. Having replenished fuel and rations, Lieut.-Colonel Evans and his men continued the march next morning and reported in at El Adem twenty-four hours later.

COEFIA GROUP

The mixed force trapped at Coefia comprised elements of 1 Welch Regiment, 4/16 Punjabis and Central India Horse, as well as detachments of Sappers and Miners, "B" Echelon transport drivers and a variety of details. When Lieut.-Colonel Lavender gave the order to destroy transport and to break away on foot, a party of approximately 100 officers and men kept together. Before dawn broke they managed to slip across the coastal plain and to find cover in the undergrowth beyond the Dahar el Ahmar escarpment. Next morning they marched south until they encountered the Barce-Benghazi railway, which they followed to the east. Here fortune smiled. A Sepussi of 4 Libyan Arab Force, which had dispersed in the Benghazi area, joined the party and led the fugitives from one Bedouin camp to another. To these Arabs the group owed their eventual escape. In three days they had covered more than 60 miles. On the afternoon of January 31st they arrived at Borgo Tortelli on the lower Djebel road, 15 miles east of Barce. Firing could be heard from the direction of d'Annunzio, on the upper road, eight miles to the north-east. (4/6 Rajputana Rifles were dealing with the Germans who attempted to interrupt their withdrawal). Before the escape party could cross these few miles, the firing ceased. The fugitives continued to tramp eastwards along the broken valley between the two main highways. They were then in a position to join up with British rearguards on either side.

On February 2nd Arab scouts brought word that Maraua was in German hands. By-passing the danger point, the party reached Slonta, 20 miles further east. Here again distant firing could be heard as the enemy strove to dislodge 11 Brigade from Carmusa. It was now necessary to proceed with the greatest caution, as the Djebel was filled with enemy troops who would not have hesitated to visit reprisals upon the Senussi encampments which provided food and shelter. The party therefore struck away from the habitable valleys into the mountain block to the south-east of Cyrene. By February 5th they had negotiated these rough uplands. Before them stretched the rolling ridges and innumerable wadis which marked the beginning of the desert. Here they met Lieut.-Colonel Peake's party. Both groups had made their way across 125 miles of enemy-held country and had reached the same point at the same time.

Lieut.-Colonel Peake felt that he had walked far enough. With two other officers and a number of men of the Welch Regiment, he turned into the north for the purpose of capturing a vehicle on the Martuba road. The remainder of both parties continued on into the east. Having entered open country it was now possible to move only by night. On February 9th they lay hidden all day within sight of an enemy leaguer. Arabs from a nearby village, in spite of great risk, brought food and water. The next night's march carried them to Temrad, only 9 miles east of the Allied lines at Alam Hamza. Enemy artillery groups were located on all sides and during the forenoon a shoot drew counter-battery fire. It was observed with satisfaction that British gunnery was exceedingly good.

As soon as darkness fell the party moved off on the last lap of their journey. Having encountered trip wires the escapees boldly essayed to cross the minefield. On the opposite side they were challenged. Replies in English resulted in a fusilade. Hails in French (possibly not of the best) drew redoubled fire. The disheartened fugitives picked their way back across the minefield. Fortunately a French patrol seized a straggler. Once identification was established the Frenchmen atoned for their previous reception with unbounded hospitality. The mess was opened in the middle of the night and, as Captain Chase of the Punjabis put it in his report, "A gallant session to which we did full justice from 0300 hours to 0600 hours non-stop compensated us for all our difficulties. Our only regret was that our splendid Arab friends were not with us to share the celebration."

INDIVIDUAL ESCAPES

It is hoped that in due course a book of escapes will be compiled which will do justice to the daring and hardihood of scores of British and Indian soldiers who for months afterwards continued to trickle back to safety. These stories display epic resolution and resource and reveal morale that no misadventure could daunt. Undoubtedly the friendship of the Libyan Arabs and Senussi was responsible for many escapes. This friendship was not entirely disinterested, since the RAF furnished all pilots with *ghoulis*—chits in Arabic which promised payments on safe delivery into the British lines. As a result British soldiers had a "money on the hoof" value to the nomads, who sometimes adopted extreme measures to protect their vested interests. A Mussulman naik was delivered to safety in truculent temper, eager to wreak vengeance on his saviours. When picked up he had been rushed hurriedly into a Bedouin encampment and concealed in the pig-sty. Swarms of fleas left the pigs for a tenderer host. In justification of his anger the naik exhibited his grossly irritated skin.

The story of Sowar Deep Chand of Central India Horse has been told before but deserves repetition as a typical instance of persistence and ingenuity. On attempting to escape from Benghazi with Headquarters Group, his truck had blown up on a mine. His two comrades were killed. Deep Chand hid in a wadi until daylight. Next day in an Arab village he obtained a burnous, Italian boots and a rug, and started to walk towards the sunrise. He wandered from one Arab encampment to another, travelling only by night. He rapidly improved his Arabic and passed muster as a nomad. Near Barce he could not forbear to creep up and gloat when a brace of Hurricanes beat up an enemy convoy, setting a number of petrol carriers alight. Then his feet gave out and he lay up in the underbrush within sight of Derna airfield, where he observed the nightly bombing with the utmost satisfaction. He was robbed by one Arab, but taken in hand by others for the last stage of the journey. The party was captured and sent back to a nearby headquarters for questioning. Once again the RAF staged a performance for Sowar Deep Chand's benefit. Aircraft machine-gunned the German headquarters, allowing the suspects to escape. Next day in another encampment a Mahratta walked in, armed with a tommy gun. This was Havildar Babu Jadhao who had strayed from Captain Oldham's raid on Martuba airfield. (See Page 154). Sowar Deep Chand cannily induced the Arabs to open the conversation, but was assured by them that the havildar undoubtedly was an Indian soldier. Disguises were then provided for Havildar Babu Jadhao and for his companion, Sapper Ram Chadgra Chag. That night all three Indians were delivered to a South African reconnaissance patrol, whose officer paid the requisite bounty. Sowar Deep Chand had left Benghazi 34 days before.

Lieut.-Colonel Roger Peake and Lieut. Willis of 4/11 Sikhs struck off from the Benghazi by-pass together. After lying up throughout the day in sight of enemy leaguers along the foreshore, they commenced the long walk eastward in better case than most—with five tins of bully beef, two lbs. of chocolate, a bottle of whisky and a compass. Avoiding the settled areas the two officers marched for five days and nights before falling in with a friendly Senussi who declared British troops to be holding Carmusa. On the sixth day a party consisting of four officers and four other ranks of 4/16 Punjabis and the Welch Regiment were encountered, who were making good time eastward under the guidance of a member of Libyan Arab Force. Lieut.-Colonel Peake, Captain McKinley of 4/16 Punjabis, Lieut. Willis and Private Daniels of the Welch Regiment, decided to move to the north-east into the Gazala area for the purpose of waylaying a German vehicle. After watching the highway for two days from the shelter of metal piles, this plan was abandoned when an accosted vehicle refused to accept the simulated surrenders. The party thereupon marched on into the east, meeting with great kindness from the Arabs and evading the enemy without difficulty. On February 17th an R.A.M.C. medical orderly with two sepoys of 4/16 Punjabis joined the party. On the next night the fugitives organised to pass through the enemy lines. In the lead went an advance guard of seven Arabs on foot who made no attempt at concealment, but bickered loudly in quarrelsome fashion. Then came the escapees on camels and Arab ponies. A flock of sheep and goats brought up the rear. In the morning intermittent gunfire was heard and the Arabs, who had gone out to reconnoitre, returned with a South African armoured car officer who escorted the party into the British lines.

When the remnants of 1 Welch were cornered on January 30th, Lieutenant V. R. P. Sylvester, although hampered by a wound in his knee, obtained permission to make his getaway. Accompanied by two privates, one of whom spoke Arabic, he slipped between enemy detachments and reached a Senussi area. His party was treated with the greatest hospitality. They were guided from encampment to encampment, and often were shown *"ghoulis"* of recommendation supplied by other British troops who had passed that way. Many Senussi had relatives in the Libyan Arab Force and they were willing to take risks to help British escapees. They hated the Italians. The Germans, who shot them out of hand, they greatly feared. One of Lieutenant Sylvester's anxieties was the feeling of security engendered by his uneventful passage through enemy territory. Nevertheless he was destined to have adventures; he was shot at by Arabs and on one occasion dived under blankets in a tent only seconds ahead of Germans who entered to bargain for eggs. Twelve days after escape he was gladdened by the distant sight of the anti-aircraft barrage over Tobruk. When picked up by the Poles on February 12th, it was estimated that he had averaged 25 miles a day in his march eastwards.

Many escapees had not reached safety when Rommel attacked at the end of May. They crossed the Djebel only to find that they were still 350 miles from the British lines. Two Mahsoud transport drivers arrived in the New Zealand sector at El Alamein in August, having taken more than six months to negotiate their escape. These drivers—cheerful and intelligent frontiersmen—had devised a deception which served to allay enemy suspicions. One had painted a large sore on his leg. He limped on his brother's arm; the brother in turn abused and buffeted him, exhibiting the sore as the cause of his burden. The pair had kept their eyes open. By means of dots on the hem of their burnous they had kept tally of the dumps, leaguers and guns in the areas through which they passed.

Ten months after the fall of Benghazi, a number of sepoys and South African Basuto labourers were recovered when the victorious Eighth Army entered Mersa Matruh. These Basutos told a strange story which South African Headquarters in Cairo pased on to Indian Army Public Relations. The African natives had been part of a labour gang in Benghazi docks. There two Indian sappers had joined them and had gained their confidence. These Indians endeavoured to persuade the Basutos to place explosives in the hold of an ammunition ship which they were unloading. The Basutos refused, but a Zulu in the gang took the bomb aboard. The ship blew up with a prodigious crash. Later this dock party was brought to Mersa Matruh. From some source the Indians again obtained explosives, with which they decided to destroy an ammunition train in a siding 15 miles east of the port. They proposed to insert sticks of explosive with detonators attached in the links of the couplings while the train stood in the station. From this enterprise the Indians never returned. In the opinion of the Basutos they had blown themselves up with the train. *

*Lieut.-Colonel Stevens of Indian Army Public Relations did his utmost to authenticate this story, but without result. South African officers who questioned the released prisoners on his behalf were certain that Indian sappers had incited the Basutos to sabotage and had taught them to use explosives. Prior to the battle of Alamein an enemy ammunition train had blown up at a siding to the east of Mersa Matruh. The RAF entered no claim for it.

The balance sheet of the Benghazi break-out revealed the striking success of the operation. Headquarters Group had lost a platoon of Punjabis and two anti-tank guns. Gold Group had lost no one. Silver Group had incurred 38 casualties during the series of air attacks. On the credit side the Royal Sussex carriers had cost the enemy 14 dead and 35 prisoners. The missing platoon of Royal Sussex and the troop of 25-pounders made their way across the desert unescorted and arrived at Tobruk on February 1st.

The Tiger Kills well summarises the operations:

"The break-out from Benghazi showed British and Indian troops at their best. From the moment that Brigadier Briggs gave the command, every heart rose to the tonic of a bold decision. They were audacious and it paid handsomely. Gold Group leaguering for the day in the midst of hostile forces; Headquarters Group cutting across the Agedabia-Antelat trails in the midst of the swarming enemy transport; Silver Group turning to strike venomously at a careless enemy; these were the daring acts which won their reward. High resolve was allied to good practical management, and every man responded with a supreme effort. General Auchinleck made courage the keynote of his short stirring speech on March 7th, when he reviewed the refitted 7 Brigade. 'You got through because you were bold. Always be bold', he said."

Chapter 12

THE STORM GATHERS

SOLDIERS must fight sometimes but they must dig always. On arrival at Acroma the tired troops ate hot meals and slept for the first time in three days. Then the picks and shovels were issued.

The new Eighth Army front, which existed only on paper, ran west from the sea coast to Alam Hamza, a distance of 15 miles. Thence it swung south-east for 35 miles. It embodied no natural features which lent strength. The defences as planned consisted of continuous minefields, guarded in part by static forces in strong points and in part by mobile groups which patrolled the mined areas. Infantry was responsible for the strong points, armoured forces for the intervening spaces. 1 South African Division held the coastal sector as far as Alam Hamza, where "L" Force took over. 5 Brigade continued the line on the left of the Poles and Frenchmen. 11 Brigade occupied a reserve position 4,000 yards to the rear of 5 Brigade, from whence it supplied mine-laying details and mobile columns. 1 Armoured Division patrolled the left flank as far as Bir Hacheim, where a desert fortress position was planned as the southern bastion of the defences.

To thoughtful soldiers the Gazala Line had little to recommend it. At this period the technique of desert warfare and the employment of desert fortresses was the subject of marked controversy. Isolated garrisons in such strong points were very vulnerable even behind wired and mined perimeters. Armour remained the decisive weapon and the minefields which covered and connected fortress positions were no more than a nuisance to well-handled mobile forces. Gaps in minefields could be cut quickly and unless the garrisons of desert strong points maintained sufficient mobility to sally against encroaching enemies a short period of siege was usually sufficient to reduce ammunition, water and food reserves to the danger point. Thereafter a panzer rush at any time might make an end. Such inherent weaknesses led experienced soldiers to regard the defence of isolated patches of sand with misgiving.

7 Brigade after escape from Benghazi had moved back to railhead on the Egyptian frontier to refit. On February 16th orders arrived for relief of the remainder of Fourth Division. 50 Northumbrian Division would take over. As conclusion to the tour a party of 2/5 Mahrattas staged an audacious enterprise. On the night of February 22nd Captain

A. J. Oldham, MC, with ten riflemen and two sappers set out in two trucks to raid Martuba aerodrome, sixty miles behind the enemy's lines. Without incident this party navigated on a compass bearing to within a few miles of their objective. It was found impossible to attack during the night of February 23rd; all next day the raiders lay in covert within sight of the airfield. When darkness fell they crawled across the landing ground. Only one 'plane occupied the strip; the Mahrattas therefore returned to hiding for another day. Next evening three new fighters were found pegged down for the night. Having fixed charges, the raiding party scurried away; in a series of heavy crashes the planes and an adjacent bomb dump went up. At the rendezvous Havildar Babu Jadhao and Sapper Ram Chandra Ghag were missing. Food and water were left behind and the remainder of the detachment without incident returned to the British lines.

Ten days later the missing men arrived back. En route they had picked up Sowar Deep Chand of Central India Horse, who had walked from Benghazi. They had traversed the entire distance without food and with only such water as they found in puddles. They turned up clean, shaven and smiling.

On relief 5 and 11 Brigades joined 7 Brigade in the frontier area where they were entrusted with the construction of fortified positions near Hamra, a trail junction on the escarpment 36 miles to the southeast of Salum. Here PLAYGROUNDS and KENNELS redoubts were designed to cover the southern routes into Egypt. They consisted of areas of commanding ground surrounded by mine belts and aprons of wire, fortified with dug-in gun positions, slit trenches and strong points. These large-scale cages had been christened "cowpats" by the practical-minded British soldiery. This name gave offence to official nostrils and they were re-named "Boxes". That description afterwards stank so profusely that it was proscribed and gave way to the euphemistic legalism "defended localities". The last name was worse than the first.

On March 15th when the Hamra positions were nearing completion, Fourth Division relieved 2 South African Division in the Salum Box. A battalion of Royal Yugoslav Guards came under command. The routine duties of traffic control, guarding of stores, salvage and local administration, although undoubtedly necessary, impressed the Divisional Staff as a waste of time. Fourth Division had completed a hard campaign, had 4,500 recruits to absorb and badly needed a breathing space. Unfortunately all hope of concerted training and reorganization ended in early April, when 7 Brigade with 12 Field Company and 17 Field Ambulance was ordered to Cyprus, 5 Brigade despatched to Palestine to work on defences along the Syrian frontier, and 11 Brigade moved to the Canal Zone to train in Combined Operations.

The dispersal of the brigades was attended by a number of changes in the battle order of the Division. 1 Field Regiment, 57 LAA Regiment and 65 Anti-Tank Regiment passed to other commands. (Fortunately the first two of these fine gunner units were destined to return). 1 Welch Regiment, on the other hand, did not rejoin 5 Brigade, nor did 1/1 Punjab Regiment, which was detailed with 31 Field Regiment for a tour of duty at Giarabub. Another loss was Central India Horse, attached to an armoured formation for training prior to despatch to Iraq, where forces were assembling to meet a possible enemy irruption over the Caucasus. As replacements 5 Brigade on arrival in Palestine received 1/4 Essex (Lieut.-Colonel Arthur Noble), drawn from garrison duties in Syria, and 3/10 Baluch Regiment (Lieut.-Colonel A. C. Taylor, DSO) one of the original battalions with 8 Indian Division in Iraq. Concurrently with these changes Fourth Indian Division undertook to relinquish two veteran battalions to Tenth Army, in order that garrison units in PAIFORCE might benefit from their battle experience. With great regret 4/11 Sikhs (Lieut.-Colonel R. Bamfield) and 1/6 Rajputana Rifles (Lieut.-Colonel J. R. West) were selected for this exchange. The Divisional Commander made a strong plea for Gurkha units as replacements, with the result that 2/7 Gurkha Rifles (Lieut.-Colonel A. W. Orgill) joined 11 Brigade in the Canal area and 1/2 Gurkha Rifles (Lieut.-Colonel O. de T. Lovett) was incorporated in 7 Brigade soon after its arrival in Cyprus. The latter unit had been General Tuker's own battalion.

This dispersal of his men to all points of the compass was a bitter blow to the Divisional Commander. Ever since assuming command his mind had been engrossed with the problems of desert warfare. The trend of his thinking was summarised in a letter to the Deputy Commander-in-Chief, India:

"I have always opposed the pernicious infantry brigade group system. It does for small wars but it is rubbish for modern war. It leads to confusion, dispersion, unbalancing of forces and chaotic planning".

That this sweeping assertion was no hasty judgment is evidenced by a list of no less than nine papers on improved battle tactics which he and his staff officers prepared in the first quarter of 1942. These papers explored such subjects as the use of bulldozers in putting columns to ground, the mounting of 25-pounders on lorries, battle group drill and staff tables, the organisation of infantry leaguers, the handling of columns, the essentials of fortress positions and the makeup of their establishment. Even more radical innovations were in his thoughts. He was by no means happy with the generally accepted concept of a war of positions in the fluid expanses of the desert, particularly in view of German superiority in armour. He strongly urged the Corps Commander to exchange the linear Gazala position for a fortress defence of the Tobruk area, creating a secure base from which mobile forces might sally in a battle of manoeuvre. To this end he urged that Fourth Indian Division should be entrusted with a role similar to that of 90 Light Division in Afrika Korps, with employment as lorryborne troops in close support of tank operations.

Unfortunately Middle East commitments were too far flung and the hour too critical to permit consideration of these proposals. The eyes of the world rested on southern Russia, where Hitler's spring offensive might prove one of the most momentous events in history. Should the Wehrmacht drive the Red armies headlong, as in the previous campaign, the enemy might burst over the barrier of the Caucasus and reach into the beckoning East, with its vast resources of men and materials. If this occurred the defenders of Egypt would be caught between giant pincers closing from north and west. 8 and 10 Indian Divisions were busily fortifying northern Iraq. It was necessary to take similar steps to protect the Eastern Mediterranean. Under instructions from GHQ, Middle East, General Tuker therefore followed his brigades to Palestine and Cyprus to examine the existing defences and to devise plans for their improvement.

In Palestine the lie of the land permitted him to site defences on his favourite model—fortress positions which would be occupied as soon as the enemy's true thrust line was ascertained, with a force of manoeuvre operating either in support or independently of such positions. The line of the hills, Carmel - Mus Mus - Jenin - Nablus - Jericho, would provide the main bastions of the fortifications between the Dead Sea and the Mediterranean. Mobile forces on the plain of Esdraelon were designed to lead the enemy to assault the centre of the line, where in General Tuker's words, "If I could induce him to get his head properly buried into one of these north forts I could force him into most costly assaults. I would not be hurried in dealing the counter-stroke, since time would favour me in wearing him down". It is interesting to note that this plan was identical with that adopted by the Crusaders more than eight centuries before, in their endeavours to pin back the infidel hordes from the Holy Land. The remnants of this system can be seen to this day in the ruins of castles perched on pinnacles in the southern Lebanons and in the magnificently preserved Krac de Chevalier which covers the Homs gap.

The previous scheme of defence for Cyprus had scattered the defenders in small groups covering the ports and beaches. In such dispersal the garrison represented little more than a liability to the Royal Navy. General Tuker proposed to concentrate his forces in a central position, to provision and munition the colony to withstand siege and to use the Tröodos mountain block in the west of the island for a "keep" defence. A diverging system of roads linking the central plain with all possible beachheads would allow reserves to be hurried against any invader. (Many of these roads afterwards were built as a contribution to the Cyprus war effort by the engineers of an American mining company).

5 Brigade arrived in northern Palestine early in May and at once began detailed siting of the defences. Under the direction of 4 Field Company the work was placed with civilian contractors, whose lethargy and evasiveness sorely tried the supervising officers. On June 8th when Rommel's offensive recalled 5 Brigade to

Egypt, this task was handed over to Ninth Army. 7 Brigade enjoyed a longer tour in Cyprus and through the medium of anti-invasion exercises was able to indulge in an extended period of training on the Cypriot mountainsides. These manoeuvres were destined to pay handsome dividends before a year had passed. In one such outing Jemadar Loganathan of 12 Field Company proved himself a man of lively and alert mind, scoring heavily over the infantry. His Company chronicler tells the story with manifest satisfaction:

"The engineer tasks for the anti-invasion exercises were chosen by an infantry officer without engineer advice, and consisted of road craters, railway bridge demolitions, mined chambers in rock and similar jobs, all of which could be accomplished in an hour or two by the planting of notice boards. This having been done, the section commander (Jemadar Loganathan) captured an enemy despatch rider, put on his Stetson and signal armbands, toured the enemy lines on his motor-cycle, and brought back a most interesting report on strengths and dispositions. As a result, in the closing hours of the battle the sapper section captured a 25-pounder, the enemy HQ mess truck, two Fifth Columnists, three innocent ration-drawers and a carrier platoon complete".

During the spring and early summer of 1942 a number of changes of command occurred. In March Brigadier R. Mirrlees, DSO, MC, was recalled to an important post in India. As replacement Brigadier H. K. Dimoline, MBE, an outstanding Territorial gunner, was appointed CRA. He was a soldier of immense drive, a man of enterprising and untrammelled mind. He was blessed with two receptive superiors: Brigadier Hornby, CCRA 13 Corps and Brigadier Meade Dennis, CCRA 30 Corps were both outstanding artillery Officers, the latter being one of the most distinguished gunner commanders of the war. In April Lieut.-Colonel D. R. E. R. Bateman, DSO, OBE, departed to the appointment of Commandant, Middle East Training Centre. Lieut.-Colonel James Showers, a Gurkha officer, replaced him briefly as GSO 1; thereafter Lieut.-Colonel K. Shepheard, a sapper officer who had previously been brigade major of 161 British Infantry Brigade, began his long service with the Division. In May Brigadier H. R. Briggs, DSO, was notified of his well-earned promotion to the command of 5 Indian Division. Brigadier J. A. Finley, MC, replaced him. Lieut.-Colonel J. H. Blundell, OBE, a well-known officer of the Roorkee Sappers and Miners, took over from Lieut.-Colonel H. P. Cavendish, DSO, OBE, as CRE of the Division. During 7 Brigade's tour of duty in Cyprus, Major W. W. Stewart began his long tenure as Brigade Major of 7 Brigade.

While General Tuker planned and his brigades laboured at their routine tasks, the build-up for the next phase in Western Desert developed into a race to determine who would strike first. Early in May it became evident that shortage of ships, diversions to Russia, and the long haul around the Cape would retard the delivery of British tanks and anti-tank guns sufficiently to afford the enemy the opportunity to open the battle. In renewing the offensive it was certain that he would exploit his armour to the utmost. He had been reinforced by 164 Infantry Division from Crete and by a number of mobile Italian formations. Afrika Korps became in effect two corps. The villages of the Djebel were crammed with fresh enemy troops and Benghazi was landing 2,000 tons of war material daily, a four-fold increase in under two months. A drunken German officer in a Balkan capital divulged the opening date of the new offensive. Rommel would strike on May 27th.

General Tuker returned to Cairo in the third week of May to discover that his comments upon the indefensibility of Bir Hacheim had borne fruit. He was entrusted with command of the Eighth Army forces which held the desert flank, consisting of a Free French brigade under General Koenig, 29 Indian Infantry Brigade, 7 Motor Brigade of 7 Armoured Division, 3 Indian Motor Brigade, comprising three mechanized cavalry units and 2 Field Regiment, Indian Artillery. He hurried to the desert with one dominating idea—to get his command on wheels, and by making it mobile to save it from destruction. Thereafter it would operate as a threat to the Axis flank and rear. He lost out by a matter of hours. On arrival at 30 Corps Headquarters on May 26th the battle was imminent. Next morning, Rommel rounded Bir Hacheim with three armoured divisions in line, fell on 3 Indian Motor Brigade and crippled it, besieged the Frenchmen, forced 29 Brigade to withdraw from El Gubi into El Adem, and by the weight of his assault caused the recall of 7 Motor Brigade to 7 Armoured Division. General Tuker's mobile command had melted away like snowflakes on a hot stove and the Divisional commander returned to Salum to organize the frontier defences. There he found 11 Brigade, which had recently arrived from the Canal area and had been placed under command of 5 Indian Division.

The opening days of the new battle were characterised by the same high hopes which had been in evidence during the first phase of the British offensive in the previous November. On June 1st the intelligence summary declared: "Evening fell with the enemy in utter disorder as a result of air and ground attacks". Unfortunately this was not an accurate picture. Rommel was fighting according to plan. In the opinion of many it was a bad plan, which invited a quick and decisive counterstroke. General Tuker was not alone in urging that Eighth Army should crash through the Gazala front and should fall on the enemy's rear at the entrance to the Djebel. General Briggs of 5 Indian Division, General Ramsden of 50 Division and General Dan Pienaar, the eccentric but able South African commander, all proposed similar solutions. Instead, Eighth Army remained on the defensive. On June 1st Rommel cut two lanes through the centre of the British minefield. He then surrounded and captured 150 Brigade of 50 British Division near Knightsbridge. Four days later he exploited these lanes to destroy 9 and 10 Indian Brigades of 5 Indian Division and to overrun the combined headquarters of 7 Armoured and 5 Indian Division. General Tuker decided that the situation was such that he should personally report to General Auchinleck. He raced to Cairo and through the medium of the CGS, General Corbett, urged the Commander-in-Chief to take personal control of the battle, to concentrate his forces and to move to the attack before the enemy had destroyed Eighth Army in detail. Although Middle East Headquarters was anxious, no one deemed the situation sufficiently serious to modify the over-all plan. As a result General Tuker and his headquarters remained in Cairo as spectators of the unfolding disaster.

Chapter 13

DESTRUCTION OF 11 BRIGADE IN TOBRUK

SHORTLY after arrival at Salum on May 24th, 11 Brigade received orders to send 2 Camerons with a battery of 25 Field Regiment to Bel Hamid, a defended locality on the second or inland escarpment 18 miles south-west of Tobruk. Five days later 21 Indian Brigade took over responsibilities in the frontier area, and the remainder of Brigadier Anderson's men moved forward. On June 25th (the Camerons having rejoined) 11 Brigade relieved 20 Indian Brigade on the Tobruk perimeter and passed under command of 2 South African Division.

The three infantry battalions, with 25 Field Regiment, 18 Field Company, 19 Field Ambulance, ancilliary transport sections, workshops company, anti-tank and machine-gun detachments, occupied the eastern quadrant of the outer Tobruk perimeter. Its sector ran from the sea coast to the El Adem road, a distance of 13½ miles. The original defences of Tobruk consisted of two concentric perimeters. Due to insufficient troops the inner perimeter was unmanned. The outer perimeter was only garrisoned by a series of isolated section posts, whose positions were plainly identified by the belts of concertina wire which surrounded them. The outer perimeter originally had been covered by an extensive minefield. Many gaps now existed owing to mines having been raised for use at Gazala. Moreover, the majority of the mines laid around Tobruk had been of the simple "soup-plate and plunger" type which tended to deteriorate and to silt up rapidly. After initial reconnaissance Brigadier Anderson asked for 20,000 additional mines to complete his aprons. Only 4,000 could be provided.

11 Brigade Headquarters was located near King's Cross, the junction of the El Adem and Bardia roads on the foreshore overlooking Tobruk harbour. 25 Field Regiment had deployed its guns in the same area. 2/7 Gurkha Rifles occupied the sector astride the Tobruk-Bardia road, with its left flank resting on the cliffs above the sea. 2/5 Mahrattas held the centre and 2 Camerons carried the line to the El Adem road. Beyond that road "Beer" Battalion, a composite unit from 1 South African Division, held the forward area. 4 and 6 South African Brigades with 201 Guards Brigade and 32 Army Tank Brigade occupied the western half of the perimeter, an unusual distribution of strength when it is remembered that the high eastern foreshore of Tobruk had always been recognised as the weak spot in the defences. The Guards Brigade

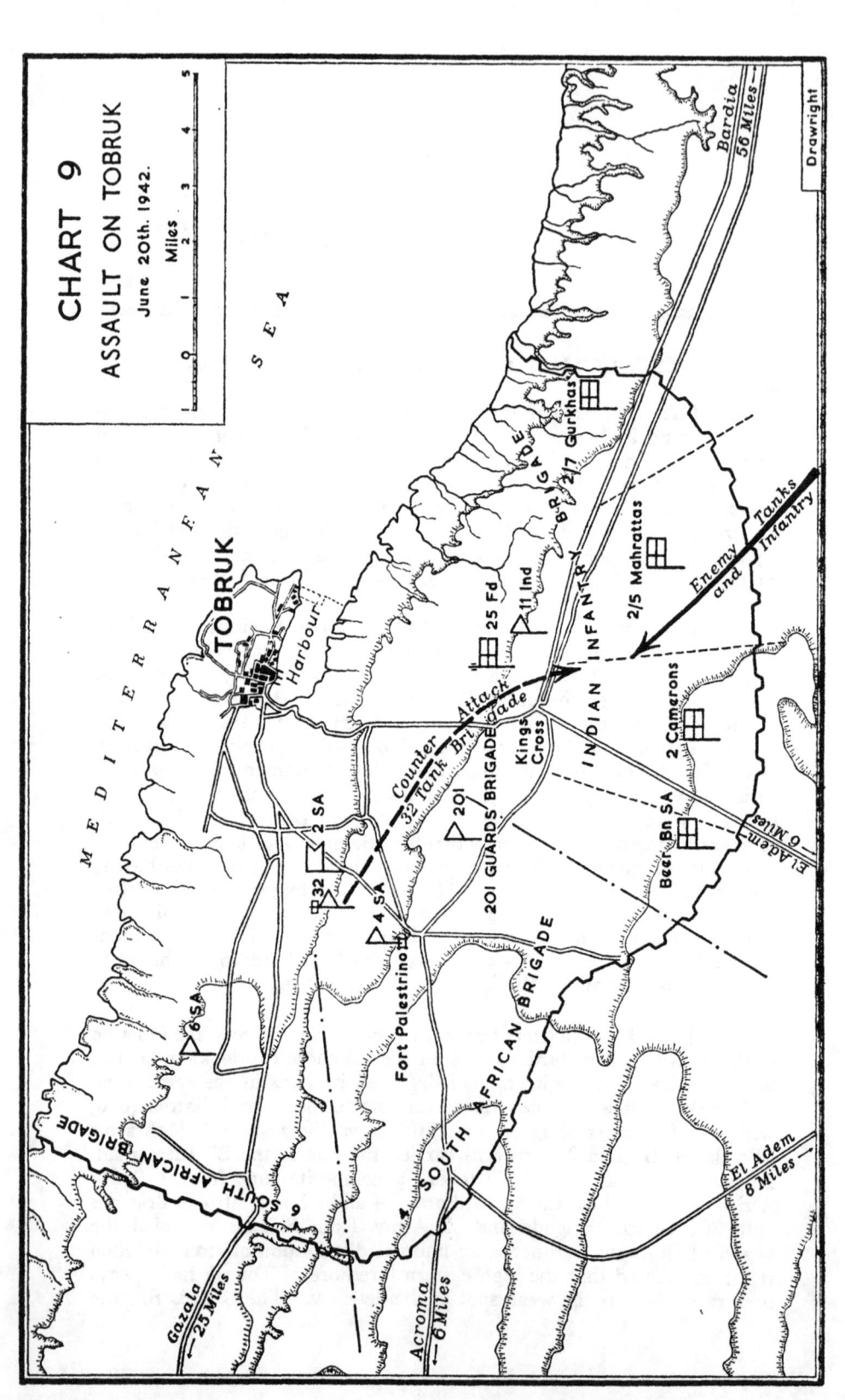

had come in from Knightsbridge on June 14th, much reduced in numbers after heavy fighting, and consisted of battalions of Coldstream Guards, Worcesters and Sherwood Foresters. 32 Army Tank Brigade comprised 4 and 7 Royal Tank Regiments and mustered 60 runners in all.

In addition to defensive duties, 11 Brigade was expected to supply three columns to co-operate with 7 Armoured Division in a mobile rôle outside Tobruk. These columns consisted of companies of lorried infantry, troops of field guns and platoons of anti-tank gunners. They remained in the desert for as much as ten days at a time. Their absence manifestly weakened the garrison, particularly in the artillery arm. If all three columns happened to be out, only one battery of twenty-five pounders remained to cover thirteen miles of front. A windfall reinforcement arrived in the shape of 250 released Indian prisoners of war who had been recovered from an enemy column intercepted in the Acroma area. These men were organised into a composite battalion for duties in the rear areas and for coast watching. Unfortunately they had not been armed or equipped when the German attack opened.

On the night of June 13th, the mounting wastage of British armour in non-decisive encounters compelled the abandonment of the Gazala positions. 1 South African Division passed through Tobruk and continued to the east. 50 Division, finding the roads blocked, withdrew by an attack to the west, bursting through the Axis defences and motoring to safety in a wide detour through the enemy rear areas. Headquarters 13 Corps, which had been located in Tobruk, hurriedly left for the frontier, where 10 Indian Division, as it arrived from Iraq, manned the escarpment defences.

On June 14th, the Tobruk fortress commander, Major-General H. B. Klopper, DSO, held a conference attended by all brigade commanders and heads of services. General Klopper was the recently appointed commander of 2 South African Division. In view of the controversy that has since arisen, it is worth recording that in Brigadier Anderson's opinion General Klopper was a stout-hearted and able soldier, and that any different judgment maligns a brave man. At his first meeting with his subordinates he announced that the Army Commander had decided to stand on the line Tobruk-El Adem-El Gubi, and that supply columns would operate across the desert from Maddalena, on the frontier wire 50 miles south of Salum. There was sufficient food in Tobruk to sustain the garrison for three months, but artillery ammunition was in short supply. The Royal Navy would not undertake to keep ocean communications open. Supply dumps would be divided between the constituent brigades of the garrison. The general feeling of the conference was that a successful defence of the port could be maintained.

Meanwhile the tide of battle outside the perimeter flowed rapidly into the east. On June 16th Captain Wilson of 2/7 Gurkhas, acting as Brigade Liaison Officer, paid a routine visit to effect contact with 29

Indian Brigade in the El Adem box. On arrival he found the Brigade gone and the Germans in occupation. He was captured but managed to escape. He returned to Tobruk to inform the Fortress Commander of the situation. This was General Klopper's first intimation that the garrisons of El Adem and Bel Hamid had withdrawn. The enemy was closing up on three sides, and that same evening the mobile columns serving with 7 Armoured Division re-entered Tobruk. A re-grouping of artillery followed which gave 11 Brigade two batteries of 25 Field Regiment, one South African twenty-five pounder battery and two medium guns. The anti-tank screen however remained thin—indeed almost non-existent. At some points the light guns were 1200 yards apart.

On the morning of June 18th, armoured car patrols reported a strong enemy column of all arms to be approaching Tobruk from the east. 25 Field Regiment engaged the advanced elements of this force, which dispersed into the desert to the south-east, leaving a number of burning vehicles behind. During the night strong battle patrols were sent out by each of Brigadier Anderson's battalions with instructions to harass the enemy and to determine his numbers and dispositions. On the following night (June 19/20) the same tactics were pursued. The patrols returned to report contact with substantial groups of the enemy, as well as a heavy movement of hostile vehicles along the eastern perimeter.

At 0400 hours on June 20th General Klopper warned all formations that an attack on Tobruk was imminent. No indication as to its nature and direction was given, but from the dispositions it was evident that the main assault was expected from the west or south-west. Nevertheless it appeared obvious that either a feint or the real thing would be directed against the eastern perimeter, where a comparatively shallow penetration would bring Tobruk harbour and peninsula under fire. All units were warned to stand to. At 0600 hours flight after flight of Stukas swept in from the south. 110 aircraft participated in this strike, bombing and machine-gunning the minefields and outposts on the centre and left of 11 Brigade's position. A heavy artillery concentration followed, smothering the same front with high explosive and smoke shell, reducing visibility to nil. The Stukas and artillery then lifted to targets behind the outer perimeter, while 1000 *Sonderverbond*, special troops trained for assault on fortified areas and containing a proportion of sappers, drove up under cover of a smoke screen, debussed and moved forward to raise the unexploded mines. These specialists carried smoke candles to cloak their labours, should the original fog dissipate. Behind them came groups of tanks from 21 Panzer Division, German infantry from 90 Light Division on foot, with Italian troops embussed in the rear.

The weight of the first assault fell on 2/5 Mahrattas, but also involved the left-hand company of the Camerons. Shortly after 0700 hours Lieut.-Colonel Lancaster of the Mahrattas advised Brigade Headquarters that German infantry was within 400 yards of his Battalion Headquarters. He was launching an immediate counter-attack with his reserve rifle company and carrier platoon. This gallant rush of a handful against a host (in which the carrier platoon of 2/7 Gurkhas under Lieutenant Stonehouse participated) succeeded in halting the penetration, but it could not regain the forward posts. On receiving news of the attack General Klopper advised 11 Brigade that an immediate counter-attack would be launched by 4 Royal Tank Regiment, with one company of Coldstream Guards and a number of anti-tank guns under command.

Brigadier Anderson with his Tactical Headquarters immediately moved to meet this counter-attack group on the Tobruk-Bardia road, with a view to stating his requirements and suggesting a plan of battle. Until now there had been no report from the Mahrattas which suggested that tank forces had entered the gap in the minefield. 18 Field Company stood ready with mines to reclose the gap. Everything depended on speed. With deepening anxiety Brigadier Anderson counted the minutes as he waited and the counter-attack force did not appear. From the Mahratta front Major Tower, forward observation officer of 25 Field Regiment, was providing the Brigade Commander with a running commentary on the fighting. Until 0900 hours the Indian counter-attack had stoppered the hole. Then bad news came through: 20 panzers burst through the gap, split into two groups and swung into the rear of the Cameron and Gurkha positions. A second clump of tanks of approximately the same strength overran the forward companies of Mahrattas and continued towards Lieut.-Colonel Lancaster's headquarters and the gun lines of 25 Field Regiment. At this juncture Major Tower went off the air and communication with the firing line ceased. It was evident that a serious penetration had occurred. Reports from the Camerons however stated that the tank foray against their left had been roughly handled: that the enemy had withdrawn leaving behind a number of disabled panzers.

At 0930 hours—more than two hours after General Klopper had ordered the counter-attack—the first of the "I" tanks from 32 Army Tank Brigade reached Brigadier Anderson. They arrived in groups of twos and threes throughout the next half-hour, and immediately moved forward to a rendezvous arranged with Lieut.-Colonel Lancaster. The Coldstream Guards and anti-tank guns never turned up. (It was later ascertained that they had been given the wrong rendezvous). This delay proved fatal. In the two lost hours the panzers had punched a hole and had destroyed the Mahrattas. The officer commanding 7 Royal Tank Regiment went forward to reconnoitre and on his return reported that the leading "I" tanks had arrived too late to close the gap but that they had occupied a defensive hull-down position where they would fight it out with the German armour. The situation was held to be serious but not hopeless.

Between 1100 and 1200 hours another 20 panzers entered the perimeter through the gaping hole in the Mahratta sector, and approximately 60 enemy tanks thrust northwards against the vital road junction at Kings Cross. This force advanced slowly and dogged fighting ensued. The defensive screen of "I" tanks was battered to pieces by the heavy guns of the Mark IIIs and Mark IVs. On approaching the Bardia road the panzers fanned out, one column moving to the north to engage South African guns which had put in some excellent shooting, while another group crawled westwards against 25 Field Regiment. At 2000 yards the tanks opened fire, supplementing their cannons with long range machine-gun fire. The gunners lay on the ground waiting for the range to close. They then smashed back, scoring hit after hit. One troop claimed eight tanks disabled. One by one the guns were knocked out until only two out of sixteen twenty-five pounders were firing. Three batteries were overrun and the last two guns blown up before the enemy reached them. Major Pope and his men had fought magnificently. A number of gunners slipped away in the confusion and went to ground out of the path of the enemy armour.

With 25 Field Regiment silenced, the tanks turned towards Kings Cross and 11 Brigade Headquarters. Between 1300 and 1400 hours heavy fighting continued as 11 Brigade anti-tank gunners desperately strove to ward off the mortal thrust. The weight of metal told; the tanks burst through and reached Brigadier Anderson's headquarters. All documents and equipment had been destroyed; the personnel, with the exception of the anti-tank gunners, took cover in a wadi and evaded capture. Brigadier Anderson immediately established an emergency headquarters to the north of the Bardia road, on the high ground above the harbour. The panzers did not pursue in this direction, but turned east along the foreshore into the rear of 2/7 Gurkhas. Here the agile hillmen had the advantage of broken ground, with numerous deep-cut wadis. In these hideaways they evaded the enemy and refused to be mopped up. 18 Field Company had less luck and went into the bag, but not before they had fired their vehicles, several of which were loaded with anti-tank mines. A number of Germans, rushing in to salve or to loot, were blown to pieces as the loads exploded. 18 Workshop Company and 19 Field Ambulance likewise disappeared in the wake of the panzers. 11 Brigade Transport Company withdrew into the western sector of Tobruk where it remained intact until the general surrender.

Throughout the late afternoon bitter fighting continued around Kings Cross as 7 Royal Tank Regiment met the German armour head on. Shelling and bombing had increased in intensity; a number of panzers, having by-passed the opposition, circled the west end of the harbour and thrust into Tobruk town. The Royal Navy had thrown a smoke-screen over the harbour and with greatest gallantry small craft were braving an inferno of artillery and machine-gun fire to take small parties off the beaches. The area commander ordered all installations destroyed, and incessant explosions added to the din and fury of the scene. As night closed, General Klopper shifted his headquarters farther west into 6 South African Brigade's area.

During this period Brigadier Anderson had been striving to re-open communications with his battalions. Leaving a signal officer to continue calling, he visited General Klopper's headquarters to give the fortress commander a first-hand account of the battle. While there he arranged to use the Divisional No. 11 sets for the purpose of regaining touch with his men. It was evident that resistance was continuing and it seemed possible that under cover of darkness a way might be found to organise cohesive defences.

That night Tobruk town and harbour lay under a pall of smoke. The eastern foreshore was lit by the flickers of scores of burning dumps and vehicles. The western perimeter however was intact, and in that area three brigades had not yet entered the battle. Moreover, reports indicated that "Beer" Battalion of South Africans and the Camerons were still in place and full of fight. Communications with 2/7 Gurkhas had been broken—a misfortune, indeed, for the morale of Lieut.-Colonel Orgill's men might have stimulated others. A Gurkha officer wrote:

"The men were fairly bursting with confidence. Things were a bit chaotic, but it was war and it was fun. They had knocked everything for a six that had come up against them and had received almost perfect battle inoculation. Their overwhelming sense of superiority did not leave them until the end. They met panic, the most devastating of battle influences, with steadfastness and watched streams of demoralised troops passing through their positions with amused tolerance."

"Battalion headquarters was in the front line, protected by runners, signallers and one sorry looking South African six-inch howitzer. The Subedar Major and Subedar Marasindu with the aid of the handbook hurriedly unpacked and assembled a recently arrived spigot mortar. The German tanks which approached us were just as afraid of the spigot bombs as we were of firing them. To fire a spigot mortar, one jams the canister onto an instrument which resembles a blunt marline spike. The bomb hits some unpredictable distance away, precipitates itself along the ground like a prehistoric monster, belching fire as it goes, until it finishes its career in an ear-shattering explosion. At least, that is the way they behaved for us. They scared off any tank that looked as though it wished to try conclusions with us."

At 2000 hours Brigadier Anderson decided to move his headquarters into the Cameron's sector. An hour later he was summoned to a conference. The Fortress Commander stated that he had reported the situation to the Army Commander and had proposed a break-out. General Ritchie had asked that Tobruk should be held for another twenty-four hours. General Klopper thereupon planned to reconstitute a truncated defensive perimeter by deploying 201 Guards Brigade plus two South African battalions between the left of the Camerons and the sea to the west of Tobruk. Instead of semi-circular, the defended area would be triangular, with the Mediterranean as its base.

At 0400 hours next morning (June 21st) Major Abbot of 11 Brigade proceeded to Fortress Headquarters to obtain the latest situation report before Brigadier Anderson left for the Camerons' area. He returned shortly to report that General Klopper had decided to surrender. Brigadier Anderson immediately interviewed the Fortress Commander. General Klopper stated that information received during the night indicated that 150 tanks of 15 Panzer Division had concentrated on 4 South African Brigade's front in the Acroma area and would attack at dawn. His CRA had advised him that the Brigade dumps only held enough ammunition for one hour's fighting. He had notified the Army Commander of the situation and had been instructed to use his discretion. It was now too late to organize a breakout before daylight. He believed the situation to be hopeless and that the end must come during the day. He therefore had decided to surrender in order to save unnecessary bloodshed. He had issued instructions to all units to destroy their equipment but he was willing to permit anyone who wished to try to escape to retain vehicles for that purpose. At dawn a white flag would be raised on the wireless mast at Fortress Headquarters.

Having learnt of this decision Brigadier Anderson and the officers of his Tactical Headquarters decided to go to ground, in the hope of slipping through the German net that evening.

To this sad drama 11 Brigade was destined to add a gleaming epilogue. Long after Tobruk had surrendered officially, two of Brigadier Anderson's battalions fought on. 2/7 Gurkha Rifles blew back the enemy until the last round was spent. Throughout the forenoon of June 21st isolated Gurkha posts without food or water held out under intense fire. The panzers waited for the kill a few hundred yards away. "It had become very one-sided" wrote Subedar Major (afterwards Captain) Sherbahadur Limbu with magnificent under-statement. At 1300 hours Lieut.-Colonel Orgill ordered resistance to cease. The word failed to reach Subedar Balbir, or perhaps he had ideas of his own. He and his platoon fought on until evening.

2 Camerons wrote an equally shining page. When General Klopper's orders reached Lieut.-Colonel Duncan and his men through the adjoining battalion of South Africans, they were received with derision. The Highlanders shifted "C" Company to cover the rear of their position and waited for what the day would bring. At 0800 hours three Italian tanks approached from the Tobruk side. A two-pounder gun in "B" Company's posts held its fire until the last tank was within 200 yards. It then disabled all three in quick succession. As the crews tumbled out they fell to Cameron snipers. Five minutes later three more tanks appeared and walked into the same trap; then a last tank, with an officer standing in the turret studying the battlefield with his binoculars. He was sniped, and the two-pounder put seven rounds into his vehicle, smashing it to scrap metal. After this highly successful ambuscade the Camerons took the precaution of burning all seven tanks. Throughout

the day their positions were pelted with mortar and machine-gun fire while field guns sniped at any movement. The enemy meanwhile continued to use the El Adem road. Later in the afternoon a three-ton lorry attempted to pass within fifty yards of the Cameron positions. When this vehicle went up in flames, aircraft dive-bombed the Highlanders viciously. Dauntlessly they replied, and an ME 109 disappeared with smoke pouring from its engine and losing height. When night fell on June 21st they were still fighting and in good heart. They had not even sustained serious casualties.

After dark Germans approached a Cameron outpost. A spokesman hailed the sentry. "Kamerad English, you are safe now. The war for you is over." A reply was given in short bursts. Later in the evening a South African soldier crossed from "Beer" Battalion to advise that a German officer had sent him to contact the commander of the resistance group. Captain McKenzie sent for the German and conducted him to Lieut.-Colonel Colin Duncan. It was then learned that Tobruk had fallen that morning. The Germans demanded acceptance of General Klopper's capitulation. Lieut.-Colonel Duncan promised a reply by 0500 hours next morning. The Germans offered to postpone attack if the Camerons would undertake to parade on the El Adem road at that hour ready to march to the prison cages. Lieut.-Colonel Duncan gave his assurance that he would be there but he added that he expected very few of his battalion to be on parade at such an early hour. When all weapons, stores and documents had been destroyed, fifteen officers and approximately 200 men disappeared into the night in an endeavour to reach safety in the east.

Few made more than the first miles, for the enemy was swarming across Libya in chase of Eighth Army. On June 23rd a column of prisoners drew up to the cage on Tobruk airfield. The column halted, came to attention; the skirl of the pipes arose and the Camerons with dauntless bearing played themselves into captivity. The German guard turned out to honour the gesture; that night a fellow prisoner, conscious of the dark hour, wrote in his diary "Their example strengthened the weak". Only six of the Scotsmen eluded capture. Lieutenant T. A. Nicol, MC, after fantastic adventures reached the enemy positions at El Alamein in a truck which he had obtained at the pistol point near Mersa Matruh. Waiting his chance he followed a German staff car through the minefields. After spending some time with an Italian division in the midst of a battle he reached the British lines 26 days after leaving Tobruk.

Four officers and 60 gunners of 25 Field Regiment walked 400 miles to safety—the only considerable body to escape. Two havildars and three Gurkha riflemen came in at Alamein—one of the havildars riding a camel which he had hired from the Arabs.* For months afterwards men arrived in ones and twos, having felt their way through the desert in some extraordinary fashion—each a proof that the longest shots sometimes come home. But they were a handful which stood for what had been one of the finest brigades in any army. **

Brigadier Anderson was one of the luckless. He was captured in attempting to pass through the enemy lines on the night of June 21st. Next day while awaiting disposition he saw Rommel arrive in Tobruk in a Feiseler Storch. The Axis Commander appeared pleased with himself—and with good cause. In 24 hours Eighth Army had lost 25,000 men. The shock of the disaster spanned the world. Mr. Churchill who received the news while at the White House as a guest of President Roosevelt, later described himself as "the most miserable Englishman in America since Burgoyne surrendered at Saratoga". A battle had turned into a débâcle in such manner as to leave soldiers with a sick, hopeless feeling. Fourth Indian Division, like many others, could not understand it. A strong confident brigade had gone under, as though submerged by a tidal wave. To no one was the blow more acute than to General Tuker. He was shocked by the accuracy of his own prophecies concerning the danger of field fortifications to an army weak in armour and in mobile reserves. The world had witnessed the greatest defeat of British arms since the destruction of Gough's army on the Somme in 1918. The odds against Gough had been 37 to 13 Divisions, whereas Eighth Army had been defeated by forces of more or less equal strength, largely because of the inherent weaknesses of its deployment and dispositions.

*Havildar/Clerk Bhuwan Chand Tewari of 2/7 Gurkha Rifles, who was taken at Tobruk, surely must be one of the most travelled men of his race. Imprisoned in Poland, he was released by the Russians and rejoined his unit in Italy by way of Odessa.

**The Assistant Military Secretary, Middle East, sponsors the following story:

One morning soon after the fall of Tobruk, three young officers of 2/7 Gurkhas, who were at the reinforcement camp, asked for an urgent appointment. The AMS saw them and estimated their combined service at 18 months. They requested that they should be allowed to form a new battalion of 2/7 Gurkha Rifles to take part in the re-capture of Tobruk. They quoted as precedent the first Great War when their Second Battalion was taken at Kut-el-Amara and the newly raised unit was in the force which eventually regained the Turkish stronghold. The AMS was so impressed with the young officers' earnestness that he recommended to GHQ, India, that their request be granted. The officers were 2/Lieuts. Clay, Tait and Taylor.

Chapter 14

5 BRIGADE — MERSA MATRUH, RUWEISAT AND ALAMEIN

ON the night of June 5th, 1942, when the working detachments of 5 Indian Brigade in the Palestine passes had stacked their picks and shovels, the officers eagerly tuned in on Cairo for the latest news of Rommel's offensive.

The communiqué proved vague and unsatisfactory and with good reason. That day the enemy had struck fiercely at 7 Armoured Division and 5 Indian Division, inflicting heavy losses. Next morning 5 Brigade was placed on notice to proceed to Egypt. Four days later Brigadier Russell's men had concentrated at Amiriya, the gateway to Western Desert. Instructions on arrival presumed a stay in this area until re-equipped. Such orders remained in force for less than twenty-four hours. On June 11th the Brigade moved forward under direct command of Eighth Army. Rail parties from Palestine were routed through to Mescheifa without leaving the trains. On June 14th 5 Brigade came under command of 5 Indian Division and next day moved into KENNELS defensive position on the Libyan escarpment to the south-east of Salum.

On June 17th 5 Brigade shifted further south to PLAYGROUNDS in order to make room for 1 South African Division, which had arrived from Gazala. The South Africans stated that they had no intention of remaining on the frontier—Brigadier Russell's first intimation that the battle had veered against Eighth Army. On June 18th the move to PLAYGROUNDS had been completed, but before defensive plans could be placed in train the Brigade was ordered to return to Salum where it would pass under command of 10 Indian Division. On arrival next morning it was discovered that 2 Free French Brigade had received no orders to leave Salum Box. A dual occupation continued for the next two days. To increase the complexity some high-level authority selected this moment for the issue of anti-tank guns to the infantry battalions, at a time when none could spare even minutes for instruction in a new weapon.

On the afternoon of June 21st came the black tidings of the fall of Tobruk. Towards evening Major-General Nicholls, a British service officer, arrived to announce that he had taken over command of 10

Indian Division, that no stand would be made on the frontier, and that Salum and Halfaya would be evacuated on the following night. At 2000 hours on June 22nd, 5 Brigade less 4/6 Rajputana Rifles, with anti-tank and Royal Horse Artillery gunners under command, left Salum Box and moved into Egypt by way of Conference Cairn and the Railway Gap. Rommel's panzers were driving across the desert in full cry and the escarpment was crowded with columns heading eastward. The RAF flew an unprecedented number of sorties and gave superb rearguard cover. As a result the withdrawal proceeded without incident. On the evening of June 24th 5 Brigade reported in at Sidi Haneish, continuing under command of 10 Indian Division.

4/6 Rajputana Rifles remained at Salum until the evening of June 23rd. The switchback road over the escarpment was then blown and the rearguards moved eastward by way of Capuzzo and Conference Cairn. The scene recalled the early days of Auchinleck's offensive, with enemy leaguer flares soaring in a crescent to the south and east, while flashes of gunfire stabbed the western horizon. Halting for the night the Rajputana Rifles despatched detachments ahead to explore next day's line of march. One patrol overran an enemy scout group and took 9 prisoners. At dawn the battalion turned into the south-east, and soon sighted the streams of Eighth Army traffic withdrawing from Libya by way of the foot of the escarpment. Joining the throng, 4/6 Rajputana Rifles, after a few brushes with enemy armoured cars and roving panzers, safely reached Mersa Matruh.

This small watering place was the scene of feverish activity as a mixed force of 2 New Zealand Division, 50 Division and 10 Indian Division sought to organize its defences. At 2000 hours on June 25th, 5 Indian Brigade relieved 5 New Zealand Brigade along the southern perimeter of the Matruh box. 4/6 Rajputana Rifles held the left sector, 1/4 Essex the centre, with 3/10 Baluchis on the right. The Essex detailed one company with supporting arms under Major Dudley Smith to patrol the minefields. 5 Brigade units were no more than in their places when advanced elements of Afrika Korps closed up. 100 panzers with 3,000 attendant transport were reported from Charing Cross, seven miles to the west. That morning British covering forces had withdrawn through the minefields, and the gaps had been sealed behind them. A last train with heavy equipment left Mersa Matruh during the afternoon.

Unknown to the troops on the spot, the High Command had already reviewed the situation and had decided to substitute mobile operations for a fixed defence. But before withdrawal could be organised the enemy struck. At 1500 hours on June 26th, enemy panzer columns well supported by guns burst through the minefield on the front of 29 Indian Brigade, which had been incorporated in 10 Indian Division's front. One of Brigadier Reid's blocking columns was destroyed. That evening 5 Brigade was ordered into the gap between 25 Indian Brigade and what remained of 29 Brigade. First casualties were sustained when a reconnaissance patrol of 3/10 Baluchis was ambushed. Early next morning 5 Brigade moved forward from the Matruh Box towards its new positions on the line of the escarpment. At 1030 hours the Essex and Baluchis came under heavy artillery fire. Efforts to dribble forward failed when the high ground was found to be firmly held. At 1600 hours word was passed that 50 Division and the New Zealanders were moving to the attack. Whereupon Brigadier Russell's men again thrust for their objectives and gained the crest of the escarpment. Before consolidation could be effected, intense artillery fire made the newly-won position untenable.

On the morning of June 28th—five months to a day after 7 Brigade had found itself bottled up in Benghazi—Mersa Matruh was ominously quiet. The desert to the south was stippled with thousands of enemy vehicles moving past into the east. Major Dudley Smith's roving column of Essex had shot up some unwary detachments and 4/6 Rajputana Rifles had ambushed the enemy guard at a gap in the minefield. In midafternoon the significant code word BENGHAZI was flashed to 5 Brigade. This meant in effect that a Divisional break-out would be attempted. Before the plan could be placed in train, a second code word arrived. It conveyed *sauve qui peut,* or as an officer put it, "break away any old how". As a result of this latter instruction the Brigade was divided into four groups, consisting of the three battalions and Brigade Headquarters and was given a rallying point to the south of Fuka, 43 miles east of Mersa Matruh.

At 2100 hours the general movement began, with all columns heading south in cruising formation. Unfortunately the moon was nearly full, and no dispersal could hide the long lines of vehicles. As units cleared the defences a ring of enemy leaguer flares soared and fell ceaselessly to the south, the south-east and to the east. Only to the west and south-west was the horizon silent and dark. All columns therefore tended to bear in that direction.

5 Brigade Headquarters group with 350 vehicles had no sooner entered the desert than it bumped a panzer leaguer. Sheering off to the west the columns reached the Hamsa escarpment only to find more enemy armour in their path. Again bearing west the columns brought up against an airstrip on which a twin-engined bomber rested for the night. The guard opened fire as the leading vehicles swung away. Turning east along the base of the escarpment Brigadier Russell's group continued for ten miles without detection. Transport, presumably of enemy origin, could be seen in the gloom on either side, moving in parallel columns. Then another tank leaguer barred the way; while attempting to by-pass it several vehicles were knocked out. By 0430 hours Brigade Headquarters group, like a shifty runner in a broken field, had evaded all tacklers. Having reached the rendezvous area the men were about to outspan when they discovered that they were not alone. The enemy was already there. Headquarters Group hurriedly swerved off, again feeling for the east. At 0900 hours contact was

established with a mobile force of 2 Rifle Brigade operating under 7 Armoured Division. When Brigadier Russell reported in at the El Alamein checkpost he was ordered to concentrate immediately in front of the defended area. The enemy however was in such close pursuit that a better sorting out ground was chosen behind Deir El Shein, a bowl in the desert five miles inland from the Mediterranean.

"A" and "D" Companies of the Essex commenced the break-out together, but ran into trouble immediately. Captain D. A. Beckett thus describes the scene:

"As the leading elements reached the wadi 800 yards ahead of our battalion position, the enemy opened fire with machine-guns, tank guns and other artillery. The spectacle that met the rearguard was one of unbelievable chaos. Some of the trucks and guns were stuck in the soft sand of the wadi bed. Others had crashed over the steep sides in an endeavour to escape from the merciless fire of enemy guns. The flames from burning vehicles lit up the columns racing to safety and the groans and cries of the wounded added to the din of battle".

This encounter scattered the Home County men. In groups small and large they set out to sift between the enemy's fingers. They navigated to such good effect that of 400 men in the two companies, 260 reported in at El Alamein. Major Smith's "B" Company, already on column with a troop of field guns and anti-tank guns under command, moved east in its own time, shooting up the enemy, taking prisoners in a daring onset on an enemy leaguer, raiding a landing strip, and destroying aircraft. Falling in with the New Zealanders, SMITHCOL on June 28th joined 19 New Zealand Infantry Battalion in a spirited charge which burst through enemy forces which blocked their way.

"C" Company of the Essex had been sent direct from Salum to the Delta under a plan for the organisation of reserve battle groups. That company was destined to find a place in military history.

Before sallying from Mersa Matruh, Lieut.-Colonel Lawrenson of 4/6 Rajputana Rifles had split his battalion into small parties—a wise move which brought his wily veterans through enemy territory with small losses. 3/10 Baluchis experienced a more adventurous passage. In column of companies Colonel Taylor's men in their vehicles charged the enemy cordon at 30 miles an hour. Although beaten up from front and flanks they burst through, the gallant carrier platoon immolating itself against anti-tank guns which sought to bar the way. Naik Mian Gul in his tiny caterpillar destroyed two guns and made his getaway. Momentum carried the Baluchis over entrenched troops who panicked as the trucks surged past; enemies sprang from slit trenches offering to surrender. Entrapped on a minefield, harassed by panzers, the columns broke up and fled to safety in small parties, reporting in at El Alamein with the moderate losses of 5 officers and 129 men.

5 BRIGADE — MERSA MATRUH, RUWEISAT AND ALAMEIN

All told, 60 per cent of 5 Brigade reached safety within 24 hours of the break-out. Others came in later. As they arrived the groups were despatched to the Delta to be sorted out. Without rest all re-equipped in great haste, for the situation at El Alamein was too critical to spare any cohesive formations. After a retreat of 400 miles Eighth Army had arrived not in sanctuary but at a defensible position. Lashing his panzers in pursuit, Rommel drove all-out, with the vision of Egypt in his eyes. Mussolini in his white uniform, with brass bands and orientalists in train, had already left Italy for the triumphal entry. If the tenuous British dyke was to hold the oncoming flood, it was essential within a space of hours to devise new stop-gaps and to conjure reserves out of nothing.

Reinforcements were on the way from other parts of Middle East but the first shock must be taken by the battle-weary men on the spot. General Auchinleck, who had assumed personal command at El Alamein, was guaranteed a firm coastal flank by 1 South African Division, strong and full of fight. Deep in the desert, where under the blinding glare of midsummer the horizon danced all day with mirages, the tough New Zealanders blocked the enemy's line of advance along the black cliffs of Qattara Depression. Between the Springboks and Kiwis a gap of 15 miles intervened. In the centre of this gap a long finger of high ground rose gradually out of the west until it overlooked both the sea coast and the deep desert. At its eastern extremity this ridge—Ruweisat on the map—ended in an abrupt promontory. It was the key to the battlefield. Unless Ruweisat was firmly held, the Alamein defensive system was untenable.

18 Indian Brigade—first element of 8 Indian Division to arrive from Iraq—had hurried from the trains to construct a "box" at Deir El Shein, under the western tip of Ruweisat. On July 1st, before the defences could be organised, the panzers closed under cover of a sand-storm, overran the position and destroyed the Brigade. Rommel's armour need only mount the ridge for 10 miles eastward to split the British defences. But even while the Essex, Sikhs and Gurkhas of 18 Brigade were being rounded up, a blocking force had been assembled and was hurrying forward along Ruweisat to meet the challenge.

The long association destined to ensue permits the story of 11 Field Regiment (Lieut.-Colonel A. C. McCarthy, MC) at El Alamein to be incorporated in this history. At the outbreak of war these gunners had been stationed at Meerut, where under the leadership of Lieut.-Colonel B. J. Fowler they had already established an outstanding reputation. They accompanied 8 Indian Division to the Persian Gulf. On June 15th, when in Northern Iraq, 11 Field Regiment received orders for Western Desert. It covered 1500 miles in 11 days and marched straight into the mêlée at Mersa Matruh. After an exciting disengagement Lieut.-Colonel McCarthy and his men found their way back to El Alamein, picking up enough straggling guns to repair their losses. On July 1st, strong and fresh, they hurried forward with "C" Company of 1/4 Essex to form ROBCOL under Brigadier R. P. Waller, CRA, 10 Indian Division, and to dispute the passage of the panzers across the rocky saddle-back of all-important high ground.

Shortly after 1000 hours on July 2nd, from a position near the tip of the ridge, 11 Field Regiment began to hammer masses of enemy transport in the Deir el Shein area. A German lorried infantry group threw in a quick attack, apparently to test the strength of the blocking forces. Enemy artillery found the range and searched the crest of the ridge. The panzers followed forward to mount the high ground. They were beaten back. As they swung to flank the steady fire of the 25-pounders followed them. The Essex in their covering positions sat tight all day under continuous bombardment. Casualties mounted. By nightfall 7 guns had been knocked out and ammunition was all but exhausted. But for the first time since Tobruk, Rommel's armour had broken off action and had retired into the west.

Early next morning ROBCOL thrust forward to Point 97, where Ruweisat merges into the desert plain. A furious artillery battle raged throughout the forenoon; the panzers took a mauling whenever they attempted to close. That afternoon, guns of Royal Horse Artillery stiffened the blocking force. Lieut.-Colonel Noble brought forward a composite rifle company and the Essex carrier platoon. Thereafter supporting arms hourly reached ROBCOL. It became WALCOL and continued to carry the battle to the enemy. Elements of 1 Armoured Division arrived, blocked the gaps on either side and gave firm flanks to the force holding the ridge. Furious gun duels and tank combats continued, but the crisis had passed. Afrika Korps had foundered against the rock of Ruweisat.

Slightly to the south of the main ridge, Lieut.-Colonel Noble and his men found a wrinkle of high ground, named it Essex Ridge and prepared to live up to General Auchinleck's exhortation to harass the enemy without ceasing. In the next week they blew up a gun position, killing 9 Germans, raided and burnt an enemy leaguer, captured some stray transport and took prisoners. Deploying his full force, Rommel endeavoured to by-pass the New Zealanders in the south. Thwarted in this attempt, he shifted his attack and struck at the South Africans on the seashore. Again he took a beating. As a war correspondent put it, "The Alamein line, fluid one day, elastic the next, in one short week became an iron wall against which the invaders battered in vain".

That week was sufficient to bring 5 Brigade back into the field. After two days of reorganisation at Wadi Natrun, Brigadier Russell's men took over lines of communication; but this task was less than 48 hours old when orders came to proceed to the battlefield under command of 1 Armoured Division. As it took to the roads 5 Brigade received a welcome reinforcement in the form of 6 Rajputana Rifles Machine Gun Battalion (Lieut.-Colonel F. G. Cuerdon) which had arrived in Middle East on June 11th. This fine unit was destined to

COMMANDERS—CYRENAICA, TUNISIA, ITALY

Major-General (afterwards Lieut-General) F. I. S. Tuker CB, DSO, OBE.

Major-General A. W. W. Holworthy DSO, MC.

ROYAL ARTILLERY COMMANDERS

Brigadier W. H. B. Mirrlees DSO, MC.

Brigadier H. K. Dimoline CBE, DSO, TD.

Brigadier H. C. W. Eastman DSO, MVO.

MEMORABLE JOURNEY

OFF TO THE WEST.

MARBLE ARCH.

OUTSIDE GABES—
PRISONERS FROM WADI AKARIT.

EL DJEM—ROMAN RUINS.

KARIOUAN—HOLY CITY.

THE END OF THE TRAIL.

GROUP OF SAPPERS AND MINERS OFFICERS KILLED AT BATTLE OF WADI AKARIT — (From left to right) Lieut.

GENERAL VON ARNIM, COMMANDER-IN-CHIEF, AXIS FORCES IN AFRICA, AFTER SURRENDER TO 7 INDIAN BRIGADE, MAY 13th, 1943.

FOURTH INDIAN DIVISION MEMORIAL—ENGLISH CHURCH, TUNIS

SPECIAL OCCASIONS

PARADE IN TRIPOLI, JUNE, 1943.

VISIT OF FOURTH INDIAN DIVISION PARTY TO UNITED KINGDOM. RECEPTION BY LORD MAYOR OF OLDHAM.

remain with Fourth Indian Division throughout the war. On July 9th, with 4 Field Regiment and 149 Anti-Tank Regiment under command, 5 Brigade relieved 24 Australian Brigade in the Point 97 area, where ROBCOL had made its first stand. Here the Essex returned from their filibusters farther south. On July 13th Brigadier Russell's men came under command of 5 Indian Division, which after re-equipment entered the line to exact compensation for its rough treatment at Knightsbridge. The remainder of General Briggs' force consisted of a re-formed 9 Indian Brigade and 161 Brigade (Brigadier F. E. C. Hughes), in which three Essex battalions originally arrived in Middle East. This formation now consisted of 1 Argyll and Sutherland Highlanders, which had seen service under Fourth Division at Sidi Barrani, 3/7 Rajput Regiment and 3/14 Punjabis, formerly of 11 Indian Brigade. 161 Brigade had been brought from the Sudan during the critical period after the fall of Tobruk.

5 Indian Division got to work at once. There had been no greater traitor than time in this desert fighting. Rommel's overworked Germans were nearing exhaustion and they must be given no rest. Rebound strategy was the order of the day. Every stroke must elicit an immediate counter-stroke. On July 14th orders were issued for 5 Indian Brigade to attack that night in conjunction with a New Zealand brigade on its left. The New Zealand infantry had been equipped with six-pounders and it was the general impression that this attack had been ordered in order to incite the enemy to a counter-stroke in which the value of the new weapon might be demonstrated. On the map the proposed operation looked like a finger poked into the enemy's midriff, a liberty which invited reprisal.

5 Brigade's attack was entrusted to 3/10 Baluchis and 4/6 Rajputana Rifles, with their objectives respectively Point 63 and Point 64 on the flanks of the high ground to the west. Shortly after midnight the two Indian battalions filed through the belts of wire covering the British minefield and thrust towards the tip of Ruweisat Ridge from the south-east. Fighting broke out and the advance proceeded only after breaking the resistance of successive enemy outpost lines. By dawn the Baluchis had reached the Ridge slightly to the south of their objective but the Rajputana Rifles had been held up by machine-gun nests and dug-in panzers.

At 0930 hours the Baluchis renewed their advance. With tanks in close support they overran a battalion of the Brescia Division. At 1120 hours 4/6 Rajputana Rifles swept forward anew. In front of Point 64 sappers from 4 Field Company blew gaps in the wire; the infantry flooded through and stormed the redoubt. By nightfall the assault battalions had collected nearly 1,000 Italian prisoners.

On the New Zealand front the right flank battalion was held up by a strong point. 1/4 Essex came forward to assist in its reduction. As the Home County men deployed for the assault the enemy garrison surrendered. By midday the New Zealanders had come up into alignment and a long slender salient intruded into enemy territory. Reaction was immediate. That evening Rommel struck with his panzers and overran the adjacent forward companies of New Zealanders. This left 5 Indian Brigade manning Point 64 at the tip of the finger of ground. As an officer put it, "We may not be bait but it certainly feels as though we were on the hook".

The enemy was ready to bite. At this period the pick-up vans on Ruweisat Ridge enjoyed the intimate discussions of their German adversaries. This privilege was partly due to almost unbelievable carelessness on the part of German operators, who often neglected code and relapsed into clear, but also in part to the presence of a number of talented young men of the Intelligence Corps, who interpreted without difficulty the somewhat clumsy *entendres* of the enemy. Through such sources precise information was forthcoming as to German intentions. 21 Panzer Regiment had been ordered to attack the New Zealand positions at 0530 hours on July 16th, with a follow-up assault that same evening by 8 Panzer Regiment and 155 Lorried Infantry Regiment against the adjoining Baluchi positions.

Support arms immediately moved to the threatened sector. 11 Field Regiment, which had been covering an Australian brigade, swung its guns half circle on to the Indian front. A British armoured brigade hurried up in close support. Six-pounder detachments from Royal Northumberland Fusiliers and the Buffs joined the Rajputana Rifles and Essex near Point 64. Rajputana Rifles and Northumberland Fusilier machine-gunners and 149 Anti-Tank Regiment likewise deployed in 5 Brigade's support.

Throughout the afternoon of July 16th Stuka attacks and enemy artillery fire gradually increased. At 1805 hours, as the level sun struck the eyes of the defenders, movement began in the Deir el Shein depression to the west and north-west of the Indian positions. (The attack had been expected on the opposite side of the exposed salient). 25 minutes later clouds of dust broke over a low ridge less than 2,000 yards from 5 Brigade's forward lines. As the panzers streamed into sight they were engaged by British armour from a hull-down position and by the six-pounders which had been dug in flush with the northern rim of the ridge. A furious engagement followed over the heads of the infantry who received little harm in their sangars and slit trenches. As dark fell, light tanks and armoured cars skirmished out to meet in individual engagements. A remarkable pyrotechnic display ensued. Streams of interlacing tracer marked the clashes, the flat trajectory of the Breda guns easily distinguishable from the bouncing golden balls of the British fire. For three hours the armour battle continued, heavily supported on both sides by artillery. At 2100 hours the enemy broke off the fighting and withdrew.

Daylight revealed the extent of the victory. 800 yards from the Indian positions the first victims sprawled. Behind them the ground was strewn with wrecks as far back as the lip of the Deir el Shein depression. A careful scrutiny revealed some dubious derelicts; Brigadier Russell called for searching fire, whereat a number of panzers which had been shamming dead scurried away. Throughout the day detachments from 4 Field Company dealt with the wrecks. The demolition list that evening proved the enemy to have mounted a full-scale attack with all arms in close support and to have sustained substantial losses. 24 tanks including a re-captured Stuart tank had been blown up. 6 armoured cars were scrap metal. The most imposing list covered self-propelled guns. One storm gun, five 20 mm. anti-tank guns, five 37 mm. anti-tank guns, eight 75 mm. field guns, and six 88 mm. self-propelled guns had been abandoned on the battlefield. For these kills the six-pounders were largely responsible. In a day these venomous little cannon became the pride of Eighth Army. As with the jeep, for the rank and file it was a case of love at first sight.

At dawn on July 17th a strong Australian force raided across the Divisional front deep into enemy positions along the Alamein-Qattara trail. Panzers chased back the audacious intruders, who brought several hundred prisoners with them. During this operation a company of 4/6 Rajputana Rifles under Lieut. Nand Lal Kapur advanced from Point 64 through a gap in the minefield for the purpose of destroying an enemy machine-gun post 2,000 yards in front of the position. Having traversed 1,000 yards the raiding party came under fire. With one platoon Lieut. Kapur pushed on until confronted with a number of panzers which suddenly emerged from the shelter of a ridge 800 yards away. The tanks advanced and for a moment it appeared as though the small party was doomed. With great coolness Lieut. Kapur ordered his men to lie down while he walked up and down in front of them. The panzers slowly crept forward. It was evident that they suspected a trap. At 500 yards they opened fire but made no attempt to close. The Rajputana Riflemen sat tight until night fell when they withdrew, having suffered 15 casualties.

That same evening 9 Indian Brigade passed through 4/6 Rajputana Rifles' positions and continued to probe to the west. Next afternoon the West Yorkshires of this brigade in a dashing advance gained 3,000 yards. Acrid comment in the enemy's intercepts revealed that Italians no longer could be entrusted with such an active front and that German infantry was moving in. 5 Indian Brigade took over the task of patrolling the gap between the South Africans on the right and the ground gained by the West Yorkshires. 3/10 Baluchis and 4 Field Company co-operated to lay a minefield. On the night of July 20th 1/4 Essex relieved the forward troops of 9 Brigade in anticipation of the next phase of the attack. A heavy thrust by British armour was projected in conjunction with infantry assaults by 1 South African Division in the north, 69 Brigade of 50 Division and 161 Indian Brigade along Ruweisat Ridge, and 2 New Zealand Division in the south. Should a break-through occur, 5 Indian Brigade was briefed to exploit as far as Daba, the well-known marshalling ground and staging post 25 miles to the west. For the purpose of this operation 4 Field Regiment, 149 Anti-Tank Regiment, a battery of 1 LAA Regiment and a company of Rajputana Rifle machine gunners were taken under 5 Brigade command.

This ambitious operation never reached the stage at which 5 Brigade was due to make its entrance. In fluctuating fighting 161 Brigade was roughly handled and 69 British Brigade suffered heavily in attempting to force the enemy minefields. On July 28th 5 Brigade stood down from active notice and was ordered to relieve 161 Brigade on the following day.

This month of constant probing and harassing accomplished little on paper but it served an important strategical purpose. It impressed upon Rommel that Eighth Army was not content to adopt a static rôle. The time had now come when the Allies could think in terms of decisive quantities. On the highest level the termination of the African campaign had been given first priority. A supply buildup began on a scale hitherto unknown in Middle East. 44 and 51 British Divisions arrived together with sufficient new tank formations to give Eighth Army four armoured divisions. The British Prime Minister, a stocky figure in a siren suit and an-out-size solar topi, came to see for himself. He traversed the battlefield in the blinding heat of midsummer. He had decided on a clean sweep and had sent out his most highly qualified British commanders. The passing of General Auchinleck was deeply regretted by all ranks of the Indian Army, but it was conceded that changes were inevitable.

Meanwhile throughout August on Ruweisat Ridge 5 Brigade endured hell on earth. In talk of battles and high policy it is often forgotten that the chief preoccupation of any soldier in the field is his routine. On Ruweisat Ridge the daily round was well-nigh intolerable. Except in a few sandy hollows, there was no cover. A slit trench could only be cut with an air drill out of solid stone, or blasted with high explosives. A shallow saucer-shaped sangar preserved the appearance rather than the reality of protection. The sun beat upon the solid rock and the glare struck the eyes like a knife. Every passing vehicle ploughed dust into the air, to choke mouth and nostrils and to reveal movement to the enemy. Water and fuel were precious and were issued sparingly. Labour, on the other hand, was unsparing; always there were loads to carry, mines to lay, wires to string. At the rocky tip of the ridge, where stony pimples gave the enemy spy-ground, there was always bickering, always shellfire or panzers threatening, always Stukas swimming out of the west, with the rhythmic pumping of the Bofors as prelude and the monstrous blast and leaping cloud as they struck. Yet these dangers and discomforts were less than the horror of the clotted masses of flies which maintained their filthy siege as long as warmth was in the air. This living carrion pestered men to the limits of their endurance.

Towards the end of August evidence multiplied that Rommel was committed to a final bid for Egypt. A number of new German formations had arrived from Crete. A first-class Italian division (Folgore) likewise had come forward. On August 29th, in a special Order of the Day, the German commander announced the imminent destruction of Eighth Army. Afrika Korps would be in Alexandria in three days.

The main blow of the new offensive (destined to be known as the Battle of Alem Halfa) fell on 44 Division deep in the desert, but diversionary attacks also struck at 9 Australian Division on the sea coast and at 5 Indian Division on the tip of Ruweisat Ridge. Shortly after midnight on August 30th the Bologna Division attacked to the south-east against the New Zealanders, but losing direction in the darkness crashed into 9 Indian Brigade. The forward companies of the hard-fighting West Yorkshires were overrun. 46 Royal Tank Regiment immediately moved to the attack accompanied by 1/4 Essex, who re-occupied the ground and closed the gap after the ejection of the Italians. Next day "A" Company of the Home County men was visited under cover of a white flag by a German officer and his orderly. An amiable discussion over a cup of tea followed, in the course of which the German rather bashfully suggested that he had been sent to demand surrender. The Essex thanked him for his expressions of good will and saw him off the premises.

On September 2nd Montgomery's counter-stroke began with the New Zealanders shifting to the left to fall on the flank of the intruding German columns. In spite of the spreading gap to the south of Ruweisat Ridge the Indian units were left unmolested, and the only Divisional representative at the decisive encounter at Alem Halfa was Captain Jephson of 11 Field Regiment, whose battery was covering the extreme left flank of the Divisional positions. He wrote:

"In my borrowed Matilda for three days I fumed over such targets as I am sure no gunners have ever seen before or since. At least 3,000 motor transport visible, 50 panzers wandering along eastward, several batteries of self-propelled guns coming into action and ambling off, chivvied by more fortunate gunners. All alas, out of range to me, and because of our infantry responsibilities forbidden to move into range".

During this exciting week Fourth Indian Division made ready to take over from 5 Indian Division on Ruweisat Ridge. In the third week of August, 7 Brigade had been relieved in Cyprus and had arrived in Egypt. General Tuker experienced the customary difficulty in reclaiming his scattered units. To the Deputy Commander-in-Chief, India, he wrote:

"7 Brigade has two battalions here with me and one battalion near Alexandria. 31 Field Regiment is still in Cyprus and 1 Field Regiment at Amiriya. The Division as usual is dispersed over half the country, part of it under 5 Division, part under 50 Division, part under 51 Division, part under BTE direct and others under XXV Corps and a local AA Brigade. I don't think I have ever known anything so thoughtless and so lacking in foresight as the break-up of Fourth Division in March of this year. It was the most experienced Division in Middle East and all it needed and asked for was 4,500 reinforcements and two months' training *as a Division*. I am afraid the prestige of the Indian divisions has dropped sadly. The sorrow of it is that it was not their fault. They were taken from their Divisional commanders and sent here, there, and everywhere. We've got to restore the name of the Indian divisions out here".

Two days after arrival from Cyprus a shocking tragedy occurred. During the final stages of instruction in live mines of Headquarters Company, 1/2 Gurkhas, an instructor pressed a plunger, exploding a group of mines in the midst of his closely packed pupils. The specialist sections of the battalion were wiped out, 68 being killed out of a total 153 casualties. Nevertheless, when the relief of 5 Indian Division began on September 1, 1/2 Gurkha Rifles went forward with improvised mortar, carrier and anti-tank platoons. In effect this relief meant the substitution of 7 Indian Brigade for 9 Indian Brigade, since 161 Brigade remained under Fourth Division's command and 5 Indian Brigade returned to the fold. On October 14th Brigadier Finlay and Brigadier A. W. W. Holworthy, MC, exchanged commands. 7 Brigade's new leader had served as GSO 1 10 Indian Division before appointment to 10 Indian Brigade. An able soldier of charming personality, he immediately impressed his vigorous outlook upon the units under his command.

In a stirring Order of the Day General Tuker expressed the pleasure of all ranks at the return to active operations. He wrote:

"Fourth Division has taken the field again. We have much to avenge on the enemy—the losses inflicted on 7 Brigade about Benghazi and our comrades lost in Tobruk. Every single fighting NCO and man will not rest until he knows that he has killed or captured six of the enemy. Each platoon must destroy its tank, each field and anti-tank gun must have its four tanks, each light AA gun its aircraft."

"The eyes of the Army are upon us. Dominion and American troops are closely watching us. Let us show the Italians that it is of no avail to struggle against us; the Germans that they can never hope to stand against our fury in battle".

Rommel's repulse at Alem Halfa bred no over-confidence when Fourth Division entered the line. General Tuker's attention was immediately directed to the weakness of his right flank where a gap existed between the northern tip of Ruweisat Ridge and the nearest South African brigade, nearly three miles across the valley. It was rather surprising that this gap had not attracted the enemy, since penetration in this sector would have rolled up the South Africans and Australians on the seashore and turned Ruweisat from the rear. From the date of take-over all units of Fourth Division worked like beavers to improve the defences. The loosely knit front was tightened into a continuous system of strong points, each encircled by its own minefield and wire entanglements. To supplement the anti-tank screen 120 spigot mortars were dug in along the Divisional front.

Patrolling was stepped up and for the first time camouflaged clothing was issued to neutralise the glare of the desert moon. Within a few days of taking over the sector, General Tuker advised 30 Corps that his patrols had penetrated enemy territory to considerable depths without encountering resistance. In his opinion the forward zone represented no more than the screen of Rommel's real positions. He therefore proposed to "close piquet" the enemy and to contact his main defences. The patrol record for September showed no less than 80 scouting and fighting reconnaissances on the Divisional front, each of which added some item of intelligence concerning the enemy's dispositions and intentions. The climax of this harassing campaign came on the night of October 5/6 when two platoons of "B" Company of the Royal Sussex under Captain B. B. Clegg struck at the strongly defended enemy observation posts on Point 62. In a dashing assault 6 sangars were mopped up, enemy casualties being estimated at 28 in return for 9 Sussex missing and 17 wounded.*

In his customary fashion the Divisional Commander was experimenting. He got a great deal of pleasure out of the dummy figures which sentries in the forward defensive lines pulled up and down. As he put it, "We keep the Italians amused in the moonlight. The Ities are then smoked so they dont know how many are coming at them. They are then raided elsewhere. The next day the dummies are pulled up for them to look at so that they know that they are dummies. The next night they are attacked where the dummies were shown the night before".

The Divisional workshops never knew from day to day what might be demanded of them. They toiled to produce a grapnel tossed by a mortar bomb by which tanks or carriers might drag away sections of enemy entanglements. The CRA was busied with a kindred project, a chain shot which would break down belts of wire. With a score of such enterprises Fourth Indian Division, delighted to be in the field again, hastened its preparations to share in the final rout of the Axis forces in Africa.

Among the officers who found the Divisional Commander's taste for improvisation to his liking was Lieut.-Colonel G. S. N. Hughes, in command of 26 Indian Field Ambulance, which in the early autumn relieved 14 Field Ambulance with 5 Brigade. Lieut.-Colonel Hughes had been Medical Officer of Cossipore Ordnance Works and was conversant with metal work. With forward surgical teams available, he felt that his

* Mr. Winston Churchill sent congratulations to the Royal Sussex on this occasion. There is a record of the message as having been passed by the Corps Commander to the Battalion. Unfortunately a search of the Prime Minister's private papers, the War Office, the Divisional, Brigade and Royal Sussex war diaries, has failed to uncover the text of the message.

Field Ambulance should have its own operating theatre. Instead of indenting and waiting, he decided to construct his needs out of the scrap of the desert. An ingenious structure evolved, consisting of two captured Italian vehicles sawn into parts and rejoined. The operating lamp standard was fashioned from the gear lever of a derelict truck. Petrol tins appeared in a dozen guises as clinical fittings. Surgical instruments were obtained in a score of indirect ways. The Division as a whole became interested in Lieut.-Colonel Hughes' project. Workshops and Sappers and Miners provided many fixtures. From Alamein onwards emergency operations, particularly upon belly wounds, saved lives which would have been lost had it been necessary to await transportation and to move such critical cases to the rear. The first two patients treated were upon the operating table within thirty minutes of being struck. In October, when the ADMS was displaying Lieut.-Colonel Hughes' innovations to Public Relations and press representatives, a flight of Messerschmidts made a deliberate low-level attack on the plainly marked ambulance, dropping a stick of bombs across it.

Every type of material and equipment was now arriving in Western Desert in unprecedented quantities. The men of Fourth Indian Division, remembering the lean times when the tools of war were scarce, smacked their lips as the dumps mounted high and the formations multiplied in the rear of the Alamein position. After viewing this abundance General Tuker in a letter to General Hartley envisaged his dream battalion of to-morrow. It would have its own heavy and light mortars, a profusion of medium and light machine-guns, 16 anti-tank guns, a recce unit of 8 tanks and 5 armoured cars, its own porter company. No infantryman would move upon his feet. Lorryborne and mobile to the last man, such a unit would fight its own sort of battle at its own time and place.

In no field did the theories of the Divisional Commander obtain greater results than in the artillery arm. Napoleon believed that the mission of artillery was not to make a noise but to hit enemies. General Tuker was satisfied with nothing less than their obliteration. He took a dubious view of barrage programmes. The rolling wall of fire had never achieved annihilating density; in many instances it was not sufficient to break resistance. Its waste was enormous, for it treated the battlefield as homogeneous; empty desert and concentrated strong points received the same dosage of shell. As a more efficient fire plan the Divisional Commander sought something akin to pattern bombing from the air. He found the Royal Regiment ready, willing and able to give it to him.

The technique of intensified artillery fire had been worked out previously, but under conditions of desert warfare its practical application had yet to be devised. Artillery trace sheets were known to the infantry only by name. Surveys for predicted shoots were scarcely more than on the divisional level. The organisation essential to secure a quick and accurate concentration which would pulverise centres of enemy resistance, had been mapped out, but neither the establishment, the equipment, nor the training for such operations had been provided. To this immense detail Brigadier Dimoline devoted himself. The task was not unlike the expansion of a handcraft into a mass production industry, yet within a few months the energy and enthusiasm of the gunner units blended the Divisional artillery into a striking force of outstanding virtuosity, a flexible instrument trained to engage individual objectives with devastating effect, to swing from target to target with unequalled accuracy, speed and freedom. Constant training and experiment envolved a technique for crash and saturation shoots well in advance of current practice. Gun surveys and the artillery communications grid were elaborated until the CRA could sit in his battle headquarters with trace sheets which blended like a musical score, from which he could play his weapons singly, in unison or in harmony. Although only bare deserts confronted him he had worked out exhaustive details of personnel and equipment for mountain warfare. By the trial and error method he had improved Divisional performance in mobile and fixed operations, in deception and direction shoots, in the use of smoke, and above all in the rapidity and certainty of communications under battle conditions. When on the night of November 1/2, 57 LAA Regiment opened the Divisional programme with a high-angle tracer "V for Victory" sign, it provided a true portent of the great rôle to be played thereafter by the artillery units of Fourth Indian Division.*

After the September full moon the weather worsened. Sandstorms and driving rains made life on Ruweisat Ridge even less bearable than usual. But now discomforts scarcely counted. The rising tension and the imminence of a great battle engrossed all ranks. Early in October the general plan was disclosed to divisional commanders. Fourth Indian Division had not been alloted a leading rôle. The impact of this disappointment on exuberant morale is reflected in General Tuker's report: "The Division is feeling as savage as tigers. It is really hard to restrain them from going in and 'crowning him' as they put it, whenever they see the guns harassing a post near them. I must work this off soon". There was reason to believe that the enemy expected the new offensive to be launched from Ruweisat Ridge. Preparations accordingly were made to encourage this belief. To release 1 South African Division for the battle, Fourth Indian Division undertook additional responsibilities on its right flank. In this extended sector its initial task was demonstration. Raids and dummy attacks were to be employed to keep the enemy guessing.

As the full moon rose towards its zenith on the evening of October 23rd, showering the desert with silver, Eighth Army crouched tense and waiting. At 2140 hours the Alamein front erupted with the crash of

*No one in Fourth Indian Division would wish to make extravagant claims, but there is a sound basis for considering the Division's chief contribution to the winning of the war to have been the services rendered by the Divisional gunners in the elaboration and perfection of the new artillery technique. Certainly Fourth Indian Division led the way in Eighth Army. Brigadier Dimoline afterwards carried his methods to Fourteenth Army in Burma.

1,200 guns. From the Divisional positions on Ruweisat Ridge an unforgettable scene unfolded in the north. The back area was pin-pricked with continuous light flashes as the artillery smashed first in counter battery and then concentrated for a rolling barrage. Far to the west the signal flares of the enemy sprang over the tortured crescent of front, calling for aid in extremity. A great cloud of dust and smoke billowed into the shining night, to hang over the dunes and in the soft sandy valley through which the railway ran. The streaking tracer of the Bofors demarcated unit boundaries and gave the infantry direction. Far out on the tranquil Mediterranean, splinters of light twinkled along the horizon as the Royal Navy held 90 Light Division from the main battlefield by simulating a landing.

At 2215 hours Fourth Indian Division artillery, which had been embodied in the general counter-battery programme, switched onto Point 62, a fortified position at the north-west extremity of Ruweisat Ridge. This objective was well known to Indian troops who had reached it on several occasions but had never been able to hold it. Here strong stone sangars had been constructed on the slopes of a slight hillock. A belt of wire and an apron of anti-tank and anti-personnel mines girdled the knoll, which possessed exposed approaches from all sides. At 2300 hours "C" Company of 1/2 Gurkha Rifles with three tracked carriers and a detachment of 12 Field Company, passed through the British wire and headed west along the ridge. On approaching Point 62 two platoons remained in covering positions while the remaining platoons with the carriers and the sapper detachment, under command of Lieutenant N. W. Carrick, closed up in bright moonlight. The carriers, which were equipped with grapnel devices, rushed in to remove the wire. One was disabled: another having fastened its grapnels had its hawser shot away; the third managed to place its hooks and to yank loose a section of the wire, exploding connected mines and booby traps. Lieutenant Carrick led the rush through the gap, while a second platoon gave covering fire. The leading section was wiped out, and the officer with only two riflemen reached the main sangar. Here Lieutenant Carrick fell as his men leapt in with the steel. After clearing the sangars the raiders withdrew with losses of 8 missing and 17 wounded. (Lieutenant Carrick was believed to have been killed, but afterwards it was learnt that he had been severely wounded and taken prisoner). A Gurkha rifleman, shot through both legs, remained hidden in a slit trench throughout the next day, crawling painfully to safety with important information when darkness fell on the following evening.

A corresponding raid by 1/1 Punjabis, on 161 Brigade's front, failed to close with the enemy, but served its purpose in pinning down his forces. 161 Brigade likewise devoted itself wholeheartedly to a dummy attack. Deception shoots laid down fixed lines of tracer, the brigade transport moved up to forward positions and with exhausts open roared about in dervish-like musical rides. Light lanes were laid where they might be observed, while mortar and machine-guns raked the enemy forward positions.

On the opening night of the battle 5 Brigade passed into 30 Corps reserve, a move preliminary to a projected attack by 2 New Zealand Division. This assault was cancelled, and shortly after midnight on October 27th Brigadier Russell's men moved to relieve 2 and 3 South African Brigades on the right of Ruweisat. In this move 5 Brigade was supported by the Rajputana Rifles machine gunners, 1 and 154 Field Regiments, 4 and 12 Field Companies and a number of anti-tank batteries. 161 Brigade occupied the centre of the Divisional sector with 7 Brigade on its south flank, where contact was established with a Free French formation. At this stage the Divisional commitments covered 25,000 yards of front, an extremely heavy responsibility as long as the main battle in the north pivoted on this sector.

It was now apparent that General Montgomery's "crumbling" process had failed to punch a hole in the vital Kidney Ridge area, and that 10 Armoured Corps could not yet enter the fighting. Two German panzer divisions on the evening of October 28th had concentrated for attack in the rear of Kidney Ridge, and although mauled by Desert Air Force, remained in that locality to threaten the right of Fourth Indian Division's position. On the next day the Divisional Commander, after careful survey, realigned his front and shortened it by 5,000 yards. The Australian attack along the dunes had drawn 90 Light Division into the coastal area, a significant move which reduced the threat to Ruweisat. Fourth Indian Division thereupon passed under command of 13 Corps, which had been entrusted with the defensive rôle in the battle. General Tuker wrote with justifiable disappointment:

"Our part is to hold a huge front and make noises to keep the Boche interested. A poor sort of business, but someone has to do it. I don't think he has moved a man from our front".

Even while General Tuker wrote, events were in train which were destined to grant his men participation at the climax. Having gradually drawn the bulk of the Germans into the coastal area, a quick encirclement by 9 Australian Division pinned a substantial enemy force against the Mediterranean. As a consequence of this operation the thrust line of 10 Armoured Corps' break-through was shifted to the south-west in order that the mortal blow might fall mainly upon Italian divisions. At 0100 hours on November 2nd, "SUPERCHARGE" Operation began. 7 Brigade contributed a dummy attack on the southern flank which drew fire and proved significant nervousness concerning the the central sector. Further north the main armoured drive broke through the enemy's defensive lines and minefields, but 9 Armoured Brigade in the van was ambushed, losing three-quarters of its runners against a thick hedge of anti-tank guns. General Montgomery immediately ordered a subsidiary thrust to outflank this hostile screen. On the night of November 2nd, 7 Brigade relieved 5 Brigade, and the latter formation at 1030 hours next morning passed into 30 Corps reserve. At noon Brigadier Russell received his orders. 5 Brigade would

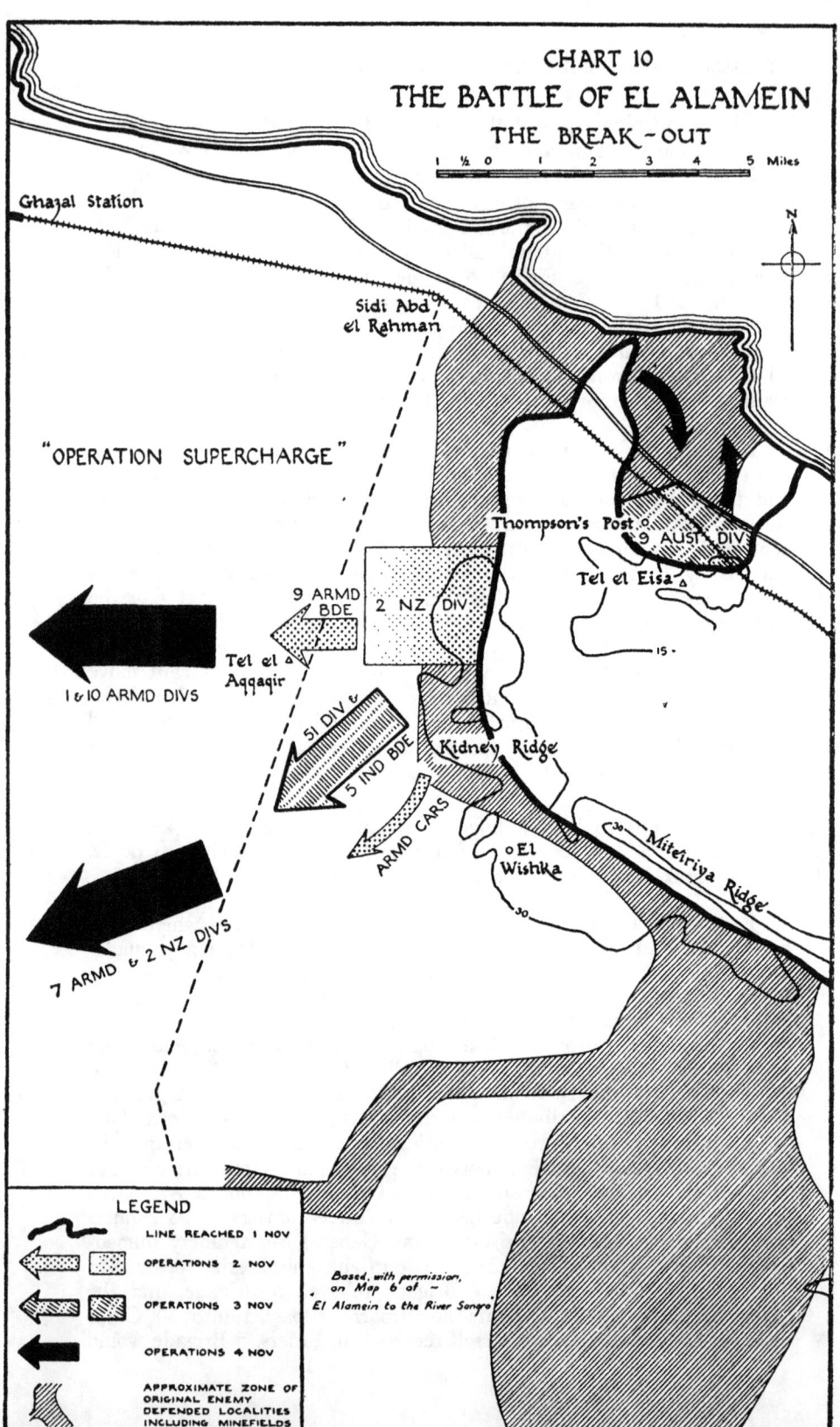

lead the new attack in conjunction with and under command of 152 Brigade of 51 Highland Division. The assault would be mounted on a very narrow front behind a heavy barrage. The intention was to cut a lane and open a gap in the enemy minefields two miles to the south-east of Tel El Aqqaqir where 9 Armoured Brigade was pinned down amid a thicket of anti-tank defenses. Through this gap 1, 7 and 10 Armoured Divisions would drive to the kill. 2 New Zealand Division would follow in a mobile rôle to mop up.

The new operation required rapid organization. 5 Brigade was faced with an approach march of 12 miles over unknown tracks. A further 5 mile night march would carry the men to their battle positions. By 1600 hours on the day of briefing the jump-off location had been selected and the formations were on the move. Enemy dive bombers spotted the columns and endeavoured to interfere. When night fell the units were trudging forward along Sun, Moon and Star tracks, rough desert trails ankle deep in powdery sand which all but stifled the marchers. When 3/10 Baluchis bogged down, 4/6 Rajputana Rifles replaced them as one of the leading battalions. By midnight Brigade Headquarters column, following lanes of cheerful "V's" cut in the shaded sides of petrol tin lanterns, had passed through the gaps in the British minefields and had reached the jump-off line. As other units arrived they were allotted their battle positions. By 0100 hours it was apparent that 5 Brigade would not be deployed in time, whereupon Brigadier Russell asked that the artillery programme should be delayed for an hour. This last-minute request was arranged without delay—a tribute to the excellence of the staff work. By 0200 hours 1/4 Essex and 4/6 Rajputana Rifles had formed up. Accompanied by detachments of Sappers and Miners they advanced on their objective, followed by brigade transport.

An Indian Army Public Relations officer has described the ensuing action vividly:

"At 0230 hours the guns began to bark and cough. Battery after battery registered with intermittent harassing fire. It was like the tuning up of a multi-engined bomber—warm up one engine, switch it off, try another, race one a bit, try two at a time, try one pair, both pairs. Until at 0330 hours, everything was switched on with a rush and a deafening roar, which for an instant pinned the men to the ground. Then plain as day, looming before them, 5 Brigade saw the Wedge."

"It looked like a cloud that had suddenly risen out of a fissure in the earth, a steady and constant thickness of smoke and dust, where 400 guns cast their shell, one gun to every two yards of ground. It was a cataract of steel which poured out of the air, churning the earth into powder. Down each side fireworks ran—Bofors guns firing tracer as flank guides. Minute by minute the crescendo heightened and deepened until at 0400 hours, slowly, inexorably, like a machine when power surges into its dead metal, the Wedge began to move. The drive had begun."

"The men who led this advance told me that in that thirty minutes while they waited for the curtain of steel to be woven, there came to them a wonderful feeling of confidence. The Wedge was so exact that they felt the barrage to be part of themselves; a weapon in their hands; as an airman feels when the earth has slipped away from him, when his engines beat sweet and true and he knows he has great power within his grasp. The Indians moved forward not as men ahead of guns, but as men behind a shield. They were the garrison, the crew of the Wedge. They moved freely without fear. 'They could have leaned against it', said their Brigadier. The first casualties, and indeed most of the casualties, were men who followed the wall of shell so closely that they became queasy from the fumes of our explosives."

"Of fighting there was little. It was more tidying-up—winkling out the dazed occupants of dug-outs and dusting off slit trenches where a few panzer grenadiers sought to sell their lives dearly. There were incidents, of course. While a German stood in a dug-out entrance with his hands raised, another crept up behind him and drew a bead on a Rajputana Rifle officer. When a subedar collared the marksman, the irate Englishman laid into the German with his fists. The subedar saw the Wedge marching on without them, and spoke to his officer with some such words as 'See, Sahib, there is our battle. Let us go on with it'. Every now and then desperate enemies, who had come unscathed through the torrent of steel, sprang up and sought to fight. Sudden deadly clashes occurred. A havildar whom the Rajputana Rifles mourn took a mortal wound in dealing single-handed with a dozen Germans. But ahead the men marched steadily with the Wedge, 35 yards in each minute, moving without hurt over ground which every device of war had made deadly. And so perfectly was the Wedge planned, that when our men had passed beyond the range of field guns, and the mediums and heavies took up the task, those who followed a stone's throw from the curtain of fire saw no gap or break in it."

"I asked a young officer of the Essex how it felt to walk forward for nearly three hours with a storm of 400 guns beating about his head, and their shells blasting a trail a few yards before his feet. 'Engrossing', he said, 'but after a while, it seemed a bit lonely. I was rather pleased when, a little before dawn, I saw some shapes in the gloom, and realized that we had somebody with us'."

"These shapes were the tank screen,—South Africans and the Royals in their armoured cars. The Wedge was all but driven. At the first streak of light in the east, the infantry came into broken ground. They saw before them the kidney-shaped contour which they had been shown on the map. The guns lifted and were done; there was quiet but for the crackle of small arms fire. Out in front little figures scuttled madly, seeking holes. A carrier platoon went out to bring them in. Then another noise, thunder out of the east, and more thunder. The roar mounted. The tanks came plunging through—hundreds of tanks, lunging to the west through the gap the Wedge had made, and wheeling north for the kill. The sun rose on the last of Alamein."

5 BRIGADE — MERSA MATRUH, RUWEISAT AND ALAMEIN

In the course of the break-through, 5 Indian Brigade took 351 prisoners at a cost of 80 casulties.

This dramatic action was less a battle than a quick and accurate manoeuvre. The Corps Commander wrote to General Tuker:

"It was a tremendous achievement to move such a distance by night and the Army Commander tells me that the captured commander of the German Africa Korps stated that one of the reasons for the success of our armoured battle on the following day was that all the Italians on the front of the break-through had been captured by your 5 Brigade; thus no information of the break-through and advance of our armour reached enemy headquarters".

As a record of a most soldierly performance, 5 Brigade's "play by play" log is of interest:

Hours—November 3, 1942.

1230 Brigadier Russell and COs arrive Headquarters 51 Highland Division.

1330 Orders received and arrangements completed for anti-tank support, for anti-aircraft direction shoot, and for sapper details.

1400 Recce group arrived at 152 Brigade Headquarters and went forward with guide.

1440 Brigade Commander and COs arrived at Headquarters 2 Seaforths and began recce for suitable forward deployment positions. Brigade Major by wireless ordered Brigade to advance to a debussing area by Sun,, Moon and Star tracks.

1600 Forward deployment position selected, gaps in minefields located, detailed barrage programme worked out. COs left to collect company commanders from Headquarters 152 Brigade. Officer sent to New Zealand Divisional Headquarters with details of barrage. Intelligence officer went for tape to mark forward deployment positions.

1800 COs and company commanders having completed recce returned for final orders from Brigade commander. Tac Headquarters opened at 152 Brigade area.

1830 Nightfall. COs leave to rejoin battalions.

1900 Supporting elements begin to arrive. Intelligence officer leaves to mark route forward with lanterns.

2200 Brigade Headquarters leaves for forward deployment position.

2400 Brigade Headquarters column and 1/4 Essex arrive in forward deployment area.

0055 Jump-off tape located. 4/6 Raj Rifs arrive. Divisional Headquarters asked to pospone programme for one hour.

0200 Battalions form up. Only one suitable gap found in minefield. Transport marshalled to move through this.

0230 Artillery programme starts. Units move forward.

0315 Motor Transport stuck in sand dunes. Tactical Headquarters moves forward.

0400 Barrage begins.

0710 Barrage finishes. Forward patrols reach objective.

0800 Essex carriers in action against enemy retiring west.

0900 Leading elements of armoured force pass through.

As the line broke, General Tuker rapidly organized both brigades for pursuit. Unfortunately others drew the honour. While the armour and the New Zealanders put an end to the resistance of Afrika Korps in the north, 13 Corps took over the task of rounding the hapless Italians, deserted by their allies. Four enemy divisions littered the southern expanses of the battlefield. Their transport had been snatched to allow the Germans to escape, their ration and water convoys discontinued. The ensuing operation therefore was less mopping-up than rescue.

At 0600 hours in November 4th, a flying column consisting of a rifle company, the carrier and anti-tank platoons of 1/2 Gurkha Rifles, a company of Rajputana Rifles Machine Gun Battalion, detachments of 32 Field Regiment, 12 Field Company Sappers and Miners, and troops of 149 Anti-Tank Regiment and 57 L.A.A. Regiment, was organized. Both Brigadier Holworthy and Lieut.-Colonel Lovett accompanied the column. It was delayed by a maze of minefields but on the morning of November 5th it encountered large numbers of forlorn Italians trudging up Rahman track from the south. The dispersed and demoralised groups made half hearted attempts at resistance, but Captain Malcolm Cruickshank led a charge of 1/2 Gurkha carriers which completed the rout. Throughout the day this flying column continued to round up prisoners, guns and equipment. Captain Abdul Qadir of 26 Field Ambulance, who came forward to deal with the casualties, found his advance dressing station submerged in suffering and exhausted enemies. At nightfall the haul consisted of General Messina (commander of the Brescia Division), 101 other officers, 2,192 men, 6 tanks, 17 field guns, many flak and anti-tank guns and motor vehicles. The sweep continued for several days, 4/16 Punjabis joining the beat on November 6th. 5 Brigade were ordered to seek out and gather in a force of approximately 3,000 Italian infantry marooned to the south-west, but before columns could be organised these castaways had been bagged by others.

On November 7th Fourth Indian Division was withdrawn from offensive operations and entrusted with the salvage of the battlefield. Nightly the radio news bulletins reported the pursuit to be crossing well-remembered terrain. When rearguard brushes were reported between Beda Littoria and Barce an officer exhibited characteristic disappointment: "Damn it" he said "that's our Djebel". The men of the Red Eagle Division felt that the task of picking up scrap was something less than they deserved; so they gave vent to their feelings by turning in 1500 tons of salvage daily—six times their assigned quota—in the hope of completing the job quickly and of catching up with the war.

On November 6th torrential rains fell, turning much of the desert into a quagmire and filling innumerable wadis with storm water. The three armoured divisions spearheading the pursuit bogged down to the east of Mersa Matruh. As a result Rommel was able to extricate a substantial proportion of his battered columns. When the ground had dried, 1 and 7 Armoured Divisions and 2 New Zealand Division continued the chase. On November 14th Tobruk was retaken. At Gazala 1 Armoured Division regrouped, leaving the pursuit to the Kiwis and the Desert Rats. By the end of the month Rommel had regained his old bolt-holes at the bottom of the Gulf of Sirte. There he prepared to make a stand. 51 Highland Division went forward, followed by 50 Division. On December 2nd Fourth Division was warned for a move. On receipt of such warning 161 Brigade left Divisional command to return to garrison duties in Egypt. On December 10th the move to Tobruk area began and five days later Divisional headquarters was established at El Adem.

On arrival Brigadier Russell was notified of his appointment to command 8 Indian Division, a promotion which brought mingled pleasure and regret to the Brigade which he had so boldly and skilfully led in many a tight corner.* The selection of Brigadier D.R.E.R. Bateman, DSO, OBE, as his successor, was a happy appointment, as there was no better known officer in Fourth Division. The new comander had joined Fourth Indian Division in December, 1939, as Brigade Major of 5 Brigade. He was appointed GSO 1 during the Keren fighting and continued in this post until, as has already been recorded, he was selected to command Middle East Training Centre. A man of meticulous mind and remarkable memory, he was highly schooled in the exacting problems of desert administration.

*In the Italian campaign 8 Indian Division earned a **magnificent reputation**. In the words of General Mark Clark, "It never put a foot wrong. It was here, there and everywhere". At one time it was known as "Fifth Army's Flying Squad". It spearheaded the break-through at Cassino, the advance on Florence and the break-through on the flood-banked river lines which ended the Italian campaign.

Chapter 15

THE DOLDRUMS

A FEELING of anti-climax pervaded Fourth Indian Division as it settled down to routine training and rear area duties on the bleak desert at El Adem.

Eighth Army, restocked with weapons and equipment so long denied, had won a great victory and had swept on towards a new theatre, leaving Fourth Indian Division behind. Every officer and man of the Division felt most keenly the change of role and all were eager to be re-included amongst the foremost troops. There was a fear among the senior officers that Eighth Army might become a purely British command, and that the new commander-in-chief might wish to leave Indian troops in rear areas and on garrison duties in the non-active zones of Middle East.

Shortly after Alamein the Divisional CRA had been loaned to 30 Corps for the period of the pursuit. Towards the end of the year, Brigadier Dimoline, who had not served with Indian troops previously, wrote:

"The Army Commander's intention is, I think, to employ Fourth Indian Division in the same manner as the rest of the Indian units in Palestine, Cyprus and Egypt, i.e. as garrison troops, useful fatigue parties for salvage, and as police; namely, in the same manner as the Libyan Arab irregulars and other second line troops are employed. Naturally the unfortunate happenings of last summer have given him and others of his way of thinking a strong case. Nevertheless it is humiliating that Indian troops should be so regarded and so treated by their Army Commander".

Earlier in the year General Rees, commanding 10 Indian Division, had written:

"Changes (in Western Desert) continue to be kaleidoscopic. Brigades are rocketed from command to command in bewildering fashion". General Tuker had protested in the strongest terms against this piecemeal and stop-gap practice. He apparently found a firm ally in General Montgomery, who on September 29th issued an order in his most concise style. He said:

"A cardinal point in my policy is that divisions shall retain their identity and esprit de corps and that they shall not be split up into bits and pieces which never see their parent formations. Divisions must fight as divisions and under their own commanders . . . There may be certain individuals and units who do not like the composition of divisions as issued and who wish for changes. There will be no changes . . . Protesting or belly-aching about this matter is forbidden".

As codicil to this order General Montgomery announced establishments for the seven United Kingdom divisions in Middle East. As he was not allowed to alter the make-up of Dominions' divisions, *the only troops which this order did not cover were the Indian formations.* Concerning them silence reigned.

General Tuker felt that he was entitled to know where he stood. He addressed the following letter to General Horrocks:

"Everyone in this Division is feeling most apprehensive as to its future. We know that this theatre of war—the Mediterranean—is becoming a theatre of United Kingdom and American armies. We feel that there is a good chance that we may thus be relegated to some peaceful theatre of war. We feel most strongly that this Division does not deserve such a fate."

"Its standard of training and its fighting spirit are probably higher to-day than they have ever been. I do not think anyone would deny that it is the most experienced Division in the Empire, having been the only formation that has fought at Sidi Barrani, has fought all through the desert and mountain campaign of Eritrea, in the Syrian campaign, in the summer attacks last year in Western Desert, throughout the Tobruk operations a year ago to Agedabia and through the withdrawal from there, as well as having had considerable elements fighting successfully in the Gazala-Alamein operations, and now having been engaged in this recent battle."

"Further it looks as though mountain fighting may yet develop. I think we have more experience than most in this sort of warfare. Our men, British and Indian, are tough. The Indians come from the high Himalayas and the Punjab and are used to extremes of cold. The Division is a very seasoned one. Among its Indian troops it has more than 1400 who have been on active service continuously for two years and over. About 75% of all its Indian troops have been on continuous active service for over a year."

"Its British troops have if anything a higher proportion of men who have seen similar periods of continuous active service."

"Lastly, perhaps I am allowed to say that Fourth Division has represented India in active operations in the Middle East for two and a half years, not without success. Should it not continue so to represent her in the Middle East?"

"I do hope that these considerations will favourably influence anyone who might consider sending Fourth Division to some peaceful area. Can we be assured that this will not happen? I should find it hard to explain to my officers and men that they are no longer needed, after all they have achieved and in view of the high spirit and expectations with which they entered these present operations."

General Horrocks forwarded the letter to General Montgomery with the following comment:

"Although this Division has only been under my command for a short time I have had the opportunity of going round a good many units. I concur with the remarks in the attached letter. There is no doubt that this is an experienced Division, more experienced probably than any other Division in the Middle East. It is imbued with a fine fighting spirit and in my opinion it would be a tragedy if this fine Division was not given a further opportunity of representing India alongside United Kingdom and Dominion forces."

"The esprit de corps in the Division would undoubtedly suffer if it was relegated to a peaceful theatre of war. What it requires is more fighting. Generally speaking the standard of training amongst the forces available here is not very high, but in the Fourth Indian Division this is not the case. It is well trained and fit for battle in every way."

It was unfortunate at this period that the Indian Army was not represented at Middle East Headquarters by an officer of high rank. The Indian section of the Adjutant-General's Branch, GHQ Middle East, was concerned only with administrative details. Tidings of high level decisions by New Delhi and Whitehall seldom penetrated to Cairo. Officers and men of Fourth Indian Division could only possess their souls in patience and hope for the best.

Towards the end of December the plan of "FIRE EATER", designed to turn Rommel out of his Sirte-Buerat position, was circulated. Fourth Indian Division was omitted from this projected operation. 5 Brigade however on December 26th received warning for a move to Benghazi, under command of 10 Corps. Early in the New Year it marched off by way of Bir Hacheim and the deep desert route. The winter had been exceptionally stormy and many soft sand expanses were sodden and soup-like. 5 Brigade managed to keep moving and took some consolation from the miseries of formations which it passed, bogged down on their way forward to participate in "FIRE EATER". On arrival at Benghazi the Brigade was allotted garrison duties which included the provision of 800 labourers daily for stevedore work at the docks. An order followed which placed much of the Divisional transport at the disposal of 50 Division. In mid-January Brigadier Holworthy was taken away to organise and command Middle East Mountain Warfare School in the Lebanons. Dispersed and stripped of leaders and personnel fears again arose that Fourth Indian Division had been relegated to non-combatant duties and its fighting prowess forgotten.

THE DOLDRUMS

Fortunately it takes much to shake the morale of men who are sure of themselves. There were certain crumbs of comfort. In spite of the cheerless camp and incessant rains, Christmas had been a happy festival—"an agreeable blend of religious exercises, hearty eating, beer and bonhomie" wrote one correspondent. NAAFI had come up to scratch for the British troops and Rich Food had been arranged for all Indian ranks. The King-Emperor's speech brought a bounteous day to a fitting conclusion. In January a full supply of Divisional flashes arrived. The men swaggered and eyed with pride the red eagles on each other's shoulders. The flashes were the gift of the ladies of Lahore who had presented them at the instance of the late Sir Sikander Hyat Khan, Prime Minister of the Punjab. About this time a reminder that even stevedores mattered reached the men in a thoughtful message from Mr. Churchill, who wrote with his customary felicity, "Tell them from me that they are unloading history".

Meanwhile General Tuker continued his battle to assemble, to train and to hold together a front-line division. When 3/10 Baluchis needed a rest 1/9 Gurkhas (Lieut-Col. Ian Roche) came from duties in Cairo to replace them. The Divisional Commander made vigorous efforts to obtain the reconstruction of 2/4 and 2/7 Gurkhas, destroyed at Knightsbridge and Tobruk. He pointed out that many Indian formations (including excellent State Force units) were now scattered over Middle East on detached duties. They would be of greater value and in far better heart if gathered into brigades which would train and care for them. A similar attempt to re-form 18 Field Company Sappers and Miners (lost at Tobruk) failed because the expansion of the Indian Army was proceeding so rapidly that every available veteran was needed at home.

The ever-increasing technical stature of all ranks of Fourth Indian Division reflected in significant fashion the march of India towards nationhood. In a thoughtful survey the News Letter of Central India Horse reviewed the progress:

"The older jawans, now seasoned veterans, are few but unmistakable. They stand out like trained ponies in a ring of raw walers. They can cook, sew, drive, maintain, navigate, work wireless, rifle, tommy-gun, anti-tank gun, mortar, machine-gun, lay mines and drink beer."

"As replacements of regular officers we have a banker, a farmer, a trawler captain, an oilfield operator, the son of a ruling house in India, a tea-planter. Yet continuity shows in a list of many relations of former officers".

"Mechanisation looms larger every day. Gone are the rough and ready sides of the desert. Jawans must now be tradesmen and pass the appropriate trade tests. No longer can Sowar Poop Singh 'baitho' by the roadside with a 'petrol stoppage' and wait the coming of a 'fitter' to diagnose the trouble and set the engine going again. The days of 'Gari thandi ho hai, Sahib' are gone forever. He must now take off his coat and repair the damage himself. The mysteries of the petrol engine have to be learnt through tears, sweat and blood—otherwise he will be 'unmechanisable'—a disgrace bordering on untouchable. As such he will have to leave the Regiment. How could he face his family after such a disgrace?"

"But one thing leads to another. The passing of trade tests requires education. Khuda Bakhsh's father said it wasn't necessary in the Army in his day, so Sowar Khuda Bakhsh never went to school. Now he sits and struggles with the alphabet. That is enough in itself—or so he thought until he tried mathematics! However, if he emerges successfully from this somewhat painful ordeal, he is richer by Rs. 45 per month. Further, if he is sensible he can park most of this with Government—where it collects 2½% interest. Provided he survives the war, he will be well equipped to enjoy the peace. So nowadays all are busy learning their trades—Crew Driver-Mechanic, Crew Motor-Mechanic, Crew Driver-Operator, Crew Gunner-Mechanic, and Crew Gunner-Operator. If only our recruits had been educated before they joined the army, how much easier it would all be!"

The long winter of slow misfeature ebbed away. Without haste and employing his now standard right jab and left hook General Montgomery ejected Rommel from one lay-back position to another. Tripoli fell without resistance: at the triumphal entry platoons of 4/6 Rajputana Rifles and 3/10 Baluchis, who were acting as Army Headquarters guards, represented Fourth Indian Division. At the end of February 10 Corps moved into Tripolitania and Fourth Indian Division took to the roads.* After the first night's leaguer they were in new country. As they passed along the Via Balbia between the marshes and the sea the desert faded behind them. The dunes began to wear a catch of grass and some of the innumerable wadis carried water. When the columns had passed Mussolini's grandoise Arch of Empire, scattered fields appeared in which the winter sowings were already showing green. Finally the road ran through a countryside checker-boarded with olive and citrus groves, the neat farms exhibiting the loving care of the Italian peasant for his land. At Tripoli the highway found that ancient town through an avenue of wattles, passed through Arab slums and emerged at the battered waterfront, where the Royal Navy and engineers laboured indefatigably to make the port servicable. 7 Brigade took over as garrison, while 5 Brigade and Divisional troops camped on the outskirts of the town.

The war was 185 miles ahead. 90 miles beyond the Tunisian frontier the Gulf of Gabes gouges deeply into the Tunisian headland. A few miles inland a large mountain block springs out of the plain. The main highway passes under the shadow of this massif, along a narrow

*The speed of this move was noteworthy. With battle calling the "tail" of Fourth Division took no heed of hours. 149 Anti-Tank Regiment, among the last to move, covered 400 miles in two days.

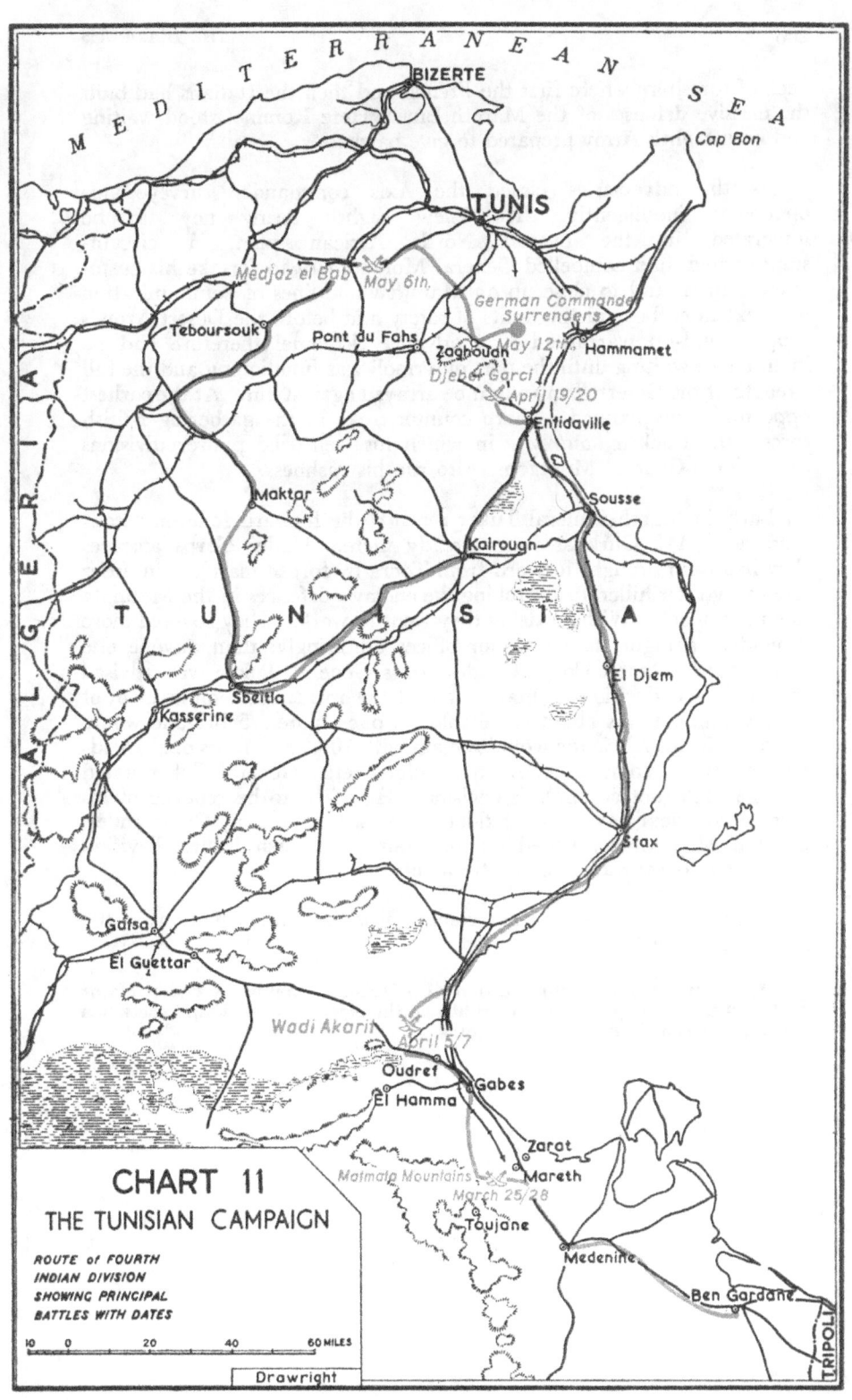

neck of foreshore where first the French and then the Italians had built the massive defenses of the Mareth Line. Here Rommel stood waiting and here Eighth Army prepared to give battle.

As the adversaries closed the Axis commander surveyed his opponents intelligently. He knew Eighth Army now to be integrated in the overall North African plan, a circumstance which had compelled General Montgomery to forsake his customary caution and to close up on Mareth while lines of communication were extended beyond the limits of safety and before the Desert Army's supply build-up warranted such advance. Rommel therefore had no intention of waiting until the port of Tripoli was functioning and the full strength of the Desert Army might be arrayed against him. At the earliest opportunity he planned a sharp counterstroke at the gathering British forces, an attack *a l'outrance* in which his well-tried panzer divisions might force General Montgomery to rue his rashness.

Early in March General Tuker reached the forward zone on reconnaissance. 1/2 Gurkhas were already there. Under Corps auspices they had been brought forward from Tocra by forced marches, in order to employ their hillcraft in probing the enemy's defences in the Matmata mountain block. Without delay they went to work. They covered more ground in a night, said a senior officer admiringly, than anyone else in a week.* At 30 Corps Headquarters General Tuker was advised that high level decisions militated against the operational employment of his division. It was about to be split up once more. 5 Brigade would go to 30 Corps, 7 Brigade would remain with 10 Corps, Divisional Headquarters would come under Army Headquarters. General Tuker stated that he could not accept this decision. He asked to be relieved of his command. Next day he was bidden to tea with the Army Commander. General Montgomery ended all uncertainty. Fourth Indian Division was to be concentrated for battle at once.

Thus India again joined her comrades of the United Nations in the forefront of the fray.

*An advanced Dressing Station of 17 Field Ambulance under Major Ved Parkash accompanied 1/2 Gurkhas on this special mission and sustained casualties when shelled by heavy guns.

Chapter 16

MATMATA MOUNTAINS

As has been foreshadowed in the preceding chapter, at the beginning of March General Montgomery was gambling on his luck. Only 7 Armoured Division and 51 Highland Division had closed up against the Mareth positions. Three enemy armoured divisions had been identified on this front. This concentration presaged a blow at Eighth Army before its build-up had been completed. 2 New Zealand Division and an additional tank brigade hurried forward and on March 5th the British forces covered Medenine, the gateway to Tunisia, with 500 anti-tank guns and 400 tanks. That day Field Marshal Rommel addressed his troops in the mountains. He told them that unless Medenine was recaptured the days of the Axis forces in Africa were numbered. Next day his three panzer divisions smashed at this vital objective. The anti-tank gunners won the battle single-handed, 52 enemy tanks being left on the battlefield. Rommel immediately faced about to meet a threat to his rear from an American corps advancing through central Tunisia; whereupon General Montgomery without delay put preparations in train for an assault on the Mareth Line.

This position was 22 miles in length, stretching from the sea at Zarat to the high buttresses of the Matmata mountains. In the rear of these defences a switch line ran north and south across the El Hamma plain, with one flank resting on the Matmatas and the other against the Chott el Fedzada, an impassable salt marsh. This switch line covered the port of Gabes and prevented approach from the west. The Matmata mountain block could be by-passed to the south-west but only after a circuitous march of nearly 200 miles through broken and waterless country. French sources had reported this route as unfeasible, but Long Range Desert Group after reconnaissance early in the year declared it to be difficult but passable.

Once again the right jab and left hook gave Eighth Army its battle plan. 30 Corps would smash frontally at the Mareth Line and the coastal corridor while 2 New Zealand Division, reinforced to corps strength by additional armour, would essay the long detour around the Matmatas with a view to bringing Rommel's panzers to decisive battle on the El Hamma switch line.

As an element in the right jab under 30 Corps Fourth Indian Division moved forward and concentrated on the left flank of the Mareth position confronting the high eastern haunches of the Matmatas. Here 7 Brigade relieved a brigade of 7 Armoured Division on March 12th. At this juncture, Lieut.-Colonel Lovett of 1/2 Gurkhas relieved Brigadier Lawrenson, whose health was not of the best. The new brigadier, affectionately known in the Division as "Os", had served throughout his military career with his regiment. A man of intense vitality and great physical strength, he possessed the tough, realistic outlook invaluable to the front-line soldier. " 'Os' is always on the ball" said one of his subordinates admiringly. Lieut.-Colonel L. C. J. Showers was recalled from duty at Allied Force Headquarters at Algiers, to take command of 1/2 Gurkha Rifles.

On the morning of March 15th this battalion returned from a successful investigation of the El Djouamea Pass, a deep cleft leading into the heart of the Matmata mountains. They had covered a great distance (estimated by one of the officers at 40 miles) and had brought back prisoners. On March 16th a preliminary operation to destroy the enemy's last covering positions on the Mareth Line involved all elements of 30 Corps. The participation of Fourth Indian Division was restricted to a raid by 1/2 Gurkhas, who under the leadership of Captain Ramsay-Brown overran a platoon position containing a nest of medium and light machine-guns. Not a shot was fired by the raiders but in an eerie scene in bright moonlight at least 9 Germans died under the kukris. One prisoner, a Viennese sergeant, was brought back to identify 164 Infantry Division. One Gurkha rifleman was killed and one wounded. The raiders were accompanied in this signal exploit by George Lait, a Californian war correspondent who wrote a thrilling if somewhat gruesome narrative of the encounter. A press agency made great play of his story, which apparently struck the American front pages on a dull day. Overnight the Indian troops became news in the United States. A number of correspondents received cabled rebukes for their neglect of such colourful allies. "Why have I not been told of these Gurkhas before?" enquired one irate editor. A month before forgotten, the spotlight now focussed on Fourth Indian Division.

The assault on the Mareth Line was due to open on the evening of March 20th. 50 Division was entrusted with the task of smashing through the main system of fortifications along the Wadi Zig Zaou, a deep and wide nullah which had been heavily fortified as outworks to the main defensive positions. For this attack 4/16 Punjabis were placed under the command of 69 Brigade on the left flank of the assault area, with instructions to hold Point 33, a knoll from which enemy machine gunners might enfilade the battlefield. The remainder of 7 Brigade was briefed under command of 23 Armoured Brigade for an exploitation role after the break-through. 5 Brigade would be employed in a similar capacity under 50 Division when a hole had been punched in the defences.

At 2200 hours on March 20th under a brilliant full moon a heavy artillery barrage heralded the new battle. 151 Brigade of 50 Division forced its way across Wadi Zig Zaou and established a bridgehead. With the battle apparently going well 5 Brigade came forward, reaching its assembly position after a fatiguing march of 17 miles. Arriving at 0200 hours amid the thunder of battle the tired sepoys endeavoured to snatch some sleep before their turn came.

The Tyneside infantry of 50 Division had gallantly stormed the enemy outworks but the barrage had failed to blast a hole in the main defences. Throughout March 21st fierce fighting continued. At this juncture the situation on the Wadi Zig Zaou gave rise to anxiety. This moat was 200 feet wide and 20 feet deep, with sheer banks on either side. Its bottom consisted of soft wet mud with a trickle of shallow water in the centre. The enemy artillery and mortars had ranged this obstacle to a yard and enfilade guns raked it from the left flank; as a result the Northumbrian sappers suffered heavy casualties as they strove to build crossings. One bridge was completed but was of such temporary nature that it was decided to send over tracks rather than wheels—a momentous decision. Instead of establishing an anti-tank screen a force of Valentine tanks crossed to support of the infantry. Under the caterpillars the crossing collapsed, and on the evening of March 22nd British infantry and light tanks were isolated on the far bank of the wadi. That same night heavy rains fell and storm water completed the destruction of the crossing. The weather bogged down Desert Air Force so that ideal conditions were created for the enemy counterstroke. On the afternoon of March 23rd 15 Panzer Division supported by a brigade of 90 Light Division and the Ramcke paratroops struck at the luckless Northumbrians and recaptured most of the bridgehead.

Until a firm crossing had been built on the Wadi Zig Zaou the coastal offensive was held up. Fourth Indian Division Sappers and Miners were placed under command of 50 Division and ordered forward to undertake this vital task. Lieut.-Colonel Blundell decided to rush through two temporary bridges of steel mesh stretched over fascines. 11 Field Park Company was given a few hours to make 150 bundles ten feet in length and two feet in diameter. On the evening of March 22nd between dusk and moonrise this material was carried to positions short of the wadi. 4 Field Company under Major Murray and 12 Field Company under Major Cameron moved forward. Sections of sappers began to break down the eastern bank for the approach ramps, while others dropped into the bed of the wadi to work on the crossings.

The enemy was alert. As the moon rose in the east the workmen on the eastern lip of the wadi were silhouetted in plain view. When fire opened British covering detachments replied. From front and rear over the heads of the sappers tracer shell, mortars and sheets of machine-gun fire streamed. The field guns joined in; between the walls of shell the engineers grappled with their task. The area around the Wadi Zig Zaou was transformed into a block of dust and fumes, shot with flames rising into the luminous sky.

On the approaches to the wadi vehicles continued to unload infantry for the coming assault. The press of transport blocked the sapper lorries carrying the steel mesh. In the wadi itself in the midst of an ear-splitting din and a hail of bullets the work proceeded calmly and steadily. Madrassi and Sikh Sappers and Miners lived up to the cool and imperturbable behaviour of their officers. Major W. J. A. Murray and Lieut. J. R. S. Baldwin of 4 Field Company, Major John Cameron and Subedar Sampangiraj of 12 Company supervised the tasks as calmly as though on exercises. Lieut.-Colonel John Blundell was everywhere, with his cheery laugh and exhortations. He pointed out how safe others must be since a man of his height remained unhit. (Actually the peak of his cap had been shot off). A Cheshire officer reached the wadi to ask for radio detectors in order to clear a way to one of his men who had been blown up on a minefield. Without hesitation Lieut.-Colonel Blundell and a sapper proceeded to the rescue. When the sapper was hit by a fixed line machine-gun Lieut.-Colonel Blundell sheltered him with his body and carried him to safety.

Hour by hour the work continued. Small groups of men dashed forward a few yards at a time to deliver material to the workers in the cleft of the Wadi. The ramps were cut, the fascines laid, the ballast spread to make firm crossings. At 0300 hours the shoot died away. Ninety minutes later enemy guns opened with extremely heavy concentrations which seemed to herald a counter-attack. Amid a torrent of shells the crossings received their final touches. Wadi Zig Zaou had been bridged.

It was now time to withdraw. The Sappers and Miners might have been pardoned had they scurried for safety. But along the wadi the assault infantry waited. Before withdrawal Lieut.-Colonel Blundell explained to his men that it might have an unfortunate effect upon these troops if men were seen running to the rear. He therefore ordered that all should move back at a casual pace, chatting and joking as if on some ordinary occasion. The CRE himself walked even more slowly than the others, stopping often to speak to infantry groups, explaining the situation. On such occasions the Sappers and Miners halted around their officer, moving on only when he moved. This cool behaviour was not wasted. After the battle a number of units testified to the heartening effect of the calm and confident bearing of the Indian Sappers and Miners.

On this same evening General Montgomery had reached a radical decision. Rommel's crack troops had been identified on the eastern flank, where the right jab had been blocked. Whereupon the Army Commander without delay switched roles and made the left hook his knock-out blow. The New Zealanders had made good time in their stealthy approach around the left flank. 1 Armoured Division now was despatched to reinforce them, with instructions to hurry. The intention was to smash through the El Hamma switch line before Afrika Korps could disengage on the Mareth front.

An alternative enterprise also presented itself. From Medenine a secondary road traversed the Matmatas to emerge at the Hallouf gap 35 miles to the west. Soon after entering the mountains this road split, with one branch turning into the north and climbing to the crests at Toujane and Techine. Thence it dropped down through Matmata village and Beni Zelten into canyons which opened on the Gabes plain in the rear of the Mareth positions. If these mountain tracks could be brought under control concurrently with the arrival of the left hook against El Hamma, 150 miles would be cut from the supply lines of the New Zealanders. In addition, there dangled a glittering possibility. The route to the plains over the tops of the mountains offered (on paper at least) the opportunity to thrust a force into the rear of both the Mareth Line and the El Hamma positions. Thereby the straight jab and the left swing would be supplemented by a short hook to the enemy's most vulnerable point. General Montgomery designated the opening of the Hallouf Pass as Fourth Division's immediate objective. Thereafter the seizure of Techine on the north-eastern spurs of the Matmatas would assure control of the mountain block. Should the main battle still be in progress when Fourth Division reached the crest of the Matmatas General Tuker decided to mask or to by-pass Toujane and to throw his brigades into the Gabes plain with the utmost expedition.

At long last a decisive and individual role had been alloted to Fourth Indian Division. General Tuker quickly picked up the threads, reclaimed his formations from their marchings and counter-marchings, secured the release of 5 Brigade from 7 Armoured Division, 4/16 Punjabis from 69 Brigade, and organised for the task of forcing the Matmatas. 7 Brigade was despatched to the south to encircle the main buttresses, passing through Khordache Gap into the Gabes plain. 5 Brigade was ordered to thrust through the mountains and to seize Hallouf, thereafter turning north to clear the crests. 7 Brigade on reaching Hallouf would enter the Pass from the west, and would follow behind 5 Brigade to assist or exploit as needed. The summits won, both brigades would resolve into mobile battle groups for the descent into the plain.

On the night of March 24/25 5 Brigade concentrated at the eastern entrance to Hallouf Pass. 1/9 Gurkhas led the advance, with 1/4 Essex closed up to take over the running. 4/6 Rajputana Rifles were detached to enter a valley four miles to the north, where a track led upwards along a deep defile. The mission of the Rajputana Rifles was to distract the enemy by simulating an advance towards Toujane and by simultaneously protecting the right flank of the true thrust towards Hallouf. The immediate task of Lieut.-Colonel Scott's men was to seize the high features overlooking Medinine which were believed to be held by the enemy.

At the entrance to Hallouf Pass a minefield was encountered. In Tunisia the technique of mine-laying had been greatly elaborated. No

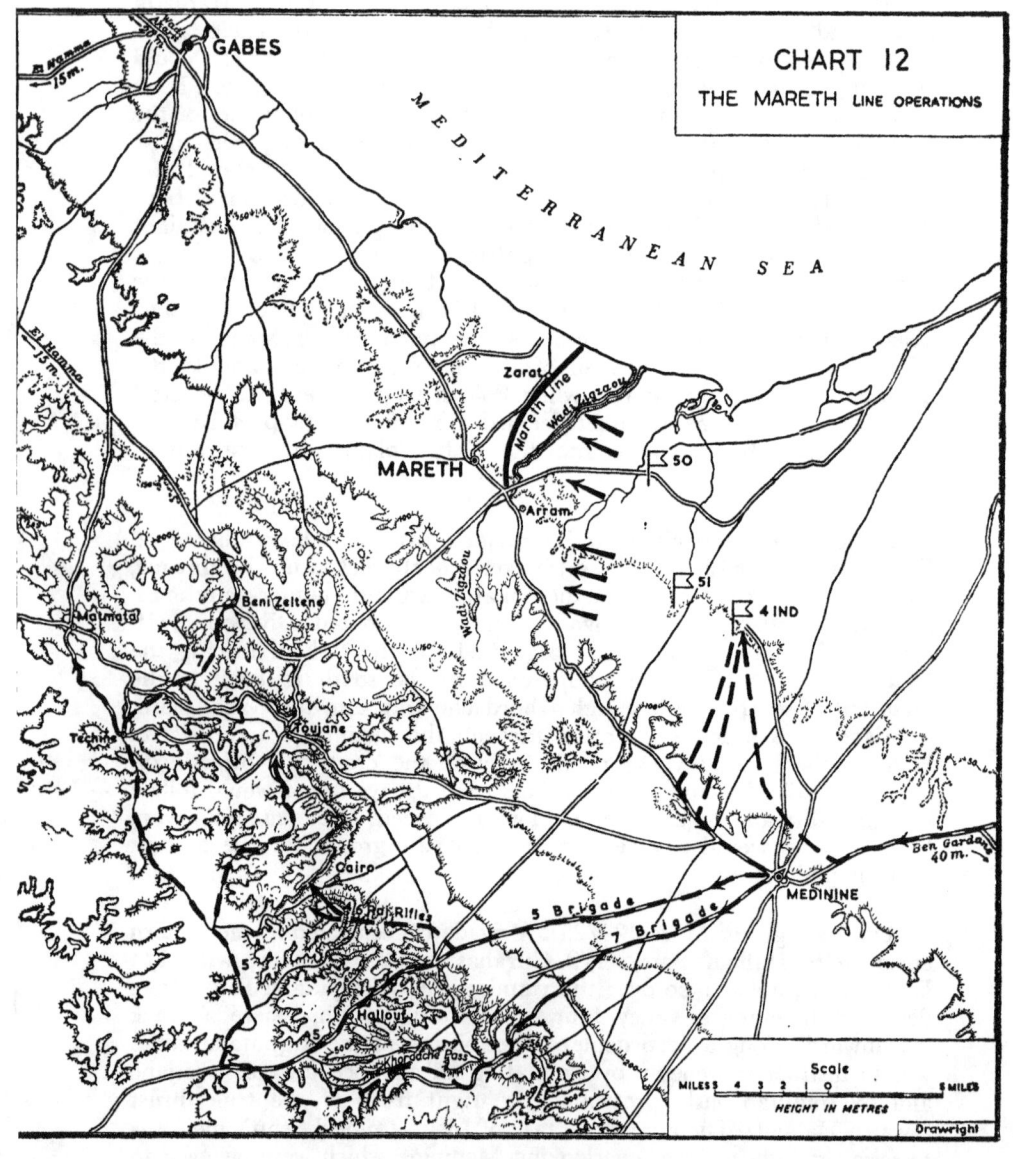

longer were regular patterns of simple soup-plate-and-plunger mines to be anticipated. Instead a fiendish variety of deadly types and a multiplicity of sowing practices complicated the task of cleansing the ground. There were the long Italian "N" mines like lengths of rail; heavy Tellermines which might be buried singly or in sets; paratroop anti-tank mines like oversized finger bowls; square French mines; shrapnel or "S" mines filled with ball bearings which sprang breast-high before exploding; limpet mines shaped like Chianti bottles. (The small schu mines, destined to be so deadly in Italy, had not yet appeared). These infernal machines were sown at depths at which prodding bayonets could not reach them. They were armed for delayed action so that a number of vehicles might pass over them before exploding. Plastic and wooden cases gave no response to the radio detectors. Trip wire and booby-trap technique had been improved until any inanimate object on the battlefield might conceal destruction. Allied Force Headquarters recently had reported two particularly foul devices—booby-traps disguised as cakes of chocolate and as field dressing packets. This elaboration in design and in sowing practices represented the enemy's efforts to develop a defensive instrument which would impose sufficient delays to permit its employers to disengage from any battlefield and to regroup without molestation.

It was not until after midnight on March 24/25 that the Sappers and Miners had cleared the entrance to Hallouf Pass. 1/9 Gurkhas thrust down the road along a narrow winding ravine. No opposition was encountered in the first few miles but the advance was slowed down by the discovery that the verges of the road were heavily mined. When vehicles passed in opposite directions they clung to every inch of safety, scraping and jostling to avoid the dangerous shoulders. All possible by-passes and turn-outs were mined. Nevertheless fair progress was made until towards morning, when a demolition completely blocked the road. Sappers came forward to clear away and reported 15 hours delay before the track could be reopened. As work began foot patrols of "B" Company of 1/4 Essex passed the block and explored ahead. At dawn the advance continued into the heart of the mountains. Early in the forenoon the enemy was located. "D" Company of the Essex in a quick attack overran a rear-guard, killing a number of Italians of Pistoia Division and taking 25 prisoners. The junction of the Techine trail and Hallouf road was reached early in the afternoon. The Essex explored the rolling foothills until they saw the open El Hamma plain before them. "C" Company of Rajputana Rifles machine gunners with a battery of 149 Anti-Tank Regiment took station to guard the western entrance of the Pass. Whereupon the Essex turned northward and upwards on the Techine trail, knocking out a number of unsubstantial rearguards and picking up 30 prisoners. In spite of mines, demolitions and enemy resistance, the Home County men covered ten miles during the afternoon with 1/9 Gurkhas following close behind them. A Sapper officer who accompanied the scout screen from hilltop to hilltop watched the Italians mining the roads after their rearguards had passed through. By pinpointing such positions he was able to accelerate the pursuit. Late in the afternoon the Essex screen reached a junction (known as Hardy Crossroads) on the crest of the Matmatas, where an east-west trail intersected the main track. Accurate artillery fire by German guns revealed the presence of enemy forces holding a crescent of crests only approachable along a knife-edged ridge.

Meanwhile 7 Brigade had struck heavy going in its detour through Khordache Gap. Minefields of unusual size and density were encountered. All available mine-sweepers were blown up. By dour navigation the columns eventually wriggled through. That evening Brigadier Lovett's leading elements reached the western entrance of the Hallouf road, and immediately pushed into the mountains on the trail of 5 Brigade.

4/6 Rajputana Rifles in their detached mission likewise had found trouble. At 2000 hours on March 25th the Battalion moved off to secure "Cairo" and "Delhi"—peaks approximately three miles to the north of the eastern entrance to Hallouf Pass. These features rose steeply on the flank of the main massif, "Cairo" to a height of 1500 feet and "Delhi" 500 feet higher. Their slopes were serrated by deep wadis and covered by loose rock and slippery shale. After an arduous climb the Rajputana Rifles reached the top of "Cairo" and found it unoccupied. When "C" Company moved through to explore "Delhi" it came under heavy mortar, machine-gun and anti-tank fire and was forced to ground. Fortunately the enemy fired on fixed night lines and few casualties resulted. When at daylight the Rajputana Rifles vehicles entered the ravine between "Cairo" and "Delhi" it was discovered that sniping guns commanded the approaches, and that mortar teams on secluded peaks could effectively barrage the entrance to the defile. Caught in this shoot, 7 vehicles were destroyed and 17 men wounded. Whereupon the Divisional artillery intervened with smoke and neutralised enemy observation. That evening the vehicles were extricated under cover of darkness. Early next morning enemy withdrawals were detected and on the night of March 27/28 three platoons occupied "Delhi" without resistance.

At 0800 hours on March 27th "A" Company of the Essex under Major H. C. Gregory, MC, advanced with artillery support against the Italian positions which covered Hardy Crossroads. The line of attack lay along the track on the crest of the razor-backed ridge. Enemy artillery opened; a number of vehicles were hit and the track blocked. Finding the advance at a standstill General Tuker came forward and ordered the road to be cleared by pushing the damaged vehicles over the cliff sides. He gave positive orders that the position must be forced by nightfall. In early afternoon the Essex dashed to the close with the bayonet. The Italians broke, leaving behind 116 prisoners and numerous dead and wounded in return for nine Essex casualties.

The Home County men pushed on and late in the afternoon reached the junction where the uplands road divided, the right fork leading to

VICTORIA CROSS

"For Supreme Valour"

HIS EXCELLENCY THE VICEROY, FIELD MARSHAL WAVELL, PRESENTS VICTORIA CROSS TO THE MOTHER OF RIFLEMAN SHERBAHADUR VC, 1/9 GURKHA RIFLES.

HIS EXCELLENCY THE VICEROY, FIELD MARSHAL WAVELL, PRESENTS GEORGE CROSS TO THE MOTHER OF SOWAR DITTO RAM, GC, CENTRAL INDIA HORSE.

Lieut. St. J. G. Young GC,
Central India Horse.

Subedar Richpal Ram VC,
4 Battalion (Outrams) 6 Rajputana Rifles.

Subedar Subramanyan GC,
11 Field Park Company, Q.V.O. Madras Sappers and Miners.

Company Havildar-Major Chhelu Ram VC,
4 Battalion (Outrams) 6 Rajputana Rifles.

Subedar Lalbahadur Thapa VC,
1/2 King Edwards Own Goorkha Rifles.

GEORGE CROSS

"For Selfless Sacrifice"

Toujane and thence across the northern spurs of the Matmatas to the Beni Zelten defile, the left fork leading to Matmata village by way of Techine. 4/16 Punjabis under command of 5 Brigade passed through and blocked the right fork, despatching patrols to Toujane. The Essex thrust along the left road and reached the queer village of Techine, where the inhabitants lived underground, with only tombs on the surface. The troglodytes entered their galleries and caves by means of shafts in the hillsides as well as by way of sheer-sided quarries and rope ladders. The enemy had already retired from the village, leaving a small blocking force covering the road to the north.

Meanwhile 7 Brigade, less 4/16 Punjabis, were engaged in reconnoitering the Beni Zelten defile, through which the Division might descend into the Gabes plain. Patrols reached the top of the pass at mid-day on March 27th. The road hung on the side of a steep ravine. There had been no demolitions but stretches of the stone abutments had crumbled and fallen away leaving wide gaps. Lieut.-Colonel Blundell and Major Murray with 4 Field Company hurried forward. Rock drills and a bulldozer were eased down to the first gap and began to cut away the overhang. 1/2 Gurkhas formed four human chains on the side of the gorge to pass up stones which the sappers built up into a retaining wall. Brigadier Lovett reported that if the work continued all night, wheeled vehicles might start down at midnight, but in view of the nature of the task, it was deemed wiser to suspend labour at dusk.

That evening Fourth Indian Division had completed two-thirds of its allotted task. It had opened a supply route to the western flank of the Mareth battlefield and it had seized the heights above the El Hamma plain. There now remained the exciting prospect of intervening in the battle below. Early in the afternoon of March 28th the leading elements of the Division began the descent of the defile. Behind the infantry the guns gingerly edged down the ravine; as a war correspondent put it, "clinging to a gossamer of road spun along the cliff side". 7 Brigade led the way. On reaching the mouth of the defile, a secure base was established and patrols were despatched to locate the enemy. It was then learned that the battle was over. On the morning of March 27th, while the New Zealanders grappled with the main body of the enemy, 1 Armoured Division had penetrated the opposite flank of the defences and had swung towards Gabes to strike at Rommel's rear. The German commander, never slow off the mark, disengaged abruptly and fled. As 7 Brigade patrols bowled across the plain towards the sea they overran an Italian rearguard of 100 men.

Fourth Indian Division had played a minor rôle in the victory. It had not been entrusted with either of the major thrusts and the opening of the Hallouf Pass had proved a mountain exercise rather than a battle. (460 prisoners were taken in return for less than 100 casualties, nearly all from mines). Nevertheless it served to demonstrate in no uncertain fashion that the Division was a battle instrument with a particular aptitude for mountain warfare. The speed and power of its thrust, the ability to surmount obstacles and to improvise, were the hall-marks of a first-class fighting machine.

Every unit had delivered the goods. 4/16 Punjabis had given a firm flank, the Sappers and Miners had built the Wadi Zig Zaou bridges. 7 Brigade had burst through minefields and had kept up with its time-table. The Rajputana Rifles had seized the heights, Gurkhas and Essex had cleared the roads at top speed, infantry and sappers had opened Beni Zelten defile in several hours under the estimated time. Each of these small successes fitted into a mosaic of achievement to which recognition was handsomely extended by the Corps commander;

"I write to congratulate you and all ranks of the Fourth Indian Division on your splendid work in the mountains during the Mareth Battle.

"You were called upon to carry out a difficult task at immediate notice. You were very short of MT and you had no time to collect mountain warfare equipment. Nevertheless, you accomplished your task with complete success, crossing difficult mountainous country, clearing extensive mined areas and driving in strong enemy resistance.

"Your advance turned the southern extremity of the Mareth Line and contributed strongly to the enemy's enforced withdrawal, a withdrawal which by a few hours only robbed your Division of a large haul of enemy personnel and equipment.

"I am very proud once again to have Fourth Indian Division in 30 Corps, and I congratulate all ranks on an outstanding performance—which could have only been carried out by troops highly trained in mountain warfare".

Confidence in the ability of Indian troops to deal with the principal enemy had been restored. The tide had turned and great days were near at hand.

Chapter 17

WADI AKARIT

HAVING been ejected from the Mareth Line Rommel may have wished to adhere to desert strategy, which had taught him to disengage defeated forces with the utmost speed and to motor out of danger. Had this been possible, his next lay-back positions would have been the ramparts of the main Tunisian mountain block, 150 miles to the north. But the much-publicised Axis commander no longer was master of his fate. He was now an element in an overall defence system and obliged to conform to the requirements of others. A battle was in progress 80 miles to his right flank rear, where II U.S. Corps was endeavouring to thrust into southern Tunisia by way of El Guettar and Gafsa. This advance, together with British First Army's assault on the western outworks of the Tunisian fortress, limited Rommel's independence of manoeuvre. The chief Axis requirement of the moment was to prevent the junction of General Montgomery's troops with the North African Allied armies. Afrika Korps and its satellite divisions therefore must give as little ground as possible. As a consequence Rommel sought a defensive position near at hand. Almost at his elbow he found it.

Twenty miles to the north of Gabes the impassable Fedjadi salt marshes extend for 120 miles inland, and a gap of less than 15 miles separates the beginnings of these soft sloughs from the Mediterranean. Across two-thirds of this gap stands Djebel Zemlet el Beida, a high puckered ridge system which divides the Gabes from the Sfax plain. As at Mareth, a neck of flat foreshore joins the plains. Here too, as at Mareth, a broad and deep nullah interposes its moat between the sea and the high ground. Five miles inland the Roumana saddleback, approximately 500 feet in height and a mile in length, runs into the north-west on a bearing roughly parallel to the coast. To the west of Roumana, the easy contours of a series of rolling hills extend for two miles before ending in the fantastic pile of Fatnassa. This freakish and outlandish agglomeration of high ground is reminiscent of a Disney drawing. A series of transverse crests merge in a labyrinthine tangle of pinnacles, escarpments, counter-escarpments, deep fjord-like chimneys and corridors. On the left of this wild tangle a ravine pierces the El Beida feature, carrying a military road which connects the two plains. Beyond the road the high ground falls away in a series of cones and ridges until five miles to the south-west the barrier ends within a mile of the oozy shore of the salt marshes.

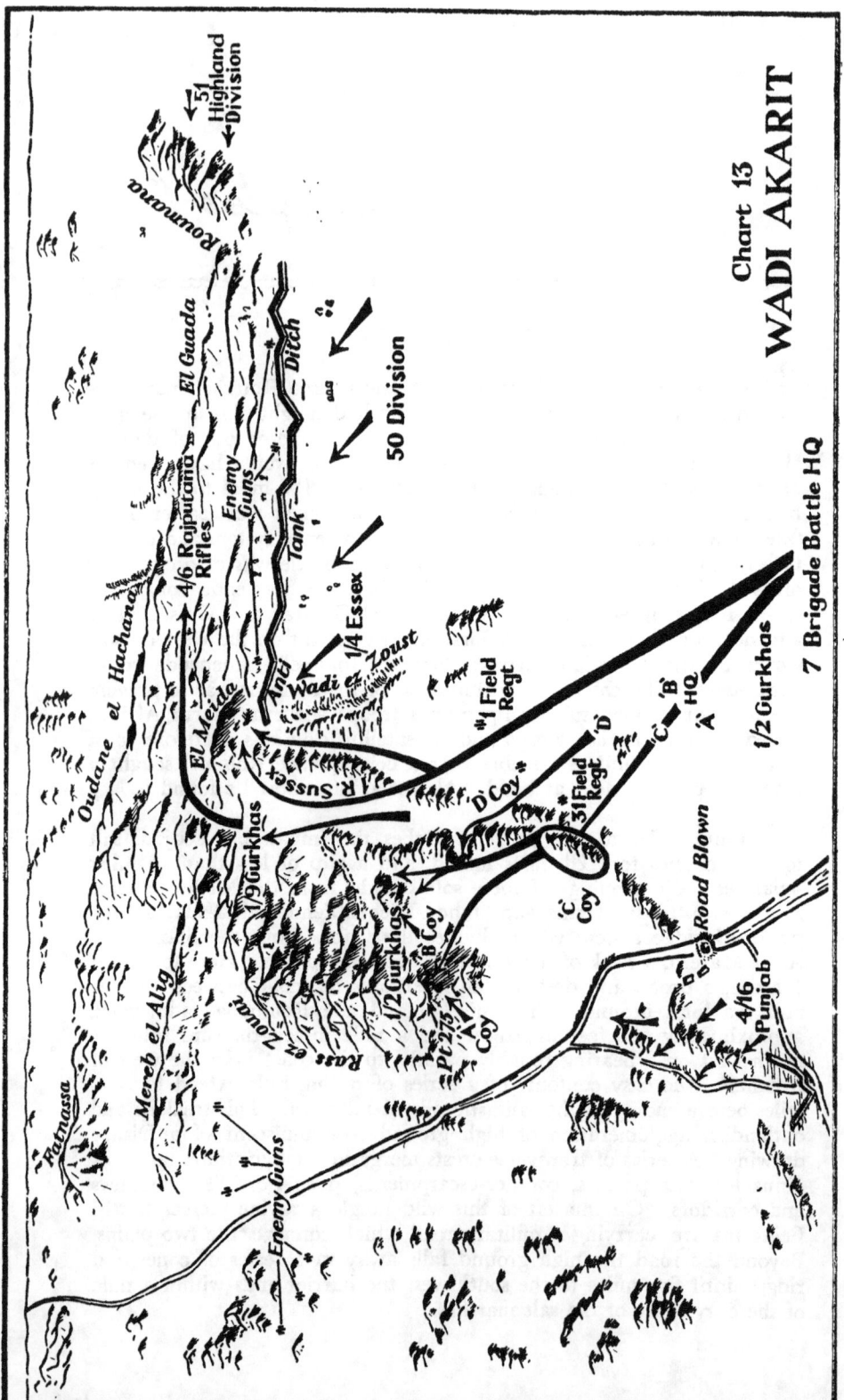

Field-Marshal Rommel recognised both the strength and the weakness of this position. Remembering the number of times that General Montgomery's mobile forces had turned his flank he must have been grateful for the quagmires on his right. He need fear no left hook here. In other directions the lie of the land left much to be desired. The barricade of high ground was shallow since a bare three miles separated the Gabes and Sfax plains. Moreover, the low rolling ridges which connected Roumana and Fatnassa weakened the position: a short advance across this easy ground brought the rear slopes of Roumana under fire. To stiffen this central sector Rommel had hastily constructed an anti-tank ditch two miles in length which continued the obstacle of the Akarit nullah across the base of the rolling ridges. On the western flank Fatnassa appeared to offer an insuperable obstacle, and it seemed obvious that Eighth Army's attack would be staged against the easier ground along the Mediterranean foreshore.

When General Montgomery began to plan his battle, he accepted this view and concentrated his strength against the coastal sector. 51 Highland Division was given the task of overrunning Wadi Akarit and of opening a passage through which tanks would plunge to complete the rupture. Fourth Indian Division would protect the left flank of the main assault by seizing Roumana and by holding it as a barrier against counter-attack from the west until the British armour had fulfilled its mission.

There were elements in this plan which General Tuker did not like. The new operation promised to be a mountain battle. One of the axioms of mountain warfare is that the second highest ground is no good at all. Roumana was commanded by Fatnassa and easily approachable from the north. Should British tanks fail to break through, Fourth Indian Division would be left sitting on the thin edge of nothing, "holding the baby". Roumana might prove another Majuba.

When the Divisional Commander voiced his fears, he was asked for an alternative proposal. He declared that the battlefield should be widened and that the entire Zemlet-el-Beida barrier should be brought under attack. With such a shallow defense system penetration anywhere would be decisive. He therefore was prepared to commit Fourth Indian Division to an assault on the twisty mazes of Fatnassa. If won, the other Akarit sectors became untenable. General Montgomery saw the force of these representations. 50 Division was brought into the battle to attack frontally against the anti-tank ditch and the rolling ground between Roumana and Fatnassa. The timing was arranged to allow Fourth Division to open the battle with a silent night attack several hours before the main assault, in order to obtain the advantages of surprise on the most difficult terrain.

When General Tuker examined in detail the battlefield which he had chosen, he may well have wondered whether he was not asking too much of his men. The configuration of Fatnassa suggested appalling difficulties, not only in the initial assault but in exploiting any gains. On the frontal approach the club-shaped pinnacle of Point 275 stood sentry over the plain. To its rear the long high escarpment of Rass Zouai ran back to Mereb el Alig, a slender peninsula of high ground which thrust into the west with precipitous boulder-strewn slopes on either side. Behind Mereb el Alig a deep *cul de sac* like a blocked canyon separated Fatnassa, the highest ground of all, from the frontal features. To the east the mountain block gradually fell into the rolling ridges, but the high kopje of el Meida stood out like a battlement on the edge of the easy ground. Against this butte the enemy's anti-tank ditch ended.

In front of El Meida a number of escarpments ran into the plain. Two of these ridges converged to form a chimney which led inwards towards the crest of the main escarpment. This narrow passage between high rocky ridges extended before the main body of the mountain, like an elephant's trunk outthrust in trumpeting. It afforded a corridor by which the dominating peak at the front of the system, Point 275, could be by-passed. It also offered a line of approach to the crest of the el Meida feature. Like a secret passage in a castle it supplied a covered way into the keep of the defences. It was obvious that this curious corridor would be strongly defended. Nevertheless General Tuker believed that he had the men to deal with it. In battle, add mountains to darkness and the sum is confusion compounded—unless the fighting men are cat-eyed, cat-footed and trained in the peculiar crafts of hill warfare.

The Divisional Commander was confident of the capacity of his troops. He was sure that he had correctly assessed the lie of the battlefield. Nevertheless he was constantly aware that he was pledging his men in a desperate enterprise which might be beyond their strength, and from which they could not easily withdraw when once they had been committed to battle. No more serious responsibility can confront any commander. It says much for General Tuker's courage that at a time when Fourth Indian Division alone represented India in the war in the west he refused to play safe and unhesitatingly planned a daring and decisive operation.*

He decided to strike not only to win Fatnassa but to win the battle. 7 Brigade was ordered to seize and hold the mountain block while 5 Brigade plunged through and punched a hole to the Sfax plains. A usable track led across the rolling ridges between Fatnassa and Roumana. If 5 Brigade burst through and British tanks followed quickly, the battle could be won in the centre, no matter what happened on the coast.

*In examining the challenging terrain of Fatnassa, General Tuker quoted to Brigadier Lovett, also a hunting man, Adam Lindsay Gordon's famous advice on tricky hurdles:

'Look before you leap,
But if you mean leaping, dont look long,
For the weakest fence will then grow stiff
And the stiffest doubly strong'.

On April 1st both Brigades of Fourth Division, concentrated in the Gabes area, were placed at four hours' notice for the move forward to the new battlefield. On the night of April 2nd they were carried up the coastal road to the small village of Oudref, pleasingly situated in the midst of extensive palm plantations. Patrols were sent out that night from both brigades. 1/4 Essex reconnoitred the anti-tank ditch while 1/2 Gurkhas explored the entrance to the corridor between the escarpments. 164 and 90 Light Divisions were reported as holding Fatnassa, the intervening rolling ground and Roumana. Italian formations from Pistoia, Spezia and Trieste Divisions were interspersed under German command. 21 Panzer Division was concentrated in close support.

The plan of battle called for the assault by 50 and 51 Divisions to begin at 0430 hours on the morning of April 6th.* 5 and 7 Brigades would begin their approach march as soon as dark fell on the previous evening. 1/2 Gurkhas would lead the silent attack, striking for the key Fatnassa features. 1 Royal Sussex would seize the el Meida kopje at the end of the anti-tank ditch. 4/16 Punjabis would remain in brigade reserve. Platoons of Rajputana Rifle machine-gunners would accompany the assault battalions.

On the evening of April 5th a slender sickle moon hung in a nacre sky. As dusk fell 7 Brigade began to move forward from Oudref with units in single file. The line of advance along Star Track crossed the main road near Divisional Headquarters, where General Tuker stood watching the heavily laden infantrymen trudge forward over the rolling crests. The night was cool with a slight ground mist. Enemy planes, well aware of the imminent attack, quartered the area with parachute flares.

Near a track junction 2000 yards to the south-east of Fatnassa Brigadier Lovett set up his battle headquarters. Tape layers moved off at once to the start line. As the leading Gurkha platoons had been over-running these guides, a halt was ordered at the cross tracks until the remainder of the Brigade closed up. "D" Company of 1/2 Gurkhas then headed directly for the double row of jagged cliffs which marked the escarpment chimney. The remainder of the battalion, with "C" Company leading, swung slightly left. Shortly after midnight the guiding peak of Point 275 disappeared behind the black shadow of the escarpment ahead. The foremost platoons of "C" Company came under the ridge and began to pick their way silently up the slopes.

The first sentry encountered was asleep. He never awakened. The leading section sprang into a sangar, cutting down the unwary Italians. Screams broke upon the night, answered by shouting from the crests

*Mr. Churchill unwittingly erred in reporting this battle in the House of Commons. While paying full tribute to the rôle played by Fourth Division, he gave zero hour for the British divisions as the beginning of the battle.

above. "C" Company hurriedly scrambled to the top of the escarpment and closed against defenders firing wildly into the darkness. The knives took toll, and to watchers in the plain below came an eerie sound—an excited whimper not unlike hounds finding scent—as the Gurkhas, swarming over the high ground, guided each other with shrill voices. Close behind "C" Company, "A" and "B" Companies plunged into the battle. "A" Company lunged at Point 275, 1,000 yards to the north-west. On reaching the base of the pinnacle the leading platoons swung left-handed, working their way onto the south-east approach where easy slopes rose from the valley which carried the military road. Clambering rapidly to the top the Gurkhas found only an artillery observation post which gave little trouble. The first objective had been won.

"B" Company meanwhile had thrust along the line of the escarpment to the right of Point 275. Here a number of ridges converged, creating a small bowl like a natural amphitheatre. In this maze of broken ground progress might have been slow had not the enemy obligingly cast light on the situation. His reconnaissance planes hung parachute flares directly over the line of advance. "This Guy Fawkes show was grand", said an officer of the Gurkhas, "for we could see exactly where we wanted to go". Within an hour "B" Company had advanced nearly a mile along the escarpment into the depths of the enemy's defences and stood well in the rear of Point 275. At 0130 hours its success signal went up.

This welcome sight was the first tidings received, for by an unfortunate coincidence both 7 Brigade and Gurkha signallers had suffered severely in the storm of enemy fire which curtained the approaches to Rass ez Zouai. A salvo of mortar bombs hit 7 Brigade Headquarters destroying both the infantry wireless sets and those of the artillery observation groups which had come forward to arrange supporting fire. Brigadier Lovett was wounded but retained command. In default of tidings Lieut.-Colonel Showers of the Gurkhas went forward to ascertain the position. An anxious hour passed in which "A" and "B" Companies had gone off the map, while from the all-important corridor between the escarpments into which "D" Company had disappeared came the crash and rattle of heavy exchanges. What happened there cannot be better described than in *The Tiger Kills*:

"The dense darkness of that boulder-studded ravine hid a great feat of arms. Under command of Subedar Lalbahadur Thapa, two sections of Gurkhas had moved forward to secure the only pathway which led over the escarpment at the upper end of the rocky chimney. This trail reached the top of the hill through a narrow cleft thickly studded with enemy posts. Anti tank-guns and machine-guns covered every foot of the way, while across the canyon, where the cliffs rose steeply for some 200 feet, the crests were swarming with automatic gunners and mortar teams. Subedar Lalbahadur Thapa reached the first enemy sangar without challenge. His section cut down its garrison with the kukri. Immediately every post along the twisty pathway opened fire. Without pause the intrepid Subedar, with no room to manoeuvre, dashed forward at the head of his men through a sleet of machine-gun fire, grenades and mortar bombs. He leapt inside a machine-gun nest and killed four gunners single-handed, two with knife and two with pistol. Man after man of his sections were stricken until only two were left. Rushing on, he clambered up the last few yards of the defile through which the pathway snaked over the crest of the escarpment. He flung himself single-handed on the garrison of the last sangar covering the pathway, striking two enemies dead with his kukri. This terrible foe was too much; the remainder of the detachment fled with wild screams for safety. The chimney between the escarpments was open, and with it the corridor through which 5 Brigade might pass. It is scarcely too much to say that the battle of Wadi Akarit had been won single-handed several hours before the formal attack began".

This magnificent achievement won for Lalbahadur Thapa the Victoria Cross. It is interesting to note, as illustrative of the high standards prevailing, that Colonel Showers recommended the dauntless Subedar for an immediate Military Cross. The Army Commander on reading the citation increased the recommendation to that of the supreme award for valour.

Immediately behind 1/2 Gurkhas 1 Royal Sussex deployed. Soon after 2100 hours the South Country men began to move forward across the plain on a bearing parallel to the Gurkhas but slightly to their right . Their line of advance took them past the mouth of the corridor and into a re-entrant of low ground which ran up to the base of the el Meida kopje. As the Gurkha attack went in, enemy defensive fire fell on the forward Sussex companies causing many casualties. The battalion radio sets, as in the case of the Gurkhas, were knocked out. By 0130 hours Royal Sussex were within 1,000 yards of their objective, but the adjutant had been wounded and the companies were operating more or less independently. Some confusion prevailed; the attack lost direction and fell behind timing. At 0230 hours Lieut.-Colonel Firth asked for a directional crash shoot on el Meida. The Divisional gunners responded by laying down lines of tracer and with a heavy concentration. At 0400 hours a second shoot pounded el Meida. Under its cover "D" Company followed by "B" and "C" Companies worked their way along the serrated and rugged lip of the escarpment. Within thirty minutes el Meida and 600 yards of the western end of the anti-tank ditch had been captured, together with 300 prisoners from Spezia Division. Lieut.-Colonel Firth went forward on reconnaissance and reached Point 152 among the ridges of Ouidane el Hachana. Here enemy armoured cars were encountered. Dawn found the Royal Sussex busily consolidating their gains, having gouged a hole in the enemy's defensive system at a cost of 8 killed and 59 wounded.

50 Division's frontal assault on the anti-tank ditch was now in full swing. The left flank Brigade of the Tynesiders had been pinned down. A platoon of Royal Sussex passed into the rear of the anti-tank obstacle

and charged with the bayonet, capturing four 65 mm. guns and a number of prisoners. These weapons were immediately turned on nearby enemy batteries and mortar teams which were shelling the attacking Northumbrian brigade.

Meanwhile 4/16 Punjabis had entered the battle. When the enemy's defensive fire came down, Brigadier Lovett ordered Lieut.-Colonel Hughes to advance and clear the line of the escarpment on the left of the defile through which the military road ran. The Punjabis had watched the fireworks on Rass ez Zouai with impatience; when the order to advance came their leading company under Capt. W. G. Popple more or less charged from its start line. Carrying parties moving up were overtaken by groups of figures dashing forward with wild yells in the darkness. An officer present paraphrased the Duke of Wellington's remarks about his recruits. "I don't know how the enemy felt about it", he wrote, "but they certainly scared me". The Punjabis raced across the military road and flung themselves at their objective, held by elements of Pistoia Division. Having cleared the first ridges "D" Company swept uphill against a high buttress. The demoralised Italians proved easy prey. Throughout the morning the Punjabis continued to mop up, delivering a tally of 800 prisoners and a number of enemy mortars, which at once went into action against their former owners.

Dawn found battle raging on a front of 12 miles between Fatnassa and the sea. On the right the Highlanders had broken into the Wadi Akarit positions and were attacking the eastern slopes of Roumana. In the centre the enemy maintained the line of the anti-tank ditch, meeting 50 Divisions thrusts with curtains of fire and local counter-attacks. On the left, penetration continued swiftly according to plan. Before dawn the leading companies of 1/9 Gurkhas passed through Lalbahadur Thapa's corridor and thrust along the crest of the mountain block, heading for the rear of the Fatnassa feature and the open plains beyond. Ridge after ridge was stormed in quick succession. In spite of mortar fire and delaying machine-gun nests, Lieut.-Colonel Roche's men raced ahead until they reached the narrow neck between Mereb el Alig and Fatnassa. Here they topped a low ridge to sight a confusion of Italians below them. They quickly put an end to resistance and found themselves burdened with an unwieldy mass of prisoners. This blow at the heart carried 1/9 Gurkhas nearly 3,000 yards into the enemy's defences and netted upwards of 2,000 prisoners at a cost of one killed and 19 wounded.

4/6 Rajputana Rifles followed closely behind. On the approach march the battalion had passed through two curtains of defensive fire. Lieut.-Colonel Scott had been wounded but had retained command. At 0800 hours three companies advanced up the corridor between the escarpments, skirted the Royal Sussex positions on el Meida, and with the support of Rajputana Rifle machine gunners broke into Ouidane el Hachana, the rolling ridge system immediately behind the anti-tank ditch. With "D" Company in the lead they drove into the enemy's rear, mopping up machine-gun nests and rounding up prisoners. "A couple of grenades and a few bursts of tommy-gun fire resulted in white flags being vigorously waved from the stone sangars. Masses of Italians came pouring out, hands well in the air", wrote an eye-witness. Throughout the forenoon "A" and "C" Companies joined in the hunt and headed for Point 152. They penetrated half way to Roumana. From the newly-seized ground the rear of that feature and the Sfax plain came under observation. Large enemy formations could be seen in movement. This dashing advance, which gouged a deep gap in the enemy's defensive system, was accomplished at the negligible cost of 3 killed and 40 wounded. More than 1,000 prisoners were sent back.

Throughout the hours of darkness 1/4 Essex had waited at its rendezvous behind the centre of the 50 Division sector, where it had been intended to bridge the anti-tank ditch on the site of a track which wandered across Ouidane el Hachana. The Home County men had been detailed to escort the anti-tank guns across the rolling ridges to meet the remainder of 5 Brigade as it wheeled towards Roumana. Thereafter the Essex task was to cover the passage of the Divisional transport through the hills. Unfortunately the Tyneside men of 50 Division had failed to win their objectives. Again the wireless sets failed and the Essex were unable to report the delay to Divisional Headquarters. Although unbriefed for battle and on a strange front, Lieut.-Colonel Noble decided to storm the anti-tank ditch—a bold yet characteristic decision. While preparations were in train for this attack, General Tuker managed to contact the Essex from his command vehicle. He ordered them to rejoin 5 Brigade. They moved to the west through the midst of the battle and only a few hundred yards behind the firing line. The Royal Sussex and Gurkhas on the high ground watched them coming and observed their steady bearing under fire. Reaching the western end of the anti-tank ditch they joined in the work of consolidating the el Meida feature. 500 yards east of the terminus of the anti-tank obstacle a second trail across the hills was discovered. The Essex rounded up groups of Italian prisoners and started them filling in the ditch preparatory to the building of a crossing by the Divisional Sappers and Miners.

At 0845 hours 10 Corps Commander arrived at Fourth Division Headquarters. With reports from all units in hand General Tuker pinpointed his positions. An Office Note supplies the following details of the subsequent conversation:

"Commander Fourth Indian Division pointed out to Commander 10 Corps that we had broken the enemy; that the way was clear for 10 Corps to go through; that immediate offensive action would finish the campaign in North Africa. Now was the time to get the whips out and spare neither men nor machines".

"Commander 10 Corps spoke to Army Commander on the telephone requesting permission to put in 10 Corps to maintain the momentum of the attack. After this telephone conversation Commander 10 Corps said that his armour was going to go through at once, using both Fourth Indian Division's crossing over the anti-tank ditch and the one on the boundary between 50 and 51 Divisions, south-west of Roumana."

"Commander 10 Corps did not give any indication that his advance forward was restricted by bounds or by timings laid down by High Command nor that there were any administrative difficulties. GSO. 1 Fourth Indian Division immediately sent a liaison officer to the Divisional crossing over the anti-tank ditch to ensure that the armour had priority over all other traffic and to hold up Fourth Indian Division traffic as necessary for this purpose".

Shortly afterwards both 5 and 7 Brigades reported British tank columns to be on the move forward. The stage seemed set for a decisive victory.

The enemy was reeling but the knock-out blow never reached its mark. At Cambrai in 1917 a single German battery held the vital Canal du Nord crossing. Something similar seems to have occurred at Wadi Akarit. Hour by hour 51 Highland Division gathered more of the coastal sector in its teeth. Roumana fell and Rommel's battle line all but collapsed. His artillery however stuck it in tenacious fashion, particularly a group of guns firing obliquely into the west from the rear of Roumana. These guns had the anti-tank ditch ranged to a yard. Although in little more than sniping strength they maintained accurate and constant harassing fire throughout the day. One salvo took a tragic toll. All three Field Companies had come forward to work on a track which would carry the Divisional wheels across the Oudane el Hachana ridges. 4 Field Company was entrusted with the completion of the anti-tank ditch begun that morning by the 1/4 Essex. The work went forward in the customary imperturbable fashion of Indian engineers. At 1600 hours when Lieut.-Colonel John Blundell was conferring with his officers, a shell struck the little group to earth. Major W. J. A. Murray MC, commanding 4 Field Company and Captain Baldwin were killed outright, together with Lieut. Allan, an American liaison officer who had first met Fourth Division in Cyprus. Lieut.-Colonel Blundell was so seriously wounded that he died in the dressing station. Thus passed a great officer and gallant gentleman. General Tuker wrote: "He died yesterday evening, mourned by thousands of humble Indian soldiers". The Commandant of Bengal Sappers and Miners declared, "He is the greatest individual loss that this Corps has so far suffered".* Major J. A. Cameron of 12 Field Company was called to Divisional Headquarters that evening and appointed CRE.

* When this history was in course of compilation, Lieut.-Colonel Blundell's sister was approached for a photograph. She replied: "A photograph of Jack in his uniform — à la Bond Street — does not exist. He could not see himself like that. He was a workman and a dreamer".

The guns which caused this tragedy may have constituted the anti-tank screen which appears to have blocked 1 Armoured Division's break-through across the ridges. All that is certain is that precious hours passed and that when night fell on April 6th the British tanks continued to occupy defensive positions in the rear of the infantry. At dawn on April 7th, when the enemy disengagement was all but complete, the Rajputana Rifle carriers reconnoitred the Sfax plain and came back to report what General Tuker had announced 24 hours before — that the door was open. Only then did the tank columns cross the ridge and take up the pursuit.

Indeed, by mid-day on April 6th the battle had ended for all but 1/2 Gurkhas on the crests and among the mazy passages of Fatnassa. Here the enemy continued to resist vigorously. (It appeared as though the German defenders on the summits were unaware of what was happening elsewhere). When dawn broke "A" and "C" Companies of 1/2 Gurkhas had occupied positions on the western ledge of the Rass ez Zouai feature, commanding the military road in the ravine below. To the north the long rocky spur of El Alig ran at right angles to Rass ez Zouai. This finger of high ground, 300 yards in width and 1,000 yards in length, lay immediately under the dominating heights of Fatnassa across a steep-sided and rugged canyon. "B" Company was ordered to advance along Rass ez Zouai and secure a footing on El Alig at the point where it merged in the main ridge system. "C" Company edged to the right for the purpose of linking up with 1/9 Gurkhas.

This move along the crests was accomplished without undue opposition. A platoon pushed down the El Alig feature destroying a number of enemy posts in brisk *shikaring* fashion. On reaching the western tip the mopping-up squads were almost out of ammunition, and found themselves under heavy fire from machine guns and mortars on Fatnassa. They therefore withdrew and consolidated at the base of the spur.

The enemy immediately returned to El Alig. Concurrently tommy-gunners began to infiltrate up the slopes of Rass ez Zouai from the military road. Lieut.-Colonel Showers' men now were scattered along the western lip of the crest for nearly 3,000 yards with "A" Company guarding the vital Point 275 feature and "D" Company protecting the flank of the Royal Sussex in their mopping-up operations around El Meida. "B" and "C" Companies therefore were distributed in handfuls. Throughout the day individual stalking matches continued between the scattered defenders and the enemy machine-gun squads which sought to win back the summit. One Gurkha section, running short of ammunition, rolled boulders down the hillside to flush the enemy out of dead ground. Rajputana Rifle machine gunners crossed the ridge and gave valuable support to the thin line.

During the same period "A" Company on Point 275 was subjected to continuous shelling and mortar fire. The Gurkhas clung to the bare rocks and endured the ordeal. During the afternoon it appeared as though a counter-attack in strength was imminent and "D" Company moved across the ridge to thicken the defenders on the heights above the military road. An equally welcome reinforcement was the arrival of an artillery line at Battalion Headquarters. (From a communications point of view Wadi Akarit had been a most unlucky battle. Brigade and Battalion signal officers and personnel seemed to attract mortar bombs. At 0830 hours the Divisional artillery had moved across the open ridges to forward positions in full view of the enemy and except for the wholesale destruction of wireless sets would have intervened in the battle at an early stage.) At 1610 hours, with communications at last established, 31 Field Regiment from positions in front of 7 Brigade Headquarters raked Mereb el Alig with a shoot which dispersed the gathering enemy. Later in the afternoon a young German officer audaciously led a gun team up a steep chimney and gained the crest of Rass ez Zouai. Fortunately he was spotted and a section of Gurkhas led by a young rifleman closed before the machine-guns could come into action, the officer being killed.

After nightfall persistent attempts to infiltrate continued. At 0100 hours "B" Company detected the enemy advancing along the El Alig feature. As figures came into view, clearly silhouetted against the night sky, a curtain of defensive fire ended the threat. A second attack against "C" and "D" Companies at 0300 hours on the Rass ez Zouai face of the cliffs likewise melted away when steady opposition was encountered. Thereafter silence reigned and no further attempts were made to dislodge 1/2 Gurkhas, who had won the key to the battlefield at the low cost of 52 killed and wounded.

The Tiger Kills describes the last phase:

"When light broke on the morning of April 7th the Gurkhas walked openly along the crests or toiled uphill with heavy loads on their head straps. Across the valley the Punjabis broke into song as they went about their tasks. Clouds of dust far across the plains showed the enemy to be in full retreat. A patrol of Gurkhas headed by Subedar Major Narbahadur Gurung* pushed down the military road and met a jeep loaded with American scouts. They shook hands, exchanged cigarettes, examined each other's weapons and grinned. Eighth Army was now part of a continuous front."

"On the ravine through which the military road ran an Italian battalion had jettisoned its equipment. A lance-naik had the luck to discover a box of regimental silver. Under the northern slopes of Fatnassa a field dressing station had stood. It was gone but its dead lay neatly swathed in blankets waiting for the victors to bury them."

On the afternoon of April 7th General Tuker wrote to the Deputy Commander-in-Chief, India:

*This rotund and genial figure was known to most of Eighth Army as "N.B.G."

"Today I have been over the battlefield. I marvel at the skill of the men who captured the bastion of hills. I think the battle is over for us. Last night I should have loosed a battalion at a 90 Light Division position but I didn't. The men were dead beat and I didn't know what today would bring forth. In fact the enemy has fled. It was a very great feat and not due to my plan in any way. I simply trusted to a kind Providence, as the operation was so near the border-line of imbecility and impossibility that the outcome could not possibly have lain in our hands."

"It has put the Indian Army on the map. Lovett's brigade was past all praise. He himself was hit three times but commanded his brigade right through the battle. He'll be out for four months. I hope you will see that he comes back to 7 Brigade when he is fit again."*

The Indian Army was not only "on the map". It was standing in relief. Comrades and Allies joined in an overwhelming ovation to Fourth Indian Division. It was tacitly recognised that only troops highly trained for modern mountain warfare could have struck such a daring blow with such power and precision. The Prime Minister, ever scanning the battlefield, led the paeans. His subsequent message to Fourth Indian Division read:

"The high renown of India's soldiers and of the redoubtable Gurkha troops has been enhanced by the outstanding performance of Fourth Indian Division in the battle of Mareth and in the recent victory of Wadi Akarit.

"I take this occasion to express to the Princes and Peoples of India and to our firm friend, His Highness the Maharajah of Nepal, our admiration and gratitude for all that the Indian Army has done in Africa, in the Far East and in India itself. We take pride that India's fighting men should now share in the successes which have crowned the long uphill contest in which they have played so valiant a part".

For the world in general the clean-cut nature of Eighth Army's victory, at a time when British and American forces in western Tunisia had struck rough sledding, made Wadi Akarit a front page story. Even the Congress press in India, which until now had more or less boycotted the achievements of Indian troops, opened their columns. New Zealand war correspondents, who ordinarily were restricted to actions in which Kiwi troops participated, were given special permission to cover the Wadi Akarit operation. Their pride could scarcely have been greater in their own men. They filed long, glowing stories featuring the "nuggety little Gurkhas" and "India's magnificent fighting men". The news-conscious North American continent likewise was avid for details. One of the first jeeps to arrive from First Army front bore an American correspondent, who ruefully displayed his editor's admonition: "Whatsa

*General Tuker under-estimated his man. The hospital held Brigadier Lovett for a bare fortnight.

matter. Your latest unnews. Shoot rapidest feature Indians. Pictures, knives, turbans. Skedaddle". When correspondents flocked to obtain first-hand narratives, General Tuker obligingly gave a press conference. An American correspondent wrote: "You have only to see these tall, proud fighting men to realise what an asset the Allied forces possess. They are not civilians fumbling towards a knowledge of war. They have battle in their bones. To me the most astonishing thing was not what they achieved on the summits of these mountains but their calm and relaxed behaviour while waiting for their turn. I asked one shy man if he realised what was ahead. I could see his surprise as the interpreter translated. 'Of course', he replied. 'We are soldiers'."

Considering the scope and decisiveness of the action, casualties were astonishingly light. Under the leadership of Lieut.-Colonel G. S. N. Hughes the Divisional ambulances, supplemented by the American Field Service, provided immediate care and expeditious evacuation. By nightfall on April 6th only 335 casualties had come back, nearly all of whom bore light wounds from rock or mortar fragmentation. Total casualties were under 400. It is interesting to note that a unit which seldom appears in the record but usually was in the thick of it—the Rajputana Rifles Machine Gun Battalion—lost more men in this battle than did some of the infantry battalions. Two of its officers—Capt. G. R. Riddick and Capt. I. B. St. R. Surita—were among those honoured for outstanding and gallant conduct.

There was one regret that the brilliance of the victory did not dissipate. Had Fourth Indian Division possessed its third brigade to continue 5 Brigade's thrust into the enemy's rear, it might have trapped Rommel's entire army. If so, the Allies would have been spared thousands of casualties.

Chapter 18

DJEBEL GARCI AND ENFIDAVILLE

THERE now remained no sanctuary for Rommel's battered forces save the inner keep of Tunisia, the great mountain mass which reared its ramparts around the Gulf of Carthage. Hurriedly extricating his remnants, the Axis commander fell back 150 miles. Spring had decked the plains with a riot of gay, warm colours. For mile after mile the wearers of the Red Eagles rode across a glowing countryside. At an overnight leaguer a Divisional botanist identified 24 different varieties of wild flowers. This clean, easy and bountiful land stirred the hearts of the sepoys. They examined it with keen eyes and pronounced it good. Their officers likewise responded to the gala dress of the landscape, the thrill of expectancy in the air. An Indian Army observer wrote:

"In the long ride northward many said to each other that the years of vicissitude were over. Eighth Army was 'clicking' at last. There was a sense of power, of timing, of intimate comprehension of battle needs, which denoted the rhythm and assurance of a great machine. Yet the thoughts of many turned back over the past three years, when gallant comrades and fine leaders had paid the price of an empire's unreadiness. Many remembered the dead men strewn over a score of battlefields whose bodies, in Kipling's fine line, 'were all our defence, while we wrought our defences'."

Along the main highways the Indian convoys moved northwards with the sea on their right hand. The roads bore along raised causeways above the low-tide mud flats, through shimmering palm plantations, dusty olive groves, past small fishing villages with crude smacks pulled up to the cottage doors. By-passing the battered Sfax waterfront the lorries rolled on past El Djem, with its Roman amphitheatre, into a countryside where the pastures and bright fields gave way to interminable olive plantations. At Msaken some of the convoys swung to the left and passed through Kairouan with its 165 mosques, a city high in the Moslem hierarchy of holiness. Others turned into Sousse, the main town of southern Tunisia, where the civilians lined the roads to give acclaim and sprightly young women ogled the passing troops. Then far ahead mountains again loomed in the sky, swinging in a long arc to the south-west. Here, as at Mareth and Wadi Akarit, the high ground arose a few miles inland leaving a narrow gap into the north along the foreshore. The sedate little market town of Enfidaville sat in the entrance to this gap. On April 16th in the groves and pastures to the south of the town the convoys dispersed and settled down to organise for the work in hand.

Of all Africa there now remained to the enemy only the abrupt headland of Tunis. His defensive positions covered 100 miles of mountain wall from 40 to 80 miles inland, between Enfidaville in the south and Sedjennane on the northern coast. On both flanks great ramparts barred the way, but at Medjez-el-Bab, 40 miles to the south-west of Tunis, the barrier declined to rolling hills guarding a low open valley which ran into the plain surrounding the Gulf of Carthage. First British Army had hammered at this gap in stubborn and fluctuating fighting. American forces had regrouped after their incursion into southern Tunisia and had taken over the northern front adjacent to the Mediterranean. Thus three armies had closed in a ring around the Tunisian fortress.

The plan for the final overthrow of the enemy in Africa has been stated by Field-Marshal Montgomery:

"On April 12 I received word from General Alexander that First (British) Army was to make the main effort in the final phase of the North African campaign and that Eighth Army's rôle would be to exert the maximum pressure on the southern sector of the enemy's front, in order to pin down as much of his strength as possible. The plain west of Tunis was the most suitable ground for the deployment of armoured forces and I was asked to send an armoured division and an armoured car regiment to join First Army. I nominated 1 Armoured Division and Kings Dragoon Guards for this rôle. In due course they joined 3 Corps."

"The Enfidaville position was admirably suited for defence, and unless the enemy could be 'bounced' out of it before he had time to organise his defences thoroughly, it was obviously going to be a very difficult undertaking to break through it. The country was generally unsuitable for tanks except in the very narrow coastal strip, and even there water channels and other obstacles existed. The enemy had excellent observation over his territory to the south; moreover he showed every indication of being prepared to stand and put up a desperate fight."

"I gave orders for 'squaring up' to the Enfidaville position. 10 Corps (now consisting of 7 Armoured, 2 New Zealand, 4 Indian and 50 Divisions) was instructed to endeavour to push the enemy out of the position before he had settled in. The attempt would be made on the coastal axis, and if successful 10 Corps would go on to the next system of defences known to exist around Bou Ficha".*

*Bou Ficha is a road junction at the northern end of the coastal corridor, 12 miles from Enfidaville.

This statement reveals the Field-Marshal's intention to interpret his orders in a forthright manner. Given a brief to maintain pressure he proposed to "bounce" the enemy out of the Enfidaville positions. Moreover he was prepared to continue the "bouncing" across a mountain block, 12 miles in depth, in which according to his own reckoning the enemy would fight desperately. It was perhaps a natural amplification. Eighth Army had come a long way and the goal was in sight. Once armour was loose on the easy tank runs of the Cap Bon peninsula, Medjez-el-Bab would have ceased to matter.

10 Corps Commander contemplated his commission with assurance. He believed the southern mountain ramparts to be lightly held and that the main enemy position lay at the northern end of the corridor at Bou Ficha. His intelligence summary identified only 6 enemy battalions in the 33 miles between Enfidaville and Point du Fahs. His battle tactics postulated hostile forces thin on the ground which could be ejected from mountain fastnesses by infiltration and local turning movements. With the enemy present in any strength his plan for a wide wheel through the mountain block by two Indian brigades, with the New Zealanders conforming in a shorter wheel on the inner flank, obviously would have been impossible. As a 'squaring-up' or 'bouncing-out' operation this scheme had possibilities: as a slogging match, none.

The first moves were to secure Takrouna, a high castellated buttress with a village on its crest three miles west of Enfidaville, and Djebel Garci, a great bald-domed mountain 4 miles west of Takrouna. 2 New Zealand Division was allotted Takrouna, Fourth Indian Division, Garci.

Neither General Tuker nor General Freyberg shared General Horrocks' optimism. On examining the overall picture of the enemy's dispositions, General Tuker again declared Medjez-el-Bab to offer the logical site for breaching the fortress; that attack elsewhere would be fraught with risks and certain to incur heavy casualties. Quite apart from other considerations the shortage of infantry constituted a major problem. Of the eight infantry divisions arrayed at Alamein, 9 Australian, 1 South African and 44 British Division no longer were available. 50 and 51 Divisions were due to be withdrawn shortly for training for the Sicilian campaign. After a pursuit of 1,500 miles, 2 New Zealand Division urgently needed rest and reinforcements. This left as relatively fresh troops for a major operation two Indian brigades and 201 Guards Brigade. The main anxiety, however, arose from divergent views of the enemy's intention. Neither General Tuker nor General Freyberg believed that Rommel would wait at the Bou Ficha keep when he might man the Enfidaville battlements. As experienced battle commanders they realised that should enemy strength in the latter area be underestimated the difficulties of the proposed operation might prove overwhelming. Nevertheless Headquarters 10 Corps adhered to the opinion that Takrouna and Djebel Garci represented no more than lightly held outposts, and at a conference General Montgomery reiterated his intention to smash through and seize the beaches of the Cap Bon peninsula. With the decision taken, the Divisional commanders turned to the task in hand.*

Djebel Garci, a spade-shaped eminence with its point thrust into the southern plain, rose to a height of over 1,000 feet at its rear, where beyond a narrow valley it merged into the main massif. On either side of the tip of the mountain a re-entrant of low ground continued for perhaps two miles. As has been noted, Takrouna stood on the right flank; on the left the high buttress of Fadeloun guarded the approach. This latter feature was held by General Le Clerc's Lake Chad Brigade, under Fourth Divisional command but in a non-operational rôle. This French formation under its highly individual commander had crossed the Sahara from French Equatorial Africa to join up with Eighth Army. It contained many men who had participated in the drive down the Red Sea littoral in February-March 1941 as part of Briggs Force. (See Chapter 4). Arriving in front of the Garci positions in advance of Fourth Indian Division, it had "bounced" out the German garrison in a surprise thrust. This Brigade was destined later to form the nucleus of 2 French Armoured Division which served with conspicuous success in General Lassigny's First French Army in Europe.

Between Fadeloun and Garci a valley nearly three miles in width ran into the north-west, carrying the main road to Pont du Fahs. Across the entrance to this valley the Wadi Boul cut a deep channel. Beyond this broad nullah the ground sloped up gradually to El Bleida, a knoll which stood like a wart on the snout of the mountain. The small village of Abd el Rahman clung to the southern slopes of the knoll above the Pont du Fahs road. Immediately behind the knoll the ground rose sharply in a series of false crests and wrinkled contours. The summit of the dome was bare, giving the mountain a deceitfully benevolent appearance, but closer examination showed the slopes to consist of a confusion of abrupt features, rocky ledges, deep scarred nullahs, protuberant pimples, precipitous approaches—a tangled agglomeration of all that in a military sense was difficult and dangerous. The approach ground to the south of Wadi Boul consisted of a series of gently rolling ridges now clad in the lush greens of the early crops. Small white farmhouses with cactus zarebas dotted the uplands and imbued the landscape with an air of pastoral serenity.

As General Tuker disposed his thin forces for the attack, three necessities presented themselves. First of all it was important to obtain more detailed information regarding enemy dispositions. Thereafter it was necessary to arrange for the replenishment of troops when they had seized this isolated mountain top. Finally it was essential that the artillery should intervene to the utmost extent in this battle, since

*When desperate fighting ensued at Takrouna and at Djebel Garci, 10 Corps admitted the original Intelligence picture to have been incorrect. At a press conference the spokesman declared the "density of the enemy to be the greatest on the Allied front". 23 battalions had been identified, or approximately 1,000 men to every mile of the active sector.

ground reinforcements were unavailable and an air target did not exist.

To satisfy the first of these necessities, extensive patrolling was ordered. To secure pack animals for a mountain train Lieut.-Colonel J. A. C. Greenwood, the efficient Divisional Quartermaster, undertook to beat the neighbourhood for all available mules. Finally, the CRA was instructed to plan an artillery battle on a formidable scale.

1/4 Essex were entrusted with the preliminary patrols.* (It is interesting to note that this Territorial battalion had concentrated on patrol training until it challenged Indian units in their own field). From positions in the rolling ground to the south of Garci the Home County men immediately began to push forward to establish contact. On the afternoon of April 17th three Essex carriers under Captain C. J. Kendrick, accompanied by an artillery observation officer, advanced across the open, explored the Wadi Boul, found a crossing and audaciously thrust up the Pont du Fahs road for a distance of approximately 3,000 yards. This incursion evoked retaliation, but the patrol escaped. Next morning Divisional artillery dealt with enemy guns which had disclosed their positions.

On the night of April 18th a platoon of "A" Company under Captain G. R. Summers raided Abd el Rahman village, snatching 7 Italians who talked freely. Garci Mountain, they said, was held by a German regiment, morose and difficult men with whom they had no contact. On the night of April 19th Lieut. C. Hailes led out 14 men of "C" Company in an endeavour to reach and mine the alternative road to Pont du Fahs which ran through the narrow valley behind Garci. This enterprise called for penetration of enemy lines to a depth of five miles. Detected soon after crossing into hostile territory, the patrol slipped away from the enveloping Germans only to be held up by a British harassing shoot across their line of advance. Fortunately the guns ceased in time for the Essex to escape through the dust and smoke. Crossing a meadow in the dark and confronted with square black shapes, they charged the suspected gun positions only to imbed their bayonets in haystacks. Beyond the haystacks on the crest of the ridge a number of silent figures stood watching. The two groups, one above, the other below, stared motionless until a man moved downhill to investigate. He was pulled down in the high grass and proved to be a German officer. The captive was guarded by Lieut. Hailes' servant. As the party continued its march, a faint cry came from the rear. A corporal rushed back to find the batman overpowered and the officer about to escape. The hunt was up. A wild scrimmage ensued in which the Essex rushed two posts, killing 5 Germans, crept on hands and knees through a wheatfield, took refuge in a deserted farmhouse, scurried along an anti-tank ditch and finally went to ground in a wadi. With dawn approaching the patrol attempted to fight its way back to the

*Lieut. J. Wilson took out a patrol from 1/9 Gurkhas from which neither he nor his men returned.

British lines. Leaving the wadi and moving in couples, yet keeping cohesion the Essex withdrew from ridge to ridge followed by sniping and machine-gun fire. They had reached the Pont du Fahs road when Lieut. Hailes fell seriously wounded. He ordered the remaining ten men to abandon him. They hid until after nightfall when they completed their journey. Three of the wounded returned three days later. Lieut. Hailes himself was recovered from a German hospital in Tunis.

In addition to these reconnaissance assignments, the Essex were entrusted with the opening assault on Garci. At 2100 hours on the night of April 19th, "D" Company under Captain J. Watts, MC, advanced with the prominent white mosque of Abd el Rahman as landmark. The village was deserted, but as the Home County men clambered up the slopes of Bleida heavy machine-gun fire opened. Swinging his men to flank Captain Watts stalked a post, capturing 14 prisoners. The other flank platoon in similar fashion overran two machine-gun nests. A Bren gunner cleared a nullah single-handed and "D" Company reached the crest of the knoll. Thunders shook the night, as devastating artillery concentrations blasted enemy positions on the upper slopes of the mountain. 50 prisoners were taken in this workmanlike operation, which had secured a jump-off position for the main assault.

At 2130 hours 4/6 Rajputana Rifles assembled on the line of the Wadi Boul. Thirty minutes later, "A" and "B" Companies passed through Abd el Rahman on their way up the mountainside. Beyond El Bleida the attack encountered heavy opposition. On a steep slope "A" Company was pinned down, but "B" Company swung to flank and destroyed the defenders. *The Tiger Kills* describes the scene:

"In the darkness men grappled and slew each other. The survivors went to earth as bombs burst about them, rose and rushed forward in the dust and smoke, and fastened upon other enemies. For four hours the Rajputana Rifles battled their way forward in one of the bitterest encounters of the war. Every gain drew a counter-attack from desperate men pledged to hold the heights at all costs. Yard by yard the assailants worked upwards, around rocky knolls, across mountain wadis, surging over crests to face other crests from which mortar and small arms fire swept down incessantly upon them."

"On the approach to the battalion's second objective, an enemy machine-gun post pinned down the advance. Company Havildar Major Chhelu Ram of 'B' Company, armed with a tommy-gun, sprang into the midst of the spurting flames, reached the sangar and killed four gunners. Ignoring his wounds he took command of his own company as well as the leading elements of 'A' Company, whose commander, Captain French, had been shot down. The attack had been brought to a halt, and the Havildar Major, working like a Trojan and disdainful of safety, began to organise the position in preparation for the next advance."

At 0300 hours Brigadier Bateman came forward to examine the situation. The leading companies of Rajputana Rifles were locked in a deadly grapple and ammunition was running short. 1/9 Gurkhas had closed up and were waiting for the word. They, too, were in a most uncomfortable position, since their forming-up areas caught the "overs" of the mortar fire showered from the crests above. Lieut.-Colonel Roche received permission from Brigadier Bateman to enter the battle at once. "D" Company under Captain Peter Jones passed through the Essex and swept uphill in the face of heavy machine-gun fire. The Germans met the hillmen breast to breast around a series of stone sangars. "A" Company under Captain Denis Donovan swept over the lower knolls on the left of Point 330. After two bitter hand-to-hand clashes, this objective was won. Both company commanders were wounded but a final rush carried the Gurkhas over the crest of Point 330. A handful of German survivors fled screaming in the darkness.

At 0400 hours a heavy counter-attack swept downhill against the Rajputana Rifles. Group by group assailants and assailed fought to the death. Ammunition gave out; the dauntless Rajputana Rifles crouched waiting, and as their enemies loomed in the darkness they hurled stones and followed in under with the bayonet. Lieut. Yates fell mortally wounded at the head of his men. Havildar-Major Chhelu Ram sprang forward, dressed his officer's wound and was hit a second time. As he turned to take command of the company, Germans dashed forward to bayonet the prostrate officer. Rifleman Harsukh Ram leapt among them striking furiously. Nearby Gurkhas sped to the rescue, plying their kukris. At this critical moment a new rush came. Havildar-Major Chhelu Ram was everywhere. Racing from point to point amid crash of bombs, rattle of musketry, yells and screams, he rallied his men, shouting "Jats and Mohammedans, no withdrawal! Forward! Forward!" Under his superb leadership and that of Subedar Mohammed Yusof of "A" Company, the Rajputana Rifles countered the frenzy of the enemy with inspired resistance. The line held and the foiled Germans fell back across the mountainside. Sprawled bodies marked the ebb and flow of this deadly mêlée. Among them lay the greathearted Chhelu Ram, who had been mortally wounded at the crisis of the fighting. Until he died he continued to command and exhort his men. For unsurpassable courage and leadership, this Jat from Dhenod village, Bhiwani, Hissar district, earned his battalion its second Victoria Cross.

While 1/9 Gurkhas consolidated their gains around Point 330, Jemadar Dewan Sing of "D" Company scouted forward to encounter one of the most remarkable adventures of the war. The story can best be told in his own report:

"I was challenged in a foreign language. I felt it was not the British language or I would have recognised it. To make quite sure I crept up and found myself looking into the face of a German. I recognised him by his helmet. He was fumbling with his weapon so I cut off his head with my kukri. Another appeared from a slit trench and I cut him down also. I was able to do the same to two others, but one made a great deal of noise, which raised the alarm. I had a cut at a fifth but I am afraid I only wounded him. Yet perhaps the wound was severe, for I struck him between the neck and the shoulder."

"I was now involved in a struggle with a number of Germans, and eventually, after my hands had become cut and slippery with blood, they managed to wrest my kukri from me. One German beat me over the head with it, inflicting a number of wounds. He was not very skilful, however, sometimes striking me with the sharp edge but oftener with the blunt.

"They managed to beat me to the ground where I lay pretending to be dead. The Germans got back into their trenches and after a while I looked up. I could not see anything, for my eyes were full of blood. I wiped the blood out of my eyes and quite near I saw a German machine-gun. I thought, 'if only I can reach that gun I shall be able to kill the lot'. By now it was getting light and as I lay thinking of a plan to reach the gun, my platoon advanced and started to hurl grenades among the enemy. But they were also falling very near me, so I thought that if I did not move I really would be dead. I managed to get to my feet, and ran towards my platoon. Not recognising me, I heard one of my men call. 'Here comes the enemy! Shoot him!' I bade them not to do so. They recognised my voice and let me come in.

"My hands being cut about and bloody, and having lost my kukri, I had to ask one of my platoon to take my pistol out of my holster and to put it in my hand. I then took command of my platoon again.

"I met my company commander, who bade me go to the Regimental Aid Post. I said, 'Sahib, there is fighting to be done, and I know the enemy's dispositions. I must stay and command my platoon'. But he firmly ordered me and I had to go. Yet before I went, one of my Bren gunners was hit, and my company commander, although wounded in the neck, took over the Bren gun and continued to fire it. Moreover, the doctor sahib, having bandaged me, refused to allow me to return to my platoon."*

Day broke with Garci mountain wreathed in smoke. On the forward slopes a heavy enemy mortar barrage played incessantly, pounding the newly-won positions. "A" and "B" Companies of Rajputana Rifles had suffered 30 per cent casualties in the night fighting; they were out of ammunition and needed re-organisation. They therefore dropped back through "D" Company. Believing the assault to have lost momentum, a counter-attack under cover of an intense mortar barrage swept against "A" and "D" Companies of 1/9 Gurkhas. As the enemy

*Which was not remarkable, as he had a dozen wounds on his head alone. This Gurkha officer was awarded the I.O.M. The Fourth Indian Division standard of recommendation for awards was very high.

appeared the hillmen counter-charged. In five minutes of deadly hurly-burly 44 Germans died under the kukris. The survivors fled uphill. Following the enemy, Lance-Naik Til Bahadur and Rifleman Khim Bahadur raced forward and destroyed two machine-gun posts which had given their assailants covering fire from the flank. A platoon of "C" Company pushed forward and consolidated the ground gained by this quick-witted pair. When Lieut.-Colonel Roche reached the forward positions he found his men in high heart. A jemadar said, "Sahib, we drove them back before we had settled down. Now nothing can move us".

During the period of this counter-attack, "D" Company of the Rajputana Rifles likewise improved its grip on the mountainside by seizure of a menacing knoll on the left flank. 80 prisoners were taken in this quick thrust. At 0635 hours the Essex, which had caught a part of the heavy mortar shoot attendant upon the Rajputana Rifles' attack, despatched "B" Company to secure the Ksaa feature, a high shoulder on the left flank of the mountain. At 0845 hours two platoons, having moved around the western slopes of El Bleida, threw themselves at this objective. They seized Ksaa, taking 30 prisoners. An immediate counter-attack surged downhill; the Essex stood firm and broke the assault after hand-to-hand fighting. The situation was too confused and the opposition too intense to exploit this gain, which nevertheless constituted an important penetration of the enemy's battle positions. Concurrently with the Essex thrust, a platoon of "D" Company of the Rajputana Rifles moved towards an isolated crest 1,000 yards in front of the battalion position. A handful of men reached and stormed this important vantage point. In the face of a heavy counter-attack that night the outlying platoon stood firm, and when the general counter-attack went in on the following afternoon, this tiny force once again threw back the enemy, taking no less than 50 prisoners.

The situation on review that forenoon showed that 5 Brigade, in the face of the fiercest opposition, had established itself on the toe of the Garci massif. Nevertheless the course of the battle had confirmed General Tuker's worst fears. The mountain was held in great strength and the enemy proposed to contest every yard of ground. Before a fresh assault could be undertaken, it was necessary to consolidate and to arrange protection for the right flank of the attack. At Takrouna the New Zealanders were engaged in fighting no less desperate than that on Garci, and there was always the possibility that the enemy might muster behind the line of the Zaghouan road for a thrust southward across the open ground between the two assault divisions. To cover this gap the Divisional Commander moved 7 Brigade forward. 1 Royal Sussex crossed the Pont du Fahs road and occupied positions on the right of Abd el Rahman; 1/2 Gurkhas covered the approaches from the east and established contact with the New Zealanders. 23 Armoured Brigade also moved up into close support, with 50 Royal Tank Regiment well forward on the right of El Bleida and 40 Royal Tank Regiment along the Pont du Fahs road. With this armoured strength at his disposal,

Brigadier Firth (who had taken command when Brigadier Lovett was wounded) was able to loan 4/16 Punjabis to 5 Brigade. Shortly after mid-day the Punjabis deployed on the plain to the south-west of Garci and advanced for the purpose of extending the battle line by seizing the lower slopes of the mountain on the right of 1/9 Gurkhas. This spectacular advance occurred in full view of the enemy, who raked the approach ground with heavy concentrations. A spectator on Garci wrote: "The 4/16th advanced across the plain in perfect open formation. They might have been on a battle drill parade. We waited breathlessly for the enemy defensive fire to fall among them. It soon came, and they were enveloped in thick dust and smoke. When it cleared away the battalion was still advancing in the same perfect formation". The Punjabis reached the hillside, clambered upwards and established themselves. The left flank company relieved the Gurkha platoon which held the ground seized by Lance-Naik Til Bahadur and Rifleman Khim Bahadur in the first counter-attack.

With these safety measures effected, the Divisional Commander could plan his next move. Four of his six battalions of infantry were now in the firing line. 5 Brigade had won perhaps one-hundredth of the mountain block which barred the way to Bou Ficha at a cost of some 400 casualties. To continue the infantry battle on the same scale invited exhaustion, if not decimation. Even with Garci won the battle was no more than begun, for the bald dome in turn was commanded by the towering ridges of Mdeker to the north. The New Zealanders were in no better case. The entire Kiwi Division had been committed to the storming of Takrouna, an objective less than one-quarter the size of Garci. These circumstances impelled General Tuker to consider two alternatives. Lacking the strength to push on, he either must take toll by smashing enemy counter-attacks or he must abandon the battle. The violence of the enemy suggested that disproportionate losses might be exacted by breaking his reckless and furious assaults. Brigadier Bateman's men therefore were ordered to stand fast and to crack the enemy's teeth in his efforts to push them off the mountain.

Worsted in their endeavours to dislodge the assault troops by lightning thrusts, the Germans during the afternoon of April 20th intensified their bombardment into a non-stop shoot which sorely harassed the British and Indian troops clinging to the slopes of this naked mountain. Little natural cover existed and it was impossible to dig trenches. The recurrent false crests allowed the enemy to creep up to within striking distance without challenge. For the first time the men on Garci heard in the sky the eerie moan of the nebelwerfers—multiple mortars fired by remote control. Sniping guns on the flanks kept up a continuous shoot whenever movement was detected. One shell crashed into Brigadier Bateman's headquarters behind the Wadi Boul. The day cost 5 Brigade 100 casualties. A few such losses would leave the gallant infantry so thin on the ground that the clumping rushes from behind the false crests might win home. The only counter was to make the Germans suffer in even greater degree. This possibility presented

Brigadier Dimoline and his gunners with their long-awaited opportunity —to take over a battle and to bend the enemy to their will.

To supplement the Divisional artillery, 57, 58, 78 and 121 Army Field Regiments had been taken under command, while 51, 64 and 69 Medium Regiments were on call through CAGRA. 222 guns were under Divisional orders. With Corps supplying emergency assistance from flanking formations, 294 guns could be incorporated in Brigadier Dimoline's fire programmes. This force could pitch shell at the rate of 8 tons in each minute and could switch from target to target in less than five minutes. These sudden pulverising shoots, both in actual damage and in psychological effect, far surpassed the creeping barrage. Their fury for the first time in the African campaign was now unleashed upon the enemy.

When the infantry went forward, numerous gallant artillery observation officers followed into the thick of the fighting. Several were struck down. Others, like Captain David Rowe of 1 Field Regiment, who encountered two Germans in a nullah and although unarmed talked himself out of capture, rapidly pinpointed the areas where defensive fire curtains should be interposed and where the enemy might assemble for counter-attacks. Thereafter, over the 19 lines radiating from his battle headquarters, Brigadier Dimoline would manipulate his fire power to meet any emergency. On the evening of April 19th, when the first attack went in, the Divisional artillery laid 13 shoots on 10 different targets in the space of 70 minutes. 7 field regiments represented the heaviest concentration. On April 20th, 12 shoots were staged, a number of targets being engaged at different times throughout the day. On April 21st the artillery began the day with a series of heavy concentrations in which 7 field and 3 medium regiments played on centres of enemy activity. At 0955 hours hostile gun positions received a similar plastering. Throughout the forenoon enemy artillery and mortar fire intensified. At 1420 hours Captain Morrison of 1 Field Regiment reported the Germans to be assembling for a counter-attack against 1/9 Gurkhas. Thereafter the CRA's log tells the engrossing story:

> "1 Field Regiment and its two affiliated field regiments told to engage, while simultaneously on the other telephone, a call was put through to all other regiments to put them on ROSE as well. Simultaneously CAGRA was rung up, told of impending counter-attack and told that we would like all three medium regiments made available."

> "Telephone rang again—defensive fire wanted urgently on LUPIN, Forward Observation Officer reports enemy seen running along crest throwing stick grenades. Three medium regiments put straight on to LUPIN, 'clear the line' multiple call to all field regiments to engage. Two minutes later, two telephones rang, defensive fire urgently on CROSSLEY, defensive fire urgently on HISPANO. Now it had to be decided which was the more

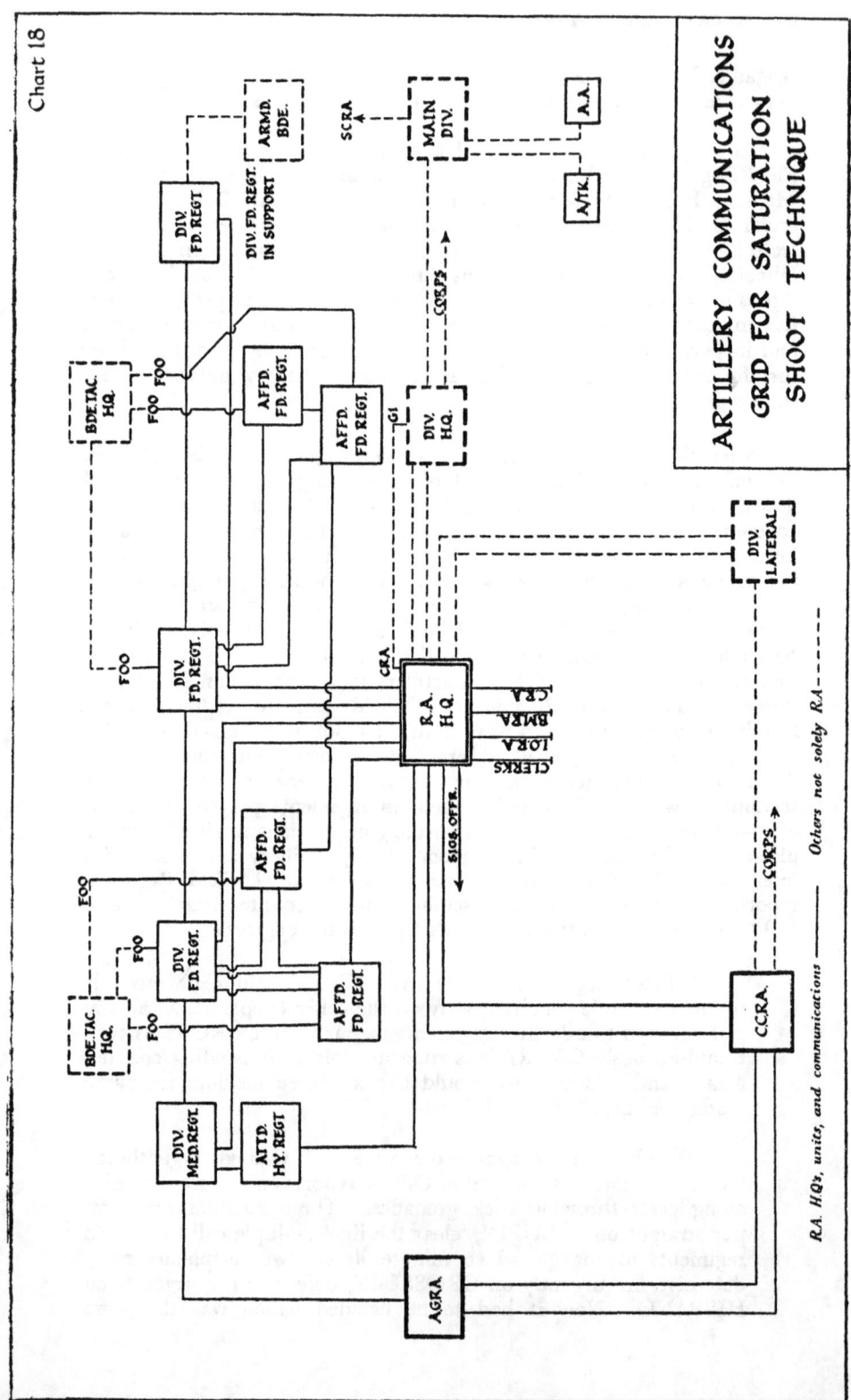

important. The medium regiments were left banging away on LUPIN, 3 field regiments were swung on to CROSSLEY, and 4 field Regiments on to HISPANO."

"GSO 1 direct line calls and asks how its going, and is told what we know. He has a copy of our DF trace, so can follow the direction of the counter-attack from the sequence in which DF is called for and fired. Every time we fire, he is notified on his direct line."

"CCRA 10 Corps rings up to know what its all about and if we need any assistance. He is told all we know, and that we have the medium regiments banging away for us and that is all the additional support we need at the moment."

"Information comes down from the mountain that the enemy counter-attacks seem heavy, but that our fire is falling right amongst them, and that our infantry have not given an inch of ground."

"The telephones now all ringing constantly, FOO'S calling for fire the whole time, now on this target, now on that. CHEVROLET came next, then CHRYSLER, then CHRYSLER again, then AUSTIN. All in rapid succession. Just as orders to all regiments had gone through to fire on one target, call for fire on another came through. Sometimes it took its turn and then had the full weight of 7 field and 3 medium regiments, sometimes two or three Regiments switched on to it instantly and the remainder came in later."

"FOO reported that enemy infantry had got within 300 yards of him, when the full weight of the Divisional Artillery came down. The DF he had called for fell slap amongst them. When the smoke and dust had cleared away nothing was seen of them afterwards. This was encouraging, and we hoped that Boche was getting a really bloody nose everywhere."

"At 1510 hours AUSTIN called for again. This time, for once, it was the only call at the time, and it had 10 regiments on to it. Then at 1515 hours a new one, AVRO on the right flank popped up, and it too had the benefit of 10 regiments, which was repeated five minutes later."

"At 1520 hours, there was an unaccountable hush. No telephone bell rang. It seemed uncanny after the last hour, when the telephones had seemed to be vying with each other as to how many times they could ring."

"To break the lull, we rang up 1 Field Regiment who had had news from its observation posts that the enemy counter-attacks, which had come in a very determined manner from two directions, had been broken up, that our infantry were still secure in their positions and that for the moment all was quiet."

Ammunition expenditure at Garci averaged 640 rounds per gun in a period of under 72 hours, more than three times the expenditure at Wadi Akarit. Artillery casualties on the other hand were considerably lighter, amounting only to 8 officers and 40 men, a small loss in view of the crushing contribution of the gunners. It is worth noting that throughout the Tunisian campaign the only Artillery officers killed were battery commanders who controlled the fire of their guns from dangerous vantage points far forward.

Scattered along the broken slopes in shallow wadis and in the lee of rocky ledges, regimental aid posts and advanced dressing stations endured the flailing enemy bombardment while the doctors and orderlies bandaged the wounded and eased their pain. Everywhere the stretcher-bearers followed the fighting; the greatly enduring infantry knew that they were not alone on this naked mountain but that their medical services stood near at hand to succour them. "The courage of the doctors" wrote an officer, "and the confidence reposed in them by the sepoys, sustained morale at its highest pitch." Lieut.-Colonel G. S. N. Hughes of 26 Field Ambulance, in his story of the magnificent work of the stretcher-bearers and advanced dressing stations, ends with a vivid paragraph:

"There had not been a minute's rest for twenty hours. Mazhar and I decided to run the night ADS so that Chaudhari and Willson could start again fresh in the morning. The stream of cases continued until midnight. Pictures come to mind of a constant stream of people. The medical corporal of the Essex scrounging tea and sugar; a visiting colonel wounded while watching the battle; a gunner brigadier asking about the shelling; a boy Gurkha proudly displaying his blooded kukri; a wounded B.O.R. blasted into near coma; constant visitors asking news of friends. Stretcher-bearers arriving exhausted with hands bleeding; reliefs sent up, young Madrassis yet to prove themselves. Dawn showed that the strain was telling. The Brigadier looked ten years older and the Brigade Major was grey from lack of sleep. Captain Holman was ordered back to get desperately needed rest, but he returned later to finish the job he had so magnificently done. Only arrest would have stopped him. We heard later that he had put out a fire on an ammunition dump. One can be truly thankful that such medical officers as he were spared, for God knows they are needed."

Although this stand-up slogging on the mountainside was proving expensive to the enemy, the battle remained little to General Tuker's liking. Approximately 500 casualties had been incurred in the first two days fighting. On April 22nd defensive fire intervened on nine occasions, breaking up two assemblies for counter-attack and raking the Garci back area until the enemy, in a desperate bid to blind the gunner observers, switched to smoke shell. Although no infantry encounter occurred, the day cost 5 Brigade 80 casualties from shell fire and mortar fire, a figure which appeared to be more or less the routine price of clinging to a few acres of worthless mountainside. At this juncture the Divisional Commander expressed his belief that the attack on Garci would never show profit. In this view he was strongly supported by General Freyberg, who had lost the best part of a brigade in costly fighting around Takrouna. Faced with such representations the Corps Commander asked both leaders to submit alternative proposals. He stated that there could be no question of abandoning the attack and that high-level policy required a continuation of the attempt to reach Bou Ficha—that "vital issues were at stake".

The Office Notes of GSO 2, Fourth Indian Division, supply an interesting account of the ensuing conversations.

"General Horrocks described the course he favoured. That was, to push through the narrow coastal plain north of Enfidaville with armour and lorried infantry while small detachments occupied the lower features on the western flank of this corridor. He agreed with General Tuker's observation that this ignored the enemy's forces firmly established on the higher ground to the west, but he hoped that success on the coastal plain and determined exploitation northwards would compel the enemy in the hills to withdraw. Time was important and this method offered best possibilities of a quick success."

"General Tuker expressed with some emphasis his opinion that if this course were followed General Horrocks would be in danger of losing his whole Corps. While the enemy occupied the higher hills he could dominate the narrow coastal corridor and inflict heavy casualties on our forces there. The correct method was to capture the enemy's positions in the hills piecemeal by a series of deliberate operations and thereby deprive him of his observation and gun positions."

"The discussion explored these two courses for some fifteen to twenty minutes. Before he left, General Horrocks said that he had decided on the plan of attacking through the corridor and was prepared to accept the risks."

"Later that day (I think it was during dinner in mess) the Corps Commander called up General Tuker and said that after discussion with the Army Commander he, General Horrocks, had decided to adopt the plan to capture the enemy's hill positions by a series of set-piece attacks before attempting to advance along the coast."

In view of this decision arrangements were made forthwith to abandon the Garci and Takrouna operations. On the night of April 22/23, 153 Highland Brigade in a holding role relieved 5 Brigade on the mountain top. The battered but indomitable Essex, Raputana Rifles and Gurkhas moved to a reserve area to the south-west of Enfidaville.

It was imperative that no rest should be given the enemy, and the new battle was timed to begin immediately. 7 Brigade moved into positions in the extensive olive groves which covered the easy hillsides to the north and north-west of Enfidaville. Here 13 regiments of field artillery had been crammed under leafy cover. The immediate objective was Tebaga, a feature of moderate height five miles to the north of Enfidaville. This crescent-shaped ridge masked a high mountain block and likewise controlled the coastal corridor, which at this point was slightly over four miles in width. The ejection of the enemy from Tebaga would allow British armour to deploy and would leave only 7 miles to be traversed to the end of the bottleneck at Bou Ficha.

Nevertheless by any reckoning the new operation remained a dubious enterprise. Tebaga was a stopper driven into a funnel. Two miles beyond it a salt lagoon ate inwards from the Mediterranean until less than 4,000 yards of open ground remained between its oozy shores and the abrupt slopes of Djebel Chabat el Akar. On both front and flank higher ground would continue to command the passage: the corridor always must be tactically insecure. Furthermore, any advance on Tebaga must pass under the lee of Point 130 on the left flank. As preliminary it was essential to neutralise this latter position. For this purpose a brigade of 56 London Division, lately arrived from Tripoli, was placed under Fourth Division's command. After a firm flank had been secured at Point 130 7 Brigade would strike against Tebaga and 201 Guards Brigade would attack along the coastal corridor.

On the night of April 29th the Londoners seized Point 130. Early next morning a quick thrust hurled them from the high ground. No reserve position had been organised, and the enemy followed up the withdrawal, driving vigorously on Enfidaville. The heavy concentration of field regiments was covered by the deployment of 7 Brigade along the borders of the olive groves, with 1/2 Gurkha Rifles and 4/16 Punjabis in the forward zone. The latter battalion was engrossed with plans for the Tebaga attack and all officers of the Gurkhas except Capt. M. A. Ormsby were absent on conference. The enemy was within 2,000 yards of the leading wave of field guns when the alarm was sounded. Delay and confusion might have been expected. Instead, Punjabis and Gurkhas reacted with precision and assurance. Riflemen took charge of sections, NCOs of companies, and the covering troops doubled forward to contact the enemy and to pin him down. What might have been a serious situation was averted by alertness and battle-readiness.

The speed and strength of the counterstroke against the Londoners undoubtedly impressed the Corps Commander. He now felt it incumbent to represent to General Montgomery that two of his veteran Divisional commanders were strongly against the optimistic plan upon which he had pinned his hopes of success. Quick action followed. On April 30th General Tuker and his staff proceeded on an all-day reconnaissance to the north of Enfidaville. That morning, General Alexander, acting as General Eisenhower's field commander, arrived by plane at

THE FIGHTING RACES

JAT

PATHAN

BENGALI

More than two hundred diverse peoples found a common identity in the old Indian Army, but ten races bore the principal burden. Stern and indomitable Jats: quick-witted, cat-footed Pathans and their brethren of the Frontier: Dogras, steady as shiresmen: Punjabi Mussalmans, outnumbering all others: Rajputs, tall and proper men of

GURKHA

MADRASSI

DOGRA

PUNJABI MUSSALMAN

princely blood: Mahrattas, sometime the restless White Companions of India: the proud imperious Sikhs: imperturbable Madrassis: Gurkhas, peer of the world's fighting men: the agile and disputatious Bengalis—these will be extolled by the British officers who led them as long as memory remains and as long as legend preserves the saga of their service together.

RAJPUT

SIKH

MAHRATTA

Eighth Army's headquarters. It is not known what transpired but it seems possible that General Alexander may have represented that the instruction of the Supreme Commander to end the Tunisian campaign by a breakthrough at Medjez-el-Bab constituted an unalterable decision, and that the Bou Ficha operation over-amplified Eighth Army's directive. Or it may be that neither for the first or last time General Montgomery accepted the view of his battle commanders in preference to those of his staff planners. In any case, at 1100 hours a signal flashed to Fourth Indian Division, 7 Armoured Division and 201 Guards Brigade. These formations would leave Eighth Army immediately and would cross Central Tunisia to join First British Army at Medjez-el-Bab, where they would spearhead the final thrust for Tunis.

Four hours after receipt of this message the first flights of Fourth Indian Division vehicles were on the roads. As General Tuker prepared to follow his telephone rang. General Freyberg had called to thank the Indian commander for his advocacy of an alternate plan of battle and to wish him and his men Godspeed as they moved to the climactic operation of the North African campaign.

Chapter 19

THE END IN AFRICA

THE departure of the original divisions of the Desert Army to another front marked a denouement in the war. There was a fine sense of justice in summoning to the kill the men who had borne the burden from the beginning. From the disengagement at Enfidaville until the end came at Ste. Marie du Zit eleven days later, events moved in ever-quickening tempo. History wore the habiliments of Drama.

The Divisional Commander's Order of the Day announced the new task:

"Fourth Indian Division is now moving over to First Army. The name of our Division stands at the very top of Eighth Army, mainly because of the great dash and courage of our fighting men and our refusal ever to give an inch of ground that we have won, even if we have had to fight with fists and stones.

"Let us now place our Division at the very top of all of First Army. We shall probably meet the Hermann Goering Division very soon. They are the people who shot British prisoners in cold blood.* Let us of Fourth Indian Division teach them a lesson once and for all."

Throughout the afternoon of April 30th, column after column of vehicles emerged on the main road, picked up their timing and fell into place with that absence of fuss and bother that only seasoned troops attain. In the twenty-mile long column moving to the south-west Divisional Headquarters led, followed by 5 Brigade and the artillery regiments, with 7 Brigade in the rear. It was only after darkness fell that 7 Brigade was fully disengaged and embarked on the long trek. Provost and IEME detachments had raced ahead to establish control posts and road patrols. Capt. Unni Nayar, an Indian Army Observer recently returned to duty after wounds at Wadi Akarit, thus described the passage:

*Troops of the Hermann Goering Division on First Army's front overran the Headquarters of a British tank brigade. Four clerks and the Brigade Major were put up against a wall and shot. The Brigade Major escaped by throwing himself flat on his face on hearing the command to fire and remaining there while his would--be executioners rifled his pockets and stole the watch from his wrist.

"When darkness fell on April 30th, a steady stream of vehicles was passing through the holy city of Kairouan, on the long southern route to Sbeitla, where ruins of the old Roman city still stand. Headlights were allowed but after years of blackout only one vehicle in five had bulbs. Driving steadily through the night at a regulated pace, they passed Sheiba and came into the fertile valleys of central Tunisia, with trim, tidy crops mounting to the hill crests, neat villages reminiscent of the Midi girt about with almond and fruit orchards, or with rich pasture land in which contented sheep continued to graze as the unending convoys bowled past."

"After a short halt for a 'brew-up' at dawn, the traffic quickened to day pace. The Division was now in new country, filled with civilians who stood along the road, thrusting up their fingers in the 'V' sign, while children wearing berets raced beside the trucks shouting in voluble French to the uncomprehending jawans, who twirled their moustaches and examined the lively scene with deep interest. The scuttle-helmeted Americans began to line the roads to stare at men whom they had only known previously on the pages of books: bearded Sikhs in their pugarees, Rajputs, Jats, Punjabi Mussulmans, and squat little Gurkhas. The Yanks gave the 'thumbs up' sign, and friendly jests crackled as the lorries lumbered past. So throughout the day, up the long valley from Le Kef to Le Krib, through the Provencal town of Teboursouk on its hillside, and past the great monastery of the White Fathers at Thibar, Fourth Division drew nearer to the bastion which the enemy defended so desperately—the Medjez-el-Bab gateway into the open plains of Tunis".

"Here British First Army appeared. The contrast was extreme. With their new vehicles, camouflaged in dark colours to blend with the trees and fields, this other Army might have belonged to another nation. Into its ordered scene swept the battered old trucks of Eighth Army, painted a light sandy grey, with never a windscreen, rarely a hood, with mudguards tied on with bits of wire; scratched, rusty veterans of an advance of two thousand miles."

On arrival at Teboursouk General Tuker reported to 9 Corps Headquarters. Here General Horrocks was in command, having taken over from a former corps commander who had been wounded. The overall picture showed 1 and 4 British Divisions to be engaged in heavy fighting on the high ground on both sides of the Medjez-el-Bab gap. On the right the village of Montmarnaud, on the left the broken ground around Bou Huaker, constituted the principal obstacles. Between these positions there stretched a low valley, almost like an arena, completely exposed, covered by breast-high new crops. The plan of battle called for 1 British Division to secure Bou Huaker. Thereafter at dawn on May 5th 4 British Division on the right followed by 6 Armoured Division, Fourth Indian Division on the left followed by 7 Armoured Division, would smash through behind a monumental barrage of 1917-18 type on a front of 3,500 yards and would drive on Tunis, 30 miles away.

As General Tuker examined the proposals in detail he might have been pardoned if he had rubbed his eyes. The weapons and formations available for his support far surpassed anything that Eighth Army had ever been able to provide. 400 guns stood ready to blast his front. 25 Army Tank Brigade with the new Churchills would support his infantry. Troops of Scorpions, the armoured mine-sweepers, were available with their flails to cleanse deadly ground. A seventeen-pounder regiment and an additional six-pounder regiment would be available to thicken the anti-tank screen. A number of spigot mortar groups stood ready to meet panzer counter-attacks. This positive luxury in supporting arms was climaxed by the air programme. The assaulting Indian brigades were given no less than 20 squadrons of fighter bombers and tank busters on their private tentacles. (It was a far cry from the old days in Eritrea, where the commander of 7 Brigade, when asked what air support he required, humbly requested three Gladiators.)

General Tuker, while welcoming this mighty array of support weapons, had his own ideas for their employment. Once again he did not like the plan of battle. His men had been trained to save lives and to demoralise the enemy by infiltration and by the seizure of positions under cover of darkness. The Divisional Commander had learnt that First British Army had not employed night attacks to any extent. Consequently Fourth Division's tactics would be enhanced by surprise. The first week of May was moonless, and therefore advantageous for night operations. Moreover from personal reconnaissance and from sapper reports General Tuker believed the enemy positions to be lightly mined—a circumstance which made it more advantageous to force foul ground by night than to incur losses in cutting lanes by day. He therefore suggested that the Corps Commander should simplify his plan of battle by a break-in on the front of a single division. Fourth Indian Division would lead the way, would burst into the enemy positions by night and establish a hedge of support weapons through which 4 British Division could pass to exploit the gains by day.

After considerable discussion the Corps Commander agreed that the attack might begin under cover of darkness. Zero hour was set for 0300 hours. He insisted upon an assault by both divisions, shoulder to shoulder, but Fourth Indian Division was allotted the heavier task and the deeper penetration.

The artillery programme likewise failed to please General Tuker. To thrust through a gap commanded by hills on either side without a thorough blasting of enemy positions, meant that the assault troops would be harassed by field gun, mortar and machine-gun fire over every furlong of advance. With massive artillery support available the Divisional Commander felt that the fire plan should not merely neutralise, but should destroy or paralyse. At El Alamein a monumental barrage had cast one shell on each ten yards of front. General Tuker demanded a five times tighter shoot—that is, one shell to every six feet. No straight barrage programme could secure such concentration. It was therefore necessary in the Garci fashion to choose the enemy's main defensive positions, submit them to stunning weights of metal, switch rapidly from one target to another and return to deluge key areas with repeated torrents of shell. 450 rounds per gun had been allotted. General Tuker demanded 1,000 rounds per gun. He guaranteed to fire that quantity. In the face of his confident attitude there was a tendency to meet his wishes. In the end his main points—concentration shoots and a night attack—were conceded.

There was likewise need for an adjustment of views when 25 Army Tank Brigade passed under Divisional command. The tank commander expected to be told to pursue the traditional rôle of armour in that theatre and to lead the attack. General Tuker had no intention of allowing his tanks to immolate themselves against a *cheval de frise* of anti-tank weapons. When artillery had cleared the way and infantry had punched the hole, the tanks, he said, would barge through to wreak destruction. Until such time as the door was open they would stay hull-down—out of sight and out of trouble.

At dusk on May 5th, after a ferocious bombardment, 1 British Division stormed Bou Huaker. With the left flank secured, 5 Brigade at 2300 hours moved forward, 1/9 Gurkhas leading. A company of Rajputana Rifles machine-gunners accompanied the hillmen. 4/6 Rajputana Rifles and 1/4 Essex followed: then came 7 Brigade with 1/2 Gurkhas in the lead, 1 Royal Sussex and 4/16 Punjabis closing up. 145 Royal Tank Regiment was attached to 5 Brigade and 142 Royal Tank Regiment to 7 Brigade. Six successive objectives had been selected, three of which were allotted to 5 Brigade and three to 7 Brigade. Thereafter 7 Armoured Division would crash through for the *coup de grace*. The armour was expected to break loose as soon as possible after daybreak.

Captain Nayar's narrative supplies an interesting account of the approach march:

"We had a nine-mile march ahead of us. The men bent under the weights they carried, for besides their arms and extra ammunition they brought digging implements, wireless sets and signalling equipment. We passed the dimly-lighted signs of Tac Divisional and Brigade Headquarters and plodded uphill towards 'Z' track. We passed three German dead, presumably killed when out on patrol, and then came to a fork. We were wondering which fork to take when a voice hailed us. 'Fourth Indian Division?' it asked. 'This way Sir, first left, first right'. It was a Divisional policeman."

"We were only a mile from the first objective which we could see dimly across the cornfields. We were guided by a Bofors gun which fired three red tracer shells on a fixed line every five minutes."

"Our artillery barrage now opened. The twenty-five pounders and the mediums deafened us with their roar. Thousands of shells streaked over our heads towards the enemy positions. From the German lines Verey lights went up. The enemy obviously had been surprised by the intensity of the barrage."

"Wading through ripening grain breast high, the aroma of crushed corn and wild thyme came to us mingled with the acrid smell of cordite. About 0320 hours we heard the roar of tanks on our left and right. The Churchills were closing up."

The apt timing of the attack enabled the assault troops to escape the enemy's defensive fire which fell well behind 1/9 Gurkhas as they drew up to Ragoubet Souissi, a low ridge on the right flank of Fourth Division's front. Three companies deployed and swept uphill. After a short sharp encounter the success flare rose. 4/6 Rajputana Rifles crossed their start line at 0400 hours, and having made contact with the reserve company of the Gurkhas, deployed "C" and "D" Companies as a covering party while an anti-tank screen, facing west, rapidly organised behind them. The Rajputana carrier platoon reconnoitred the front while the armour rolled forward to battle positions. As a slate-grey streak of dawn showed in the east, the British tanks, slightly too far forward, drew a deadly fusilade from 88 millimetre guns dug in along the sides of the valley. Remembering General Tuker's admonition the armour withdrew to hull-down positions. At 0440 hours 1/4 Essex closed up to find the Gurkhas well established on Point 145, their second objective. As the sky lightened overhead, to the thunder of the guns was added a deeper roar. Squadron after squadron of fighter bombers and tank busters streaked out of the south and struck in venomous low-level attacks. The weight of metal, the perfect timing, gave irresistible power to the blow. The enemy line began to sag and crack. A number of German artillery groups fought to the death, while forward posts of enemy machine-gunners continued to indicate targets with white tracer. They took toll as the Churchills rolled through to the kill—a last venomous exaction as doom closed on them.

The tide of battle quickly receded from Ragoubet Souissi where 1/9 Gurkhas, their part played, took their ease. Many slept despite the thunder overhead. Others had unslung their brew cans and were busied with breakfast. Burial parties were picking up the sprawled dead. Casualties had been light—less than 50 in all. As 1/4 Essex passed through the Gurkhas they veered to the right, across the front of 4 British Division. The tanks had closed up and the Home County men moved on their final objective with an escort of 30 Churchills. The confident spirit of this great battalion was reflected by their transport, of which some 70 vehicles followed less than 800 yards behind the firing line. "C" Company with carriers raced off their front and overran a battery of 5 *nebelwerfers* in action against 4 British Division—the first occasion upon which these weapons had been captured. 7 Brigade, following close behind, deployed and swept forward. Brigadier Firth's men found themselves in the midst of a rout and a chase. The line had broken. The road to Tunis was open as the Axis forces in Africa fled from their last battlefield. At a cost of 137 casualties Fourth Indian Division had punched the hole.

7 Armoured Division, close on the heels of their old comrades, were on the move at 0730 hours. At 0845 hours the Desert Rats reported that they were abreast of the Indian objectives. They were not permitted to go through until Fourth Division had "loosened up" the defences. At 0925 hours Lieut.-Colonel Shepheard GSO. 1 on behalf of General Tuker advised 9 Corps that as far as could be judged defences had ceased to exist, 7 Armoured Division could "go as fast and as far as it liked". At 0940 hours General Tuker, in a conversation with the Corps Commander, repeated these assurances and was told that 7 Armoured Division would be loosed for Tunis as soon as Point 157 was secured. At 1030 hours the Royal Sussex reported themselves as established on this objective, with total casualties of 5 wounded. There was no longer any conceivable reason for delaying the view halloo: the time had come to ride hard to the kill. Yet throughout the day, as the broken enemy streamed away in search of a last sanctuary, 7 Armoured Division was only allowed to plod cautiously forward, and was eventually halted in the late afternoon for maintenance. At 1700 hours General Tuker implored Headquarters 9 Corps to despatch at least an armoured car squadron into the north-east to block the lines of retreat. He was informed that this was not possible.

11 Hussars won the race for Tunis, a well-earned entry in the game book of this great regiment. Of Fourth Indian Division only 12 Field Company advanced beyond the battle positions and then only as far as Bord Frendj, where a shell had punctured a wine vat and 8,000 gallons of potable beverage was running to waste. The pursuit had been sufficiently delayed to allow substantial enemy forces to crowd eastwards into the mountain block to the north of Enfidaville, where 90 Light Division and Folgore Division stood grimly at bay. Across the world the query hung on all lips—would the Cap Bon beaches spell Dunkirk or débâcle? On May 9th General Tuker in his observation plane carefully reconnoitred the ground between Tunis and Zaghouan on the northern slopes of the Enfidaville mountain block. (While confirming his impressions on foot, the Divisional Commander and Brigadier Dimoline flushed a German artillery observation group on top of the Djebel Cust, which fortunately did not stand to argue but incontinently fled). The value of these reconnaissances was demonstrated on the same day, when Fourth Division was instructed to join in the cordon around the Cap Bon area. Both brigades moved off to the east and took up positions by night, with 5 Brigade along the Zaghouan-Tunis track and 7 Brigade on their left to the north of Djebel St. Zit. The brigades were deployed on two sides of a square, 5 Brigade facing east and 7 Brigade south. On May 11th the beat began. Rearguard groups occasionally disputed the advance, but on the whole the operation represented no more than a round-up of the remaining Axis forces in Africa. Across the countryside columns of smoke poured into the air from burning dumps and transport. On the night of May 11th, fighting

patrols from 4/6 Rajputana Rifles and 1/9 Gurkhas gathered in 2,000 prisoners. The next day the entire Italian Superga Division surrendered to a Rajputana Rifles carrier patrol. Even the company cooks of 1/4 Essex brought in prisoners, taking care to fetch them in captured transport. By the afternoon of May 12th 5 Brigade had effected contact with French forces advancing from Pont du Fahs.

Meanwhile 7 Brigade had been working through the rolling ground to the south of the Gulf of Carthage. At 1400 hours on May 12th, Royal Sussex encountered an organised position to the north of Ste. Marie du Zit, where 80 feet of roadway had been blown away and strong rearguards, supported by artillery and mortars, maintained resistance. An attack led by the carriers overran the infantry positions, taking 150 prisoners. Mortar and artillery fire continued and no further progress was possible that night. 200 Gurkhas aided 12 Field Company in rebuilding the roadway. During the evening an officer of 10 Panzer Division arrived at Royal Sussex headquarters to arrange for the surrender of a Panzer Grenadier Regiment. Lieut.-Colonel Glennie ordered him to bring in his men next morning. At 0630 hours 3,000 Germans arrived to lay down their arms.

During the forenoon the Royal Sussex reached Ste. Marie du Zit, where another 500 prisoners were rounded up. Here a German staff car bearing a number of officers arrived, with Colonel G. S. Nolte, Chief of Staff Afrika Korps, as spokesman. This officer bore a personal letter from General von Arnim, the Axis Commander-in-Chief, to the officer commanding the Allied troops in that area. The emissary was forwarded under escort to General Tuker's headquarters near Ain el Aakar. The letter, on examination, proved to be an offer on the part of the German Commander-in-Chief to surrender himself, General Kram, Commander of 5 Panzer Army, and his Headquarters Staff. General Tuker immediately advised General Allfrey, Commander of 5 Corps, and arranged to proceed to General von Arnim's headquarters.

Before formal negotiations could ensue, 1/2 Gurkhas took a hand. This battalion had been mopping up to the south of Ste. Marie du Zit. Lieut.-Colonel Showers, who had accompanied his forward companies, climbed a ridge to reconnoitre. In a near-by hollow he spotted a staff car with a German officer beside it waving a white flag. He had stumbled upon von Arnim's headquarters. Covered by his orderly tommy-gunner, Rifleman Sargahna Limbu, he walked down into the camp, where upwards of 1,000 Germans had fallen in on parade. In Prussian fashion they were immaculately clad, clean-shaven, with accoutrements polished as for ceremonial. Lieut.-Colonel Showers, in ragged shorts and bush shirt, found himself marching along a rigid line of beautifully turned out enemies. As he approached the Commander-in-Chief's caravan, a staff officer, speaking English, advised him that Colonel Nolte had already left to arrange surrender. Lieut. Colonel Showers with this officer proceeded to Brigade Headquarters. On their way they met Lieut.-Colonel Glennie coming forward to post guards over von Arnim's camp.

General Tuker and General Allfrey arrived soon afterwards. In von Arnim's caravan, a large vehicle camouflaged with bushes and grass, conversations began in French. General von Arnim stated that even if he possessed the authority and wished to do so, he could not order the surrender of the Axis forces. He had lost touch with his troops and had no means of giving effect to his commands. General Tuker pointed out that any further bloodshed would be a German responsibility. The German Commander thereupon offered the surrender of his own Headquarters and that of 5 Panzer Army under General Kram. This was accepted.

General Tuker has described the remainder of the proceedings:

"The senior German staff officers then formed up outside their Commander's caravan, and the two generals walked down the line saying good-bye. A salute, a *heil* and a handshake—but no mention of Hitler was heard.

"The two generals, their chiefs of staff, ADCs and a German interpreter, got into their cars and drove away slowly under a guard of the Royal Sussex. Von Arnim stood up in the front seat of his car as he passed down the track between groups of Germans who were standing in their lines to say farewell to the commander of all Axis forces in Africa. They raised a cheer as he passed and then slowly formed into a long column to follow him into captivity."*

At 1800 hours that evening all organised resistance ceased. 220,000 prisoners crowded the cages, with more to come. In the mountains around Enfidaville 90 Light Division, doughtiest of enemies, had surrendered to the New Zealanders. Fourth Indian Division's take, in addition to the Axis Commander-in-Chief, ran into so many thousands that count was lost. Two years and 336 days after Italy had declared war, final and complete victory had crowned Allied arms in Africa.

*General Tuker claimed von Arnim's caravan on behalf of Fourth Indian Division. It was subsequently displayed in various parts of India in aid of military charities.

Chapter 20

AFTERMATH OF VICTORY

THE destruction of the Axis armies in Africa ranks with the recession of Hitler's armies from Stalingrad as a turning point in history. After nearly four years of war the Allies had won a victory so complete, so fraught with profound possibilities, that freedom-loving nations could gratefully re-echo Mr. Churchill's phrase, "Westward the land is bright". Of the felicitations attendant upon such an auspicious event Fourth Indian Division drew its full share.

Without recourse to the invidious vice of comparison, it could fairly be claimed that General Tuker's men had played a leading rôle in the victory. No other division in any of the three armies could quite match the Matmata—Akarit—Garci—Medjez-el-Bab series of battles. Neither 7 Armoured Division nor the New Zealanders, mighty men though they were, had been committed in all these operations. It was natural therefore that Fourth Indian Division should have received its full meed of the paeans which were showered on the victors. The capture of the German Commander-in-Chief, although only a fortuitous episode, inevitably put the capstone on the edifice of success and drew world attention to the part played by the wearers of the Red Eagle. The headlines were sufficiently fulsome for General Tuker to declare on May 15th in a letter to the Deputy Commander-in-Chief, India:

"BBC and others have said so much about Fourth Indian Division lately that there is a danger of some swollen heads and over-confidence. I shall have to drop heavily on that. We have a lot to learn yet".

From far and wide the congratulations flowed in. The Viceroy and General Hartley on behalf of Commander-in-Chief, India, wired warmest congratulations. Mr. Churchill's message as usual was felicitously phrased. Sir Firoz Khan Noon, Defence Member, telegraphed, "The whole of India is proud of your achievement in the defence of the freedom of India and of the world". Prince Mohammed Ali, Heir Apparent to the Egyptian throne, wired, "Please transmit my congratulations and admiration to all officers and troops of Fourth Indian Division. As an oriental Prince I think it my duty to tell them how happy and proud we feel to see them fighting with such stubborn courage". From old friends and new came a spate of congratulations: from Lieut.-General Sir Oliver Leese, Major-General Blaxland of 10 Indian Division and

AFTERMATH OF VICTORY

Major-General Russell of 8 Indian Division. Lieut.-General Sir William Platt, the former East African Commander, extolled "the final Dunkirking of the Axis out of Africa". On behalf of 2 New Zealand Division General Freyburg signalled: "We count it an honour and a privilege to have served beside you and trust that such will be our fortune again". General Anderson commanding First British Army wrote: "What a glorious climax to your long campaign in Africa!"

The senior Allied commanders each in his own way paid tribute to the prowess of India's fighting men. Perhaps the happiest contribution came from General Alexander, who on meeting General Tuker on May 14th promised him his third brigade and a reconnaissance regiment. General Montgomery now had no doubts; in a lecture to officers of Eighth Army at Tripoli on June 3rd, apropos of instructions to transfer troops to First British Army, he said, "I gave them my best—7 Armoured Division and Fourth Indian Division". General Eisenhower arrived for a visit bursting with high spirits and confidence. The Supreme Commander provided an enduring picture of a great man—simple, sincere and dynamic.

The last and greatest honour was to come. It was necessary to relieve the congestion in Tunisia as quickly as possible. On May 17th Fourth Division began to trek back to Tripolitania. A week later it had concentrated at Misurata, on the sea coast 120 miles east of Tripoli. Here a fortnight's complete rest was ordered with routine duties restricted to a minimum. After months of fighting it became possible to provide a few amenities. (In matters of soldiers' comforts Fourth Indian Division had long been off the map. The British troops had had one bottle of beer per head in three months, the Indian troops no rum tots at all). NAAFI canteens and welfare vans opened up: with sea-bathing, games and concert parties the days slid past.

Light training began early in June. When that month was ten days old, rumours of an important occasion began to circulate. It appeared that Fourth Indian Division would participate in a highly ceremonial parade for inspection by the Chief of the Imperial General Staff, the Secretary of State for War and GENERAL LYON, whose name neither roused a chord in memory nor was to be found in the Army List. It was all very high level. Senior officers dashed about in staff cars with portentous looks on their faces. Quartermasters grew as lenient as they were usually parsimonious; they issued lavishly while their clerks attended to fittings with all the care of West End tailors. The dhobis worked overtime. Polish and Blanco were laid on until spotless accoutrements shone. The NCOs threatened Gehenna for unclicking heels, for shoulder sockets which did not rattle with the snap of the salute. There was a corps rehearsal. On June 13th Algiers wireless broke the news. His Majesty the King-Emperor was in Africa and would review Fourth Indian Division.

Jawans will boast to their grandchildren of this day, which will stand in their memory even above great days of victory. Each unit has its own story of the occasion; in this history one must stand for all. The chronicler has chosen the narrative of 4 Field Company, Sappers and Miners, because of its intimate glimpses:

"As the evening draws on on June 18th one can feel the air of excitement which prevails. Songs break out as it gets dark. The British gunners are singing. 21 Company Sikhs are singing lustily. It catches on, our Hindus start singing and then the Sikhs and Pathans strike up on the far side of the road, and the Madrassis in 11 Field Park Company just next door start a weird noise accompanied by clapping. The general air of merriment, excitement and expectancy, is like that which surrounds the shoppers in a big city just before Christmas, or like children as they help decorate their homes on Christmas Eve. Tomorrow will be one of the greatest days in the lives of everyone here and in the history of the Indian Army."

"The sun rises at 6 o'clock into a cloudless blue sky. As the day wears on it gets hotter, but a breeze prevents the heat from becoming oppressive."

"The Company has to be fallen in by 1400 hours, so markers are called at 1340 hours and the Company at 1345 hours. First Platoon Commanders carry out their inspection and then O. C. carries out his inspection."

"The Company is drawn up in two ranks on either side of the main road from Castel Benito to Tripoli, immediately south of the 10 Kilo stone. NCOs and men with the longest service occupy the front rank and the rear rank covers off the gaps in the front rank. 'A' Platoon (Pathans) and 'B' Platoon (Sikhs) are on the west side of the road. 'C' Platoon (Hindus) and HQ Platoon (Mixed) are on the east side of the road. Officers and VCOs are one pace in front of the front rank of their platoons, with the O.C. in the centre on the east side."

"The CRE, Lieut.-Colonel J. A. Cameron, holds one final practice. Then the parade is stood easy."

"About 1450 hours we hear distant cheers to our south. The Review must have begun. These must be the cheers of Divisional Headquarters.

"We are honoured to be on the right of the line, immediately after the Royal Artillery. Hence we are the first Indian unit to be inspected by the King-Emperor.

"The cheers draw closer as the King passes each Field Regiment. The atmosphere is one of tense military pride as the great moment draws close. Then comes the CRE's order 'The Sappers will come to attention!' followed by the O.C.'s order 'Four Field Company attention!'

"The Royal car passes 12 Field Company, 11 Field Park Company and stops opposite the CRE, who is presented to the King-Emperor. The CRE shakes hands with His Majesty and then says, 'May I present

Subedar Narinder Singh'. Subedar Narinder Singh then took a pace forward to the car, saluted and shook hands with the King-Emperior. His Majesty then asked the CRE 'How many years service has he got?' to which the CRE replied 'Eighteen years, Sir'. His Majesty then asked the CRE 'Can he speak English?' and the CRE replied 'Yes, Sir.' The King-Emperor then checked up on the accuracy of the CRE and said to Subedar Narinder Singh 'How many years service have you got?' Subedar Narinder Singh said 'Seventeen years, Sir'. The King remarked 'A good lot'. The CRE then took a pace to the rear and ordered, 'Sappers and Miners, three cheers for His Majesty the King-Emperor!'

"As the Company cheered, the officers raised their hats and the men their right hands. Everyone was able as they cheered to look towards the Royal Car, where the King-Emperor was standing up acknowledging the cheers. He was dressed in the uniform of a Field-Marshal and was wearing a bush shirt without medal ribbons. In spite of being told that the King would be dressed in uniform there were still men who expected to see him in an ermine mantle wearing a crown."

"As the last of the cheers died away the Royal car moved off, passing slowly between the men, with His Majesty scanning the ranks as he passed".

General Tuker and General Montgomery accompanied the King. At each unit the Royal car stopped. At 1/2 Gurkha Rifles General Tuker introduced Lieut.-Colonel Showers. His Majesty then asked to be introduced to Subedar-Major Narbahadur Gurung, an officer of 23 years service, an outstanding personality and one of the most popular figures in Eighth Army. Subedar Lalbahadur Thapa then stepped forward and His Majesty pinned the ribbon of the Victoria Cross on the Gurkha officers sturdy chest. "You did a very brave act. I am proud of you" said the King, who expressed his pleasure at being able to perform this investiture. Lieut.-Colonel Showers replied that it was a great day for his battalion, since it was the first occasion upon which the King had presented a decoration to a Gurkha soldier. His Majesty, noting the ring of photographers, expressed the hope that the battalion would receive a generous supply of photographs.* Wishing all the best of luck he drove on.

The 4 Field Company narrative supplies an interesting glimpse of the close of this great day:

*The King-Emperor's reference to photographers was particularly felicitous, since the ciné record of the ceremony, taken by Capt. Gerald Ingram MBE, was one of the best Fourth Division films of the war. It was obtained only after personal intervention by General Montgomery. All publicity coverage of the King's tour was in the hands of the War Office and Middle East officers were accorded no facilities. On discovering this Capt. Ingram, greatly daring, paraded to General Montgomery, who said, "My boy, this is not a War Office area. This is Eighth Army area. You may take all the pictures of his Majesty that you wish".

"In the evening General Tuker came around to see the Company. The CRE had given everyone a bottle of beer with which to drink the health of the King-Emperor. The Company sat around in a circle and each man charged his drinking vessel. (In many instances this was the bottle). The Pathans filled their mugs with tea. We all stood to drink The King's health. After that the General walked around, chatting to each man. He caused great astonishment and amusement by telling each man from which district he came. In four out of five cases he was right. He was particularly good with Hindus but tailed off somewhat with the Sikhs and Pathans. Finally the General left. We gave him three cheers."

"We stayed in the circle long after he was gone. Various men came forward to sing and to do conjuring tricks. We were all terribly proud that the Subedar had been presented to the King-Emperor. Many men said, "As the Subedar has been presented I feel as though the King-Emperor has shaken hands with me"."

The truism that adversity welds friendships but success divorces comrades was pleasingly refuted in Fourth Indian Division. At the end of a period in which adulation might have bred arrogance General Tuker's men remained modest and unspoiled. One half were British, one half Indian; their diverse threads blended perfectly in the texture of the Division. The men were proud of each other. Many instances of mutual confidence and admiration have been quoted in the course of this narrative. The infantry swore by its gunners. The gunners declared that there was no infantry comparable with theirs. The Sappers and Miners, always in the van, sharing all dangers and working untold hours at backbreaking tasks, the sleepless signallers whose lines tied the Division together, the medical units encamped on every battlefield with their stretcher bearers following the fighting line, the supply, transport, ordnance and IEME formations which met every emergency with deft improvisations—each in time of peril had earned the wholehearted gratitude of its comrades. The sense of integration, of being part of a splendid community, which General Montgomery had laboured to instill in all ranks of Eighth Army, needed no elaboration in Fourth Indian Division. That outlook was ingrained in all ranks.

The team spirit of Briton, Indian and Gurkha was illustrated on countless occasions. When the BBC instituted unit recordings for home transmission, many British units insisted on including an Indian spokesman. Indian units in turn always asked for a British comrade to speak a few words. An American war correspondent visited 4/6 Rajputana Rifles while Colonel Scott and his men were making ready to move forward to the desperate grapple on the Djebel Garci. The pressman asked a havildar if he knew what the war was about. "Certainly" said the havildar, "it is our friends war; therefore it is ours." When the unkempt and rather hairy Eighth Army reached Medjez el Bab and mingled with the trim and well-equipped First Army the jawans said, "This is indeed a well-found land but the soldiers are in no sense the equal of our soldiers". If enemy planes flew high it was because they dare not face 57 LAA Regiment. If they flew low it was because these gunners were not in the neighbourhood. A British signaller after fourteen months with Fourth Indian Division wrote from hospital:

"The Indian soldiers are among the best fighters in the Allied armies. Their good qualities do not stop there. They are wonderful and loyal comrades. For example they get a better issue of tea, sugar and milk than we do. Every time they brew up we get dozens of invitations to cups of tea. Sometimes we would be kept busy until well past mealtime, but regardless of the time of day or night the Indian cooks could be counted upon to prepare a jolly good meal for us."

"The most outstanding thing that I noticed about them was that they could keep perfectly clean under the most appaling conditions. I have many friends among them, many of whom could speak English. I was learning Urdu. I am fervently hoping that my wound will heal quickly so that I can get back to the Division."

An Indian Army Observer reported a characteristic incident:

"'S' Battery of 149 Anti-Tank Regiment had its initial testing at Wadi Akarit, where it supported the Gurkhas. Afterward it moved with the Gurkhas all the way to Tunis. Nothing further apart could be imagined that Gurkhas and the men of this battery, who had been drawn from a territorial battalion of Gordon Highlanders. Yet a sentimental attachment grew up between them. In the quiet hours when the hillsmen were serving hospitable 'cha' to anyone who could visit them, they would enquire of their guests 'Anti-Tank Top Khana Hai?' and when the inevitable confirmation came they would smile and say softly, ' "S" Battery'. It is high praise to identify a regiment with a battery, and higher praise still from the lips of a Gurkha."

"With the campaign over 'S' Battery was ordered to return to the Delta. The general regret felt at the loss of gunners which had now become old friends was crystallised by a gesture from the Gurkhas. They lined the road and cheered as the battery drove away. Into the middle of the road and in front of the Battery Commander's car strode the rotund impressive figure of a famed Subedar Major. He signalled the car to halt, and to the astonished Major made a final gesture of admiration. He presented him with a kukri on behalf of the Gurkha battalions. Then the Gurkhas sprang forward, attached ropes to the car. To the music of a Gurkha pipe band they manhandled the car in true artillery fashion for a short distance along the road."

" 'S' Battery were about to form a new regiment. That kukri to them must always symbolise the profound conflict-tested mutual admiration, trust and understanding between men of two races, though they come 'from the ends of the earth'."

This remarkable brotherhood was no fortuitous circumstance. It represented under General Tuker's leadership the labours of a group of intelligent and devoted officers. The principal staff appointments were held by outstanding men. Lieut.-Colonel J. K. Shepheard DSO, a Sapper officer who after seven years' service with Indian field companies had come to Middle East as Brigade Major of 161 (Essex) Infantry Brigade, was a highly trained soldier of steady mind and inflexible resolution. The GSO 2, Major A. E. Cocksedge, DSO, of 2/5 Mahrattas, a man of charming personality and considerable literary attainments, possessed a meticulous mind and a passion for detail which served the Division in excellent stead. Lieut.-Colonel J. A. C. Greenwood OBE, a Bombay business man attached to 4/11 Sikhs, brought to the onerous office of Divisional Quartermaster an alert intelligence, a flair for organisation and unfailing ability to improvise in emergency. Colonel F. R. H. Mollan, MC, ADMS, a veteran Medical Officer, infected all his subordinates with his vigorous Irish personality. Lieut.-Colonel J. A. Cameron, CRE, an efficient Scotsman, led the Sappers and Miners in the magnificent tradition of their Corps. Lieut.-Colonel P. L. Gray, OBE, drove his tandem team of British and Indian Signallers with the deft touch of long experience. Lieut.-Colonel C. W. G. Thorpe, CRIASC, kept the supply services on their toes and ready for any emergency. Lieut.-Colonel C. H. Sanderson, OBE, the tireless and resourceful CIEME, daily performed miracles with his ever-labouring workshops.

The field commanders magnificently implemented the work of the staff. Brigadiers Bateman, Lovett and Dimoline each were outstanding men in their field—Brigadier Bateman with conspicuous attainments as a staff officer, Brigadier Lovett as an unexcelled battle commander and Brigadier Dimoline as a technician of high capacity and flexible mind. Their right-hand men, Major G. H. Carr, IAC, Major W. W. Stewart, MC, 1/2 Gurkhas, and Major E. J. Wyld, RA, brought enthusiasm and energy to their tasks. The unit commanders likewise were officers of experience and resource. Lieut.-Colonel A. Noble, DSO, of 1/4 Essex had assumed command in December 1941 and had led his battalion in every battle in the campaign. Lieut.-Colonel R. B. Scott, DSO, whose quiet cold courage was a byword in his battalion, had come to Africa with 4/6 Rajputana Rifles. Except for his unscheduled tour of Europe as a Vichy prisoner he had been with them ever since. Lieut.-Colonel Ian Roche, DSO, a veteran officer, had brought 1/9 Gurkha Rifles to Middle East. Lieut.-Colonel C. E. A. Firth, who succeeded to the command of 7 Brigade when Brigadier Lovett was wounded, had handed over command of 1 Royal Sussex to Major J. B. A. Glennie, an officer of conspicuous service. Lieut.-Colonel H. A. Hughes, MBE, able soldier, genial wit and great companion, endowed 4/16 Punjabis with the high spirits of a Varsity rugger side.* Lieut.-Colonel L. J. G.

---

*Among many memorable bon mots Colonel Hughes' admonition to a somewhat arrogant brigadier, a casual visitor from New Delhi, deserves to be enshrined: "I think you should remember, Sir, that every brigadier carries a bowler hat in his knapsack".

Showers, DSO, who took over 1/2 Gurkhas on Brigadier Lovett's promotion, had previously held an important staff appointment and had proved an exceptionally able leader in the field. Lieut.-Colonel F. G. Cuerden and his men of the Machine Gun Battalion, 6 Rajputana Rifles, on account of serving under other formations and seldom appearing as a unit, never emerged in the limelight to the extent that they deserved; yet those whom these aggressive and well-trained gunners covered or supported never failed to pay tribute to them.

Lieut.-Colonel H. Thorne-Thorne of 1 Field Regiment, Lieut.-Colonel A. H. E. Howell of 11 Field Regiment, Lieut.-Colonel C. H. Norton, OBE, of 31 Field Regiment (the latest in a series of outstanding commanders), Lieut.-Colonel G. L. Hildebrand of 149 Anti-tank Regiment and Lieut.-Colonel E. D. Howard-Vyse of 57 LAA Regiment all maintained their units at a high stage of efficiency and delivered them at full potential in the execution of Brigadier Dimoline's programmes.

No list of outstanding officers in the Division would be complete without mention of Lieut.-Colonel H. J. R. Thorne, DSO, RAMC, and Lieut.-Colonel G. S. N. Hughes, DSO, IMS, who commanded 17 and 26 Indian Field Ambulances. Together with their devoted doctors and staff they followed the fighting men everywhere, bringing prompt succour to the wounded and confidence to all ranks. Nor would it be out of place to mention a unit which never showed on the Divisional establishment and yet was claimed as its own with pride and admiration. The young volunteer ambulance drivers of American Field Service had first been encountered in Syria in 1941. During the Tunisian campaign a section joined Fourth Indian Division and immediately in wholehearted American fashion identified themselves with their British and Indian colleagues. Tireless and daring, they roamed the battlefields until their name became a by-word for energy and ingenuity. In turn they found a home in the Division, establishing the happiest relationship with all ranks. Their pride in Fourth Indian Division was boundless and as a result of their admiration a number of these attractive college men later accepted commissions in combatant units of the Indian Army.

The glow of excitement engendered by the visit of the King-Emperor still hung over the Division when on June 22nd the move to Egypt began. Day by day the columns wound back through well-remembered scenes—Agheila, Benghazi, Cyrene, Derna, Tmimi, Tobruk, Salum and Mersa Matruh—a 1500 mile trek which ended when Divisional Headquarters and 7 Brigade found camp on the outskirts of Alexandria among the sand dunes along the Mediterranean. 5 Brigade was allotted a dusty and uninteresting encampment near Burgh el Arab village, 25 miles to the west. Here Fourth Indian Division passed under command of GHQ, Middle East with the customary discouraging accompaniments. Even as it settled down to static garrison duties Eighth Army had leapt into Sicily with 50 and 51 Divisions in the van. Once again the fighting front receded leaving Fourth Indian Division with a stranded feeling. Officers and men felt that they had earned something better. Once again the struggle began between General Tuker, who wished to keep his Division together and to train it for battles to come, and GHQ, who wished to scatter it thither and far on a variety of errands. "Since we have only two brigades I doubt if we can be dispersed over three continents" wrote the Divisional Commander.

On the credit side, there remained another signal honour to come. Early in August the War Office asked that a representative party from the Division should be detailed for a tour of Great Britain. The following were chosen:

British Officers.

Lt. Col.	R. B. Scott, DSO.	4/6 Rajputana Rifles
Major	J. H. Gibson, MC., RA.	31 Field Regiment R.A.

British Warrant Officers.

R.S.M.	F. E. Harwood, DCM.	149 Anti-Tank Regiment R.A.
RQMS	A. Taylor	Royal Signals
B.S.M.	W. Riddle	1 Field Regiment R.A.
C.S.M.	J. Downes	1st Bn. The Royal Sussex Rgt.
C.S.M.	R. H. Cox	1/4 Bn. Essex Regiment

Viceroy's Commissioned Officers.

Sub.Maj.	Agandhar Khandaka, IOM.	1/9 Gurkha Rifles
Sub.Maj.	Gulab Singh	7 I.B.T. Coy. R.I.A.S.C.
Sub.Maj.	Vishwambar Ghadge, IOM.	2/5 Mahratta Light Infantry
Sub.	Lalbahadur Thapa, VC.	1/2 Gurkha Rifles
Sub.	Bir Singh	4/11 Sikh Regiment
Sub.	Mohd Bashir	4 Ind. Div. Signals
Sub.	Sampangiraj, IOM.	12 Fd. Coy. Madras S. and M.
Sub.	Redkar	17 Fd. Amb. I.A.M.C.
Jem.	Mian Mohamed, IDSM.	4/16 Punjab Regiment
Jem.	Zaristan Khan	3/10 Baluch Regiment
Jem.	Bhima Ram, IOM., IDSM.	1/6 Rajputana Rifles
Jem.	Harnath Singh, IDSM.	3/1 Punjab Regiment
Jem.	Habib Khan, IOM.	4/6 Rajputana Rifles
Jem	Mohammed Shafi	I.A.O.C.

British Other Ranks.

Gnr.	Holmes, R. J.	57 LAA Regt. R.A.
Pte.	Mackinlay, N., MM.	1st Bn. The Royal Sussex Rgt.

Indian Other Ranks.

Rfm.	Deda Ram	1/6 Rajputana Rifles
Sep.	Mohamed Nawaz, IDSM.	4/16 Punjab Regiment
Spr.	Sher Rehman	4 Fd. Coy. Bengal S. and M.
Dvr.	Sewa Singh	4 Ind. Div. H.Q. M.T. Section
Rfm.	Daibir Thapa	1/2 Gurkha Rifles

Followers.

Cook	Ram Saran	5 I.B.T. Coy. R.I.A.S.C.
Cook	Bhom Singh	1/6 Rajputana Rifles
Cook	Mohamed Yakub	4/16 Punjab Regiment
Water Carrier	Zakir Hussain	I.A.O.C.
Sweeper	Parsadi Ram	Bombay Sappers and Miners

A Correspondent wrote:

"Not a section of the Indian Army had been left out; Sikhs, Pathans, Jats, Punjabi Mussulmans, Mahrattas, Rajputs, Dogras, technicians from Madras, Bengal and Bombay. Among them were Britishers. It was perhaps that aspect of an Indian division—that Indians and British fight together—which left the deepest impression wherever the contingent went. Men of the Royal Sussex and Essex, gunners and a signaller bronzed from the desert, took their places in the parades, on the platforms, in the factories, in the theatres. They offered visual evidence that dangers and hazards shared make for great comradeship".

For a crowded fortnight the United Kingdom paid whole-hearted tribute to these straight fine soldiers whose deeds had won such accolades. There were "brass hat" functions when the fighting men were surrounded by the great names of the land; on one such occasion Field-Marshal Lord Birdwood stirred inspiring memories by his speech in Hindustani. But the daily round of sight-seeing and visits also was designed to introduce the representatives of India's great army to the working people of Great Britain, who had endured rigours not less than those of the battlefield. At Shoreditch, in the heart of East London's bombed area, a crowd of ten thousand gathered to give acclaim to the men who had won through in North Africa. Everywhere the British public took these simple dignified soldiers to its heart; in spite of the austerity of war the warmth of welcome made every occasion memorable.

The reactions of the visitors were no less favourable than those of the hosts. Subedar Lalbahadur Thapa, VC, naturally ran the gauntlet of exceptional publicity. He was photographed with the Lord Mayor of London's sword, playing ping pong, accepting a bottle of whisky from a Lancashire publican, endlessly scribbling his signature in autograph books; yet when asked what had impressed him most in a new country and strange social system, he designated the nurseries in which women war workers left their children while at the factories. Jemadar Zaristan Khan similarly gave pride of place to the rehabilitation of wounded by means of physical training; Subedar Mohamed Bashir to bathing pools in which tots of three learned to swim; Jemadar Bhima Ram to the escalators in the tube stations; Subedar Sampangiraj to the employment of blind workers in an aircraft factory; Sapper Sher Rehman to the food rationing which "gave enough for all"; Subedar Mian Mohamed to the endless excitement of "jolly small boys and girls together waving flags. They fill me with wonder". These were mature judgments, befitting men who had come to own no peers on a world battlefield.

On August 17th the Sicilian campaign ended. Before dawn on September 3rd the leading elements of Eighth Army were ashore on the continent of Europe. Italy surrendered, but the Germans stemmed the Allied advance from the toe of Calabria by rushing heavy reinforcements to man the Gustav line to the north of Naples. The relief map showed central Italy to be a mass of mountains; ergo, it was the proper place for Fourth Indian Division. In spite of disparaging rumours concerning the employment of Indian troops in Europe it was known that they were on call. (General Alexander in mid-August in Sicily gave a Public Relations Officer precise dates of arrival in Italy for all three Indian divisions in Middle East). There was much to be done and every reason for making ready; yet General Tuker encountered continuous obstacles in his endeavours to re-equip, reinforce and train his men.

Throughout the summer the Divisional Commander had been hammering away in an endeavour to obtain his long-promised third brigade. There were in Middle East a considerable number of detached Indian battalions, many of them with a core of veteran personnel. Until September no action had been taken to re-form 11 Brigade. During a lecture tour in England in September/October General Tuker interested the Chief of the Imperial General Staff in the matter. On his return to Middle East General Maitland-Wilson advised him that the brigade was being assembled as rapidly as possible. In line with his recommendations a British, Gurkha and Indian batttalion would be included. The Indian battalion was to be 4/6 Rajputana Rifles which had been replaced in 5 Brigade in July by 1/6 Rajputana Rifles (Lieut.-Colonel J. R. West) in order that Lieut.-Colonel Scott's men might have the opportunity to reorganise. When Fourth Division was warned for service in Italy General Tuker was informed that it would be necessary to retain 11 Brigade on Middle East establishment. The loss of one of his most prized units led the Divisional Commander to a sharp and vehement protest. He wrote:

"4/6 Rajputana Rifles has fought in every single battle that Fourth Indian Division has fought anywhere throughout the war. It has earned two Victoria Crosses in this Division and is the very pith and core of the Division. It is unthinkable that this battalion should ever wear the badge of any other division. Every single officer and man under my command knows of its past and deeply regrets its absence".

These representations led to re-consideration and 11 Brigade was re-allotted to its original Division. By a happy circumstance its other battalions were reconstitutions of units lost at Tobruk. 2 Camerons was fresh from Britain and 2/7 Gurkhas had been rebuilt around a sprinkling of old hands.

Similar difficulties arose over the provision of a reconnaissance regiment. It will be remembered that the Divisional Cavalry, Central India Horse, after the withdrawal from Gazala in February 1942, had departed for a long tour of duty in PAIFORCE. For more than a year General Tuker had been seeking a replacement. Finally in July 1943 the Divisional Commander took the initiative and organised a Recce Group for each brigade out of its own resources. These groups were trained and equipped by Middle East but when ready to take the field GHQ India refused to recognise them. The tussle over these formations continued and it was only at the last moment before sailing (December 15th) that General Tuker was advised that Central India Horse would be restored to him at some later date in Italy.

The difficulties over units and training was re-enacted in the provision of men and equipment. As late as mid-November Fourth Indian Division was 4,500 men under strength. British personnel, particularly gunners and signallers, had been drained off to other divisions. The field regiments were 600 men under strength. Equipment was equally hard to come by. When 2 New Zealand Division sailed for Italy it took 4,000 vehicles. Fourth Indian Division although recognised as a mountain division was given a transport establishment of 3,200 and even this number was not to be had. With some justice General Tuker wrote on the eve of departure for Italy:

"As a Divisional Commander I have always done a great deal more fighting to keep my Division in existence and to obtain equipment and the opportunity to train them than I have ever done against the enemy. I feel that if divisional commanders were spared the former battles we could win more of the latter".*

He added a strong recommendation that an officer of high rank should be sent to GHQ Middle East to act on behalf of Indian divisions in the field. He pointed out that Australia, New Zealand and South Africa, all with contingents smaller than those of India, had lieutenant-generals to speak for them. It was not a matter of neglect or ill-will towards Indian formations. It was simply that in an operational theatre peopled by diverse entities, those units which could not support their claims on the highest levels would not receive the priorities essential to fit them for service in the field.

Fortunately the rank and file knew nothing of the travail attendant upon the rebirth of the Division. For them it had been a great year. It began by re-admission to the select circles of the battlefield. In a

*Lieut.-Colonel W. W. Stewart, MC, comments:—

"The comparison with 2 New Zealand Division perhaps is a little unfair to GHQ M.E.F. Once it became known that we were going to Italy they accepted our recommendations for a mountain division establishment of vehicles and did their best to provide them. When we got to Italy our establishment of vehicles was the envy of 8 Indian Division and other British divisions and A.F.H.Q. did their best to cut us down".

series of smashing blows Indian troops had won world-wide acclaim and ascendancy in the hierarchy of fighting men. The King-Emperor in person had come far to thank them. Lazy weeks of rest beside the Mediterranean had been followed by long treks, beloved of all soldiers. Then autumn in the Lebanons—a valiant season with hard training, a tensing of the muscles and a quickening of the pulses as a new theatre and fresh battles beckoned.

In late November Fourth Indian Division took to the southering roads through Palestine. The units mustered at Suez, where the dazzle-painted transports filled the harbour. On December 2nd the convoy emerged in the open Mediterranean. The troopships hoisted their guardian balloons and eight destroyers raced to station. Drivers of 1 and 11 Field Regiments were in the stokehold of one transport, replacing stokers who had struck at Alexandria. They gave as their opinion that stoking in four hour shifts was light duty after the customary hours of labour in Western Desert. Four days later the high cone of Aetna was picked up. On December 7th the convoy anchored off Taranto.

Chapter 21

ITALY — THE FIRST PHASE

FOURTH Division disembarked on December 8th in raw, blustery weather and marched to improvised camps among the olive groves outside Taranto. Soaking winter rains had transformed the ground into a quagmire. Colds and bronchitis lengthened the sick parades but in a remarkably short time the troops became acclimatised. There was nothing approaching the mass sickness which laid low Indian troops in France during the winter of 1914—a tribute to improvements in training, clothing, equipment and medical care.

The inconveniences and discomforts of the first weeks in Italy were enhanced by the non-arrival from Middle East of a second flight of 1,500 specialists and their vehicles. 2 Polish Corps, moving from Egypt concurrently, apparently received priority in shipping space. Then difficulties arose over the new establishment as a mountain division, which had been accepted by GHQ Middle East at the completion of training in Syria. AFHQ Italy was sceptical as to the necessity for any changes from normal infantry division establishment and the essential alterations in personnel and equipment were only approved after a sharp struggle.

The Division had no more than found its land legs when General Tuker was ordered to detail a brigade group for employment in the forward area, and also to supply a battalion for guard duties at Bari. As 11 Brigade was yet to arrive, this left Fourth Indian Division with two battalions of infantry. Moreover, from the nature of their demands, it was clear that Allied Force Headquarters Italy was not properly cognisant of the problems of caste, race, food and language which existed in an Indian Division. General Tuker protested with such vigour that a staff officer was sent from Eighth Army Headquarters, who settled matters to the Divisional Commander's satisfaction.

In mid-December Fourth Division moved to the Potenza area, 75 miles west of Taranto and approximately half-way to Naples. Training began in the hilly country to the north-west of the town. Here Fourth Division spent its fourth Christmas abroad. Most units were able to celebrate the festival in fitting fashion, with 4/16 Punjabis perhaps luckier than the rest. An officer of that battalion wrote:

"We spent Christmas in a village graced by a mediaeval castle. Our billets in the past had received the patronage of the kings of Albania and of certain scions of the House of Savoy. We had stocked ourselves with turkeys and various other kinds of poultry while local resources obliged with lamb and pork. Rum issues and meat on the hoof for the sepoys were available. Snow arrived appropriately to complete the atmosphere. Even mistletoe and holly were there to give the feast a nostalgic quickening."

The first snow was followed by blizzards. January opened with freezing rains, hail and wet snow flurries. 5 Brigade moved out on exercises only to encounter fresh falls which blocked the roads. Motor transport froze and troops were scattered over the countryside, in some instances finding billets in farms and in other cases being obliged to abandon their vehicles and to return on foot. 1/6 Rajputana Rifles had to be dug out, some of their men being isolated on hilltops with drifts six feet deep blocking all tracks. This battalion found a friend in need in the person of an Italian farmer who only appears in the records as "Jimmy". He had lived in America, spoke what passed for English and was imbued with hustle. He arranged accommodation, supplied firewood, organised shovel parties and led rescues. A narrow gauge railway was opened and a number of Italian snow ploughs enlisted to clear the roads.

Meanwhile General Tuker with his brigade and battalion commanders had gone forward to survey the battlefield. Eighth Army's drive northward through Calabria, Basilica and Puglia had encountered its first serious opposition in the previous October on the line of the River Trigno, which discharges into the Adriatic 165 miles north-west of Taranto. Here 8 Indian Division under the command of Major-General Dudley Russell, the former 5 Brigade commander, began its glorious fighting career. Thereafter the enemy fell back a further 25 miles to man defensive positions in the Gustav Line. This massive system crossed Italy from the Adriatic to the Tyrrhenian seas. In a series of bitter battles between November 27th and December 30th British, Canadian and Indian troops had broken into the enemy defences along the Adriatic. The Germans fought desperately to hold the line of the Ortona-Orsogna highway since the town of Orsogna, 18 miles inland, represented a key bastion of the Gustav system. Here on December 7th the newly arrived New Zealanders attacked with two brigades and fought their way into the centre of the town. A heavy counter-attack flung them back. In a battle of rising intensity the Kiwis and 5 British Division struck again and again. On December 31st a raging blizzard with intense cold ended the general offensive against the Gustav positions.

On January 9th Mediterranean weather returned; zephyrs and a warm sun sped the snow. The next day the call came to Fourth Indian Division to move forward under command of 13 Corps, led by Lieut.-General Miles Dempsey, soon to proceed to Europe as commander of British Second Army. 13 Corps at this juncture consisted of 2 New Zealand Division and 78 British Division, which had distinguished itself

ITALY — THE FIRST PHASE

in the North African campaign. On January 13th General Tuker conferred with the Corps Commander and learned that on arrival in the forward area Fourth Division would relieve the New Zealanders in the Orsogna sector. Thereafter it would be expected to storm the town and to break the enemy front.

Having reconnoitred the position both on the ground and from the air the Divisional Commander realised that his men faced a formidable task. Orsogna, strong and well built, was situated in a commanding position on the ridge between the Moro and the Arielli rivers. General Tuker described it as "an island with steep approaches on all sides except to the north-west". To the difficulty of the terrain was added the uncertainty of the weather. (With an eye to all possibilities the Divisional Commander visited the Canadians in the coastal sector and obtained a drawing of an improvised snowshoe. From this model he arranged with General Leese, who at the end of 1943 had replaced General Montgomery as Eighth Army commander, to have 4,000 pairs made.) On account of the situation on Fifth Army's front (where the Anzio landing was imminent) it was essential that Eighth Army should maintain the utmost pressure against the enemy. Plans therefore were expedited for a major assault against Orsogna in which under General Tuker's command Fourth Indian Division would be supplemented by a Canadian infantry brigade group, a Canadian armoured brigade, 36 Brigade of 78 Division and a Canadian motor battalion.

On January 14th 7 Brigade moved forward in drenching rain and relieved 5 New Zealand Brigade on the right of Orsogna in a sector which ran down to the Arielli river. The line followed the reverse slopes of narrow hills and consisted of linked-up strong points. Headquarters and most formations occupied farmhouses with outlying dug-in positions which were manned at night or in case of alarm during the day. As long as groups in the open kept below the crests of the knife-backed ridges, they were moderately safe. Behind the front, the roads for a considerable distance were under intimate observation by the enemy and any extensive movement drew fire.

Of this tour of duty Brigadier Lovett wrote:

"The left sector of 7 Brigade front was particularly unpleasant, due both to the extremely bad weather and to the close proximity of the enemy. Men coming back from a spell in the line were much exhausted by the heavy shelling and by the constant vigilance necessary to keep on top of the Germans".

An Indian Army Observer described the situation in greater detail:

"Fighting on the Indian front in Italy nowadays consists of nightly hide-and-seek around houses in No-Man's Land. When dusk comes patrols go out to investigate localities where movement had been detected during the day. It is a nerve-racking business with patrols creeping with blackened faces through the mud—undoubtedly the sort of thing which was prevalent in the last war in Flanders. The enemy is constantly active with 'rustling' raids aimed at snatching identifications. Several such forays have been beaten back with losses.

"Although it is a period of comparative inactivity on the Eighth Army front artillery and mortar shoots are to be expected at any hour of the day or night. Our harassing fire programme is designed, as an artillery officer put it, 'to make the Boches keep their heads down and to pin their ears back'. The Germans respond to this hate but their fire is nothing in comparison with ours. Twenty-five pounders from time to time crack as rapidly as machine-guns and life for the Germans must be extremely noisy and uncertain."

This view of Allied artillery activity was confirmed by a captured letter from a batch of outgoing mail of 2 Company, 146 Grenadier Regiment, then on the Adriatic front:

"Dear Brother: The sweat of fear was streaming down my face last night. Thank God my guardian angel was looking after me. I was on sentry when Tommy opened up on us good and proper. I was filled with fear as you can well imagine. Dear Josef, you tell me you don't want to become a parachutist but would like to get into the S.S. Neither of these branches is any good to you. You get into the heavy artillery. That's what I recommend. You see, the heavy artillery is well to the rear and if you are with it you aren't so likely to get a shell lobbed alongside you."

"The lice are at me now and I haven't washed or shaved for a fortnight. We daren't show ourselves in daylight. In the night Tommy often opens up suddenly and we are liable to get a packet. The best thing is to sit on your backside in the dug-out and watch until you see a Tommy to shoot at. All I am doing is waiting for the war to end."

On the night of January 18th 1/4 Essex led 5 Brigade into the line on the right of 7 Brigade. This tour of duty was of short duration as the Canadian formations which were to serve under General Tuker in the assault on Orsogna were moving into the front line. Nevertheless both Royal Sussex and 1/2 Gurkhas clashed with the enemy in patrol encounters, the Royal Sussex capturing 9 prisoners in an attempted raid on one of their outposts. On relief a company of Rajputana Rifles Machine Gun Battalion remained behind with the Westminster Motor Battalion. On January 22nd Lieut. A. J. V. Samuels and 20 men of 1/9 Gurkhas in the course of a patrol sustained 9 casualties. On January 21/22 the Perth Regiment of Canada, the Cape Breton Highlanders and the Irish Regiment of Canada relieved the Essex, the Royal Sussex and 1/2 Gurkhas. 11 Canadian Armoured Regiment arrived to train with 5 Brigade for the coming assault. On January 25th Fourth Division returned to the line, 1/9 Gurkhas and 1/6 Rajputana Rifles relieving Canadian troops in the Salarolo and Bianco sectors. This date is memorable for a remarkable coincidence. On the morning of that day the new 11 Indian Infantry Brigade arrived at Taranto. In the evening the old commander of 11 Brigade, Brigadier A. Anderson, DSO, MC, who had been captured at Tobruk, arrived at Fourth Divisional Headquarters after an adventurous escape.

4/16 Punjabis, who had remained in the line on the relief of the Royal Sussex and Essex, had devoted themselves to making life unpleasant for the enemy around the Carloni feature. Here on January 21st a platoon established itself. The occupying force was stepped up to a company before the enemy struck back. On the night of January 25/26 the same procedure was followed on a two company front. One platoon failed to gain its ground but brought back six prisoners of 334 Division. Heavy artillery exchanges followed and next day under cover of a smoke screen the Punjabis withdrew.

On the night of January 28th a 45-minute fire fight ensued when enemy patrols endeavoured to infiltrate between 1/6 Rajputana Rifles and 1/9 Gurkhas. At the end of the month, Lieut.-Colonel Ian Roche, DSO, handed over command of the latter battalion to his second-in-command, Lieut.-Colonel G. Nangle.

The battle for Orsogna was expected to open on February 7th when the main assault to turn the town would be mounted from the northwest, together with a subsidiary attack against the eastern approaches. No one was happy over the prospects. The spongey fields confined armour to a few congested roads. Even infantry bogged down in the sodden morasses along the swollen streams. The attack represented an attempt to break the enemy at his strongest point. On January 21st while at church service General Tucker received an urgent summons to Corps. There he was instructed that the assault on Orsogna had been abandoned and that Fourth Indian Division would move to join Fifth Army at once.

"Shades of Tunisia" said one of his officers. General Tuker was devoutly thankful. He wrote: "I must say that I think Providence has been kind to this Division. Each time when we were about to be cast at some awful fortress something has intervened to help me fight the battle of stopping a needless sacrifice of life. I hope it is not Fifth Army's intention to use us against some impregnable place."

The Divisional Commander's fears were not without foundation. Fourth Indian Division had been ordered to Cassino.

Chapter 22

CASSINO — THE LINE UP

TWENTY miles inland from the Tyrrhenian Sea a buttress of stone as high and abrupt as Gibraltar abutted into the junction of the spacious Liri valley and the confined sac of the Gari/Rapido valley. This great boss, the most southerly promontory of the Matese massif, was Monte Cassino. It constituted the central bastion of the Gustav Line and represented a classical example of the control exercised by height on terrain.

The Gustav Line crossed Italy in the narrowest and most mountainous region of the Kingdom. As has been noted previously, the spurs of the Maiellas extended to within a few miles of the Adriatic beaches. On the Tyrrhenian coast the flat foreshore to the north of Naples was gradually squeezed out by the bluff limestone masses of the Aruncis, a mountain block which interposed its barrier as far as the sea immediately to the north of the mouth of the Minturno. The two main north-south roads in western Italy diverged after leaving Capua, 25 miles to the north of Naples. Route 6 turned inland, following the right flank of the Aruncis for 40 miles to Cassino; Route 7 felt westwards across the Pontine marshes and reached Rome along the foreshore. Any invasion must follow one or the other of these routes. The coastal road although traversing easier terrain offered more obstacles. For long distances this road was raised above low-lying water meadows and the adjoining fields were checkerboarded with drainage canals. A few blown bridges could effectively block advance across these reclaimed marshlands. Route 6 therefore with its solid footing and negotiable terrain represented the road to Rome.

At the beginning of 1944 three corps of Fifth Army stood arrayed against the enemy. As no further progress northward was possible save by consent of Cassino, a massive attack was mounted along the Garigliano, Gari and Rapido rivers.* On the left 10 British Corps endeavoured to thrust northward along the line of the Aruncis. II

---

* It is all Minturno water in each of these rivers. The Gari and Rapido join a mile north of Cassino and become the Gari. The Gari and the Liri join six miles south of Cassino and become the Garigliano. Two miles from the sea the Garigliano joins the Ausente and becomes the Minturno. As Fourth Indian Division was not concerned in operations south of Cassino, the river and its valley will be known as the Rapido in this narrative.

U.S. Corps assailed Cassino in a frontal attack. The French Expeditionary Corps struck across the Matese massif to the north of the principal obstacle.

The first American attack broke down in the face of devastating fire from the Cassino defences. A second assault forced the Rapido and established American troops on the mountainside, 4,000 yards to the north of Cassino. From this foothold on the night of January 29/30 II American Corps made a supreme effort to carry Cassino by storm. 36 U.S. Division struck southward along the valley of the Rapido while 34 U.S. Division endeavoured to break through the mountain defences and so reach the valley of the Liri, thus amputating the tip of the Cassino promontory. Ten days of terrific fighting followed in the course of which 36 U.S. Division along the Rapido managed to reach the edge of Cassino town. 34 U.S. Division gained ground across the boulder-strewn hogbacks which gradually merged into the main rocky cape; elements reached the rear of the Cassino position approximately half way between the Rapido and Liri valleys. In the face of fiercest opposition, foul weather and all but impassable terrain, it captured much of Monte Castellone and turned south along Albaneta ridge in an all-out attack to secure the Monastery on the crest of the heights. The fluctuating tide of battle flowed to within 300 yards of the final objective, but as always in the Cassino fighting it was the Monastery or nothing. After gallantry beyond all praise the American assault petered out on the bare hillsides. The survivors of 34 U.S. Division clung grimly to their hard-won ground, buffeted day and night by the elements and by the foe. They had done all that men could do.

On the abandonment of Eighth Army's offensive on the Adriatic three divisions crossed the mountains to take over the battle for Cassino. 2 New Zealand Division led the way followed by Fourth Indian Division and 78 British Division. On arrival the New Zealand Corps was formed. The new corps' commission was to co-operate with II U.S. Corps and to exploit any successes gained. The exhaustion of the Americans made it obvious that little further fighting could be expected from them. On arrival 5 New Zealand Brigade at once relieved the American force on the outskirts of Cassino. 34 U.S. Division in the hills, although driven back from the Monastery walls, still held a firm grip on commanding ridges 1,500 yards in the rear of the great Benedictine hospice.

Headquarters of the newly formed New Zealand Corps consisted of General Freyberg's Divisional staff, a circumstance which put an unfair weight on officers who continued to do double duty. Nevertheless by February 4th the new organisation was in working order and on that day a planning conference was held. The first New Zealand plan represented a continuation of the first American plan. A turning movement would develop through the mountains well to the north of Cassino, with a view to cutting through the enemy's rear positions and avoiding the necessity of an assault on the frontal heights. The tactical "rough" of the projected assault placed one New Zealand brigade in a holding capacity around the base of Monte Cassino, a second Kiwi brigade at the top of the Rapido valley four miles to the north, and the principal elements of Fourth Indian Division in the foothills at the top of the Rapido basin. From this deployment position the indicated thrust line of Fourth Indian Division was in the rear of the great cone of Monte Cairo, five miles to the north of Cassino. 4 New Zealand Armoured Brigade would concentrate behind Monte Trocchio, a pyramidal ridge in the centre of the Rapido valley, 4,000 yards east of Cassino. Its role would be to burst into the Liri valley when a decision had been reached in the mountains. 78 British Division would remain in Corps reserve to exploit the break-through.

This plan was satisfactory to General Tuker. It avoided his *bete noire*, the commital of flesh and blood against undamaged field defences. He was however aware that Cassino must be stormed by someone sooner or later and with characteristic thoroughness he began to study the subject.* He then discovered to his astonishment that no one in the Allied forces knew very much about the Monastery, which represented the nodule of the defences. On February 12th he wrote to General Freyberg:

"1. After considerable trouble and investigating many bookshops in Naples, I have at last found a book, dated 1879, which gives certain details of the construction of the Monte Cassino Monastery.

"2. The Monastery was converted into a fortress in the 19th Century. The Main Gate has massive timber branches in a low archway consisting of large stone blocks 9 to 10 metres long. This Gate is the only means of entrance to the Monastery.

"3. The walls are about 15 feet high, or more where there are Monks' cells against the walls. The walls are of solid masonry and at least 10 feet thick at the base.

"4. Since the place was constructed as a fortress as late as the 19th Century it stands to reason that the walls will be suitably pierced for loopholes and will be battlemented.

"5. Monte Cassino is therefore a modern fortress and must be dealt with by modern means. No practicable means available within the capacity of field engineers can possibly cope with this place.

* The Monk who in the 6th century built an abbey 1,700 feet above the Roman town of Casinum was the founder of the Benedictine Order. His hospice rose on the site of a former temple of Apollo. In the 7th century it was sacked by the Lombards. Rebuilt in 720 A.D., the Saracens destroyed it 164 years later. It was later sacked by the Germans in the 13th Century, and by Napoleon's armies. In the 19th Century the Monastery was converted into a fortress but afterwards returned to its owners.

"It can only be directly dealt with by applying 'blockbuster' bombs from the air, hoping thereby to render the garrison incapable of resistance. The 1,000 lb. bomb would be next to useless.

"6. Whether the Monastery is now occupied by a German garrison or not, it is certain that it will be held as a keep by the last remnants of the garrison of the position. It is therefore also essential that the building should be so demolished as to prevent its effective occupation at that time.

"7. I would ask that you would give me definite information at once as to how this fortress will be dealt with as the means are not within the capacity of this Division.

"8. I would point out that it has only been by investigation on the part of this Division, with no help from 'I' sources outside, that we have got any idea as to what this fortress comprises, although the fortress has been a thorn in our side for many weeks.

"When a formation is called upon to reduce such a place, it should be apparent that the place is reducible by the means at the disposal of that Division or that the means are ready for it, without having to go to the bookstalls of Naples to find out what should have been fully considered many weeks ago."

His reference to "blockbusters" brought into the open a line of thought which General Tuker had developed extensively since arrival in Italy. He had thus described the fortress of Italy to the Deputy Commander-in-Chief, India:

"Here is a country with a long coastline and a spine of mountains. To conquer Italy is easy if one looks at Italy from the west or from the east. One has a wide front at which to launch a concentrated blow, and terrain on which one can easily isolate that blow and divert one's enemy. If one looks at Italy all the way up its length one sees it to be impossible of conquest except in one tedious manner. No commander who is not either unimaginative or a time-server would accept the last direction of attack without the one and only means of conquest, great air power on the battlefield, close in.

"In 1914-18 in France, though the Boche had no mines and no anti-tank guns, we could *not* break through in spite of our huge mass of artillery of all types. There the Boche was not blessed with mountains. When his morale collapsed, we went through, mainly due to our tanks, to which he had no proper answer at that time. Our artillery never won us a break-through battle in four years of war. To-day, in Italy, we have less and lighter artillery as a whole: the Boche is in steel and concrete: he has anti-tank and anti-personnel mines and plenty of anti-tank guns. Virtually the whole break-through of his positions must be done by infantry. The front of attack on which we can put in infantry with a hope of later using out tanks is narrow. He is ready for us on it. If we intend to put infantry through we have only one means to do it and that is by the surprising weight of our fire. 1914-18 proved that artillery weapons will not give this effect. The only effect left to us is the weight of our air power and that *must* be used in its *fullest* weight and concentrated and co-ordinated with artillery and ground small arms. The blow *must* be in depth, division following division, armoured and infantry, and carried through *fast* by this great fire power, for the enemy has position after position on which to fall back."

From the tower at Castel Frentano near Orsogna General Tuker had shown both the Corps Commander and the Army Commander how the old Italian fortress towns dominated the landscape and controlled the roads, which offered the only lines of approach. These compact heavily-built towns were perfectly sited for defence. The most satisfactory manner of dealing with them was by obliteration from the air. He asked that tests be made to determine essential concentrations. It was in line with this programme that on February 12th he gave General Freyberg his views on the conduct of the new operation:

"1. It is apparent that the enemy are in concrete and steel emplacements on Monastery Hill.

"From a wide experience of attacks in mountain areas I know that infantry cannot 'jump' strong defences of this sort in the mountains. These defences have to be 'softened up' either by being cut off on *all* sides and starved out or else by continuous and heavy bombardment over a period of days. Even with the latter preparation, success will only be achieved in my opinion if a thorough and prolonged air bombardment is undertaken with really heavy bombs a good deal larger than 'Kittybomber' missiles.

"2. We have complete air superiority in this theatre of war but the 'softening' of the Monastery hill has not been started.

"An attack cannot be undertaken till this 'softening' process is complete.

"Already, three attacks have been put in and have failed—at some considerable cost. Another attack without *air* 'softening' will only lead to a similar result. The Monastery feature is a far more formidable obstacle than Takrouna, and resembles the higher part of Garci, which was rightly deemed inaccessible to infantry attack once initial surprise had passed. At Garci the enemy was in field defences and not in concrete emplacements.

"3. If proper air 'softening' is not possible then the alternative remains: to turn Monastery Hill and to isolate it.

HIS MAJESTY THE KING REVIEWS FOURTH INDIAN DIVISION
OUTSIDE TRIPOLI, JUNE 19th, 1943.

HIS MAJESTY THE KING MEETS MEMBERS FOURTH INDIAN
DIVISION AT AREZZO, JULY 25th, 1944.

DISTINGUISHED VISITORS
GENERAL MONTGOMERY AND SIR SIKANDER HYAT KHAN

MR. L. M. S. AMERY,
SECRETARY OF STATE FOR INDIA.

GENERAL DEVERS (U.S.A.)

CONTACTS WITH ALLIES

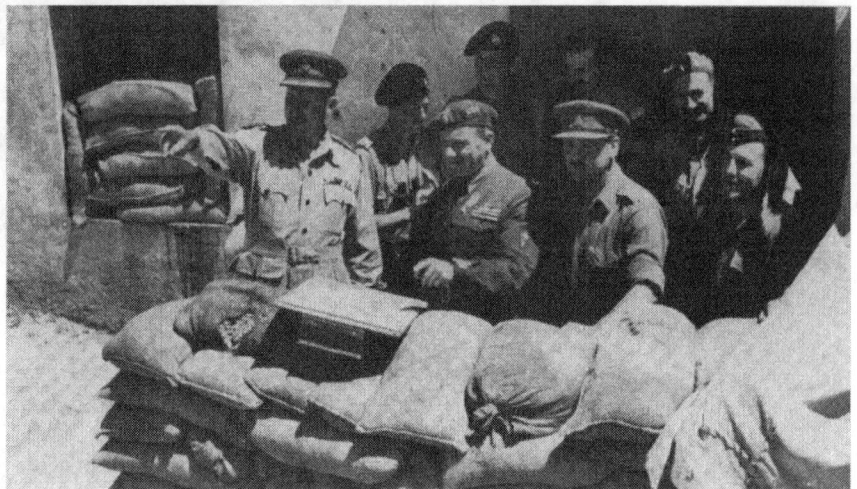

BRIGADIER LOVETT AND POLISH COMMANDER—
LOWER ADRIATIC FRONT.

INDIAN AND NEW ZEALAND
SAPPERS—TOBRUK

FREE FRENCH FORCES—
TUNISIA.

GURKHAS AND AMERICANS MEET—GAFSA ROAD, TUNISIA.

GENERAL AUCKINLECK

GENERAL MONTGOMERY

FIELD MARSHAL ALEXANDER

CAMOUFLAGED GUN-PIT, WESTERN DESERT.

25 POUNDERS IN ACTION, WADI AKARIT.

57 LAA REGIMENT, LOWER ADRIATIC FRONT.

NIGHT ACTION—CASSINO.

INDIAN MEDICAL SERVICES
FIRST AID TO PRISONER—SIDI BARRANI.

FIELD DRESSING STATION—ERITREA.

LIEUT-COLONEL G. S. N. HUGHES DSO, IMS AND MOBILE OPERATING THEATRE BUILT BY DIVISIONAL PERSONNEL OUT OF SALVAGED VEHICLES AND DESERT SCRAP.

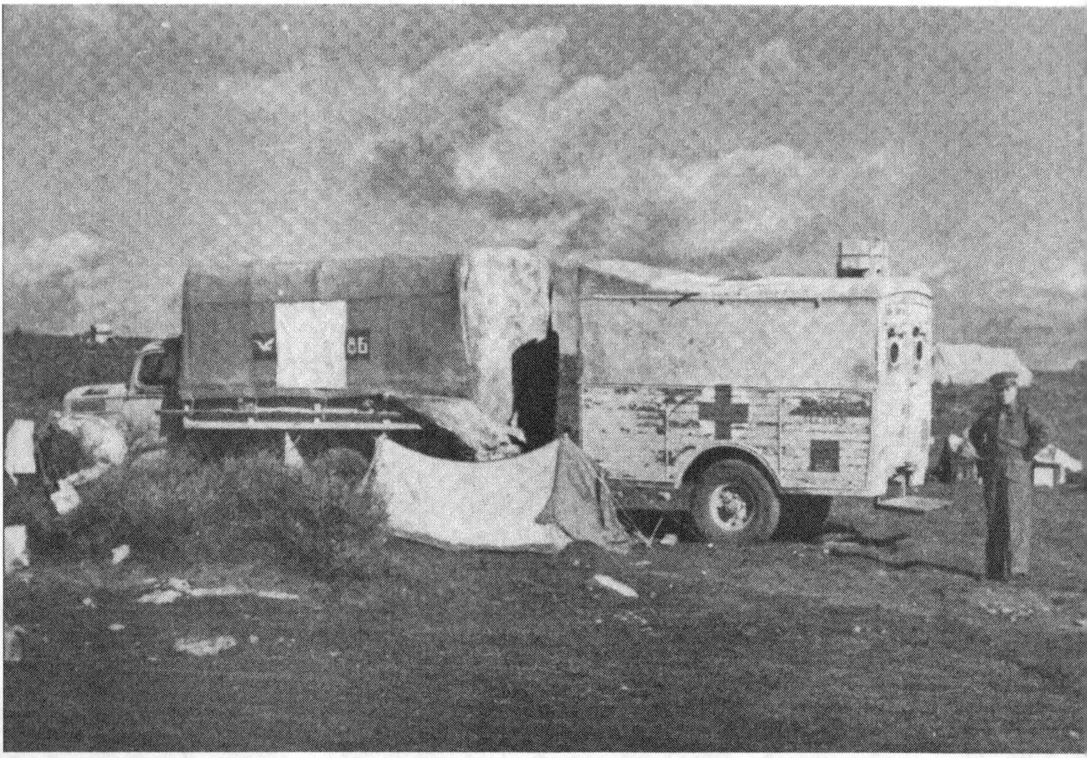

INDIAN STRETCHER-BEARERS UNDER FIRE, MARETH LINE

"This course I regard to be possible as the enemy is, I believe, still only in field defences in the mountain areas to the west and south-west of Monte Castellone. Using Monte Castellone and the area now held by the U.S. II Corps as a firm base, we can attack in fast short jabs to the west and south-west of Monte Castellone and cut No. 6 Highway west of Monastery Hill. With this and an attack on Cassino to keep that place quiet the river can (I feel) be crossed lower down and the crossing joined up with the cutting from the north of No. 6 Highway, thus isolating Monastery Hill.

"4. To go direct for the Monastery Hill now without 'softening' it properly is only to hit one's head straight against the hardest part of the whole enemy position and to risk the failure of the whole operation."

When the Divisional Commander penned this appreciation he was a sick man. A long-standing ailment was about to force him into hospital. On February 4th he gave over command of Fourth Division to Brigadier Dimoline.* This change on the eve of a critical operation was a severe blow to the Division. At a time when, as never in its history, Fourth Indian Division needed a commander of sufficiently wide experience and standing to insist on the acceptance of his findings, it was bereft of its leader.

In General Tuker's absence modifications in the plan followed. Instead of the wide detour through the mountains combined with a holding attack on Cassino and a blow in the Liri valley, a compromise was forced upon the Division. The new plan meant little less than a frontal assault on Monte Cassino. Indeed New Zealand Corps in Operation Instruction No. 4 of February 9th defined Fourth Indian Division's task as: "Attack and capture Monastery Hill and Point 593; exploit south to cut Highway 6 and capture Cassino from the west."

---

* General Tuker, although ill, remained in his caravan during the planning stages of the Cassino battle and later re-visited the Division from hospital. As a point of medical interest he was the first man in the Division to receive treatment with penicillin.

Chapter 23

CASSINO — THE FIRST ASSAULT

GENERAL Freyberg had determined to strike at Cassino from front and rear, the frontal attack to be carried out by his New Zealanders from south of the town, the rear attack by Fourth Indian Division from the American positions on the ridge crests 1,500 yards west of the Monastery.

More than one observer, in describing the approach to Cassino, mentions the eerie feeling of imminence as the numbers of the milestones decreased. When only a few kilometres remained Highway 6 curved across a last hogsback and startlingly close at hand lay the panorama of the battlefield. In the foreground the thickly populated Rapido valley thrust into an enclave of mountains dominated by the great snow-clad cone of Monte Cairo, towering to a height of 5,000 feet. From this eminence the scarred ridges flowed down to merge in the Cassino promontory, with the still unscathed Monastery esconsced upon its tip. The once substantial town of Cassino nestled around the base of the mountain, with a castle and numbers of better-class villas standing out on its lower slopes. Highway 6, after cutting across the Rapido valley, swung to the left through Cassino town, and followed the base of the mountain into the open expanses of the Liri valley. Far across that valley, against the Arunci mountain wall, two converging trickles of silver marked the junction of the Liri and Gari rivers.

Not the great height of Monte Cairo but the aloof commanding outwork of Monte Cassino caught the professional eye. This bastion allowed the enemy to intrude his nerve centre into the forefront of the battlefield. From thence he observed every move, controlled every critical occasion. Monastery Hill was the master key, the fountainhead of the defensive system, the natural bulwark which made Cassino a classical model of impregnable terrain.

Seen from afar the mountain block appeared bare and smooth, with little natural cover. Detailed examination revealed it to be a merger of ridge systems, a jumble of scoured hollows and narrow crests. A still closer view discovered a savage surface of rough boulders, rocky outcrops and stony escarpments. Small farms dotted the upper slopes with patches of pasture and orchard. Towards the summit there grew a heavy fuzz of scrub and undergrowth.

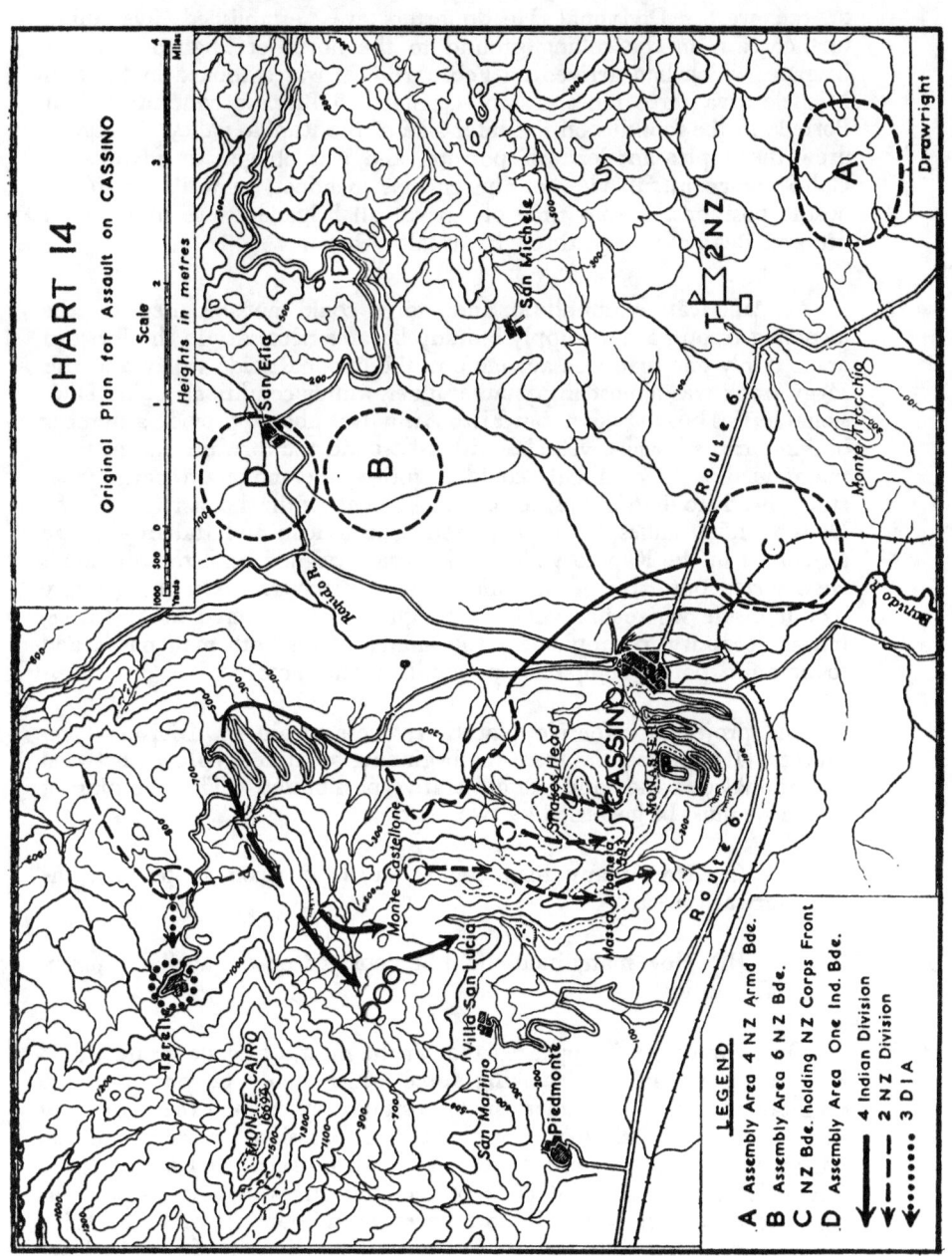

Fourth Indian Division's concentration area lay in the upper Rapido valley, immediately under the eyes of the enemy on the heights to the west. Divisional Headquarters was established five miles further east, in the rolling ground to the north of Highway 6. 11 Brigade, which had arrived on February 6th, was stationed in the San Michele area three miles east of Cassino. 5 Brigade concentrated at Portella in the foothills on the safer side of the Rapido valley. 7 Brigade drew the unpleasant lead-off position and was obliged to advance to Cairo village in full view of the enemy; in effect, to walk up to the hostile positions. From time of arrival all brigades were under shell fire and steady wastage through casualties began.

As American ammunition and stores could not be used by the incoming troops, a new supply buildup became necessary in the forward area. Only one road was available in the upper Rapido valley and this soggy track was almost impassable under winter conditions. The Divisional lorries bogged down but Fifth Army was able to provide a number of American six wheel vehicles with whose aid the forward dumps were maintained. Only animals could negotiate the mountain paths from truck head to battle positions. Coincident with the arrival of the Division 1,500 mules — Indian, French, American and Italian — were assembled in the Rapido valley. Confusion reigned until these animals were sorted out. But even mules were not enough. On the slippery mountainside where harassing fire might be encountered at any time, it was necessary to supplement the animal trains with man packs and to organize porter companies as auxilary transport.

The projected offensive placed a severe strain on Divisional resources. It was essential from the beginning to strike a balance between operational demands and administrative possibilities. The planning of the battle must be governed by two factors:

(a) How many men could Fourth Division support in the forward areas?

(b) How many men could be deployed on the available jump-off positions?

On examination it appeared that at the most a brigade group would comprise the maximum striking force which could be put into and maintained in action. American dispositions represented the equivalent of six British brigades, four on the Cassino massif, one on Monte Castellone and one on the northern outskirts of Cassino town. These formations had lost 80% of their effectives in a series of fruitless encounters in which it had never been found possible to bring the maximum assault strength to bear. In the light of this experience Fourth Division's plan called for a comparatively modest test of strength against the dominant feature of Point 593, followed by an all-out bid by 7 Brigade to reach the Monastery in a single bound.

As immediate reinforcements 1/9 Gurkha Rifles and 4/6 Rajputana Rifles were placed under Brigadier Lovett's command. 12 Field Company, "B" and "C" companies Rajputana Rifle Machine Gun Battalion, one troop of 57 LAA Regiment and two companies of 2/7 Gurkha Rifles (the latter for porter duties,) completed the Brigade group. Brigade Headquarters moved into the hills approximately halfway between Cairo village and the firing line.

On return from his first reconnaisance of the forward positions Brigadier Lovett expressed himself in strong terms. The Americans had fought magnificently but they were finished. He urged that their relief should be expedited as he did not consider them to be in condition to face counter-attack. First contact with these allies elicited mixed admiration and astonishment. A 4/16 Punjab officer who accompanied the Brigade reconnaisance party provides an interesting picture of the men of the Western World:

"We had already been impressed by the efficiency of the American organization on their lines of communication. At their mobile baths you could get a brand new uniform. Their equivalent of our ENSA was well up to the front line. Their cigar-smoking negro drivers, when called 'Sambo' maintained courteously that they were 'citizens of the United States of America'. We were impressed with the downrightness and cheerfulness of our new friends."

"We were now to meet their fighting men. The Regimental Commander of 168 Infantry Regiment was a character. If ever he should read these words it is hoped that he will take no offence. He looked like one of Snow Whites Seven Dwarfs and he seemed to be a mixture of all of them, reflecting their various moods in turn. His headgear was of a type which one associates with an engine driver on the C.P.R. Steel rimmed spectacles surmounted a face which bore a fortnights greyish stubble. His 'combat pants' were drawn up close under his armpits by a very serviceable pair of suspenders. He smoked many cigars and when he wasn't expressing an opinion, making a decision or rating someone over the telephone he disappeared into the dark corner of the Command Post where he immediately began to snore."

"His conversations on the telephone were better than anything recorded by Metro-Goldwyn-Mayer. We proudly informed him that our Brigade was going to take the Monastery. He thought it possible if we threw enough people at it. First of all, we said, we were going to destroy the Monastery with American bombers. This caused him to push his cap to the back of his head, bite his cigar and with his hands on his knees regard us sympathetically over his steel-rimmed spectacles. 'Waal' he said, 'If it is incumbent arn you to depend on our barmers, and I wuz in your shoes, I'd hie me back to dear old Pittsburgh.'

Our optimism slumped. We smiled wanly and muttered that we had the greatest faith in American bombers."*

By midnight on February 11th 7 Brigade had concentrated on the lower eastern slopes of Monte Castellone above Cairo village. From this assembly area a rough trail climbed for 4,000 yards along the crests to the American positions on the northern slopes of Point 593. Relief had been planned for the night of February 12/13th. Before leaving the line 168 U.S. Regiment had mustered its exhausted handfuls for a last attempt to win Albaneta House and Point 593. The attack failed. In the course of this fighting an enemy outpost was over-run and a machine gunner and signaller sepoy of 10 Indian Division recovered. These prisoners had been captured at Mersa Matruh in 1942 and were being used by the enemy as porters.

In the early morning of February 1st the enemy in a counter stroke drove heavily against the American group holding Monte Castellone. While this attack was in progress a second German force infiltrated into the top of the Rapido valley. American troops hastened to restore the situation but by first light hostile elements had reached Manna feature, 2,500 yards to the north-west of 7 Brigades assembly area. This threat led Brigadier Lovett to deploy 1/2 Gurkhas and 4/16 Punjabis in covering positions and the relief at Point 593 was posponed until the following evening, when 1 Royal Sussex led the climb up the mountain. Shell and mortar fire searched the route, causing casualties. In the early hours of February 14th the much enduring American garrison was relieved. Less than 200 men remained of the equivalent of a British brigade. Of this number 50 were so exhausted that it was necessary to carry them out on stretchers. Dead were strewn everywhere, 150 of the enemy being counted on a single company front. The Royal Sussex occupied approach positions below Point 593 while 4/16 Punjabis came forward on the left, facing the Monastery along the southern slopes of that feature. 1/2 Gurkhas remained in Brigade reserve further back on the ridge while 4/6 Rajputana Rifles waited on call in the Cairo village area. On account of maintenance difficulties 1/9 Gurkhas remained temporarily near San Michele.

On the right flank of 7 Brigade 36 U.S. Division held the high ground 1,000 yards to the north-west of Point 593. On the left 133 U.S. Regiment with 100 Nisei (Japanese-American) Battalion under command, carried the line back to the valley of the Rapido along the

---

* The American officers involved in this handover, including Colonel Mark W. Boatner, commander of 168 Infantry Regiment, Lieut.-Colonel Burton Barr S-3 (Operations Officer), Major Hansen, Intelligence Officer and Major Rickard, U.S. Artillery, have placed on record a heart-warming tribute to the courage and initiative of Brigadier Lovett, Lieut-Colonel Packwood and Capt. Popple of 4/16 Punjabis and Major Shore, 7 Brigade Machine Gun Officer. On finding 7 Brigade to be without a FOO in the forward area, Major Rickard voluntarily remained behind for 24 hours to direct American artillery support should it become necessary.

northern slopes of Monte Cassino. 7 Brigade therefore represented the point of a spear thrust into the heart of the German defences, with American forces on either side completing its broad gouging blade.

When dawn broke 4/16 Punjabis looked across the intervening falling ground into the rear walls of the Monastery—"almost within touching distance" as one of the officers put it. Every window peered into the Indian lines. The Royal Sussex were even less comfortably situated. Immediately in front of their foxholes and shallow sangars loomed the rocky crest of Point 593, with the ruins of a small fort upon its summit. The slopes were shaggy with great boulders, sharp ledges and patches of scrub. These natural hideouts sheltered German spandau teams and bomb squads. Enemy outposts were less than 70 yards distant. The slightest movement drew retaliatory fire. No reconnaisance was possible, nor was there any method of ascertaining the enemy's strength. There was no elbow room for deployment, no cover behind which to concentrate effectively, no opportunity to withdraw in order to obtain space for manoeuvre. 7 Brigade therefore was committed to battle without knowing the lie of the land nor the strength of enemy which held it. Neither artillery nor air could intervene. The infantry must make its way alone.

The weather had turned clear and cold and on February 14th the Luftwaffe came to life. Flashing down the Liri valley a series of hit-and-run raids struck at the crowded artillery lines behind Monte Trocchio. Here the guns of two corps were arrayed almost wheel to wheel. The air onslaught did little damage but it afforded 57 LAA Regiment the opportunity of bringing down its hundredth plane of the war—an achievement which elicited congratulations from all sides. 10 enemy tanks and more than 300 planes damaged in the air completed the game book of these great marksmen.

With the delay of the infantry attack the air assault on the Monastry likewise had been posponed. Some failure in liaison ensued and 7 Brigade Headquarters was not notified of the new hour of the strike. At 0930 hours on the morning of February 15th a dull roar was heard in the sky. Brigadier Lovett wrote: "At that moment I was called on the blower and was told that the bombers would be over in 15 minutes. I started to blow up myself but even as I spoke the roar drowned my voice as the first shower of eggs came down". The diarist of 4/16 Punjabis continues the story:

"We went to the door of the command post, a derelict farmhouse, and gazed up into the cold blue sky. There we saw the white trails of many high level bombers. Our first thought was that they were the enemy. Then somebody said, 'Flying Fortresses'. There followed the whistle, swish and blast of the blockbusters as the first flights struck at the Monastery. Almost before the ground ceased to shake the telephones were ringing. One of our companies was within 300 yards of the target and the others within 800 yards; all had received a plastering and were asking questions with some asperity. We could not offer any explanation, we just had to grin and bear it. Luckily our casualties were under the thirty mark and were mostly bodies bruised by pieces of the Monastery hurled many yards through the air."*

Twelve bombs from the Fortresses fell in 7 Brigade's area. One stick of four fell far behind in 1/2 Gurkhas "B" echelon lines. After the first strike the Sikh company of 4/16 Punjabis withdrew to safer ground. An intercepted enemy message in clear reported "Indian troops with turbans are retiring". After four groups of Fortresses had bombed from 18,000 feet medium bombers struck at 1100 hours and 1330 hours from 10,000 feet with considerably greater accuracy. The roof of the Monastery was blown away and the interior of the building reduced to a shell. Unfortunately the thick outer walls resisted the blasts and although breaches appeared none of them reached to ground level. This unintegrated employment of air power therefore did nothing to lighten the task of the infantry, which was unable to take advantage of the confusion and destruction by staging a correlated attack.**

While the bombing was in progress the Divisional Commander held a conference at 7 Brigade Headquarters at which Brigadier Lovett expressed the view that it was impossible to perservere with the main attack until Point 593 had been neutralized. The capture of this latter position should be regarded as a separate operation. In the light of this recommendation the main attack therefore was posponed for 24 hours and the Royal Sussex were instructed to move against Point 593 in the preliminary assault.

On the night of February 16th, before the opening of the attack, a massive artillery concentration pounded Monte Cassino. An Indian Army Observer wrote:

"I walked through the gun lines. The crews were standing to. From battery to battery I heard every conceivable English accent—American, British, New Zealand. Elsewhere orders crackled in Polish and in French. Then like the opening phrase of a colossal symphony the guns roared in unison. The night was pricked with belching flames; across the valley stabs of light against the mountainside showed where the shells struck. Sudden glares and steady fires marked exploding dumps and burning houses. The enemy began to loop white flares onto the lower slopes of Cassino. Lines of tracer cut across the sky. Then came the distant staccato crackle of small arms fire as the infantry went

---

* This attack on Cassino was the first occasion upon which bomber groups from Great Britain struck at an Italian target and continued on to North Africa to re-arm for a similar strike on the way home.

**Examination after capture revealed that in spite of the devastation caused by two major air attacks the Monastery continued a fortress to the end. A curious feature was that the only entrance, a mounting arched corridor about 15 feet high and about 30 yards in length, at the south-east corner of the building, remained completely undamaged.

in. The Rapido valley filled with smoke, soft as ermine under the moon. On the soar of every flare we strained our eyes, praying that each mounting light would prove to be the success signal and that our men had won home."

When the leading company of the Royal Sussex formed up for the assault the enemy was alert and detected the movement. The South Country men groped forward but when only 50 yards from their start line an impassable palisade of boulders was encountered. Intense fire at close range lashed the advance mercilessly. After several unsuccessful attempts to outflank and by-pass this obstacle the Royal Sussex withdrew, having lost two officers and 18 men.

This failure again set back the main attack. At 2320 hours on the following night (February 17th), the Royal Sussex, with "D" Company in the lead, again assailed the black crest ahead. The forward platoons worked around the barricade of boulders and gained a footing on the slopes of Point 593. From the cover of sangars and from foxholes dug under rocky ledges the defenders buffeted their assailants with bursts of spandau fire and with showers of grenades. While the leading platoons struggled doggedly ahead, Lieut. Dennis Cox with the consolidation platoon dashed around the flank to the crest and destroyed two spandau nests. With many of his men struck down and himself severely wounded by a grenade, this gallant young officer crawled forward and established himself in a ditch outside the broken walls of the fort. His company commander, Capt. Harry Hawkes, also wounded, likewise reached the summit, but incessant fire prevented the platoons from following their officers. A signal for reinforcements brought "A" Company up the slopes; again sheets of spandau fire took heavy toll and swept the attack to ground. "C" Company came surging into the fight to add its weight to the thrust and for a few minutes it seemed possible that sheer valour might win the day. Unfortunately at this critical moment three green Verey lights, the Sussex signal for withdrawal, soared aloft. These lights—fired by the enemy—succeeded in their purpose. A stretcher bearer dashed to the summit, returned with Lieut. Cox flung across his shoulders, and "D" Company relinquished its tenuous grasp on the all-important crest. On detecting the ruse "B" Company formed up for a fresh assault, but intolerable fire thwarted every effort to gain ground. At the end Royal Sussex fell back to their original jump-off positions, having lost 7 officers and 63 men.

Two failures by an outstanding battalion to seize a preliminary objective unmistakably indicated the magnitude of the task and the need for greater strength in the striking force. On February 17th the battle became a Corps instead of a Brigade operation. All the resources of Fourth Indian Division would be thrown into an assault *a outrance* and 2 New Zealand Division simultaneously would attack on a separate front. The new plan called for 4/6 Rajputana Rifles with three companies of Royal Sussex under command to put an end to resistance on Point 593 and thereafter to strike downwards along the ridge to Point 444 in the rear of the Monastery. Two hours later, 1/2 and 1/9 Gurkhas would smash through on the left of the opening assault and storm the Monastery. Thereafter they would exploit downhill to the south of Cassino town until Highway 6 had been brought under fire. Concurrently 2 New Zealand Division would force the lower Rapido and drive for the entrance of the Liri valley, where contact would be effected with the Gurkhas. 1/4 Essex and 1/6 Rajputana Rifles of 5 Brigade would move to the attack on the north of Cassino town, thus pinning its defenders between two fires. The uncommitted battalions, 2 Camerons and 2/7 Gurkha Rifles, would supply porters and support companies for the assault groups.

Dispositions for the new operation were completed on the night of February 18/19 when 4/6 Rajputana Rifles and 1/9 Gurkhas clambered up the rough mountain trail and moved forward to enter the fray. (1/2 Gurkhas had reached battle positions on the previous evening.) The enemy swept the approach with harassing shoots, causing many casualties; out of a train of 200 mules which accompanied Rajputana Rifles, only 20 animals reached the forward zone. Nevertheless timing was preserved and at 2359 hours "B" and "C" Companies of the Rajputana Rifles scrambled forward across the scrabbly slopes in a third bid for the defiant crest of Point 593. Intense fighting followed. It was 45 minutes before the situation could be pieced together. Then it was learned that groups of gallant riflemen had gained the summit. Along the parapeted ditch reached by Lieut. Cox on the previous evening a grenade battle raged. But the main strength of the companies was held back by incessant small arms fire less than 100 yards from the final objective. At 0140 hours Lieut.-Colonel Scott called for a five minutes artillery concentration on the summit; under cover of this bombardment "D" Company swung wide and endeavoured to reach the crown of the knoll from the left flank. 90 minutes of bitter fighting followed. At 0315 hours all three forward companies reported that they were pinned down and that counter-attacks appeared to be imminent. Major Markham-Lee was missing and two other company commanders were wounded; only two British officers remained on their feet. At 0430 hours Colonel Scott sent his last company into the battle, but to no avail. On the vital half acre of shaggy crest the panzer grenadiers bared their teeth and stood like the rocks themselves.

After the fall of Cassino the bodies of Major Markham-Lee, Jemedar Maru Ram (who was posthumously awarded the IOM) and a number of riflemen were found inside the ruined fort. They had died in the heart of the enemy defences. Rajputana Rifles casualties amounted to 196 of all ranks.

Despite failure to win the vital Point 593 objective the battle continued according to plan. At 0215 hours, while the Rajputana Rifles strove for the crest, less than 300 yards away 1/9 Gurkha Rifles with "A" Company in the lead advanced from 4/16 Punjabis positions, skirted the fringe of the fighting and struck downhill towards Point 444, an intervening ridge only 300 yards from the rear walls of the Monastery. As the hillmen passed through a small orchard they came under heavy converging fire from Point 593, looming quarter right, and from Point 450, a knoll 500 yards to the left, which represented the extreme flank of 7 Brigade's attack. "A" Company's thrust line opened a gap between the Gurkhas and Rajputana Rifles; into this gap "B" Company drove, pushing up the eastern slope of Point 593 towards Point 569, 300 yards on the left of the Rajputana Rifles objective. Capt. Arthur Bond of "C" Company with one of his platoons joined in the rush and disappeared in the darkness. When the assault companies thinned out under the murderous fire "D" Company threw its weight into the attack, but all to no avail. The crossfire beat the assailants into the ground and the advance was brought to a halt with the loss of 94 of all ranks.

On the left flank, 1/2 Gurkha Rifles, also from jump-off positions in the 4/16 Punjabis sector, deployed with "A" and "B" Companies in the lead, their left flank resting on Point 450. At 0330 hours the hillmen began to work towards a low intermediate wrinkle of ground beyond which the slopes fell away into a hollow beneath the north walls of the Monastery. Beyond this false crest aerial photographs had shown a belt of scrub. It was impossible to reconnoitre this area, but as such undergrowth had proven negotiable elsewhere it was presumed that it did not constitute a serious obstacle. As a result the leading companies walked into a death trap. This scrub proved to be thorn thicket seeded with anti-personnel mines, its outskirts threaded with trip wires linked to booby traps. Behind this deadly barrier storm troopers lay in wait, in machine gun posts less than 50 yards apart. Between these nests foxholes sheltered enemy tommygunners and bomb throwers.

As the Gurkhas closed up on the scrub a shower of grenades arced out of the night. Lieut.-Colonel Showers instructions had been explicit —to close on the enemy at all costs. The leading platoons dashed into the undergrowth and blew up almost to a man. Colonel Showers fell shot through the stomach. Two-thirds of the leading company was struck down within five minutes yet the survivors continued to force their way ahead. Riflemen were found afterwards with as many as four trip wires around their legs, Naik Birbahadur Thapa, although wounded in many places, managed to burst through the copse and to seize a position in the midst of the stormtroopers. Stretcher-bearer Sherbahadur Thapa made 16 trips across this deadly ground before he was killed. An unscathed handful battled on until ordered to withdraw. 7 British officers, 4 Gurkha officers and 138 other ranks had fallen.

After 15 minutes fighting in which both "B" and "C" companies had been reduced to platoon strength, the survivors of "C" Company under Major Ormsby, who was wounded, gained the meagre shelter of a shallow nullah. "B" Company, under Major Ramsay-Brown, was recalled to dig in behind the fatal belt of scrub. When "A" Company came forward to reinforce the firing line Lieut. Loftus-Tottenham, of a family of long Indian Army associations, was killed in a fearless rush at a spandau post. "D" Company likewise closed up and began to consolidate a position around Point 450, with Battalion Headquarters more or less in the firing line. Major G. S. N. Richardson came forward and took over command.

Dawn broke with Rajputana Rifles, Royal Sussex and the two Gurkha battalions pinned down in front of their objectives. A little ground had been gained in the centre where "A" and "B" Companies of 1/9 Gurkha Rifles were embedded in the enemy's defensive system; on the right and left flanks there had been no gain. Three companies of Rajputana Rifles were astride Point 593 but withheld from the crest. Behind them, echeloned on their left flank, lay three companies of the Royal Sussex. "C" and "D" Companies of 1/9 Gurkhas were in touch with the Sussex on their right and with 1/2 Gurkhas on their left. The latter battalion after extrication from the death trap on their immediate front had spread to flank and "A" and "D" Companies now held Point 445, 300 yards on the left of Point 450 and approximately 500 yards from the north-east corner of the Monastery Walls. With the recall of the two forward companies of 1/9 Gurkhas 7 Brigade stood almost in its original jump-off positions. No ground had been gained, no hole had been punched in the defences.. Within bowshot the battered Monastery walls towered, aloof and impregnable.

There seems to be little basis for the report that groups of Gurkhas fought their way up to the walls. Capt. Nayar of Indian Public Relations, who accompanied 7 Brigade, was told that a jemedar and three men had reached the Monastery and had returned. Capt. Arthur Bond of 1/9 Gurkhas penetrated the enemy defences with a few men about him, but all save one died with their leader in charging a spandau nest. The survivor, a wounded signaller, crawled back to declare that the group had reached the Monastery. It seems more likely that Capt. Bond and his men fell on the approaches to Point 569. Items of Indian equipment were found in the Monastery by the Poles after the final assault in May, but no graves were discovered nor have any prisoners returned who were taken so far forward. The evidence of Colonel Egger, a pompous and conceited paratrooper, who declared after his capture that he had ejected Indian troops who had penetrated the Monastery, likewise must be discounted.

While Fourth Indian Division smashed at the rock-ribbed defences on the mountain-top 2 New Zealand Division had thrown in a heavy assault in the valley below. On the evening of February 19th the Kiwis had crossed the Rapido to the south of Cassino town, striking for the key sector around the railway station, 1,000 yards from the foot of the mountain. 28 Maori Battalion in a magnificent feat of arms stormed this heavily fortified and desperately defended position. Consolidation of this area would have opened the way into the Liri valley and would have left Cassino town untenable for the enemy. Throughout the night bitter fighting continued; at dawn the crossings of the Rapido had not been completed and the Maoris were left to face the day without tanks or anti-tank guns. At 1600 hours on February 19th after heavy artillery preparation the enemy struck back with panzers in the van. The forward Maori companies were overrun and it was necessary to withdraw the survivors to the opposite bank of the river.

Everywhere, therefore, the fortunes of the day rested with the dour and unyielding defenders. Nor was there any reason to believe, with the strength which could be arrayed on the start lines, that a renewed assault would fare better. Until the ring of master crests at Points 593, 569 and 575 had been neutralized any attempt to burst into the Monastery invited destruction. Fourth Indian Division commander represented to the Corps Commander that before renewing the offensive he must re-organize with two brigades forward. General Freyberg agreed with this decision. 7 Brigade's front was defined as from Point 593 to Point 450, a distance of 800 yards fronting the main enemy defences. 5 Brigade would take over on the left of Point 450 and would carry the line along the Majola ridge system above the valley of the Rapido.

After a night's rest 1/2 Gurkhas relieved 4/6 Rajputana Rifles in their forward positions. 1/9 Gurkhas established a chain of posts between Point 450 and Point 445. 2 Camerons and 149 Anti-Tank Regiment undertook to supply porters and stretcher bearers for 5 Brigade while 2/7 Gurkhas and 57 LAA Regiment acted in a similar capacity for 7 Brigade. The Sappers and Miners immediately began the construction of a jeep track along the Majola feature into the forward area.

Chapter 24

CASSINO — THE SECOND ASSAULT

THE thrust at the heart had failed. The assault divisions had become involved in desperate fighting in which they did not support each other, in which neither artillery nor air power could aid them. The battle needed realignment and a fresh balance. Yet every hour was precious for the situation in the Anzio bridgehead remained desperate; such radical expedients as a break-through in the Liri valley or a turning movement through the mountains could not be considered in the time at General Freyberg's disposal. The new battle plan therefore only modified (and simplified) the existing operations. The enemy's positions were recognised as mutually supporting. They could not be stormed simultaneously; therefore they must be rolled up progressively. It was likewise recognised that it was next to impossible to deploy on the exposed summits sufficient forces to destroy the defenders.

The new scheme envisaged a single thrust line by both assault divisions southward along the Rapido valley and across the hillsides which mounted into Monte Cassino. By the employment of colossal air power, General Freyberg hoped to destroy resistance in Cassino town at a single stroke. Thereafter the unleashed New Zealand armoured brigade would sweep around the base of Monte Cassino and exploit up the Liri valley. Fourth Indian Division meanwhile would protect the right flank of the armoured thrust by seizing the slopes of the hill above Cassino town. When the New Zealanders had broken through and had turned the position, the Monastery could be dealt with at leisure.

Fourth Division's new battlefield possessed an extraordinary configuration. It comprised a boulder-strewn hillside approximately 1,200 yards in length which could be entered only from the northern end, and through a narrow bottleneck between Cassino town and a long winding ridge which ran upwards into Monastery Hill. This narrow passage was blocked by a high knoll which stood immediately above the town with a ruined castle on its crest. (Someone aptly described it as a pulpit above the Cassino congregation). To the north a deep gorge furrowed the mountainside; to the south, the sturdily constructed stone buildings of the town mounted the hillside to meet the outworks of the Castle. Before Fourth Division could enter the battle Castle Hill must be secured. This task devolved on the leading New Zealand assault brigade .

From the southern fringe of Cassino town a road crossed and recrossed the slopes in five switchbacks as it wound up to the Benedictine hospice on the crest. Two of these hairpin bends stood immediately in front of the Castle on the line of approach to the Monastery. The lower switchback, Point 165, was only 300 yards from the Castle gateway. Another 300 yards above it the second hairpin bend, Point 236, supplied an ideal covering position. These strong points blocked a frontal attack on the Monastery from the north.

600 yards beyond Point 236 and high on the shoulder of the mountain a rocky knoll stood out with steep boulder-strewn approaches. On the crest of this outcrop rose the gibbet-like concrete pylon of the aerial ropeway which formerly connected the Monastery with Cassino town. On the maps this feature was shown as Point 435. To soldiers it was Hangman's Hill. Its flat acre of platform was less than 300 yards from the towering front walls of the Monastery—so close that in part it was dead ground. Hangman's Hill therefore constituted the obvious start line for the final surge to the Monastery walls.

The new battle planned to employ artillery and air power to the full. For 7 Indian Brigade's attack 351 tons of bombs had been dropped. For 6 New Zealand Brigade (which would head the assault on Cassino town) 1150 tons of bombs would be used. Thereafter the artillery of three corps, totalling 610 guns in all, would deluge the target area with 1,200 tons of shells over a period of four hours. A heavy barrage would march ahead of the infantry assault on Castle Hill. As soon as that objective had been secured 5 Indian Brigade would move forward and release the New Zealanders for their drive through Cassino town. From Castle Hill Brigadier Bateman's men would thrust forward across the slopes, first to storm the hairpin bends and thereafter to seize Hangman's Hill.

In conjunction with the main assault a somewhat unusual diversion was projected. The Sappers and Miners had laboriously built Cavendish Road, a jeep track which mounted from Cairo village, gained the crest of the massif and led into the forward areas. This track afforded entry to a long narrow valley which traversed the Monte Cassino ridge system by way of Massa Albaneta, between the razor-backed summit crowned by Point 593 and the next high ground to the west, Point 575. The defile was sickle-shaped, curving into the east and offering a covered passage almost to the western walls of the Monastery. Little more than a hollow between the ridges, it seemed likely that it would be commanded by guns. It was decided that when the main attack on the Monastery opened a filibustering force would thrust down this ravine from Massa Albaneta for the purpose of creating confusion in the enemy's rear. The foray was designed as a demonstration and the force commander was allowed considerable discretion as to the extent of commital of his men and tanks to battle.

While these preparations were in hand the enemy likewise made ready for a supreme effort. In January Hitler had deemed the defence

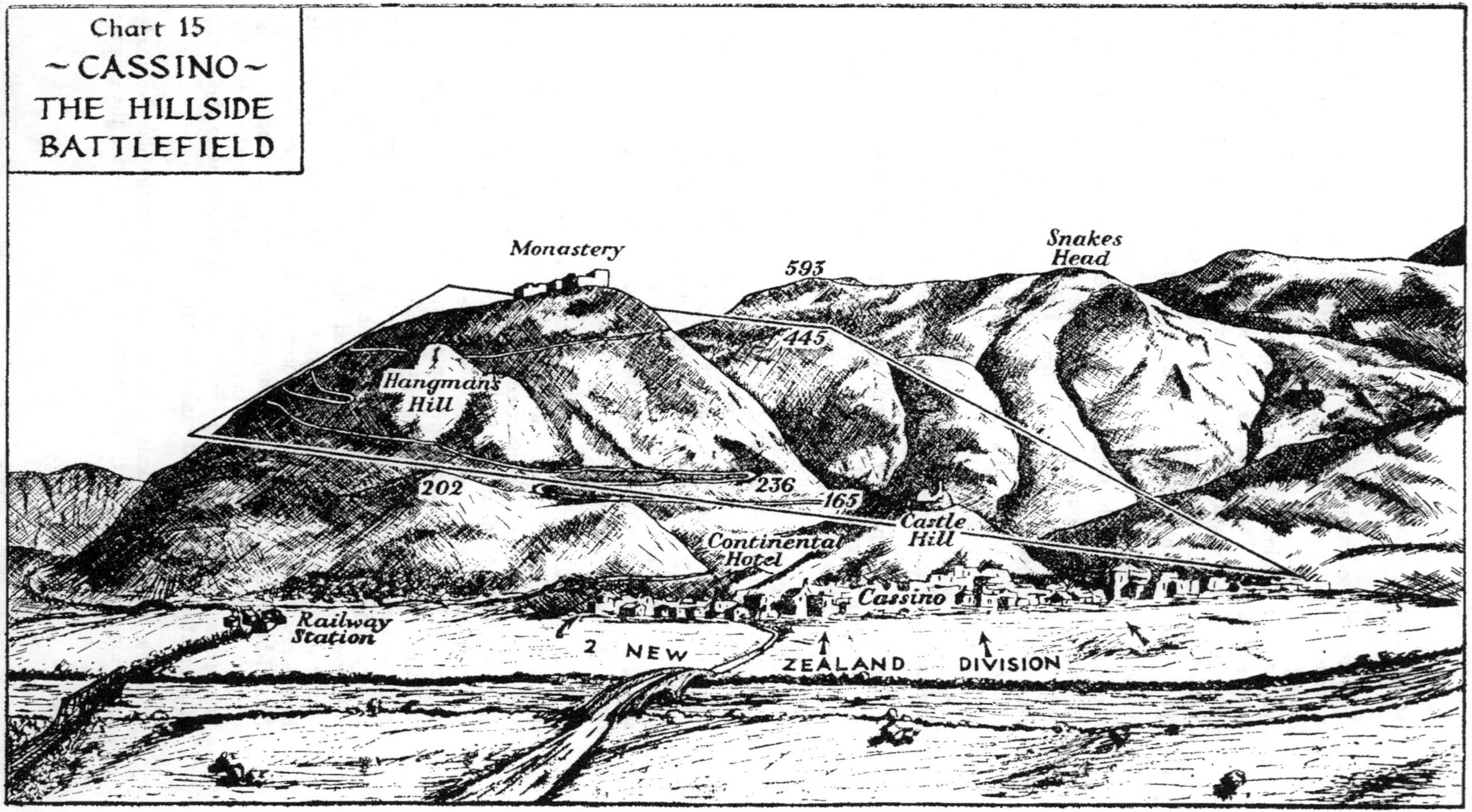
Chart 15
~CASSINO~
THE HILLSIDE
BATTLEFIELD
Monastery
593
Snakes
Head
445
Hangman's
Hill
202
236
165
Castle
Hill
Continental
Hotel
Cassino
Railway
Station
2 NEW ZEALAND DIVISION

of Cassino sufficiently vital to issue a special directive in which he declared that even if no military purposes were served, it was necessary on political grounds to hold this key bastion to the death. Such drastic dictum drew to the defences the elite of fanatical Nazi manhood. In the German military heirarchy 1 Parachute Division stood at the top. At the end of February this *corps d'elite*, one of the greatest fighting formations ever to take the field, relieved 15 Panzer Grenadier Division in the Cassino sector. 7 battalions defended Monastery Hill and Cassino town. Three battalions held Monte Castellone on the flank of the active front. 180 guns supported the paratroopers. The hills behind the Monastery were thickly seeded with mortar groups including some 20 Nebelwerfers. Substantial air support was on call.

The new battle was timed for February 24th. As soon as reorganisation had been completed 5 Brigade battalions were relieved in order to rest and to prepare for the encounter. Before relief on the night of February 23rd 1/9 Gurkhas endeavoured to complete the occupation of Point 445. Unfortunately a supporting shoot by heavy mortars ignited the scrub and exposed the direction of the attack. Heavy resistance developed and the assault force was withdrawn.

In placing the new battle in train New Zealanders relieved the American-Japanese battalion on the northern outskirts of Cassino town. French colonial troops moved in on 7 Brigade's right flank. The Allied alignment therefore on New Zealand Corps' front ran from 3 Algerian Division on Monte Castellone through 7 Indian Brigade to 6 New Zealand Brigade on the northern outskirts of Cassino. 5 New Zealand Brigade faced west along the Rapido and 78 Division took up the line at the entrance to the Liri valley.

By February 24th the redeployment had been completed and New Zealand Corps stood ready for the stroke. At this juncture the weather broke completely. From day to day the assault was postponed.* For three weeks while winter gales, driving snow and freezing rain pelted the exposed infantry, Fourth Division dourly waited, enduring an average daily toll of 40 to 50 casualties. No hour passed in which the crump of mortars, the whine of shells or the crack of a sniper's rifle did not herald the call for stretcher-bearers. A proud death in this period was that of Subedar Subramanyan, of 11 Field Park Company, Queen Victoria's Own Madras Sappers and Miners. On February 24th a British officer was trapped on an enemy minefield near railhead at Mignano. A second British officer, Subedar Subramanyan and five other ranks undertook to extricate him. As the sappers cleared the ground one trod on the prongs of a shrapnel mine. In the four seconds which elapsed before the mine sprang Subedar Subramanyan threw

*An unfortunate and rather inexplicable state of affairs as a result of which inter-brigade reliefs were not possible. A postponement for a week would have given the Indian brigades a rest. It must have been known that after the weather mended a few days must elapse before the airstrips would be dry enough for use by the heavy bombers.

himself upon it and saved the lives of his comrades by absorbing the burst. His gallantry and self-sacrifice was recognised by the award of the Division's first George Cross.

It had recently been decided that the description "gallantry in the presence of the enemy" which is the requisite qualification for the Victoria Cross, did not cover feats of consummate bravery on minefields. To many this appeared an invidious distinction, since rescue from minefields required the coldest kind of courage and involved the utmost risk.

On the ridge crests and along the hillsides the infantry of 7 Brigade clung to their meagre shelters under the continuous buffeting of the elements. When darkness fell the men emerged from the freezing cramp of their foxholes to prepare for the next miserable day. The enemy likewise came to life, searching the trails and assembly areas with mortars and artillery fire in the hope of intercepting supply columns. Paratroopers crept forward to strike down unwary sentries. With abysmal ignorance of British psychology they tried propaganda—shouting the names of prisoners taken and promising creature comforts to all who would surrender. They likewise dropped leaflets. Often the Urdu leaflets reached the Royal Sussex and the English leaflets 4/16 Punjabis; or else they both reached 1/2 Gurkhas who could read neither. In spite of their aggressiveness the Germans were feeling the strain. An officer of 31 Field Regiment picked up six prisoners on Point 593 who were only too willing to be brought in while 4/16 Punjabis every now and then found outpost sentries in a mood to surrender.

The interminable flights of shells which passed overhead brought confusion and unrelenting labour to the rear echelons of Fourth Division, cooped in the upper Rapido valley. Porters and mule trains assembled nightly at the dumps, signallers moved out to repair or to lay new wires, field companies shouldered their tools and squelched off through the freezing mud, ambulance convoys crept forward to pick up the day's wounded. For these workers the searching bombardments supplemented the enmity of the weather and the difficulty of the terrain. Along the slippery ice-covered ridges little groups with endless delays made their way forward. Parties scattered as the shoots came down and never re-assembled. Some lost touch in the darkness and took the wrong turnings. The mixture of French, American, Italian and Indian mules was perhaps the greatest trial of all. No one knew how these temperamental animals would behave or to what tongue they would respond. The bleak nights wore away in noise, confusion and back-breaking toil. If dawn caught the work parties in the open or in the forward areas swift retribution followed.

Yet in spite of every ordeal, every mischance, the spirit triumphed. Minds retained their composure, bodies their resiliency. A war correspondent stood one night at the crossing on the Rapido as exhausted men who had portered supplies up the mountainside trudged back.

Two soldiers retained sufficient vigour to describe their mules with such original maledictions that the pressman took notes. At that moment a concentration shoot crashed against the slopes of Monastery Hill. The tired porters paused to survey the cone which towered behind them, now spangled with the splashes of innumerable shells. One of the soldiers chortled: "Lumme, what a Christmas tree," he said.

Major Clements of 11 Field Regiment vouches for a delightful anecdote in the best Bairnsfather vein. He had ended a long and exhausting tour in a spandau-swept artillery observation post a few hundred yards from the rear walls of the Monastery. On his return to his battery he found a letter from his mother who besought him, should he ever be in the neighbourhood, not to fail to visit the famous Benedictine hospice.

Of all Divisional units perhaps none endured greater exposure, served longer hours and contributed more to the organisation that made maintenance possible than Major Cook's Fourth Divisional Provost Company. His men were stationed at points certain to attract the attention of the enemy. Their tasks were manifold. Road control, vehicle control, the demarcation and marking of tracks, the supply of information, the sorting out of priorities, the reporting of casualties, the maintenance of security, the custody of prisoners, the direction of stragglers and a score of unclassified employments engrossed these efficient pointsmen for 24 hours in each day. A mixed British-Indian formation, the red caps and red band turbans no longer represented the insignia of resented authority. Instead, they stood for assistance in any emergency.

In the second week of March the weather began to mend. On March 9th Major-General A. Galloway, CBE, DSO, MC, assumed temporary command of the Division. General Galloway was commander of 1 Armoured Division which had recently arrived in Italy from North Africa. On March 14th the long awaited signal flashed, "Bradman will be batting to-morrow". "DICKENS" operation was under way. That night New Zealand troops withdrew from the fringes of Cassino. Next morning broke fair and warm. (The diarist of 4/16 Punjabis remembered it to be the anniversary of the final attack on Keren). At 0830 hours the dull thunder of groups of heavy bombers was heard high overhead.

In the next 3½ hours 514 heavy and medium bombers crashed 1100 tons of bombs on the target area. The base of Monastery Hill disappeared in erupting smoke and dust. One battalion of 3 Parachute Regiment is believed to have died to a man in the ruins of Cassino town. Nevertheless with such unmistakable target indicators as the snow-clad cone of Monte Cairo and the junction of the two valleys a number of heavy groups went astray. Army Headquarters in Venafro (nearly 20 miles away) received a stick of bombs. Fourth Division's "B" Echelon in the upper Rapido valley received a thorough plastering, 50 men and 100 mules being hit. Three 500-pound bombs fell within 50 yards of

4/16 Punjabi Headquarters. An officer wrote: "No lives were lost but shaken figures emerged from their foxholes covered in fine white dust, like ghosts in a fantastic graveyard". On the stroke of noon the air was rent by an ear-splitting crash as 600 guns spoke as one. Behind a wall of steel 6 New Zealand Brigade advanced to the attack.

In spite of the devastating weight of metal fierce resistance was encountered as the Kiwis moved forward. Their immediate objective, Castle Hill, was strongly held. Neither bombing nor artillery had neutralised Continental Hotel, a fortress position on the hillside above the town 500 yards to the south of the Castle. In Cassino town the completeness of the destruction defeated its purpose. With the area a vast rubble heap the Kiwi tanks could not penetrate to mop up. Four hours after the opening of the attack the New Zealanders won Castle Hill and were able to exploit their gain by a downhill assault into Cassino town. By this time groups of tough paratroopers had emerged from deep tunnels and from caves cut into the hillside and had occupied last stand positions. From cellar windows, angles of broken houses, foxholes dug under rocky ledges, spandau teams disputed the advance. It now seems possible that had two brigades struck at Cassino simultaneously from different directions the town might have been captured. The air programme however had raised too great hopes and the uncommitted New Zealand formations were standing by for pursuit into the Liri valley.

At dusk rain descended in torrents. 5 Indian Brigade began to close up as soon as night fell. The downpour, the pitch darkness and blasts of enemy fire slowed up the advance but by 2330 hours 1/4 Essex had reached Cassino and had relieved 25 New Zealand Battalion. "C" Company held the Castle, "A" Company its approach on the outskirts of the town, "D" Company Point 175 across the ravine behind the Castle, and "B" Company a reserve position on the road along the hillside to the north. At 0300 hours on March 16th Lieut.-Colonel Noble despatched a company which seized the lower hairpin bend at Point 165, on the hillside 300 yards above the Castle. The Essex thus established a grip on the bottleneck through which Fourth Indian Division would enter the battle.

Behind the Home County men 1/6 Rajputana Rifles had followed down the Rapido in impenetrable darkness. On the outskirts of Cassino town heavy defensive fire caught the trudging files. "A" Company made its way to the Castle followed by "B" Company. The other companies were scattered by the artillery blasts and never reached their destinations. At 0245 hours "A" Company sallied across the hillside in an attempt to capture Point 236, the second hairpin bend. Much hung on the seizure of this position. Its possession opened the slopes for a drive upwards towards Hangman's Hill and ended intimate enemy surveillance of the Castle area. By 0430 hours the Rajputana Rifles had closed up on their objective. With less than 150 yards to go their presence was detected. Small arms fire swept the slopes and defensive shell fire searched the mountainside. "A" Company found it impossible to gain ground and withdrew to the Castle.

Lieut.-Colonel Nangle at the head of 1/9 Gurkhas arrived on the outskirts of Cassino shortly after 0100 hours. His instructions were to support 1/6 Rajputana Rifles and thereafter to continue the attack towards Hangman's Hill. On finding that only two of Lieut.-Colonel West's companies had reached the Castle area, Lieut.-Colonel Nangle sent his "C" and "D" Companies forward. "C" Company under Captain Drinkall skirted the fringes of Cassino town, gained the hillside and disappeared in the darkness. "D" Company was ambushed by an enemy spandau team, losing 15 men within a minute. Dawn broke before this company could be re-organised for a further advance.

During the night Lieut. Murray of 4 Field Company accompanied by Sergeant Morris of 19 New Zealand Armoured Regiment carried out a daring reconnaissance of Fourth Division's battlefield for the purpose of discovering if it would be possible to move tanks across the hillside. Having evaded the strong points at the hairpin bends they examined the winding road which led to Hangman's Hill, thereafter audaciously descending into Cassino town. They found themselves in the midst of Germans. In a dugout in a ruined building Sergeant Morris captured a prisoner. While exploring an underground passage he fell riddled with bullets. A Wild West pistol duel followed in which Lieut. Murray killed three Germans. In a running fight in the early dawn he outfooted his pursuers and returned safely to the Castle.

Thus of 5 Brigade only 1/4 Essex, two companies of 1/6 Rajputana Rifles and one company of 1/9 Gurkhas had managed to reach the forward positions. The Essex were firmly established in the Castle and on Point 165. The Rajputana Rifles likewise were on Castle Hill. Captain Drinkall and his men had disappeared, leaving no trace. The remainder of 1/9 Gurkhas had formed a rough perimeter in the rear of the Castle area within 100 yards of 1/6 Rajputana Rifles' headquarters. The two remaining companies of this latter battalion were scattered in small groups along the northern approaches to Cassino town.

March 16th dawned on bitter battle. The New Zealanders slogged ahead, rubble heap by rubble heap. General Heidrich, commander of 1 Parachute Division, from his eyrie on the heights above could follow every move below him as intimately as a player above a chess board. The Nazi commander concentrated all his strength to hold the vital area around Castle Hill. Fresh paratroop formations were brought in from Monte Castellone and stood ready to stiffen the line should it sag. All enemy-held sectors could be reinforced without difficulty, the Monastery hillside by way of the wadis and the ravine to the north of Castle Hill, Cassino town by way of Highway 6. The enemy concentrated his artillery and mortar strength to play on the northern approaches to Cassino town and the paratroopers were told that they were to stand firm man by man until death closed on them.

At 0830 hours Allied guns laid a smoke screen below Point 236 and 1/6 Rajputana Rifles for the second time flung themselves at this vital strongpoint. They came under devastating fire from all sides as soon as they emerged from shelter. While their attack was in progress a mortar bomb hit their battalion headquarters. Five officers including Lieut.-Colonel West and his adjutant were knocked out. Major P. R. Inwood assumed command. During the day Major Marshall extricated the two Rajputana Rifle companies scattered along the northern outskirts of Cassino. They withdrew to the upper Rapido valley for reorganisation.

Throughout the morning British and Indian troops strove to consolidate their positions and to make ready for the next phase of the battle. Progress was slow; every boulder, every block of broken masonry, seemed to harbour a paratrooper. The artillery thundered on in counter battery and in softening-up programmes. (In the first 24 hours of the attack shell expenditure averaged 800 rounds per gun). During the morning New Zealand Corps asked if it would be safe to shoot on Hangman's Hill. The gunners held their fire while the disappearance of Captain Drinkall's company of 1/9 Gurkhas was investigated. Early in the afternoon the New Zealanders reported that they could discern figures below the gibbet platform and shortly afterwards a faint wireless signal brought electrifying news. In some extraordinary fashion Captain Drinkall and his men had threaded their way across the hillside, had evaded enemy defences and before dawn had reached and seized the all-important knoll almost in the shadow of the Monastery walls.

This exciting success made it imperative that the battle should be carried to a decision without respite to the enemy. First priority was the reinforcement and replenishment of the men who had won Hangman's Hill. For the night of March 16/17 the plan called for "A" and "B" Companies of 1/6 Rajputana Rifles to make a third attempt to seize Point 236, the upper hairpin bend. Concurrently the remainder of 1/9 Gurkhas would emulate their pathfinder company and would squirm through to Hangman's Hill. The New Zealanders undertook to engross the garrison of Continental Hotel during these operations.

At 1900 hours concentration shoots began to batter the hillside. Two hours later "A" and "B" Companies of 1/6 Rajputana Rifles under Captain P. A. Scaife thrust up the slopes from Point 165 and after an hour's stiff fighting stormed the upper hairpin bend. Unfortunately casualties and shortage of ammunition prevented exploitation higher up the hillside, where a covering position afforded a rallying point for enemy counter-attack forces. While this fighting was in progress 1/9 Gurkhas debouched from the Castle and began to thread their way between their battling comrades—Rajputana Riflemen above and New Zealanders below. As they crossed the lower hillside they came under fire but plodded steadily onwards. Proceeding with the utmost caution they took upwards of eight hours to sift through the enemy defences. Shortly before dawn the leading elements reached Hangman's Hill. The battalion deployed with "C" and "D" Companies holding the platform of the knoll, "A" Company covering the road bend on the left and "B" Company the northern slopes of the pimple. The reinforcements arrived in time to intercept a counter-attack from the Monastery, which fortunately struck at the centre of the Gurkha positions and was easily blown back.

At dawn a counter-attack also struck and with greater success at 1/6 Rajputana Rifles in their newly won positions on the upper hairpin bend. Captain Scaife's men were too thin on the ground and they were forced to withdraw to the shelter of the Castle.

Once again the hillside was under enemy control. On the other hand a substantial force had been established on Hangman's Hill. The purposes of the adversaries now were unmistakable. Fourth Indian Division must support and replenish 1/9 Gurkhas; 1 Parachute Division must seal up the bottleneck at Castle Hill. The first move came from the enemy. In spite of the utmost efforts of the New Zealanders, sniping and spandau groups continued to infiltrate into ruins along the northern fringe of the town. Here they could sweep the slopes above them and could bring the Castle gateway under fire. These persistant assailants continued to encroach until it was only possible to leave the Castle in single file and at the double.

It had become urgently necessary to despatch a supply train to 1/9 Gurkhas, whose "C" Company now had spent 48 hours on the battlefield with only one day's water and rations. Shortly after dark on March 17th porters from a pioneer battalion escorted by "A" and "D" Companies of 4/6 Rajputana Rifles moved down the Rapido valley. Defensive fire caught the column en route causing 19 casualties. It was not until 2210 hours that the supply party reached the Castle. Another 90 minutes intervened before it passed out across the hillside. The enemy was on the alert and threw a strong raid against the lower hairpin bend at Point 165. This assault was blown back but mortar and artillery fire continued to search the slopes. At 0145 hours on March 18th Lieut. J. R. M. French, MC, reported that owing to the heavy bombardment the porter personnel had refused to proceed beyond the Castle. On receipt of this news 4/6 Rajputana Rifles were ordered to fight their way through to Hangman's Hill. The infantry shouldered as much of the porters' loads as could be carried and moved off to run the gauntlet. Three hours later a welcome message reported that with the loss of eight men the supply party had got through. It was too late to return before dawn so the Rajputana Riflemen spread out among the Gurkhas and spent the day on Hangman's Hill.*

To supplement the portered supplies, on the afternoon of March 18th 48 aircraft, guided by coloured smoke, dropped containers on

---

*A party of gunners from 11 Field Regiment under Sergeant Parfitt volunteered for porter duty to Hangman's Hill, and successfully negotiated the passage. On his return the following night Sergeant Parfitt brought out a wounded Gurkha officer.

Hangman's Hill. Although the dropping was reasonably accurate many of the containers bounced down the steep hillsides out of reach. Sufficient supplies were retrieved to support the garrison on restricted rations.

Throughout March 18th the dogged clearance of Cassino continued. On the previous day 26 New Zealand Battalion had stormed the railway station. Thereafter Corps artillery swathed Cassino town and the lower slopes of the mountainside with a thick pall of smoke, to protect the Kiwi sappers who laboured on the Rapido crossings. This smoke shell was cast with less accuracy than was the gunners' wont. An artillery observation officer who had joined the Gurkhas on Hangman's Hill wrote: "The smoke nuisance now became acute. Our shelling continued throughout the afternoon with such accuracy that the Gurkha commander's sangar received three direct hits from shell itself. Attempts by the battery commander urged by the Gurkha CO to shift the target proved fruitless. . Relations in all directions assumed an atmosphere of strain. The galling aspect of the whole business was that the smoke so placed screened nothing from nobody."

Enemy artillery and mortars shelled the obscured area viciously. Long range guns chimed in and howitzers lobbed heavy metal into the New Zealand assault positions. The pertinacious paratroopers took advantage of the smoke mantle to establish themselves still more strongly above and below Castle Hill. During the previous night enemy groups had crept down the wadis from the rear of the Monastery and had reinforced the strong points and weapon pits on the upper hillside. These German outposts undoubtedly had suffered severely from the Allied bombardment. 4/16 Punjabis from its lookouts on the ridge crest reported 50 enemy stretcher-bearers under Red Cross flags to be picking up wounded around Point 445. The steep slopes where Castle Hill met the town now were infested with snipers and bomb squads. A conspicuous twin-towered building was reoccupied by the paratroopers as a key centre of resistance. 26 Field Ambulance, which had established a forward post in the cellar of a ruin on the outskirts of Cassino, was asked to vacate its premises while the New Zealanders dealt with an enemy machine-gun nest on the top floor. It had previously been possible to reach the Monastery hillside by way of the northern outskirts of Cassino town, but now the paratroopers managed to seal off this approach and the only remaining route led directly through the Castle. In an endeavour to clear up the situation New Zealand tanks moved up and shelled the infested area at close range. Unfortunately a number of "overs" caused casualties among 1/4 Essex on Castle Hill.

In spite of increasing difficulties every effort was bent to destroy the enemy resistance by the only decisive method—the storming of the Monastery. On the evening of March 18th the Machine Gun Battalion, Rajputana Rifles, arranged to take over porterage duties to Hangman's Hill. The remaining elements of 1/6 Rajputana Rifles were merged into a composite company and placed under command of 4/6 Rajputana

Rifles with instructions to relieve 1/4 Essex in the Castle area and at the lower hairpin bend. These reliefs were to be completd by 0400 hours on March 19th. Thereafter the Essex would move forward to join 1/9 Gurkhas on Hangman's Hill. At dawn both battalions would race across the intervening 300 yards and strike for the supreme prize—the battered ruins on the crest. Concurrently the tank diversion in the rear of the Monastery would be launched. 24 New Zealand Battalion would cross the lower hillside and assist the advance by assaults on enemy strong points at Continental Hotel and Point 202.

This plan involved timing and speed of movement which asked a great deal of the participants. The Castle bottleneck was increasingly constricted by the attentions of the enemy on the upper fringe of Cassino town. 1/4 Essex were expected to complete an involved relief, to traverse the danger zone and to arrive in time to attack from Hangman's Hill at dawn. It was indeed a bold decision to stake everything on a blow at the heart at a time when Fourth Indian Divisions' hands were tied by the situation in the Castle area.

That night the Rajputana Rifle machine-gunners made a trip to Hangman's Hill with supplies and returned without incident. "A" and "D" Companies of 4/6 Rajputana Rifles brought in wounded from Hangman's Hill and also returned with supplies. It was not until well after midnight that the remainder of 4/6 Rajputana Rifles arrived at the Castle to take over from 1/4 Essex. One platoon under Lieut. Gopal was sent forward to relieve a similar force of the Home County men at the lower hairpin bend. While these reliefs were in progress "B" and "D" Companies of the Essex started across the slopes towards Hangman's Hill.

As night thinned in the east heavy machine-gun fire from the summit of Monte Cassino and from spandau teams in Cassino town raked the slopes of the mountain. After a short but sharp artillery and mortar shoot a battalion of 1 German Parachute Regiment launched a heavy attack down the hillside by way of the upper hairpin bend. The Essex and Rajputana Rifles platoons at the lower hairpin bend disappeared in a smother of enemies. (Two Essex men, Privates Wise and Horseley, lay undetected for 48 hours in a slit trench and then managed to escape). Without pause the attack swept on against the Castle.

Two companies of 1/4 Essex less one platoon, one company of 4/6 Rajputana Rifles, two platoons of 1/6 Rajputana Rifles, some Sapper and Miner details, together with Major Ronald Oswald of 1 Field Regiment and his artillery observation group, garrisoned the Castle. Six German paratrooper prisoners including a sergeant-major also were present, awaiting evacuation. The defending force in all numbered 150 rifles under the command of Major Frank Kettley, MC, of the Essex.

When the German shoot came down it was impossible to call for defensive fire because of uncertainty concerning the fate of the detachments at the lower hairpin bend. With reckless daring the Germans came swarming in while snipers on the hillside picked off defenders who showed on the battlements. Grenades were showered over the walls into the courtyard. The garrison met the onset doughtily. Through arrow slits light machine-guns swept the approaches with bursts of fire. At the north-west corner Corporal Parker of the Essex broke up two attacks single-handed with genade and Bren gun. He was killed soon afterwards.

After 20 minutes brisk fighting the paratroopers were pinned down. A flare recalled them but only for long enough to reorganize. At 0700 hours a second attack swept up under cover of a smoke screen. Major Kettley while passing messages was mortally wounded and Major D. A. Beckett took command. In full view paratroopers endeavoured to climb the walls. Once again the attack broke down in the face of a blaze of defensive fire and once again after a brief lull the stubborn paratroopers leapt to the assault. By this time supporting mortars and artillery had established fire lines; defensive curtains of shell intervened to hold off the assailants. Major Beckett while spotting for the mortars was wounded a second time. During a pause in the fighting he sent a number of Rajputana Riflemen outside the gateway with instructions to find cover on the hillside and to counter the incessant sniping.

The situation at the Castle was now serious. Only three officers and 60 men remained on their feet. The expenditure of ammunition had been enormous. Machine-gunners had fired more than 8,000 rounds and the Essex mortars more than 1,500 bombs. Mortar barrels had grown red hot, had curled and bent. During the fighting RSM Rose, DCM, of the Essex had carried load after load of bombs to the mortar pits. A party of 8 men had run the gauntlet across the ravine and had brought sand bags of ammunition. At 0900 hours the enemy began to work up from Cassino town against the lower walls of the Castle; spandau teams hosed the gateway with streams of bullets. In reply Essex and Rajputana Rifle mortars and machine-guns from across the ravine curtained the western wall with fire and New Zealand tanks laid a similar barrage in the path of the attack from Cassino town. This protection halted the assailants who sent a stretcher-bearer under a white flag to ask for a truce to pick up wounded. General Galloway granted an armistice of 30 minutes during which time a number of Essex casualties were dug out from under the collapsed castle wall. (Capt. Douglas Beach, MC, was extricated alive nearly 24 hours afterwards). The truce was broken by enemy snipers, but during the interval Castle casualties were evacuated and preparations made to meet the next assault. At 1200 hours "A" Company of 2/7 Gurkhas under Major Denis Drayton, a German speaking officer, reached the Castle.

During the afternoon a party of 8 Germans led by an officer managed to insert a demolition charge under a buttress of the northern battlements. The explosion breached the wall, burying two officers and 20 men of "A" Company of the Essex. As the Germans leapt through the gap they were riddled. One wounded paratrooper crept in to surrender. He stated that out of 200 men launched in the dawn assault only 40 remained on their feet. In the defence of the breach in the walls Major Beckett was wounded a third time.

The repulse of this audacious assault ended the ordeal of the Castle defenders. On the next and last alarm curtains of defensive fire held the enemy from the close. During the afternoon, while accompanying General Galloway in a survey of the battlefield, Lieut.-Colonel Arthur Noble of the Essex was wounded and his long period of command ended. Major L. W. A. Chappell, MC, took over.

During these tense assaults the behaviour of the paratrooper prisoners was noteworthy. They acted as if they were members of the garrison. All except the Sergeant-Major volunteered as stretcher-bearers. Two were killed while bringing in wounded. When the wall was breached a sniper drew a bead at close range on Major Beckett. One of the paratroopers sprang forward and threw him out of the line of fire. The Sergeant-Major, disdaining cover, walked in the open with the air of a supervisor of events. When the attack was beaten off he congratulated Major Beckett on a soldierly performance and presented the Essex officer with his fur-lined paratrooper gauntlets as a trophy of the occasion.

When the assault on the Castle began, "B" and "D" Companies of the Essex were little more than started on their trek to Hangman's Hill. Some men of the rear company retraced their steps in order to aid the defenders. With the paratroopers flooding to the attack only a few managed to regain the Castle walls. The remainder followed the leading company to Hangman's Hill. Day broke with the Home County men in full view as they toiled across the bare slopes. It was not until 1015 hours that 75 survivors reached the Gurkhas around the rocky platform. High above the battle the garrison of Hangman's Hill watched attack after attack surge to the Castle walls and ebb back. The gallant handful of Essex, in spite of their mauling, were in no mood to stand by and see their comrades assailed. They asked permission to strike down the slopes from Hangman's Hill onto the rear of the paratroopers. Permission was refused, for the assault upon the Monastery had been set for 1400 hours. By noon however it was apparent that it would be folly to commit the Hangman's Hill force, thin on the ground and with scanty replenishment, to a major assault while a critical battle raged on its lifeline of communication. The culminating attack therefore was abandoned and the Essex were ordered as soon as night fell to return to the Castle. That evening they once more crossed the fire-swept slopes and took a pummelling from enemy outposts. Shortly after 2200 hours, some reached the Castle; others, finding the way blocked, returned to Hangman's Hill.

When 5 Brigade's bid for the Monastery was abandoned in the face of the enemy's all-out assault on the Castle, it might have been expected that stand-fast orders would have been despatched to the auxiliary force entrusted with the minor role. Research historians doubtless will be puzzled by the fact that 7 Brigade's diversionary filibuster in the rear of the Monastery was allowed to proceed. This force consisted of 7 Brigade Reconnaissance Squadron reinforced by 19 Shermans and 21 light tanks from "D" Company, 760 U.S. Tank Battalion and from "B" Squadron, 20 New Zealand Armoured Regiment. It moved off from Madras Circus in the upper Rapido valley at 0600 hours that morning. Passing along a nullah to the west of the Majola feature, the intruders followed the new jeep track to Massa Albaneta. Thence they encircled Points 479 and 593, shooting up outposts on the western slopes of these ridges. Having crashed through a thinly held defence line the tanks wheeled and pushed on along a shallow defile into the rear of the Monastery. This unexpected blow completely upset the enemy. Had it been integrated with infantry attacks it seems possible that the Cassino defences might have collapsed. But once again one fist struck while the other arm hung idle. The local German commander revealed his apprehension in a series of excited and exaggerated wireless reports in clear. He advised the Wehrmacht High Command that an infantry attack must be expected in conjunction with this armour thrust.

At 1020 hours, with this evidence before him, the Corps Commander decided that if the tanks reached a position from which the Monastery could be brought under effective fire, the force on Hangman's Hill would strike for the crest. Once again the "if" factor intervened. An integrated effort was made conditional upon an individual success. At midday, the tank columns having safely encircled the main enemy defences, encountered a narrow defile with precipitous slopes. This passage was mined and under heavy mortar and machine-gun fire. A leading vehicle brewed up and blocked the track. When the Shermans could not negotiate the steep going, they withdrew and the light tanks pushed on. All afternoon the armour gallantly endeavoured to force its way up to the rear walls of the Monastery, although it is by no means certain that had the tanks arrived in commanding positions their guns would have been heavy enough to do much damage. At 1730 hours, when a dozen tanks had been knocked out, the raiding forces were ordered to withdraw under cover of darkness.

March 19th thus proved to be the decisive day of the battle. None of New Zealand Corps' various enterprises—the destruction of enemy forces in Cassino town, the assault on the Monastery, the tank filibuster—had succeeded. On the other hand, the single enemy purpose of blocking the Castle bottleneck was within a hair's breadth of success. An appreciation of the situation revealed that the harassed forces besieged in the Castle, like the isolated groups at Hangman's Hill and Point 202, were incapable of offensive action. It was therefore necessary to re-direct attention to the sector which had engrossed the enemy commander from the first—the entrance to the battlefield. Until this vital corridor was dyked and widened, the assault forces fought with nooses round their necks.

On the evening of March 19th 6 Royal West Kent Regiment (Lieut.-Colonel P. E. O. Bryan, DSO, MC), borrowed from 78 Division, relieved the battered but indomitable Essex in the Castle area. One unwounded officer and less than 200 men marched out. The first task of the newcomers was to regain the lower hairpin bend. In conjunction with this assignment, 7 Brigade undertook to drive downhill from holding positions to the north of the Monastery, on the opposite side of the deep ravine which ran behind Castle Hill. If both forces made their ground, it would constrict and perhaps close the gap through which the enemy paratroops crept down to reinforce their blocking groups on the northern fringes of Cassino town. For 7 Brigade's operation 2/7 Gurkhas were briefed to lead the way.

When darkness fell on March 20th, the leading company of Royal West Kents slipped out through the Castle gateway, deployed and moved against the lower hairpin bend. The advance was no more than under way when a tremendous explosion—probably a series of newly-planted land mines—shook the hillside. The leading platoons suffered casualties and the advance came to a halt. Reorganising on the start line a second attempt came to grief in the neighbourhood of a small mound between the Castle and Point 165, where a recent sowing of anti-personnel mines caused a number of casualties. The mountainside was now awake and bickering and continuous shoots searched the Castle area. The attack therefore was abandoned. The downhill advance of 2/7 Gurkhas on the opposite side of the ravine likewise failed. A blaze of fire greeted the hillmen, who attempted for two hours to infiltrate towards Point 445. After 20 casualties, including a company commander, the Gurkhas found progress impossible.

The failure of both prongs of this operation emboldened the enemy to further efforts to seal up the Castle. In the 500 yards between the Castle entrance and Point 165 a group of paratroopers infiltrated and endeavoured to link up with detachments in Cassino town. Concurrently other enemy groups thrust down the deep ravine in an equally bold attempt to isolate the Castle from the rear. A composite company of 4/6 Rajputana Rifles and "A" Company of 2/7 Gurkhas guarded the supply lines and linked up with 4/16 Punjabis on the hillside above. At 2300 hours on March 20th, after harassing artillery and mortar fire, an enemy force estimated at company strength struck at the right flank of the Rajputana Rifles. Thirty minutes of brisk fighting broke up the attack but soon after midnight an even heavier group smashed at the centre of the Indian positions. This time it took an hour's fighting to discourage the paratroopers in their persistent attempts to establish themselves in the ravine behind the Castle. These sharp thrusts cost the Rajputana Rifles 32 casualties.

At 0615 hours on March 21st, in the dense darkness before dawn, a substantial enemy force estimated at battalion strength moved down the hillside in a further effort to storm the Castle. The approach was detected and the Royal West Kents called for defensive fire. The entire

Corps artillery as well as battalion mortars and machine-guns were brought to bear and the attack disintegrated in face of devastating blasts of fire. Groups of paratroopers doubled forward to gain the shelter of the Castle walls and thereafter to surrender. Approximately 40 prisoners were taken.

On the same morning (March 21st) a Corps Conference examined the situation. The initiative had passed to the enemy. General Heidrich had appreciated from the first that to enter a room one must pass through a door. He had concentrated his strength to keep the door closed. To date it had been swinging on its hinges—sometimes open, sometimes slamming shut. Now it must be wedged open in such manner as to place it beyond the power of the enemy to turn the key.

The long overdue step of constructing a well-defended corridor was approved. 4 Field Company came forward to site wire barriers and to lay out a defensive minefield which would link the Castle area with the upper Rapido valley. Major Rawson-Gardiner of the Rajputana Rifle machine-gunners arrived to install his guns in defensive positions. Mutually supporting strong points were established. With an impregnable perimeter Castle Hill would constitute a fortress from which mobile forces might sally to take up a battle of manoeuvre on the slopes.

The enemy immediately detected the altered plan. A week of fierce fighting had thinned out the paratroops but General Heidrich ruthlessly decided to bid once more for victory. At dawn on March 22nd he assembled his sapper companies for use as infantry. In a final attempt to storm the Castle the engineers raced down the hillside from the hairpin bends. The attempt had been anticipated and the gunners were standing ready. Defensive fire swept the slopes and caught the improvised force as it surged to the close. The attack disintegrated with heavy casualties, leaving 30 prisoners behind.

The battle now had reached stalemate. Assailants and defenders alike were staggering from weakness. All reserves had been committed and no possibility remained of a knock-out blow. 7 Brigade, which has appeared little in the narrative of the second assault, had reached a state of exhaustion almost equal to that of Brigadier Bateman's men. For six weeks without relief Royal Sussex, Punjabis and Gurkhas had confronted the enemy on the high ridges under constant strain in all but indefensible positions. Continuous harassing fire took a toll only less than that of actual battle. Nor had 11 Brigade been more fortunate. All units had been employed in one capacity or another. The New Zealanders were in no better case. Two Kiwi brigades had been worn thin in constant yard by yard struggles in Cassino town. In his report to the New Zealand Government General Freyberg pointed out that the operation had been planned into three phases—the break-in battle, the encounter battle and the break-out battle. The second phase had proved interminable because the first phase had never really succeeded.

On March 23rd the New Zealand Corps offensive was abandoned.

The next necessity was to withdraw Lieut.-Colonel Nangle's force from Hangman's Hill. After the initial attack on the morning of March 17th the enemy had ignored this area, probably considering that if the battle were won elsewhere the troops on Hangman's Hill would constitute a prize of victory. It also probably suited the enemy commander to regard the reinforcement and replenishment of this force as a bait which would cause Fourth Indian Division to disperse its strength. Nevertheless the gallant garrison, isolated in mid-air with battle on all sides, paid a daily toll in casualties, enduring alike the malice of the enemy and of the elements. From their advanced lines along the Rapido the New Zealanders watched Hangman's Hill with anxiety. A New Zealand non-commissioned officer wrote:

"If we weren't altogether happy about our own position we at least realised that it was infinitely preferable, with its slit trenches and firm base of supply, to the undefined area among the barren rocks of the hill where our Indian friends grimly held on under a hail of mortar and shell. Our own twenty-five pounders appeared to rake most of the hillside. One wondered how men could live in such a place."

"On the night of the 18th the Indians suffered a most ferocious bombardment. In the darkness shells and mortars crashed among the rocks, burst in spraying red circles of flame on their flinty surfaces, and sent their echoes rolling down the hillside. Our own guns from behind and before Trocchio replied with a hurricane of steel that rushed over our heads and plastered the face to the south and west of Hangman's Hill. I thought I could see the occasional flash of grenades. As the storm subsided through the comparative silence came the rip of an occasional spandau and—by contrast—the slow rattle of a Bren in reply. The Indians were still there!"

Lieut.-Colonel Nangle was an equally anxious spectator of the New Zealand attack below him. Of the fighting on March 18th he wrote:

"The battle in Cassino town went on all day but with reduced violence. The smoke screen of which we were the point of origin, continued. Canisters, shell cases and base plugs continued to fall amongst us and to cause casualties. One Essex man hit by a base plug ran about forty yards downhill before falling dead. We watched, in one interval in the smoke, the New Zealanders below clearing one of the streets of Cassino. From our detached viewpoint we could appreciate the subtleties of the technique of both sides. The careful approach of the tanks, the searching for them by the German mediums, the blasting of each house in turn, the withdrawal of the Germans from house to house always covered by fire from another or from the street, the quick dashes of the supporting New Zealand Infantry and the use of smoke by both sides."

The last attempt to reach Hangman's Hill overland had occurred on the night of March 18/19. On the two following nights porterage parties assembled at the Castle but the situation on the hillside was too precarious to allow them to proceed. Thereafter one or two air droppings per day kept the isolated force in a reasonable state of replenishment. About 50% of all canisters dropped were recovered. The enemy attempted to confuse the low-flying supply planes by reproducing the coloured signal smokes over other positions. The German commander also regrouped his anti-aircraft guns to harass the supply planes. The only essential replenishment which failed to arrive were radio batteries. Out of 50 dropped only 4 were recovered. As a result communications with Hangman's Hill were hampered. When plans for withdrawal were drafted it was deemed unwise on security grounds to risk wireless transmission.

Officers were asked to volunteer for the task of reaching Hangman's Hill and of delivering orders by word of mouth. Captain Mallinson of 1/4 Essex, Captain Normand of 1/9 Gurkhas and Lieutenant Jennings of 4/6 Rajputana Rifles were chosen. On the night of March 24/25 these messengers (each with a carrier pigeon) set out across the hillside.* At 0340 hours on March 25th Captain Mallinson arrived and arranged a system of three signals (by radio code word, by groups of Verey lights, by Bofors bursts), any one of which would constitute orders to evacuate. At 0515 hours Captain Normand likewise reached Hangman's Hill. Lieut. Jennings was intercepted and forced to return to the Castle. At 1220 hours on March 24th the code instruction "ROCHE" was received and acknowledged by Hangman's Hill.

At 2015 hours the withdrawal began, following the route traversed by the messengers of the night before—down the hillside towards Point 202 and thence along the lower slopes above Cassino town. Lieut.-Colonel Nangle has described this tricky passage:

"Once over the ridge a weird scene came into view. It was a clear fine night with visibility quite good. The Castle could be seen standing up on its knob in the distance. Thee Brown House (Continental Hotel) stood bold and desolate between us and the Castle.. Above the Brown House there was a line of bursting shells stretching right across the face of the hill, their flashes making a queer glow in the clouds of smoke and rock dust they threw up. Just before us a similar curtain of shells was drawn across the hill above the town itself. Between these walls of fire lay the way to the Castle. We continued to move slowly across the face of the hill. The artillery fire quite covered any noise we made as we stumbled over the loose stones. A slight deviation allowed us to give the Brown House a wide berth as we were uncertain whether it was held or not. No sound came from this ruin and we continued, hardly believing our good luck, to the Castle. We filed up the narrow path and were challenged by the West Kents."

*Mallinson was an Englishman, Normand a Scot and Jennings a Welshman. Their pigeons were named St. George, St. Andrew and St. David.

BRIGADE COMMANDERS

Brigadier (afterwards Major-General)
O. de T. Lovett CBE, DSO.

Brigadier J. C. Saunders-Jacobs CBE, DSO.

Brigadier H. J. C. Hunt CBE, DSO.

CASSINO

MONASTERY FROM POINT 445.

MONASTERY FROM SNAKES HEAD.

CASTLE HILL—MONASTERY IN BACKGROUND.

INDIAN AND AMERICAN TROOPS ON TRACK TO SNAKES HEAD.

ITALIAN OPERATIONS

CARRIER PATROL, SAN VITO VILLAGE, LOWER ADRIATIC

7 BRIGADE RECONNAISANCE SQUADRON ADVANCING ON PESCARA,

CENTRAL ITALY—TYPICAL ATTACK AGAINST WOODED SUMMIT, BEHIND SMOKE SCREEN.

SAN MARINO

WHITE CROSSES CUT IN CHALK ALONG STATE BOUNDARY.

SMOKE SCREEN COVERING ADVANCE ON VALDRAGONA.

CASTLE ON CLIFFSIDE IN UPPER TOWN.

GOTHIC LINE BATTLES

TAVOLETO IN FLAMES

MULE TRAIN PASSING THROUGH MONTESUEDO

ATTACK ON MONTE CALVO.

GEMMANO RUINS

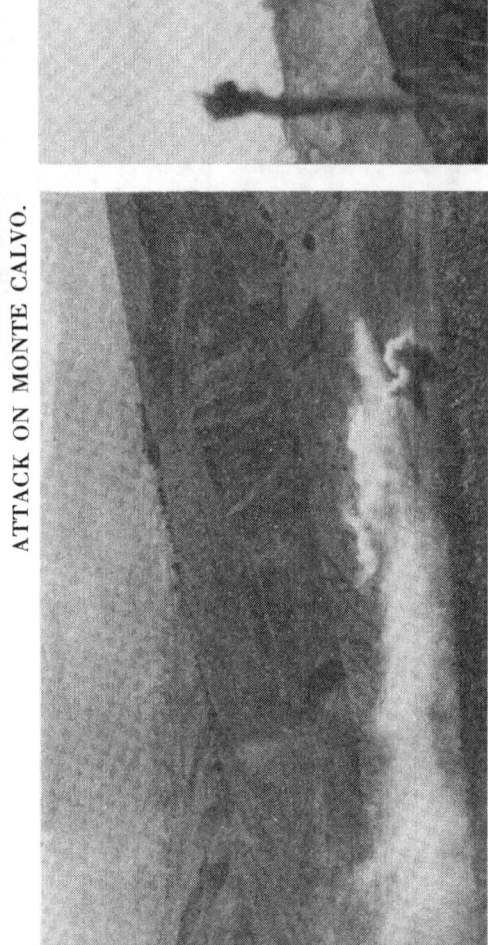

WOODCUT PRESENTED TO FOURTH INDIAN DIVISION BY THE CITY OF URBINO IN REMEMBRANCE OF ITS LIBERATION. THE INSCRIPTION READS:

"The Division gave of its best and by its victories at Monte Calvo, Auditore and Tavoleto, ensured our safety from bombardment by the German artillery."

The march back from Hangman's Hill occupied three hours. To engross the enemy during the withdrawal a heavy shoot was laid on the Monastery. Royal West Kents raided from the Castle area and the New Zealanders demonstrated at various points on the outskirts of Cassino. Two gunner officers and 4 other ranks, 8 officers and 177 men of 1/9 Gurkhas, 2 officers and 30 men of 1/4 Essex and 40 men of 4/6 Rajputana Rifles returned. A number of wounded were left on Hangman's Hill for evacuation next day. The last stretcher party was given a card by an enemy patrol which stated that thereafter facilities for the evacuation of casualties under the Red Cross would not be allowed by the German Divisional Commander.

Despite their ordeal all ranks returned in good heart. The Gurkhas on being warned for withdrawal enquired who would relieve them. One of the gunner officers who kept an informative diary wrote: "The most noticeable hardships of life on Hangman's Hill were hunger and cold. We had one great blessing in the shape of tea. Mugs were irreplaceable kit".

On the night of March 25/26 11 British Brigade of 78 Division began the relief of both 5 and 7 Brigades. 8 Argyll and Sutherland Highlanders assumed responsibility in the Castle area while 5 Northamptonshire Regiment relieved 1 Royal Sussex, 1/2 Gurkhas and 4/6 Punjabis along the hillside between Point 593 and the deep ravine. 2 Lancashire Fusiliers took over on Point 175 and the hillsides above the Rapido. The relief was carried out during a blizzard of unexampled severity. In the storm some units were unable to complete the handover and many detachments came in later. The diarist of 4/16 Punjabis wrote:

"The quickening dawn saw many of us still in the Rapido valley. Men who had spent long days in foxholes and whose knee joints and muscles had weakened through lack of normal exercise had to move carefully. The blizzard was still just thick enough to hide us from view. As we neared the transport that was to carry us away, the smoke screen cleared and the shape of the now shattered Monastery loomed out dressed in a mantle of snow as if to hide from us her scars of battle. It was a fitting farewell".

For the infantry Cassino was the supreme ordeal. What it might have been if the medical services had not risen to the challenge must remain to the imagination. In six weeks more than 4,000 men of Fourth Indian Division were killed or wounded. To cope with this overwhelming emergency Colonel R. L. Raymond, ADMS, who had replaced Colonel F. R. H. Mollan, OBE, MC, on the latter's retirement at the end of 1943, brought 17 Field Ambulance (Lieut.-Colonel H. J. R. Thorne, DSO, RAMC), 26 Field Ambulance, (Lieut.-Colonel G. S. N. Hughes, DSO, IMS), 32 Field Ambulance (Lieut.-Colonel C. W. Greene, IMS), which had arrived with 11 Brigade, and 2 Indian Mobile Casualty Clearing Station (Lieut.-Colonel C. Reed, RAMC), together with a group of volunteer ambulances of American Field Service, onto the battlefield. Whether from the crests behind the Monastery or from the mountainside below it, or from the Rapido valley, the rescue, evacuatiion and care of casualties proceeded in full view of the enemy. Many British and Indian soldiers are alive to-day because no danger was sufficient to deter the devoted stretcher-bearers, doctors and orderlies from their day and night struggle against imminent death.

7 Brigades opening assault along the bare fire-swept summits in the rear of the Monastery imposed a severe strain on the medical units. Captain E. Bowmer, 17 Field Ambulance, organised the evacuation route down the hillside. Many officers and men owe their lives to this gallant doctor. A motor ambulance Car Head and an advanced dressing station under Captain Minford was established in the ruins of Cairo village. For several miles to the rear the road was under fire. A medical officer who traversed this track daily paid a tribute to the American Field Ambulance which was equally applicable to all ambulance drivers:

"The river crossing—Windy Corner—received an unhealthy amount of shelling. Jeeps did not tarry there. Yet in full daylight, an American volunteer halted his ambulance, rescued a wounded man, dressed his wounds, took him to the advanced dressing station under continuous fire, and classified it as 'all in the day's work'. Another driver lost his ambulance when a near miss ditched it, but continued on foot and brought in four Indians under a hail of fire. Day and night, and nonstop if necessary, these American boys would carry on. They could always be trusted to get through, no matter how sticky the situation".

From the advanced dressing station jeep ambulances negotiated a rough and difficult mountain track for nearly a mile along the slopes of the massif. At "Ambulance Jeep Head" Captain Aslam, IMS, operated a forward dressing station. Here during the early fighting 16 stretcher-bearers were knocked out by a single shell. Thence a steep narrow and winding mule path continued for 2 miles towards Point 593 where the most advanced dressing station was set up by Captain Bhatia and Captain Ghaznavi (26 Field Ambulance) in conjunction with regimental aid posts of Royal Sussex (Captain Reilly), 1/6 Rajputana Rifles (Captain Karney), 1/2 Gurkhas (Captain Jones) and 1/9 Gurkhas (Captain Sonnic). These casualty assembly points, possessing only the sparse cover afforded by a bleak mountainside, received a full measure of attention from the enemy. The Royal Sussex and 1/9 Gurkha posts were hit no less than fifteen times by mortar or shell fire.

The hand-carry route for casualties therefore covered a distance of nearly four miles. While ambulance mules with litters and cacolets were available, the steepness and slipperiness of the slopes and the danger of animals stampeding under shell fire, prevented their use. Four hundred stretcher-bearers, ambulance and jeep drivers were constantly moving up and down in the service of the wounded. Lieut.-

Colonel G. S. N. Hughes, DSO, was in command; his abounding energy and unfailing resource surmounted every difficulty. The medical units were reinforced by a flow of volunteer stretcher-bearers—from 57 LAA Regiment, 149 Anti-Tank Regiment, from the pioneer companies, even from the followers. Baz Mir, a dhobi, won the IDSM for repeated trips to Hangman's Hill. Sepoy Chet Singh, a jeep driver from 4/16 Punjabis, covered the route to the Rapido more than 100 times. Mortally wounded, he died while helping a wounded comrade to safety. Towards the end of the battle when the ranks of the battalion stretcher-bearers had been depleted by casualties, groups from the advanced dressing stations went forward to search the forward lines and to bring in the wounded from where they fell.

Between the first and the second battles casualties continued at the rate of nearly 100 daily. When 5 Brigade entered the battle in the Castle area, the work of the medical services doubled, since there was no diminution in the flow of wounded from the crests behind the Monastery. (In the first two days of fighting, 5 Brigade evacuated 213 casualties; in its static section 7 Brigade lost 150 men.) 26 Field Ambulance set up an advanced dressing station at the foot of Castle Hill, and sent its groups scouring forward to find and to fetch in the stricken. Naik Mohammed Yusef, IOM, IDSM, organised the evacuation of the wounded along a track continuously under shell fire. He was afterwards presented to the King-Emperor, who complimented him on his courage. Lance-Naik Maiappa Ral, after being buried for six hours in debris on the edge of Cassino town, continued on duty for five days and repeatedly braved German snipers to rescue men who had fallen in tthe open. The battle evolved into a mêlée in which some of the medical personnel saw even more of the enemy than did the fighting troops. On March 18th Captain Sonnic and Captain Bhatia sallied from the Castle with their stretcher-bearers in broad daylight to bring in 24 wounded from the lower hairpin bend. Encountering the enemy, they were allowed to pass, one officer being detained as hostage. Thereafter stretcher-bearers were permittd to proceed on similar errands of mercy, but only in small groups. Sergeant Roche of 26 Field Ambulance led a party to Hangman's Hill, bringing in 30 wounded and taking back first-aid supplies and blood plasma. The garrison of Hangman's Hill was under medical charge of Lance-Corporal Edmond Hazle, DCM, of 1/4 Essex, who with Lance-Corporal Leonard Piper of the same battalion, handled upwards of 200 casualties in the eight days of isolation. Major operations and even amputations were performed by Hazle from the slender resources of his first-aid haversack. To bring the wounded down the precipitous and slippery slopes, avoiding the mined footways, it was necessary to rope sling from one foothold to another, with the wounded tied to the stretchers by fish netting.

At the main dressing station, in a nullah near San Michele, the Indian units were supplemented by 28 British Field Surgical Unit, 6 New Zealand Field Surgical Unit and a blood transfusion team. Here the long suffering and exhausted casualties found beds, if only briefly before evacuation. Yet even here there was no safety. On March 16th the area was systematically shelled. Casualties to medical personnel included Captain Seth, whose arm was severed while he attended a patient. 32 Field Ambulance, less companies on forward evacuation, operated a main dressing station at Piedmonte d'Alife, from which the wounded flowed to 2 Indian Mobile Casualty Clearing Station at Pressenzano.

It is impossible in the space at disposal to give individual credit to all who met and triumphantly encompassed the greatest medical emergency in Divisional history. As all shared the dangers, so all earned the bays.

At Cassino Fourth Indian Division lost more than a battle. It lost some of its very substance in the form of the men who had moulded it. On March 15th General Tuker wrote from hospital:

"Alexander (C. in C.) is coming to see me. C. in C. India has cabled for me to go to U.K. on leave and then return to India to take up another appointment. I dont think I could face good-byes. The Division has made the whole of my life worth living. It has shown me what my old battalion showed me, but on a huge scale in varied colours—courage, daring, utter devotion, utter endurance until death. May God bless them all in their supreme nobility and selflessness".

In his farewell message General Tuker said:

"For two years and a quarter it has been my good fortune to serve with you. Now the time has come for me to go. I can never forget you.

"You have built a brotherhood in arms such as has seldom been equalled in our long history.

"Your great battles are carved deep on the tablets of this war. I have never known you to falter. I have only seen your courage, your tenacity and the skill and fierceness of your attack, that has won you victories which have astonished the rest of the Army.

"May God speed you and bear you with good cheer and hope through every test which lies before you to the final victory."

Fourth Division replied:

"Affectionate greetings from all ranks of Fourth Indian Division. Sincere thanks for your gallant and far-sighted leadership during two very happy, memorable and eventful years. We trust and expect you will become an army commander and hope sincerely that we shall be in your army."*

*General Tuker upon recovery served for a time under SEAC in Ceylon. In the closing stages of the Burma campaign he commanded 4 Corps. Thereafter he was appointed GOC.-in-C. Eastern Command, India. He was knighted in the New Year Honours in 1946.

Two of General Tuker's ablest adjutants, officers whose skill and resource had charted success on many battlefields, likewise were seen no more. Brigadier D. R. E. R. Bateman, DSO, OBE., after upwards of four years' field service relinquished the command of 5 Brigade and after long leave passed to well-earned preferment at General Headquarters, India Command. Brigadier H. K. Dimoline, CBE, DSO., the quiet technician who had developed the Divisional artillery into a master weapon, left on long leave to England before reporting for duty in the Burma theatre.

On March 25th, Major-General A. W. W. Holworthy, DSO, MC., arrived to take command. It was deemed good fortune that Fourth Indian Division should retrieve one of its own as its new commander. General Holworthy, himself of 3 Gurkha Rifles, at the beginning of the war had organised 7th Gurkha Regimental Training Centre. He afterwards served as GSO 1, 10 Indian Division, from whence he succeeded to the command of 7 Indian Brigade in Western Desert. In the winter of 1942 he left to take charge of the Middle East School of Mountain Warfare in the Lebanons. His next appointment was as GOC, 6 Indian Division in Iraq, where he successfully maintained the keenness of his units in spite of the tedium of garrison duties. His charming yet forceful personality, marked courage and keen brain combined to provide the essential qualities of leadership.

Brigadier J. C. Saunders-Jacobs, former commander of the hard-fighting 3/18 Garhwal Rifles, which had suffered bitter losses with 11 Brigade in the Keren battle, replaced Brigadier Bateman. Brigadier Claude Eastman, DSO, the commander of 25 Field Regiment with Fourth Indian Division in Western Desert, and a man of many adventures, took over from Brigadier Dimoline as CRA.

There was a sad gap in the Divisional battle order.

4/6 Rajputana Rifles had fought its last battle with the Red Eagles on its shoulders. Concerning this great battalion the historian can state with assurance that no unit in the Allied armies had seen more fighting. In the surge through the perimeters of the Tummars, in the mêlée in the darkness at Acqua Col, on the heights of Keren, in the battered shell of Mezze House, along the thirsty ridges of Alem Hamza, at the road blocks in the Djebel, on the escarpment of Mersa Matruh, in the tense hours when history was made on the evil brown whaleback of Ruweisat, when the wedge was driven at El Alamein, when the hole was punched at Wadi Akarit, in the death grapple on the bald dome of Garci, when Africa was cleansed of the last Huns at Medjez el Bab, Outram's splendid battalion never found lesser place than the forefront of the fray. Two Victoria Crosses, a thousand acts of daring and self-sacrifice, had marked its odyssey. Now it was going home, to due rest and honours. The hearts of many who had known these great fighting men leapt in pride when in March, 1946, they swung past in the Victory Parade at New Delhi, in their red airborne berets, with Lieut.-Colonel R. B. Scott, DSO, still leading them.

3 Royal Battalion, The Frontier Force Regiment (Lieut.-Colonel H. W. McDonald, DSO,) with a long record of service in 5 Indian Division and one of the two Indian units which had participated in the Sicilian campaign, now joined 11 Brigade. The long anticipated reconnaissance regiment likewise materialised with the return of Central India Horse after two years absence from the Division. Following the Benghazi breakout in which a squadron was lost, the cavalrymen had joined 10 Indian Motor Brigade. In September, 1942, they marched from Egypt to north-western Iran, where they were incorporated in a blocking force designed to meet the enemy should he burst over the Caucasus. In January, 1943, they moved into south-west Iran where miscellaneous duties included protection of British oil installations, the shepherding of restless tribesmen and a locust extermination campaign. On rejoining Fourth Indian Division, Lieut.-Colonel Richard George after a long period of command was succeeded by Lieut.-Colonel Ralph Peters.*

*The Monastery was stormed by the Polish Corps on May 16th after 8 Indian Division and 4 British Division had broken the Gustav Line along the Liri River. The Poles approached by way of Point 593 on the same thrust line as 7 Brigade in the first assault. Desperate fighting ensued at Piedimonte, 4 miles west of the Monastery, before the enemy was finally hurled from the high ground. Upwards of 1,000 Polish dead are buried in their cemetery on the slopes of Point 444.

Chapter 25

LOWER ADRIATIC

THE last blizzard on Cassino heights was succeeded by balmy airs. Spring was creeping up from the south. Spring meant new battles. April therefore brought no rest to Fourth Indian Division. The convoys began to wind back across the mountains to the Orsogna sector, where 8 Indian Division, destined to play the leading role in the next and final Cassino offensive, awaited relief. On the nights of April 7/10 the change-over was completed and the fourth day found Fourth Division in the sectors occupied in its previous tour of this front.

11 Brigade held from Crecchio to the rail junction at Point 280, 5 Brigade from Arielli to Orsogna and 7 Brigade from Orsogna to Guardiagrele. The left flank of the continuous Adriatic sector ended at the Maiella massif, from where a gap of over 20 miles stretched across the rolling foothills and high crests of the mountain block. To assist Central India Horse in guarding this open front 11 KRRC and 5 Reconnaissance Regiment were taken under Divisional command. A number of Italian partisan groups also operated quasi-independently. Divisional Headquarters again was in Lanciano, 8 miles to the east of Orsogna. Central India Horse was already on duty, having taken over responsibilities under command of 8 Indian Division.

During 8 Division's tour, Indian and Canadian troops had co-operated in a series of offensive enterprises which had shaken the enemy. As a result, a discomfited seccond-quality division had been withdrawn and 334 Division, a highly aggressive formation, had entered the line. The newcomers were looking for trouble—they made it and found it. On the day of Fourth Division's arrival their artillery fired over pamphlets which commiserated with the Indian troops on their hard lot. The leaflets declared that the New Zealanders, who had shared the Cassino ordeal, had been more favourably treated, and they promised a warm reception to the newcomers on the Adriatic front. Such immediate identification illustrated the difficulty of maintaining field security in a countryside swarming with civilians and recently liberated from the enemy.

An Indian Army Observer furnishes a good description of the front:

"The bleak-looking farmhouses, which dot the countryside, are the scene of many quick, murderous encounters. Both Indian and German detachments live in much the same fashion. Downstairs, in the toolsheds and cattle stalls, the infantry platoons are quartered. The cellar serves as a bolt-hole in emergency. The upper storeys, reached by outside staircases, which give excellent observation, house the machine-gunners, signallers, and other specialists. Everyone moves discreetly during the day to avoid unwelcome attention from enemy guns. When darkness falls, the danger mounts. These farmhouses nearly all have blind walls, behind which a raiding party may approach unseen. Throughout the night, therefore, sentries are stationed on all sides in slit trenches. Alarm wires are strung and likely approaches are mined or booby-trapped. The technique of surprise, like the precautions against it, demand courage and resourcefulness of a high order, as well as skill in battle tactics which are a mixture of gangster and Red Indian practices."

On the night of April 15/16 a platoon of 1/2 Gurkhas in an exposed position engaged in an all-night fracas with enemy raiders. On the same evening near Chiamato Royal Frontier Force Regiment bumped an enemy fighting patrol estimated at 40 strong and in a fire fight incurred 11 casualties. Three enemy bodies were picked up. Shortly after midnight on April 18/19 2 Camerons in a skirmish in Arielli bagged some interesting specimens—15 men of 412 Ostland Regiment, a unit consisting of ex-Russian prisoners of war and boys too young to be in the Russian Army, who had been evacuated to Germany as civilians. Technically these men were volunteers and traitors. In point of fact they were conscripts with no stomach for battle. As a result of their capture a welcome in Russian was broadcast on Fourth Division's front. This had excellent results: deserters came in almost every night. Among those taken was a wounded Italian child of seven who stated that he was the only survivor of a party of 16 civilians who had taken shelter in a cave during an artillery shoot. The Germans had pelted the cave with grenades.

On Hitler's birthday (April 20th) Orsogna was draped with flags. A notice board displayed on Fourth Division's front read: "British must give cheer for our leader, Adolf Hitler". The notice board drew an artillery shoot and as if in retaliation 10 Focke-Wulf 190s bombed Lanciano scoring direct hits on a crowd of soldiers waiting to enter an ENSA show and on 26 Indian Field Ambulance. 30 were killed and 150 wounded.

The enemy likewise visited 11 Brigade forward positions with intensified mortar and artillery fire. On April 22nd and again on April 25th parties of approximately company strength dashed in on 2/7 Gurkhas under cover of bombardment. In each case the assaults were beaten back from close range. A similar attack at midnight on April 21/22 on 5 Brigade's front broke up before the fire of "B" Company of 1/6 Rajputana Rifles. The same day however "C" Company Headquarters of 1/4 Essex received a direct hit which killed everyone, including Major M. S. Mallinson, one of the gallant officers who had carried orders to 1/9 Gurkhas on Hangman's Hill.

On April 3rd Central India Horse in the Maiella gap had taken over from 6 Lancers of 8 Indian Division as the chief component in Dawnay Force, which was entrusted with the security of this open front. Here among the peaks which rose around the central massif of Monte Amore—a rounded snow-capped cone 9,000 feet in height—the reconnaissance regiment established outposts in villages on pinnacles and in the ruined *palazzi* of 15th century robber barons.* From these strong points they endeavoured to keep tab on enemy movements and to interfere as much as possible with German observation posts and outlying pickets. Lama, on Route 84 half-way through the mountains and Fara, 5 miles further north, were spots where trouble usually could be found. In this area Central India Horse received considerable aid from a partisan group of 40 men under the command of the local building contractor. These guerillas proved invaluable as guides and unhesitatingly shared the fighting. An enemy ambush at Lama was countered by an attack to the north of Fara upon a German ropeway by which outposts on the pinnacles were replenished. In the course of this operation an Indian reconnaissance party was cut off by German ski troops. Recourse to a classical ruse saved the patrol. Using their greatcoats and gas capes as the Romans once used their shields the detachment cascaded to safety at the bottom of Fara Gorge.

On May 1st 11 KRRC under command of Lieut.-Colonel John Hunt (who was destined to know Fourth Division better) raided Pissavini, an uplands village 7 miles south-west of Orsogna. Prisoners were taken. On May 4th Captain Ditmas of Central India Horse and his patrol were snatched in return. A few days later a King's Dragoon Guards outpost was rescued by Central India Horse mortar and machine-gun detachments. Indian patrols reported German ski troops on the snowbound crests as late as May 6th, when the Italian plains were basking in summer sunshine.

On the night of May 3/4, 3/10 Baluch Regiment (Lieut.-Colonel L. V. Sherwood, DSO,) which joined 7 Brigade on the 22nd April, before being transferred a few weeks later to 5 Brigade, carried out a successful patrol. This operation was typical of the confused fighting which occurred on some part of the Divisional front on almost every night. A platoon from the garrison company at Chiamato, under command of Major J. M. Forster, had explored a ridge over two miles long to the south-west of Orsogna. Returning before dawn the patrol searched a group of suspected farm houses within a thousand yards of the company positions. Here after a sharp scrimmage two German artillerymen were ferreted out and captured; with their wireless set these gunners had been operating an observation post behind the Indian lines. The platoon had no more than reformed when 20 Germans, a mine laying

*A palazzo is neither a castle nor a squire's manor but a little of each. It consists of an immensely strong central residence with smaller houses clustered about it. These small compact communities were impervious to all but the heaviest bombing or gun fire. They constituted the chief problem of offensive operations in Italy. They were less effective on the isolated Maiella peaks than on the rolling foreshore.

party returning from the rear of the Indian positions rushed out of the darkness shouting in Hindustani "white troops, do not fire, Subedar Sahib". There was momentary confusion but the Baluchis twigged the ruse and opened fire. A brisk scrimmage followed in the course of which a third German was taken. The enemy was driven off into the north, having sustained further casualties.

At 0600 hours on May 5th two enemy companies swept against 1/9 Gurkha Rifles at the head of a ravine a mile north of Orsogna. The outposts were driven in but the attack was not pressed against the main positions. On May 10th 1/4 Essex reported a patrol clash and on the next night 4/16 Punjabis ejected German detachments which had worked their way into their lines to the north of Arielli. This bickering flared into serious fighting on May 14th, when Royal Frontier Force Regiment, in charge of a difficult sector to the north of Orsogna, sustained a full-scale attack. The forward companies of the Frontier Force held a ridge overlooking three convergent valleys, which offered concealed approach from different directions. At dawn a sharp artillery shoot crashed on these exposed positions. With tanks in close support the enemy, estimated at battalion strength, overran the forward platoons and company headquarters. At 0930 hours a reserve company supported by tanks of 23 Armoured Brigade counter-attacked but failed to re-take the ground. At 2000 hours 2 Camerons, in three waves of a company each, drove on the lost positions and ejected the enemy. Their casualties were 21, and the Frontier Force Regiment lost 131 of all ranks in this sharp encounter. Captain P. G. Francis, MC, of 11 Field Regiment, a veteran gunner officer who had been involved in the defence of Castle Hill, was killed in this fighting.

In the chill mists of early morning on May 11th a great battle opened between Monte Cairo and the Arunci mountains. Three corps struck at the Cassino positions. Forty-eight hours later 8 Indian Division, which spear-headed the assault in the Liri valley, had punched a hole in the main defences. Cassino fell after a week's bitter fighting and a general enemy withrawal on the Adriatic front became a possibility. Fourth Indian Division was instructed to maintain intimate contact everywhere in order to intensify pressure if any thinning-out was detected. Almost immediately a lessening of enemy activity occurred. Explosions were heard behind the German lines and there was a perceptible reduction in the number of patrol and outpost encounters. Divisional scouts sometimes penetrated the enemy positions for some distance without challenge. Minefields unfortunately caused many casualties during these reconnaissances. On May 24th patrols from 3/10 Baluchis reached the top of the ridge above Guadiagrele, a location known to have been held previously by the enemy in strength. Pennapiedimonte, a strong position three miles to the south, likewise was reported unoccupied; but when a combined reconnaissance patrol of 9 Lancers and Central India Horse investigated the area, it was ambushed.

10 Indian Division, which held the coastal sector, discovered in the course of a raid that a new German formation was expected on the

Adriatic front. To test dispositions and to secure identifications 1 Royal Sussex on the night of May 25/26 with tanks and artillery in support raided Le Piane taking a number of prisoners from 334 Division. A similar probing thrust four miles further south on 11 Brigade's sector was less successful. Two platoons of Royal Frontier Force Regiment and a platoon of 2 Camerons were trapped on a minefield covered by concentrated crossfire from enemy machine-guns. 24 men were killed and wounded before the platoons could withdraw.

By the end of May it was apparent that the battered and retreating German forces on Fifth Army's front would not be able to stand in front of Rome and that a long retreat to the main wall of the Apennines might be anticipated. With mountain fighting imminent arrangements were made to relieve both Fourth and 10 Indian Divisions for a period of intensive training. 10 Division was first to go. As the plan for pursuit called for the heaviest pressure to be exerted in the coastal sector, Fourth Division undertook to relieve 10 Division as soon as its own relief was effected. On May 30th a number of Italian formations arrived to take over on the Orsogna-Maiella front. The new Allies exhibited more enthusiasm than common sense; their advanced parties arrived with flags flying and bands playing. As a result they attracted a heavy shoot. Utili Gruppo occupied the right of the Divisional front, CIL Gruppo the left. The Italian artillery was uncalibrated and it was necessary to leave behind the Divisional gunners. 11 Brigade Commander (Brigadier H. G. Partridge, DSO, had recently relieved Brigadier V. C. Griffin) with his Brigade major and staff captain also remained in an advisory capacity.

During June 2/3 7 Brigade led the relief of 10 Indian Division, taking over from 20 Indian Brigade in the centre of the coastal sector. The enemy was on the alert and the newcomers suffered a number of casualties in the course of the relief. 5 Brigade relieved 25 Brigade in Villa Grande, the scene of desperate fighting during the previous December. 11 Brigade occupied the foreshore to the north-west of Ortona. To allow 10 Division to withdraw its field regiments 3 Carpathian Division loaned its divisional artillery. A *lingua franca* of French and Italian provided a sufficient medium for communications with the quick-witted and well trained Polish gunners.

Fourth Division were no more than established in their new lines when the long expected German withdrawal began. On the early morning of June 6th, presumably as cover for the disengaging movement, the enemy attacked in strength on both 5 and 7 Brigade fronts against 3/10 Baluchis and 1/2 Gurkhas. A Baluchi fighting patrol was driven in and one of the forward companies surrounded. The enemy endeavoured to infiltrate into the rear positions, but without any great success. At dawn the assault troops withdrew. The Baluchis suffered 9 casualties. Similar tactics against 1/2 Gurkhas were frustrated by the timely intervention of the Polish artillery.

On June 7th a deserter from 278 Division stated that the enemy proposed to retreat for a distance of 25 miles. Parols were immediately despatched to investigate. By the morning of June 8th clever and persistent probing on all Brigade fronts proved the Divisional flanks to be clear of the enemy. Only the main Adriatic highway continued to be held by a blocking force. Plans for the pursuit called for a rapid thrust along the coast with the Italian groups more or less conforming in their own time. The case began with 11 Brigade following the foreshore and 7 Brigade advancing on a parallel axis inland. 5 Brigade was instructed to move up to the line of the Arielli, the first water barrier; thereafter to maintain contact with the Italian groups if and when they advanced.

11 Brigade was disposed with Royal Frontier Force Regiment on the right and 2/7 Gurkhas on the opposite flank. Owing to extensive demolitions and deep minefields little progress was made on the first day. On June 10th Royal Frontier Force Regiment reached Francavilla, a small outpost half-way to Pescara. At noon on the same day a rifle platoon of 2 Camerons with a pioneer detachment landed by DUKWS to the north of Francavilla beyond the Alento river. This platoon, hearing that 7 Brigade had made good time inland, hastened along the coast in order to add Pescara to its game book. Concurrently the remainder of the Camerons arrived in Francavilla but found it impossible to cross the Alento until a detour had been constructed.

Meanwhile 7 Brigade had covered more ground at a faster pace. With 31 Field Regiment, self-propelled guns and anti-tank guns under command, Brigadier Lovett and his men drove into the north. The advance was so rapid that a number of mined bridges were captured before the enemy could demolish them. 1/2 Gurkhas in the lead encountered mild resistance at the Arielli river and a somewhat stiffer fight on the outskirts of Tollo, where an enemy strong point included the unusual defences of dug-in flame throwers. Tollo, one of 8 Indian Division's main objectives in the fighting of the previous December, had been smashed flat. The Gurkhas forged ahead, crossed the Foro, turned west and headed for Chieti, a sizeable market town 8 miles south of Pescara. En route they bumped an enemy rearguard at Ripa Teatina. With bad judgment the Germans counter-attacked. In a fire fight 7 enemies were killed and one prisoner taken. Meanwhile Captain Ramsay-Brown with a Gurkha fighting patrol approached Chieti by a circuitous route, entered the town before the Germans had cleared off and established contact with the local partisans, who promised to take care of any enemy rearguards which might attempt a last stand.

Next morning (June 9th) the drive continued. The countryside was up and the partisans had taken the field. On one occasion the irregulars chased a number of Germans into the Indian lines. On June 10th 1/2 Gurkhas entered Chieti, receiving an hysterical welcome. It now became a race between the two forward brigades to decide who could claim Pescara. Lieut.-Colonel Hill of the Camerons did not wait to see his battalion over the Alento. With his Intelligence Officer he cycled off into the north. Brigadier Lovett in turn sent the Brigade Reconnaissance Squadron and a detachment of sappers, with instructions to hurry. This force found all the bridges over the Pescara river down but nevertheless on June 10th it made its way into the town from the west at 1530 hours.* During the entry a Sherman tank picked off two German self-propelled guns in quick succession. Cameron patrols arrived along the coastal road at about the same time. Pescara was deserted and had been stripped by the enemy.

On the night of June 10/11, 4/16 Punjabis took over the lead on 7 Brigade's front while the Camerons continued their advance along the coast. A Bailey bridge had been hurriedly flung over the Pescara river. Next day both brigades exploited as far as the Salino river, 10 miles to the north of Pescara. 4/16 Punjabi patrols by noon on June 12th had reached Citta San Angelo having captured five heavy guns on the way. Lieut.-Colonel Packwood and his men were thrusting on with a tank escort when they encountered an extensive minefield along the line of the Piomba, a small stream which reaches the Adriatic 12 miles north of Pescara. Before a passage could be swept, orders arrived to return to Citta San Angelo where a stabilised line was established pending relief by the 3 Carpathian Division. As a last stroke the Camerons that night (June 12th) seized Monte Silvano Marina on the coastal highway, taking a number of prisoners in a rearguard scuffle.

The speedy and exciting chase of the enemy acted as a tonic to all ranks of Fourth Indian Division. The second tour on the Lower Adriatic had been anything but peaceful; the Division had suffered 633 casualties without the semblance of a set piece battle. Nevertheless it had been a give-and-take period in which the last memories of the desperate deadlock at Cassino had been erased. All were in high heart when on June 13th two Polish brigades arrived to take over.

5 Indian Brigade already had moved back to Campobasso, 80 miles to the south-east, where the rugged Abruzzo spurs provided suitable terrain for training in mountain warfare. Here a delightful fortnight was spent amid ideal surroundings. The diarist of Central India Horse wrote:

"It is difficult to imagine any really good reason for the entry of the Italians into the war. They have a wonderful country of their own with the last word in summer weather. It would be almost impossible to improve on the climate for the purpose of living in the open. The fruit

---

*General Lovett comments: "Tanks, self-propelled guns and the incomparable 31 Field Regiment all found their way across the Pescara before the bridge was up. The infantry was not allowed to go far without the tanks. 7 Hussars were very dashing and a joy to work with. It all sounds easy but in reality it was a tricky business advancing along a heavily mined and booby-trapped 'one way' road without losing the momentum of the pursuit".

crop is varied and appreciated by us all. The harvest has been very good but hard work for the depleted population—men seem in short supply and those that are here are not as hardworking as their womenfolk. Heavily laden vines will soon produce a bumper yield of 'vino'.

"The *jawans*, having acquired a smattering of Arabic and Persian in their travels, have now mastered the local *'bat'* and can converse freely with the people round about. They appreciate the agricultural potentialities of the land here and several are said to be considering the establishment of an Indian agricultural settlement here after the war. All are very fit here and the rations are good".

For a month after their resounding defeat in the Liri valley the Germans steadily gave ground before Fifth Army. Rome fell and there followed a rapid withdrawal through Central Italy. In the van of the advance went 8 Indian Division, covering 225 miles in less than four weeks. The pursuit columns thrust across the gracious Umbrian countryside until the rolling ridges stiffened their contours and increased in substance and the high rounded crests of the Apennines showed to the east of the Tiber valley. In positions covering Perugia and Lake Trasimeno the enemy stood and bitter fighting ensued. At the end of June Fourth Division was warned for transfer from 5 Corps to 10 Corps, which was conducting the operations in Central Italy. 11 Brigade and Central India Horse remained behind to rejoin the Division upon completion of training.

Two other units were left behind. 1/6 Rajputana Rifles and 4/16 Punjab Regiment, two original battalions of Fourth Division, after bearing the heat and burden of four years of war, were despatched to well-earned rest in Middle East. Shortly afterwards they followed 4/6 Rajputana Rifles to India. Each had made history on many occasions and each will be remembered beyond its generation. 3/10 Baluchis, until now a "Swinger" battalion between Fourth and 8 Indian Divisions, returned to its old brigade of desert days and 2 Royal Sikhs (Lieut. Colonel R. A. d'E. Ashe) after a long period of garrison duty in Middle East entered 7 Brigade.

On July 2nd 7 Brigade led the move from Campobasso into Central Italy. 5 Brigade followed two days later. A three days' trek through the glowing Italian *campagna* brought Fourth Indian Division to its new battlefield. On July 8th General Holworthy's men took over 10 Indian Divisions responsibilities west of the Tiber vallley, south of the Nestore river, 15 miles north of Lake Trasimeno.

Chapter 26

CENTRAL ITALY AND "VANDAL" OPERATION

THREE intentions dominated German strategy in Italy during the summer of 1944. The enemy planners wished to deny ground to the Allied armies until it could be sold at an incommensurate price in blood. They wished to make progress more difficult as the nature of the terrain progressively favoured the defenders. Finally, they wished to hold back the advancing Allied forces from the High Apennines until the mighty wall of the Gothic Line defences had been completed.

In pursuance of such plan the Wehrmacht had dropped back rapidly in Central Italy and more slowly on the Adriatic front. In June the withdrawal reached the Umbrian mountain block in which the Arno and Tiber rivers find their sources. Some sixty miles of rugged highlands intervened in front of the transverse spine of the main Apennine massif, along which forced labour toiled at the fortifications of the Gothic Line.

To the north of Lake Trasimeno the contours of the Umbrian landscape thickened. Ridges grew higher and narrower, valleys deeper and more abrupt, high vantage points crowned with villages or *palazzi* more numerous. The fertile soil wore a heavier dress, with fields of breast-high grain interspersed among orchards and vineyards. Groves and patches of woodland decked the hillsides and summits. The crests and valleys tended to bear to the east and west, across the Allied line of advance. Each valley carried a brawling stream which fed down towards the Arno or the Tiber. Almost all roads bore east and west along the meandering defiles of these tributaries, affording the enemy an admirable system of transverse communications.

Such terrain prevented the concentration of forces and lent itself to surprise—two tactical advantages which might have eased the task of the defenders. Fortunately the Wehrmacht High Command had nullified these advantages by leaving holding troops in the line for long and exhausting periods. Enemy formations usually were thin on the ground. Counter-attack forces would fight fiercely to regain lost vantage points, but initial penetration and seizure of German positions was often easier than the lie of the land deserved. *The Tiger Triumphs* describes the technique of battle on such terrain:

"In a war of automatic weapons an advance through a wooded countryside with few tracks and little visibility constituted a hazardous enterprise. The first necessity was to locate the enemy, the second to by-pass his fixed positions. The final task was to mop up. The routine of infiltration varied with conditions, but the usual method was to send reconnaissance patrols of not more than three or four men to explore the ground ahead. Within close supporting distance a fighting patrol approximately one platoon in strength lay in wait. Within equally easy reach of the fighting patrol a force of one or two companies, with machine-gunners, mortar teams and an artillery observation officer remained on call. The screen of reconnaissance patrols would infiltrate between the enemy posts, or in some instances would bump into them. From these contacts a pinpointed picture of German dispositions would emerge, from which objectives would be allocated. These objectives were key sectors which when seized would force the enemy to withdraw from his other positions."

"This type of warfare suited Indian troops. It retained something of the character of the endless little squabbles of the North West Frontier. The deep patrols brought out military qualities inherent in the blood of men whose ancestors have been soldiers for a thousand years. Keen sight, silent movement, quick decision and abounding courage were the counters to win in this sort of game, and those abilities Indian troops have always possessed in full."

The foregoing description, while supplying an accurate picture of infantry operations, fails to do justice to the roles played on such terrain by artillery and armour. In well-chosen coverts the enemy had stationed groups of guns and tanks which exploited the grain of the ground to take toll of the attacking infantry as it appeared over the far crests, descended to the valley bottom and thereafter toiled up the opposite slope to the assault. In order to counter such dispositions it was necessary to cover the advance with similar groups of field, medium, self-propelled and anti-tank guns, which of necessity moved in close contact with the attack formations. Only by Herculean labours could such weapons be worked across the steep hillsides and broken defiles and only by magnificent management could the guns and their crews keep pace with the infantry's progress.

Fourth Indian Division, whose previous experience with Italian troops in the Lower Adriatic had not inspired them with any particular confidence, now found the local patriots useful. With their aid German outposts and concentration areas could be pinpointed for surprise attacks. Partisan patrols were often sent ahead to instruct farmers in possession of dogs to take their animals indoors and thus prevent any alarm being given during night operations. These irregulars usually were unwilling to operate outside their own districts since capture in an unauthorized area meant not only death for themselves but reprisals against their families.

On July 8th Fourth Indian Division relieved 10 Indian Division and at once prepared to take up the running. For this operation each brigade took a company of Rajputana Rifles machine-gunners under command.* 10 Indian Brigade, 9 Armoured Brigade, a squadron of Skinner's Horse, and 165 (Jeep) Field Regiment remained under Divisional command. 7 Brigade entered the forward zone when 1/2 Gurkhas relieved 4/10 Baluch Regiment on Monte Bastioala, three miles west of the Tiber and the same distance south of the Nestore river. 2 Royal Sikhs took over the left sector of the Brigade front. On its western flank 7 Brigade was in touch with SACK FORCE, a flexible formation which linked 10 Corps with 13 Corps, now battering its way towards Arezzo. Fourth Divisional Headquarters was situated at Badia, less than a mile across the Tiber from 10 Divisional Headquarters.

By the morning of July 9th both forward battalions of 7 Brigade with tanks of Warwickshire Yeomanry in close support had reached the high ground around Monte Alvieri, overlooking the re-entrant bend of the Nestore river. Here the battalions separated, 1/2 Gurkhas pushing into the north while the Royal Sikhs wheeled into the west. A mile beyond Monte Alvieri Lieut.-Colonel Richardson's men drew first blood. British Commando Corporal Björman, attached to the Gurkhas as an interpreter, discovered an enemy observation post on an isolated knoll. A fighting patrol commanded by Jemadar Pirthilal Pun, MC, stalked the position, attacked with the kukri, killed 6 and brought back one prisoner, the only damaged Gurkha having sustained a broken nose.

On the same day 2 Royal Sikhs reached the Nestore river at Volterrano. With the occupation of this village 7 Brigade established a front four miles in width.

In the first advance the gunners had a taste of what awaited them. The guns and vehicles of 31 Field Regiment had followed up with great difficulty along an upland track which was little more than a footpath. After labouring all night on a wellnigh impossible trail, a three tonner overturned. No breakdown vehicle could reach the casualty. Some forty gunners however got their shoulders underneath and righted the lorry. By dawn the guns were in position.

At 2100 hours on July 10th under bright moonlight 1/2 Gurkhas crossed the Nestore and in a silent advance won the summit of Monte Civitella, 2,500 feet high, on the left flank of the battalion line of advance. At dawn they swung right-handed and chased a few Germans out of Mucignano. In a number of clashes with "penny packets" of the withdrawing enemy, heads were taken. The Gurkhas pushed on to the valley of the Aggia, a stream two miles to the north of the Nestore. Here the escorting tanks bogged down in the soft gravel. Beyond the river a long ridge ran into the north-east, rising steadily towards Monte

*On June 25th Lieut.-Colonel D. G. Ryan had replaced Lieut.-Colonel F. G. Cuerden in command of the Rajputana Rifle Machine Gun Battalion.

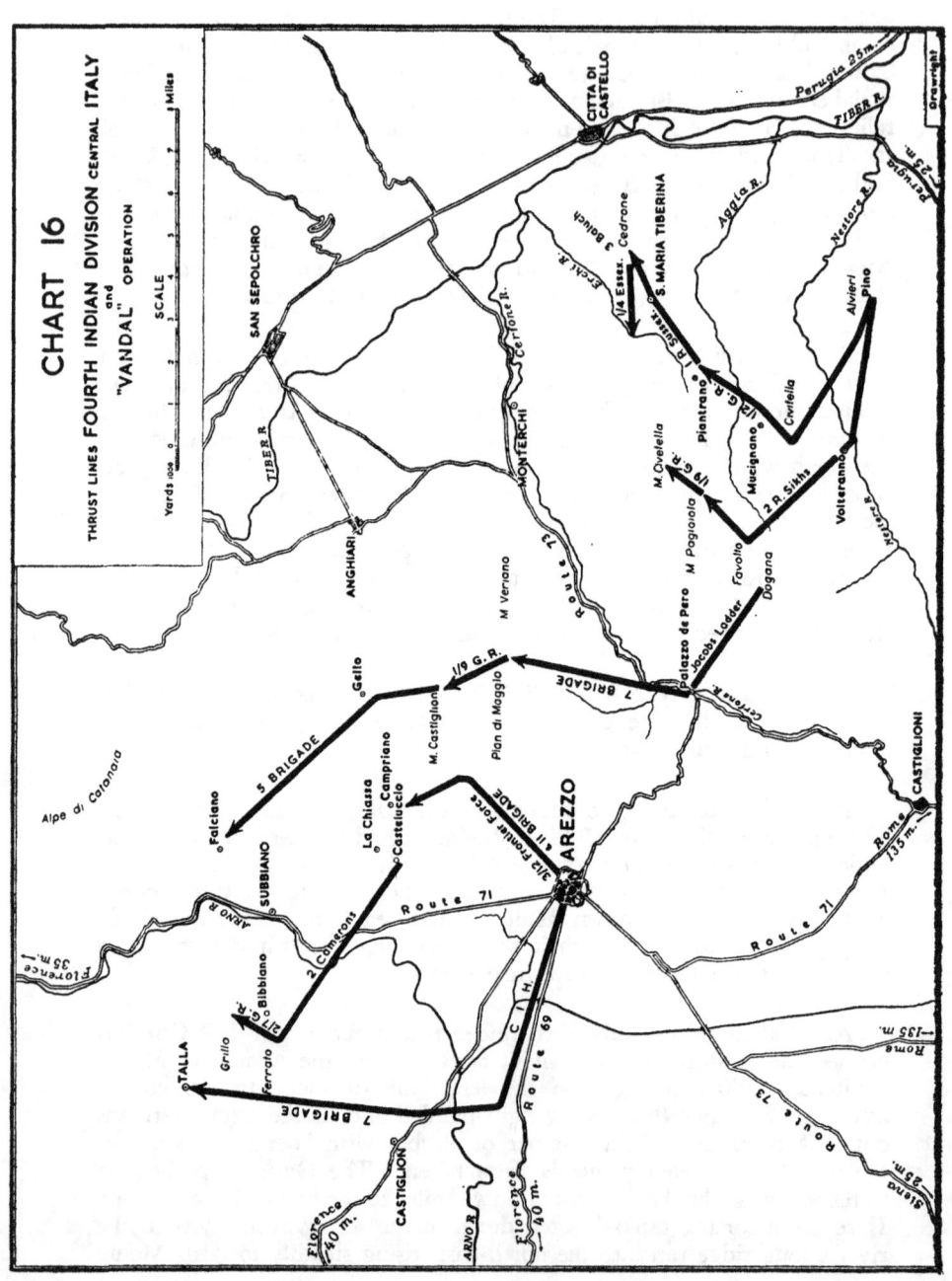

San Maria di Tiberina, a picturesque village on an isolated pinnacle high above the countryside. This eyrie-like hamlet commanded the ground as far as the Tiber and it was known to be held by the enemy in some strength. The Gurkhas immediately organised for attack upon Piantrano, on the south-westerly extremity of the ridge. On the afternoon of July 11th the hillmen supported by Sherman tanks from Wiltshire Yeomanry advanced on this objective. Artillery exchanges followed and during the night all four companies established themselves in the Piantrano area. Roving through the undergrowth the Gurkhas destroyed a number of outposts. In one instance the hillmen chased their quarries for 1,000 yards before bringing them down.

During the previous day (July 10th) 2 Royal Sikhs had climbed a narrow, steep and wooded spur which rose 2,000 feet in less than 3,000 yards. On its summit they seized Poggio Civitella, a companion position to that held by the Gurkhas three miles to the south-east. Next morning the Sikhs turned further west and in a double thrust seized Monte Pagliaiola and Monte Favalto, the latter peak rising to a height of 3,600 feet. The enemy held Monte Pagliaiola in some strength and brisk fighting ensued, in which "A" Company in the lead was held up by machine gun fire from the undergrowth. Sepoy Kartar Singh in a most gallant individual attack silenced three enemy posts, killing five Germans before being shot down. He was afterwards awarded a posthumous I.O.M.

The Sikh drive widened 7 Brigade's front, which now covered more than six miles. It therefore became necessary to bring other troops into the line. 1/9 Gurkhas from 5 Brigade moved up on the left while 1 Royal Sussex came forward to support 1/2 Gurkhas.

During the night of July 9/10 a German counter-attack had endeavoured to oust the hillmen from their grip on San Maria di Tiberina ridge. The attempt broke down with an estimated 25 casualties to the enemy. In the late afternoon next day "B" Company Royal Sussex under Major Cavalier passed through the Gurkhas and advanced along the crest of the ridge. Divisional and Corps artillery supported the thrust, supplying smoke cover in the more exposed positions. The village itself was bombarded but the buildings proved so compact that only plunging fire took effect. By 2200 hours the Royal Sussex were within a mile of their objective and were encountering intense opposition. "A" Company came into the fight; its commander, Major D. H. Brand, a gallant officer with a fine fighting record, was killed, and the advance halted. At dawn a patrol discovered the enemy to have withdrawn. San Maria di Tiberina was occupied and a platoon was despatched 3,000 yards to the north-east to seize Monte Cedrone, an important lookout which blocked the advance of 10 Brigade along the western bank of the Tiber.

On the opposite flank of the Divisional front 1/9 Gurkhas on a mule-pack basis (under command of 7 Brigade) had passed through 2

Royal Sikhs on Monte Pagliaiola on the previous night, had descended 2,000 feet to the Scarzola valley and had climbed the same distance above the northern bank to capture Monte Civitella at dawn. The seizure of this peak gave 7 Brigade observation over route 73, one of the principal east-west highways in the mountain block. Thereafter enemy traffic between Arezzo and the Tiber valley could be harassed by long-range fire. This advance established the left flank of 7 Brigade in the heart of the highlands, somewhat ahead of the general line of 10 Indian Division on the right and of SACK FORCE and 13 Corps on the left.

On the right flank the enemy had reacted vigorously to the seizure of Monte Cedrone. Counter-attacks at dusk on July 13th in company strength were repulsed but because of their insecure position the occupying detachments of the Royal Sussex were withdrawn that night.

4/10 Baluchis of 10 Brigade, which was closing from the east, encountered considerable opposition while endeavouring to regain Monte Cedrone. 1/4 Essex meanwhile had come forward on the left of the Royal Sussex, and had entered the gap between the right and left forks of the Divisional advance. The Home County men trickled forward to seize a strong position on the high ground astride the Erchi river. This move, which established a continuous Divisional front, likewise served to constrict the manoeuvre area of the enemy on the west bank of the Tiber. The Essex position threatened Monterchi and Citerna, twin centres which controlled any movement into the northwestern highlands.

By the night of July 14th a more or less stablised line existed between Monte Cedrone and Monte Favalto—a distance of eight miles. It was now necessary to give priority to the ejection of the enemy from Monte Cedrone. 1 Durham Light Infantry of 10 Brigade advanced from the south-east while 3/10 Baluchis of 5 Brigade moved up to attack from the south-west. There had been little time for reconnaissance and the approaching battalions found themselves in difficult country. The attack opened at 0200 hours on July 15th. An hour later heavy enemy fire had brought it to a halt. Rather than risk the exposure of the assault troops at first light on the forward slopes, Brigadier Saunders-Jacobs ordered a withdrawal. On the following night 10 Brigade after a two-hour concentration by 200 guns, smashed with all three battalions at Monte Cedrone and at the neck of falling ground between this ridge system and the Tiber. 4/10 Baluchis and 2/4 Gurkhas broke through on the right. The Durhams' assault by good fortune coincided with an enemy relief on Monte Cedrone and the position was secured without difficulty. After a series of counter-attacks had failed to shake 10 Brigade's grip the enemy gave up the fight.

At this juncture, when a thrust along the easy reaches of the expanding Tiber basin might have turned the north eastern flank of the mountain block, over-riding considerations made it necessary to slow down the advance in the east and to concentrate on the left flank where

7 Brigade confronted a succession of almost insurmountable obstacles. This shift in thrust line occurred because of the strenuous resistance encountered by 13 Corps in its drive to reach Arezzo and the upper Arno valley. To relieve the pressure 10 Corps was instructed to wheel into the west and to seize the Alpe di Poti massif, an abrupt mountain ridge system five miles to the east of Arezzo. The capture of this dominating height would interpose a barrier between enemy forces in the Tiber and Arno valleys.

The main crests of the Alpe di Poti massif towered some seven miles to the north-west of the Divisional positions at Monte Civitella and Monte Pagliaiola. The immediate problem was to cross this distance, particularly the first four miles to Route 73, the main highway which followed the Cerfone valley from Arezzo to the Tiber. A succession of cliff-sided canyons and heavily wooded razor-backed ridges intervened which made the terrain impassable to all formations which moved on wheels. It was therefore essential that some sort of roadway should be opened as preliminary to the Alpe di Poti operation.

As early as July 12th, Major Patinson of 7 Brigade Reconnaissance Squadron and Lieut. Murray of 4 Field Company had been instructed to survey a cross-country line of advance. With the aid of a spotter plane from the Division O. P. Squadron a route was selected which defied rather than circumvented obstacles. On July 14th the work began. Italian labour companies cut a path through the undergrowth. Canadian mining squads followed with explosives, blasted major obstacles and shaped a rough trail. British sappers with groups of bulldozers pushed and scraped until a semblance of a track grew behind them. The Divisional Sappers and Miners followed to complete the roadway. Central India Horse provided the covering parties.

After 28 working hours a jeep and tank track had emerged from Monte Dogana, on the left of Monte Favalto, and was feeling towards Palazzo del Pero, the nearest point on Highway 73. Palazzo del Pero at this time was believed to be held by the enemy. Before the track was completed Major Patinson and Lieut. Murray, still exploring ahead, crossed the intervening two miles to Route 73 on collapsible parachutist motor-cycles. On nearing Palazzo del Pero it was discovered that 13 Corps had gained ground and was shifting eastwards to link up with 10 Corps. New Zealand armoured cars were first to contact Fourth Division patrols. Next day Arezzo fell and Route 73 was open for approach to the Alpe di Poti. This circumstance however did not detract from the constructional achievement of "Jacob's Ladder", as the trans-mountain track was named. The speed of its building and the extraordinary difficulties overcome were bruited abroad. When His Majesty the King visited Italy during the summer he asked to be driven over it.

It was now necessary to regroup for the drive on Alpe di Poti. Although Palazzo del Pero had been cleared the enemy was clinging to the line of Route 73 to the north and east. 1/2 Gurkhas crossed from the right to the left flank of the Division, despatched patrols along the highway and provided a jeep-borne company to support Royal Wiltshire Yeomanry in clearing enemy road blocks. In this operation a Madrassi bulldozer driver, Sapper Benglase, distinguished himself. He completed three diversions on the scene of road blows and proceeded to construct a fourth under heavy shell, mortar and spandau fire. He continued at work until severely wounded. Central India Horse, which had rejoined the Division on July 14th, relieved 2 Royal Sikhs in the Monte Favalto area in order to allow the infantry to move forward for the projected assault. With a gap of 12 miles between the new objective and the Divisional right flank it was decided to divide responsibilities: as a consequence on July 18th 5 and 10 Brigades passed under 10 Indian Division's command. On the same day 11 Brigade, which had arrived from Campobasso, began to move forward to join 7 Brigade in the new operation.

On the night of July 17/18, 7 Brigade crossed Route 73 and moved against the looming mass of Alpe di Poti, 2 miles north of the highway. 2 Royal Sikhs on the right headed for Point 966 on the eastern flank of the mountain. 1/2 Gurkhas climbed towards Point 974 on the track which led across its crest. Intense resistance had been expected but by 0300 hours the Gurkhas had seized their objective. For some reason probably not unconnected with the fall of Arezzo the mountain top was not held in force, but the Sikhs while clambering along its eastern face came under heavy mortar fire and did not arrive on the summit until noon. Within 24 hours 7 Brigade Reconnaissance Squadron and tanks from the Royal Wiltshire Yeomanry had worked their way to the crest and the stage was set for a continuation of the advance. 3,000 yards to the north of Alpe di Poti the crescent-shaped ridge of Piane di Maggio covered Verazzano, the terminus of a road from Anghari in the Tiber valley. Any substantial advances to the east along this road would place enemy forces west of the Tiber in jeopardy.

Moving by night and in silence, 1/2 Gurkhas before dawn on July 20th had secured Point 864 in the centre of the Piane di Maggio hogsback. During the forenoon a company seized Point 775, 1,000 yards to the north-west. This sudden incursion with its double threat to Verazzano took the enemy by surprise but rallying quickly German troops threw in a succession of heavy assaults in an effort to regain the lost ground. Throughout the afternoon counter-attacks followed in quick succession. The thick scrub and fir groves enabled the enemy to concentrate close to the Gurkha positions. The defenders would have been critically placed had it not been for the magnificent work of 31 Field Regiment and the support of the Wiltshire Yeomanry's Shermans. The gunners fired 800 rounds, the tanks 450 rounds. Never since Garci did artillery deal with enemy threats in such summary fashion. In spite of heavy and continuous mortar fire the Gurkhas managed during the afternoon to extend their gains. A swift pounce afterwards described by the Corps Commander as "brilliantly successful" carried Major the

Hon. L. C. F. Shore and his company to a further objective. Unfortunately this officer, whose family connection with his regiment began in its first campaign 135 years before, was mortally wounded. The day's fighting cost the Gurkhas substantial casualties and the Germans left 60 dead on the ground.

While the hillmen tightened their grip on the centre and left of the Piane di Maggio, 2 Royal Sikhs despatched strong fighting patrols along the right flank as far as Monte Verrano, while Royal Sussex worked into the north-east along Route 73. These parallel thrusts drove the enemy towards the Tiber valley. Concurrently 11 Brigade moved up to occupy the left flank of 10 Corps frontage, which had been extended to include Arezzo and the highway to Florence by way of the Arno valley. Here on July 18/19 Brigadier Partridge's men relieved SACK FORCE but retained King's Dragoon Guards under command. 3 Royal Frontier Force Regiment moved into a defensive position to the north of Arezzo, with 2 Camerons on its left astride Route 71, south of the westering bend of the Arno river. 2/7 Gurkha Rifles remained in reserve. The Royal Frontier Force Regiment effected contact with the enemy at Torricellino, and at dusk on the evening of July 20th ejected the local garrison after a brisk scrimmage which cost the Germans three killed and four prisoners.

5 Brigade, which had been relieved on the Tiber flank, now came into Divisional reserve at Antria, in close support of 11 Brigade. Fourth Division was then concentrated for twin thrusts northward: on the right, along the western slopes of the Alpe di Catenaia, the next mountainblock to the north of Alpe di Poti; on the left, along the eastern slopes of Prato Magno, the opposing massif to the west of the Arno. Central India Horse emerged from reserve around Monte Favalto and took over patrol duties under 10 Indian Division along Route 73, on the Tiber flank of the Corps front. Here on the night of July 23rd Lieut. St. J. G. Young led a patrol of Dogras to occupy a ridge. When nearing the objective Sowar Ditto Ram and Sowar Shiv Pershad were blown up on schu mines, each losing a leg. . Lieut. Young ordered his men to stand fast while he crawled across the minefield towards the wounded men. He dug up three mines with his hands and reached the stricken sowars unharmed. On lifting one of them to carry him to safety he trod on a mine. Both his feet were blown off. He despatched a messenger for sappers and stretcher-bearers and bade everyone remain without movement until day broke. Five hours later when the rescue parties arrived, Lieut. Young was still conscious and in command. He died from loss of blood before reaching hospital. Ditto Ram likewise died after having crawled to his wounded comrade and bandaged him. For their outstanding gallantry and self-sacrifice both officer and man received posthumous awards of the George Cross.

The shift in Fourth Division's front carried the forward troops out of range of the corps artillery groups. For the next stage of the assault the Divisional CRA had under command 165 Jeep Field Regiment, 5

Medium Regiment, 32 Heavy Regiment, 1 Royal Horse Artillery and a battery of self-propelled guns from 57 Anti-Tank Regiment. A survey troop, an OP flight and a meteorological section also came under command. Throughout this most difficult advance men and animals were frequently frustrated by the malevolence of the terrain. Yet the gunners, who moved on wheels, never failed to reach their positions nor to play their full role in the operations. An officer of 7 Brigade wrote admiringly:

"A feature has been the work of 31 Field Regiment supporting our Brigade. The guns, hauled over tracks which had never seen wheels before, reached positions which totally surprised the enemy. The gunner O. P. parties, always heavily laden, climbed up and down the mountains with the rest. They were rewarded with many perfect targets. A special word of praise is due to the O.P. signallers who kept communications going under all sorts of conditions. On many occasions the O.P. wireless set was the only communication between battalions and Brigade".

On July 23rd 2 Royal Sikhs advanced to the east of 1/2 Gurkhas on Piane di Maggio to secure the Divisional right flank. After brisk fighting Monte Verrano was seized, lost and regained. 10 Division had reached Monterchi, five miles to the east, while 9 Armoured Brigade dominated Route 73, half-way between the two positions. 10 Division's line of advance had now veered into the west to conform with the swing of the Tiber valley. Hereafter Fourth Division pivoted on its right flank in conformity with the progress of 10 Division.

On the night of July 23/24, 11 Brigade moved against Campriano, five miles to the north of Arezzo in the rolling ground along the haunches of the eastern massif. At 1900 hours on July 25th the attack opened, with three companies of Royal Frontier Force Regiment working forward across undulating ground, closely supported by tanks of the Royal Warwickshire Yeomanry. 11 Field and 5 Medium Regiments supported the assault; the enemy likewise had guns in support and an artillery duel of unusual intensity ensued. Night fell with Royal Frontier Force Regiment battling forward against bitter opposition, followed from ridge to ridge by the tanks, which speedily engaged targets indicated by the red Verey lights of the infantry. The reserve company of Royal Frontier Force Regiment passed around the left flank to continue the battle but encountered a minefield before reaching its objective. At dawn the situation on the right was precarious and one company of 2/7 Gurkha Rifles came forward to make secure the ground gained. On the left the Brigade objectives finally were overrun and the battle died away with Royal Frontier Force Regiment firmly holding both flanks and the enemy still in possession of the crest of the ridge behind the village. This sharp fighting had cost 138 casualties. 84 German dead were counted and 20 prisoners taken. While the operation was in progress the remaining three companies of 2/7 Gurkhas advanced on the left flank of Royal Frontier Force Regiment and without difficulty established themselves at Castellaccio, 3,000 yards west of Campriano.

Throughout the day, while the guns thundered, Divisional units uncommitted to battle gathered along the roads leading from Arezzo. His Majesty the King had come to pay a brief visit to Fourth Indian Division. At Palazzo del Pero he talked to Divisional representatives and from an observation point at Arezzo he watched a concentration shoot by 1 Field Regiment, 5 Medium Regiment and 32 Heavy Regiment, fired in support of 11 Brigade at Campriano.

That night (July 25th) 5 Brigade from its concentration area to the north of Arezzo thrust across 7 Brigade's front in a surprise attack which won commanding ground with negligible losses. At 0530 hours next morning 1/9 Gurkhas stealthily approached Monte Castiglione, two miles to the north of the 1/2 Gurkhas positions on the Piane di Maggio. When the men from Nepal went in with the kukri the Germans scuttled for safety, dropping their weapons in flight. Two hours later 3/10 Baluchis on the left of 1/9 Gurkhas seized positions on a narrow neck of high ground 1,000 yards further north. That same evening, when 1/4 Essex was about to exploit this gain, a counter-attack swept against the Baluchis who, after a brisk fire fight, ran out of ammunition. It was not until next day that the Essex passed through and against light opposition advanced two miles to Gello, almost in the shadow of the Alpe di Catenaia massif.

These rapid thrusts upset the enemy's plans for orderly withdrawal. Together with 10 Division's advance along the easy ground of the upper Tiber basin they left the German forces in the main mountain block hemmed in on both flanks. Operations now became fluid, and several successful patrol actions ensued. Far out on the left flank on the Prato Magno spurs, 2 Camerons were enjoying themselves. One of their officers wrote:

"During the first two weeks, we had only four or five casualties, against which we inflicted thirty on the enemy and took twenty-eight prisoners. There was no real front, although it could be taken roughly as the line of the Arno, which with its steep banks and its little villages nestling among the trees, provided an ideal playground for grim games of hide-and-seek. A German sauntering into the village of Casteluccioni in search of *vino* suddenly drops dead in the road. Two Germans hanging out their washing at a house in Balze are brought down by Corporal Cameron before they can regain the safety of their building. A German sergeant, taking a Sunday afternoon nap in a house which he considered well behind his own lines, is spirited away by some Jocks without disturbing the Sabbath's harmony."

On the night of August 29th, 2/7 Gurkha Rifles took over Campriano and Royal Frontier Force Regiment patrolled forward and occupied the small hamlets of Terrio and Perrieccia. The enemy still stood stubbornly and any attempts to improve positions led to retributive fire. Suspicions were aroused that the German guns were being directed from within 11 Brigade's area. A search resulted in the discovery in the village of San Pola of an Italian colonel who had been controlling the enemy artillery with his wireless set. Royal Frontier Force Regiment in their new positions overlooked the Arno valley and the market town of Subbiano, which patrols reported to be empty. 2/7 Gurkha Rifles in their turn on August 2nd seized Monte Castelaccio, where an enemy observation group had been using the chapel tower of a monastery for artillery observation. As if expecting ejection the edifice had been abundantly booby-trapped.

In a patrol clash near Giuliano 1/4 Essex had shot up an enemy detachment. Next morning the villagers were rounded up, told that they were responsible for the casualties and the village burned. This senseless proceeding deprived the Germans of their billets. Many other brutalities and stupidities betrayed the exhaustion and tension of troops who could not hope for reinforcement or relief. Of the German divisions on this front 5 Mountain Division and 305 Division could only assemble battle-worthy formation by merging units. 114 Jaeger Division was two-thirds under strength and 44 Division was reported as possessing less than 800 riflemen. Deserters frequently came in to testify to the demoralisation of the once proud Wehrmacht.

On the left flank of Fourth Indian Division 13 Corps continued to veer into the north-west. This wheel again opened the Divisional flank, which as from July 29th had been covered by LINDFORCE, a flexible formation including Central India Horse, Kings Dragoon Guards, tanks of Royal Warwickshire Yeomanry, 152 Field Regiment and a battery of self-propelled anti-tank guns. The mission of this independent command was to penetrate deeply into the Prato Magno mountain block and to maintain a link between the diverging axis of the two corps.

On July 31st the Corps commander announced a general offensive for the purpose of securing Bibbiena, on the main Florence highway 20 miles north of Arezzo. Here the Arno valley swung into the west around the northern shoulders of Prato Magno. At this point a valley also came in from the north-east, running down from the main spine of the High Apennines, on whose slopes the Gothic Line was under construction. The capture of Bibbiena therefore would open the road to Florence and would allow 10 Corps to close up against the main German defences.

The new operation (to be known as VANDAL) called for 10 Indian Division to storm the mountain block between the Arno and Tiber valleys, while Fourth Division gave a firm western flank and in similar fashion ejected the enemy from the Prato Magno massif. The general plan for both divisions was to thrust ahead at top speed in a series of infiltration movements which would by-pass the principal centres of resistance, leaving them to be dealt with at leisure. A start line would be found for 5 Brigade two miles to the north-west of Gello, at Poggio Alto on the flank of the towering buttresses of Alpe di Catenaia. 11 Brigade on the left would jump off from Monte Castelaccio, two miles north of Campriano. 7 Brigade would be concentrated to the north of Arezzo, to exploit any opening which might develop on the Divisional front.

Prior to the main operation adjustments were necessary which involved a number of minor operations. To the west of the Arno Central India Horse and those old friends of Western Desert days, Kings Dragoon Guards, after a series of brisk scrimmages broke into the San Giovanni area, among the southern outcrops of the Prato Magno. In three days Colonel Peters' men reached Monte Ferrato, four miles west of Subbiano, in the heart of the massif. These advances afforded 11 Brigade the opportunity of turning into the west to deal with enemies on its flank. On August 2nd 2 Camerons advanced on Monte Altuzzo while Royal Frontier Force Regiment, after ejecting an enemy rearguard, pushed into Subbiano. 5 Brigade in turn took advantage of 11 Brigade's infiltration to thrust forward along the base of the Alpe di Catenaia. These advances ousted the enemy remaining on Fourth Division's front to the east of the Arno and allowed General Holworthy to concentrate on the problems of Prato Magno. The immediate Divisional objective was defined as Castel Focognano, on the north-eastern haunches of the mountain block, three miles south of Bibbiena.

At 2130 hours on August 3rd the forward brigades moved to the assault. On the extreme right 1/9 Gurkhas advanced for 2,000 yards along the base of the Alpe di Catenaia. In a series of clashes on the wadi-ribbed hillside the hillmen overran a series of enemy outposts, killing 12 Germans and taking three prisoners at a cost of 21 casualties. 1/4 Essex on their left kept pace and seized Falciano 2,000 yards east of the Arno. On the opposite bank of the river 2 Camerons after an approach march by moonlight secured Bibbiano and Monte Ferrato. Thereafter "A" Company of the Highlanders pushed on to seize Poggia del Grillo, a mile to the north. This position stood on the eastern arm of a bare, V-shaped mountain which overlooked the Arno valley to the east and on its western slope dominated the only road of importance leading into the Prato Magno mountain block.

The capture of Poggio del Grillo ended the easy acquisition of enemy territory. Shortly after dawn on August 5th two companies from 115 Panzer Grenadier Regiment supported by assault engineers struck viciously at "A" Company of the Camerons. Tanks of the Warwickshire Yeomanry had reached Monte Ferrato and intervened as soon as battle was joined. Nevertheless the enemy attacked with great determination, overran a forward platoon and used the prisoners to screen an assault on Cameron headquarters in a large farmhouse. The German sappers blew in the doors with pole charges and fighting ensued from room to room. The Company Commander, Major Underwood, eventually was taken, but as he was led away tank fire distracted his captors. He made his escape—the only survivor of the action. The Cameron losses totalled 3 officers and 60 men.

That night under a bright moon "C" Company of the Camerons moved forward from Bibbiano to retrieve the situation. Armoured cars of Central India Horse followed in close support. Stern fighting followed. One platoon won a hilltop but another found itself embedded in a German position. Central India Horse, unable to reach the battle with their armoured cars, dismounted their machine-guns and hurried forward. They were ambushed, losing a number of prisoners. The defenders were too numerous for the assault force and the attack was abandoned. Next evening (August 5/6) 2/7 Gurkhas struck at Grillo in full battalion strength. After a promising start the battalion was held up. On the right flank of the Camerons Royal Frontier Force Regiment attacked silently by night against Poggio Pinale, commanding ground which stood above the western bank of the Arno two miles east of Grillo. The assault was held up on a spur slightly short of the objective. The Camerons shifted into the east, linked up with Royal Frontier Force Regiment and fused a continuous line across the mountain block east of the Arno. Heavy artillery exchanges followed, in the course of which Lieut.-Colonel Hill of the Camerons was mortally wounded.

Meanwhile 7 Brigade had come forward on the left flank of 11 Brigade, in the uncharted territory previously patrolled by LINDFORCE, and had moved up to Castiglione on the road which skirts the southern spurs of the Prato Magno. On August 5th 1/2 Gurkhas and 2 Royal Sikhs supported by Sherman tanks of King's Dragoon Guards moved into the mountains. The Sikhs found Talla, 2,500 yards to the north of Grillo, to be strongly held. Before the enemy could be chased away and the ground consolidated Major Key and 12 men had been wounded. At this juncture Lieut.-Colonel P. S. Mitcheson, DSO, took command of the Royal Sikhs. 1/2 Gurkhas, on a parallel line of advance three miles to the west, chased German outposts from Poggio la Cesta and established contact with Skinner's Horse and Lovat Scouts on the open front beyond the Divisions left flank.

VANDAL operation had opened well. After fierce fighting 10 Indian Division had destroyed the defenders on the crests of Alpe di Catenaia. On Fourth Divisions front all three brigades with moderate losses had bitten deeply into enemy territory. Half the distance to Castel Focognano had been traversed. By dint of exceptional efforts both armour and artillery had circumvented the difficult terrain and were intervening effectively in support of the infantry. The drive promised to take increasing toll of the scattered German forces as the Indian divisions ejected the harried enemy from position after position.

Nevertheless on August 10th VANDAL operation was abruptly suspended. A weakness had been discovered in the enemy defences further west, where New Zealand, Canadian, South African and Indian divisions had broken through to Florence. As a consequence of this advance a thrust eastwards of a few miles along the Arno valley would turn both the Prato Magno and the Alpe di Catenaia from the rear. There was no longer any necessity to battle forward ridge by ridge, pinnacle by pinnacle.

In the 32 days operation Fourth Indian Division had advanced 25 miles as the crow flies and probably twice as far by actual march distance across terrain which might have been designed to protect the defenders, to frustrate the assailants. In continuous contact with the enemy, with occasional eruptions of savage fighting, the Division had incurred 1,043 casualties. German casualties are unknown. Perhaps they were no greater than those of the attacking forces. But the Wehrmacht suffered a mortal loss of morale and of fighting efficiency, as the Indian divisions battered their way through these mountain fastnesses. As *The Tiger Triumphs* puts it:

"By the end of August, 1944, not only the German High Command but the rank and file knew that the war could not be won. Month after month of unremitting defeats, with the strongest positions torn from their grasp, with stop-gap successes fewer and fewer, brought home to the Nazi cannon-fodder the certainty that they were battling in a lost cause".

Already the Allied formations were mustering for the autumn offensive against the Gothic Line. In grand plan this operation called for converging assaults, into the north-west along the Adriatic coast, into the north-east across the High Apennines. These thrust lines squeezed out 10 Corps front and freed its divisions for employment elsewhere. On August 11th, 10 Indian Division began to spread out in a holding capacity across both mountain blocks. To conceal the suspension of the offensive, armour and artillery continued to stage demonstrations and patrol activity was stepped up. Behind this deception screen Fourth Indian Division removed all Divisional flashes and signs (except road signs), sealed its radios and unostentatiously slipped back through Arezzo to the Lake Trasimeno area. 1/4 Essex were left behind with instructions to display freely the Red Eagles on their shoulders.*

By August 14th Fourth Division had concentrated to the west of Perugia. For three days only were the officers and men able to enjoy the amenities of this playground countryside. On August 17th the Division passed under command of 5 Corps (Lieut.-General C. F. Keightly, CB, DSO, OBE,) and next day commenced to trek towards a new battlefield.

*1/4 Essex were absent for three months. Their place in 5 Brigade was taken by 4/11 Sikhs, (Lieut.-Colonel D. M. Cornah) one of the original battalions of 7 Brigade, which returned after a long tour of duty in Iraq and Middle East. The Essex, ostensibly left behind to reorganize, had no more than a months rest. In September they were incorporated in Wheeler Force and participated in sharp fighting in opening up the main highway to Florence. Thereafter they switched to the Polish Corps area and engaged in operations on the Adriatic foreshore. Lieut.-Colonel Chappell was wounded and the battalion remained under command of Major H. C. Gregory, MC, until the appointment of Lieut.-Colonel V. C. Magill-Cuerdon on November 11th. Three days later the Essex rejoined Fourth Indian Division.

Chapter 27

THE GOTHIC LINE

IN mid-June, after Fourth Indian Division had handed over on the Adriatic coast to the Polish Corps, the enemy withdrawal to the north continued. The Poles followed up closely; when 278 Infantry Division elected to stand in front of Ancona a sharp attack netted 1,000 prisoners. Thereafter the enemy once more retired across the rolling ridges until his right flank elements encountered the foothills of the Apennines. As the foreshore narrowed, resistance stiffened. At Pesaro, 42 miles to the north of Ancona, the Foglia river slipped into the Adriatic through a broad gravel watercourse. This river bed had been chosen as a moat to front the Adriatic outworks of the Gothic Line.

At Pesaro the coastal plain is only about 15 miles in width. It is less a plain than a succession of rolling ridges which separate gently-contoured valleys. Here the main Apennine mountain block diminishes towards the Adriatic in continuously mellowing terrain. From the towering main summits innumerable rivers seek the sea, their watercourses divided by high narrow hogbacks well inland, softer and rounder crests along the foreshore. On the easy ground along the Adriatic the enemy held continuous positions; 18 miles inland, on the line of the Foglia, the mountain system of garrisons in key positions began. When Fourth Indian Division moved forward it was directed towards the junction of the coastal and the mountain defences, in the foothills of the Apennines.

In this advance there was an air of stepping into the unknown. The intelligence concerning the Gothic Line was contradictory. Air photographs showed piecemeal fortifications with many gaps. British and Canadian patrols reported unoccupied outposts, uncoiled wire, unlaid mines. On the other hand the voluminous partisan intelligence insisted upon feverish activity everywhere, with convincing details of the number of labourers, count of guns, even the thickness of concrete walls. It seems probable that the Italian reports magnified particular instances into an erroneous overall picture, a rather curious circumstance, since these irregulars had been to a considerable degree responsible for the weaknesses of the Gothic Line. The Todt organisation had conscripted thousands of Italians without effective screening and the German press gangs had netted many patriots who supplemented the natural lethargy of forced labour by clever and effective sabotage. A poor quality of cement had been supplied by Italian manufacturers. Emplacements did not cover all approaches. Indeed in many respects the Gothic Line exhibited a quite un-German attitude towards detail—a circumstance which reflected the exhaustion and war-weariness of many of the enemy formations.

To accentuate the uncertainty General Holworthy was given considerable latitude in his instructions. He wrote:

"The Army Commander did not wish the left-hand Division of the Army to move any distance into the hilly country, but 5 Corps commander felt that a wide movement was more likely to find weakness and so enable the line to be pierced. He therefore gave me full discretion as to how far into the difficult country I should go. There was no restriction, provided the left flank of Eighth Army was protected."

"5 Corps plan called for 46 Division on the right and ourselves on the left to burst open the Gothic Line by advancing on as broad front as possible and by pushing in as far as possible without regard to protected flanks. In this opening attack all risks were to be taken. It therefore was essential for the Division to 'get off on the right leg', a circumstance which caused me many anxious moments. The prohibition of liaison enforced by higher authority to ensure secrecy was even extended to personal reconnaissance by commanders. Air photos for the same reason were not available and it was impossible to obtain accurate information concerning enemy dispositions".

In spite of rigorous security measures General Holworthy realised that it was next to impossible to maintain secrecy in any part of Italy. The enemy was well aware of the massive assembly on Eighth Army's front; indeed Canadian intelligence had reported that even the names of individual battalions arriving on the Adriatic front were being broadcast by the enemy. Under such circumstances it was inconceivable that the Germans would not keep a wary eye on their exposed inner flank. Resistance might be met well in advance of the enemy's main battle positions. General Holworthy therefore decided to rely on speed to achieve surprise. This proved a most fortunate decision. As it happened, 5 Mountain Division, entrusted with the defence of the enemy flank in the foothills, had been withdrawn into reserve to make room for the reorganisation in the Gothic Line of 278 and 71 Divisions, both of which had been roughly handled by the Poles in the drive northward from Ancona. It was against these battered formations that Fourth Indian Division moved. Should the attack be launched before they were ready for battle the prospects of success would be greatly increased.

By August 18th the Division had concentrated at Sigillo on Route 3 (Flaminian Way) on the eastern slopes of the Apennines 25 miles north-west of Perugia. There it prepared to advance behind a covering screen provided by CIL Gruppo. There was no liaison with the Italian formations except through Corps. The Italians seldom sent in situation reports and their movements in screen remained vague and unpredictable. This circumstance, together with the heavy congestion and poor condition of the Trans-Apennine roads, slowed down Fourth Division's approach to the battlefield. It quickly became apparent that a common D-Day for Eighth Army would find the left flank 20 miles in the rear of the divisions in the coastal sectors. It was therefore planned to give Fourth Division a day's start, with the consequent honour of opening the battle.

At 0600 hours on August 25th the leading formations advanced from Sigillo. 7 Brigade moved along the axis of Route 3 while 5 Brigade with the Divisional jeeps and a mule train proceeded on a parallel axis across country, along a track reconnoitred by Brigadier Saunders-Jacobs and his Brigade Major on commandeered Italian bicycles. One battalion of 11 Brigade went forward to patrol the left flank. Central India Horse covered the ground between the two brigades. It was discovered that the enemy had excelled himself in his demolitions along the Flaminian Way. In many places it was simpler to build a diversion than to attempt road repairs. Every bridge had been blown and the road blocked by craters, trees, demolished houses and concrete slabs. The Divisional Sappers and Miners laboured incessantly to effect sufficient repairs to let the traffic through and it was only due to their dour and sustained labours that Fourth Indian Division was able to keep up with its timing.

In addition to regular battle order 6 Royal Tank Regiment, 58 Medium Regiment, 85 Mountain Regiment and a battery of 165 Field Regiment (jeep-drawn guns) moved with the Division. A detachment of American Field Service ambulances also had reported for duty in the ensuing operation.

By nightfall 1/9 Gurkhas, jeep-borne on the right flank, had reached the line of the Metauro near Fossombrone, where Route 3 turns into the east towards the Adriatic. 4/11 Sikhs had covered 20 miles on foot to arrive 10 miles south of the river, an excellent performance on a hot and exhausting day. Both battalions had contacted the Italian screen but had not encountered the enemy.

7 Brigade moving northward on the axis of Route 3 was delayed by an exasperating series of demolitions. At Aqualagna, 2 Royal Sikhs, in the van of the advance, caught up with the enemy rearguards. The engagement was characteristic of the difficulties encountered when co-operating with Italian irregular forces. 2 Italian Brigade, after a telephone conversation with the adjutant of their San Marco battalion in the town of Aqualagna itself, reported the enemy to have withdrawn and that except for minefields, the line of advance was clear of the enemy.

On a two-company front the Royal Sikhs pushed ahead. On entering the vineyards which extended up to the town walls they were met

COMMANDERS IN GREECE

Major-General C. H. Boucher CB, DSO, MC.

Major-General T. W. Rees CB, CIE, DSO, MC.

7 BRIGADE LANDING AT SALONIKA.

STREET FIGHTING, PIRAEUS

PATROL AT MOUNT ATHOS MONASTERY.

OPENING OF BRIDGE BUILT BY DIVISIONAL SAPPERS AND MINERS ACROSS ALIAKMON RIVER.

DURBAR—3/10 BALUCH REGIMENT—GREECE.

SUBEDAR HARAKBAHADUR THAPA IDSM, 1/2 GURKHA RIFLES LEADS FOURTH INDIAN DIVISION ASHORE AFTER MORE THAN FIVE YEARS SERVICE ABROAD.

with a hail of fire from mortars and guns on the heights which overlook Aqualagna on three sides. The company commander (Major J. L. Key, MC,) and all three platoon commanders of the left company were killed; the right hand company commander (Major D. Farr) was wounded. A third company, under command of Major D. Pim, was sent forward to clear the town, only to be met at point blank range with fire from Italian troops in Aqualagna. Heavy shelling and mortaring of all three companies continued until night fell, when the battalion consolidated the ground gained. Next morning, when Royal Sikhs prepared to renew the attack, the enemy was gone. This sharp encounter cost the battalion two company commanders and 70 other ranks. The death of Major Key, who already had been twice wounded and whose family possessed long standing associations with the Royal Battalion, was most keenly felt by all ranks.

On the night of August 26th 1/9 Gurkhas crossed the Metauro and seized the southern end of Monte Cesena, a narrow-backed ridge system which stood 1,500 feet above the northern bank of the river. 4/11 Sikhs closed up to the line of the river at Calmazzo. On 7 Brigade's front 2 Royal Sikhs reached Formignano, also on the Metauro river 4 miles south of the ancient market town of Urbino. On August 27th, 4/11 Sikhs passed through 1/9 Gurkhas and pushed forward. Light opposition was encountered from elements of an enemy mountain regiment, but with the help of Sherman tanks of 6 Royal Tank Regiment the Sikhs consolidated on the north-eastern spur of Monte della Cesena to the north-east of Urbino. 3/10 Baluchis likewise moved up throughout the day. On the left, 1 Royal Sussex passed through 2 Royal Sikhs and entered Urbino. The 20,000 inhabitants lined the streets and gave voice in an excited welcome.*

5 Brigade was now in touch on the right with 139 Brigade of 46 British Division—a first acquaintanceship which was destined to ripen in another theatre. Both divisions had closed up against the outworks of the Gothic Line. These defences followed the north bank of the Foglia six miles beyond Urbino, where the river described a series of back-and-forward meanders along the base of a long ridge which ran for four miles into the east. On a spur in the centre of this ridge, with river loops on either side, stood the hamlet of Monte della Croce. A mile farther north on still higher ground stood Monte Calvo in Foglia. Behind Monte Calvo a white ribbon of road wandered along the rising crest of the hills for three miles to Tavoleto, where the spur merged into a transverse east-west ridge system. On this main spine Monte San Giovanni, three miles west of Tavoleto and Monte Gridolfo, five miles to the east, marked the enemy's main battle positions.

On both sides of Tavoleto the advantage of ground had been studiously exploited by the enemy with a variety of fortification devices—anti-tank ditches, wire obstacles, machine-gun pits, forward

*Urbino is perched on a pinnacle high above the surrounding ridges. It was the birthplace of Raphael.

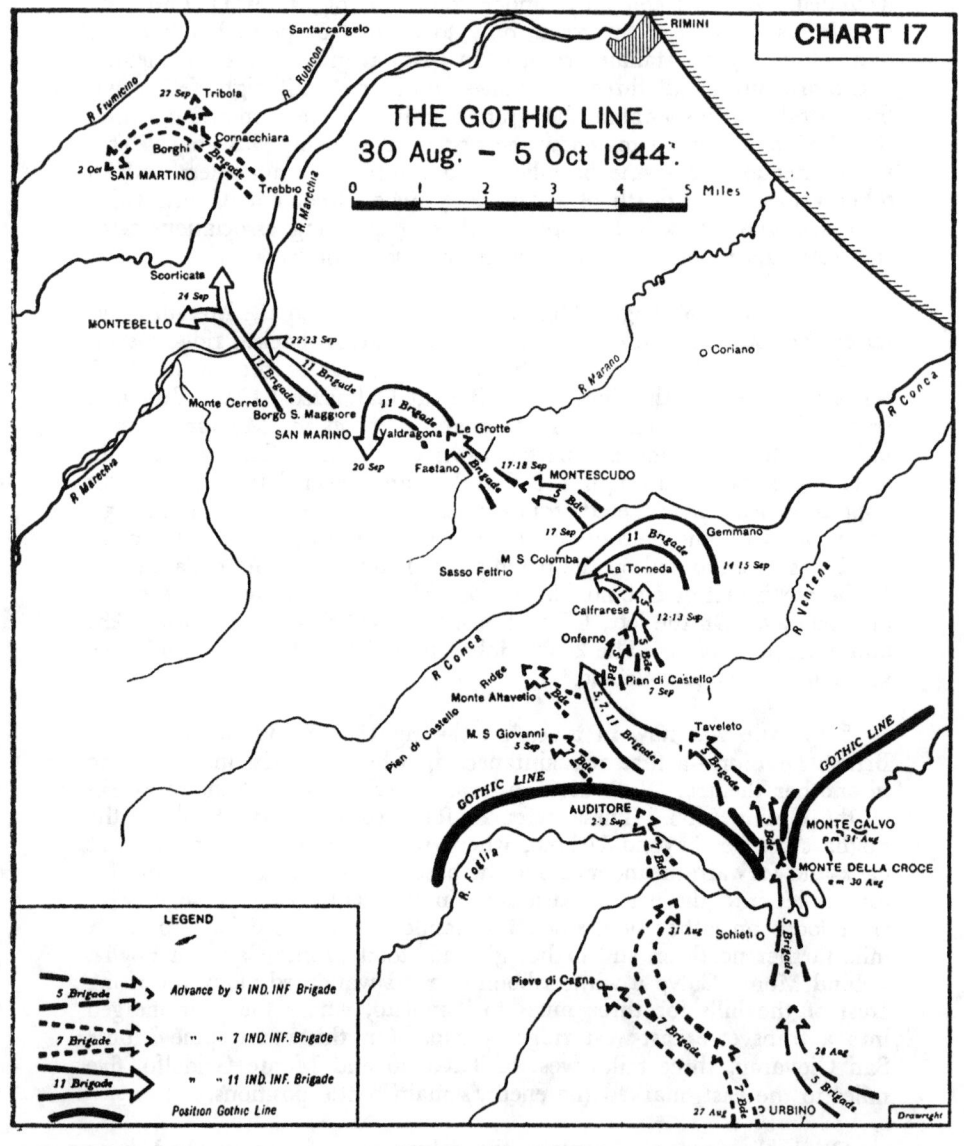

sniping guns and trench systems. The glacis had been cleared to provide an open field of fire. Thickly sown minefields covered all approaches. On the left of Monte Calvo the enemy defences were organised on a mountain basis; instead of fixed and continuous lines the forward positions were held by outpost groups protected by intricate defensive fire lines. German counter-attack forces waited in sheltered reserve areas in the rear.

As Fourth Division thrust forward from Urbino only rearguard resistance was encountered and all brigades continued to edge into their battle positions. 5 Brigade reached the meanders of the Foglia in front of Monte Calvo. Echeloned on the left 11 Brigade moved forward less rapidly while 7 Brigade as the extreme left hand formation of Eighth Army clashed with watchful flank guards. The Royal Sussex in particular ran into trouble. The South Country men, after passing through Urbino, had been ordered to seize the Piepi di Cagna Ridge and Monte Calende, in order to protect the flank while the remainder of the Brigade "squared up" to the Gothic Line positions. Heavy and accurate artillery fire from across the Foglia greeted this move, and in a series of short savage fights well dug-in defenders disputed the advance. In these encounters Corporal White and Corporal Horwood greatly distinguished themselves and the battalion was saddened by the deaths of Captain Sinclair-Thomson and the Chaplain, the Reverend C. H. Bingham. The supporting armour likewise was roughly handled, losing seven tanks.

During daylight on August 29th, 3/10 Baluchis despatched patrols who explored the southern bank of the river. When no resistance was encountered Brigadier Saunders-Jacobs determined to test the degree of the enemy's reputed readiness with a silent night attack. Before dawn on August 30th two companies of Baluchis boldly crossed the Foglia and climbed the spur to Monte della Croce. To their astonishment the hamlet was reached without a shot being fired. Attempts to exploit beyond Monte della Croce drew immediate retaliation, and on the left flank the enemy was discovered to be holding as far forward as the line of the river.

At 1500 hours the forward Baluch companies reported a light counter-attack which was thrown back. During the afternoon tanks crossed the river followed by 4/11 Sikhs. At 1800 hours the Baluchis thrust 1,000 yards to the north seizing Point 332, half way to Monte Calvo. On the right the Sikhs conformed to the advance. 1/9 Gurkhas on their way forward became involved in the deployment of a fresh British brigade on the immediate right of Fourth Division, and were delayed in reaching their jump-off positions.

That night a colossal bombardment crashed on the enemy defences between Monte Calvo and the Adriatic. Three corps (2 Polish, 1 Canadian and 5 British) moved to the assault. By dawn 46 British Division on the right of Fourth Indian Division had broken into strongly fortified and desperately defended positions to a depth of over a mile. At 0400 hours 4/11 Sikhs had pushed two companies forward on the right of Monte Calvo, had gained fresh ground and had taken 40 prisoners. At first light 1/9 Gurkhas closed up and were ordered to encircle Monte Calvo while Sikhs and Baluchis mounted a frontal attack against this strong position. At 1115 hours the assault began with a crash shoot by Divisional artillery and affiliated units. Fighter bomber groups added their metal to the concentration and afterwards searched the ruins with cannon fire. The enemy resisted fiercely. 3/10 Baluchis, profiting by a certain amount of dead ground, worked up the crest of the spur. The supporting tanks were disabled on minefields. On the Baluchis' right 1/9 Gurkhas made rapid progress and early in the day seized commanding positions well to the rear of the main objective. At nightfall 5 Brigade securely held Monte Calvo and had established a protective flank to the west. A spur astride the Tavoleto road a mile to the north of the village represented the deepest penetration. 40 prisoners had been taken from 71 Infantry Division. An eyewitness wrote:

"As the attack developed on Monte Calvo the enemy probably realised that he was not going to be allowed to make his getaway under cover of darkness. To his east, 4/11 Sikhs began to make their presence felt by pushing against the left flank of the village. Beyond them, 1/9 Gurkhas, moving up the valley, threatened to cut the enemy line of withdrawal a mile to the north of Monte Calvo. At nightfall the enemy artillery admitted defeat by opening fire on the village. By this time, the Baluch and Sikh battalions were searching amid the ruins."

"The village was a shambles. Wire obstacles had been crushed by the tanks. Broken shutters, window frames and drainpipes swung in the breeze. Tileless roofs allowed clouds of dust and smoke to rise above the village. A bell from the church tower lay in the rubble but the altar was still intact. Piles of barbed wire and rail dumps revealed that the Germans had not finished work on their defences."

While the main battle thundered on into the night on 46 Division's front, the hours of darkness passed without alarm for 5 Brigade. It seems probable that the rapid enveloping move had shaken the enemy's confidence in his ability to regain Monte Calvo. At 0930 hours on September 1st, 1/9 Gurkhas took up the battle and again thrust into the north. 46 Division had mounted a full-scale attack against Monte Gridolfo, at the eastern extremity of the long barrier ridge which fronted the Foglia. Intense fighting ensued throughout the day. A Hampshire battalion finally won the position against desperate resistance. Conforming to the British advance, 1/9 Gurkhas registered gains along the axis of the Tavoleto road. By nightfall they had reached a track junction on the crest of the ridge 1,000 yards to the south-east of Tavoleto village. 2/7 Gurkhas, who had closed up on Monte Calvo at 1300 hours, came forward under 5 Brigade's command on the left of 1/9 Gurkha Rifles, and 4/11 Sikhs moved up into close support at the road junction. These moves were in anticipation of relief of 5 Brigade by 11 Brigade. Soon after dark that evening an enemy counter-attack dislodged the forward elements of 1/9 Gurkha Rifles. Nevertheless by 0100 hours on September 3rd 4/11 Sikhs had completed the relief of Colonel Nangle and his men and had passed under command of 11 Brigade for the ensuing operation.

The enemy had now recovered from 5 Brigade's sudden incursion into his defences and had rushed forward substantial reinforcements, including self-propelled guns and mortar groups, to buttress his threatened right flank. 7 Brigade, which had closed up on the left of 5 Brigade but south of the Foglia, encountered a well-defined defence line. Royal Sussex and 1/2 Gurkhas clashed with outposts in sharp encounters. When Monte Calvo fell the enemy relinquished these outlying positions and withdrew across the river towards the main flank bastion of Monte San Giovanni, whose eminence afforded detailed observation over the battlefield. 278 Infantry Division was identified as holding this sector.

On September 2nd, while 1/9 and 2/7 Gurkhas were battling their way towards Tavoleto, a platoon of 1/2 Gurkhas crossed the Foglia and stealthily approached Auditore, a heavily fortified village 1,000 yards to the north of the river and the same distance east of Monte Calvo. The patrol was confronted by an eerie situation—a battle position silent, deserted, and apparently untenanted. Jemadar Bharti Gurung after distributing his small force in covering positions, worked into the rear of the village and detected enemy detachments lurking in houses. When these hideaways were flushed the main German positions along the south and east of the village opened fire, revealing a carefully baited trap. Jemadar Bharti Gurung despatched an appreciation of the situation by wireless and called for artillery support. He and his men remained near at hand throughout the day reporting the progress of the shoot. This artillery programme prevented the enemy from reinforcing the Auditore garrison. That night two companies of 1/2 Gurkhas crossed the Foglia, closed in and overran Auditore with slight losses—largely as a result of the canniness and battle instinct of the Jemadar. Sappers came forward and opened lanes through the minefields along the river. Mule trains and tanks crossed over and 7 Brigade established a firm bridgehead from which to strike for Monte San Giovanni, 3,000 yards to the north-west.

Throughout September 3rd, patrols from 11 Brigade probed to ascertain the strength of the enemy, whose dispositions were affected by the rapid advance of 46 Division on the right. The thrust line of the main battle was swinging from north-west into the west thus crowding the enemy on Fourth Division's front against the mountains. The night attack on Tavoleto had been entrusted to 2 Camerons. At 2130 hours Divisional artillery reinforced by two field regiments from 56 British Division, laid down a heavy deception shoot off the projected line of attack. The Germans responded with a counter attack against 2/7

Gurkhas on the southern outskirts of the village. Defensive fire broke up this assault. As the enemy fell back, "C" Company of the Gurkhas, in a spontaneous move under Lieutenant Smith, followed the retiring enemy groups into Tavoleto village and there fell on the garrison with an unheralded close-quarters attack. Camerons and Sikhs, waiting for the signal to advance, heard bedlam break out among the ruins of the village. Artillery officers went forward and reported that the Gurkhas had overcome all opposition. Two 88mm. guns and a number of prisoners were taken. Less than 30 men of "C" Company of 2/7 Gurkhas were still on their feet.

The Tiger Triumphs comments on the work of the gunners during this action:

"The log of the artillery for this night's work affords a characteristic illustration of the intricacy, speed and flexibility achieved by Divisional gunners in fire programmes. The plan called for a deception shoot wide of the infantry objective, a concentration shoot on Tavoleto, protective fire in case the deception shoot achieved its object, and a barrage programme for the Sikhs' and Camerons' attack. When the Gurkhas took unpremeditated action, it was necessary to cancel these schedules and to improvise new shoots. Yet throughout the night the guns answered every call, thanks to intrepid forward observation officers who kept the batteries informed from minute to minute of the course of the fighting".

At 0430 hours on September 4th, 7 Brigade moved to the assault on San Giovanni. 2 Royal Sikhs and the remaining companies of 1/2 Gurkhas had forded the Foglia on the previous evening and the two battalions advanced abreast, with the Sikhs on the right and the Gurkhas astride the road which led westwards from Auditore. From the outset the Gurkas encountered stiff resistance in the cemetery area to the north of Auditore and afterwards on the slope of Point 581, where enemy self-propelled guns raced forward and engaged "A" Company at a range of 300 yards. At 0700 hours the first tanks arrived and occupied hull down positions in support of the dourly fighting infantry. Forward observation officers of 31 Feld Regiment moved with the leading companies, indicating many targets which were immediately engaged by guns hidden among the vineyards on the approaches to the battle positions. On Point 581 the spotter for a medium regiment obtained a direct hit on one of the enemy's self-propelled guns. Throughout the day against similarly stiff resistance 2 Royal Sikhs fought their way forward to the outskirts of Poggio San Giovanni. At sunset 7 Brigade was firmly established in approach positions to the principal objective. As soon as darkness fell the Gurkhas moved off in an attempt to win the crest of Monte San Giovanni by a silent approach. At dawn a heavy artillery concentration played on Poggio San Giovanni and when the Royal Sikhs entered they found the enemy gone. The villagers stated that the Germans had carried away 50 wounded. The Sikhs pushed on to secure Baldo, a tiny hamlet on the next ridge to the north, while 1/2 Gurkhas continued their slogging ascent of Monte San Giovanni. A spotter plane brought useful details of enemy dispositions on the summit and by 1545 hours that afternoon the Gurkhas had dealt with the last stubborn defenders and were exploiting along the high razor-back crest which ran northward towards the valley of the Ventano. On the slopes of Monte San Giovanni 50 enemy dead were picked up. Next morning Sikh and Gurkha patrols flushed a German observation post which had failed to withdraw. Twelve Germans scurried for safety and all were bagged by snipers before they could reach covert.

So far the battle had gone well for Eighth Army. The enemy had been caught on the wrong foot and under the massive flails of air and artillery concentrations had yielded valuable ground. 46 and 56 Divisions had made rapid progress and in their wheeling movement had reached the Conca, nearly 8 miles ahead of their start line. This thrust, as has already been noted, had tended to pivot on Fourth Indian Division so that the battle front was now almost due north and south. At this juncture the enemy hurriedly reinforced a number of his key positions including Gemmano, a strongly organised ridge system four miles north of Tavoleto and immediately in the path of 56 Division. Here the battle rose to fresh heights of fury. British brigades were thrown back in assault after assault. The failure to break enemy resistance at this point altered Fourth Division's thrust line. Instead of continuing to the north the Indian brigades were obliged to bear into the west, where rising ground and abrupt features imposed a succession of formidable barriers to their progress

The first of these major obstacles was the Pian di Castello ridge to the north of the Ventano river. This high ground represented a characteristic Adriatic defensive position. From its crest the approach of attacking troops could be observed for some miles. On its reverse slopes mortar groups found cover to impose a continuous curtain of fire on the river crossings. Minefields everywhere blocked the advancing infantry. Sniping guns had ranged the roads to a yard. The breaking weather augmented and implemented all other adverse circumstances.

On the night of September 5/6, 11 Brigade struck at Pian di Castello with Royal Frontier Force Regiment on the right and 2 Camerons on the left. Castelnuovo, a compact village on the slopes of the ridge, was by-passed by both thrusts. At first light "A" and "D" Companies of Royal Frontier Force Regiment under Major Finnis had seized the village of Poggiale, while the Camerons worked up another spur to Valle. The enemy held high ground in strength and the assault resolved into a slow and expensive slogging match. Major Finnis and his men threw back a counter-attack which had penetrated into Poggiale and both 11 Brigade battalions retained their initiative in dogged fighting. During the day tanks made their way across the flooded Ventano and a combined infantry and armour assault struck at Castelnuovo. By 1530 hours Royal Frontier Force Regiment had won this objective, taking 28 prisoners of 5 Mountain Division. Four full-scale counter-attacks followed, each of which was thrown back, the last with the aid of captured spandaus. A German intercept revealed a concentration against the right flank of the position, whereupon 11 Field Regiment intervened effectively. Soon after first light on September 6th, a company of German infantry was caught in the open advancing against 2/7 Gurkha Rifles, who had sent up a support company on the eastern slopes of the village. All weapons were brought to bear and this foolhardy force was dispersed with heavy losses. 11 Brigade consolidated pending the arrival of 5 Brigade, which was due to pass through and continue the attack. Soon after dawn a counter-attack was thrown at Royal Frontier Force Regiment and fierce fighting ensued before the Germans gave way. By mid-afternoon Royal Frontier Force Regiment had encircled Castelnuovo and had pincched out the village from the rear. Night fell with 11 Brigade firmly established on the Pian di Castello feature, but at a cost of substantial casualties.

The same morning 7 Brigade advanced on the western terminus of Pian di Castello, thrusting against the village of the same name on the road which ran northward across the ridges. Once again stiff opposition and heavy shell fire was encountered. "B" Company of Royal Sussex lost nearly a score of men including 2 officers killed. "D" Company of the same battalion was trapped on a schu mine field. The tanks failed to close up on 11 Brigade's front and at dusk Brigadier Partridge's men were short of their objective. Throughout the night the enemy repeatedly endeavoured to regain Castelnuovo, Royal Frontier Force Regiment repulsing no less than four assaults. During these counter-attacks 2/7 Gurkhas sent forward two companies to reinforce the firing line.

The fighting had been sufficiently severe to impair 11 Brigade's ability to continue effective pressure on the enemy. That evening 5 Brigade passed through to seize a ridge system to the north and west of Pian di Castello. 1/9 Gurkhas on the right and 4/11 Sikhs on the left struck vigorously at this objective: by dawn on September 8th the enemy had been compelled to withdraw, losing a number of prisoners. An enemy self-propelled gun knocked out two of the tanks supporting this attack.

September 8th proved a miserable day, with high driving winds and incessant cold rains. Mopping up and consolidation occupied both forward brigades. Before dawn next morning vicious counter-attacks struck at 1/9 Gurkhas and at Royal Sussex on the right and left flanks of the Divisional sector. The assault infantry reached the Gurkhas and a hand-to-hand mêleé ensued before the enemy was ejected. A platoon of "C" Company of the Royal Sussex was cut off but Lieut. R. A. Roach completed a field day of achievement by beating off in a single-handed grenade battle all attempts to overrun the isolated sections. Another miserable day of howling winds and pelting showers followed. An icy downpour soaked and chilled the forward troops as they crouched in their battle positions along the sodden ridges.

On the night of September 9/10 "D" Company of the Royal Sussex advanced from Pian di Castello village to seize Cemetery Hill, 1,000 yards to the north. A heavy bombardment which preceded the attack failed to shake the enemy. As soon as dawn broke "B" Squadron, 6 Royal Tank Regiment, moved forward to intervene in the battle. It proved an eventful assignment. The leading tank struck a mine and blocked the line of advance. A second tank in endeavouring to extricate itself shed a track. The remainder of the squadron cut across country, missed the rendezvous with the infantry, but came under heavy fire from a self-propelled gun. A tank was destroyed; in turn the remainder of the troop knocked out the gun. 50 Germans raced into the shelter of a near-by house. The tanks blew it to pieces killing most of the occupants. Advancing across a cornfield, weapon pits were discovered under the stooks. 20 Germans including 5 bazooka men were captured. A chaplain took 20 prisoners while attending the wounded tank men.

That night two troops of tanks followed by "C" Company of the Royal Sussex in carriers closed up behind a Corps barrage which marched northwards towards Onferno, 1,200 yards beyond Cemetery Hill. The tanks followed a track which led over a steep declivity. In the darkness the leading Sherman executed a complete somersault and continued on its way undamaged. The next three disabled themselves as they tumbled down the slope. The remaining three with tracks reversed slid down and pushed on to reinforce the Royal Sussex, who had seized their objective and were busily consolidating against an imminent counter-attack. Working at top speed the position was organised on the crest of a knoll which fell sharply into the north. A defensive fire zone was plotted to protect the approaches; a mortar fire curtain was arranged to cover the adjacent slopes where the angle of descent created dead ground for the artillery. The tanks took hull-down positions behind the infantry and waited. As anticipated an enemy force (estimated at battalion strength) struck again and again in an endeavour to dislodge the South Country men. Each time the attack broke down under the combined fire of the guns and mortars. The Browning machine-guns of the tanks remained in action until the barrels were red. After five attempts the enemy gave up the fight. Royal Sussex casualties were negligible.

While Fourth Division in the face of abominable weather and fierce resistance had continued to break into the enemy positions the advance of the British divisions on the right had ended abruptly against the bastion of Gemmano. Here the principal obstacle consisted of a bare ridge 1,300 feet high at the junction of the Ventano and Conca rivers. The high ground extended from east to west for 4,000 yards and constituted a barrier which could not be by-passed. For five days (September 5/10) 56 British Division again and again assailed this rampart, sometimes winning a grip on the vital crest but always forced back by fierce counter-strokes. On September 10th, when 46 British Division took over the battle, Fourth Division was ordered to shift its thrust line farther to the north, with a view to clearing Monte San Colomba, on the western flank of the Gemmano position.

5 Brigade relieved 11 Brigade on Pian di Castello that night and organised for an attack 3,000 yards to the north of the present Fourth Division positions. This objective would give jump-off ground for an assault on Gemmano from the left flank. The two Sikh battalions were allotted the place of honour in the new advance.

On the night of September 11/12, 4/11 Sikhs advanced in order to secure Cafrarese, a cluster of farmhouses on the north bank of a narrow steep-sided gorge. By 0600 hours this objective had been stormed, but before support arms could arrive a heavy counter-attack with tanks in the van dislodged the Sikhs, who fell back across the ravine.

2 Royal Sikhs advanced from behind the Royal Sussex screen to the north of Cemetery Hill, with orders to clear Onferno, a village in a hollow between ridges running up to Monte San Colomba, and thereafter to exploit towards the main objective. "B" Company under Major Franklin was directed along one of the bare ridges while "A" Company under Major Collins dealt with the village. After an advance of 1,000 yards the enemy was encountered in force and "B" Company was held up. "A" Company found scrub and a series of streams in its path and failed to make progress. "D" Company came forward to assist but by 0200 hours it was apparent that the objectives could not be reached during the hours of darkness. The leading companies therefore consolidated on the ground won. At first light tanks came up into close support and throughout the day an intense artillery duel continued. Enemy tracer set fire to a haystack near Lieut.-Colonel Mitcheson's battle headquarters; the blaze supplied a ranging mark and enemy guns and mortars continuously pounded the area. Towards evening a German observation post in the rear of the Royal Sikh positions was detected and destroyed by a tank. In spite of heavy casualties the Sikhs stood firm, holding all but indefensible terrain for a full day. On September 13th, they finally were forced to withdraw before a fierce enemy counter-attack.

The night of September 12/13 had been chosen for a major attack on the entire Eighth Army front. 1 Canadian Corps and 1 British Armoured Division had been ordered to smash through and to cross the Marano. 46 Division's role was to make an end to Gemmano and to exploit as far as Montescudo, two miles further north. Fourth Indian Division was briefed to assist by a continuation of the Sikh assaults on Cafrarese and Onferno. 3/10 Baluchis were ordered to conform to the advance of the left flank battalion of 46 Division.

At 2300 hours the Baluchis moved forward. They immediately struck heavy going, the mud and slippery steep slopes being almost as great impediments as enemy fire. Before dawn a first objective had been reached but it was found impossible to exploit beyond it. 4/11 Sikhs were in trouble from the beginning. One company was mauled by enemy defensive fire and two other companies halted by a vigorous counter-attack as they approached Maite, 1,500 yards east of Monte San

Colomba. On the left of the Divisional front 2 Royal Sikhs gained Schiano to the north of Onferno but their advance on their main objective encountered unbearable artillery and mortar fire. 46 Division on the right had been held from Gemmano but had made considerable progress towards Monte San Colomba. The dawn situation report on September 13th therefore showed a number of subsidiary gains but with the key bastion still firmly in the enemy's grasp. 46 and 56 Divisions now had attacked Gemmano eleven times.

The Corps Commander at this juncture decided to commit Fourth Indian Division against this position. On September 13th 2 Camerons were placed under command of 46 Division and took over a sector on the Farneto spur between Gemmano and the right flank of 5 Brigade. On September 14th, 11 Brigade occupied the left sector of 46 Division's front and 7 Brigade extended to the north to cover the gap, 5 Brigade remaining in Divisional reserve. The new assault was set down for the night of September 14/15. The main objective was Point 449, a steep-sided kopje with a large wooden cross upon its summit. When this key position had been won the assault troops would exploit into the west towards the valley of the Conca.

The artillery organisation for this attack was noteworthy. The 260 guns enrolled in the shoot ranged from Bofors to 7.2 howitzers. Each calibre was accorded specialist employment. The high angle weapons undertook to deal with hostile mortar groups and at the same time to search enemy concentration areas with harassing fire. The other guns collaborated in a series of crash shoots on the principal objectives. Ninety minutes before the Cameron attack Zollara, a tiny hamlet on the left of Gemmano, would receive the full blast of 2,000 shells. Forty minutes before zero hour Bofors guns would lay deception lines of tracer well to the left of the main thrust line of the attack. Five minutes later a series of crash shoots would switch rapidly from target to target on the Camerons' front while other groups of guns duplicated such concentrations on deception targets. At 0300 hours all field guns would join in a barrage behind which the Camerons would advance across the crest of the spur to the south of Gemmano.

Supported in such impressive fashion the attack won home with surprising ease. An indirect route to Point 449 afforded a covered approach. By 0350 hours the leading Highland platoons had reached Zollara. Here the attack halted, reorganised and waited for the tanks to come up. By 1000 hours with armour in the van the Camerons were firmly ensconced on the crest of Gemmano ridge. Utter desolation marked the scene; the torn and tormented ground, the sprawling dead, recalled the battlefields of the First World War. It was reported that 900 Germans had perished in the defence of this key position. Without detracting from the magnificent work of Camerons and artillery it seems probable that the easy Gemmano victory must be attributed (in part at least) to the cumulative effect of ten days of intolerable bombardment and furious assault.

The capture of this bastion was reflected in marked gains elsewhere. 2/7 Gurkhas seized Monte San Colomba without opposition, thereafter despatching patrols across the Conca who brought back 40 prisoners from 100 Mountain Regiment. Only at Trebbio and at Monte Altavelio, on the extreme left of the battlefield, did the enemy cling to his original positions. At Trebbio on September 15th a platoon of 1/2 Gurkhas under Havildar Kulbahadur ejected the enemy in masterly fashion. Having first located the hostile outposts the hillmen overran them killing 12 Germans without loss. A similar manoeuvre at Altavelio resulted in a furious fire fight. In the face of overwhelming opposition the Gurkhas withdrew section by section. Fourth Division picked up an agitated intercept which ordered an enemy reserve battalion 9 miles from Altavelio to force march to the relief of a garrison besieged by a single platoon.

Beyond the Conca 46 Division had seized the road junction at Montescudo, a gain which opened highways to the north and west. The left flank of Eighth Army now was able to expand and to widen the battlefield. Fourth Division was directed towards the unmistakable skyline of San Marino, whose castle-crowned crest towered above the western countryside. The weather and the condition of the roads precluded movement of all brigades. 7 Brigade therefore stood fast, pinning down the enemy in the Altavelio area, while Central India Horse accompanied by mountain artillery patrolled and raided into the foothills on the exposed flank.

On September 17th, 5 Brigade closed up on Montescudo where 3/10 Baluchis had already arrived under command of 46 Division. Patrols were despatched towards San Marino State, reputed to be the oldest republic in the world. White crosses cut in the chalk along the western bank of the Marano identified the boundaries. San Marino had formerly supported a population of 14,000 of which more than half inhabited the solidly built and attractive town on the western slopes of the mountain. At this stage its population had been swollen by 120,000 refugees from adjoining battle areas. Until the Gothic Line offensive became imminent, the Germans had respected San Marino's neutrality. At the beginning of September Field-Marshal Kesselring had demanded the use of State territory and had occupied the unequalled observation posts along the eastern cliffsides on the mountain.

Two Allied assault divisions were pushing to north and west through the Montescudo bottleneck. Owing to the foul weather and congestion on the roads the advance even of an additional brigade was achieved with the utmost difficulty. On the night of September 17/18, 3/10 Baluchis established a bridgehead across the Marano in the loop of the road near Faetano. (This crossing was unopposed and it seemed possible that the enemy was withdrawing from San Marino). Soon after midnight 1/9 Gurkhas moved through in order to seize Points 345 and 366, two commanding knolls on the crest of the next high ground. Point 343 stood immediately above a nullah with steep cliff-like sides. Stiff resistance was encountered and it was not until 0515 hours that Point 343 was won. Pressing on against Point 366 the fighting increased in intensity. The supporting tanks had bogged down near Faetano and there was delay in inaugurating the defensive fire programme. The forward company of Gurkhas ran out of ammunition and was compelled to fall back on Point 343.

During this action there occurred one of those shining acts which live on to inspire by force of their magnificent example. Rifleman Sherbahadur Thapa and his section commander stormed an enemy strong point, killing the machine-gunner and putting the remainder of the garrison to flight. A group of Germans struck back and the section commander fell wounded. Single-handed Sherbahadur Thapa charged his assailants, swept them before him and gained the top of the ridge, where he brought his Bren gun into play against groups of the enemy on the reverse slope. For two hours he bore a charmed life under a hail of fire, destroying numerous detachments which sought to regain the crest. When his platoon had spent its last round and was virtually surrounded, the intrepid rifleman covered their withdrawal. He then dashed forward under heavy fire and brought in two wounded men lying on the forward slopes. While returning a second time in full view of the enemy he fell riddled and joined the sublime company of those who have not lived to know of the accolade of a Victoria Cross.

As the Gurkhas fell back on Point 343 they took shelter on the clay cliffs behind the knoll, as one observer put it, "clinging to the sides of the gully like flies on the wall". 1 Field Regiment with high explosive and smoke laid down a defensive fire curtain. When enemy pressure increased, a multiple "clear all lines" call to Corps swung the guns of fifteen field and four medium regiments onto this threatened sector. This overwhelming concentration dispersed the enemy and enabled the Gurkhas to maintain their meagre bridgehead.

Throughout the day work continued on the crossing of the Marano. The enemy kept the ford under fire; the Red Cross jeeps, in spite of their plain markings, were machine-gunned, causing a number of casualties. By evening tanks had made their way forward. During the same evening 4/11 Sikhs, swinging wide round the right flank, reached Corianino, a mile north of Faetano; from thence they thrust rapidly into the west towards Valdragona, immediately under the northern buttresses of San Marino. Heavy fire was opened from the summits above them—the first intimation that the enemy held the town in strength. The sheer precipices on the eastern face of the mountain precluded attack from that side and the only possible approach was from the rear of the mountain, where the main highway mounted to the summit in a series of switchbacks through the serried terraces of the town.

At this juncture 7 Brigade, in the course of a series of clashes, found the enemy thinning out on the southern flank of the battlefield. Brigadier

Lovett's men moved north, crossed the Conca and took over the front of 2/7 Gurkhas at Sasso Feltrio, 4,000 yards south of Faetano. 11 Brigade was now free to pass through 5 Brigade and to continue the encirclement of San Marino. 2 Camerons from the front of 4/11 Sikhs drove on Valdragona, and with artillery and armour support captured the village at 1300 hours on September 19th. That evening patrols were despatched around the northern haunches of the mountain into the lower streets of the city. In a series of clashes Lieutenant Ellis of "D" Company killed 6 Germans and captured 6 others without loss.

On September 20th with the aid of smoke cover the Camerons closed up under the cliffs and closely beleaguered the town. An AMGOT lorry which attempted to reach San Marino with a load of foodstuffs blew up on a tellermine and the Camerons enjoyed supplementary rations. At 0800 hours on September 20th "A" and "C" Companies of the Highlanders began to dribble forward for the final phase of the assault. "C" Company was checked by machine-gun nests at the north-western corner of the mountain, where the main road turns upwards into the town. Tanks came forward and shot up Borgio Maggiore, a lower suburb. "D" Company passed through and began to work up the winding streets towards the palaces and castles on the summit. By 2000 hours resistance had ceased. In a driving rainstorm the Camerons searched the city, picking up 20 dead and 54 bedraggled and miserable prisoners. The Highlanders sent out patrols to the west and despatched a company to the north to contact 46 Division. The capture of San Marino, which turned the enemy's defences on the coastal plain, cost the Camerons 4 killed and 32 wounded.

Early on September 21st General Holworthy accompanied by Brigadier Saunders-Jacobs of 5 Brigade made an official entry. General Holworthy has provided a lively account of the proceedings:

"I was taken to the Governor's Palace where I was met by the San Marino Military Guard and escorted into the sanctum sanctorum. The Captain Regent was seated beside a large table. He wore a tail coat, butterfly collar, pepper and salt trousers and elastic-sided boots. I was in shorts, khaki shirt, battle-dress blouse and coat duffle. With the aid of an 'American-speaking' local girl, we discussed matters. I told him that refugees had to be kept off the roads until military movement was finished. We wanted local labour to mend road blows. We had come to kick out the Boche and not to take over the Republic."

"We then adjourned through the Council Chamber to a dining-room where I signed my name in the Golden Book. We had some wine. I was asked to state what I desired. I said I wanted headquarters for myself and one for Brigade, and some stamps. I was allotted a villa and was told that all the stamps of the Republic were at my disposal. I could have anything I wanted. The Captain Regent expressed his gratitude to the Allies for their restraint in not bombarding the town.

We then shook hands warmly and I went back to see how the battle was going."*

"There was a thick mist and some rain, with visibility nil. The 3/12 (Royal Frontier Force Regiment) were getting their objectives beyond the town without trouble. I booked a room in the Albergo del Tritorno and had a first-class lunch—wonderful muscato wine—some ham and olives—macaroni—superb steak (due to cattle killed by our artillery fire) and sweet omelette. The hotel was crowded with civilians, mostly rich refugees from Rimini and neighbouring towns, who had hoped to find sanctuary in the neutrality of the State. It was strange in the middle of a battle to find ourselves seated at a nice meal among a civilian community of all ages and sexes. The *padrone* of the hotel was very obliging and good. He had been a waiter at the Carlton in 1902."

At 0700 hours on September 21st 11 Brigade continued the Divisional thrust into the west. Royal Frontier Force Regiment seized Monte Cerreto, between San Marino and the wide winding valley of the Marecchia, capturing 20 prisoners who were found asleep. On September 22nd patrols reached the river 4 miles to the north-west of San Marino. German artillery searched the roads as the Division closed up; during a conference in the forward area General Holworthy, Brigadier Partridge, Brigadier Defonblanque, CCRA, and Brigadier Eastman, CRA, were driven into the roadside ditches, Brigadier Defonblanque being seriously wounded. It was decided to force the Marecchia and to seize a shaggy tableland approximately 2,000 yards in length in the loop of river valley which sagged towards San Marino. A number of small hamlets were strewn along this summit, with Scorticata on the river bend to the north, and Montebello similarly located to the south. This platform of high ground continued for two miles into the west until intersected by the valley of the Rubicon.

At 2300 hours on September 22nd, 2/7 Gurkhas advanced on Point 460, high ground slightly to the south-west of Scorticata. Royal Frontier Force Regiment at the same time moved against Montebello. After the fall of San Marino the harassed and dispirited 278 Division had been replaced in the line by 114 Jaegar Division, tough, surly and truculent. "B" Company of the Gurkhas secured Point 362, an objective 800 yards to the south of Point 460; "D" Company had closed up and "C" Company was passing through, when murderous fire opened from all sides. At dawn the three forward companies found themselves on bare slopes amid a ring of enemies. Three counter-attacks were repulsed but it was impossible to reach the firing line with replenishments of ammunition. It was therefore necessary to withdraw to the river bank, where the dogged Gurkhas immediately reorganised for a fresh assault. The morning's fighting had cost them 130 casualties, of whom almost half were killed.

*Two days later when the Army Commander, General Leese, and Sir Harold MacMillan, Resident Minister in North Africa, called on the Captain Regent, the Cameron pipers provided the flourishes for the occasion.

Royal Frontier Force Regiment in an advance on Montebello endured similar buffeting. "B" Company had reached an intermediate objective and "C" Company had passed through before the ambush was disclosed. At daybreak both companies were short of ammunition and as in the case of the Gurkhas it was found impossible to bring supplies through the enemy curtain of defensive fire along the flooded river. Nevertheless Royal Frontier Regiment clung grimly to its gains. A counter-attack against "B" Company was flung back. Throughout the day harassing fire continued to take toll but that night "A" and "D" Companies after a thunderous two hour concentration reinforced the firing line and made good the crests of Montebello. Simultaneously 2 Camerons crossed the river and joined the battered Gurkhas in the capture of Point 460, thus consolidating the Divisional bridgehead to the west of the Marecchia.

The Corps Commander at this juncture announced the general retirement of the enemy on the Adriatic front. The Germans nevertheless stood stubbornly along the Apennine foothills and 7 Brigade was brought forward on the right flank of 11 Brigade to fill the gap between Fourth Indian and 46 Divisions. On the night of September 24/25 a company of 1 Royal Sussex crossed the Marecchia and seized Gemmiano on the western bank. On the next night a second company with tank support pushed through to Cornacchiara, two miles to the west of the river. At this juncture Brigadier Lovett received instructions to alter 7 Brigade's axis of advance and to strike into the north-east along the diminishing Borghi ridge in order to relieve pressure on 46 Division's left brigade, which was in difficulties. Shortly after midnight on September 26/27 Royal Sussex and Gurkhas advanced. The Gurkhas after bitter fighting seized Point 160, 30 German dead being found on the feature. After 30 minutes bombardment by the Corps artillery the infantry, supported by 6 Royal Tank Regiment, thrust on. Intense opposition developed and only Major Malcolm Cruickshanks company was able to keep direction. Pinned down on the approaches to Tribola, fierce and costly fighting ensued. The supporting tanks bogged down and the thirty gallant survivors of the leading company drove off one counter attack after another. It became necessary to withdraw, but the enemy, exhausted by successive failures to hold strong positions, relinquished Tribola and Reggiano-Tribola next day. On the same evening (September 28) 2 Camerons from their positions to the south despatched a strong fighting patrol across the Rubicon to San Giovanni in Galilia, 4 miles deep in enemy territory. After a series of crash shoots 2/7 Gurkhas occupied this village, whereupon 7 Brigade organised for further penetration and took 2 Camerons under command.

At 0100 hours on October 1st, with the Camerons on the right and Royal Sikhs on the left, a fresh attack opened behind a barrage in which 306 guns fired 22,000 shells in three hours. By 0330 hours the Camerons had reached their objective at Eight Trees and were enjoying sniping practice at numerous Germans who bolted like rabbits across their front. 2 Royal Sikhs reached Borghi at 0730 hours and the Royal Sussex on the right seized Reggiano. The Camerons took over Borghi during the day in order to release the Sikhs, who undertook to extend the Divisional front.

On the night of October 1/2 two platoons of 2 Royal Sikhs reached San Martino, the latest Brigade objective. After a fire fight they were forced to withdraw. "A" and "B" Companies reached Point 337 and "A" Company a second time approached San Martino. Next morning in a driving mist, before consolidation could be effected, a strong counter-attack forced the leading company to fall back on "B" Company, 1000 yards in the rear.

Like a vehicle that ploughs forward, in heavy going, gradually losing speed until it finally bogs down, Fourth Indian Division's drive slowed and came to a halt. For the last ten days of September the hostile elements had excelled themselves. Autumnal gales from the Adriatic brought torrential rains. The watercourses had risen to dangerous levels. On the western flank Central India Horse patrols were marooned on the wrong side of the rivers; men were drowned in endeavouring to rejoin their units. Lieut.-Colonel Peters and his men finally extricated themselves and their mountain guns by means of aerial ropeways. Everywhere the low ground was a sodden morass, ankle-deep in freezing mud. The slopes were greasy and slippery, the crests wind-swept and storm-beaten. For the assault troops life was misery; in the back areas continuous day-and-night labour barely managed to keep minimum supplies moving to the firing line.

It was now 37 days since Fourth Indian Division had moved out of Sigillo and 32 days since it had opened the battle. In this period the three brigades had advanced more than 60 miles, of which the last 25 miles had been in constant contact with a desperately resisting enemy. Casualties had been heavy, amounting to 1,892 of all ranks, including an unusually high percentage of junior officers. The average strength of companies was now less than 30 rifles. The battle had been of the most wearing type—no set piece assaults on the grand scale with intimate preparation and subsequent relief, but an unrelenting series of small bitter clashes, with thrust plied on thrust, in which the evenly balanced strength of assailants and defenders exacted a substantial toll of casualties for each acre of gained or lost ground. Companies seized limited objectives; other companies passed through to register gains or to be flung back; the enemy fought with frenzy throughout the hours of darkness to be gone at dawn—but only as far as the next crest behind. Always a dominating ridge barred the way; when won, a swollen stream curtained by mortar fire lay behind it. To advance up a fire-swept hillside, surge over the crest, descend the reverse slopes in full view of the enemy, pick paths across deadly mined ground along the river banks, splash through icy torrents scarcely colder than the pelting rains, work up another slope against another crest stiff with enemies; with support arms, sappers, medicals and supply services following up; battling by night and day against abominable terrain and foul winter weather—such was the recurrent log of Fourth Indian Division's five weeks' drive along the Apennine foothills.

It had been felt and said—sadly by friends, casually by others—that Fourth Indian Division had been destroyed at Cassino and never would be the same again. To this opinion the Gothic Line battle supplied abundant and eloquent refutation. The record of this operation is rich in characteristic performances by all ranks of the Division—great courage in extremity, indomitable doggedness, quick improvisation, the ability to make war and to win through against every stress of circumstance. The new units bore themselves with the same pride and resolution as their predecessors. The battle-worthiness of the Red Eagles lived on.

All ranks had won renown, but it is perhaps permissible to accentuate the outstanding role played by the Divisional Commander in these last fierce battles. General Holworthy had taken over Fourth Indian Division when it was still shaken by the tragedy of Cassino. Fortune was kind and his men were vouchsafed the opportunity to regain their wonted dash and resilience in a series of operations of rising severity. For the opening of the Gothic Line battle the Divisional Commander had been entrusted with a task which required exact perspective, unrelenting drive and dogged perseverance. These qualities General Holworthy communicated to all who served under him and his personal example played no small part in creating a potent instrument of victory.

At the end of September it became known that 10 Indian Division was on its way forward to take over. Relief was almost as great nightmare as battle. With only three one-way roads to carry three divisions, with rivers everywhere in spate and sodden ground churned to quagmires, the disengagement and substitution of units constituted a slow and arduous operation. 5 Brigade, which was in reserve, extricated itself with the least difficulty and headed back to Perugia. 11 Brigade was relieved by 20 Indian Brigade on October 3rd. 7 Brigade got away two days later. One by one the gunner, sapper and service units were released. Fourth Indian Division reassembled in the Lake Trasimeno area in the hope that sufficient time would be available for a thorough rest followed by a period of training and reorganisation. Thereafter everyone expected to return for the last phase and the final destruction of the enemy.

It was the fortune of the Division never to know what next week held. At Lake Trasimeno, as at Sidi Barrani, as at Keren, as at Enfidaville, dramatic news arrived. The tour of duty in the Italian theatre had ended. Fourth Indian Division would proceed forthwith to Greece.

Chapter 28

GREECE — THE BACKGROUND.

IN Africa, in Syria, in Italy, Fourth Indian Division had been occupied with normal military employments. The implications of its victories were the affairs of others. But in modern warfare, in which the total economy of the state is pledged in support of the military effort, in which civilians perish, are enslaved, ruined or starved as the natural consequence of hostilities, no triumph at arms restores peace and normal living. Instead, if the victor is not to share the miseries of the vanquished, he must shoulder the responsibility of reorganising communities in chaos, of nursing sick peoples back to health. As if to complete an unparalleled war experience, Fourth Indian Division took over such duties in its last operational theatre. The record of the Greek campaign is less that of enemies destroyed than of services rendered—services not less worthy of honour than achievements on the battlefield.

To appraise such services correctly, it is necessary to examine the background of the Grecian scene.

This small poor country, the source of one of the world's mightiest civilisations, possessed at the beginning of the twentieth century few vestiges of its former grandeur. In the Balkans it could claim no friend among its neighbours. Among the great powers, Great Britain stood as sponsor, and any diminution of British world prestige awakened greedy appetites and restless ambitions beyond Greece's loosely held and tenuous frontiers.

In pursuance of the "Mare Nostrum" aspiration, Mussolini was eager to forestall Hitler's threatened occupation of the Balkans. Without consulting his senior partner at the end of October 1940 he attacked Greece on ludicrous pretexts. The Greeks proved as agile of body as of mind, and justified their lively and unconcealed contempt for Italian pretensions by containing the invaders easily among the ridges and ravines of western Epirus. Graziani's resounding defeat at Sidi Barrani followed and the Rome extremity of the Axis began to wobble. Whereupon Hitler intervened. On April 6th, 1941, advanced German elements crossed the Greco-Bulgarian frontier. British, Australian and New Zealand troops arrived from Western Desert and fought valiantly, but in three weeks the panzer columns were in Athens, and Greece had passed under the conqueror's heel. In the wake of the invasion a Bulgarian rabble flooded into Macedonia, ferociously extirpated the local population and annexed much of the province. With equal callousness the Germans set about the devastation of the remainder of Greece. Nearly two thousand villages were destroyed, thousands of Greeks shot, imprisoned or deported, schools closed, the press and radio muzzled. With less than ten thousand square miles of arable land in the Kingdom, it was essential to import three million tons of foodstuffs annually. The Germans made no effort to meet this requirement. Famine stalked the land. Infant mortality rose to 90% of all births. But for the efforts of Great Britain and her Allies, who managed to supply cargoes of foodstuffs through neutral channels, at least half the population of Greece would have died of hunger.

If a man must die he usually prefers to die fighting. Thousands of Greeks fled into the mountains, formed guerilla bands, collected arms and began to take toll of enemy detachments along lines of communication. Italian troops, who formed the bulk of the occupation forces, proved incapable of dealing with these implacable partisans. It became evident that the Greek resistance movement might influence the Mediterranean campaign. Whereupon under direction of Middle East command, Force 133 came into being. British officers and signal personnel were parachuted into Greece to organize and to correlate the operations of the independent bands. When arms and equipment arrived, a state of war was established in the Greek highlands. The wretched Italians moved in terror of their lives, and the Germans were forced to take cognizance of a sticky situation. Instead of employing the Wehrmacht, the Nazis economised by raising a number of German led "Security battalions". The Greeks who volunteered for such service were by no means confirmed traitors. Many joined in order to eat, and many more in order that they might live long enough to square accounts with their employers. Unfortunately they had been recruited largely from the gendarmerie and political police which had bolstered the royalist, nationalist and repressive Metaxas dictatorship. This circumstance nullified British plans for a unified guerilla campaign. The most active and best organised partisans came from left-wing groups whom Metaxas had suppressed; the "Security Battalion" recruits were the men who a few years before had hunted these groups to ground. The Metaxas men had been close to the King of the Hellenes, now the nominal director of the resistance movement from his sanctuary in Cairo. It was asking too much of those who were republicans at heart to render more than lip service to a monarch whom they suspected of a foot in either camp. Thus the ELAS groups, as the left wing guerillas were known, tended more and more to go their own way, to disregard Cairo directives, and to fight private wars after their own fashion. *

*For the purpose of this narrative there is no point in distinguishing between the actions, attitudes and individuals of the various left wing groups in Greece. EAM/KKE are therefore described as ELAS in this narrative. EAM represented the left wing coalition; KKE its predominant Communist bloc; ELAS its armed forces.

This attitude revived the latent hostility between ELAS and EDES, a partisan organisation which drew its main strength from the west and north-west of Greece, and whose personnel was strongly monarchist. The basic schism between King's man and Republican had only lain dormant because of the extremity of the times. With bellies and bandoliers full both sides now prepared to devote themselves to feuds rather than to assaults on the common enemy. Lack of communications abetted distrust; it was simple for German agents to foster tales of ELAS atrocities in Thrace, of EDES misbehaviour in Epirus. Each party believed the worst of the other, and even minor misunderstandings were translated as betrayal and treason. British officers began to report the disappearance of arms and ammunition supplied by the Allies; they had gone underground against the day when domestic differences would be debated. The destruction of the Axis armies in Tunisia accelerated this private munitioning, for it seemed as if the liberation of Greece might be imminent. Sir Henry Maitland-Wilson, Commander-in-Chief, Middle East, eventually lost patience and peremptorily summoned the Greek leaders to Cairo. They arrived in irreconcilable mood. General Sarafis, representing ELAS, and General Zervas, the EDES commander, agreed to an armistice that amounted to little more than a pious wish that future differences might be settled without fighting. Any hope of unity was stifled by the conditions on which ELAS agreed to collaborate. Left-wing representatives would be sent to Cairo only when the King's cabinet was reconstituted in line with their wishes; moreover the King must undertake not to return to Greece until a plebiscite had decided on the future of the monarchy. King George attempted to placate the irreconcilables with a half-promise; his Ministers, realising that in effect ELAS was asking for their heads, ignored the provisos. Whereupon ELAS arbitrarily set up a "Political Committee" of Communist tinge, arrogated to themselves the right to speak for the Greek people, and established relations with Marshal Tito, the recognised leader of the Communist forces in Yugoslavia.

This summary action put an end to prospects of peace in Greece. Throughout the early months of 1944 ELAS and EDES were at war with each other; Greek slew Greek and wrought reprisals indistinguishable from those of the Bulgarian and German invaders. In this internecine strife ELAS established ascendancy, partly by virtue of superior numbers and organisation, partly by the efficacy of Communist propaganda and partly because of the failure of the King of the Hellenes and his Council of Ministers to give a lead to the best and most stable elements. As the summer wore away, and crashing blows on all fronts presaged the doom of the Fascist powers, it became apparent that if liberation was not to be a signal for civil war, a fresh effort must be made to secure Greek unity. In September, with the Gothic Line battle in full swing, a second conference was held at Caserta under the authority of the Supreme Allied Commander of the Mediterranean Theatre. Somewhat surprisingly the rival factions committed themselves on paper to an entente which if observed would have ensured a peaceful settlement. Both groups bound themselves to sink their differences during the period of liberation, to accept orders from the Allied High Command, and to obey the dictates of the Greek Provisional Government until such time as it was replaced by more representative authority. It was concurrently agreed by both parties that British troops should enter Greece, and should operate in the terms of the following limited objectives: (1) to eject the enemy; (2) to maintain law and order; (3) to repair communications; (4) to distribute civil relief; (5) to remain strict political neutrals. In this agreement nothing was said about the nature of the provisional government, which in lieu of other definition could only be the expatriate government in Cairo. There is every reason to believe that at the time of the Caserta meeting ELAS was prepared to wait out events and to act constitutionally, confident that its leaders would be returned to power at the first election.

The Conference was scarcely completed when the anticipated Axis withdrawal began. The Germans disappeared from the Aegean Islands, pursued by British commando and special service troops. By early October they had withdrawn all garrisons to the mainland. As they moved northwards they scorched the countryside. Communications were destroyed, railways torn up, rolling stock burned, bridges blown. The harbour channels were studded with scuttled blockships. Any food discovered was carted away. In many villages key men were shot as a last act of vengeance. Less than one-third of the farm animals and one-sixth of the farm equipment remained. Devastated fields and a starving countryside were the victors' inheritance.

In mid-October 2 Independent Parachute Brigade and 23 Armoured Brigade landed near Athens. The capital acclaimed the British troops hysterically. Four days later the designated British Commander, Lieut.-General Scobie, together with the Greek Prime Minister and his Cabinet, arrived from Cairo. They too received a tumultous welcome. The occupation of Salonika and other outposts followed without incident, although an early message from Macedonia reported the existence of an ELAS-sponsored government in that province. On October 20th, Fourth Indian Division was ordered to proceed to Greece. On October 21st Brigadier Lovett of 7 Brigade flew ahead on preliminary reconnaissance. Movement of the Division was ordered to begin during the first half of November. First priority was a brigade group for Salonika, followed by a brigade for Patras and the Ionian Islands. The remaining brigade would move to Crete a little later, when the attitude of the 12,000 German and Italian troops in that island had been ascertained. Divisional Headquarters would be established at Salonika.

The Corps instruction issued to General Holworthy early in November amplified the Caserta decisions, and indicated some of the more obvious powder barrels that lurked under the surface. Insofar as the ELAS-EDES fend was concerned, it was hoped that the presence of British troops, even in small detachments, would restrain the Greeks from waging war on each other. No distinction was to be made between rival factions, nor was the projected British garrison in any way to interfere with political activities. The occupation forces would only intervene on the request of Greek authorities, or to prevent bloodshed. Force or violence must not be used before force or violence had been employed against British troops. On the thorny question of the "Security Battalions", it was decided to disarm and imprison them as German collaborationists, but to take precautions against mob violence by guarding them with British troops. It was recognised that political motives mitigated their treason in many instances, and it was left to the Greek government to decide the measuure of their guilt. The Corps instruction in conclusion declared that the sooner communications were opened, food distributed and normal intercourse restored, the sooner Britains task would be completed. In the restoration of civilian services British troops were enjoined to treat all Greeks similarly, and to intervene only to prevent exploitation or victimisation.

This fair and moderate directive established the British forces of occupation not as an umpire but rather as a buffer between two groups determined to have each others blood. It contemplated the use and not for the abuse of liberty. But freedom is a heady draught, and a volatile people could scarcely be expected to assuage their thirst in sips. There were too many dead to be avenged; too much pent-up eloquence; too many inflammatory newspapers. Moreover, it was beyond the goodwill of soldiers to settle the paramount problem of King or no King. One party or the other saw itself delivered to its enemies, bound for the burning.

Of all this, Fourth Indian Division, accustomed to inscrutable moves, happily knew nothing. Another theatre beckoned. Red Eagles have wings, and so they are chosen to fly far.

Chapter 29

7 BRIGADE IN MACEDONIA

As its portion of the Greek theatre, 7 Indian Infantry Brigade drew the stormy cockpits of Macedonia and Thrace.

For a thousand years these north-eastern provinces have known little peace. A polyglot population has made feuds its first industry. Envious and vengeful neighbors have glowered across the frontiers. An unstable economy has fostered unrest. Poor communications have hampered administrative control. During the war years, starvation, violence and the Bulgarian influx accentuated the traditional turbulance and inspired the quasi-nomadic Macedonians with a fierce and justifiable craving for retribution.

As in other parts of Greece, the Nazis had recruited local forces to quell the hungry and hostile peasantry. These so-called "Security Battalions" proved of little value to the Germans. As soon as armed and organised they asserted their independence, establishing local controls over groups of villages and stretches of countryside. Having drawn defensive cordons they ejected Germans, Bulgarians and neighbouring Greeks alike.

This policy brought them less into conflict with the Nazi forces than with their fellow Greeks, particularly with the well-organised OMM, the Communist-sponsored Macedonian Corps which served as the ELAS spearhead in north-eastern Greece. This force drew its strength from Salonika, where its authority had been sufficient to establish a measure of underground government during the German occupation. Under command of General Bakirdzis, the Macedonian Corps was well equipped with artillery, small arms, vehicles and ammunition. Nominally this officer took orders from ELAS General Headquarters, Athens, but he had become adept in acknowledging receipt only of such instructions as he wished to carry out. It was in part due to his caution and good sense that the tragedies which supervened in other parts of Greece were not enacted in Macedonia.

On the night of November 3rd, 7 Indian Brigade sailed from Taranto. Its transports made rendezvous at the island of Skiathos in the northern Aegean, where an advanced base had been established by British special service troops. Minesweepers cleared a channel in the infested waters of Thessalonika Bay, and on November 11th the Brigade group began to disembark at an emergency bridgehead adjoining the Salonika power station. A British agent had reached the city before the enemy withdrawal, and had been able to bribe the German demolition squads. As a result the waterworks, electricity supply and other public services were intact. The dock installations however had been thoroughly demolished and the port was unusable.

By November 12th 7 Brigade had been lightered ashore, and was busily organising its area. 1 Royal Sussex undertook guard duties, 2 Royal Sikhs manned the bridgehead, 11 Field Park Company had begun a survey of the docks, 12 Field Company Sappers and Miners were at work on the roads, 1/2 Gurkhas and 31 Field Regiment had deployed as garrison in the town. Fourth Indian Division took over command of elements of 2 British Parachute Brigade and 9 Commando Group which had screened the landing. On the next day representatives of the Greek National Government arrived from Athens, together with the Governor-Generals of Salonika and of Western Macedonia, and General Avramadis, the newly-appointed military Governor of Salonika. A parade was held in which representatives of ELAS participated. It was characteristic of Macedonian mentality that even at this juncture, in the midst of devastation and famine, the Governor-General's speech should have been punctuated with recurrent shouts of "Sofia—Sofia—On to Sofia".

From the beginning it was obvious that while ELAS might tolerate the British occupation, little cooperation in the rehabilitation of Macedonia could be expected until local feuds had been satisfied. Priority objective for ELAS was the liquidation of the "Security Battalions" at Kozani, Kilkis, Poliyiros and Drama. To prevent bloodshed 7 Brigade despatched detachments of 1/2 Gurkha Rifles and 31 Field Regiment to these centres. They arrived in time to forestall a clash, although at Drama the situation remained tense for some days. In Kozani bickering between the Greek partisans could not be entirely suppressed and the small detachment under Major Calvert had an anxious time. On November 20th General Holworthy visited this market town but failed to compose the differences. By the end of the month ELAS had dispersed or cowed its opponents in this area.

In the meantime symptoms of trouble developed in Salonika. On November 16th, General Avramadis reported ELAS to be making unauthorised arrests, particularly of Greek Reserve officers who might be called to the colours by the Provisional Government. At the same time Greek interpreters serving with 7 Brigade reported attempts to intimidate them and to compel them to quit their employment. On November 19th the Bishop of Kozani, a notorious cleric, preached a violent and treasonable sermon. The Salonika populace reacted to his incitement and staged hostile demonstrations. The excitement was at its height when Fourth Indian Division received orders to re-form the Salonika National Guard and to proceed with the disarmament of ELAS as from December 10th.

Such orders could only be construed as a direct challenge to the Macedonia Corps. ELAS had no intention of surrendering its arms to anyone. General Bakirdzis refused to vacate the Salonika barracks in spite of direct orders from General Sir Ronald Scobie, Commander Land Forces, Greece. An officer of General Avramadis' staff gaoled by ELAS was released on intercession of British officers; when an ELAS detachment undertook to re-arrest him they were disarmed and placed in custody. A large crowd demonstrated in front of Fourth Division Headquarters. The Governor-General of Western Macedonia fled to Athens. By the end of November the situation had deteriorated sufficiently for General Holworthy to fly to Athens for conferences with the Commander of 3 Corps.

The arrival of Central India Horse and the Rajputana Rifles Machine Gun Battalion strengthened the Salonika garrison sufficiently to permit 1 Royal Sussex, together with elements of 1/2 Gurkhas and gunners, to relieve the Commando force in Drama. This first incursion into the Greek countryside proved an engrossing experience. At both Drama and Kavalla ELAS forces were in control and the arrival of small British detachments did nothing to diminish the tension. The resentment of the left wing partisans was scarcely less than that of their enemies, the Royalist bands in the hills, who expected the British troops to join them in the extermination of ELAS. A series of incidents followed which greatly angered the fair-minded men of the Royal Sussex. Ration cards were only issued to ELAS supporters. Shopkeepers who refused to pay ELAS levies had their goods confiscated and they were thrown into jail. Parents were ordered to assemble their children for a procession in which each child was given a stone to hurl at the Royal Sussex Headquarters. A football match between a British minesweeper and a Greek team was interrupted by ELAS tommy gunners, who marched the crowd away to participate in a political demonstration. When at Kilkis a general strike forced the Royal Sussex to take over all public services they found themselves obstructed by partisans at every turn. Nevertheless their sense of humour prevailed, as witness the battalion chronicler's report upon a tense moment in Drama:

"The QM and 'B' Echelon found themselves where, in a more orthodox tactical lay-out, a forward rifle company would have been. The QM assuring us (as usual) of his best attention at all times, promised that 'B' Echelon would provide another Verdun. It would be easier, he said, for anyone to get something from him without signature than for ELAS to pass through his lines".

Meanwhile events moved swiftly in other parts of Greece.

On December 3rd a general strike was declared in Athens and the police opened fire on the demonstrators. Next day ELAS forces attacked British and Greek naval headquarters at Piraeus. On the same day ELAS detachments entered the civilian administration buildings in

Salonika, ejecting the Governor-General and his principal officials. General Holworthy immediately interviewed General Bakirdzis and besought him to co-operate in preventing incidents. General Bakirdzis was well-disposed and with the British Consul-General in Salonika acting as a cool, cheerful and adroit intermediary, the coup d'état was effected without clash with the occupation troops. 7 Brigade, however, with unmanned perimeters and troops scattered throughout Macedonia and Thrace, remained in an unenviable position. The Salonika garrison was heavily outnumbered and its first necessity was to concentrate the units scattered throughout the city. Unostentatiously the various formations shifted into two main areas, one covering the Eastern Mole, and the other the southern foreshore of Thessalonika Bay. The latter was designated as the main concentration area and its perimeter was known as the Iron Ring. Dispositions were of such nature that the area could be sealed off at short notice. At the completion of this operation General Holworthy, who had been in ill-health for some time, handed over command of Fourth Division to Brigadier O. de T. Lovett, DSO, and left for England and a period of recuperation.

R.A.F. Squadrons arrived and took possession of Sedes airfield. This occupation was accomplished without active intervention on the part of ELAS, but in the face of certain ominous preparations. Salonika was thronged with donkey carts bringing in ELAS supplies and supporters from the countryside. The local newspapers shrieked hysterical vituperation and the streets rang with loud speakers inciting the populace to resist "British intervention". On December 8th an intelligence summary estimated 4,000 ELAS troops to be massed in Salonika, with as many more on call on the outskirts of the town. A number of guns had been hauled in from country districts. On December 10th General Bakirdzis dissolved the Salonika National Guard in bloodless but effective fashion by picketing all approaches to its barracks and refusing to allow the militia, who slept at home, to enter the cantonments. Moving swiftly 7 Indian Brigade managed to recover the National Guardsmen's arms. By this time issue had been joined everywhere in Macedonia between ELAS and the forces of occupation. With heavy fighting proceeding in Athens any hour might bring battle in the north. In view of such possibility the Indian garrisons were withdrawn from all points east of the Styrmon river and concentrated at the port of Kavalla, from whence communications with Salonika by sea could be maintained. Thanks to the firmness and tact of Brigadier Lovett and Mr. Rapp, the British Consul, the expected blow never fell. There is ample evidence that ELAS headquarters in Athens had ordered General Bakirdzis to attack, and that with great good sense that officer had chosen to turn his deaf ear to the instruction. Each day ELAS newspapers trumpeted vast victories in Athens—too vast, it seems, for General Bakirdzis to credit. He chose to wait out events and by shrewd negotiation to obtain some crumbs of compromise. Conferences between this astute soldier and the representatives of Fourth Indian Division became the order of the day. For more than a month the uneasy peace hung on tenterhooks from meeting to meeting.

British and Indian participants will long remember these conferences. Their minutes, with the interruptions, fiery denunciations, soothing irrelevancies and plain and fancy lying, make engrossing reading. High tragedy and low comedy stare from adjoining lines. One of the chief British props was Major Dodson, a Force 133 officer who was very much at home with the Greeks. This officer's suavity was in sharp contrast to the tumultuous belligerence of Markos Viafides, General Bakirdzis' political adviser. While the others sat back, British soldier and Communist agitator plied thrust and counter-thrust; but they were never entirely sure of each other's strokes, since the rival interpreters, each wedded to his master's cause, distorted questions and answers to suit themselves. An unvarying item on every agenda was the activities of a Scarlet Pimpernel organisation, concerning which ELAS complained loud and long. Under the direction of Brigadier Claude Eastman, DSO, CRA, Fourth Indian Division, who had acquired a remarkable influence over the Greeks, hundreds of those proscribed on ELAS black lists had been spirited to safety in Athens. General Avramadis, who had remained at his post when the Governor-General fled, was Brigadier Eastman's stout adjutant in this rescue work. Scarcely a night passed in which in true Baroness Orczy fashion prominent citizens were not smuggled under the eyes of ELAS sentries on to waiting ships in the harbour. Mr. Gwynn, the American Consul-General at Salonika, gave valuable assistance in these "snatch parties". The succession of impudent and daring escapes infuriated ELAS intensely, since many of the intended victims bore valuable information to British Headquarters. Nearly 1,000 members of the former Macedonian gendarmerie, police officers who had remained at their posts during the Axis occupation but who had been obliged to go underground when ELAS took over control, were among those evacuated. Their intimate knowledge of Macedonia was destined to prove invaluable when the rehabilitation of Northern Greece began.

To the incessant complaints, protests and accusations General Lovett replied in all truth that he knew nothing about the matter. It is seldom that a divisional commander has taken greater pains to avoid knowledge of the activities of one of his officers. With the aid of a modest expenditure of cash, Brigadier Eastman managed to penetrate into the inner enemy councils, and there learned that following a mammoth demonstration on December 15th ELAS would move to the attack. In view of this contingency, Royal Sussex, Gurkha and Sikh detachments were recalled from Kavalla; despite threats and clamour this reinforcement of the Salonika garrison was accomplished without incident. Fortunately a blizzard blew on December 15th; the demonstration fizzled out in wintry weather, and with it the projected assault.

With the returning Indian formations from Thrace came Colonel Keown Boyd and his British Military Mission. Colonel Boyd immediately took charge of intelligence work in Salonika, and dealt ELAS a succession of embarrassing blows. Brigadier Eastman in a last coup evacuated a record number of escapees, including no less than a dozen officers of ELAS headquarters as well as General Bakirdzis' Chief of Staff. Following these desertions, two of the constituent parties of the left-wing coalition withdrew their representatives. On January 11th a truce was signed in Athens. Next day General Hawkesworth, Commander 3 Corps, flew to Salonika and in a pointed interview informed General Bakirdzis that the terms of truce would apply to Macedonia. ELAS was in a hopeless position. The partisans were given four days in which to concentrate in defined rural areas. The evacuation of Salonika began immediately. Unfortunately the terms of the truce permitted ELAS to take hostages with them. In bitter wintry weather these wretched prisoners were marched away, under conditions of greatest brutality. Many succumbed to callous treatment, and the fate of others is still unknown.

On January 18th, two battalions of the Greek National Guard arrived from Athens to take over police duties from Fourth Indian Division. As elsewhere these recruits proved quick on the trigger and prone to private settlements with their opponents. In order to hold the scales in even balance, the gendarmerie was accompanied for some time by Indian detachments.

7 Brigade was now free to undertake the urgently needed rehabilitation of Macedonia. Patrols pushed out to make the country roads safe. Once given the "All Clear" Sappers and Miners, medical sections and transport formations moved off to bring succour to the starving countryside.

On January 19th Major-General C. H. Boucher, CBE, DSO, arrived to take command of Fourth Indian Division. After regimental service with 3 Gurkha Rifles and a period as BGS to General Quinan, Commander 10 Army Iraq, General Boucher had commanded 10 Indian Brigade during the ill-fated Knightsbridge Cauldron action in June 1942. Captured when Rommel's panzers overran his headquarters he escaped after the Italian surrender and made his way through the German lines. He took command of 17 Indian Brigade in 8 Indian Division during heavy fighting on the lower Adriatic, at Cassino and on the Gothic Line. General Boucher's small alert figure, quick glance and cheery grin, betokened a tough yet human fighting man of the type that soldiers follow and serve willingly. He was an immediate success with the Greeks.

Day by day the situation in Macedonia eased. British-trained police gendarmerie relieved the National Guard, whose belligerent propensities undoubtedly proved a deterrent to pacification. The British Resident Minister arrived, and supressed two firebrand newspapers which had continued to insult and vilify the forces of occupation. The Governor-Generals of Salonika and of Western Macedonia returned and were re-installed. ELAS forces accepted the restriction of their movements; their adherents as a consequence lost much of their proselytising fervour. A sure indication of the trend of events was the efforts of the Bishop of

Kozani to turn his coat. Through a series of intermediaries this turbulent priest in best cloak-and-dagger fashion made it known to General Boucher that in return for certain perquisites he was prepared to desert ELAS and to support the Government. The negotiations progressed to a point where a direct contact was essential; whereupon the Bishop sent his secretary to Salonika. Unfortunately the Bishop's mistress chose to travel to the same destination on the same day. The secretary enlivened the journey with unwelcome advances. The lady returned to Kozani to complain, and the negotiations ended abruptly, for nothing would induce the almoner to return and to face the wrath of his lord.

The arrival of two British divisions in Southern Greece now permitted Fourth Indian Division to extend its authority throughout Northern Greece. A date was set on which Indian formations would cross the truce boundary and complete the occupation.

Before recording this development it is necessary to report the vicissitudes of 5 and 11 Indian Brigades during the first stormy months of their service in other parts of Greece.

Chapter 30

5 BRIGADE IN ATHENS.

ON November 17th Brigadier Saunders-Jacobs left Taranto to reconnoitre the Aegean Islands, where 5 Brigade was to be dispersed in garrison.

The original plan for the occupation of Greece had allotted Crete to 5 Brigade, but when the German withdrawal on the mainland began, a new Nazi commander flew to that island with instructions to continue resistance. As an enemy force of divisional strength occupied Crete, and as its fate would be settled elsewhere, it was decided not attempt landings. The destination of 5 Brigade was altered to the Dodecanese and Cyclades groups, where commando forces were operating against the various German garrisons. 3 Corps in Athens gave Brigadier Saunders-Jacobs wide latitude. He was instructed to work out all details of defence and rehabilitation. The problems of putting troops ashore and maintaining them on groups of small islands presented a number of posers, and it was not until the end of November that the commander of 5 Brigade returned to Athens with his plan.

By that time, trouble was imminent. On December 3rd, the police opened fire on left-wing demonstrators in Athens. ELAS armed formations appeared on the streets, and surrounded British Headquarters in the Hotel Grande Bretagne. Concurrently British and Greek Naval Headquarters in Piraeus were invested and the harbour area isolated. The outbreak of hostilities found only skeleton British forces in the Greek capital. 2 Parachute Brigade, which had effected the occupation, was at the point of returning to Italy. Only 23 Armoured Brigade and a Greek Field Army Brigade remained near at hand to support the Provisional Government. Reinforcements therefore were flown in; the first to arrive, 2/5 Leicesters and 16 Durham Light Infantry of 139 Infantry Brigade established a tiny perimeter around naval installations at Piraeus. In view of the critical situation Brigadier Saunders-Jacobs was advised that the deployment of 5 Brigade in the Aegean Islands had been cancelled. His men would be brought to Piraeus and incorporated in BLOCK FORCE, which had been entrusted with the task of clearing the harbour area and of maintaining sea communications with the beleaguered Greek capital.

The guerillas were no mean opponents. Nearly 75,000 men had been mobilised under ELAS command in southern Grece. Toughened by underground warfare, embittered by adversity and fanatically devoted to their cause, the Communist recruits comprised first-class fighting material. Their organisation was of standard military design, from corps down to companies. Their equipment was modern and reasonably complete, consisting in part of British arms supplied to the resistance movement, and in part of weapons of German and Italian origin. They possessed little artillery but plentiful supplies of sub-machine guns, grenades and other arms useful in street fighting. They knew the ground and they had few scruples. They were well aware that they were the political protegées of a great Ally. It was necessary to handle them carefully in order to avoid complications, yet the outside world must not gain the impression that British soldiers were unable to deal with them. Much depended on the dexterity and restraint with which the ensuing operations were conducted.

Piraeus, a harbour of great antiquity, is situated on the Saronic Gulf five miles southwest of the centre of Athens. Here the Kallipolis promontory thrusts a blunt cape two miles into the waters of Faliron Bay. To its north the outer, middle and inner basins of the harbour, from 300 to 700 yards in width, intrude into the centre of the town. On the southern side of the promontory, a small landlocked basin (Limin Zeas) bites into the land and creates the Aktion peninsula, so that the Kallipolis promontory narrows to a bare six hundred yards between the two waterfronts. To the northwest of Limin Zeas a pimple of commanding ground rises above the dingy streets. This is Lofos Castella, whose summit is 300 feet above the harbour area. This high cone originally had been fortified against the Germans, who during the occupation of Greece used it as a fortress area to protect the harbour. Situated on the base of the peninsula, one flank of Lofos Castella was secured by the sea. On the land side, a series of fortified strong points, including a railway station, a refrigerator plant and a tobacco factory completed the investment of the quays. Numerous barricades sealed off the streets; as many as twenty road blocks could be counted in a single thoroughfare. The intention of ELAS was to hold the harbour under siege until the British forces in Athens had been defeated.

Quay 8, British and Greek Naval Headquarters, was situated at the tip of the Kallipolis promontory. Prior to the arrival of 5 Brigade, 2/5 Leicesters had courageously endeavoured to extend their tiny perimeter by working up the peninsula. 16 Durham Light infantry had landed on Faliron Bay to the east of Kallipolis in order to protect fuel installations there. Fortunately ELAS had remained passive, content with bottling up the small garrisons. On the night of December 9th 1/4 Essex came ashore at Quay 8. Next morning they passed through the left flank of the Leicesters, and began to clear the surrounding built-up area. Sporadic resistance in the form of snipers and bomb squads disputed the advance but by nightfall the Home County men had gained about 1200 yards and had reached the area of a school on the road Kharikou Trikoupi, which crossed the peninsula at its narrowest point, linking the middle harbour with Faliron Bay. Next morning at 0400 hours, the remainder of 5 Brigade began to disembark. As Brigadier Saunders-Jacobs could not be ferried to Kallipolis on account of the stormy weather, Lieut.-Colonel J. C. Hudson, MC, of 1/9 Gurkhas took temporary command on the peninsula. The Brigade Commander arrived that afternoon.

The plan called for the first operation to be conducted in five stages. The road Kharikou Trikoupi, already reached by the Essex, would be cordoned. Thereafter a beat would mop up all ELAS elements caught behind this barricade. With the lower peninsula secured a second bound would carry the advance to the road Yeoryiou, a main thoroughfare 800 yards further north, which ran across the base of the penisula between the main quay on the inner harbour and Lofos Castella. It would then be necessary to storm Lofos Castella. The final phase of the operation would carry 5 Brigade forward to the line of the railway which skirted Faliron Bay. Here the advancing troops would link up with 16 Durhams and open the road to Athens. Thereafter a second operation would be necessary to clear the main enemy forces from the northern or opposite side of the harbour.

On December 11th 1/4 Essex, working along the line of the road Kharikou Trikoupi, erected a belt of wire across the peninsula. A corvette came into position off Quay 18 to keep the roadway illuminated with its searchlights throughout the night. At 1330 hours on December 12th, 3/10 Baluchis and 1/9 Gurkhas began to search the lower peninsula, routing out ELAS pockets. Resistance at times grew stiff, with mortar squads and machine gun nests active. Companies of Royal Greek Marines accompanied the battalions of 5 Brigade in this advance. These ardent monarchists were intensely bitter fighters and something of a liability, as they tended to shoot at all and sundry; nevertheless their local knowledge was of value. By nightfall on December 13th all ground up to the Essex cordon had been cleansed of the enemy. The Leicesters moved forward to take over the barricade and so release the Home County men for the second phase of the operation, the advance to the road Yeoryiou.

On the morning of December 14th, 1/9 Gurkhas were withdrawn from the sweep, in order to prepare for the assault on Lofos Castella. Essex and Baluchis continued the tedious if dangeraus task of rooting out the opposition. A number of Sherman tanks had been landed; in spite of limited fields of fire they greatly eased the task of the infantry. Corner houses with area entrances which commanded the streets in two directions gave considerable trouble, but the tanks bored in with mopping up squads close behind, and dealt with the defenders before they could do much damage. Lieutenant R. J. W. Craig and Jemedar Sakhi Mohammed of 3/10 Baluchis achieved particular success in the tricky technique of street fighting. Even with tanks in action the advance fell behind its timing. At nightfall the Baluchis were still involved in scuffles in the Limin Zeas area and the Essex, who had battled their way forward along the harbour water-front, likewise were short of their objective. 1/9 Gurkhas' assault on Lofos Castella therefore was postponed for twenty-four hours.

Next morning resistance stiffened, but with armour in the van both battalions continued to make headway. 3/10 Baluchis overran the local ELAS headquarters; the tanks in turn blasted a number of street barricades, opening the way for the infantry. At 1700 hours the welcome bark of 25-pounders was heard. 1 Field Regiment had arrived and had taken up gun positions on Psittalia, a small island in Faliron Bay. The field guns opened on Lofos Castella, which had endured a heavy bombardment on the previous day from naval vessels in the harbour. Unfortunately ammunition supplies were short, and only a preliminary shoot prefaced the Gurkha attack. With guns of necessity silent a composite battery of 1 Field Regiment undertook to fight as infantry in the ensuing assault.*

At 1800 hours that evening (December 15th) 1/9 Gurkhas took over from the righthand company of 3/10 Baluchis along Faliron Bay. The high cone of Lofos Castella stood before them. Concrete emplacements and underground dug-outs gave ample shelter to the garrison; without artillery preparation the stronghold promised to prove a serious obstacle. A silent night attack had been proposed; the Corps Commander approved such plan with the proviso that the Gurkhas should not use their kukris. At 0140 hours on December 16th "C" and "D" Companies, with the gunners of the 1 Field Regiment, made contact with advanced ELAS posts at the foot of the hill. Heavy fire was opened as the infantry began to work up the steep slope. Fierce fighting followed in which the Gurkhas found the light No. 36 grenade a passable substitute for their knives. By dawn they had cleared the western slopes of Lofos Castella, and had obtained a footing on the summit. Captain R. F. P. Harrison of the 1 Field Regiment, although wounded led his men with great gallantry in the final assault. By 1000 hours the position was won.

The crest of Lofos Castella afforded excellent observation over the southern Athenian suburbs and the high ground at the top of the inner harbour. During the forenoon 1/4 Essex relinquished the left sector on the waterfront to 2/5 Leicesters and passed around Lofos Castella to come up on the right of 1/9 Gurkhas. Their carriers pushed out along Faliron Bay and at last light linked up with Durhams, who had extended their perimeter sufficiently to deny ELAS the use of the main road to Athens. Both intentions of 5 Brigade now had been realised—the Kallipolis peninsula had been cleared, and communications had been established between the port and the capital. From ships in

*The time spent in Taranto by 1 Field Regiment had been employed very profitably by Lieut.-Colonel G. Thompson, DSO, in intensive infantry training, with particular reference to close combat in built-up areas. This training had been carried out under the direction of Major Boulton, DSO, 1/9 Gurkhas. Such forethought now reaped a rich reward.

the outer harbour vehicles of 4 British Division began to roll ashore and to proceed in convoy to the Faliron airfield, where the first flights of their infantry awaited them.

The inner harbour alone remained under ELAS control. There was always the possibility of interference from that quarter, and the Royal Navy was insistent that the enemy should be driven out of small arms range of the unloading jetties. A number of British detachments had already established themselves on the north side of the harbour, including 57 LAA Regiment, which was enlarging its already varied war experience by a defence of the power station on St. George's Bay, 2,000 yards to the north. These infiltrations did not necessarily foreshadow the easy ejection of the enemy, who was firmly entrenched in the adjacent suburbs. Behind the devastated quays the built-up area stood on higher ground with a cemetery, a cigarette factory and the Powder House area as the nodal points in the defences.

The thrust across the harbour involved all the problems of a full-scale amphibious operation. On the afternoon of December 19th Brigadier Saunders-Jacobs reconnoitered the northern quays within a few hundred yards of the enemy positions. The Brigade chronicler records that he moved "as nonchalantly as possible". On the following night ELAS heavily attacked 57 LAA Regiment in the Power Station on St. George's Bay. Major Finlay and his gallant gunners spent the hours of darkness in staging a miniature Stalingrad defence.

At dawn the attack died away and the day was calm. That evening low-flying aircraft began a dusk-to-dawn patrol over the waterfront. The roar of their engines was designed to cover the noise of the landing craft and the occasional test-runs of the tanks. Throughout the night without alarm or interference all three battalions of 5 Brigade were ferried over and established in the northern dock area. To create a diversion a naval craft patrolled offshore to the west and simulated activity with a pyrotechnic display.

The infantry in assault waves secured immediate objectives without resistance. It developed that ELAS troops in the neighbourhood, after the attack on Major Finlay and his men of 57 LAA Regiment on the previous night, had slept soundly. A company of 3/10 Baluchis moved off in an endeavour to link up with the anti-aircraft gunners. Detachments of 1/9 Gurkhas silently seized forward posts in an engineering shop and an oil refinery on the ground above the docks. The Indian Docks Operations Company, which had been isolated on this side of the harbour for more than a week under frequent sniping, having covered the landing of 1/4 Essex on the main terminals began to prepare the quays for use. Just before dawn five Sherman tanks arrived and ELAS awakened to find three battalions of infantry well established in a bridgehead a mile and a half in length and a quarter mile in depth.*

*This was Fourth Division's first and only amphibious operation. In the early months of 1942 a Brigade group had been briefed for a landing behind the Axis positions on the Gulf of Sirte; throughout the spring of that year 11 Brigade trained in the Canal area for a similar expedition. Neither project came to fruition.

Recovering from their surprise the enemy lashed out furiously. During the afternoon of December 22nd the stiffest fighting of the Piraeus operation ensued. The Sherman tanks proved invaluable and rocket-firing Beaufighters, working against strong points pinpointed by 5 Brigade, intervened with devastating effect. At 1300 hours after 3½ hours hard fighting all three battalions had advanced to an average depth of 800 yards and were holding the line of the Avenue Dhionisiou across the top of the inner harbour. The Greek Marines dealt effectively with last stand resistance in the rear of the advance.

Throughout that night three further counterattacks fell on 3/10 Baluchis, who held the left flank position adjacent to the tiny Foron inlet. Hand to hand fighting followed in which one company of the Gurkhas was involved. Gurkha and Essex mortar teams from positions across the harbour supplied remarkably accurate concentrations which held up and dispersed the guerillas.

On December 23rd when the advance was resumed progress was slow. Heavy and sustained machine-gun fire from strong points commanding the Brigade position compelled slow and careful infiltration. The battalions battled forward from factory to tenement, from one strong point to the next, driving the defenders before them. Panic-stricken civilians scurried like rabbits ahead of the beat; as the left wing irregulars wore little or no uniform, it was usually necessary to hold fire in order to identify enemies.

For ELAS it was a tragic hour. The tide had turned in Athens and the Communists fought for the survival of the revolution. Their reserves had been rushed in from country districts to make a last bid for victory. On the night of December 23rd they again struck at 3/10 Baluchis, but heavy mortar concentration effectively held them from the close.

At 0900 hours next morning, 5 Brigade again took up the running with an attack on the Powder House, a strong point which had blocked progress to the north of Avenue Dhionisiou. This area consisted of a group of concrete buildings which were held by a force of the enemy estimated at company strength. Heavy mortar and artillery concentrations preceded the assault and Beaufighters with rockets and cannon struck at the ELAS shelters. Demoralised by the hammering the defenders fled. On the following afternoon two companies of the Essex with tank support seized the Papastratos Cigarette Factory, a strong point at the north-east corner of the harbour. Here they took 300 prisoners and found the cellars crowded with 600 women, children and old men, starving and filthy. Strong patrols pushed out around the head of the inner harbour and linked up with 16 Durhams. Thereafter a continuous line nearly three miles in length pinned back the ELAS forces in the southern Athenian suburbs.

On Boxing Day Mr. Churchill and Field-Marshal Alexander arrived in Athens. The latter visited BLOCKFORCE headquarters in Kallipolis accompanied by 3 Corps Commander. There Brigadier Saunders-Jacobs explained his plan for the final clearing of the harbour. It was necessary to drive the enemy from the Evyenia suburb, which blocked the link-up with 57 LAA Regiment. Thereafter an advance of 1000 yards would cut Leoforos Saliminos, the main highway connecting Athens with northern Greece.

At 0900 hours on December 30th 2/5 Leicesters under 5 Brigade command attacked towards the power station on St. George's Bay. The assault proceeded like an exercise. Machine gunners of 3/10 Baluchis from the tops of factory buildings maintained effective overhead covering fire. The mortar sections laid a curtain of shell along the south wall of the Anatasis Cemetery, protecting the right flank of the attack. Dominating ground and communications centres were smothered by concentrations, while the infantry steadily worked forward and winkled out the defenders. At first light next morning the attack was renewed by the Leicesters, with Essex and Baluchis opening fire on their fronts as deception measures. Air and artillery again dealt with the strong points. Shortly after noon the power station on St. George's Bay was reached and the investment of 57 LAA Regiment ended. Following up behind the infantry advance the tanks caught ELAS groups as they fled in disorder into the broken ground to the north of Leoforos Salaminos. An armoured car patrol raced along the highway and established a road block in the open country.

Thus ended 5 Brigade's participation in the Athenian operations. In a three weeks' campaign Piracus had been relieved and the port opened. Casualties had been very light—18 killed and 175 wounded. Enemy casualties were unknown since on most occasions ELAS managed to carry away their dead and wounded. Many guerillas undoubtedly perished under the rubble heaps. 847 prisoners were taken, together with a wide range of weapons and military stores.

On January 5th the general withdrawal of the ELAS forces from Athens began. 5 Brigade patrols thrust forward and found only a few snipers who remained to seek martyrdom. The end of the fighting however brought no rest. On 5 Brigade devolved the task of evacuating and feeding thousands of starving civilians. Piraeus had been heavily damaged during the German occupation and many homeless people had taken up residence in public buildings and factories. When such buildings were battered down the victors inherited the task of finding food and cover for these unhappy refugees. A Brigade Clearing Centre was opened and reserve ration dumps used to feed the starving population. 22,000 meals were served daily by 5 Brigade to the 10,000 civilians under disposition. 26 Field Ambulance set up first aid posts to treat the sick and injured, while the Sappers and Miners constructed water points and latrines.

At the conclusion of active operations Lieut.-General J. L. I. Hawkesworth, 3 Corps Commander, sent the following message to 5 Brigade:

"I wish to send a special message of congratulation to your soldiers from India. Their skill and courage have contributed in very large measure to the successful issue of the recent operations. The bravery of your men and their restraint under great provocation are worthy of the finest warrior races. I am proud to have such gallant and skilful soldiers under my command".

On January 5th 139 Brigade received orders to withdraw the Leicesters and the Durhams, who were to proceed immediately to Patras to reinforce 11 Indian Brigade. 5 Brigade thereupon assumed command of the Piraeus area, and began the construction of a wire barrier from St. George's Bay to Athens, for the purpose of preventing ELAS forces in the country districts from infiltrating into the built-up areas. In connection with this operation nine battalions of National Guards were placed under Brigade command. On January 11th Greek forces took over responsibility for the cordon.

Four days later a truce was signed in Athens and 5 Brigade was ordered to leave for Volos, an important outpost on the east coast of Greece, 150 miles (by road) to the north of the capital. Here ELAS garrisons when repatriated from the Aegean Islands were landed, on their way to a concentration area near Larissa. In Volos ELAS were in complete control. 5 Brigade's stay in this area is thus described in *The Tiger Triumphs*.

"The Volos attitude to the occupation troops evolved in characteristic fashion. During the first few days the Greek press—blatant windy inflammatory broadsheets which passed for newspapers—ignored the garrison, and gave themselves over to scurrilous abuse of Mr. Churchill. When this drew no response, alleged atrocity stories from returned ELAS prisoners of war were played up, with flaring wood block headlines and a wealth of gruesome detail. Once again the lethargic British ignored the insults. This apathy was unendurable. Delegations began to pester the Brigade Commander with every conceivable complaint, fortified by the most impudent falsehoods. The Greeks talked and talked; British officers listened and listened. Towards the end of January fatigue set in and wronged parties grew less plentiful. A newly recruited battalion of the National Guard arrived in time to save the situation. In a trice the alleged abominations of Indians and British were forgotten in a spate of venom directed against the Greek soldiers who sided with law and order".

When Fourth Indian Division early in March crossed the truce boundary in Macedonia, 5 Brigade handed over its responsibilities in Volos to elements of 4 British Division, and moved north to share in the last task set for the wearers of the Red Eagle — the rehabilitation of Northern Greece.

Chapter 31

GREECE — 11 BRIGADE IN THE PELOPONNESE

AT the end of September, 1944, when the Germans began to withdraw from the rocky and detached southern headland of Greece, British forces were on their heels. Special service troops under Lieut-Colonel Lord Jellicoe * landed on the outskirts of Patras, the principal port on the straits which separate the Peloponnese from the Greek mainland. After desultory fighting they cleared the town and established Allied authority before either of the principal Greek factions could set up any form of government.

There had been less tension and privation in the Peloponnese than in any part of Greece. The peninsula is one of the chief food growing areas of the Kingdom, and for much of the war it had been administered by Italians in lenient fashion. The fundamental political schism existed, but the gulf of Corinth separated the EDES on the mainland from the predominantly left wing highlands of the Peloponnese. Western Greece therefore was not regarded as a critical area and the initial plan for 11 Brigade group called for a wide dispersal of small garrisons, whose task would be less to restore order than to inspire confidence through the presence of British troops.

At the end of the Italian campaign Brigadier Partridge had relinquished command of 11 Brigade to Brigadier H. C. J. Hunt DSO, the former commander of 11 KRC, which co-operated with Fourth Indian Division in the Maiellas during the 1944 tour of duty on the Lower Adriatic. Brigadier Hunt was no stranger to India having been born at Simla. At one time he was seconded to the Indian Police for special intelligence duties in Bengal. A young and vigorous officer, he was particularly qualified for the diversified problems of command in Greece.

While 11 Brigade awaited transport at Taranto, Brigadier Hunt instructed his officers in the nature of their new task. Guarantee of internal security, support of the Provisional Government and political neutrality epitomised his brief. On November 1st the Brigade commander and his reconnaisance party proceeded by sea to Athens and thence onwards by road to Patras, where they arrived on November

*Three years before, Central India Horse had picked up this gallant young officer (then a subaltern in the Coldstream Guards) on the Agheila road in a state of exhaustion, after escape from the Germans.

5th. After a five days' detailed examination of the area, Brigadier Hunt returned to the capital and voiced his uneasiness over the tactical insecurity of the area and the wide dispersal of his forces. The plan called for 11 Brigade to find garrisons for four sectors. The northern sector, covering the Greek mainland as far as and including Corfu, was allocated to Lieut.-Colonel D. M. Connel-McDowell DSO and his 2/7 Gurkha Rifles. The central sector comprised Missolonghi area, on the northern shore of the straits, where Lieut.-Colonel R. B. Reford MC took charge with 3 Royal Frontier Force Regiment. In the Peloponnese proper Lieut.-Colonel A. J. Noble MC with 2 Camerons provided the garrison, with company detachments at Pyrgos and Aiyon, outposts on either side of Patras. Lieut.-Colonel I. G. Clarke MC and 149 Anti-Tank Regiment was allotted command in the southern Ionian islands of Kephallinia and Zante.

On November 17th the leading flight of 11 Brigade group sailed for Patras. 2 Camerons were first to arrive and found the situation less favourable than had been hoped. As elsewhere the disarmed "Security Battalions" were a bone of contention. The British special service troops, in an endeavour to avoid friction, had removed these collaborationists from the port. The local irregulars, consisting of elements of 3 ELAS Division, having been robbed of their principal prey, were fostering reprisals against the gendarmerie, the Patras police and a long roster of political opponents whom they denounced as traitors. The situation possessed an air of unreality. The civil population, if unmolested, exhibited almost undue enthusiasm for their British guests. On arrival the local ELAS leaders likewise were voluble in their offers of cooperation. But thereafter day by day, as with the coming of winter, a chill grew between the partisans and the forces of occupation. British and ELAS minds did not move in the same groove, nor were their aims convergent. This bleakness found a focal point when on November 24th the Greek Government called the 1936 class to the colours as recruits for the newly commissioned National Guard. Colonel Tsikliteras, the commander of ELAS troops, offered full facilities in the formation of the local battalion and arranged to find billeting space for the conscripts in the barracks of one of his regiments. This manoeuvre was accepted in good faith, although it placed the recruits at the mercy of the well-armed ELAS contingent.

On November 29th Brigadier Hunt presided at a conference of the principal Greek Government officials and ELAS representatives. It was arranged that the National Guard should assume responsibility for Patras as from December 1st. Thereafter it would extend its authority bit by bit into the country districts. When the question of handing over arms was raised Colonel Tsikliteras declared that he had direct orders not to relinquish his weapons and that these orders were of later date than the instructions from British Land Forces Greece. The matter was referred to Athens for adjustment but on December 1st ELAS refused to honour their previous agreement to hand over duties in Patras, claiming again that no instructions had been received to this effect from their own headquarters. Colonel Tsikliteras insisted that a fresh agreement between the Greek Government and ELAS had been consummated.

It became evident that the local Communist forces were playing for time. In Missolonghi the ELAS commander went further and informed the British representative that he did not recognise the existing Greek Government, would not hand in his arms, nor would he disband his forces. Faced with these menacing attitudes Brigadier Hunt issued an operational directive, outlining plans for both offensive and defensive action throughout the Peloponnese. It specified that any operation in support of law and order should be undertaken initially by British troops and that only when the British units were exhausted numerically would Indian formations be employed.

On December 3rd the ELAS commander in Patras assured Brigadier Hunt that his forces would be disbanded in conformity with instructions. This assurance constituted an example of deliberate double dealing, for that night the National Guard detachments in Patras and Pyrgos were surrounded and disarmed, the men being taken into the mountains. Next morning the ELAS commander impudently denied all knowledge of the occurrence. In Pyrgos Lieut.-Colonel Noble was negotiating with Major Mandukos, a two-faced officer who followed up the disarming of the National Guard with broadcasts to the effect that the Greek Government had fallen and that the Communists had assumed power in all parts of the country. When the Camerons commander called Mandukos and his political commissar to account a stormy interview followed. A general strike was declared next morning but the garrison, with the aid of Lieutenant Riley and a detachment of the R.A.F. Regiment, effectively countered the truculent partisans and maintained the public services. In Patras a similar strike produced 300 volunteers from the professional classes who operated the town services under British protection.

The Royal Frontier Force Regiment and 11 Field Regiment had begun the move from Patras to their garrison station at Missolonghi. On December 12th S.S. "Empire Dace" on its eighth trip across the straits, struck a mine in a previously clean channel. 70 were killed and 40 wounded. Three days later a landing craft was blown up on almost the same spot. Although no proof was forthcoming it seems tolerably certain that ELAS had mined the channel. Thereafter landings were transferred to Krioneri, a small wayport ten miles to the east of Missolonghi.

On report of this disaster 3 Corps Headquarters Athens ordered the arrest of all ELAS commanders and political advisers in the Peloponnese. It was decided to establish martial law as from 2000 hours on December 6th and to make the arrests at that hour. Unfortunately a B.B.C. news bulletin two hours earlier announced that the Greek Government had resigned. Hard on its heels a "stand fast" signal arrived from

3 Corps. This tardy advice made it impossible to countermand the arrest orders in outlying areas and it became necessary to make releases, to return arms, and to proffer apologies. Such admissions of error did nothing to quieten the truculent partisans. Faced with a critical situation in Athens, 3 Corps modified its instructions to 11 Brigade a second time and again the concessions were regarded as signs of weakness. From day to day demonstrations and inflammatory newspaper articles whipped up excitement. It became evident that it would be unsafe to disperse detachments over a wide area. Orders to garrison Corfu and the northern mainland were rescinded and 2/7 Gurkhas, en route from Italy, were directed into Patras. "D" Company of the Camerons was withdrawn from Pyrgos and the R.A.F. detachments from Araxos airfield. ELAS forces in the neighbourhood of Patras were now estimated at the strength of a division. Communist families moved into the countryside as the partisans began to fortify commanding ground and key buildings.

For a week a precarious equilibrium was preserved. Daily the ELAS leaders voiced their desire for peace; nightly they prepared for battle. Each morning scurrilous broadsheets preached hatred; each afternoon British, Indians, ELAS and civilians flocked amicably to the stadium to watch sports programmes and football matches. Only the sang-froid and self-possession of the occupation troops kept the spark from the tinder. Brigadier Hunt wrote:

"One of the reasons why the whole affair did not explode in our faces was the stolid good humour of British and Indian soldiers, who refused to be rattled by the most obvious provocations".

On December 14th, in the course of transferring detachments of Royal Frontier Force Regiment and gunners from Agrinion to Krioneri a truck was ambushed. Three British officers and four other ranks were seized as hostages. Another officer, sent under a white flag to negotiate, likewise was imprisoned. An intercepted telephone message revealed plans for an attack upon the small garrison in Krioneri. That evening an impudent demand for surrender of that port was received and refused. At dawn on December 15th ELAS opened the assault with a shower of mortars. Two platoons of Royal Frontier Force Regiment were driven in from the high ground; harassing fire accounted for approximately 20 casualties throughout the day. A naval craft offshore came to the rescue and obtained direct hits on at least one hostile mortar group. The attack was not pressed home and that evening the garrison was withdrawn.

Among other detachments ordered into Patras was Major Russell and a few men of 149 Anti-Tank Regiment, who had proceeded on reconnaissance to Kephallinia, the largest of the Ionian Islands. Here the ELAS commander had disowned the Central Government and had seized power. He disarmed the reconnaissance party by treachery and imprisoned them. A caique sent from Patras to evacuate this group likewise was seized.

By the middle of December, therefore, Patras remained the only foothold of British troops in Western Greece. The partisans, excited by their small successes, sought a trial of strength in the main centre of occupation. The civilian population of the port remained friendly; several thousand Greeks proffered deepest sympathy and risked reprisals by attending the funerals of the Krioneri victims. The patience of British and Indians alike now had worn thin. They had borne insults, they had seen their dead; their commanders, leaning backward in an effort to maintain peace, found it necessary to confine all ranks to barracks. Once again forebearance was construed as pusillanimity. On December 27th the local ELAS leader confronted Brigadier Hunt with a series of impertinent demands and indicated that he would no longer respect the status quo. A heavy infiltration of ELAS troops into Patras began and all evidence pointed to an imminent attack. The occupation forces, however, having made prudent dispositions, kept their heads and waited. A series of Christmas entertainments was arranged to which the ELAS officers were invited. £200 was subscribed by the British forces to the Mayor's fund for the relief of the poor. Children's parties, games, concerts and dances maintained the spirit of the season and at least the outward appearance of peace and goodwill. December 25th passed with the latently hostile partisans sharing the festivities. In the hope of further easing the tension Brigadier Hunt on Boxing Day promulgated a training plan to occupy the next three months, making it clear that such training implied the early re-deployment of his men against the Germans or the Japs.

The holiday spirit swiftly dissipated. On December 28th, as the first detachments of the garrison moved out of Patras in search of training areas, they were stopped by ELAS pickets. This action was perhaps due to misunderstanding but the incident re-established the tension and the streets once more rang with loudspeakers blaring denunciations and abuse of the occupation forces. The news sheets excelled themselves in vituperation yet in the same week half the voting males of Patras invited trouble by signing a testimonial to the Brigade Commander, thanking him for the conduct of his troops. Such tribute, welcome as it was, was not sufficient to alleviate the strain on the British units who had borne the brunt of the provocation. Reports had arrived of the fighting in Athens. Men learned of comrades killed or spirited away as hostages. A number of British and Indian soldiers had been assaulted and robbed. In Patras the Krioneri funerals and the disappearance of the Kephallinia party contributed their quota of bitterness. Confident of their ability to deal with their arrogant and treacherous adversaries, the British soldiers walked more lightly, arms at the ready. Fortunately no incident occurred and the New Year opened with peace hanging by a thread.

The end of the tension was near. On January 2nd 3 Corps advised Brigadier Hunt that the meeting with the ELAS representatives had proved abortive and that 11 Brigade must make all preparations to defend Patras. Brigadier Hunt thereupon made a strong appeal for permission to take the offensive. In reply 3 Corps extended him full discretion, provided that he act in conformity with broad British policy in Greece. The Corps instruction added the welcome news that 139 Infantry Brigade with two squadrons of 50 Royal Tank Regiment and one brigade of the Greek National Guard would soon be on their way to Western Greece.

On January 5th the interminable and futile series of conferences with ELAS ended. A state of armed truce began. On January 9th a convoy of transports and warships appeared off Patras. Disembarkations began immediately, with tanks first to land. At sight of them the Bishop of Patras and the Mayor hurried to Headquarters to offer their services as mediators. Brigadier Block of 139 Brigade, who had been instructed to take over command, had dealt with Communist negotiators before. He peremptorily ordered all ELAS formations to evacuate Patras within forty-eight hours. The partisans' commanders, bursting with indignation at such summary treatment, demanded a conference. They spoke much of their honour and blustered. Two hours before the expiry of the ultimatum they phoned to state that rather than submit Patras to the horrors of Athens, they would withdraw.

11 Brigade immediately emerged from its wired-in beach-head, pushed out to the edge of the town and despatched patrols into the countryside. Substantial ELAS forces were discovered four miles to the southeast in the neighbourhood of the village of Klaus, where they covered the mountain line of withdrawal into the southern Peloponnese. At 2200 hours on January 13th Brigadier Hunt issued orders to intercept and disarm all ELAS troops in 11 Brigade's area, which had been defined as a mountainous pocket approximately forty miles in depth along the Gulf of Corinth. In spite of bad weather and deep snow three columns moved off at first light next morning, happy to be at work after the strain of waiting.

2 Camerons traversed the southeast boundary of the pocket and in spite of patrol clashes and inclement weather reached its objective at Kalavrita on the third day. The Royal Frontier Force Regiment moved eastwards along the Gulf of Corinth and made excellent progress after brushing aside ELAS rearguards at a number of road blocks. At Kamarais, seventeen miles to the east of Patras on the coastal road, a Greek destroyer cooperated by shelling the retiring partisans. On January 15th "C" Company of Royal Frontier Force Regiment, after an arduous 15 mile march under full pack, closed the cordon by junction with the Camerons at Kalavrita. Thereafter patrols systematically began to quarter the mountain areas, disarming the scattered irregulars and bringing in quantities of military stores.

2/7 Gurkhas were given the task of dealing with the defiant concentration in the villages around Klaus. They passed across the mountains by night and at dawn on January 14th arrived in the rear of the ELAS positions. Concurrently a mobile column from 139 Brigade with a troop of tanks advanced frontally against the partisans. It was hoped that if surprised and surrounded the enemy would surrender. The mobile column from 139 Brigade was delayed by road blocks and before negotiations could take place fighting broke out between the Gurkhas and ELAS groups in the hills behind the village. Throughout the morning a series of encounters occurred but by early afternoon the Gurkhas had dispersed the irregulars, who left 22 killed, 32 wounded and 84 prisoners behind them. Two Gurkhas were killed and two wounded. On January 15th when the truce was signed in Athens Brigadier Hunt received orders that no further action was to be taken against ELAS, who were to be allowed to withdraw from his area, taking their arms, ammunition and equipment with them. On January 19th patrols reported that all partisans had complied with the armistice terms. Preparations at once began for the move to rejoin Fourth Indian Division. By January 25th 11 Brigade had concentrated at Patras, awaiting transport.

The final episode of the Peloponnese operation dealt with the recovery of the reconnaissance group from 149 Anti-Tank Regiment, which had been seized as hostages on Kephallinia. This party together with the crew of the captured caique had been taken to Astakos, on the mainland to the northwest of Missolonghi. Thereafter they were marched for 100 miles on foot through the snowy mountains, to be imprisoned in Tatana monastery under appalling conditions. Fortunately an UNNRA detachment was able to supply food and clothing. Following the truce in Athens successive delays occurred and it was not until January 30th that the party was released. Thereafter in the face of considerable hardship Major Russell and his men made their way overland to Missolonghi and thence along the Gulf of Corinth to the village of Eppalion, where they were picked up by Brigadier Hunt on February 15th.

Thus ended an episode in which British and Indian troops were tried almost beyond endurance, yet by forbearance and discipline achieved their ends. No sterner test confronts the soldier than to be obliged to accept without retaliation the insults and threats of his enemies. 11 Brigade endured such ordeal, and emerged triumphant.

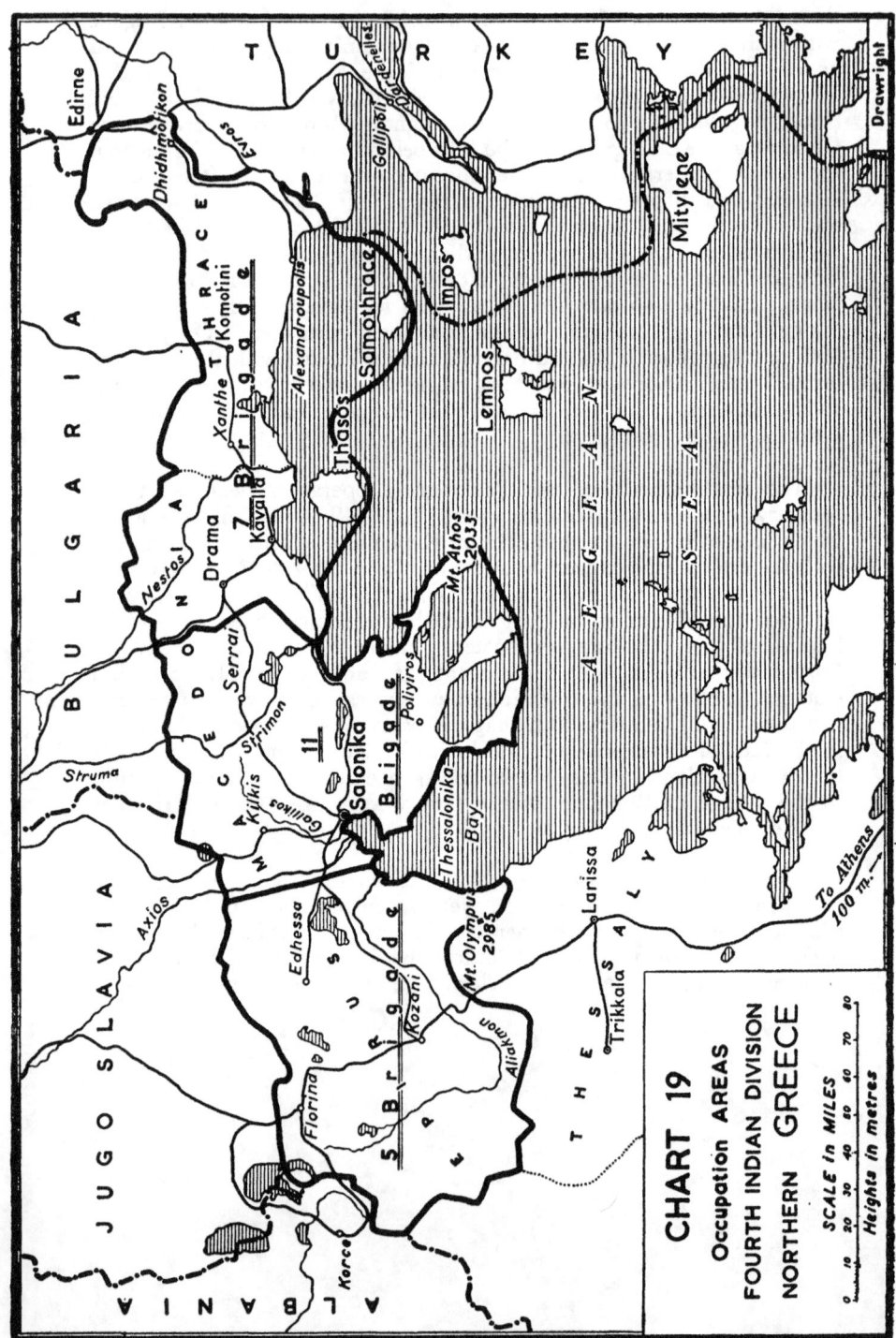

Chapter 32

GREECE — THE LAST PHASE —
REHABILITATION OF NORTHERN GREECE

ON February 19th, 1945, the Divisional Commander outlined the future rôle of Fourth Indian Division. Its primary task was to extend the authority of the Provisional Government into all parts of Northern Greece. The National Guard battalions, then in course of recruitment, would be the instrument of such authority. British troops after inducting these formations would be held in reserve to support them in emergency. The sooner Greek forces could accept responsibility the sooner British troops would go home.

Fourth Indian Division was instructed to cross the truce boundary on March 2nd. The occupation thereafter would proceed in stages. One week after the British forces had moved into any area, National Guards units would follow. A week later British troops would begin to collect arms; on the same date the Greek authorities would call up local classes for service in the National Guard. A fortnight later equipment and clothing would be issued to the conscripts and their training would begin. When this routine had been completed in one area the process would be repeated elsewhere.

On March 2nd 7 and 11 Brigades moved out of Salonika leaving the Rajputana Rifles Machine Gun Battalion, 1 Field Regiment and a squadron of 40 Royal Tank Regiment in garrison. The truce line was crossed without incident and both brigades spread out over the *nomes* (departments) of Khalkidike, Thessalonica, Kilkis and Pella. In almost all centres the occupying troops were well received by the inhabitants. The National Guards units in turn followed in. Progress was sufficiently smooth to allow the timing to be stepped up and in the middle of March the occupation of a second area began. 7 Brigade turned eastward into Thrace and took over successive departments of that turbulent province. By March 29th 1/2 Gurkhas had reached Alexandroupolis near the Turkish frontier. The arrival of the National Guards in this out-of-the-way spot led to a faction fire-fight which necessitated the intervention of the armoured cars of Central India Horse and of a company of Gurkhas. Approximately 300 German prisoners were gathered up along the Turkish frontier.

With the arrival of 5 Brigade from Volos, 11 Brigade relinquished all responsibilities west of the Axios river. The deployment of Fourth Division therefore was completed with 7 Brigade in Thrace and Eastern Macedonia, 11 Brigade in Central Macedonia, 5 Brigade in Western Macedonia. Patrols and garrison detachments pushed out as far as the Bulgarian, Yugo-Slav and Albanian frontiers. Divisional Headquarters remained in Salonika. 5 Brigade Headquarters was situated at Verroia, forty-five miles to the west of Salonika, with 1/4 Essex at Edhessa and at Florina on the Yugo-Slav frontier. 3/10 Baluchis dropped a company at Naousa while the remainder of the battalion joined 1/9 Gurkhas in garrison of the notorious Kozani area. In the central sector 3 Royal Frontier Force Regiment reinforced the Salonika garrison; 2 Camerons occupied Serres and 2/7 Gurkhas Kilkis, unruly centres to the south of the Bulgarian frontier. In the east, in addition to the Royal Sussex at Drama and Kavalla, 1/2 Gurkhas held the central area at Xanthe, with 2 Royal Sikhs at Komotini in the much disputed tongue of eastern Thrace. 7 Brigade also provided garrisons for the island of Thasos in the northern Aegean.

In their introductory sweeps through the countryside the officers and men of Fourth Division discovered the magnitude of their task in the Macedonian hinterland. Living had sunk to brute level. The scorched earth policy and the Bulgarian influx had left the inhabitants starving, houseless and naked. Communications had broken down. Authority had disappeared or if maintained was engrossed with reprisals against neighbours. The hungry wasted for want of a handful of grain; the sick died for lack of the simplest remedies. The mountains were devils' cauldrons in which hate stewed, in which violence and disorder represented the normal routine. The political fanatics drew support in their feuds from gangs of hooligans intent upon plunder. Every man was a partisan who regarded the occupation forces either as partners or as enemies. Either rôle promised equal complications to troops whose only interest was to maintain law and order. As one officer put it:

"We were involved in the business of fair play, of having to impose a reasonable way of life, a system of justice and of fair trial upon everyone. But neither side could see it like that. To the National Guard ELAS and Communism was a fatal malignant disease which must be cut out. To suggest justice for a Communist, they said, was an absurdity, a contradiction of terms. ELAS on their part cried 'Fascists' even more loudly. The National Guard, they said, were stormtroopers and the forerunners of another dictatorship. When we arrested a Nationalist officer ELAS hailed it as a victory. The Nationalists were equally jubilant when an ELAS member got into trouble".

The lawless elements usually avoided contact with the British and Indian troops, and except for occasional patrol clashes and a certain amount of long-range sniping few incidents were reported. In the towns political eruptions sometimes led to military intervention. The normal aftermath of such a disturbance would be a strike, which usually petered out in a rowdy demonstration. Calm would follow and for a season everyone would be angelically reasonable; then the wrongs, the intrigues and the slights would be resuscitated and after a spate of wild harangues the factions again would spring at each other's throats.

The induction of the National Guard battalions provided British and Indian officers with many headaches. The arrival of the Guardsmen often emboldened the Royalist groups to undertake reprisals against the Communists. It took a great deal of patient tutelage to convince the newcomers that they must enforce order with equal justice on all factions. In ELAS areas the National Guards were inclined to discover disturbances; in Royalist areas to condone them. On more than one occasion they reported naively that they had been obliged to fire in the air and that casualties had resulted. Right wing bands sometimes were allowed to roam unmolested. The ELAS forces for their part drew succour from over the frontier. The Macedonian Autonomist Movement, fostered by Yugo-Slavia and led by the notorious guerilla leader Gotsis, maintained a reign of terror in central Macedonia. The National Guards were powerless until the Essex with Central India Horse and tanks took a hand. In a full scale sweep they hunted Gotsis out of reach but never managed to bring him to book.

The situation improved when the local age groups were trained, but at no time could the National Guard be regarded as a satisfactory substitute for a police force. Fortunately the provision of such a force was not long delayed. In the spring of 1945 a group of British officers drawn from the Metropolitan Police, Royal Ulster Constabulary and the Palestine Police arrived in Greece to reconstruct the gendarmerie. The personnel snatched from ELAS by Brigadier Eastman's Scarlet Pimpernels provided an experienced nucleus for the reconstituted Macedonian and Thracian Divisions. When these active and impartial officers returned to duty they quickly made their presence felt, and relieved Fourth Indian Division of many onerous responsibilities.

One military duty Fourth Indian Division retained — the collection of arms. ELAS had evaded their undertakings and had buried weapons and equipment all over the countryside. When National Guardsmen were entrusted with recovery missions they reverted to regrettable practices to elicit information. When they uncovered *caches* the weapons more often than not were reissued to friends. British and Indian troops therefore indulged in many engrossing games of hunt the thimble and of searching the right haystacks for the illicit needles. Greek methods of concealment, wrote one officer admiringly "are as many and as varied as on the Northwest Frontier". A Camerons chronicler thus described the arrival of a search party at a village on the Bulgarian frontier:

"While the reception was cold it was not silent. The people lined the street, gathered in the main square, and cried 'Zito ELAS, Zito

KKE,' intending us to comprehend their Communist solidarity. We chose to misunderstand, beamed at all and sundry and joined in with loud 'Zitos'. This could not have pleased the ELAS organisers of the demonstration, nor could the disarming way in which the Jocks stuck up their thumbs and saluted with their fists, with complete impartiality and disregard of its political significance. As a result in this town there was shortly to blossom a new one-fingered salute, a cross between an Elizabethan pulling of the forelock and the hi-de-hi of a Harlem dance hall".

Lovat Scouts (who with 2 Highland Light Infantry joined Fourth Division in July) on a similar raid encountered a fascinating gallery of queer characters. There was the Vice-President — "wears a multi-coloured shirt, black knicker-bockers that have lost one knee, with yellow and red striped pyjamas as underwear and a fashionable lounge coat of vivid Glen Urquhart check with wasp waist and padded shoulders". With him was Hatchet Face, "a cold killer type"; "Constantinos, a heavy-jowled burly brute with two revolvers and an ugly knife dangling between his ample buttocks, with a German stick grenade nestling snugly against his bulging paunch".

The scene is vividly drawn:

"Late in the evening we sat around a small table beneath the village tree; the Interpreter, the Headman, a wild-eyed corporal and myself. An omelette drenched in grease lay in a communal plate. We picked at it negligently with tiny forks. Ouzo is brought. The light is gradually fading. Village belles feeling safe in their numbers and increasing darkness walked up and down peering at us and giggling".

"Then through the night came The Informer. He sidled up to our table and whispered hoarsely in the Headman's ear".

These searches, at first barren, soon became profitable. Arms, ammunition, motorcycles, and a wide range of military stores were conjured out of open fields, ditches, manure heaps, hollow trees, lavatories and barns. On one occasion the Camerons unearthed quantities of food, sugar and clothing in a hungry and ragged village. The inhabitants had not dared to examine the ELAS *caches*.

Expeditions by British and Indian troops assisted the Greek Government in the compilation of the new electoral register. Patrols visited isolated villages and by checking with the Headman satisfied themselves as to the impartiality of the lists. Registrars were instructed to enroll everyone, even including ELAS fugitives on the run in the mountains. The following characteristic return reveals the pathetic devastation of war:

VILLAGE OF ....
1. Communications—None.
2. Education—School burned by Bulgars.
3. Religion—Priest killed by Bulgars.
4. Employment—None.
5. Food reserves—None.
6. Clothing—Rags.

Comment: Supplies of everything urgently needed.

In the wake of such patrols the Divisional services moved out to repair damage and alleviate suffering. When the truce boundary was crossed, Lieut.-Colonel L. A. B. Paten, CRE, had only 12 Field Company, 11 Field Park Company and 5 Bridging Section under his command. (On February 28th 21 Field Company arrived from Patras and on March 19th 4 Field Company moved from Volos to Kozani). There was scarcely an undamaged bridge in Northern Greece and roads of all classes had deteriorated to a common state of disrepair. On the main road to Athens a bridge 800 feet long over the Gallikos river had been destroyed. This site received early attention and a level timber deck bridge was in operation as early as January 29th. The Axios, the next river to the west, offered an even more formidable obstacle: out of fourteen steel spans totalling 1834 feet in length, five had been demolished together with the three central piers. With the aid of the invaluable Bailey sections the Indian engineers manfully pushed repairs to completion. Local labour was employed to some extent but in the words of Colonel Paten, "They wanted more pay than the rules in force allowed us to give and they were not prepared to work either in the morning or in the evening or when the wind blew, which was frequently". After the opening of these main bridges the Sappers and Miners steadily moved further afield. In each of the brigade areas the Field Company became responsible for bridge building, road maintenance, and salvage of industrial plant. Bridging operations were mostly in the west, where six permanent masonry bridges were constructed to raise the category of the Verroia-Kozani road. The broad Aliakmon watercourse, crossed by two main roads to Athens, was bridged at Yidha and near Servia, the latter bridge being opened by His Beatitude the Bishop of Macedonia and appropriately named "Red Eagle" Bridge. Month by month the work went on. The following tabulation summarises the splendid contribution of Fourth Indian Division Sappers and Miners to the task of rehabilitation:—

Class of Structure	Number	Total Foot Run
1. Permanent structures in masonry or concrete	15	398
2. Temporary timber bridges	5	996
3. Temporary Bailey bridges	13	1000
4. Semi-permanent Bailey bridges	5	1040
5. Semi-permanent Flambo bridges	6	844
Total:—	44	4278 ft.

The sparse forage of Macedonia compels constant flock and herd migrations. When the interruption of communications penned cattle and sheep in local grazing areas they died in thousands. While bridges were under construction over the Axios, Strymon and Aliakmon rivers, 4 Field Company in Western Macedonia and 12 Field Company in the central area undertook to build and to operate flying ferries in order to serve essential traffic. A Sapper diarist supplies a lively picture of the day's work at these crossings:

"Civilian vehicles arrive burdened to breaking point with an odd assortment of merchandise and livestock—black market goods. Perched precariously on top of these swaying loads is a seething mass of humans ranging from babes in arms to venerable greybeards — all champing at the bit, to get across the ferry. Shepherds with great flocks of sheep and goats make their way from the south into Western Macedonia. To date several hundreds of thousands of animals have been safely transported across. Gypsies are always on the trek. These picturesque and colourful Romanys roll up to the ferry in large numbers with their horses and donkeys. Their animals are always loaded to capacity with gaily coloured bundles of rugs and blankets. Romanys seem to be the same the world over: whenever they arrive, a fierce altercation arises between them and the shepherds as to who shall cross first. Fights are not uncommon and the rival dogs start their own private wars in sympathy. To help the traveller find the ferries, the approaches to the sites have been well marked with road and bridge signs. These signs invariably disappear. It is understood that they make ideal frying pans".

Between Verroia and Kozani the main highway to Athens traversed a high pass on the slopes of Mont Olympus which customarily was snowbound between December and March. The sparse forces at the disposal of 3 Corps made it imperative that road communications with Northern Greece should be maintained throughout the winter season. Fourth Division thereupon established detachments on this stretch of highway which kept the road open, recovered ditched vehicles and cared for stranded travellers. Signallers, recovery sections, ambulance sections, engineer and postal sections and welfare officers in charge of rest rooms and transit camps, were among the Divisional personnel enrolled in this enterprise.

British and Indian signallers followed the Sappers and Miners everywhere. The Germans had completely destroyed the Greek telephone system. The dispersal of small detachments over an area three times the size of Wales imposed a heavy task upon Lieut.-Colonel Taylor and the Divisional signallers. Trunk lines to Athens and Salonika were supplemented by feeder services into the hinterland. The linking up of outlying detachments on frontier patrol and in the mountains enabled the Greek authorities to obtain a rapid and comprehensive over-all picture of the day-to-day situation.

With communications opened the Divisional medical services moved swiftly to the succour of the civilian population. 26 Field Ambulance already had been at work in Volos, where thousands of prisoners of war and hostages had been found in deplorable condition. Under an arrangement with the Communist commander the Field Ambulance took over ELAS patients, returning them under Red Cross protection when cured. More than 400 Greek out-patients were treated daily and the Field Ambulance evolved into a General Hospital, employing and paying its own civilian specialists.

In Macedonia and Thrace the medical situation was at its worst. Many villages had been burned out and the wretched peasants exposed to the rigours of winter. Weakened by cold, hunger and ill-treatment, they sickened and died by hundreds. Under Lieut.-Colonel H. J. R. Thorne, DSO, ADMS, (formerly commander of 17 Field Ambulance and one of the veteran officers of the Division) the medical services undertook a health survey of Northern Greece. (While engaged in the compilation of the electoral register patrols also had assembled vital statistics.) 17 Field Ambulance was based on Kavalla, 26 Field Ambulance on Verroia, 32 Field Ambulance on Salonika. Detachments of 15 Field Hygiene Section, 2, 3, 12 and 131 Dental Sections and a number of malaria control units were under command. Outlying detachments were stationed in thirteen centres. To these Samaritans the civilians flocked in thousands, until the medical officers were of two minds — whether to be resentful of the overwork or grateful for the wealth of unusual medical experience. UNRRA provided medical supplies with the aid of which a number of epidemic diseases, due to malnutrition and exposure, were brought under control. The training of the newly organised National Guard medical detachments likewise devolved on the Divisional officers. The Field Hygiene Section, consisting of two officers and 100 men, laboured unceasingly to inculcate the principles of modern hygiene in a countryside which had never heard of sanitation. A museum was established as a training centre in which the Greeks were shown the chain of development of infectious diseases and modern methods of eradication. Three officers and a handful of men, in addition to attending to the teeth of 18,000 troops of the Division, gave free dental services to the civilian population.

The Malaria Control Sections, mustering a few score workers, laboured in one of the most difficult areas in the world. Macedonian mosquitoes had taken a prodigious toll of the Allied forces during the First World War. In 1916 one out of every four men in the Salonika command had contracted malaria; in 1917 two out of every five; in 1918 every other man on service in this theatre was the victim of this unpleasant and debilitating fever. By rigid camp discipline and the use of modern methods of control Fourth Indian Division reduced the malaria toll to one case in every 50 British troops and one in every 125 sepoys — a magnificent achievement which if repeated in the home villages of India would go far to repairing the health of the subcontinent. The ADMS could say proudly, when only 173 cases of fever were reported in 1945, "This malaria campaign should be regarded as one of the great battles which this Division has fought and won". The success of the Malaria Control units in Macedonia drew widespread attention and the Supreme Allied Commander sent a message of congratulation in which the magnitude of the achievement was properly recognised.

British, American, and British Dominions Red Cross teams arrived in Macedonia to supplement the efforts of the Indian Medical Services. These young women in a sense joined Fourth Indian Division, to mutual pleasure and advantage. A number of the unit diaries voice pride in these gallant girls who penetrated into every corner of the Macedonian hinterland on their errands of mercy. The Cameron diarist wrote:

"British Red Cross women helped us magnificently by bringing food and clothing to the distressed villages which we visited. On arrival of the Red Cross team of thirteen girls our patrols were mixed so that the search for arms and the distribution of food, clothing and medical supplies went on simultaneously. Perhaps this was contrary to the Geneva Convention — we wouldn't know. Certain it was, however, that the girls added a glamour to our work which was stimulating both to the villagers and to ourselves. This one Red Cross team was worth another battalion of infantry".

An allotment of 120,000 Red Cross parcels, no longer needed for distribution to prisoners of war, was offered on the condition that Fourth Division should undertake distribution. This was no mean task, the weight of the consignment alone being almost prohibitive with the transport available in the Division. An officer of 1/2 Gurkha Rifles thus describes a characteristic distribution:

"A nominal roll divided the village families into two queues, one on each side of the square. Town ushers were produced to call out the names. The first, a severe elderly gentleman with spectacles, and a shrill piercing voice, subjected each applicant to a most searching scrutiny before allowing him to receive a parcel. The second, a brawny rascal with a 'gor-blimey' cap and a four days' growth of beard had a sharp remark for each man and a slap on the bottom for each girl as they came up to receive their gifts from the Gurkhas".

Fourth Division units came to the aid of UNRRA officials who arrived during the summer to broaden the basis of assistance to the distressed Macedonian population. Once again an intimate and cooperative association resulted. The diarist of 1/9 Gurkhas declared:

"It would be unfair to exclude from an account of the work of this battalion mention of some of the people with whom we have been proud to serve. In Colonel von Spach, a retired American Army officer, UNRRA had a representative without equal. He worked sixteen hours a day seven days a week. His area was large, supplies often short and transport difficulties manifold. Fortunately, to the Colonel difficulties existed only to be solved. By his unflagging energy, his fearless denunciation of incompetence and above all, by his rough but likeable personality, much of the initial distress has been alleviated and firm foundations laid for future relief work".

This admiration was not one-sided. In his official report to the Chief of the Greek Mission Colonel von Spach wrote:

"Before leaving Greece I wish to report to you on the outstanding co-operation I have received in operating our programme in Western Macedonia from Fourth Indian Division of the British Army commanded by Major-General Charles Boucher.

"To gain my objective I was constantly calling on various units of this Indian Division for assistance which they most willingly gave. We used their transportation — all kinds, from jeeps to three-ton trucks, to haul supplies to every part of Western Macedonia. We used their gas, oil, and repair services to keep our own transportation in operation. We used their staging area to park our large convoys which remained over-night guarded by their soldiers. Officers and men helped us in fair distribution of our supplies to villages far up in the mountains. We used their quarters to house and feed truck drivers. The officers' messes were always open to UNRRA personnel. We used their ambulances to haul people to and from hospitals. Their doctors were a big factor in our public health programme.

"We used their barracks to store our supplies, at times even drawing upon them for rations to keep our soup kitchens going. They built our public baths and disinfectant centres and soup kitchens, and provided us with materials to rebuild hospitals and schools.

"Without the help and co-operation of the above it would have been impossible for us to get even a small part of our programme over in Western Macedonia. I assure you that I am most grateful for what they have done".

As the vast jumble of displaced peoples began to sort out, a further task devolved on the overworked and never resting Divisional transport services. It became necessary for convoys to proceed to the Bulgarian and Yugo-Slav frontiers and to bring back prisoners of war, dispossessed Greeks, and a wide range of lost and vagabond humanity of whom the Bulgars wished to be rid. This service began early in the year when ELAS was still in control of the frontier areas. At that time Divisional convoys were obliged to obtain passes from the partisans and to travel without arms. These expeditions had a comic opera air about them. Negotiations at the frontier were prolonged while interpreters squabbled in Greek, English, Russian, Italian, Bulgarian and French. At every halt hitchhikers mingled unobtrusively with the prisoners of war. These unsponsored travellers had to be sifted out before the convoys could proceed. The ELAS detachments, booted, spurred, bewhiskered and bandoliered, having insisted on the disarmament of the escort, sometimes rearmed their guests with shotguns and automatic pistols in order to stage hare hunts. Communist parties invariably ended in fellowship all round, with gifts of wine, sheep, poultry and eggs, a striking testimony to the ease with which good relations could be maintained when political motivations were absent.

During the year several Divisional units participated in interesting outings. 3 Royal Frontier Force Regiment and a detachment from Central India Horse had the good fortune to visit Mount Athos, the isolated monastery which stands on the tip of the third finger of the Khalkidiki peninsula. As the monastery was unapproachable by land the Indians coasted southward by caique until a magnificent scene burst upon them. "The Moni Vatophedhiou" wrote an officer, "stands at the foot of high cliffs in a secluded bay. The building itself is huge and square, grim and forbidding as a mediaeval castle. Its entrance is the archway and portcullis door of a Norman stronghold, rising straight from the water's edge, with cream coloured stone and red turrets set against a background of green jungle vegetation. Below it a deep blue sea. The scene was one of astonishing beauty".

In this romantic setting the Indian detachments received an overwhelming welcome. Each jawan was treated as an honoured guest. As at San Marino, a monk was found who could speak Hindustani. As reciprocal hospitality Jemadar Nauroz Khan, MC, prepared an Indian feast, at which the black-habited monks squatted in a circle, scooping up dhall with chapattis while holding back their long beards with the other hand. When the patrol's radio set was switched on to give this isolated community the world news the voice of a woman announcer came through — a unique occurrence since nothing female, not even cows or hens, is tolerated by the Mount Athos communities.

An equally interesting locality was the scene of the Divisional mountaineering school on Mount Olympus. Excellent training was obtained by climbing the sheer pinnacles. Here it was revealed that a number of Gurkhas were reasonably proficient on skis, a puzzling discovery until it was remembered that 2/7 Gurkha Rifles had been detailed for training as a ski battalion and that parties of Indian troops had visited Colonel Head's school at The Cedars in the Lebanons. The Gurkhas took to the sport as though born to it and streaked down the snowy hillsides with broad grins and gurgles of delight.

In a miscellany of tasks, some tedious, some engrossing, the first year of occupation drew to a close. Week by week the situation in Macedonia and Thrace improved. The easy tolerance, good humour and impartiality of British and Indian troops had brought quiet to a tormented countryside. The Divisional services had wrought magnificently in mending the devastation of war. All in all, Fourth Indian Division had set the feet of the Greeks in the path of rehabilitation. It now remained to see whether they would walk forward diligently, emulating the behaviour of their sponsors, or whether the age-old hatreds again would drive them into by-paths, into vendettas and an anarchy of greed and fear.

The saner Greeks realised how greatly they had been befriended. These British soldiers, foreign men of curious tongue, who moved steadfastly about their tasks, yet always found time for a grin, a chuck under the chin and a slap on the shoulder, were seeking nothing for themselves, nor were they the servants of any devious policy. They were in Greece to help out, to put the house in order. They neither robbed nor raped nor flogged — unusual soldiers indeed. The hearts of the common people warmed to them and they sought to show their feelings to British and Indians in many ways — by shy courtesies, by simple gifts, by timely warnings; a garland, a sheep, a flask of ouzo — small tributes meaning much. The Greeks who co-operated with the forces of occupation knew that one day Fourth Indian Division must go. For them today's intimacy might count as tomorrow's treason. Nevertheless these officers, administrators and clerics did not hesitate to put their gratitude on record. The Regent of the Kingdom said, "We are indeed fortunate in the friends who have hastened to help us". General Bitsanis, a Greek commander in Central Macedonia, in thanking General Boucher for participation in a parade commemorating the Italian declaration of war, poured praise on the Divisional representatives, enumerating their virtues — "their order and rank discipline, their virile and smart countenance, their irreproachable dress and the regularity of their pace during the march before the Officials". When Lieut.-Colonel L. V. Sherwood DSO of 3/10 Baluch Regiment was killed in a tragic incident, the Mayor of Verroia asked permission to name a street in his memory, at the same time bestowing on Brigadier Saunders-Jacobs and three other officers the Freedom of Citizenship. "Extraordinary and conscientious services on behalf of Greece" read the citation — a tribute which well epitomises the work of Fourth Indian Division.

In December, when General Boucher was chosen to command India's first airborne Division, Major-General T. W. Rees, CB, CIE, DSO, MC, arrived to take over. In its new commander Fourth Indian Division retrieved one of its own, for General Rees, a Rajputana Rifleman, had been the second GSO 1 of the Division, at Sidi Barrani far back in 1940. Thereafter he had commanded 10 Indian Brigade in Eritrea and 10 Indian Division in Iraq and Western Desert. He then assumed command of 19 Indian Division in the Burma campaign. In 1944 General Rees and his men formed the spearhead of the drive through Central Burma, when his "Dagger" Division was recognised as one of the outstanding formations in Fourteenth Army. He usually managed to be near the tip of the spear. "I saw the small intense figure of General Rees prowling in the firing line" wrote an officer in a characteristic appreciation. Once again the men who wore the Red Eagles were fortunate in the selection of their leader.

Likewise in December came echoes out of yesterday. General Freyberg after a memorial service on the field of Alamein sent a last warm greeting from great-hearted comrades of 2 New Zealand Division, now on their way to their island homeland after five years of service. 7 Armoured Division, mounting guard among the ruins of Berlin, also sent remembrances on the anniversary of Sidi Barrani. It was a proud thing to know that Fourth Indian Division stood among such peers.

At the end of the year it was confirmed that the Division would soon take ship for India. One of the war's great partnerships was about to be wound up. At the beginning of July 1 Royal Sussex and 2 Camerons had departed, leaving behind records of long service and fine comradeship. These great British battalions were bone and flesh of the Division. It was a sad moment when they marched away — the departure of kinsmen, the dispersal of the family. Soon to follow them (at the beginning of August) was 57 LAA Regiment, whose marksmanship will be vaunted by the jawans for years to come. In January 1946 the remainder of the artillery left — a sorrowful parting indeed. Among the saw-toothed mountains of Eritrea, in the glare of the Western Desert, on the drive to Damascus, among the flower-spangled Tunisian pastures and the fruitful Italian valleys British gunners and Indian sepoys had answered to each other's need until they were of one piece — the warp and woof of an unsurpassable fabric of military brotherhood. Last of all, 1/4 Essex, those splendid Territorials from Loughton and the New Forest, who had matched their regular comrades stride for stride on every battlefield, said sad goodbyes. "We shall be lost without the Indians", wrote an Essex officer. "We belong with them". *

On January 22nd the first of four troopships arrived in Salonika harbour bearing the men and vehicles of 4 British Division who were destined to take over responsibilities in Northern Greece. The relief was complicated by bitterly cold weather and deep snow. Over a month passed before the last troopship sailed. One by one the liners reached western Indian ports where with absence of ceremony the units entrained for their regimental centres.

The odyssey was over. In five years Fourth Indian Division had fought nine campaigns, had travelled more than 15,000 miles, had suffered over 25,000 casualties and had captured upwards of 150,000 prisoners. Except for the battle of El Alamein in which it played a minor rôle, and the destruction of the German armies in the Po valley after it had left for Greece, every operation in the Mediterranean theatre had found Fourth Indian Division in the van. Its fame had gone round the world. The Red Eagle flashes were a portent of welcome wherever soldiers of the United Nations met.

For the British troops, service in this Division was a memory to be cherished always. For the Indian personnel it was something more. It represented a coming of age, an assurance of manhood. Indian officers and men had proved full partners in a prodigious adventure.

* 1/4 Essex was one of the first units to be re-constituted in the post-war Territorial Forces, with Lieut.-Colonel Arthur Noble DSO again in command.

Chapter 33

EPILOGUE—"PUNJAB BOUNDARY FORCE"

Had the intent been other than to compile a historical record, the story of Fourth Indian Division might have provided a fascinating study in the development of the character of India's fighting men. Five years Grand Tour on overseas service had converted volunteers of limited outlook and attainments into professional soldiers of wide general knowledge and proficiency. Month by month the stresses of a global conflict impelled all ranks into broader commitments and increasingly intricate enterprises. Training in specialist weapons, new tactics in battle, travel in strange lands, contact with diverse social regimes and the employment of numerous foreign languages had served to acquaint the rank and file with an ever-widening knowledge of the world. It seemed as though the capstone upon this edifice of experience had been set by the Macedonian occupation, when the reclamation of a wracked and devastated province became a Divisional responsibility.

Yet the fates held a further climatic experience for the officers and men of Fourth Indian Division. As the successive echelons reached India they discovered their homeland to be in travail. The throes of vast change had begun. Some units disembarked at Bombay and Karachi to find the streets draped in black and the Royal Indian Navy in mutiny. In the midst of steadily growing communal strife Lord Louis Mountbatten, six years before a destroyer commander, arrived to announce independence for one-fifth of the people of the world. His high birth, great charm, sincere speech and direct fighting man's approach supplemented the compulsion of his mandate and earned him a hearing in the snarling arena of Indian politics. The new Viceroy declared that within a matter of months the British Raj would relinquish authority and that the only task which remained to Great Britain was to lend friendly assistance in the establishment of the new order.

Confronted with such ultimatum, the tragic expedient of the partition of India became inevitable. The splitup postulated among other things the division of the Punjab. To the British community in India this necessity brought particular pain and dismay. Generation after generation of soldiers and administrators had built this province into a great property — a proud monument to their devotion, wisdom and integrity. It had served as the crucible for many of the most successful experiments of the British Raj and its development in many respects was well in advance of that of the rest of India. From its fat lands had come the bulk of the recruits who sustained the high prestige of the Indian Army.

The acute danger in partitioning the Punjab centred around the problem of the Sikhs, that proud and self-sustained people whose colonies are found not only everywhere in India but also in many other parts of the world. This race of ultra-orthodox warriors, of high intelligence and exceptional endowments, although numbering only 6,000,000 of Punjab's 75,000,000 inhabitants, played a preponderant part in the economy of the province. Any scheme of partition was bound to split this most homogenuous and cohesive of all Indian communities. Had this fact been faced realistically a great tragedy might have been averted. Unfortunately communal leaders in the Punjab had adopted the Irish political expedient of saying more than they meant. Prominent Sikhs undoubtedly believed that by canny jockeying of rival factions their people might win a measure of autonomy and a preferential position in the new India. In addition there did exist in the Punjab a long and acrimonious history of dispute on the parochial level between Sikhs and Muslims. These divergences had been exacerbated by irresponsible controversy until arrogant Sikh and firebrand Mussalman alike preached recourse to violence. Spark was set to tinder in March 1947, when a communal clash at Rawalpindi developed into a three-weeks massacre of non-Muslims at various centres in Northern Punjab. While the communities were still stirred by these atrocities the plan to partition the sub-continent was proclaimed. Whereupon the Sikhs opted for inclusion in India, announced their intention to oppose by force any boundary award which did not satisfy them and began to organize for the day of vengeance upon their enemies.

Against this background of growing menace Fourth Indian Division, throughout the year following its return from Greece, strove earnestly to prepare for its role in the new Indian Army. On disembarkation its principal constituents had proceeded to the Punjab. Divisional Headquarters was established at Lahore and re-organization began. Leave, demobilization, new recruitments and re-equipment proceeded apace, but before peacetime routine had settled into its stride a re-allocation of territory ensued and the Division shifted to the Deccan, with Headquarters and 5 Brigade at Poona, 7 Brigade in Bombay and 11 Brigade at Deolali. As replacements of British components 1 Indian Grenadiers, 2/5 Mahrattas, 5/6 Rajputana Rifles, 1/15 Punjab Regiment, 4 Kumaon Regiment and 3 Mahar Machine Gun Battalion joined the Division. (No artillery units were allotted as due to the general re-organization of the Indian Army this service was in flux.) Training commenced and in spite of the usual post-war difficulties the units soon began to exhibit their customary soldierly proficiency.

In December, 1946, when the Commander-in-Chief, India, visited Fourth Division, he witnessed tactical exercises with live ammunition on an impressive scale. In March, 1947 full-scale Combined Operations were staged at Madh Island, in conjunction with Royal Navy, Royal Air Force, Royal Indian Navy and Royal Indian Air Force. Marked efficiency characterized the infantry performances and soon afterwards Field-Marshal Auckinleck announced that Fourth Division had been selected as the experimental formation of the new Indian Army—a decision stimulating to all ranks, since it promised exceptional opportunities to keen soldiers.

Unfortunately outbreaks of communal hostility already had intervened to dislocate re-organization and training schedules. In Bombay Presidency relations between Muslims and Hindus worsened until 7 Brigade was on constant call. Throughout these commotions the willingness and cheerfulness of all ranks and their impartial behaviour towards all communities deeply impressed the authorities and led to excellent relationships between the troops and the civil population. Elsewhere in India the situation continued to deteriorate and from time to time other Divisional units were placed under warning to move. 5 and 11 Brigades showed the flag in the Deccan. At one time it appeared as if the entire Division might be called to Eastern Bengal, where the garrison troops were fully extended as aftermath of outbreaks in the autumn of 1946. The Rawalpindi massacres, however, made it necessary to deploy the strongest available forces in Central and South-Eastern Punjab and in May, 1947, when General Rees was attending a staff conference at Camberley, Brigadier D. J. T. Turnbull CBE, DSO, CRA as officiating commander received instructions to move Fourth Division, less 7 Brigade retained in Bombay, to Jullundur. On arrival in the Punjab 5 Brigade was despatched to Amritsar.

August 15th, 1947, had been set as the date on which British authority in India would cease. As the time for the handover approached the situation in the Punjab cannot be better described than in terms of General Rees' report:

"The civil administration had been deteriorating for some time. During the war there had been no intake either of Europeans or of Indians of suitable calibre. Every area had become understaffed, with an inevitable drop in efficiency. British officers strove to maintain a high level of performance but they were not getting the same support from their subordinates. . Indian officials and police also realized that within a short period they would be scattered to various parts of India or Parkistan. In addition communalism was eating deeply into the services. These causes made for lessened responsibility, weakened discipline and possible sanctions."

The transference of authority on such a vast scale—far surpassing any similar attempt in history—was to be accomplished through the instrumentality of a Partition Council and a Defence Council, both the joint creations of the dominions-to-be. Under instructions of the Joint Defence Council Field-Marshal Auckinleck became Supreme Comman-

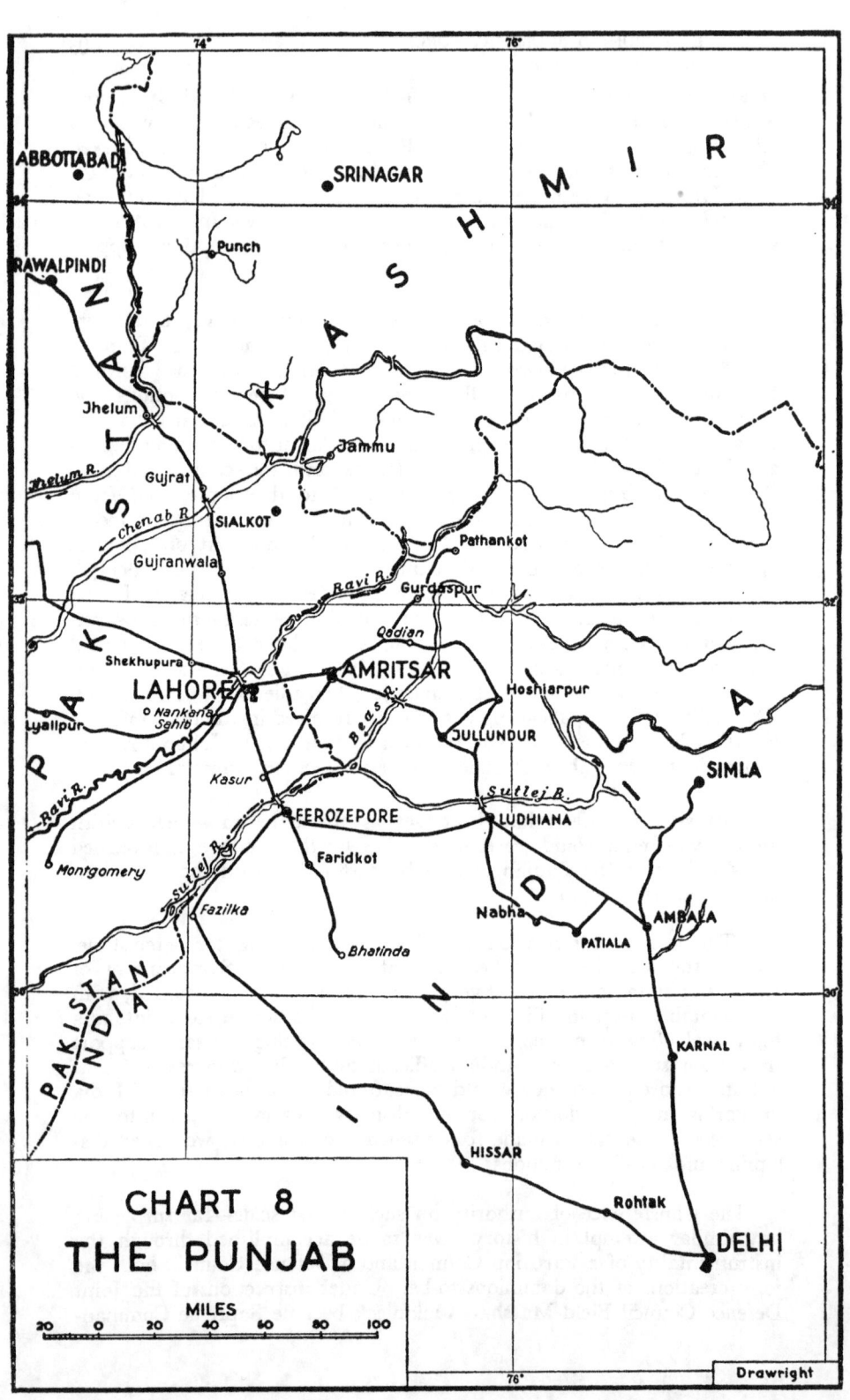

der of both India and Pakistan, with his principal function the proper division of the armed forces and the military stores and equipment of the dying Indian Empire.

As the Boundary Commission proceeded with its task it became obvious that if the demarcated frontier followed its rumoured and likely course (in general along the line of the Sutlej River) some 37,500 square miles of Central Punjab surrounding the capital city of Lahore would be the scene of serious disturbances. This territory, from Sialkot in the north to Montgomery in the south, from Ludhiana in the east to Lyallpur in the west, held 14,500,000 tough and pugnacious inhabitants, given even under ordinary circumstances to a high ratio of crimes of violence. Approximately half this population was Muslim, one-quarter Hindu and one-fifth Sikh; but the Sikhs, by reason of their substantial land holdings were distributed throughout the entire area and were particularly strong in the Montgomery and Lyallpur canal-colonies—districts almost certain to be awarded to Pakistan. These circumstances made it imperative that before the withdrawal of the British troops and the announcement of the Boundary Award the authorities in the Punjab should have at their disposal military forces competent to deal with wide-spread unrest.

In July, 1947—a scant month before the relinquishment of British authority — Punjab Boundary Force came into being, with Fourth Indian Division as its nucleus and General Rees as its commander. 5 Brigade (Brigadier N. J. B. Stuart) and 11 Brigade (Brigadier Tyrrhit-Wheeler, soon to be succeeded by Brigadier R. C. B. Bristow OBE) were supplemented by 14 Parachute Brigade (Brigadier R. B. Scott DSO) consisting of 3/7 Rajputs, 3/10 Baluchis and 4/13 Frontier Force Rifles; 43 Lorried Infantry Brigade (Brigadier J. Keenan) comprising 1/2 Punjabis, 2/7 Rajputs, 1/10 Baluchis, 3/17 Dogras and 2/8 Gurkha Rifles; and by 114 Infantry Brigade (Brigadier H. W. D. McDonald DSO, the former 7 Brigade commander) which included 4/10 Baluchis, 5/13 Frontier Force Rifles and 2/17 Dogras. Supplementary arms, ancilliary troops and miscellaneous formations already located in Central Punjab brought up the total strength of General Rees' command to more than two divisions. The Force Commander was given as advisors Brigadier Brar of India and Brigadier Ayub Khan of Pakistan. At a later date Brigadier Thimayya of India and Brigadier Nasir Ahmed of Pakistan also joined his staff.

During the last weeks of July, when the burning heat of mid-summer mounted to unusual and terrifying intensity, a fever of excitement and hysteria spread across Central Punjab. The fanaticism engendered by months of wild talk and rabble-rousing was coming to a head; individual acts of violence increased and terror like a pestilence began to stalk abroad. In a dark alley or a lonely path a wayfarer would be accosted and asked his name. If of "the other community" a knife thrust, a bludgeon stroke or a twisted scarf left a sprawled corpse as the murderers sauntered on. When the stories of such deeds spread vengeance was sworn above the wails of the women; more and more groups went on the prowl, to slay or to be slain. A newer Thuggee, callous and terrible, had returned to haunt the lands from which *Pax Brittanica* had banished it more than a century before.

The rapid emergence of armed murder gangs suggested that to some extent this eruption of violence had been planned in advance. Certainly the Sikh Jathas were more than extempore organizations. General Rees thus describes them:

"Jathas were of various kinds, in strength from twenty to thirty men up to five or six hundred, or more. When an expedition was of limited scope the Jatha usually did not increase beyond the numbers which had originally set out; but if the projected operation was to attack a village, a convoy or a train, the local Sikh villagers would join and swell the assailants to several thousands. They had recognized leaders, headquarters which constantly shifted about and messengers who travelled on foot, on horseback and even by motor transport. The usual method of attack, apart from assaults on villages, was from ambush. Information as to the movements of trains or convoys was relatively easy to obtain. As the crops were high it was simple to ambush marching columns of refugees. The attackers would remain concealed until the last moment and then would pour in a stampeding volley, usually in North-West Frontier fashion from the opposite side from where the shock assailants lay in wait. In spite of the best efforts of the escorts to hold them together the refugees would scatter in panic; whereupon the ambush parties would dash in with sword and spear. With attackers and attacked inextricably intermingled the escort usually was unable to protect its charges.

"The Sikh use of horsemen as scouts was sound and enterprising. On many occasions mounted swordsmen and spearmen were used in shock action against the refugee columns."

Superiority rested with the Sikhs not only in organization but in weapons. The *kirpan* — the token sword which is one of the five characteristic Sikh possessions — had metamorphosed for the purposes of vengeance into a formidable cutlass or dah. It was supplemented by home-made spears, hatchets and battleaxes, by crude bombards and mortars and also by shields and armour. (It will be remembered that at Keren Sikh troops constructed shields for protection against the small Italian percussion grenades.) In addition, both during and after the war there had been heavy smuggling of modern arms into India from the various battlefronts. The Jathas therefore possessed hard cores of skilled fighters armed with rifles, grenades, tommy guns and machine guns. Although the Punjab Mussalmans also possessed firearms and trained men, and a nuclear military organization in the Muslim League National Guards, they lacked the cohesiveness of the Sikhs. Moreover, they had not reckoned on a blood feud as the consequence of the Rawalpindi massacres. They therefore were by no means as well prepared to

EPILOGUE — "PUNJAB BOUNDARY FORCE" 407

strike as their adversaries; often the Mussalmans turned out to meet their foes like a rabble of mediaeval peasants, armed only with flails, scythes and other crude weapons shaped from the implements of the field. Under heavy punishment their gangs assumed a more formidable character but at the opening of the black month of August only Muslim preponderance in numbers countered the superior arms and battle-readiness of the Sikhs.

Both sides had skilled arson squads, operating with the equipment of all centuries, from fire-arrows to inflammable suitcases with time fuses.

The influential Hindu community, although suffering heavily at times, played a relatively minor role in this war of vengeance. Extremists of Rashtarya Swayam Sevak Sangh — the Hindu society afterwards outlawed because of complicity in the murder of Mahatma Ghandi—participated to a limited extent in garottings and street fighting in the principal towns.

From the outset Punjab Boundary Force was beset by almost insuperable difficulties. In an area as large as Ireland the civil authority was at point of collapse. One administration was dying; two successions, each in swaddling clothes, snarled at each other but lacked power to enforce their edicts or to control their followers. Wherever arms were available and mobs could assemble mass murder and widespread destruction only could be halted by the drastic intervention of the troops. The task of maintaining law and order demanded more men than General Rees could deploy, yet this primary duty was less exhaustive than the rescue, protection, provisioning and transportation of the endless streams of refugees which flowed to the east and to the west in search of safety. More than two million hapless and dispossessed wayfarers cluttered the roads; for their succour and segregation no agency existed except Punjab Boundary Force. As an additional responsibility the guarding and in some instances the operation of the railways devolved upon General Rees and his men, since the constant threat of attack had led many of the operating staff to desert their posts. (In Lahore the railway workers consented to remain on duty but only after military guards had been detailed to protect their homes.) Thus as the internecine struggle mounted to its tragic culmination Punjab Boundary Force was revealed as the sole restraining influence, the only effective control and regulating medium, of maddened and terror-stricken millions. Its five brigades faced a general conflagration with fire buckets.

Like point and counterpoint of a devilish harmony, the dark alleys and squalid warrens began to re-echo each other, as knives took toll of Sikhs in Lahore and grenades blasted Mussalmans in Amritsar. In early August sections of both these cities were in flames. In the key Sikh area of The Manja, the fruitful triangle of countryside between the junction of the Sutlej and Beas rivers, the first Jathas appeared in the field and began to exterminate the Muslim population of the villages. Day by day killings mounted to peak ferocity. At Gujranwala to the north of Lahore the Mussalmans struck back and hundreds of Sikhs were hunted to the death. From all parts of Central Punjab there flowed fearful tales of destruction. In the principal cities Punjab Boundary Force went into action, striking at mobs ruthlessly; but both in towns and in countryside the murder gangs were strong enough or fanatical enough to fight back and the troops sustained casualties. The widely dispersed military detachments represented little more than local dykes in an overwhelming flood of violence. In the words of General Rees:

"The killing was pre-mediaeval in its ferocity. Neither age nor sex was spared. Mothers with babes in their arms were struck down, speared or shot. The Sikhs cried "Rawalpindi" as they struck home. Both sides were equally merciless."

Lieut-Colonel P. S. Mitcheson DSO, who had taken over as GSO 1 Fourth Indian Division in the preceding April, thus describes a characteristic scene:

"Motoring from Beas to Lahore, at a time when 100,000 Mussalmans on foot were making their way westward through Amritsar, in the course of fifty miles I saw between 400 and 600 dead along the road.

"One attack on the refugees went in from thick crops while I was near by. In a few minutes fifty men, women and children were slashed to pieces while thirty others came running back towards us with wounds streaming. We got up a tank of 18 Calvary which killed six Sikh attackers and took three prisoners. The latter proved most useful as under interrogation they gave the names of the villages responsible for the ambush. These villages were immediately searched and collectively fined."

On August 8th the special train carrying Pakistan government officials and their families from New Delhi to Karachi was derailed. Two days later canal employees began to desert their posts; as sabotage of barrages and headworks would have constituted a crowning catastrophe, one more responsibility was dropped on Punjab Boundary Force's doorstep. On August 10th the Indian Deputy Police Commissioner designate at Amritsar ordered his Muslim constables to be disarmed. As four-fifths of all Punjab police were Mussalmans this action denuded East Punjab of protection; in Jullundur District alone, 7,000 policemen relinquished their posts and demanded safe conduct to Pakistan. On August 12th fighting continued throughout the day in Amritsar; Lahore and Gurjranwala were in flames; in the Sialkot-Wazirabad area three attacks on refugee trains took the lives of many non-Muslims. On August 13th troops beat back a heavy attack on the Gurdwara in Lahore; on the same day 43 non-Muslims were stabbed in Moghulpura Railway Workshops. On August 14th, in the midst of continuous fighting (35 Sikhs were knifed that day in Lahore Railway Station)

EPILOGUE — "PUNJAB BOUNDARY FORCE"

Field-Marshal Auckinleck, returning from Independence Day celebrations in Karachi, landed at Lahore airfield for a brief conference with General Rees and with Sir Evan Jenkins, the distinguished governor of the Punjab, who was relinquishing his post in two days' time. (It is fitting to interpolate that the last days of the old Indian Civil Service revealed the same splendid pattern of service as that of the old Indian Army. The brilliant administrator of the Punjab and his devoted colleagues fought to the end to contain the catastrophe and to re-establish security and the processes of authority.) At this conference the Supreme Commander learned that 10% of the houses in Lahore had been destroyed; that such police as remained on duty had become partisan-minded and unreliable; that supplementary organizations to deal with refugees were greatly hampered by the lack of experienced administrators, since all British officials were in course of replacement. General Rees further voiced the opinion that the use of troops, even in prohibitive numbers, would fail to mend the situation. With communities millions strong completely out of hand only the intervention of national and parochial leaders, would halt the campaign of extermination.

That night a mob burned the Lahore Gurdwara. A score of Sikhs perished in the flames. The Lahore civil authorities had explicitly guaranteed the safety and protection of the temple and had resisted attempts to install non-Muslim guards. Strong Muslim police and military piquets stationed within 80 yards of the Gurdwara failed to take action against the mob. Early next morning General Rees surveyed the still smouldering ruins and the charred bodies. He was able to bring home to local Muslim leaders the tragedy of this breach of faith and they forthwith declared their intention of regaining control of the city. With this undertaking in hand General Rees left for Amritsar in an effort to obtain reciprocal assurances from the Sikhs. Before his arrival a shocking counterpart of the Lahore atrocity occurred. A number of Muslim women were paraded naked through the streets. Some were raped, murdered and their bodies publicly burned; others were rescued and borne to sanctuary in the Golden Temple. General Rees and the Superintendent of Police arrived too late to intervene but this abominable crime gave the Punjab Boundary Force Commander a forcible text for his interview with Master Tara Singh and the other Sikh notables. As a result they agreed to endeavour to pacify their followers; that night they traversed the city, proclaiming their decision by beat of drum and calling on all Sikhs to desist from further reprisals. Steps were taken to carry their exhortations into the countryside. Nevertheless the situation remained critical in Amritsar where only 200 police, of which 150 were Sikhs, remained out of a normal force of 800 constables. At the request of the local authorities Punjab Boundary Force took over control and patrolled the city with mixed detachments.

On August 16th, on his return to Lahore, the Muslim authorities reiterated to General Rees their resolve to bring their community under control. On the same day the Punjab Boundary Force Commander convened a meeting of his Commanding Officers and Subedar Majors. They and their men, said General Rees, representatives of the old Indian Army, now constituted the sole stable element, the last bulwark against chaos. The future of India depended upon their steadfastness and fidelity.

On August 17th Prime Minister Nehru of India and Prime Minister Liaqat Ali Khan of Pakistan, their advisors and the Governors of East Punjab and West Punjab met the Deputy Supreme Commander and General Rees at Ambala in a momentous conference. The Dominions statesmen, deeply alarmed, undertook to support the pacification efforts of the local leaders, as placed in train by the Punjab Boundary Force Commander. On the same day the announcement of the Punjab Boundary Award touched off fresh outbursts of violence. Reports from provincial towns emphasized the increasing tendency of the police to identify themselves with their own communities. Although every effort had been made to route the streams of refugees by different roads, sometimes they met; on August 18th at Kasur, near Lahore, Muslim and non-Muslim throngs clashed in a vicious mêlée. Nevertheless there were gleams of light. Lahore and Amritsar had turned the corner; in these centres violence was decreasing and at long last the civil authorities were able to assist Punjab Boundary Force in caring for the refugees. In outlying districts Mussalmans and non-Muslims were rescued from behind their barricades and were escorted into organized concentration areas. There were even a few heartening reports of occasions on which individuals had intervened to rescue victims from assailants of their own community.

Nevertheless the general picture remained sombre. In spite of isolated instances of common humanity the outlying towns and their surrounding districts continued to erupt, spewing hate and death. On August 20th Punjab Boundary Force troops fired on a Muslim mob between Gurdaspur and Batala, causing 84 casualties. Next day there was bitter fighting along the flaming streets of Ferozpore, where the Mussalmans kindled their houses before they fled. On the Ferozpore-Batinda line a Dogra train guard repeatedly fought off Sikh attacks and saved all passengers who would leave the train. There was likewise report of the outstanding behaviour of a Sikh major in charge of a train escort, who took nine wounds, including six spear wounds, in repelling attacks by men of his own race. As offset to this steadfast behaviour ominous evidence began to accumulate that military detachments were beginning to falter when employed against their own brethren. Under extreme tension ties of blood and race fostered the illusion that punishment was the portion of one community, licence of the other. Even leaders who should have known better preached this view; Master Tara Singh complained that the troops were unduly severe in dealing with the Sikhs, quite forgetting that the well-organized Jathas had attacked military formations with the utmost fury and had suffered accordingly. On August 24th Muslim troops who had slain looters were challenged by non-Muslims of their own unit. On the same day advices from

EPILOGUE — "PUNJAB BOUNDARY FORCE" 411

Sialkot revealed that Mussalmans seized while harrying the other community had been released by troops of their own faith and had been permitted to continue their attacks.

These grave developments caused the Supreme Commander to summon General Rees post-haste to New Delhi. On August 25th the Boundary Force Commander rendered a full report to the joint Defence Council. He declared the situation to be critical. No fighting between Muslim and non-Muslim troops had as yet occurred, but any small incident might set match to train. Whereupon Field-Marshal Auckinleck reminded the Joint Defence Council that he had created Punjab Boundary Force at the request of the Partition Council. Partition now had been accomplished; the sooner both dominions assumed full responsibiiity within their boundaries, the better. A further meeting of the Joint Defence Council was convened for August 29th, at Lahore.

The intervening days witnessed rising tension and a steadily deteriorating situation. Ludhiana District was completely out of control and troops were in action all over the area. 150 non-Muslims were slain in two attacks on mail trains. Punjab Boundary Force units smashed mobs at Sialkot, and at Skeikhupura; at the latter centre 200 Sikhs fell before resistance ceased; the town was gutted and panic prevailed. When such rough justice sobered an area, fresh outbreaks immediately occurred elsewhere. On August 27th the day's reported casualties — usually only a fraction of the actual casualties — mounted to 1,200 killed and wounded. In Montgomery district Muslim gangs began to breach the canal banks in order to flood the countryside and so trap the escaping Sikhs. Near Batala 250 refugees were cut down by Muslim League National Guards. Heavy rains had fallen and the rivers were in spate; with the fords impassable the shifting throngs were immobilized; huddled beside the swollen streams and blocked bridges the refugees offered easy prey to the murder gangs. In the flooded areas it became necessary to move refugees in opposite directions on the same roads. As they passed the homeless wanderers fell on each other and expended their last strength in throttling their enemies.

The crisis swelled towards catastrophe and Punjab Boundary Force was inundated with appeals for aid and protection from every corner of the countryside. Twenty-three battalions and a handful of ancilliary units were expected to control the forces of destruction in a province gone mad. In this desperate hour General Rees, cool, fearless and indefatiguable, led a magnificent team. His British officers laboured under the knowledge that their service had come to its end. They were the last of a splendid line which had served its homeland and the country of its adoption with equal devotion. In the old Indian Army they had achieved a mission unmatched in the imperial story. They had persuaded diverse communities to walk in step, to sit down together and to keep each others backs in times of peril. In the war but lately won they had recruited, trained and led in battle more than 2,000,000 Indian volunteers — a formidable and perhaps decisive contribution to the Allied cause. On many of the races of India they had stamped an image which would not pass.

The last of those who had moulded this great instrument, who had given India a model for her future, were now to go. In a matter of days they would take ship for home, to rejoin their families and to begin life anew. At the eleventh hour a catalclysm had engulfed them. They did not flinch, saying that there was now no proud purpose to sustain them. Instead, they flung themselves upon their tasks. They fought their last fight for the India they had served so long and so well; they kept faith with the Indian soldiers whom they had led for seven generations. By sheer determination and infectious force of example they mastered an incredible situation, kept the wheels turning and the processes of government functioning. Snatching a few hours sleep in the stifling nights, with the telephones tinkling incessantly through their slumbers, hurrying out at first light to patch and revet the tattered fabric of authority, accepting new tasks hourly, improvising ceaselessly, these British officers defied the odds and circumvented every mischance. They wove golden threads in the tapestry of two hundred years service and the historian who delves into the records of Punjab Boundary Force may well turn to Mr. Churchill's great phrase for his epitome. "This was their finest hour".

Senior Indian officers, moulded in the tradition of the old Indian Army, vied with their British colleagues in meeting the challenge. The younger Indian officers, thrust in a twinkling into the communal cauldron, required a period of conditioning in which to gain the outlook and balanced judgment of their seniors. The Viceroys Commissioned officers, non-commissioned officers and men of long service, those who were literally the bone and flesh of the old Indian Army, endured perhaps the gravest tension of all. Inured to battle abroad, they had returned to be confronted with devastation at home. Many lacked tidings of their families, but daily the endless streams of refugees brought wild rumours and fearful tales. Sometimes an old soldier added his testimony, as in a typical case reported by Lieut.-Colonel Mitcheson:

"A Sikh Sardar who retired in 1921, after 28 years service, who had won an MC in Mesopotamia, came to me with tears streaming down his face.

"He said, 'Sahib, I am the last Sikh left in my village. If you do not get me out tonight I shall die there.' He had a wife and small son; being zaildar of the village he was a man of consequence and of considerable possessions. I sent an officer and a section of men to bale him out. On return the officer confirmed all that the old Sikh had said. Even while they were moving off what remained of the Sardar's house was being broken up."

For Indian veterans there can be no finer tribute than to record that for the most part they continued to bear themselves steadfastly and to live up to their oaths in the face of direst provocation and under almost unbearable incitements to retaliation. Special mention should be made of the Corps of Clerks, whose members shared the unending vigils of their officers and whose fidelity and unwearying labours contributed in no small measure to the maintenance of authority. Of other ancilliary units none failed to play its part.

Thus the last challenge found all ranks of Fourth Indian Division sustaining its unbroken record of service and achievement. Perhaps its greatest contribution had been the preservation of the link between East Punjab and West Punjab. General Rees and his officers, tireless and impartial intermediaries, kept open the lines of communication between the rent and all-but-warring segments of the province. They provided the stitches which eventually closed a gaping wound in the body of India. Seldom has a military force bridged a more momentous gap. Throughout these crucial weeks Punjab Boundary Force made history.

On August 29th, the Joint Defence Council decided to hand over complete responsibility at once to the Dominions. As from midnight on September 1/2 troops of Punjab Boundary Force would revert to the control of their respective governments. Of the old Indian Army eight regiments had been allotted to Pakistan. Ten battalions of these regiments were included in Punjab Boundary Force. Of this number eight Muslim battalions together with ancilliary units would report forthwith to General Gane, Commander Lahore Area. Two battalions would remain temporarily to guard Muslim concentrations in East Punjab. The remainder of Punjab Boundary Force would constitute the troops of East Punjab Area, with General Rees retaining command temporarily. He would preserve liaison with Pakistan by setting up his headquarters in Lahore beside General Gane's headquarters.

The dispersal of Punjab Boundary Force marked the final sundering of the old Indian Army. In its ranks Hindus, Sikhs, Muslims, and the two hundred diverse races of the sub-continent had answered a common call and had served a common cause. In many ways it had been the only truly Indian entity in the Indian Empire. It had quelled jungle law, it had enforced unity; behind the guardian hedge of its bayonets men had been free to build towards nationhood. In its last service its great actuating tradition prevailed. To hold India from chaos; to sustain the faltering hands of the new regimes; to succour the homeless and the dispossessed—such was the proud legacy bequeathed to the armed forces of the new Dominions.

Nor was the legacy disdained. There were still fearful days to come, when the crazed communities wasted the tormented countryside. September was a month of intense anxiety. But the new order rose magnificently to the challenge. When Major-General K. S. Thimayya DSO, a gallant and distinguished officer, took over command of East Punjab Area from General Rees, he exhibited the same impartiality, courage and energy as his predecessor. He dared the Amritsar hotheads to interfere with the passage of Muslim refugee columns through that city. "He is a fizzer—an absolute fizzer" enthusiastically wrote a British officer who remained to serve under him. In Pakistan, while British officers retained command temporarily, their Muslim brother-officers displayed equal vigor and resource in the tasks of pacification, in the restoration of authority and in the protection of non-Muslim minorities. The old spirit of Fourth Indian Division lived on.

There remained one final function—the transfer of Muslim personnel from their old regiments to Pakistan formations and the return of Sikhs and Hindus from Muslim units. In the case of the infantry this transfer was comparatively simple, since it could be arranged by companies. The Sappers and Miners and the specialist cadres required more sorting out. Of the remaining British officers, some elected to remain with the Indian and Pakistan forces. Others obtained transfers to the British Army. Still others sought new careers at home or in the Empire and Commonwealth beyond the seas.

Thus dispersed the great company which was known as Fourth Indian Division.

THE END

APPENDICES

1. Combined order of battle and periods of service of exchangeable formations, Fourth Indian Division.

2. Divisional, Brigade, Royal Artillery Commanders and principal Staff Officers, Fourth Indian Division.

3. Casualties sustained by units while serving with Fourth Indian Division.

4. Honours, Awards and Citations.

1. COMBINED ORDER OF BATTLE AND PERIODS OF SERVICE OF EXCHANGEABLE FORMATIONS, FOURTH INDIAN DIVISION

HEADQUARTERS
Headquarters Fourth Indian Division....
Headquarters 5 Indian Infantry Brigade.
Headquarters 7 Indian Infantry Brigade.
Headquarters 11 Indian Infantry Brigade.

ARMOURED CORPS
Central India Horse....................August 1940—April 1942:
                                            February 1944—March 1946
5 Indian Infantry Brigade Reconnaissance Squadron..........................
7 Indian Infantry Brigade Reconnaissance Squadron..........................
11 Indian Infantry Brigade Reconnaissance Squadron....................

ROYAL ARTILLERY
Headquarters Royal Artillery Fourth Indian Division....................
1 Field Regiment RA..................October 1939—January 1946
4 Field Regiment RA..................August 1939—August 1940
11 Field Regiment RA..................July 1942—January 1946
25 Field Regiment RA..................October 1940—June 1942
31 Field Regiment RA..................August 1940—January 1946
32 Field Regiment RA..................June—October 1942
3 Royal Horse Artillery (Anti-Tank) RA.May—December 1940
65 Anti-Tank Regiment RA............September 1941—April 1942
149 Anti-Tank Regiment RA............July 1942—January 1946
57 Light Anti-Aircraft Regiment RA....September 1941—August 1945
Fourth Indian Division Counter-Mortar Battery RA.........................

ROYAL INDIAN ENGINEERS
Headquarters Royal Indian Engineers Fourth Indian Division.............
4 Field Company, K.G.O. Bengal Sappers and Miners........................October 1939—March 1946
12 Field Company, Q.V.O. Madras Sappers and Miners........................October 1939—March 1946
18 Field Company, Royal Bombay Sappers and Miners........................August 1939—June 1942
21 Field Company, Royal Bombay Sappers and Miners........................September 1940—March 1946
11 Field Park Company, Q.V.O. Madras Sappers and Miners.................September 1939—March 1946
5 Bridging Platoon, Sappers and Miners.

SIGNALS
Fourth Indian Divisional Signals.........

INFANTRY

5 INDIAN INFANTRY BRIGADE

1 Battalion The Royal Fusiliers..........August 1939—July 1941
1 Battalion The Buffs (East Kent Regiment)...............................October—December 1941
1 Battalion The Welch Regiment.........January—April 1942
1/4 Battalion The Essex Regiment.......April 1942—January 1946
1 Battalion 1 Punjab Regiment..........January—April 1942
3 Battalion 1 Punjab Regiment..........October 1939—January 1942
4 Battalion (Outram's) 6 Rajputana Rifles...............................October 1939—July 1943:
               January—April 1944
3 Battalion (Queen Mary's Own) 10 Baluch Regiment....................April 1942—February 1943:
               June 1944—December 1946
1 Battalion 9 Gurkha Rifles.............April 1942—September 1947

7 INDIAN INFANTRY BRIGADE

1 Battalion The Royal Sussex Regiment..October 1939—July 1945
2 Battalion The Highland Light Infantry.July 1945—January 1946
2 Royal Battalion 11 Sikh Regiment......June 1944—September 1947
4 Battalion 11 Sikh Regiment............December 1940—August 1942:
               August 1944—November 1944
4 Battalion 16 Punjab Regiment.........October 1939—June 1944
1 Battalion 2 King Edward VII's Own Goorkha Rifles......................April 1942—September 1947

11 INDIAN INFANTRY BRIGADE

2 Battalion The Queen's Own Cameron Highlanders........................August 1939—July 1945
2 Battalion 5 Mahratta Light Infantry...February 1941—June 1942
1 Battalion (Wellesley's) 6 Rajputana Rifles...............................August 1939—April 1942:
               January—June 1944
4 Battalion 7 Rajput Regiment..........October 1939—December 1940
3 Royal Battalion 12 Frontier Force Regiment...............................April 1944—September 1947
3 Battalion 14 Punjab Regiment.........January—March 1941
2 Battalion 7 Gurkha Rifles.............April—June 1942:
               January 1944—September 1947
Lovat Scouts..........................July 1945—January 1946

INFANTRY (MMG)

1 Northumberland Fusiliers Machine Gun Battalion............................April—December 1940
Machine Gun Battalion 6 Rajputana Rifles...............................June 1942—March 1946
5 Indian Infantry Brigade MMG Company
7 Indian Infantry Brigade MMG Company
11 Indian Infantry Brigade MMG Company...............................

SUPPLIES AND TRANSPORT
Headquarters Royal Indian Army Service Corps Fourth Indian Division
Fourth Indian Divisional Troops Transport Company RIASC
5 Indian Infantry Brigade Transport Company RIASC
7 Indian Infantry Brigade Transport Company RIASC
11 Indian Infantry Brigade Transport Company RIASC
220 Indian DID RIASC
18 M.A. Section

MEDICAL
14 Indian Field Ambulance............October 1939—September 1942
17 Indian Field Ambulance............November 1940—March 1946
19 Indian Field Ambulance............October 1939—June 1942
26 Indian Field Ambulance............September 1942—March 1946
32 Indian Field Ambulance............January 1944—March 1946
15 Indian Field Hygiene Section.........

ELECTRICAL AND MECHANICAL ENGINEERS
Headquarters Indian Electrical and Mechanical Engineers Fourth Indian Division
117 Indian Mobile Workshop Company IEME
118 Indian Mobile Workshop Company IEME
119 Indian Mobile Workshop Company IEME
Fourth Indian Divisional Recovery Company IEME
Brigade and Unit Light Aid Detachments and Workshop Sections

ORDNANCE
Fourth Indian Divisional Ordnance Field Park IAOC

PROVOST
Fourth Indian Divisional Provost Company

POSTAL
Fourth Indian Divisional Postal Unit

MISCELLANEOUS
8 Camouflage Training Unit

2. DIVISIONAL, BRIGADE, ROYAL ARTILLERY COMMANDERS AND PRINCIPAL STAFF OFFICERS, FOURTH INDIAN DIVISION

DIVISIONAL COMMANDERS

September 1939—January 1940	Major-General The Hon. P. G. Scarlett CB, MC.
January—August 1940	Major-General P. Neame VC, CB, DSO.
August 1940—April 1941	Major-General N. M. de la P. Beresford-Peirse DSO.
April 1941—January 1942	Major-General F. W. Messervy CB, DSO.
January 1942—March 1944	Major-General F. I. S. Tuker CB, DSO, OBE.
March 1944—January 1945	Major-General A. W. W. Holworthy DSO, MC.
January—December 1945	Major-General C. H. Boucher CB, CBE, DSO.
December 1945—Sept'ber 1947	Major-General T. W. Rees CB, CIE, DSO, MC.

COMMANDERS 5 INDIAN INFANTRY BRIGADE

September 1939—June 1940	Brigadier T. J. Ponting CSI, CIE, MC.
July 1940—July 1941	Brigadier W. L. Lloyd CBE, DSO, MC.
July 1941—December 1942	Brigadier D. Russell CBE, DSO, MC.
December 1942—April 1944	Brigadier D. R. E. R. Bateman DSO, OBE.
April 1944—February 1946	Brigadier J. C. Saunders-Jacobs CBE, DSO.
July—August 1946	Brigadier C. H. B. Rodham DSO, OBE, MC.
September 1946—June 1947	Brigadier P. R. Macnamara DSO.
June 1947	Brigadier K. S. Thimmaya DSO.
July—August 1947	Brigadier N. J. B. Stuart

COMMANDERS 7 INDIAN INFANTRY BRIGADE

October 1940—May 1942	Brigadier H. R. Briggs CBE, DSO.
May—October 1942	Brigadier J. A. Finlay MC.
October 1942—January 1943	Brigadier A. W. W. Holworthy MC.
January—March 1943	Brigadier R. Lawrenson DSO.
March—April 1943	Brigadier O. de T. Lovett, CBE, DSO.
April—June 1943	Brigadier C. E. A. Firth DSO.
June 1943—December 1945	Brigadier O. de T. Lovett, CBE, DSO.
December 1945—August 1947	Brigadier H. W. D. McDonald, DSO.

COMMANDERS 11 INDIAN INFANTRY BRIGADE

August 1939—March 1940 ..... Brigadier A. B. Macpherson CBE, MVO, MC.
March 1940—September 1941 ... Brigadier R. A. Savory DSO, MC.
September 1941—June 1942 .... Brigadier A. Anderson DSO, MC.
January—May 1944 .... Brigadier V. C. Griffin.
May—October 1944 .... Brigadier H. F. C. Partridge DSO.
October 1944—February 1946 ... Brigadier H. C. J. Hunt CBE, DSO.
April 1946—May 1947 .... Brigadier R. H. H. Scott.
June 1947 .... Brigadier P. B. Tyrrwhit-Wheeler
June—August 1947 .... Brigadier R. C. B. Bristowe OBE.

COMMANDERS ROYAL ARTILLERY

August 1939—June 1940 .... Brigadier N. M. de la P. Beresford-Peirse DSO.
June—September 1940 .... Brigadier P. Maxwell MC.
September 1940—March 1942 ... Brigadier W. H. B. Mirrlees DSO, MC.
March 1942—April 1944 .... Brigadier H. K. Dimoline CBE, DSO, TD.
April 1944—February 1946 .... Brigadier H. C. W. Eastman DSO, MVO.
March 1946—August 1947 ...... Brigadier D. J. T. Turnbull CBE, DSO.

G.S.O. 1

September 1939—June 1940 .... Colonel W. L. Lloyd MC.
June 1940—March 1941 .... Colonel T. W. Rees CIE, DSO, MC.
March 1941—April 1942 .... Lieut-Colonel D. R. E. R. Bateman DSO, OBE.
April—September 1942 .... Lieut-Colonel L. J. G. Showers.
September 1942—May 1944 ..... Lieut-Colonel J. K. Shepheard DSO.
May 1944—March 1945 .... Lieut-Colonel P. L. A. Hill OBE.
March 1945—April 1947 .... Lieut-Colonel W. W. Stewart MC.
April—October 1947 .... Lieut-Colonel P. S. Mitcheson DSO, OBE.

A.A. & Q.M.G.

September 1939—January 1941 . Colonel H. F. C. McSwiney CBE, DSO, MC.
January—October 1941 .... Colonel J. B. Dalison OBE.
October 1941—August 1942 .... Lieut-Colonel S. W. Bower OBE.
August—October 1942 .... Lieut-Colonel Sheodatt Singh.
October 1942—June 1944 ...... Lieut-Colonel J. A. C. Greenwood OBE.
June—September 1944 .... Lieut-Colonel B. A. W. Hooper MBE.
September 1944—July 1945 .... Lieut-Colonel J. L'A. Bell MBE.
July 1945—August 1947 .... Lieut-Colonel Altaf Qadir MBE.

3. CASUALTIES SUSTAINED BY UNITS WHILE SERVING WITH FOURTH INDIAN DIVISION

Note: In spite of repeated efforts, it has been impossible to obtain exact or complete casualty returns for the following units.

Headquarters Fourth Indian Division
Headquarters 5 Indian Brigade
3 Royal Horse Artillery
1 Royal Fusiliers
1 Buffs (East Kent) Regiment
1 Welch Regiment
1/4 Essex Regiment
1 Northumberland Fusiliers Machine Gun Battalion
14 Field Ambulance
19 Field Ambulance

UNIT	KILLED AND DIED OF WOUNDS OFFICERS	OTHER RANKS	MISSING OFFICERS	OTHER RANKS	WOUNDED OFFICERS	OTHER RANKS
HEADQUARTERS FORMATIONS						
HQ 7 Ind Inf Bde	1	3	—	—	—	—
HQ 11 Ind Inf Bde	1	—	—	—	2	7
ARMOURED AND RECONNAISSANCE UNITS						
Central India Horse	3	44	—	11	1	58
5 Ind Inf Bde Recce Sqn	—	1	—	—	—	—
7 Ind Inf Bde Recce Sqn	1	6	—	—	3	11
ROYAL ARTILLERY						
1 Fd Regt RA	4	17	—	2	12	104
11 Fd Regt RA	2	51	—	1	12	111
25 Fd Regt RA	5	35	—	1	7	47
31 Fd Regt RA	10	67	—	9	23	149
65 Anti-Tank Regt RA	4	86	—	—	16	157
149 Anti-Tank Regt RA	7	92	—	35	17	227
57 LAA Regiment RA	9	76	—	—	7	208

UNIT	KILLED AND DIED OF WOUNDS		MISSING		WOUNDED	
	OFFICERS	OTHER RANKS	OFFICERS	OTHER RANKS	OFFICERS	OTHER RANKS
ROYAL INDIAN ENGINEERS						
HQ RE 4 Ind Div	1	4	—	—	1	7
4 Fd Coy RIE	5	69	—	1	10	202
12 Fd Coy RIE	1	54	—	—	—	145
18 Fd Coy RIE	—	11	—	—	1	22
21 Fd Coy RIE	1	26	—	—	2	56
11 Fd Park Coy RIE	—	4	—	—	3	17
4 Ind Div Sigs	1	8	—	—	3	39
INFANTRY						
1 Royal Sussex	35	276	—	12	62	590
2 Cameron Highlanders	16	307	—	—	27	389
3/1 Punjab Regt.	8	263	—	3	16	589
2/5 Mahratta L.I.	3	146	—	34	4	430
1/6 Rajputana Rifles	7	205	—	3	18	1020
4/6 Rajputana Rifles	7	238	—	9	17	1385
4/7 Rajput Regt.	—	2	—	—	—	19
3/10 Baluch Regt.	4	92	—	6	4	353
2/11 Royal Sikh Regt.	2	58	—	2	7	334
4/11 Sikh Regt.	1	107	—	—	10	553
3/12 Royal Frontier Force Regt.	6	124	—	1	5	459
3/14 Punjab Regt.	1	43	—	*88	3	169
4/16 Punjab Regt.	4	190	—	2	11	871
1/2 Gurkha Rifles	6	296	—	—	29	584
2/7 Gurkha Rifles	5	165	—	10	14	441
1/9 Gurkha Rifles	5	228	1	11	11	930
*Drowned at sea while POW						
MACHINE GUN UNITS						
Rajputana Rifles MG Batt'n	—	66	—	2	8	462

UNIT	KILLED AND DIED OF WOUNDS		MISSING		WOUNDED	
	OFFICERS	OTHER RANKS	OFFICERS	OTHER RANKS	OFFICERS	OTHER RANKS
SUPPLIES AND TRANSPORT						
4 Ind Div Tps Tpt Coy	1	4	—	—	1	19
5 Ind Inf Bde Tpt Coy	—	8	—	—	1	4
7 Ind Inf Bde Tpt Coy	—	13	—	—	—	6
11 Ind Inf Bde Tpt Coy	—	6	—	—	1	11
220 Inf DID	—	2	—	—	—	—
18 M.A. Sec	—	1	—	—	—	4
MEDICAL SERVICES						
17 Field Ambulance	—	8	—	—	—	29
26 Field Ambulance	—	10	—	—	4	126
32 Field Ambulance	—	5	—	—	—	17
15 Field Hyg Sec	—	1	—	—	—	4
INDIAN ELECTRICAL AND MECHANICAL ENGINEERS						
117 Ind Inf Wksp Coy	—	2	—	—	—	1
118 Ind Inf Wksp Coy	—	5	—	—	—	1
119 Ind Inf Wksp Coy	—	6	—	21	—	19
4 Ind Div Rec Coy	—	4	—	—	1	—
LAD	1	—	—	—	—	11
MISCELLANEOUS						
Divisional Ordnance Company	—	6	—	—	3	—
Divisional Provost Units	—	14	—	—	1	7

4. HONOURS, AWARDS AND CITATIONS

Note: In spite of repeated efforts, it has been found impossible to obtain the Honours, Awards and Citations for the requisite periods for the following units:

3 Royal Horse Artillery

1 Northumberland Fusiliers Machine Gun Battalion

1 Royal Fusiliers

HEADQUARTERS FORMATIONS
HEADQUARTERS FOURTH INDIAN DIVISION

		NUMBER
KBE	(Knight of the Order of the British Empire)	1
CB	(Commander of the Order of the Bath)	3
CBE	(Commander of the Order of the British Empire)	1
DSO	(Distinguished Service Order)	4
	Bar to DSO	1
OBE	(Order of the British Empire)	4
MBE	(Member of the Order of the British Empire)	4
MM	(Military Medal)	1

HEADQUARTERS 5 INDIAN INFANTRY BRIGADE

CBE	(Commander of the Order of the British Empire)	1
DSO	(Distinguished Service Order)	4
	Second Bar to DSO	1
OBE	(Order of the British Empire)	1
MBE	(Member of the Order of the British Empire)	1
MC	(Military Cross)	2
	Bar to MC	1

HEADQUARTERS 7 INDIAN INFANTRY BRIGADE

CBE	(Commander of the Order of the British Empire)	2
DSO	(Distinguished Service Order)	2
	Bar to DSO	1
MBE	(Member of the Order of the British Empire)	2
MC	(Military Cross)	2

HEADQUARTERS 11 INDIAN INFANTRY BRIGADE

CBE	(Commander of the Order of the British Empire)	1
DSO	(Distinguished Service Order)	1
BEM	(British Empire Medal)	1

ARMOURED AND RECONNAISSANCE UNITS
CENTRAL INDIA HORSE

GC	(George Cross)	2
OBE	(Order of the British Empire)	2
MBE	(Member of the Order of the British Empire)	3
MC	(Military Cross)	7
IOM	(Indian Order of Merit)	2
IDSM	(Indian Distinguished Service Medal)	9
MM	(Military Medal)	7
Foreign—Bronze Star (U.S.A.)		1

7 INFANTRY BRIGADE RECONNAISSANCE SQUADRON

		NUMBER
DSO	(Distinguished Service Order)	1
MC	Bar to Military Cross	1
DCM	(Distinguished Courage Medal)	1
MM	Bar to Military Medal	1

ROYAL ARTILLERY

1 FIELD REGIMENT RA

DSO	(Distinguished Service Order)	3
MBE	(Member of the Order of the British Empire)	1
MC	(Military Cross)	1
DCM	(Distinguished Courage Medal)	1
MM	(Military Medal)	11

11 FIELD REGIMENT RA

DSO	(Distinguished Service Order)	2
MC	(Military Cross)	5
DCM	(Distinguished Courage Medal)	1
MM	(Military Medal)	8

25 FIELD REGIMENT RA

DCM	(Distinguished Courage Medal)	1
MM	(Military Medal)	13

31 FIELD REGIMENT RA

DSO	(Distinguished Service Order)	2
	Bar to DSO	3
MC	(Military Cross)	9
DCM	(Distinguished Courage Medal)	2
MM	(Military Medal)	13

65 ANTI-TANK REGIMENT RA

DCM	(Distinguished Courage Medal)	2
MM	(Military Medal)	6
	Bar to MM	1

149 ANTI-TANK REGIMENT RA

DSO	(Distinguished Service Order)	3
MBE	(Member of the Order of the British Empire)	1
MC	(Military Cross)	10
DCM	(Distinguished Courage Medal)	3
MM	(Military Medal)	7
BEM	(British Empire Medal)	1

57 LAA REGIMENT

MC	(Military Cross)	11
	Bar to MC	1
DCM	(Distinguished Courage Medal)	2
MM	(Military Medal)	22
BEM	(British Empire Medal)	2

ROYAL INDIAN ENGINEERS

HEADQUARTERS ROYAL INDIAN ENGINEERS

DSO	(Distinguished Service Order)	3
OBE	(Order of the British Empire)	1

4 FIELD COMPANY RIE

		NUMBER
MC	(Military Cross)	6
	Bar to MC	1
IOM	(Indian Order of Merit)	4
IDSM	(Indian Distinguished Service Medal)	6
MM	(Military Medal)	2

12 FIELD COMPANY RIE

MC	(Military Cross)	1
	Bar to MC	1
IOM	(Indian Order of Merit)	3
MM	(Military Medal)	1
GM	(George Medal)	1

18 FIELD COMPANY RIE

OBE	(Order of the British Empire)	1
MBE	(Member of the Order of the British Empire)	2
MC	(Military Cross)	2
	Bar to MC	1
IDSM	(Indian Distinguished Service Medal)	3
Foreign—Croix de Guerre (France)		2

21 FIELD COMPANY RIE

MBE	(Member of the Order of the British Empire)	1
MC	(Military Cross)	4
MM	(Military Medal)	1

11 FIELD PARK COMPANY RIE

GC	(George Cross)	1
IDSM	(Indian Distinguished Service Medal)	2
MM	(Military Medal)	1

ROYAL SIGNALS

FOURTH INDIAN DIVISION SIGNALS

DSO	(Distinguished Service Order)	1
OBE	(Order of the British Empire)	2
MC	(Military Cross)	2
IOM	(Indian Order of Merit)	1
IDSM	(Indian Distinguished Service Medal)	2
MM	(Military Medal)	3

BRITISH INFANTRY

1 ROYAL SUSSEX REGIMENT

DSO	(Distinguished Service Order)	6
MBE	(Member of the Order of the British Empire)	3
MC	(Military Cross)	8
DCM	(Distinguished Courage Medal)	1
MM	(Military Medal)	20

2 QUEENS OWN CAMERON HIGHLANDERS

DSO	(Distinguished Service Order)	5
MBE	(Member of the Order of the British Empire)	1
MC	(Military Cross)	17
DCM	(Distinguished Courage Medal)	6
MM	(Military Medal)	24
BEM	(British Empire Medal)	2

1 BUFFS (EAST KENT REGIMENT)

	NUMBER
BAR to DSO (Distinguished Service Order)	1
MBE (Member of the Order of the British Empire)	1
MC (Military Cross)	1
MM (Military Medal)	2

1 WELCH REGIMENT

MBE (Member of the Order of the British Empire)	1
MM (Military Medal)	2

1/4 ESSEX REGIMENT

DSO (Distinguished Service Order)	4
MC (Military Cross)	10
Bar to MC	2
DCM (Distinguished Courage Medal)	5
Bar to DCM	2
MM (Military Medal)	21

INDIAN INFANTRY

3/1 PUNJAB REGIMENT

DSO (Distinguished Service Order)	1
MBE (Member of the Order of the British Empire)	1
MC (Military Cross)	10
Bar to MC	1
IOM (Indian Order of Merit)	8
IDSM (Indian Distinguished Service Medal)	25
Foreign—Croix de Guerre (France)	5

2/5 MAHRATTA LIGHT INFANTRY

DSO (Distinguished Service Order)	2
MC (Military Cross)	1
Bar to MC	1
IOM (Indian Order of Merit)	3
IDSM (Indian Distinguished Service Medal)	14

1/6 RAJPUTANA RIFLES

DSO (Distinguished Service Order)	1
Bar to DSO	1
MBE (Member of the Order of the British Empire)	1
MC (Military Cross)	6
IOM (Indian Order of Merit)	10
IDSM (Indian Distinguished Service Medal)	20
MM (Military Medal)	2
BEM (British Empire Medal)	1

4/6 RAJPUTANA RIFLES

VC (Victoria Cross)	2
DSO (Distinguished Service Order)	4
OBE (Order of the British Empire)	1
MBE (Member of the Order of the British Empire)	3
MC (Military Cross)	9
IOM (Indian Order of Merit)	18
IDSM (Indian Distinguished Service Medal)	36
MM (Military Medal)	1
Foreign—Croix de Guerre (France)	4

4/7 RAJPUT REGIMENT

		NUMBER
MC	(Military Cross)	1
IDSM	(Indian Distinguished Service Medal)	2

3/10 BALUCH REGIMENT

	Bar to DSO (Distinguished Service Order)	2
OBE	(Order of the British Empire)	1
MC	(Military Cross)	8
IOM	(Indian Order of Merit)	1
IDSM	(Indian Distinguished Service Medal)	3
MM	(Military Medal)	5

2/11 ROYAL SIKH REGIMENT

DSO	(Distinguished Service Order)	1
MC	(Military Cross)	4
IOM	(Indian Order of Merit)	1
IDSM	(Indian Distinguished Service Medal)	4
MM	(Military Medal)	5

4/11 SIKH REGIMENT

DSO	(Distinguished Service Order)	2
MC	(Military Cross)	3
	Bar to MC	1
IOM	(Indian Order of Merit)	3
IDSM	(Indian Distinguished Service Medal)	7
MM	(Military Medal)	2

3/12 ROYAL FRONTIER FORCE REGIMENT

DSO	(Distinguished Service Order)	1
MBE	(Member of the Order of the British Empire)	2
MC	(Military Cross)	7
IDSM	(Indian Distinguished Service Medal)	1
MM	(Military Medal)	6
Foreign—Bronze Star (U.S.A.)		1

4/16 PUNJAB REGIMENT

DSO	(Distinguished Service Order)	2
	Bar to DSO	1
MBE	(Member of the Order of the British Empire)	3
MC	(Military Cross)	15
	Bar to MC	1
IOM	(Indian Order of Merit)	8
IDSM	(Indian Distinguished Service Medal)	33
MM	(Military Medal)	18

1/2 GURKHA RIFLES

VC	(Victoria Cross)	1
DSO	(Distinguished Service Order)	3
	Bar to DSO	1
MBE	(Member of the Order of the British Empire)	3
MC	(Military Cross)	15
	Bar to MC	1
IOM	(Indian Order of Merit)	8
IDSM	(Indian Distinguished Service Medal)	33
MM	(Military Medal)	19
Foreign—Bronze Star (U.S.A.)		1

2/7 GURKHA RIFLES

		NUMBER
DSO	(Distinguished Service Order)	2
MBE	(Member of the Order of the British Empire)	1
MC	(Military Cross)	7
IOM	(Indian Order of Merit)	1
IDSM	(Indian Distinguished Service Medal)	3
MM	(Military Medal)	10

1/9 GURKHA RIFLES

VC	(Victoria Cross)	1
DSO	(Distinguished Service Order)	5
OBE	(Order of the British Empire)	1
MC	(Military Cross)	12
IOM	(Indian Order of Merit)	9
IDSM	(Indian Distinguished Service Medal)	21
	Bar to IDSM	1
MM	(Military Medal)	14

MACHINE GUN UNITS

MACHINE GUN BATTALION 6 RAJPUTANA RIFLES

OBE	(Order of the British Empire)	1
MC	(Military Cross)	3
IOM	(Indian Order of Merit)	1
IDSM	(Indian Distinguished Service Medal)	4
MM	(Military Medal)	2
Foreign—Bronze Star (U.S.A.)		1

7 INDIAN INFANTRY BRIGADE MMG COMPANY

IDSM	(Indian Distinguished Service Medal)	1

SUPPLIES AND TRANSPORT

HEADQUARTERS RIASC

MBE	(Member of the Order of the British Empire)	1

FOURTH DIVISION TROOPS TRANSPORT COMPANY

MBE	(Member of the Order of the British Empire)	1

5 INDIAN BRIGADE TRANSPORT COMPANY

MBE	(Member of the Order of the British Empire)	1
IDSM	(Indian Distinguished Service Medal)	1
MM	(Military Medal)	2

7 INDIAN BRIGADE TRANSPORT COMPANY

MBE	(Member of the Order of the British Empire)	1

11 INDIAN BRIGADE TRANSPORT COMPANY

MBE	(Member of the Order of the British Empire)	2
IDSM	(Indian Distinguished Service Medal)	1
BEM	(British Empire Medal)	1

18 M. A. SECTION
NUMBER
    Foreign—Bronze Star (U.S.A.) 1

MEDICAL SERVICES
17 FIELD AMBULANCE
    DSO (Distinguished Service Order) 1
    MC   (Military Cross) 6
    IDSM (Indian Distinguished Service Medal) 3
    MM   (Military Medal) 7

26 FIELD AMBULANCE
    DSO (Distinguished Service Order) 1
    MC   (Military Cross) 3
    IOM (Indian Order of Merit) 1
    IDSM (Indian Distinguished Service Medal) 4
    MM   (Military Medal) 1

32 FIELD AMBULANCE
    MC   (Military Cross) 2
    MM   (Military Medal) 4

INDIAN ELECTRICAL AND MECHANICAL ENGINEERS
HEADQUARTERS IEME
    OBE (Order of the British Empire) 1

118 INDIAN WORKSHOP COMPANY
    IDSM (Indian Distinguished Service Medal) 1

119 INDIAN WORKSHOP COMPANY
    MBE (Member of the Order of the British Empire) 1
    BEM (British Empire Medal) 1
    Foreign—Bronze Star (U.S.A.) 1

FOURTH DIVISIONAL ORDNANCE SECTION
    OBE (Order of the British Empire) 1
    BEM (British Empire Medal) 1

FOURTH DIVISIONAL PROVOST UNIT
    IDSM (Indian Distinguished Service Medal) 1
    MM   (Military Medal) 5
    BEM (British Empire Medal) 1
    Foreign—Bronze Star (U.S.A.) 1

COMMANDER-IN-CHIEF'S COMMENDATION CARDS
    Central India Horse 22
    57 LAA Regiment RA 2
    17 Field Ambulance 2
    26 Field Ambulance 3
    32 Field Ambulance 2

MENTIONED IN DESPATCHES

	NUMBER
Headquarters Fourth Indian Division	20
Headquarters 5 Indian Brigade	4
Headquarters 11 Indian Brigade	3
Central India Horse	58
5 Indian Brigade RECCE Squadron	2
1 Field Regiment RA	9
11 Field Regiment RA	6
25 Field Regiment RA	4
31 Field Regiment RA	19
65 Anti-Tank Regiment RA	2
149 Anti-Tank Regiment RA	22
57 LAA Regiment RA	29
Headquarters Royal Indian Engineers	4
4 Field Company RIE	20
12 Field Company RIE	11
18 Field Company RIE	7
21 Field Company RIE	14
11 Field Park Company RIE	7
Divisional Signals	17
1 Royal Sussex Regiment	31
2 Cameron Highlanders	11
1 Buffs (East Kent) Regiment	5
1 Welch Regiment	2
1/4 Essex Regiment	24
3/1 Punjab Regiment	54
2/5 Mahratta Light Infantry	20
1/6 Rajputana Rifles	39
4/6 Rajputana Rifles	76
4/7 Rajput Regiment	2
3/10 Baluch Regiment	17
2/11 Royal Sikh Regiment	13
4/11 Sikh Regiment	16
3/12 Royal Frontier Force Regiment	16
3/14 Punjab Regiment	3
4/16 Punjab Regiment	34
1/2 Gurkha Rifles	38
2/7 Gurkha Rifles	23
1/9 Gurkha Rifles	33
Machine Gun Battalion 6 Rajputana Rifles	27
7 Brigade MMG Company	1
Headquarters RIASC	3
Divisional Troops Transport Company	6
5 Brigade Transport Company	8
7 Brigade Transport Company	3
11 Brigade Transport Company	10
18 M. A. Section	2
17 Field Ambulance	8
26 Field Ambulance	7
32 Field Ambulance	7
15 Field Hygiene Section	5
Headquarters IEME	3
118 Workshop Company	4
119 Indian Workshop Company	8
LAD Workshop Section	2
Divisional Ordnance Section	8
Divisional Provost Unit	17

www.ingramcontent.com/pod-product-compliance
Lightning Source LLC
Chambersburg PA
CBHW061923220426
43662CB00012B/1785